RIVAL LEGALITIES

This book offers a wholly new way of thinking about the ideas, struggles and practices that constituted the 'historical' Cold War. In particular, it seeks to redescribe and defamiliarise what we might think of as Cold War international law in order to bring out a rich but now obscured plurality of law and legal forms during the period and to make visible the ways in which we live and work in the aftermath of this legal order. This book challenges the dominant myths about the history of the Cold War, arguing that far from being defined only by ideologically rivalry, the US and the Soviet Union were engaged in a conjoint project of world ordering.

MATTHEW CRAVEN is Professor of International Law at SOAS, University of London. He is author of *The Decolonisation of International Law* (2007), which won the inaugural European Society of International Law prize in the same year, and has authored or edited a number of other books including *International Law and the Cold War* (2019). He is currently working on a project on international law and geopolitics exploring the interconnections between the two traditions of thought and practice.

SUNDHYA PAHUJA is Melbourne Laureate Professor and ARC Kathleen Fitzpatrick Laureate Fellow, Director of the Laureate Program in Global Corporations and International Law. She is the winner of the Max Planck–Cambridge Prize for International Law. She is known for her work on the encounter between plural forms of international law and the legal, historical, political and economic dimensions of the relations between Global South and North. Sundhya is the author of the prize-winning book, *Decolonising International Law: Development, Economic Growth and the Politics of Universality* (Cambridge 2011) and the co-editor of *International Law and the Cold War* (2019).

GERRY SIMPSON is Professor of Public International Law at the London School of Economics and Political Science. He is the author of *Great Powers and Outlaw States* (2004), *Law, War and Crime: War Crimes Trials and the Reinvention of International Law* (2008) and *The Sentimental Life of International Law: Literature, Language and Longing in Global Politics* (2021). Gerry is currently writing a book on nuclearism entitled: *The Atomics: My Nuclear Family at the End of the Earth.*

CAMBRIDGE STUDIES IN INTERNATIONAL AND COMPARATIVE LAW: 200

Established in 1946, this series produces high quality, reflective and innovative scholarship in the field of public international law. It publishes works on international law that are of a theoretical, historical, cross-disciplinary or doctrinal nature. The series also welcomes books providing insights from private international law, comparative law and transnational studies which inform international legal thought and practice more generally.

The series seeks to publish views from diverse legal traditions and perspectives, and of any geographical origin. In this respect it invites studies offering regional perspectives on core *problématiques* of international law, and in the same vein, it appreciates contrasts and debates between diverging approaches. Accordingly, books offering new or less orthodox perspectives are very much welcome. Works of a generalist character are greatly valued and the series is also open to studies on specific areas, institutions or problems. Translations of the most outstanding works published in other languages are also considered.

After seventy years, Cambridge Studies in International and Comparative Law sets the standard for international legal scholarship and will continue to define the discipline as it evolves in the years to come.

Recent books in the series can be found at the end of this volume.

RIVAL LEGALITIES

International Law During the Cold War

MATTHEW CRAVEN
SOAS, University of London

SUNDHYA PAHUJA
University of Melbourne

GERRY SIMPSON
London School of Economics and Political Science

CAMBRIDGE
UNIVERSITY PRESS

CAMBRIDGE
UNIVERSITY PRESS

Shaftesbury Road, Cambridge CB2 8EA, United Kingdom

One Liberty Plaza, 20th Floor, New York, NY 10006, USA

477 Williamstown Road, Port Melbourne, VIC 3207, Australia

314–321, 3rd Floor, Plot 3, Splendor Forum, Jasola District Centre, New Delhi – 110025, India

Cambridge University Press is part of Cambridge University Press & Assessment, a department of the University of Cambridge.

We share the University's mission to contribute to society through the pursuit of education, learning and research at the highest international levels of excellence.

www.cambridge.org
Information on this title: www.cambridge.org/9781108841269

DOI: 10.1017/9781108893756

When citing this work, please include a reference to the DOI 10.1017/9781108893756

First published 2026

Cover image: History of San Francisco mural War and Peace by Anton Refregier / Alpha Stock

A catalogue record for this publication is available from the British Library

Library of Congress Cataloging-in-Publication Data
Names: Craven, Matthew C. R. author | Pahuja, Sundhya author | Simpson, Gerry J. author
Title: Rival legalities : practices of international law during the Cold War / Matthew Craven, School of Oriental and African Studies, University of London; Sundhya Pahuja, University of Melbourne; Gerry Simpson, London School of Economics and Political Science.
Description: Cambridge, United Kingdom ; New York, NY : Cambridge University Press, 2026. | Series: Cambridge studies in international and comparative law (CSIL) | Includes bibliographical references and index.
Subjects: LCSH: International law | Cold War–Law and legislation
Classification: LCC KZ3410 .C73 2026 (print) | LCC KZ3410 (ebook)
LC record available at https://lccn.loc.gov/2026015480
LC ebook record available at https://lccn.loc.gov/2026015481

ISBN 978-1-108-84126-9 Hardback
ISBN 978-1-108-81019-7 Paperback

This book is dedicated to Gerry's sister, Sheena, and nephew, Ruaraidh, to Sundhya's sister Monica, and to Janine.

CONTENTS

EPISTOLARY INTERNATIONAL LAW: A PREFACE

If the introduction that follows offers an explicit catalogue of the ideas, methods, assumptions and inclinations that provide the book's ordering principles and theoretical contribution, in this preface we want to give a flavour of the time. Letters, telegrams and notes were a striking part of the diplomacy of the period, so we have chosen a number of epistolary exchanges – some iconic, others more obscure – through which we hope that our reader might find herself listening to the voice(s) of the Cold War, acquiring a sense of its atmospheres or a curiosity for discerning some of its themes. It is a fragmentary archive, but one that we hope helps set the scene for the account to follow.

Fanon, 1961: 'A 'Third Country of the World'

When Ali Shariati, a member of Dr Mossadegh's National Front, was a student in Paris, he would regularly visit a barber's shop run by a member of the FLN where he came into contact with the Algerian resistance.[1] During this period, he befriended Frantz Fanon and entered into a correspondence with him. Shortly before Fanon's death in December 1961, Shariati received a final letter from his friend. In it, Fanon diagnoses the relationship of a familiar commitment on the part of 'sectarian' Islam and anti-colonial national liberation to various forms of sovereign statehood, and shares his own belief in a transcendent Third World 'nation' in which national boundaries themselves would wither. Fanon recognises Islam's radical potential, the centuries of harm inflicted on it by Europe and its anti-colonial credentials. And yet, when it comes to self-determination, he warns against adopting

[1] Mohammed Mossadegh was Iranian Premier from 1951 to 1953 before being deposed in a US–UK-sponsored coup.

'methods and solutions coming from Europe' and calls for the 'founding of another humanity'.[2]

Fanon places the struggle between international law's foundation in territorial statehood and this 'other humanity' at the centre of his thinking when he recalls his hope that Islamic self-determination (in Iran and elsewhere) might not necessarily be incompatible with 'my aim to build a united and harmonious nation in this country of the third world – instead, I might say, this third country of the world'.[3] Here we see Fanon caught between three conceptions of international ordering or world-making: the first, a national liberation; the second, a new humanity; and the third, a 'third country of the world', or to put it in less poetic language, a 'Third World'.[4] This letter – a valediction to the struggle – is suffused with a kind of anxious hope that the state-making of Jomo Kenyatta and Julius Nyerere can somehow co-exist with and strengthen the world-making of Bandung and revolutionary socialism.[5]

> As for myself, although my path diverges from, and is even opposed to, yours, I am persuaded that both paths will ultimately join up towards that destination where humanity lives well.[6]

W. E. Du Bois 1921: 'In General Terms'

But the matters Fanon alludes to had their precursors in earlier struggles. On 27 May 1921, W. E. Du Bois wrote to Winston Churchill, then minister for the Colonies, about the First Pan African Congress convened in Paris two years previously and invited him to send a representative to the Second Congress to be held in London later that year. 'I should like best to have a representative of the British Colonial Office to speak to our Congress and state in some general terms the main idea of Great Britain towards her negro subjects.'[7] The Foreign Office replied unenthusiastically. The main idea, after all, was to hang on to the colonies for as long as possible, an idea – in this book we call it anti-anti-colonialism – that

[2] Frantz Fanon, 'Letter to Ali Shariati' in Jean Khalfa and Robert J. C. Young (eds.), Stephen Corcoran (trans.) *Alienation and Freedom* (London: Bloomsbury, 2018), 644.

[3] Ibid.

[4] Ibid.

[5] See Chapter 6.

[6] Fanon, 'Letter to Ali Shariati', 645.

[7] Records of the Colonial Office, Commonwealth and Foreign and Commonwealth Offices, Empire Marketing Board and related bodies, UK National Archives, CO323/878.

continued to hold sway in the early years of the Cold War and that is still there in the UN Charter.

What side of history was Du Bois on here? On one hand, he seemed to be calling for, in a heavily mediated language, a managed transition to independence. The Foreign Office's failure to respond positively places it out of step with a Cold War in which the decolonisation of much of Africa and Asia was to be one of the two or three salient events. On the other hand, Du Bois's vision of pan-African politics seems to have given way to national self-determination.[8]

In a sense then, Churchill and Du Bois represent two failed Cold War projects: anti-anti-colonialism and pan-African decolonisation. Or maybe we can say that these two projects each *half*-succeeded? During the end of empire, anti-anti-colonialism morphed into various forms of co-option, privatised extraction and proxification that go under the general name: 'neo-colonialism'. Equally, or perhaps, unequally, Du Bois's pan-African decolonisation became decolonisation without pan-Africanism. Each would look out onto a world in which their world-making dreams had withered, the Cold War becoming a passage of history, an assemblage of practices, in which there is an amalgam of failure and success.

Khrushchev, 1962: 'Other Laws'

At the height of the Cuban Missile Crisis, on 27 October 1962, John F. Kennedy received a letter from Nikita Khrushchev warning the US president that there could be no safe conclusion to the stand-off unless the Soviet Union and the United States chose to administer the world together as equals. The letter was cc-ed to U Thant the then acting Secretary-General of the UN who had assumed the role of a mediator between the two States. In the letter, Khrushchev pleads with Kennedy to avoid any measures that would lead to 'irreparable and fatal consequences'. A military conflict he warns will bring into play 'other laws – the laws of war'. It was time, then, instead, to 'normalise the situation' and 'clear up the international atmosphere'.[9]

8 See, for example, Chapter 4.

9 'Letter From Chairman Khrushchev to President Kennedy, October 27, 1962' LS NO. 46236, JFK Library, T-94/T-24, https://microsites.jfklibrary.org/cmc/oct27/doc4.html.

Khrushchev's letter is notable for the faith it places in international institutions as a framework for consolidating norms and agreements authorised *elsewhere*. The Security Council, he proposed, was to ratify an exchange agreed to previously under an Amero-Soviet framework. The international legal protections (territorial integrity, inviolability of borders) enjoyed by States such as Cuba and Turkey would be respected by the superpowers but on a *reciprocal* basis. These pledges based on a mutuality of obligations might be understood as a 'really existing international law' underlying and sometimes flatly contradicting the norms found in the UN Charter, or perhaps a 'proxy' international law. Turkey's sovereign rights would be exchanged for Cuba's.

Later that day in Washington, there was confusion. This letter had not yet been received and instead a discussion was taking place on the basis of a letter sent the previous day by Khrushchev in which there was no mention of Turkey's Jupiter missiles but instead a suggestion that the US abandon its 'piratical' quarantine of Cuba in exchange for a Soviet promise to ship no further weapons to Cuba. This letter, which ends with an expression of gratitude to Bertrand Russell, too, positions the breach of international rights of navigation as a kind of world-ending failure in which 'there would be no peaceful co-existence' but instead the exercise of 'necessary measures of a defensive nature which would protect our interests in accordance with international law'.[10]

In the period between the two letters, Khrushchev receives a further letter from Fidel Castro written in a spirit of radical revolutionism combined with a kind of annihilatory reliance on international law. If the imperialists invade Cuba 'in violation of international law and morality' (as Castro clearly expected would be the case), then international law would demand that the danger be eliminated forever 'through an act of clear legitimate self-defence, however harsh and terrible the solution would be'. The letter ends on a valedictory note conveying a sense of gratitude on the part of the Cuban people to 'the Soviet people who have been so generous and fraternal to us' (note the ominous past tense)[11] but there is no doubt that this was a 'ruthless total wager': imperialism would finally be destroyed forever (as would planetary life).[12]

In the end, back in DC, McGeorge Bundy makes a suggestion: 'I would answer back saying I prefer to deal with your – with your interesting

10 'Department of State Telegram Transmitting Letter From Chairman Khrushchev to President Kennedy, October 26, 1962', Moscow, 26 October 1962, 7 pm, https://microsites.jfklibrary.org/cmc/oct26/doc4.html.

11 Fidel Castro's Letter to Nikita Khrushchev, Havana, 26 October 1962, https://nsarchive2.gwu.edu/nsa/cuba_mis_cri/621026%20Castro%20Letter%20to%20Khrushchev.pdf.

12 Slavoj Žižek, *In Defence of Lost Causes* (London: Verso, 2008) 214–16.

proposals of last night.' Richard Reeves, *President Kennedy: Profile of Power* (New York: Simon & Schuster, 1994) 413. There could then be a secret side agreement to remove the Jupiter missiles at a later date: an uncoupling followed by a re-coupling. Of course, there had already been a prior secret agreement between the Cubans and Russians to place the missiles on Cuba, an agreement whose secrecy was the very quality that provoked the US response in the first place.[13]

JFK:	'Have we had any conversation in Turkey, with the Turks?'
DEAN RUSK:	'We've not actually talked to the Turks?'[14]
(LATER) ROBERT MCNAMARA SAYS:	'We need to have ... ready: a government for Cuba.'[15]

In the end, JFK answered the first letter.

As we shall suggest, this combination of joint administration, UN governance, international legalism, crisis and an implicit acceptance that another set of norms applied when it came to spheres of influence was not at all atypical of the Cold War.[16]

George Kennan, 1946: 'Backward Peoples'

The Cold War has many parents and many competing points of origin, of course, but for the American post-war foreign relations elite it began at ten minutes to four on 22 February 1946. This was when the US Department of State received an incoming telegram from George Kennan, one of its diplomatic staff in Moscow, answering what he described as the 'Department's questions to the Embassy of February 3rd', questions 'so intricate, so delicate, so strange to our form of thought'. The questions required lengthy answers and a 'burdening of the telegraphic channel' (hence the famous characterisation of his letter as 'The Long Telegram').[17]

[13] Žižek, *In Defence of Lost Causes*, 225.

[14] Barton J. Bernstein, 'Reconsidering the Missile Crisis: Dealing with the Problems of the American Jupiters in Turkey' in James A Nathan (ed.), *The Cuban Missile Crisis Revisited* (New York: Palgrave Macmillan, 1992) 85.

[15] The National Security Archive, The George Washington University, 'The Cuban Missile Crisis, 1962', Saturday, October 27, 10:00 P.M., Oval Office and Cabinet Room, The White House', https://nsarchive2.gwu.edu/nsa/cuba_mis_cri/audio.htm.

[16] 'Our people ... are concerned solely with having our country develop and occupy a worthy place among all the peoples of the world.' Department of State, LS No.46236, T-94/T-24, 27 October 1962.

[17] See George Kennan, 'Long Telegram', 22 February 1946, Moscow, National Archives and Records Administration, Department of State Records (Record Group 59), Central

In at least one respect, Kennan's telegram bears a striking resemblance to Soviet diplomat Nikolai Novikov's later message. Though he is often said to have "announced" the Cold War with his clear-eyed assessment of aggressive Soviet intentions, Kennan, like Novikov, articulates the Cold War as a departure from what he calls 'permanent peaceful coexistence' and 'an avowed community of aims'. For Kennan, Stalinist dogma and a traditionally neurotic Russian insecurity had led to a post-war misdescription of the capitalist world (hobbled by contradictions and committed to the encirclement of the Soviet Union) in which the 'peaceful and hopeful concept of international life' (represented by the UN) receded in significance.

But Kennan's view from Moscow is also essentially a view from the North Atlantic. 'Colonial areas' – to be regulated partly through trusteeship arrangements – are simply a domain of contestation in which advanced Western States resist Soviet 'penetration' and in relation to which 'particularly violent efforts will be made to weaken the power and influence of western powers [on] colonial backward, or dependent peoples'.[18]

And, in the end, Kennan's telegram is a description of a joint Amero-Soviet project of administration and proxification, the two 'weird sovereigns' united in their division of the world. Even Kennan's characterisation of the Soviet Union will be uneasily familiar to students of American Cold War foreign policy ('unceasing pressure' on foreign countries, 'removal' of [unfriendly] foreign governments, support for 'puppet political machines' in newly independent countries, and 'penetration' of international organisations).[19]

'[The] greatest danger that can befall us in coping with this problem', as Kennan puts it at the conclusion of his letter, 'is that we shall allow ourselves to become like those with whom we are coping'.[20] But perhaps it was too late for that as the twin giants of (colonial) modernity went on to rule together.

Nikolai Novikov, 1946: 'Unity of Those Countries'

In September 1946, Nikolai Novikov, the Soviet Ambassador to Washington, wrote a letter to his superiors in Moscow responding to

Decimal File, 1945–1949, 861.00/2-2246. Also reproduced in: *Foreign Relations of the United States, 1946, Eastern Europe, The Soviet Union*, Volume VI (Washington: United States Government Printing Office, 1969) document 475, https://history.state.gov/historicaldocuments/frus1946v06/d475.

18 Ibid.

19 Ibid.

20 Ibid.

Kennan's 'Long Telegram'.[21] In it, he warned them that American monopolistic capitalism was essentially imperialistic and that this imperialism was expressing itself in an expansionist foreign policy in which the establishment of an encircling network of military bases was central. Curiously, though, Novikov was nostalgic for a post-war Great Power settlement marked by what he called 'the unity of those countries'. This 'unity', he regretted, was being eroded by American exceptionalism and by talk of a 'Third War', that is, the Cold War. Along with mutual respect, the Soviets longed for a unified front. Indeed, the term 'Cold War' was either not used in Soviet official discourse or was placed in quotation marks to indicate its American provenance or its artificiality (a practice we do not observe in the book where the quotations marks are nevertheless implicit in one of its central arguments).[22] The authentic or default arrangement of power for the Soviets was not a class struggle relentlessly fought across different global sites but a joint administration through 'coexistence' of a terrifyingly dangerous world.

Cabinet Secretary Burke Trend, Letter to Prime Minister: 'Anglo-American Nuclear Relations'

To a certain extent, Novikov's telegram proved the more prescient. And from a certain perspective, the problem was not so much dangerous contestation but joint administration.

At 10 am on 10 August 1972, Sir Thomas Brimelow and Patrick Nairne met with Henry Kissinger and other senior US officials in Washington to discuss the growing rapprochement between the Soviet Union and the United States. In the UK, there was growing alarm about a mooted US–Soviet Declaration proposing to renounce the use of nuclear weapons. In a letter to Ted Heath, the British PM, sent the day after, a Whitehall advisor describes these discussions of an initiative codenamed (by the British) 'Hullabaloo' (a codename 'not known to Dr Kissinger').[23] The reports of the conversation betray an anxiety about US–Soviet joint projects like this (an anxiety not unlike the one experienced in 2025 by

[21] Nikolai Novikov, Soviet Ambassador to the United States 'The Novikov Telegram' Washington, DC, 27 September 1946, http://slantchev.ucsd.edu/courses/ps142j/documents/novikov-telegram.html.

[22] Sheila Fitzpatrick, 'Not Corrupt Enough', *London Review of Books* (2025), 15.

[23] See [Cabinet Secretary] Burke Trend, Memorandum to the Prime Minister, 'Anglo-American Nuclear Relations', 11 August 1972, Top Secret, National Security Archive, PREM 15/1362.

the Starmer Government in relation to the Putin-Trump Alaskan summit). Kissinger, himself, it is made clear, agreed that there would be no 'unqualified renunciation of the use of nuclear weapons'. But the letter reporting (and quoting verbatim from the meeting) also reveals that Kissinger does not want Nixon simply to reject the Soviet proposal, noting that the Russians are attracted to any 'demonstration of "Super-Power partnership" in the nuclear field'.[24]

The British were pushing for a firmer rebuff, but Kissinger reminded them that 'the condition for their being able to act firmly as occasion demanded was that they should be seen to be ready to work for détente'.[25] The UK, meanwhile, wanted to 'make clear the continuing loyalty of the US Government to their obligations under the United Nations Charter and their other treaty commitments'.[26]

Patrice Lumumba 1960: 'Trusting International Law'

For the UK in 1972, the UN was there to tame US–USSR relations in the name of a heavily managed, executive-led multilateralism. For the Global South, international law played a more ambiguous role. On 11 November 1960, several months after the Congo became independent,[27] Patrice Lumumba made his last stand. This was not a stand for revolutionary socialism but for parliamentary democracy and international law. It pitted itself against an Amero-Sovietism of one-party rule and violent kleptocracy, against also the covert machinations of a former colonial power (Belgium) with a history of often horrifying violence and now seeking to secure its interests in the Union Minière du Haut-Katanga. In a letter to the President of the UN General Assembly, Lumumba calls for the re-establishment of law and order and a return to a 'legally constituted government'. 'Messrs Kasavubu and Mobutu' are accused of having 'trampled into the dust' the 'Fundamental Law drawn up by the former colonial power [Belgium]'.[28] But it is the United Nations too that draws Lumumba's ire. Its inability to protect the Congo's independence (and his government) and its failure to find a

[24] Ibid.
[25] Ibid. Underline in original.
[26] Ibid.
[27] Patrice Lumumba, *The Truth about a Monstrous Crime of the Colonialists* (Moscow: Foreign Languages Publishing House, 1961), 50–52.
[28] Ibid.

solution to the crisis leads Lumumba to call for its withdrawal. No one could then accuse it of partiality or 'interference', he goes on to say. But there remains in the letter a faith in law and a chastened faith in the United Nations (which he continues to call on to send observers to ensure 'free and fair' elections). Indeed, Lumumba's letter (with its references to parliamentary elections and constitutional provisions) is hardly the work of (or at least is not articulated in the language of) a radical Marxist. He wants to send the UN home while continuing to serve 'the mission undertaken by the United Nations in our country'.[29]

Che Guevara once said of Patrice Lumumba that he had been a victim of his own mistakes: 'he had trusted international law' as Guevara put it.[30] But Lumumba had the kind of belief that many of the great colonial leaders possessed in a world of institutions and law that had, by then, begun to declare an inalienable right to independent statehood through a process of decolonisation. What he had perhaps not fully understood is that the United States was uninterested in parliamentary democracy and more concerned to facilitate the violent elimination of (or directly eliminate) any possible Third Way in African and Asian affairs. Yes, there was a mobilisation of US intelligence and aid against 'communist influence', but Lumumba was a victim of the Kissinger principle that the US (and to a certain extent the Soviet Union) had more to fear from freely elected socialist parties than violent communist cells or market authoritarianism.[31]

Had Lumumba survived and stayed in power, however, his problems would have been far from over. Nkrumah reported in his address to the Ghana National Assembly on 22 March 1965 that since Belgium had extracted £464 million from the Congo prior to independence, it was faced with a national debt of £40 million, which, when coupled with the debts apparently owed to US and Belgian monopolies, amounted to a total debt of $900 million. As Nkrumah put it, the 'tragic-comedy continues'.[32]

[29] Ibid.

[30] Piero Gleijeses, *Conflicting Missions: Havana, Washington and Africa 1959–1976* (Chapel Hill: University of North Carolina Press, 2002), 77.

[31] Kissinger is reported to have feared not that Salvador Allende would cease to hold elections and declare himself a dictator but that he would continue to stand for election and receive a mandate for progressive change.

[32] Kwame Nkrumah, *Neo-colonialism: The Last Stage of Imperialism* (London: Thomas Nelson & Sons, 1965), 156.

Che Guevara, 1965: 'Doctors'

Guevara was of course committed not to the UN or forms of international legalism but instead to disruptive war tactics. He was also capable of appealing to Cuba's doctrines of humanitarian intervention. On 5 November 1965, while, fighting in the Congo 'in the name of proletarian internationalism', he conceded, in a letter to Fidel Castro, that there was a very small prospect of success. He asked for supplies to be sent from Cuba and in particular, '50 doctors who will give the liberated area of the Congo an enviable proportion of "one per a thousand inhabitants"'.[33]

Letters to the Editor, *New York Times*, 1976: 'A Complete Misunderstanding of Sovereignty'

The international law relied on by Lumumba and the officials in Whitehall was never as stable as either seemed to assume. On 4 July 1976, three Israeli aircraft landed without permission at Entebbe, Kampala's main airport. This was the beginning of a mission in which Israeli commandos freed hostages from a hijacked Air France jet en route from Tel Aviv to Paris and now on the tarmac in Uganda. All the hijackers were killed and all but three of the passengers were saved (one, Mrs Dora Bloch, was murdered by Ugandan security agents after being taken from her hospital bed in Kampala where she was receiving treatment). One Israeli commando (Benjamin Netanyahu's brother) was killed in an operation the legality of which was debated across the pages of the *New York Times*.

The first letter of 16 July was sent from New Haven a week earlier by two of the doyens of American Cold War international law, Myres McDougal and Michael Reisman. In it they accused opponents of the Israeli raid of Orwellian forms of Newspeak or what they call 'Opposite-Speak'.[34] In particular, they argued, there had been a misunderstanding of international law and sovereignty, each of which was more than flexible enough to permit such behaviour. The hijackers were after all pirates subject to universal jurisdiction, the Israeli action 'would appear justified as a humanitarian intervention, a doctrine whose roots go back,

[33] Letter dated 5/10/65. See Ernesto Che Guevara, *Congo Diary: Episodes of Revolutionary War in the Congo* (ed. Che Guevara Studies Centre, New York: Seven Stories Press, 2022).
[34] Letter to the Editor, *New York Times*, 16 July 1976.

at least, to Hugo Grotius' and this was, in any case, a matter of 'self-help'. This contestable combination of arguments was underpinned by a conception of sovereignty that allowed it to be exercised only by States fully complying with international law. William B. Lloyd from Rochester, Vermont, responded with the very reasonable point that this make-shift set of would-be norms could hardly be deployed by, say, Cuba in, say, Uruguay. 'Professors', he went on, 'would undoubtedly conclude that things had gone too far'.[35] He was right. It was a Cold War article of faith in Western Europe and North America that the West was law-abiding and the East cynically careless of law, no matter what the facts actually suggested.

Letter from Krushchev to Fidel Castro, 31 January 1963: 'The Crisis Has Left Some Trace'

Of course, it had already become clear that international law had its limits when it came to protecting the sovereignty of States in the Global South or, for that matter, in Eastern Europe. Shortly after the end of the Cuban Missile Crisis, Premier Khrushchev wrote to Fidel Castro in an attempt to 'dispel a trace, almost imperceptible' in relations between Cuba and the USSR following what Castro thought was a Soviet capitulation. In a sense, the letter concerned the relationship between the Amero-Soviet project to administer the globe through a series of spatial configurations and technical agreements, on one hand, and the class solidarities and anti-imperialist sympathies of the Soviet regime itself, on the other. Little wonder that Khrushchev could not decide whether the breach is made up of 'some fissures (how deep they are is difficult to determine)' or 'light marks that could be easily erased'.[36] He had found himself caught between co-existence and class struggle. The letter is an expression of that decades-long dilemma. Khrushchev wants to reassure the Cubans (and other Third World allies) that the Soviets will stand up to the 'powerful, aggressive, and merciless force' of American imperialism and support the 'powerful global socialist network'. Yet the letter is peppered with references to the deep structure of Amero-Soviet relations. At one point, Khrushchev invokes the Monroe Doctrine (in order to reject it) but refers to the American argument that the Cuban Missile imbroglio has its roots in the Soviet invasion of Hungary and the implicit

[35] William Lloyd, Letter to Editor, *New York Times*, Editorial Pages, 27 July 1976.
[36] Nikita Krushchev, 'Letter to Fidel Castro', 31 January 1963.

division of the world. This division, in the end, has more power over Khrushchev than the 'path of revolutionary words'.[37] He implores Castro to visit Moscow and begin again to build a friendship between their two countries. Castro is of course worried that any visit will be used as an opportunity by the US to invade Cuba. In response to this, Khrushchev refers to the non-aggression pledge made by Kennedy. What, though, is the status of such a pledge? It is not an absolute guarantee but nor can it be ignored altogether. It has, after all, 'become a sort of international document that has been formalised by the UN'. Khrushchev ends on a double note: 'we say both "Long Live peaceful-co-existence" and "Long live Communism"'.[38]

The order is telling.

[37] Castro had announced: 'The homeland or death!' Khrushchev rather half-heartedly describes this as 'an absolutely correct revolutionary slogan' (in fact, neither the homeland nor death are central to Marxist-Leninist thinking). But he soon turns to the question of 'peaceful co-existence'.

[38] Krushchev, 'Letter to Fidel Castro'.

ACKNOWLEDGEMENTS

This book was the work of many hands and minds, a collaborative project in more than one way. We would like to thank all of those who joined us as we tried to understand the Cold War and its relations to international law. We held a series of meetings, Cold War I–V, in London and Melbourne over many years. These meetings yielded an edited volume (*Cold War International Law*), which was an obvious influence on our thinking here. The project also led to the volume on the 'International Law during the Cold War' of the *Cambridge History of International Law*, and we are indebted to the authors of those chapters as well. Throughout the writing of the book, we were assisted by research assistants in Melbourne and London. Towards the end of the project, Caitlin Murphy led a team of researchers as we searched for footnotes, re-ordered material, caught grammatical and historical inaccuracies, corrected solecisms. She was indispensable in the completion of the task of writing. Thank you, Caitlin, and to the whole team. Lucy O'Connell hunted down references in the British Library. Thank you too to the Academic Research Service at the Melbourne Law School led by a talented group of librarians. Librarians and archivists have been crucial to this work, as they are to so much scholarly endeavour. Cait Storr, Martin Clark, Anna Saunders, Nadia Gahnecke, Jasmin Ali and Conor Foley have also all generously and expertly supported this work in different ways.

We are also deeply grateful to six friends who read the book in its near-final draft. Jeremy Baskin, Ruth Buchanan, Chris Gevers, Adil Hasan Khan, André Dao and Dino Kritsiotis offered us such wise and incisive (and learned) thoughts on a book already informed by their own work.

Our editors at Cambridge University Press were patient and conscientious. Thanks also to Finola O'Sullivan who encouraged us as we began.

The universities we work at provided research support and an intellectual community. Gerry enjoyed two periods of research leave (in Manhattan and Melbourne) during which this work was presented and discussed. Sundhya has been supported by colleagues and students at the Melbourne Law School, as well as at places where she has been lucky enough to work in visiting capacities, including SOAS, Birkbeck, Cambridge, Harvard and STIAS. Matt has benefited from various stints of research leave from SOAS, University of London and from the wonderful support of colleagues at the Wissenschaftskolleg zu Berlin.

The project as a whole has been supported financially by the Australian Research Council, the UK Arts and Humanities Research Council and the Leverhulme Trust.

Finally, there are our families. The project has lasted for so long, we thank them for their patience and forbearance, especially when we seemed to be enjoying the work altogether too much. To Esther and for Rosa and Hannah. To Asha, Om and Monica and to Ananya and Jeremy. To Janine, Elodie and Hamish.

A NOTE ON THE COVER IMAGE

The cover image is one part of a set of twenty-seven murals on display in the former Rincon Annex Post Office painted by Anton Refregier, a Russian-born artist, in 1948. The murals, one of the largest federally funded public works of art in the United States, were commissioned as part of the New Deal and were intended to portray the history of Northern California. The image on the cover records the signing of the UN Charter at San Francisco and is one part of a triptych that includes also an image of Roosevelt's Four Freedoms. The murals were controversial, not least because, as works of social realism, they depicted the history of California as one marked by racial and class violence. They became, indeed, the object of a campaign for their removal in the early 1950s led by, amongst others, Vice-President Richard Nixon, and their merits were debated at a congressional hearing (a so-called trial) in 1953. Refregier was accused of anti-American subversion and the promotion of racial hatred and class warfare. He was also suspected of involvement in both communist and peace organisations. Criticism of the cover image included its excessive use of the colour red, the portrayal of a hammer and sickle on the Soviet flag and the addition of what looked like 'mule ears' on the head of the US representative. In the event, the murals were spared.

Introduction

1.1 The Project and the Period

This book is about the practice of international law during the Cold War. It seeks to redescribe and defamiliarise what we might think of as Cold War international law in order to bring out a rich but now obscured plurality of law and legal forms during the period and to make visible the ways in which we live and work in its aftermath. Against a common narrative of the Cold War as a long aberration or interruption in the development of international law,[1] we counterpose a rethinking of the Cold War as a time of rivalrous but mutually constitutive accounts of the 'international', understood as a set of ideas, practices and intellectual and political manoeuvrings, and of international law itself. What emerges from this depiction of the Cold War is both a better understanding of the techniques and ways of thinking and imagining we have inherited from it and a more acute sense of what has been lost. These paths not taken and forgotten memories of the future can perhaps then be recuperated as imaginative resources in the present.

In one sense, the 'Cold War' is shorthand for a period that dates roughly from 1945 (the 'Iron Curtain' falls) to 1989 (the breach of the 'Berlin Wall'). The contest between East and West, or between the rival political-economic traditions of communism and capitalism is usually what springs first to mind when we hear the phrase. But this is a moment of encounter between more than these two European projects of world-making. Familiar enough is the third, 'other', project, of anti-colonial world-making.[2] But the neatly symmetrical frame of this three-worlds

[1] Matthew Craven, Sundhya Pahuja and Gerry Simpson, 'Reading and Unreading a Historiography of Hiatus' in Matthew Craven, Sundhya Pahuja and Gerry Simpson (eds.), *International Law and the Cold War* (Cambridge: Cambridge University Press, 2019) 1–24.

[2] Adom Getachew, *Worldmaking after Empire: The Rise and Fall of Self-Determination* (Princeton: Princeton University Press, 2019); Vijay Prashad, *The Darker Nations:*

vision is also problematic.[3] Not only does it overstate the uniformity of the world-making projects of the Third World (in which China, for example, assumes an ambivalent place), but it also obscures from view an equally important fourth rival project that was also in play. That fourth project – the antithesis of the third – is the older world-making project of the European empires, still being violently waged even as the 'Cold War' started. We refer to this as the anti-anti-colonial project. It had a complex relationship to the rivalry between the Cold War's more familiar protagonists. Our point is not to insist upon the necessity of a four-world rather than a three-world vision but rather to observe that paying attention to the plurality of rival world-making projects both generates and demands a different conceptual frame than one that begins and ends with American–Soviet rivalry. It also offers a different lens than one in which the period is understood as a 'global' Cold War, or as a 'Cold' War with hot global proxies. This is particularly important in the context of international law, which looks very different in each of the rival accounts.

When we speak of 'rival' forms or legalities, we are not (necessarily) talking about a conscious competition. Instead, we use the term to suggest different explanations of the *whole*. In other words, there are ways of looking at the world that each make sense as a complete picture and that may be underpinned by different knowledge systems.[4] When two 'whole pictures' exist, they offer complete accounts of the world, which may be mutually incompatible or may overlap but are likely in competition with one another as explanatory narratives. They are not points on a spectrum that can be 'balanced'. They are 'rival' worldviews,

A People's History of the Third World (New York: The New Press, 2007), many countries in Eastern Europe would also have a different story to tell.

[3] A very different account of the three-world's thesis was offered by Mao Zedong in the 1970s. For Mao, the first world consisted of the United States and the Soviet Union; the second of Japan, Europe and Canada; and the third the rest (which included most of Asia, all of Africa and Latin America).

[4] The Kombumerri-Munaljahlai jurisprudent, Christine Black, describes this existence of radical plurality using the language of 'cosmology' in which each people has its own story of creation, which defines their belief and knowledge systems: C. F. Black, 'The Camp of the Talngai-Gawarima' in *The Land Is the Source of the Law: A Dialogic Encounter with Indigenous Jurisprudence* (London and New York: Routledge, 2011) 15. Western accounts of knowledge do assert themselves as universal, whereas others may be able to abide difference. And yet for the purposes of the heuristic in this book, it makes sense to hold onto the sense of rival worlds. For a different way of understanding this sense of a non-unitariness of knowledge, see Massimiliano Tomba, *Insurgent Universality: An Alternative Legacy of Modernity* (Oxford: Oxford University Press, 2019).

whether or not the adherents themselves are consciously competing. When two rival world-views come into contact, relative power is important in understanding what might happen and how that contact might be staged. In the context of particular polities (like States) meeting other forms of association, power will shape the attitude of one to the other, not only in terms of dominant versus subordinate actors but also in relation to how different groups within the weaker or subordinated entity may relate to the dominant world-view or knowledge system. So, for instance, ruling elites in a less powerful entity may be more willing to take on aspects of the more powerful entity's world-view than non-elites (like workers or peasants) of the same entity.[5] In some cases, though, the apparently weaker or subordinated rival will assert its system of thought so powerfully that the world shifts on its axis – think decolonisation here. But even if that doesn't happen, traces are left, even after the specific world-making project fades from view.

1.2 Practice

There were certain ways of 'doing' international law during the period of the Cold War. These included ways of thinking and writing about international law, acting in diplomatic and institutional contexts, building institutions, bringing cases, drafting treaties, creating conventions and more. Each of the chapters in this book relates to a way of doing something with or around international law. Each chapter focuses on different actors and groups of actors making and using international laws in different circumstances and contexts. The sites, rubrics, rituals and institutions we have chosen are all recognisable to the international lawyer today as part of the raw material out of which international law's normative architecture is built. These ways of doing things, and the rivalrous forms with which they are associated, are part of the historical object of the Cold War 'itself'. By noticing that there were particular ways of speaking about and practising international law during the Cold War, however, we want to soften the idea that 'Cold War' and 'international law' were two independent or stable sites of thought and practice. Indeed, even placing them in 'relation' to one another risks reproducing the style of thought that was central to the Cold War itself (that, for example, law could be counterposed to power politics, or that law was merely a

[5] Sometimes rival forms of association are symbiotic, like company and State. But that is a question for another day.

technique for the pursuit of certain political ends). At the same time, by taking up an idea of practising international law, we don't want to attribute to law a special straightforwardly causal role in the politics of the Cold War. But we do want to explore and highlight how this particular field of expertise contributed to building the Cold War and post–Cold War worlds.

As well as treating practices of international law as our main object of enquiry, we also think of law 'itself' as a set of practices. We could even say as 'nothing more' than a set of practices, though that might imply that we underestimate its importance. But by 'nothing more', we mean that rather than thinking of law as a system, or 'pure' set of norms, we treat international law as something that emerges in the doing and that does not exist outside that body of activity. In other words, there is no 'international law' as such, there is only people doing and experiencing international law. If we stop practising, or 'doing' international law, it will no longer exist. But even while we do it, it continues only to be a practice and does not transcend that practice into being something permanent, or even securely defined. Making the claim that law *does* transcend its practice – that it 'is' universal – is itself part of the practice of Western jurisprudence. The same caveat is true for 'authority'. There is no 'authority' as such, only practices of authorisation. We will say something more about this in the section on method, which comes later in this chapter (Section 1.6), but for now, it is important to notice that law is (always, only) practice because nothing external to it secures it 'as such'. The international laws of the Cold War are no different in this regard.

1.3 International Laws

When we look back, we sometimes imagine that there was a settled body of international law and institutions that stretched back to some inaugural event, whether 1648, 1873 or 1945.[6] In each case, whether we imagine it to have been a tool of oppression, language of justice, technical system or procedural surface, the point is that we tend to think it was already constituted. But even if we start from 1945, this law was less solid than is typically understood from a twenty-first-century vantage point. When we look more closely, it seems that none of its content, procedures,

[6] These dates refer to the Treaties of Westphalia, the establishment of the Institut de droit International and the establishment of the UN, all attributed with originary force in familiar Western narratives of international law.

institutions or actors were stable.[7] Instead, in the late 1940s, what international law seems to have offered more than settled law, institutions and practices was what we might call 'resources of ambiguity'.[8] By emphasising international law as a resource of ambiguity, we are refusing a definitional approach. A definitional approach would attempt to qualify or settle terms and depart from there. But definition is itself a juridical technique of authorisation that disallows radical plurality.[9] Instead, we have concentrated on examining practices that are familiar to international lawyers and legal scholars today as international law in a vernacular sense. The resources of ambiguity available at the time provided a contested and contestable juridical idiom through which lawful encounters between different groups of people and 'nations' were taking place and being remade. The various leaders of many independence movements understood that a particular kind of international law may have played an important role in the perpetuation of colonialism, but now, a new international law was both urgently needed and in a process of formation. And yet their use of international law was always strategic.[10] In describing the strategic use of international law by the South, we want to correct both the romanticised impression of the Third World as naïve and idealistic about international law in the aftermath of Empire and the cynical impression that the Third World consisted of autarkic and sovereigntist States who rejected international law in favour of raw, or 'primitive', politics.

We are also interested in the images of law, lawlessness and lawfulness that attended the encounters between East and West and North and South. The retrospective accounts of a lawful North and lawless South or East prove to be almost invariably misleading, indeed, mischievous.

[7] See our introduction to Cold War international law for the argument about historiographies of hiatus, which explains this: Craven, Pahuja and Simpson, 'Reading and Unreading a Historiography of Hiatus'.

[8] Kenneth Burke, *Language as Symbolic Action: Essays on Life, Literature, and Method* (Berkeley: University of California Press, 1966).

[9] Cf Friedrich Nietzsche, *On the Genealogy of Morals* (London: Penguin Books, 2013) 53, 'only that which has no history is definable'.

[10] We use 'strategic' in a colloquial sense here as a counter to naïve or idealistic. Whether particularly uses were themselves better thought of as strategic or tactical in bellicose terms is a slightly different question. See Rob Knox, 'Strategy and Tactics' *Finnish Yearbook of International Law* 21 (2010) 193–229; and John Reynolds and Noura Erakat, 'We Charge Apartheid' (2021) TWAILR Reflections, https://twailr.com/we-charge-apartheid-palestine-and-the-international-criminal-court/. Western usages were, of course, also strategic.

Lawful initiatives, to change or use law by the South, in particular, were often, perhaps invariably, met with illegal, non-legal and extra-legal conduct by the North. The narrative of the lawless South is enabled by the myth that a liberal(ish) international law was imagined and institutionalised in 1947 but was suspended by the Cold War. For a brief moment between 1989 and 2001, history was said to have ended, and the liberal promise able to be fulfilled. The dystopia of the present has put paid to half the myth – of a progressive move towards a liberal international order – but not to the idea that some 'thing' was inaugurated in 1947, which was 'fulfilled' at the end of the Cold War. This is one idea – and one account of international law – into which this book is trying to insert a wedge.

1.4 The Argument

In its clearest terms, our argument is that the 'Cold War' was a particular form – indeed, entire field – of international relations imagined and projected from a certain place. But even hegemony was a claim and not an effect, so the project did not 'make' the world in a straightforward way. Instead, it encountered rival projects and often sought to unmake them. This book tells the story of some of those projects and encounters. As the reader will notice (and may regret), we are trying to slow the story right down. Slowing down is necessary to see plurality and its displacement and then to notice the retrospective erasure of plurality in the ways we talk about international law today. The political economy of knowledge production and the persistent Eurocentrism in how international law has been practised (including teaching, theorising and writing about it) means that the solidification and globalisation of the world-view shorthanded as the 'Cold War' has happened retrospectively. As a putatively global phenomenon, it seems more solid looking back from today than 'it' was in the contemporaneous moment.

We begin our story with the idea that the Cold War is less about the performance of an ideological confrontation that sought to divide the world and more of an outward symptom of a common, albeit conflictual, form of governmentality: in other words, an 'Amero-Soviet' project.[11] What we describe is not only what appeared to divide or distinguish the

[11] For a similar idea in slightly different terms, see Susan Buck-Morss, *Dreamworld and Catastrophe: The Passing of Mass Utopia in East and West* (Cambridge, MA: MIT Press, 2000) x, xiii, 2–39.

powers but also what they retained in common; identifying the shared forms of knowledge-power and practices of authorisation that made competition meaningful or rivalry necessary. At the same time, we describe the conditions for the emergence of this discursive and jurisdictional formation (e.g. the fact that it was instituted from the privileged vantage point of Moscow and Washington or, more broadly, the North). This is not to insist that the effects of these formations were localised but to note that those effects can be understood as consequential to the operationalisation of a particular, locationally specific, way of thinking about the world. This is the idea, to paraphrase Slavoj Žižek, that anyone can think global and act local, but only powerful actors can 'think local and act global'.[12]

This first strand of argumentation invites us to imagine the 'Cold War' as a particular form of international relations imagined and projected from a certain place. The surprising part of this is perhaps the idea that at least by the late 1960s, the two opposing forces of US capitalism and Soviet communism seemed to have created, in their own imagination, a world unified by its rival polarities. With the arrival of *détente* in the 1970s, the maintenance of that Cold War world could be understood as having (almost explicitly) become a joint US–Soviet project. This is a story, then, of unexpected unity between 'East' and 'West' that also generated the understanding that East/West rivalry was globally determinative. Struggles elsewhere were understood as simply proxies for it.[13] Indeed, 'proxification' was central to this vision of the Cold War world and central also, retrospectively, to the idea of the Cold War as a period of history. Warfare itself was rendered impossible in the nuclear North Atlantic but redistributed across the equator. In this redistribution and sublimation, the anti-colonial struggles within which the rival powers engaged came themselves to be reinterpreted and redescribed as merely symptoms of the dominant rivalry of the North. This Cold War rendered

[12] This was Slavoj Žižek, 'Knee-Deep: Leftish Platitudes' *London Review of Books* 26(17) (2004). See also Nermeen Shaikh, *The Present as History: Critical Perspectives on Global Power* (New York: Columbia University Press, 2007).

[13] For an early articulation of this argument, see George Padmore, *Pan-Africanism or Communism? The Coming Struggle for Africa* (London: Dennis Dobson, 1956) 15 – discussed in Chris Gevers, 'International Law in Africa during the Cold War' in Matthew Craven, Sundhya Pahuja and Gerry Simpson (eds.), *The Cambridge History of International Law Vol XI: International Law during the Cold War (1945–1990)* (Cambridge: Cambridge University Press, forthcoming).

itself 'global' in part through the hegemonic assertion of a monopoly over political and juridical agency.

From the perspective of many in the South, that interplay of rivalry and unity was perfectly comprehensible as an internecine struggle between rival European political-economic and legal traditions. For many in both East and West, that internecine struggle combined with a racialised Eurocentrism to occupy the whole field of jurisprudential vision. It was a continuation of colonial modernity. But for the rest of the world, the interplay created a certain level of flux in the meaning and understanding given to international law. This flux meant that, for them, 'international law' was (still) not a settled thing, not even a settled language, but a domain of struggle in which 'resources of ambiguity'[14] might be taken up in resistance to both North Atlantic unity and to the old imperialism. Decolonisation was central to that struggle, but alongside it was an explicit attempt to assert a new international law appropriate to a world after (formal) Empire.

When we refuse to forget about the anti-anti-colonial battle as part of the Cold War picture, a less familiar answer to the question of why international institutions were so important to the Global South during the middle of the twentieth century starts to emerge. From the perspective of the South – or what was referred to then as the Third World[15] – the emerging international institutions were a vital stage for political – and legal – contestation. Various interpretations have been given to the use of this theatre. These range from assumptions about the idealism, naiveté or hope of Third World actors, to the potential that lies in the 'universality' of liberal international law, or with a different inflection, in

[14] Kenneth Burke, *A Grammar of Motives* (Berkeley: University of California Press, 1969) xix ('instead of considering it our task to "dispose of" any ambiguity by merely disclosing the fact that it is an ambiguity, we rather consider it our task to study and clarify the *resources* of ambiguity. For it is in the areas of ambiguity that transformations take place; in fact, without such areas, transformation would become impossible. Distinctions, we might say, arise out of a great moltenness, where all is merged. They have been thrown from a liquid center to the surface, where they have congealed.')

[15] This could be a much longer footnote, but in the first instance, see Alfred Sauvy, 'Trois Mondes: Une Planète' *L'Observateur* (1952) 118; Hani Sayed, 'The Humanization of the Third World' in Luis Eslava, Michael Fakhri and Vasuki Nesiah (eds.), *Bandung, Global History, and International Law: Critical Pasts and Pending Futures* (Cambridge: Cambridge University Press, 2017) 431–49; Vijay Prashad, *The Darker Nations: A People's History of the Third World* (New Delhi: LeftWord, 2007); Raewyn Connell, *Southern Theory: Social Science and the Global Dynamics of Knowledge* (Cambridge: Polity Press, 2007).

the instability of international law's universal assertion.[16] But the declassification of archives in recent decades and the work of historians shows us that the internationalisation of the anti-colonial struggles in most of the world was a more complex affair than we might remember. This was an affair with both political and juridical dimensions. Those juridical dimensions were, in turn, both doctrinal and institutional. In institutional terms, the new bodies being established by the Great Powers in the aftermath of the Second World War were soon theatres not just for decolonisation but for the encounter between the four rival projects of world-making.[17] And in these encounters, international law 'itself' was being (re)formed. The strategy became available in part because of the 'resources of ambiguity' available in the extant lexicon of international law and, in part, also as a consequence of the necessarily public dimensions of the ideological rivalry that made powerful States vulnerable to moral and juridical argumentation in ways that have since largely been lost.

1.5 Outline of the Book

The book has seven substantive chapters, each of which relates to a field of practice of international law. The argument is both cumulative and iterative in the sense that elements of the whole argument are repeated in each chapter, but the chapters are better read together to see the whole. Perhaps we could think of it as a series of stories within a story, or something like a series of essays and a story at the same time. This introduction is more guide than encapsulation, so we encourage our readers to at least dip into the whole. The same might be said for the book itself. It is not a book about 'international law and the Cold War', at least not in the strong sense of that phrase. We don't aspire to anything that could be described as a complete picture or comprehensive coverage. Such aspirations could well be understood from our perspective to be part of the problem. Instead, the book is a guide, or a series of suggested openings into a different sort of Cold War international law scholarship that we very much hope others will take up and carry forward.[18]

[16] Sundhya Pahuja, *Decolonising International Law: Development, Economic Growth and the Politics of Universality* (Cambridge: Cambridge University Press, 2011).

[17] At least four. Remember this is a heuristic. Others would see more plurality still.

[18] In fact, have already begun to take up: Matthew Craven, Sundhya Pahuja and Gerry Simpson (eds.), *International Law and the Cold War* (Cambridge: Cambridge University Press, 2019) 1–24.

We begin our story in Chapter 2 where we revisit the founding document of the post-war period – the Charter of the United Nations. This was not so much an aspirational institutional order that was derailed by ideological competition, as an instrument that provided the juridical architecture for an Amero–Soviet Cold War as it was to develop over the following decades. We describe the Charter as inaugural in two senses. In the first place, it introduced a new institutional vision for global order, replacing the League of Nations with a more muscular, coercive alternative. In the second place, however, it also inaugurated the Cold War itself. By this we mean that it institutionalised the shared outlook of the rival powers, formalising the terms and stakes of their rivalry while at the same time providing a space for that rivalry and a joint division of and administration of the world to be actively conducted and secreted (often surreptitiously) in the terms of the Charter itself. So, on one hand, the Charter gave textual force to a particular vision for global order meditated through the legal form of the sovereign State. This was to pattern the form through which decolonisation would take place. On the other hand, it created space for disagreement over the medium through which the sovereign State would be represented internationally – that is, in the form of its government. It was here, in the silent presupposition of the Charter – that the people of a State were to be represented internationally through their freely chosen representatives – that a version of the Cold War would be acted out. This was evidenced in the ensuing battles over membership, representation and intervention that were to mark the early years of the post-war period. So, in the context of the wider United Nations and the rival worlds in formation, the Charter institutionalised the ambiguous relationship between the United States, the Soviet Union and the European imperial powers – a relationship that was itself both rivalrous and arranged around alliances. This institutionalisation globalised the nation-state form and stabilised legal forms of property ownership established during the imperial period. But it also opened up space, not only for ideological competition but for the articulation of rival political and juridical agendas. This was to bear fruit as decolonisation was increasingly channelled into formal statehood and the new States became members of the UN.

We follow this in Chapter 3 with a description of what we call the 'Amero–Soviet Cold War'. In contrast to emphatic and confident accounts of ideological rivalry and institutional stasis, here we offer an argument that the Amero–Soviet relationship of the time could be understood as a joint project of global ordering or world-making enacted, both through the Charter and around it, in jurisdictional projects of co-imperium, peaceful coexistence, détente and 'proxification'. This project was divided by ideology but, in our argument, unified by the shared traditions of colonial modernity and the European forms of knowledge production that those rival ideologies shared. From the perspective of most of the world, it was a local, internecine dispute. The international law consummated in that relationship was narrowly understood by the Great Powers and their allies as the sole really existing international law. But at the same time, because of the rivalrous nature of US–Soviet relations and the open-endedness of the style of law that made for itself a universal claim, there was an unsettledness of existing international legal rules, precepts and doctrines and an openness around international law as an intellectual and political project.

In Chapter 4, we consider the practice of diplomacy during the Cold War. The 'Cold War' is sometimes thought of as a diplomatic struggle. In this chapter, we describe it as a struggle over diplomacy itself, one that plays out in terms of a divide between those who understand diplomacy as a practice in which different groups can meet only when they adopt the same legal form – statehood – and agree on basic overarching rules and those who understand diplomacy as the patterns and rituals of lawful encounter between those who must engage with each other but who share no common law. We offer three examples of this. The first example concerns the Amero-Soviet sphere and the question of secrecy. Both the US and the USSR had reason to value secret forms of diplomacy, both within their spheres and between themselves. This is true even as it sat uncomfortably with the putative turn in the post-war era to the denunciation of 'secret' alliances, which were thought by scholars and statesmen alike to have contributed to the two world wars. In the chapter, we describe the lines between public and secret forms of diplomacy in the East–West engagement, and their relationship to international law and institutions. It is a pattern in which legal forms frame a secret world, an idea to which we return in Chapter 7 on the legality of 'peacetime' espionage. We contrast this with the very public diplomatic practices of the Third World. These are practices that treat diplomacy as a site of lawful encounter. We describe the way that anti-colonial world-making takes form through diplomacy as theatre, symbolic engagement, pluralistic assertion and solidarity building. Collectivities, whether conference, movement or institution, are central to these practices. These endeavours are met by the West with what we call 'anti-diplomacy', a style of engagement that refuses the diplomatic overtures of the South as forms of lawful encounter and meets and treats them as something else. The strategies engaged to misrecognise and redescribe these invitations to meet as equals and draw on the hierarchies patterned in the imperial period, whether racial, civilisational, cultural or developmental. They are repatterned and stabilised through force and coercion. This forceful repatterning takes place in a frame in which the meaning of neutrality is also at play. We take this then as the third example of diplomatic struggle in the chapter. Here there are three strands of diplomatic practice and interpretation at work. The first is found in the readjustments to the doctrine of neutrality in times of war that occurred as a result of the advent of the UN Charter and the nature of Cold War conflict. The second is the 'neutralism' of the Third World and the struggle to remain outside the superpower conflict. This was the catalyst for 'Non-Alignment', a project full of political and juridical content. It was full, too, of variety but by necessity was positioned in diplomatic terms by reference to what it was not – not 'of' a Cold War, understood from that position precisely as an Amero-Soviet project. The third strand of practice is the Amero-Soviet response to this, which condemns the neutralism of the South as a moral failure in a time of existential choice between good and evil. We weave this third strand of diplomatic practice through the account of the second. The point is to tease out the way that the rival projects of world-making were enacted in diplomatic terms. Obviously, this chapter – like this book – is a series of snapshots, and there are many other forms of diplomatic practice that could be treated in this way. We invite readers to consider the practices of the many jurist-diplomats[19] not described and to think about them in terms of rival worlds and their laws.

In Chapter 5, we turn back to the question of legal doctrine and project the unsettledness of international law and institutions into the spaces of juridical experimentation it allowed. We follow three such legal experiments to consider the ways in which the most basic propositions of international law were being struggled over during the Cold War. Each situation – the Algerian struggle, the Anglo–Iranian Oil case and the establishment of the UN Commission on Transnational Corporations – is described in detail to show what kinds of substantive and formal claims could be and were being made in a juridical language. The foundational

[19] This is a term coined by Shaun McVeigh and Adil Hasan Khan. See 'Offices of the Southern Jurist-Diplomat', Melbourne Law School, https://law.unimelb.edu.au/centres/iilah/research/projects/offices-of-the-southern-jurist-diplomat.

disagreements about where authority lay were broad and substantive rather than procedural. And yet the response of the powerful was to assert an existing body of law and cast the disputes as procedural matters rather than substantive clashes. The disputes included what counts as 'national' or 'international', who could exercise authority over what and the legality of anti-anti-colonialism 'itself'. As each example shows us, for the Third World, the struggles were grounded in plural rather than universal ideas of international law. The chapter also interrogates what happened to these legal experiments as an effect of the overlap between formal decolonisation, the anti-anti-colonial struggle and the Amero-Soviet Cold War. Our stories reveal that the familiar tropes of the present about the lawless South, and law-abiding North are historically unfounded. But they may also help us to see the way such tropes are themselves part of the way the South was resubordinated as the Cold War ended – and continues to be so since.

In Chapter 6, we shift our focus from diplomacy and doctrine toward resistance and specifically to socialist and revolutionary forms of resistance and spatial reconfigurations and government as an orientations of international law. Here we tease out ideas of revolutionary and socialist forms of international lawmaking but hold them apart from both Marxist-Leninist international law and the foreign policy of the Soviet Union. Retrospective accounts of the Cold War and its popular histories have reproduced a version of communism that is highly particular and strongly associated with Stalin, the camps and the persecutions.[20] But when we look back, we see that communist thought, and the mobilisation of Marxist traditions more broadly, created a space for a wider range of revolutionary political projects. Some of these projects could be read as communist, but many involve re-alignments of political space (Pan-Africanism), the assertion of rival forms of law (Cuba), the retrieval of social democratic practices (Chile), resistance to racial hierarchy (South Africa) or even the promise of genuine "national" liberation.[21] In the chapter, we engage with several projects of the Global South. These were

[20] Jodi Dean, *The Communist Horizon* (London: Verso, 2012), 31.

[21] Of course, there were other rejections of the dominant Cold War: Mao's willingness to contemplate the 'end of humanity', Castro's ruthless nuclear wager in 1962 (each to be set against Khruschev's marvellous response to Castro's pleas for war in 1962: 'we are not struggling against imperialism in order to die' (Jeremy Friedman, *Shadow Cold War: Sino-Soviet Competition for the Third World* (Chapel Hill: University of North Carolina Press, 2015) 217) as well as '1968' and the rejections of Yankee imperialism and Soviet collusion (Immanuel Wallerstein, 'The Curve of American Power' *New Left Review* II/40

projects that had to engage with the existing conditions (perhaps with what Scott calls the 'problem-space'),[22] but which could make use of the anti-imperial inflection which underpinned the Soviet project regardless of its own conduct and foreign policy. Notwithstanding this strategic engagement, these projects were all attempts to escape the effects and injunctions of the Cold War itself. A different way of putting this is to say that, as with the Non-Alignment described in Chapter 4, these are rivalries between the Cold War 'itself' and its competitors. Such projects established the conditions for very different juridical worlds. National self-determination promised a new world of independent, free-thinking, sovereign States detached from both European empire and Eurasian/North American contestation and with a commitment to national liberation through sovereignty at its heart (the UN Charter, the inviolability of treaties, incrementalism, pacific self-determination, *uti posseditis juris*). Pan-Africanism was a bold programme for a globe organised around something other than nation-states. Cuban Internationalism and civic engagement underpinned the collective defence of new States' territorial integrity and well-being. And the promotion of revolutionary violence – arguably lawful as a different sort of "self-determination" – found its corollary in transnational – or maybe non-national – solidarity. There are other projects of the South that we could have described here, of course. One is Non-Alignment, described in Chapter 4 through the lens of diplomatic practice, but which was also a form of Third World world-making.[23] Another is the New International Economic Order (NIEO). We don't treat the NIEO as a separate topic in this book – it has been described so well by many others[24] – but perhaps our readers

(2006) 41–55, 43). See also Piero Gleijeses, *Conflicting Missions: Havana, Washington and Africa 1959–1976* (Chapel Hill: University of North Carolina Press, 2002).

22 David Scott, *Conscripts of Modernity: The Tragedy of Colonial Enlightenment* (Durham: Duke University Press, 2004).

23 See Christine Hatzky, *Cubans in Angola: South-South Cooperation and Transfer of Knowledge, 1976–1991* (Madison: University of Wisconsin Press, 2015): Cuban Internationalism and civic engagement as defence of Angola's territorial integrity. The New International Economic Order, too, was an assertion of economic liberty constrained neither by the precepts of neo-colonial capital nor command economy.

24 See the 2015 special issue of *Humanity* 6(1) on the NIEO, as well as Antony Anghie, 'Legal Aspects of the New International Economic Order' *Humanity: An International Journal of Human Rights, Humanitarianism, and Development* 6(1) (2015) 145–58; Luis Eslava, Michael Fakhri and Vasuki Nesiah, (eds.), *Bandung, Global History and International Law: Critical Pasts and Pending Futures* (Cambridge: Cambridge University Press, 2017); Umut Özsu, *Completing Humanity: The International Law of Decolonization, 1960–82* (Cambridge: Cambridge University Press, 2024); Vasuki Nesiah,

could go back and re-read those accounts re-inflecting them through the lens we offer here.

The worlds we describe in this chapter, and their accounts of revolutionary violence and radical economic vision, have long been supplanted by the naturalised discourses – and violence – of anti-terrorism, 'humanitarian' intervention and neo-liberalism.[25] The most pertinent current example as we write is found in Gaza where political resistance or self-determination is redescribed as terror. Remembering the revolutionary moments of the anti-colonial Cold War might help us think about what has displaced it and how what displaced it might itself be dislodged.[26] When international lawyers today encounter the history of revolutionary movements, the agency and heroism of the left's struggle in the colonial and postcolonial era have been erased by a history of violent endings. Lumumba, Ben Barka, Allende, of course, but so often, too, one reads of a figure intent on redistribution, or on land reform, or on performing a detachment from the superpowers or from the Cold War itself. The reader searches for biographical background only to find that x or y has been assassinated by the CIA, or removed in a coup or has sought exile in Paris or Tunis. The Cold War bequeathed us at the very least a world in which an unrepeatable cadre of revolutionary intellectuals and politicians were eliminated. This is the international legal politics we now inhabit, a legal politics in the absence of these figures and, sometimes, their projects.[27]

'The NIEO Against Racial Capitalism' (2023) Progressive International, https://progressive.international/blueprint/30202c48-1324-4831-81e5–829f588d9492-nesiah-the-nieo-against-racial-capitalism/en. See also Pahuja, *Decolonising International Law*.

[25] See Talal Asad, *On Suicide Bombing* (New York: Columbia University Press, 2007). As we wrote this there were reports in the *New York Times* that the State Department's Africa desk was to be forced to shift from its present variety of tasks to a concentration on 'extraction' and 'anti-terrorism': 'Trump Administration Draft Order Calls for Overhaul of State Department' *New York Times*, 20 April 2025.

[26] Jeffrey Byrne, 'The Romance of Revolutionary Transatlanticism: Cuban-Algerian Relations and the Diverging Trends within Third World Internationalism' in R. Joseph Parrott and Mark Atwood Lawrence (eds.), *The Tricontinental Revolution: Third World Radicalism and the Cold War* (Cambridge: Cambridge University Press, 2022) 163–190, 169.

[27] This formulation is not without risk in the sense that we risk periodising revolutionary violence in a way that changes perspective mid-stream. So, we attend to the question of revolutionary violence initially from the perspective of the revolutionaries themselves but then approach it more contemporaneously from the perspective of the discipline or an imperial counter-insurgent perspective. We choose 'displace' rather than 'replace' to hold that back. Anti-imperial revolutionary violence has, after all, existed since the end of the

Counter-revolutionary politics during the Cold War were quite frequently conducted in secret. Recolonisation had been rendered impossible by the sweep of history and Amero-Sovietism was regarded in the South as either a collage of alien ideas or a discredited diplomatic program. The Amero-Soviet response was to move the Cold War into the shadows. In Chapter 7, then, we turn back in a way, to the axis of Amero-Sovietism, to describe the practice of espionage and its relationship to international law. Espionage is perhaps the archetypal cultural and aesthetic image of the Cold War in novels and films. And in some sense, espionage and its complex legal status, particularly in peacetime, offers a concentrated instance of the international legal ambiguity of a 'cold' war itself. Classical international law – at least in its treatise form – has always pivoted on a distinction between war and peace. Much of the early codification of international law was about war, not peace. Rules on espionage were part of those efforts, so 'legal peacetime espionage' was generally a contradiction in terms. And yet the tenor of the rivalry between the United States and the USSR and its wider context meant that neither party was willing to cede the moral high ground and disregard legality per se. But the form the rivalry took produced secretive behaviour on both sides, as well as its inversion – both a hunger for information about the other and a desire to publicise the practice of secrecy. This uneasy combination invited both a turn to espionage and a great deal of disputation, argumentation and technique around its legality, sometimes involving the extending, adapting, stretching and stitching of wartime protocols into (supposedly) peacetime programs. But this form of conjoined Amero-Soviet behaviour also had the effect of redefining both war and peace themselves, creating the imaginative domain of a space between – that of a 'non-war', or a 'Cold War'. (The rechristening – happening as we write – of the US Department of Defense, as the 'Department of War' seems to evidence a re-emergence of this idea.)[28] In the chapter, we take four aspects of espionage and explore them in terms of Amero-Soviet activity. We begin with the establishment of

Cold War, and it is a specific choice to not acknowledge it as revolutionary. Some aspects of the Iranian Islamic revolution might count as an example of this.

[28] See the White House, 'Restoring the United States Department of War' (Executive Orders, 5 September 2025), www.whitehouse.gov/presidential-actions/2025/09/restoring-the-united-states-department-of-war/; Joseph Gedeon, 'Trump Signs Executive Order Rebranding Pentagon as Department of War' *The Guardian*, 6 September 2025, www.theguardian.com/us-news/2025/sep/05/department-war-defense-trump-executive-order-pentagon.

intelligence agencies, and the practice of State secrecy, and move on, through an examination of the ambivalent figure of the spy, to the question of aerial surveillance, or spying in the skies. In each instance, we tease out practices of both activity and explanation – so doing the things and speaking about them in legal terms – and the relationship between those practices. In all cases, the practices produced what we might call the 'Amero-Soviet effect', patterning an emphasis on belligerency, security and surveillance into the legal forms of statehood and sovereignty that were being generalised in the context of decolonisation and institution formation. We could say that the simple question of the legal status of peacetime espionage produces an exceedingly complex answer.

In Chapter 8, we consider another (perhaps *the* other) great change in technology that marked and defined the Cold War. Here, we turn to what we might call the atomic effect of the Amero-Soviet Cold War by describing the international legal dimensions of the invention, deployment, possession and regulation of nuclear weapons, as well as struggles against them. Our story begins with the Cuban missile crisis. We offer our version here to draw out the totalising effects of nuclear warfare and their relationship to the production of a *global* (as distinct from an international) imaginary. We describe the contortions of international jurists around the legality of nuclear weapons and the juridical effects of trying to keep law relevant in relation to weapons of total annihilation. Part of this story is intended to show how calls for peace and disarmament from both voices in both the South and North were transformed into initiatives of security and non-proliferation. Anti-nuclearism was also linked firmly for many to anti-colonialism, and in the chapter, we draw out the continuities between imperialisms of old and new forms of nuclear imperialism. Here we also see a strange new ground for universal claims. The claim to speak for the whole, in the voice of the universal, has long been a gesture of Europe and its heirs. Its post-war incarnation is a claim by the Amero-Soviets to speak for the whole on the basis of a putatively authorised capacity to destroy it. This capacity – its modes of authorisation in security and warfare, its technical features and the securitisation it is believed to necessitate – assumes an understanding of the world as 'global'. This has institutional, diplomatic and material effects that lay the ground for the globalisations to come. Holding the thought and practice of the Cold War apart from the thematics of global history helps us to remember that 'globalisation' (like any periodisation) is an argument not a fact. When we remember this, the Cold War emerges as a parochial way of thinking about the world at a particular time, the 'globalisation' of which has come about (in hindsight if nothing else) only through the suppression of both its own points of origin and of rival accounts of global ordering after its end.

1.6 Notes on Method

Our description of the Cold War and international law, or Cold War international law, rests on an orientation, a point of departure and a sensibility. We are oriented by the understanding that 'law' is a way of making the worlds we live in. We do not treat or understand international law as purely epiphenomenal – as an adjunct to a politics of power, nor as a form of instrumental or technical know-how that merely translates policy into practice, nor as something weak but virtuous. The activity of 'making' happens through particular ways of doing things, or 'techniques'.[29] The most straightforward example is the idea that we live 'in' States. The State does not come before international law. It is not a geographical or sociological fact, it is a legal form. By this we mean that 'the State' is a particular way of arranging relations between people, place and authority that is held together by different kinds of legal techniques. These techniques shape the elements of the State and bring and hold them together in particular ways (population, territory, the constitution, citizenship, the border, legislation, the legal subject . . .). Such techniques are legal or juridical and both shape and actualise legal forms. They are in essence the way law makes worlds. We won't belabour the point here but suffice it to say that law is not something that comes to a pre-constituted world. It is a practice through which worlds are made. What is 'made' does include particular laws, but it also includes law 'itself'. And so the practices that make a world include theorising – that is, arguing and writing about law in ways that authorise the claim of a particular law to be 'Law'. This includes theories and arguments about why people should regard State law as law (and above religion, culture or morality, for instance), or why a particular constitution should be understood with a capital C, as founding a nation, or even as a legal instrument at all, rather than a piece of paper. In this sense, theory is a practice, and more

[29] We could describe this first orientation as thinking with jurisdiction. The book that has brought this mode of thinking back to general attention in the Western legal academy is Shaunnagh Dorsett and Shaun McVeigh, *Jurisdiction* (Abingdon: Routledge-Cavendish, 2012). See also Shaun McVeigh, *Jurisprudence of Jurisdiction* (London: Routledge, 2023).

specifically, a practice of authorisation. Our orientation is historical in the sense that it explicitly looks to the past, but crucially, it also renders the present 'historical'[30] in the sense that there is not a moment in which the world is 'made' and from which we depart. Worlds are made as we live in them.

Once oriented by this understanding, our point of departure is that this authorisation always happens in conditions of plurality.[31] (You will notice that we are talking about the *fact* of plurality as a point of departure and not plural*ism* as a theoretical orientation.)[32] Again, the State is an example because there is always more than one type of law in any given place, and when those laws meet, they are brought into relation through juridical technique. The settler colony illustrates this most acutely. Indigenous laws continue to exist alongside 'National' law but in the practice of the settler/coloniser those rival laws are rendered subordinate to 'National' law through a range of techniques. That subordination began in the past, through an act of conquest, but continues on a daily basis in order to remain 'effective'. This continuation often requires violence, which is, in turn, authorised by the claim of national law to be 'law' properly so called and therefore to have a right to use force.[33] The claim of one law to be 'Law' proper is supported by theorisations that assert a particular definition of law and ground that definition in other forms of knowledge, such as science, history, sociology, economics or anthropology. In the context of national law, these are forms of knowledge that claim to 'prove' that State law 'is' law and that other laws are merely 'custom', for instance.[34] But there is no secure, or external,

[30] Nermeen Shaikh, *The Present as History*.

[31] Robert Cover, 'Nomos and Narrative' *Harvard Law Review*, 97 (1983) 4–68.

[32] Paul Halliday, 'Laws' Histories: Pluralisms, Pluralities, Diversity' in Lauren Benton and Richard J. Ross (eds.), *Legal Pluralism and Empires, 1500–1850* (New York: New York University Press 2013) 259–78.

[33] One could replace 'national' here with Australian, Canadian, US, Israeli, etc. but also many national laws of the Global South, which while not settler colonies in their classic sense, involve the subordination of rival laws in the project of making national law. See Peter Fitzpatrick, *The Mythology of Modern Law* (London and New York: Routledge, 1992); Sundhya Pahuja, 'Laws of Encounter: A Jurisdictional Account of International Law' *London Review of International Law*, 1 (2013) 63–98. See also Pocock on Brehon laws in 'Britain', J. G. A. Pocock, 'British History: A Plea for a New Subject' *Journal of Modern History*, 47(4) (1975) 601–21.

[34] H. L. A. Hart is a classic example here, he grounds his assertion about what law is in a made up anthropology-history about progress. See Pahuja, *Decolonising International Law*, 199; and further discussion in Fitzpatrick, *The Mythology of Modern Law*.

foundation for the proposition that the law of one culture – or indeed any given legal system – is 'truly' law. And so, in the traditions that inherit colonial modernity (Europe and its heirs), other practices and forms of knowledge-making are engaged to provide a foundation, or to 'ground' this claim,[35] usually in the form of a racialised hierarchy. We may be familiar with this observation in an historical context, but we are less used to thinking of the Cold War as a continuation of the world-making projects of colonial modernity and their often murderous displacements of other worlds. We are even less used to thinking about the present as historical in the sense that there is still no foundation for European law's claim to be 'proper' law. Many of the ways we practice and write about (European) international law continue to authorise that claim in an ongoing way. But as Pocock observed in a different context, 'the fact of a hegemony does not alter the fact of a plurality'.[36] There is always more than one understanding of law, and efforts to define it and control the meaning of law per se have always been – and remain – an element of struggles for power. This can include critical/theoretical engagements that implicitly accept an account of law in order to critique it or that write in ways that assume that *dis*placing plurality is the same as *re*placing it.[37]

In writing about law and history, we have also tried to convey a sense that political projects and projects of international law have a character or mood. Our international laws, after all, do not exist in the abstract. They are continually being argued in and out of existence, taking on different forms, being enlisted – tactically, strategically – in political and social programs. These projects and programs are the work of people with particular visions or dispositions. We have tried to capture this latter idea in our epistolary prologue and in the stories with which we begin many of the chapters. The book has a *dramatis personae* or a cast of characters, many of whom have disappeared from the scene, some of whom have also been forgotten. What might be read as an elegiac tone, at certain points connects with our broader intention to invite the recuperation and retrieval of plurality. Perhaps we *are* elegiac about what we have found in the archives to be, what we call elsewhere in the book, an

35 Peter Fitzpatrick, *Modernism and the Grounds of Law* (Cambridge: Cambridge University Press, 2001).

36 Pocock, 'A Plea for a New Subject'.

37 Some people think of this as the expansion of capitalism and understand 'law' as a providing the tools and architecture for that expansion.

'unrepeatable cadre of revolutionary intellectuals and politicians' whose presence at the heart of decolonisation and national liberation struggles gave those struggles unusual intellectual depth, cultural energy and dynamism. We see few such figures when we look around today. Indeed, one of the after-effects of the Cold War was to remove from the frame the very possibility of such figures emerging or, more pointedly, of being recognised as such when they do emerge. It is vitally important that we are not taken to be saying that radical thought and practice is no longer possible. That would be absurd. But what we are suggesting – in this sometimes rueful, sometimes angry, mood – is that a certain hegemonic world-making attended the 'winning' of the Cold War and in that world, resistance became less legible in international legal terms.

1.7 Notes on Orthodoxy

Of course, we bring these things – an orientation, a point of departure, and a sensibility – to an existing field of study. We have collectively inherited a very powerful, and resonant, idea of the Cold War as a period of history in which two global superpowers competed with one another for political and ideological ascendancy and enveloped the entirety of the globe in that struggle. This has become in the West – with relatively few exceptions – an intellectual orthodoxy and – with virtually no exceptions – an official mantra, popular truth and journalistic commonplace. As an adjunct to the conceptualisation of that struggle as predominantly political (or even political/ economic), it is usually presumed that the language of law – of right, duty, justice, privilege, immunity, etc. – had little significance. And that was especially true of international law, which was often perceived to have been a 'casualty' of that time – to have been frozen, deferred or delayed until the 'end of history' (which turned out, in the event, to be less of an end). Remarkably this was – and perhaps remains – a view in heavy circulation among international lawyers themselves. During the decade of this book's gestation, our sense has grown that this account is not only largely mistaken but is itself a product of the forms of thought to which the Cold War, as a particular way of seeing things, gave rise. It is, in other words, itself a continuation of Cold War thought – the emanation of a way of thinking about the world that was generated by those who saw themselves as participating in that struggle directly or indirectly, and which they have passed on as a history of the world.

To put it slightly differently, we have come to realise how much the period of the Cold War has become historiographically dominant as a post–Cold War extension of Cold War thinking. Contemporaneous technique becomes historiographical inflection. Proxification as a geopolitical war-making technique transmutes into historiographical orthodoxy. It's not a coincidence that that end of the Cold War is announced as the end of 'history' per se. And the perspective persists into the present. So, from this standpoint, international law, and in particular the law of the UN Charter, was that which would be rescued following the political triumph of liberalism over totalitarianism, and international law is cast backward either as an adjunct to a politics of power or as a faint utopian aspiration. But one doesn't have to travel far to realise this is a message that circulated only in certain parts of the globe, and that very different attitudes towards international law – both what it meant, and what it might become – were offered and gained traction elsewhere (and not least in the Soviet Union itself).

In order to insert a wedge into this historiographical routine symptomatic of Cold War thought, we adopt a descriptive style of explanation. We don't spend much time in the book in direct combat with accounts of the Cold War written in the present. Instead, we are more interested in critically redescribing what we have found. And so we have avoided turning the book into a dialogue between a 'mainstream' account of the Cold War and its critique. But perhaps to give the reader a taste of what that might look like, and to sketch what the retrospective depictions of the field seem to do, we could begin with something like Martin Sixsmith's popular account of the Cold War. This begins in a fairly typical mode: 'The Cold War pitted the United States and the Soviet Union against one another for the best part of fifty years.'[38] This sort of thinking has become a commonplace in international legal scholarship as well. Normative and institutional projects of the post-war era are described as 'casualties' of the Cold War (e.g. the United Nations Military Staff Committee),[39] or as having been 'postponed' (e.g. post-war international law itself)[40] or in

[38] Martin Sixsmith, *The War of Nerves: Inside the Cold War Mind* (London: Wellcome Collection, 2021) xi; John Lewis Gaddis describes it as 'the most remarkable polarisation in world history'; *We Know Now: Rethinking Cold War History* (Oxford: Oxford University Press, 1998). 'The Cold War pitted the United States .... The Cold War, both sides declared ....' Sixsmith, *The War of Nerves*, ix.

[39] For example, the United Nations Military Staff Committee: Paul Kennedy, *The Parliament of Man: The Past, Present, and Future of the United Nations* (New York: Random House, 2006).

[40] On postwar international law in general, see Ivan Shearer (ed.), *Starke's International Law* (11th ed., London: Butterworths, 1994).

'abeyance' (e.g. international criminal law),[41] or 'paralysed' (e.g. the UN)[42] or as a 'total failure' (e.g. collective security).[43] And all of this is said to be the result of 'the political struggle between the two blocs'.[44] One could point to a thousand other examples of this kind of language often accompanied by an assertion that the Cold War was unconventional or peaceful: 'The Cold War was a bitter, *usually nonmilitary*, conflict between the United States and the Soviet Union . . . for the most part military confrontations were avoided leaving the underlying friction to surface in other ways.'[45] In Sixsmith's description, the Cold War simply 'happens' – the inevitable result of the emergence of two superpowers with their respective versions of millennial politics.[46]

Here we have an itinerary of European and North American Cold War thought: the exclusion of any non-European optic, the 'absence of military conflict' (a view impossible from the perspective of South East Asia, Africa or Latin America where there are said to be merely 'local struggles')[47] not to mention the displacement of the idea that the Cold War was a neurotic event with the repression of outright violence at the core producing aggression 'elsewhere'. In a sense, such sentences evoke a certain Cold War or Cold War mentality and, at the same time, prescribe a very particular *vista* on the post-war world. The effects are manifold. So, for example, the post–Cold War world has been understood initially (from 1989 to 2001) as the suspension of this rivalry and the opening of a new form of institutional, global ordering – or at least the resumption of an order founded in San Francisco, Bretton Woods and Nuremberg – and then, more recently (from 2001 onwards), as a reversion to a competitive bipolarity (the rise of China, the new Cold War with Russia, the substitutions of, say, Al Qaeda or ISIL for the Soviet Union). We can readily see that this idea of the Cold War has been vital to understandings of the diplomatic world we now inhabit – and have been trapped in – since at least 1989.

[41] Antonio Cassesse, *International Criminal Law* (2nd ed., Oxford: Oxford University Press, 2008).

[42] Stephen Neff, 'A Short History of International Law' in Malcolm Evans (ed.), *International Law* (Oxford: Oxford University Press, 2003).

[43] On collective security, see Rosalyn Higgins, *Problems and Process: International Law and How We Use It* (Oxford: Clarendon Press, 1994).

[44] Cassesse, *International Criminal Law.*

[45] Allan Winkler, *The Cold War: A History in Documents* (London: Routledge, 2011).

[46] The opening phrase in Sixsmith ('The Cold War pitted . . .') though suggests in the other direction the presence of a mechanism ('the Cold War') for producing and reproducing rivalries, struggle, diplomatic scenes: Sixsmith, *The War of Nerves.*

[47] Sixsmith, *The War of Nerves*, 6.

It was certainly the case that Cold War ideological rivalry left its mark on the post-1945 world order and institutions in ways resonant with the typical North-Atlantic characterisations we have just mentioned. So, for instance, the Military Staff Committee envisaged under Chapter VII of the Charter was never established,[48] a stalemate emerged that subsequently froze negotiations over an international criminal court post-Nuremberg, divisions appeared over the Havana Charter and the nascent International Trade Organisation[49] and the veto power was frequently exercised in the Security Council.[50] Indeed, the emergent dissensus between East and West in the post-war occupation of Germany and Korea left a lasting mark on the regional landscape in both Europe and Asia, and led, in case of the latter to the first major conflict of the Cold War era. And beyond appearing to place a 'freeze' on a number of global initiatives, Amero-Soviet rivalry was also to make itself felt substantively in the drafting of a range of key international instruments in the following decades, including the International Bill of Rights,[51] the Genocide Convention,[52] the Refugee Convention[53] and in the drafting of the Geneva Conventions of 1949 and 1977.[54] All of these cases appeared to instance a world divided between East and West, a world

[48] Alexandra Novosseloff, *The UN Military Staff Committee: Recreating a Missing Capacity* (Abingdon: Routledge, 2018); Margot Tudor, *Blue Helmet Bureaucrats: United Nations Peacekeeping and the Reinvention of Colonialism 1945–1971* (Cambridge: Cambridge University Press, 2023); Jonathan Soffer, 'All for One or All for All: The UN Military Staff Committee and the Contradictions within American Internationalism' *Diplomatic History*, 21 (1997) 45.

[49] See Harold Jacobson, 'The Soviet Union, the UN and World Trade' *Western Political Quarterly*, 11 (1958) 673–88.

[50] Sydney Bailey and Sam Daws, *The Procedure of the United Nations* (3rd ed, Oxford: Oxford University Press, 1998).

[51] For an account, see Christopher Roberts, *The Contentious History of the International Bill of Human Rights* (Cambridge: Cambridge University Press, 2014); Erick Weitz, *A World Divided: The Global Struggle for Human Rights in the Age of the Nation-State* (Princeton: Princeton University Press, 2019).

[52] See Anton Weiss-Wendt, *The Soviet Union and the Gutting of the UN Genocide Convention* (Madison: University of Wisconsin Press, 2017).

[53] Gil Loescher, *The UNHCR and World Politics: A Perilous Path* (Oxford: Oxford University Press, 2001).

[54] Olivier Barsalou, 'Preparing for War: The USA and the Making of the 1949 Geneva Conventions on the Laws of War' *Journal of Conflict and Security Law*, 23 (2018) 49; Giovanni Mantilla, *Lawmaking Under Pressure: International Humanitarian Law and Internal Armed Conflict* (Ithaca: Cornell University Press, 2020); Boyd van Dijk, *Preparing for War: The Making of the 1949 Geneva Conventions* (Oxford: Oxford University Press, 2022).

also in which international law was buffeted, branded or hamstrung by an ideological contestation that weighed upon it from outside.

But three notes of caution need to be sounded. In the first place, it is evident that all such moments of historic struggle were not so much *effects of* a Cold War as *instances* of the Cold War in their own right. The Amero-Soviet Cold War, in other words, did not subsist independently of the means by which it came to be expressed. Instead, the legal disputes that were to surround key events, or even constitute the terms by which they were understood, were very much part and parcel of the means by which the Cold War would be practised. To put it another way, the language and practice of international law provided a means by which the scope, scale and content of the Cold War would be disclosed or evidenced to the world. Indeed, as we shall see later, one of the reasons the language of the Cold War was so 'sticky' was because it blurred – and allowed the burring of – the juridical division between war and peace. This was a juridical model of lawful warlike activities that could be adopted as the modus operandi of an ostensibly 'peaceful' ideological contestation. And it was through the deployment of this juridical model that the 'Cold War' gained substantive meaning.[55]

In the second place, when the Cold War is litanised as a sequence of ideological battles or series of Amero-Soviet conflicts, this has the effect of both understating the degree of unity between the two superpowers (missing, for example, the extent to which they jointly administered many parts of the globe through law) and overstating the centrality of Amero-Sovietism in general (by effacing non-European projects of world-making). So, to develop this latter thought further, and in the third place, a preoccupation with the facets of Amero-Sovietism in all such cases obscures from view rival visions and ideas that were in play. In other words, it stabilises a peculiarly European understanding of the politics of world-making post-1945, and in so doing, performs precisely that which the Amero-Soviets imagined for themselves: a decisive role in shaping not just the future but also the past of the world. A very different account of the Cold War, and its relationship to international law, begins to appear when one starts with the intuition or idea of a parochial Amero-Soviet Cold War, or a displaced, sublimated war between internecine rivals that operated as the functional equivalent to the European rivalry of the late nineteenth century over colonial possessions. Just as that latter rivalry evidenced itself in a singular order whose main fault-line lay, not in a dissensus within Europe itself but in the demarcation between the European and the non-European worlds,

[55] See Chapter 7.

so also may the same construction be observed in case of the Amero-Soviet Cold War.

1.8 Conclusion

In this book, we have sought to reframe the ways in which we think about the relationship between international law and the complex historical phenomenon known as the Cold War. In many accounts, the Cold War is a geopolitical confrontation between warring superpowers. Such accounts reflected particular styles of thought and argumentation that were immanent to that confrontation. But this emphasis can distract us from noticing that the confrontation did not have the paralysing effect upon international law that many might suppose. Instead, geopolitical confrontation played out in myriad ways in different fields of endeavour – both enabling and disabling international initiatives, both discouraging and encouraging creativity. Even if we understand the Cold War narrowly, as a geopolitical confrontation that juridified itself in voting blocs and in regional security arrangements, understanding it as productive rather than chilling opens space for seeing creative alternative understandings of the international and facilitating the emergence and improvisation of counter-hegemonic modes of thought and practice (non-alignment, 'third-way' thinking).

The normative significance of this book lies in its attempt to offer a new and varied descriptive account of inheritance, loss and possibility. The Cold War operated as an effective approved discourse in certain parts of the world for a certain period of time – and perhaps the 1945–89 markers capture most of this. But to explain the world-making effects of that discourse,[56] we would have not only to recognise the complex historical lineaments of the ideas and practices that came together to form the discourse of the Cold War but also direct our attention to the possibility of the survival of many of these ideas and practices after the symbolic close of virtual hostilities.[57] We still live in a world patterned by the rivalrous encounters of the Cold War, the defeat of the East, and the re-subordination of the South 'after' empire. But perhaps those of us who find this troubling can seek inspiration from half a century of a particular kind of plurality in international law.

[56] Borrowing from Said's account of Orientalism, Edward Said, *Orientalism* (New York: Pantheon Books, 1978).

[57] On Cold War temporalities, see Dino Kritsiotis, 'The Elusive Peace of Panmunjom' in Craven, Pahuja and Simpson, *International Law and the Cold War*, 49–78; Richard Joyce, 'International Law and the Cold War: Reflections on the Concept of History' in Craven, Pahuja and Simpson, *International Law and the Cold War*, 27–48.

2

A (Dis)United Nations

A Hesitant Inauguration

2.1 Introduction

In March 1946, Winston Churchill delivered his famous 'sinews of peace' speech at Westminster College, Fulton, Missouri. In that speech he brought two features of the contemporary international environment into relation with each other. First was the creation, some nine months earlier, of the United Nations, dedicated to the preservation of international peace and security. 'We must make sure', he enjoined, 'that its work is fruitful, that it is a reality and not a sham, that is a force for action, and not merely a frothing of words, that it is a true temple of peace in which the shields of many nations can some day be hung up, and not merely a cockpit in a Tower of Babel.'[1] The future of that organisation, he cautioned, was ultimately dependent not simply upon material assistance – the provision of air squadrons to the organisation by member states – but upon the 'fraternal association of the English-speaking peoples' and the forging of their 'special relationship'. Without the combined efforts of those peoples, he warned, there was not only a risk that the 'temple may not be built' but that the dark ages would 'return on the gleaming wings of [nuclear] science'.

Churchill then struck a second, more sombre note. For at the same time as he was celebrating the formation of the United Nations Organisation, Churchill warned the assembled crowd that a 'shadow' had 'fallen upon the scenes so lately lighted by the Allied victory':

> From Stettin in the Baltic to Trieste in the Adriatic, an iron curtain has descended across the Continent. Behind that line lie all the capitals of the ancient states of Central and Eastern Europe. Warsaw, Berlin, Prague,

[1] Winston Churchill, 'The Sinews of Peace', 5 March 1946, International Churchill Society, https://winstonchurchill.org/resources/speeches/1946-1963-elder-statesman/the-sinews-of-peace/.

> Vienna, Budapest, Belgrade, Bucharest and Sofia, all these famous cities and populations around them lie in . . . the Soviet sphere, and all are subject in one form or another, not only to Soviet influence but to a very high and, in many cases, increasing measure of control from Moscow.[2]

So even whilst invoking a vision of the world united under the banner of peace, Churchill was issuing a warning that this vision was being threatened by a division already evident in Europe, between the 'controlled' societies in the East and the 'open' societies of the West.

For many, the 'Sinews of Peace' speech was one of the key interventions that marked the inauguration of what was to be popularly described – at least in the West – as the 'Cold War'.[3] The speech announced the end of the precarious alliance that had tied the political weight of the Soviet Union, the United States and Britain together in the latter years of the Second World War. The agreements forged at Yalta, Potsdam and San Francisco might have been the formal expression of the ambition of the allied powers to create a unified system of global governance around themselves, centred upon the United Nations and the critical role of the 'four policemen', but Churchill's speech at Fulton gave expression to an alternative 'reality'. For Churchill, far from being united, the world was irreconcilably divided between the pernicious forces of communism and totalitarianism and the free world.

The 'iron curtain' that Churchill described was not just a metaphor but an expression of what he perceived to be the spatial dimensions of an ideological contestation that had been running through the Western world at least since the Bolshevik Revolution of 1917. This was later formalised in the aftermath of the Second World War[4] in a variety of

[2] Churchill, 'The Sinews of Peace'.

[3] It is noted that the early years of 1946 were marked by three significant speeches/communiques that have subsequently been read as inaugurating what we now conventionally call the 'Cold War'. See George Kennan's 'Long Telegram', 22 February 1946, Moscow, National Archives and Records Administration, Department of State Records (Record Group 59), Central Decimal File, 1945–1949, 861.00/2-2246; speech delivered by Joseph Stalin at a meeting of voters of the Stalin electoral district, Moscow, 9 February 1946, History and Public Policy Program Digital Archive; Winston Churchill's 'Sinews of Peace' speech, 5 March 1946, Fulton, Missouri.

[4] Lippman was to note the significance of the meeting points of the Red Army with the British and American armies in the 'heart of Europe': 'The division between east and west' he was to argue 'is at that military boundary line. The meeting of those armies caused the division. No state in eastern Europe can be independent of the Kremlin as long as the Red Army is within it and all around it. No state in western Europe is independent while it is in effect in the rear of this military frontier'. Walter Lippmann, 'The Cold War'*Foreign*

settings – in the division of Germany, Vietnam and Korea, in the establishment of NATO and the Warsaw Pact, in the Marshall Plan and COMECON, in the symmetrical policies of 'containment', in the voting bloc arrangements at the UN, in the building of walls and the construction of demilitarised zones. In all of these contexts, a Cold War geography was in the making, inscribing itself as a palimpsest on top of the formal geography of sovereignty, thereby providing an ideological supplement to the language of statehood, territorial integrity and self-determination.[5]

And yet as much as the 'Cold War' appeared to inaugurate the appearance of a new form of what Newton has called 'division space',[6] configured around an ideological struggle, it also carried a unified vision, or better, a vision of unity. The very idea of an ideological or military 'balance',[7] of 'spheres of influence', of a 'weighing' of ideological advantage or disadvantage or of a 'division' of the world between the forces of communism and capitalism/liberal democracy, spoke ultimately of a shared conception of the world within which those forces might not only oppose one another but actively work within that world together.[8] In other words, the practices of thinking, acting, speaking and imagining the world through the lens of geopolitical competition created a common point of reference. This common vantage point was expressed in the terms of the UN Charter.

Affairs, 65 (1987) 883. This article is excerpted from a series of columns originally published in the *New York Herald Tribune* in 1947 and later collected in *The Cold War: A Study in U.S. Foreign Policy* (New York: Harper & Brothers, 1947).

[5] These novel modes of spatialisation to which the Cold War gave rise have been thematised by Scott Newton under the rubric of 'Division Space'. Cold War 'division space', he suggested, consisted in the conceptualisation of space in terms of a series of doubles – the double Germanies, the double Vietnams, the double Koreas, the double Berlins, the double Chinas – that were split along the Cold War fault-line itself. Scott Newton, 'Parallel Worlds: Cold War Division Space' in Matthew Craven, Sundhya Pahuja and Gerry Simpson (eds.), *International Law and the Cold War* (Cambridge: Cambridge University Press, 2019).

[6] Newton, 'Parallel Worlds'.

[7] Kissinger notes that the US systematically opposed the old conception of a 'balance of power'. See Henry Kissinger, 'Central Issues of American Foreign Policy' (1969) Office of the Historian, https://history.state.gov/historicaldocuments/frus1969-76v01/d4.

[8] Cf. Louis Henkin et al., 'Force, Intervention, and Neutrality in Contemporary International Law' *ASIL Proc.*, 57 (1963) 150 ('While there are two giants with giant weapons, in political terms international society is hardly "bipolar" today').

In this chapter, we explore three intuitions. First, we suggest that the contrasting images evoked by Churchill – between the lawful world of the Charter and the ideological division of Europe – were not, in their essence, separate or antithetical. Rather they could be understood as part and parcel of the same world-making project. This was a project in which two rival ideological blocs, with the US and the Soviet Union at the centre, each sought to construct a world in its own image. The Charter served as an instrument to that end. But in prioritising the nation-state as the bearer of political authority and as the only available form of decolonisation, it not only provided space for ideological conflict over the terms of its representation (governments) but gave expression to the common values and legal forms that the two hegemons each sought to stabilise and globalise.

Second, and more concretely, we suggest that the Charter of the United Nations itself formalised an Amero-Soviet rivalry, not only by giving expression to common points of departure (the nation-state as central agent for political power, the superintendence of the 'great powers') but also by setting out the means and modalities by which they might compete with one another. This was enabled by a number of 'constructive ambiguities' in the Charter as well as by what may be described as 'constitutive lacunae' (or gaps, silences or deferrals). Such lacunae concerned matters that were central to the scheme of order but that could not be spoken of without fear that the order might subvert itself.[9] It was here, secreted in the dark corners of the Charter, that questions of ideology, representation, governmental control and intervention all lay.

Third, we suggest that the formalisation of the juridico-political rivalry of the Amero-Soviet order was itself prefigured in the Charter. But the Charter evoked a worldly order that was yet to be brought into being, rather than one that was already existent. This meant that the Charter was also vulnerable – and open – to the projection of rival accounts of the world and the meaning and role of international law and the UN Charter within it. Precisely the same resources of ambiguity that facilitated US–Soviet rivalry with the confines of the charter – interpretive overdeterminacy and silence – provided the opportunity for rival visions to

[9] Cf. Althusser, who commended a practice of 'symptomatic reading' as a means of discerning the latent conditions of possibility that inform the production of a text. Louis Althusser and Étienne Balibar, *Reading Capital*, trans. Ben Brewster (London: New Left Books, 1970), chapter 3.

be forged and advanced in the projects of both of anti-colonial and anti-anti-colonial world-making.

2.2 Text

In 1943, the governments of the United States, Great Britain, the Soviet Union and China declared in the Moscow Declaration that they recognised 'the necessity of establishing at the earliest practicable date a general international organization, based on the principle of the sovereign equality of all peace-loving states, and open to membership by all such states, large and small, for the maintenance of international peace and security'.[10] Conceived when the League of Nations was politically defunct,[11] if not juridically 'dead',[12] the Moscow Declaration set the stage for a series of conferences amongst the allied powers in which the post-war global order came to be mapped out. That project was carried forward first at Dumbarton Oaks (21 August 1944), then in Crimea (4 February 1945) and San Francisco (26 June 1945), leading ultimately to the adoption of the UN Charter, which entered into force on 24 October of that same year.[13]

There were two central features of this project. The first was the UN Charter's emphasis on sovereign statehood as the legal form through which political authority would be distributed globally. Whilst the League of Nations had been formally open[14] to 'any fully self-governing State, Dominion or Colony',[15] the UN Charter was much more assertive in its

[10] Moscow Protocol, Moscow, signed 30 October 1943, formalised 1 November 1943, Annex 1, para. 4, 3 Bevans 816, 822.

[11] Molotov, the representative of the Soviet Union, expressed how it 'betrayed the hopes of those who believed in it'. I UNCIO, Doc. 15, 27 April 1945, 132.

[12] The League continued to exist, formally speaking, until April 1946 following work undertaken by the Preparatory Commission established as an 'interim arrangement' in 26 June 1945.

[13] The 'original members' of the United Nations (as defined in article 3 of the Charter) included India (which had yet to acquire independence), Ukraine and Byelorussia (whose membership had been 'negotiated' at Yalta) and Poland, which had been a signatory to the Declaration by United Nations of 1942 but which had not participated in the San Francisco Conference as agreement had not been reached on recognition of a Polish Government. For a discussion, see I UNCIO, Doc. 42, 1 May 1945, 343, 346–47, 350–51.

[14] In practice, many entities such as Armenia, Georgia and Ukraine and the three Baltic States were denied membership on grounds of lack of stability or permanence. James Crawford, *The Creation of States in International Law*, 2nd ed. (Oxford: Oxford University Press, 2006) 176.

[15] Covenant of the League of Nations, Versailles, 28 June 1919, article 1(2), 225 CTS 195.

commitment to sovereign statehood. Apart from the fact that the word 'State' occurs thirty-four times in the text,[16] the United Nations Charter not only limited (new) membership to 'States' but also gave to them the exclusive capacity to bring disputes before UN Organs, to participate in the work of the Security Council and to become a party to the International Court.[17] Even the prohibition on the use of force was cast in terms of preserving the territorial integrity or political independence of 'States'.[18] Certainly, not all of its original members were recognisably independent States at the time. India and the Philippines had yet to acquire formal independence, France continued to claim authority in relation to Lebanon and Syria[19] and the 'independent' status of Ukraine and Byelorussia was very much open to doubt. The Charter nevertheless set a template for future participation in the nascent governing institutions of the world: nothing short of statehood would suffice.

The second principal feature of the United Nations was its aspiration to universality.[20] As the Great Powers had set out in Moscow, the very idea of the United Nations was inextricably linked to a form of institutional world ordering in which they envisaged that the tattered mantle of the League of Nations would be patched and adorned afresh.[21] The

[16] Many have observed this. See, for instance, Rosalyn Higgins, *The Development of International Law through the Political Organs of the United Nations* (Oxford: Oxford University Press, 1963) 25; Crawford, *The Creation of States in International Law*, 174.

[17] See, for a discussion of the historical construction of statehood and sovereignty in relation to empire Priyasha Saksena, *Sovereignty, International Law and the Princely States of South Asia* (Oxford: Oxford University Press, 2023).

[18] Article 2(4) of the Charter of the United Nations, San Francisco, 26 June 1945, in force 24 October 1945, 1 UNTS XVI.

[19] Higgins comments that in case of original members, the criteria for membership had to be regarded as 'sui generis'. She adds, 'to have denied them original membership would have been both undesirable and embarrassing'. Higgins, *The Development of International Law*, 32.

[20] The influential memorandum of US legal scholars, Manley Hudson et al., 'The International Law of the Future: Postulates, Principles and Proposals for the International Law of the Future' *AJIL Supp*, 38 (1944) 41–50, included the proposal that the United Nations should have universal compulsory membership. This was also the position of British scholars such as Lauterpacht and Brierly, see Martti Koskenniemi, *The Gentle Civilizer of Nations: The Rise and Fall of International Law 1870–1960* (Cambridge: Cambridge University Press, 2001) 391.

[21] As Mazower notes, 'despite the attempts to play down the continuities between the League and the United Nations, the UN was, despite its very different attitude to minority rights, "essentially a second League of Nations"'. Mark Mazower, *No Enchanted Palace: The End of Empire and the Ideological Origins of the United Nations* (Princeton: Princeton University Press, 2009) 149.

Powers recognised, in particular, that the greatest failings of the League had been the absence of key States (the US and, until 1934, the Soviet Union) and its inability to preserve peace. These were to be remedied in two ways. First, by centralising authority in the hands of the five permanent members of the Security Council,[22] who were to act by consensus and possess the prerogative to veto any decision and, secondly, by opening membership up to all States but only on condition that they be 'peace-loving' and willing and able to carry out the obligations in the Charter.[23] As Judge Alvarez was to put it a few years later, since the aims of the UN were 'not confined to certain States' but were 'of a world-wide nature', it made perfect sense that membership should be open to all such States as of 'right'.[24]

But the fact that the origins of the UN Charter lay in the wartime collaboration among a select community of Allied powers meant that there was always a certain dissonance between the vaunted pretensions of the organisation as a universal institution[25] and its unrepresentative character.[26] Truman's claim that the States present at San Francisco

[22] This was a modification of Roosevelt's original vision for a post-war council of 'four policemen'. John Lewis Gaddis, *The United States and the Origins of the Cold War, 1941–1947* (New York: Columbia University Press, 1972) 25.

[23] Charter of the United Nations, San Francisco, 26 June 1945, in force 24 October 1945, art. 4(1), 1 UNTS XVI. As Feinberg notes, the very existence of article 4 put in question the apparent aspiration to universality (as did, indeed, the existence of a right to withdraw from membership). Norbert Feinberg, 'L'Admission de Nouveaux Membres à la Société des Nations et à l'Organisation des Nations Unies' *Recueil des Cours* (Hague Academy of International Law), 297 (1955) 301.

[24] Marcelo Alvarez, 'Individual Opinion' in *Conditions of Admission of a State to Membership in the United Nations (Article 4 of the Charter)*, Advisory Opinion, ICJ Reports 1948, 57, 71. In the drafting of the Charter, Uruguay had made the proposal that the UN should be universal by design with an unfettered right of membership. This implied, however, that there would be no right of exit or of expulsion and would limit the opportunity to deny entry to the former Axis powers. Both those proposals were thus rejected.

[25] See, e.g., Ecuador, 1 UNCIO, Doc. 42, P/10, 1 May 1945, 343, 368-EF. Ross observed, 'An organisation such as the UN, whose purposes is to ensure international peace and security, must naturally aim at universality.' See Alf Ross, *Constitution of the United Nations: Analysis of Structure and Function* (New York: Rinehart, 1950) 41. See also Norbert Feinberg, 'L'Admission de Nouveaux Membres à la Société des Nations et à l'Organisation des Nations Unies' *Recueil des Cours* (Hague Academy of International Law), 80 (1955) 313.

[26] Even if the principles of the Charter were widely held to reflect 'the interests of the general community' (Higgins, *The Development of International Law*, 22), there was always an in-built tension between its constitutional pretensions and its form as a multilateral agreement – between, as some would put it, its 'legislative' and 'contractual'

'represent the overwhelming majority of all mankind'[27] was not even a half-truth. Not only were the Axis powers excluded (being the object of various 'enemy states' clauses within the Charter)[28] but so were powers that were neutral during the war (Afghanistan, Ireland, Portugal, Spain, Switzerland, Sweden). Less visible to the Atlantic gaze at the time, but no less significant, were the hundreds of millions of people living under conditions of colonial rule who had no representation other than through the medium of the European metropolitan powers.[29] This extended to those former colonies such as Indonesia and Vietnam that were being actively 're-colonised' in the aftermath of Japan's withdrawal in 1945 and to Korea whose fate was left in the hands of the forces of the occupying powers (the US and the USSR).

It was not the case, though, that the Charter itself was entirely silent on the question of foreign and colonial rule. In addition to the inclusion of a general reference to self-determination as one of the 'purposes' of the UN Charter in article 1(2),[30] Chapter XII of the Charter sought to give new vision and purpose to the 'soon to be defunct' League of Nation's Mandate system (focusing, in particular, on the former colonies of

dimensions (see Ross, *A Constitution of the United Nations*, 30–40; Georges Kaeckenbeek, 'The San-Francisco Charter as It Relates to International Law' *Recueil des Cours*, 70 (1947) 109–330. As a treaty, and indeed as an international organisation, participation in its activities was built upon consent – hence provision was made, not simply for the admission of new member states but also their withdrawal. Expulsion for non-compliance with the rules of the club was also envisaged. At the same time, the authority the UN sought for itself was also preemptory in the sense that member States were under an obligation to secure compliance with its dictates (relating to peace and security) on the part of non-member States and declared the Charter as prevailing over inconsistent treaty obligations. Even in conditions of something less than formal universality, thus, it aspired to a universality of effect.

[27] Documents of the United Nations Conference on International Organization, San Francisco 1945, vol. 1, 113.

[28] See Charter of the United Nations, San Francisco, 26 June 1945, in force 24 October 1945, arts 53, 77, 107, 1 UNTS XVI.

[29] W. E. B. Du Bois wrote about this in *Colour and Democracy: Colonies and Peace* (New York: Harcourt, Brace & Co, 1945) 58, noting: 'In addition to the some seven hundred and fifty millions of disfranchised colonial peoples there are more than a half-billion persons in nations and groups who are quasi-colonials and in no sense form free and independent states.' Thanks to Christopher Gevers for drawing this to our attention.

[30] The origins of this may be traced back to the terms of the Atlantic Charter (14 August 1941) the third principle of which stated that the powers 'respect the right of all peoples to choose the form of government under which they will live'. See Declaration of Principles, known as the Atlantic Charter (signed and entered into force 14 August 1941) 204 LNTS 381.

'enemy states'),[31] and Chapter XI extended the principle of trusteeship to territories euphemistically described as 'non-self-governing'.[32] On this score, the text of the Charter brought together two rival visions for the nascent global order. One vision was an old European vision of 'order through empire'.[33] This was counterpoised against the vision of a new coalition of forces (including both the USSR[34] and the US)[35] who, for different reasons,[36] wanted to unravel the old colonial system in the name of self-determination.[37] In a sense, the principle of self-determination gave expression to a transition of power from old empires to new ones.

The text of the Charter itself was a piece of sustained ambiguity.[38] Non-self-governing territories were accorded some international legibility, and independence movements could draw some hope from the

[31] The original proposal for chapters XI and XII was forwarded by the US at San Francisco. 3 UNCIO (1945) Doc 2, G/14(v) 6 May 1945, 599–600, Doc 2, g/26(c) 5 May 1945, 607–8.

[32] Defined as 'territories whose peoples have not yet attained a full measure of self-government' and described by Ross as an 'absurd', 'illogical' and 'inexact' formulation. Ross, *A Constitution of the United Nations*, 180.

[33] See Mazower, *No Enchanted Palace*. An early conference that was of some influence in the sharpening of a divide between European powers and the US was the Mont Tremblant Conference in Quebec in December 1942. Mont Tremblant Conference on the Problems of Peace in the Post-War World, Mont Tremblant, Quebec, 4–17 December 1942.

[34] The USSR had refused to participate in the League for precisely that reason. See, e.g., 'Questions and Answers: A Discussion with Foreign Delegates' by J. Stalin, Moscow, 13 November 1927. Bill Bowring, *The Degradation of the International Legal Order? The Rehabilitation of Law and the Possibility of Politics* (London: Routledge-Cavendish, 2008).

[35] Hull, for example, had proposed the establishment of an international administrative organ with jurisdiction over all colonies in order to prepare them for independence at the Moscow Conference in 1943. Cordell Hull, *The Memoirs of Cordell Hull*, vol. II (New York: Macmillan, 1948) 1304–5.

[36] The causes were plausibly various: the dismantling of a bourgeois, imperialist order; the assuaging of anti-colonial nationalism; the unravelling of the imperial preference schemes; or, more simply, a humanitarian appeal. On the Wilsonian and Leninist conceptions of self-determination, see Bowring, *The Degradation of the International Legal Order?*

[37] See Ernst Haas, 'The Attempt to Terminate Colonialism: Acceptance of the United Nations Trusteeship System' *International Organization*, 7(1) (1953) 3–4.

[38] Goodwin remarks that 'a verbal compromise was reached. But no real reconciliation was achieved and the subsequent history of the United Nations activity under these chapters largely represents the continuation of the debate at San Francisco'. Geoffrey L Goodwin, *Britain and the United Nations*, Prepared for the Royal Institute of International Affairs and the Carnegie Endowment for International Peace (New York: Manhattan Publishing Company, 1957) 349.

Charter's more general commitment to the principle of self-determination. But article 73 itself remained silent on the question of independence, mentioning only the development of 'self-government' as a possible horizon. The colonial powers, on the other hand, could rely on the Charter's simultaneous references to the principles of territorial integrity and domestic jurisdiction to maintain colonial rule. Britain, France, Belgium and the Netherlands all continued to insist that matters colonial were still essentially within their domestic jurisdiction, even whilst conceding that they may also be matters of international interest or indeed of 'concern'.[39] In contrast to these interpretations, those arguing against colonialism were soon able to mobilise the UN Charter's commitment to the cause of self-determination writ large and argue that the principle should be applied with equal force to the trusteeship arrangements in Chapters XI and XII and to all other territories under alien rule.

And so, on one level, the text of the UN Charter staged a contest between the forces of anti-colonialism, on one hand, and those of an anti-anti-colonialism, on the other. But on another level, it did this by way of universalising the sovereign State itself as both aspiration and unitary legal form and centralising the role of UN membership in that process. So, whilst the idea of the 'non-self-governing territory' had the performative effect of 'lifting the veil of empire' that also meant that the abolition of formal colonial rule could only occur by way of the formation of 'new' States. At the same time, the process of recognition – by which one might mean the formal assessment as to whether a political collective possessed the requisite attributes of statehood – was increasingly subsumed within the decision-making processes of the political organs of the United Nations in their decisions over membership.[40] Decolonisation in other words, to the extent that it was contemplated at all by the authors of the UN Charter, was only to be equated with the achievement of sovereign statehood[41] – and sovereign statehood with membership in the United

[39] See, e.g., Goodwin, *Britain and the United Nations*, 262–63 who argues that the de facto revision of the charter in the anti-colonial cause took the form of a 'regrettable' disrespect for the 'strict law of the Charter'. Ibid., 264.

[40] See, e.g., Higgins, *The Development of International Law*; John Dugard, *Recognition and the United Nations* (Cambridge: Cambridge University Press, 1987). It was always controversial as to whether admission to membership was equivalent to an act of recognition.

[41] Albert Hourani, 'The Decline of the West in the Middle East–II' *International Affairs*, 29 (2) (April 1953) 183: 'If we look into the eyes of the Eastern nationalist, we shall see there

Nations.[42] This also conveniently bypassed theoretical debates about whether recognition was 'declaratory' or 'constitutive'. In the process, both sovereignty and self-determination were not only preconfigured territorially by reference to existing colonial boundaries but institutionally proceduralised in UN political decision-making.

2.3 Membership

Even this was muddied from the outset by the political accommodations that were necessary to secure both the predominance of the United Nations as the political/legal centrepiece of this new world order and its effective universality in the political turmoil of the end of the war. For the United Nations to maintain its authority as the principal institution of the new international order, it became apparent that its membership would have to be expanded from the fifty-one Allied and Associated Powers that constituted its original membership. That was a process liable to intensify as more States obtained independence from colonial rule. Luminaries initially estimated that this might be something in the order of twenty or so extra seats.[43] That prediction was quickly proved to be wrong.

The incipient expansion of membership in the United Nations had clear implications not simply for its claim to be a universal organisation but also for its political and ideological complexion. With it would come changes in the distribution of political authority within the General Assembly and, to a lesser extent, the Security Council. This had already been evident at Yalta where, in response to Stalin's demand that all sixteen Soviet States be given independent membership,[44] Byelorussia

a distorted image of ourselves: we have shaped the form as well as provided the object of his reaction.'

[42] 'In the new nations, statehood and United Nations membership became the hallmarks of independence from colonial rule': Henkin, 'Force, Intervention, and Neutrality in Contemporary International Law', 152.

[43] Oscar Schachter, 'A Conversation with Oscar Schachter' *ASIL Proc.*, 91 (1997) 344.

[44] The claim was made pursuant to the Soviet Autonomy Decree of 1 February 1944 in which each Union Republic was declared competent to establish relations with foreign states. See Ernst Aufricht, 'Principles and Practices of Recognition by International Organizations' *American Journal of International Law*, 43(4) (1949) 679. In defence of the Soviet proposal, it might be noted that in the early years of the twentieth century, Britain had managed to pluralise its empire through the medium of gaining separate recognition and membership in both the League and United Nations for each of its former Dominions (via South Africa, Canada, Australia and New Zealand). In case of the

and Ukraine were invited to participate as 'original members' notwithstanding doubts as to their independence from the USSR.[45] It was to become a matter of increasing importance in subsequent years, as UN agencies started to involve themselves in the various crises that marked the early years of the Cold War.[46] But in the ensuing battles over the composition of the United Nations – where the overt formalities of statehood, recognition and 'willingness' to comply with the obligations of membership were overwritten by a combative 'vetting' of prospective members by reference to their political leanings[47] – an ideological supplement appeared to overwhelm all else.[48] Just as the US sought to encourage the admission of States politically beholden to it, so too did the Soviet Union seek to water down the influence exercised by the US and its allies over the General Assembly.

Formally speaking, the UN Charter spoke only of the requirements that aspirant members be 'states', 'peace-loving' and willing and able to fulfil the obligations in the Charter. This left considerable discretion in the hands of those determining applications for membership. Most of those involved implicitly assumed that the formalities of statehood per se did not require the adoption of any particular form of government. But it

League, this was somewhat in advance of the Statute of Westminster of 1931, in which formal powers were devolved to the Dominions by the Westminster government.

45 This was part of a 'deal' in which a number of 'associated' states were also invited to participate (which included six Latin American states, Egypt, Iceland and the Provisional French Government). 1 UNCIO, Doc. 1210, P/20, 27 June 1945, 612, 613, Ruth Russell and Jeannette Muther, *A History of the United Nations Charter* (Washington, DC: Brookings Institution, 1958) 508.

46 The broadening of the powers of the General Assembly under the terms of the Uniting for Peace resolution of 1950 was, if nothing else, to draw vital attention to the question of its political composition. UNGA Res 377(V) A, *Uniting for Peace* (3 November 1950), UN Doc. A/RES/377(V).

47 This was first to arise in relation to Albania, Mongolia, Transjordan, Ireland and Portugal, and then in 1947 in relation to Hungary, Italy, Romania, Bulgaria, Austria and Finland. Statement by M. Kerno (United Nations), *Conditions for the Admission of a State as Member of the United Nations (Article 4 of the Charter)*, Oral Proceedings, ICJ Reports (1948) 48. In 1948, the application of Ceylon was barred as were those of the Republic of Korea and Nepal in 1949.

48 Higgins decried the general habit of construing UN membership questions as determined by 'politics'. They were, in her view, better understood as disputes over the interpretation of the legal principles in the Charter itself. Higgins, *The Development of International Law*, 23–24. Alvarez, in his separate opinion, was to argue that 'the constitutional Charter cannot be interpreted according to a strictly legal criterion; another and broader criterion must be employed and room left, if need be, for political considerations'. Álvarez, 'Individual Opinion', 70.

was also recognised that former fascist States and their allies against whom the 'United Nations' had recently fought would be excluded from membership until they could demonstrate that they had abandoned nationalist-fascist ideologies.[49] The terms of the post-war occupation of Germany, for example, made it clear that its return to the global stage as an independent political entity would be contingent upon radical social, economic and political change, including, in particular, an active process of de-nazification.[50] The inclusion of 'enemy states' clauses within the Charter (articles 53(2) and 107) sanctified the measures taken by the Four Powers within Germany to that end.

The Charter itself designated as 'enemy states' all those that 'during World War II' had 'been an enemy of any signatory of the present Charter' – and clearly referred, in that sense, to Germany, Italy, Japan, Bulgaria, Romania, Hungary and Finland.[51] But it became clear from the time of the dispute over Argentina's participation in the San Francisco conference[52] that the list of 'suspect States' was somewhat longer. Indeed Spain, which had remained neutral throughout the war, had been denounced at Potsdam[53] and became the object of criticism in early

[49] See Gerry Simpson, *The Sentimental Life of International Law* (Oxford: Oxford University Press, 2021) 153–56.

[50] Early proposals floated in the United States, which initially had broad support, were for the 'pasturalisation' of Germany. See, e.g., Memorandum from Henry Morgenthau Jr., 'Suggested Post-Surrender Program for Germany', 1944; Morgenthau Jr, *Germany Is Our Problem* (New York: Harper & Brothers, 1945). See also Samuel Wells, *The Time for Decision* (New York: Harper & Brothers, 1944). See generally, Philip Moseley, 'Dismemberment of Germany: The Allied Negotiations from Yalta to Potsdam' *Foreign Affairs*, 28 (1950) 487–98; Warren Kimball, *Sword or Ploughshares? The Morgenthau Plan for Defeated Nazi Germany* (Philadelphia: J. B. Lippincott, 1976); Frank King, 'Allied Negotiations and the Dismemberment of Germany' *Journal of Contemporary History*, 16 (1981) 585–95. These were watered down at Potsdam where it was made clear that Germany would be subjected to five 'D's': disarmament, demilitarisation, de-Nazification, democratisation and de-centralisation. Potsdam Agreement, Potsdam, 2 August 1945.

[51] Thailand had also declared war of the UK but subsequently argued that its declaration was 'null and void'. See Nicholas Tarling, 'Atonement before Absolution: British Policy Towards Thailand during World War II' *Journal of the Siam Society*, 66(1) (1978) 22–65.

[52] See I UNCIO, Doc. 42, 1 May 1945, P/10, pp. 343–58. Further, Thomas Grant, *Admission to the United Nations: Charter Article 4 and the Rise of Universal Organization* (Leiden: Martinus Nijhoff, 2009) 25–27.

[53] At Potsdam, the allied powers included the following statement: 'The three governments, however, feel compelled to declare that they will not support any request for accession (in the UN) to the present Spanish Government, which, having been established with the support of the Axis powers, has, by reason of its origins, its nature, its history and its close association with the aggressor countries, the qualities necessary to justify that entry.' Potsdam Agreement, Potsdam, 2 August 1945.

sessions of both the General Assembly and Security Council.[54] As far as the General Assembly was concerned, since the Franco government had been 'imposed by force upon the Spanish people' and had given 'material assistance to the Axis Powers in the war', it should be barred from participating in the activities of the United Nations pending a change in government.[55]

But the assumption that there might be a direct link between the internal form, or political organisation, of the State (i.e. its government) and its claim to be either peace-loving or willing and able to fulfil the obligations of the Charter, lent the terms of article 4 itself a very complex texture.[56] What the authors of the Charter had contemplated was not so much the evaluation of States as States per se (i.e. in terms of governmental effectiveness and/or independence) but whether they were 'pathologically' incapable of becoming members by virtue of the intrinsically aggressive or undemocratic nature of their governments. But aside from the obvious example of fascist States and their sympathisers, the real challenge was to prevent this from opening up admissions decisions to ideological competition more broadly.

During the drafting of article 4 of the Charter, Committee I/2 had debated whether the UN should take account of the nature of the political institutions of an applicant State in determining admission. Despite the submission of several proposals to do so (for example, by Haiti to introduce a condition prohibiting the practice of racial or religious discrimination[57] and by the Netherlands to ensure that States properly serve the will of the people),[58] the Committee concluded that, whilst there may well be grounds for considering such matters in admissions decisions, there was also a danger that in spelling those out, the UN would risk undermining

[54] See generally, Higgins, *The Development of International Law*, 138–41.

[55] UNGA Res 39 (I) (11 December 1946).

[56] Charter of the United Nations, San Francisco, 26 June 1945, in force 24 October 1945, 1 UNTS XVI, art. 4: 1. 'Membership in the United Nations is open to all other peace-loving states which accept the obligations contained in the present Charter and, in the judgment of the Organization, are able and willing to carry out these obligations. 2. The admission of any such state to membership in the United Nations will be effected by a decision of the General Assembly upon the recommendation of the Security Council.'

[57] III UNCIO, Doc. 2, G/7(b)(1), 5 May 1945, p. 52. Cf. Japan in League of Nations, Naoko Shimazu, *Japan, Race, and Equality: The Racial Equality Proposal of 1919* (Abingdon: Routledge, 1998); Marilyn Lake and Henry Reynolds, *Drawing the Global Colour Line* (Cambridge University Press, 2012) chapter 12.

[58] VII UNCIO, Doc. 202, 10 May 1945, 18.

the fundamental principle of 'non-intervention'.[59] As the delegate from Uruguay succinctly put it, whilst democracy might widely be represented as 'the firmest and highest guarantee of the peaceful existence of peoples', to bring it into consideration in decisions over admission might nevertheless 'drift into an indirect form of intervention of certain peoples with the affairs of others'.[60]

As we shall see, the Uruguayan anxiety about intervention was to have much broader significance in later years.[61] Its immediate effect for now was to produce within article 4 a silent equivocation on the subject. Article 4 of the Charter contained no reference to 'democracy', no reference either to legitimate or illegitimate forms of government and indeed was entirely silent on the internal political conditions that were to inform decisions as to whether a State was suitable for admission. Nevertheless, the Committee deliberations also make clear that 'in passing on the admission of a new member, *considerations of all kinds*' (emphasis added) might be brought into account in order to determine whether the 'character and policies of governments' were acceptable for purposes of admission.[62] These were matters of political determination, it was said, best left to the relevant organs of the United Nations.

The apparent silence of article 4 on the question of the internal political organisation of applicant States gave rise to two radically divergent interpretations about whether it was legitimate to take account of the political or ideological profile of the State seeking membership. The first interpretation was that the 'composition' of a State (i.e. the political orientation of its government) was a matter of domestic jurisdiction: neither the UN nor individual States had any valid reason to interfere in the choices made by domestic constituencies as to who should govern them or represent them internationally.[63] Any such measure would be an

59 VII UNCIO, Doc. 1178, 24 June 1945, 324, 317.

60 As a consequence, it recommended that 'the world organization ought not to require of its members, before their respective admission, a specific form of government, but should [rather] require of them ... real respect for the liberties essential and inherent in the human person'. III UNCIO, Doc. 2, 28 Sept. 1944, 26.

61 See Section 2.6.

62 Report of the Rapporteur of Committee I/2 on Chapter III (Membership), VII UNCIO, Doc. 1178, 24 July 1945, 326.

63 A later, and somewhat controversial, statement of this principle was articulated by Friedmann in 1965. He was to assert that 'Contemporary international society is built upon a foundation of legally sovereign states which are entitled to the same degree of respect and recognition. This means the rejection of any differentiation according to their ideology, be it Communism, Fascism, imperialism, capitalism or social democracy.'

impermissible form of intervention. This subsequently became a rallying cry for States emerging from colonial rule in the 1950s. The second interpretation was that the organisation could take the political composition of States into account, particularly for the purposes of deciding whether admission would be congenial to the preservation of international peace and security. This interpretation seemed to prevail in practice in the early years of the UN at least and hinged on the terminology of the 'peaceloving state'.[64]

And so, in a way, article 4 seemed to repress the element that both divided and united the rival Cold War powers. Rather than being neutral to the political complexion of the States seeking membership, the rival powers were *intensely* interested in that question, almost to the exclusion of all others. This played out in three interlinked ways. In the first place, as we have just shown, there were debates about the character of aspirant member States. Were they "peace-loving" (in universalist Charter terms) and were they socialist or capitalist (in sectarian terms), and to what extent was the former a substantive question and the latter a permissible one? We return to this shortly in our discussion of the ICJ's attempt to adjudicate these matters. In the second place, though, all of this was folded into a larger question about the very nature of what it meant for something to be either of international concern or a matter of domestic jurisdiction – the character of a State was evidently caught between those two spaces. Finally, there was the question of the relationship between government and State. As we will see later in this chapter and throughout the book, the character – indeed, even the effectiveness – of the State ceased to matter when it came to recognition and admission. Instead, ideological competition came to focus itself upon the question of governmental representation, or 'internal self-determination', as governments were undermined, deposed in coups, coerced and proxified as part of Amero-Soviet conflict.

So, to elaborate on the second point, throughout the ensuing decades we can track a form of disputation that consistently concerned itself with either 'internationalising' the domestic or 'domesticating' the international. This was reflected in the emergent practices of subversive

Wolfgang Friedmann, 'Intervention, Civil War and the Role of International Law' *ASIL Proc.*, 59 (1965) 67.

64 It is arguable that the very inclusion of this term was to demand the bridging of the divide between state and government. After all, states per se are neither peaceloving nor warmongering.

intervention, in the dispute over China's representation within the UN and in the emergent rules of human rights and humanitarian law, to name a few. Indeed, all of the legal sites that gave expression to the inside–outside division between government and State (internal/international, political/legal, credentials/membership, order/sovereignty) were to become central points of contestation between the rival Cold War powers. The rival powers shared a common vision of building a global order of sovereign democratic States, as well as a commitment to the language of self-determination, but visibly differed in their conception of what 'self-determination', or democracy or self-rule might mean and how they might be bought into being.[65] Indeed, these ideas were to become the rubric under which the Cold War powers were to export their mutual rivalry across the globe. As we shall see, the Third World's own engagement with the recurring question of what should be considered international and what should be considered domestic criss-crossed with the lines of Amero-Soviet disputation.

2.4 Breaking the Log-Jam: From East–West to North–South

This was not to say that the Cold War rivals refused to admit the existence of an institutional architecture in which both liberal democratic and socialist States participated on an equal basis. Indeed, that was the premise of the early 'deals' over the participation of Ukraine and Belarus amongst others and the premise also of the subsequent Soviet embrace of 'peaceful coexistence'.[66] But there were more than sufficient resources in the language of article 4 to allow political preference to determine voting patterns over membership. So it was equally plausible for the US to object to the admission of the GDR on the grounds that the international character of the communist party organisation was such as to undercut

[65] As Jessup was to argue 'We resent and oppose any attempt by the Soviet Union to impose their concept of democracy upon us or to instil it into our midst by undercover propaganda. We cannot deny their right to resent and oppose any attempt of ours to impose or instil our concept of democracy upon them .... The international problem is not one of securing throughout the world an ideological uniformity which has never existed.' Philip C Jessup, *The International Problem in Governing Mankind* (Claremont: Claremont College, 1947) 38. John Grosboll, 'Philip Jessup, *The International Problem of Governing Mankind*' *Michigan Law Review*, 46(1) (1947) 38.

[66] See Chapter 3.

claims to the GDR's political independence,[67] as it was, for example, for the Soviet Union to object that the South Korean government was merely a 'puppet' conspiratorially implanted through the joint activities of the US and the UN.[68] At least in the early years of the UN, article 4 provided a stage upon which rival hegemonic ambitions could be publicly performed.

The divisions between the two blocs on the question of membership opened out in 1947 in response to a Polish proposal to consider the applications for membership of Hungary, Bulgaria, Romania, Finland and Italy on a collective basis.[69] The US and its Western allies opposed such a procedure: 'horse-trading', it was said, had no place in the Charter. Whilst they supported the application of Italy and Finland, they could not support those of Hungary, Romania or Bulgaria on the grounds that their governments were insufficiently democratic and had violated human rights provisions in the respective treaties of peace. In the face of the deadlock, the (Western-dominated) General Assembly ultimately referred the matter to the ICJ.[70] It did this in a somewhat vain attempt to draw a line between what the West was arguing to be the 'legal' considerations relevant to the membership question and the 'illegitimate' or 'political' character of the Soviet States' approach.

The Court's response was simply to re-state the problem that had been directed to it. In returning a verdict to the effect that no 'additional' conditions could be placed upon membership other than those set out in article 4(1) of the UN Charter, and that no political bartering should take place,[71] it nevertheless admitted that its advice extended only to the point of constraining what reasons a State may give for its vote. The General

[67] See, e.g., discussion in Office of the Historian (US), 'Telegram From the Department of State to the Embassy in the German Democratic Republic' (Washington, DC, 22 January 1979, 1638Z), Foreign Relations of the United States, 1977–1980, vol. XX, Eastern Europe, Doc. 124.

[68] See description of Soviet archives in the otherwise particular account of Kathryn Weathersby, 'Soviet Aims in Korea and the Origins of the Korean War: New Evidence from Russian Archives' (Woodrow Wilson International Centre for Scholars Working Papers, 1993), 29.

[69] 2 UN SCOR, PV 204–6 (1947), 2407–80. In each of these cases, the admission question arose in the aftermath of the conclusion of a treaty of peace with each of these countries, the preambles of which affirmed that the Allied and Associated Powers would 'support' their application for membership in the United Nations. As far as the US and UK were concerned, this did not constitute a binding obligation on them to admit those States to membership.

[70] General Assembly Resolution 197 A (III), 3 December 1948.

[71] ICJ Reports [1948] 57, 65; General Assembly Resolution 197 A (III), 3 December 1948.

Assembly, it said, 'can hardly be supposed to have intended to ask the Court's opinion as to the reasons which, in the mind of a Member, may prompt its vote. Such reasons, which enter into a mental process, are obviously subject to no control'.[72] As much, then, as the Court was to insist upon the exhaustive and exclusive character of the criteria set out in article 4 as the basis of decision, it was equally clear that such an admonition by the Court could neither set out how States might decide, for example, whether an applicant is 'peaceloving',[73] nor could it prevent States from vetting applicant States by reference to their ideological credentials.

From that point onwards, however, the debate took on a largely formal cast. The US opposed the admission of Albania, Bulgaria, Hungary, Outer Mongolia and Romania on grounds that none was fully independent.[74] The Soviet Union opposed membership of Jordan, Ireland, Portugal, Italy, Austria, and Finland[75] on the grounds, inter alia, that it did not have diplomatic relations with them (Jordan, Ireland, Portugal) or that they could not be described as 'peace-loving' (Italy, Austria). Each sought to locate their objections in either the substantive conditions of article 4 (that the entity concerned be a 'state' and 'peace-loving') or in the process by which those conditions were to be determined (that admission was dependent upon the recommendation of the Security Council). In all cases, though, it was evident that the overt disagreement about the formalities required under the UN Charter for purpose of determining the admission of new States veiled a deeper contest over the composition of the UN General Assembly and the extent to which one or other bloc might be able to hold effective sway.[76] As the Soviet

[72] ICJ Reports [1948] 57, 60.

[73] As the dissenting judges (Basdevant, Winiarski, McNair and Read) were to point out, in making a distinction between the actual vote and the discussion preceding it, the Court was led into a position of giving states a discretion 'to base its vote upon a certain consideration' whilst forbidding it 'to invoke that consideration in discussion preceding the vote'. *Advisory Opinion on Conditions of Admission of a State to the United Nations*, ICJ Reports [1948] 57, 83 (dissenting opinion).

[74] UN Doc. A/AC.80/P.V.31 (7 December 1955) 52.

[75] It was later to oppose the membership of Ceylon, Republic of Korea, Nepal, Vietnam, Japan, Cambodia and Laos. See generally, Position Paper Prepared for the Geneva Summit Conference, 18–23 July 1955, Foreign Relations of the United States, 1955–57, United Nations and General Matters, Vol XI, Doc. 112.

[76] See Georg Schwarzenberger, 'The Impact of the East–West Rift on International Law' *Transactions of the Grotius Society*, 36 (1950), 229–69; Ross, *Constitution of the United Nations*, 46–47.

member in the General Assembly candidly pointed out, the real underlying question was not simply one of 'interpreting Article 4 of the Charter' but of 'interpreting the political and social nature of the States whose applications for membership' were under consideration.[77]

And so, despite the initial aspirations to open up membership of the UN to the world, by the early 1950s it effectively remained a 'closed society'[78] that was internally divided by reference to the spatial and ideological demarcations of 'East' and 'West'. Indeed, between 1946 and 1955, only five States at the 'borderline of the world frontier', as Schwarzenberger was to put it,[79] obtained membership in the UN (Pakistan, Yemen, Burma, Israel and Indonesia). All other aspirant members remained locked out. The deadlock was finally broken by a momentary détente in 1955 when the US and USSR agreed, despite the ICJ's cautions against it, to a package deal leading to the admission of sixteen new members (Albania, Austria, Bulgaria, Cambodia, Finland, Hungary, Ireland, Italy, Jordan, Laos, Libya, Nepal, Portugal, Romania, Spain, Sri Lanka).[80] From that moment on, the prospect of either a Western or Soviet majority in UN organs slowly dissipated, and with it, the sense that the composition of the UN would, or could, be predominantly configured around the Cold War ideological dissensus. Increasingly, a third force would begin to assert itself within the UN, a force whose agenda was as much dictated by an outright refusal of 'bipolarism' as by a determination to steer a 'middle course'.[81] This was propelled in large part by the juridical activity in the tailwind of the conferences in Bandung in 1955 and Belgrade in 1961 and the emergence of the non-aligned movement.[82]

The accommodation that resulted in the 'log-jam' being unblocked in 1955 was achieved neither by a move from politics into law nor by way of

[77] UN Doc. A/PV.117, 153–55. This was to rehearse the minority view of the ICJ in the first admissions case in which it was held that a member in voting for the admission of a State 'is participating in a political decision and is therefore legally entitled to make its consent to the admission dependent on any political considerations which seem to it to be relevant' and that it was therefore entitled to decide that the admission of one State should be made conditional upon the simultaneous admission of another.

[78] Schwarzenberger, 'The Impact of the East–West Rift on International Law', 235.

[79] Ibid., 234.

[80] UNGA Res 995(X) (14 December 1955), *Official Records of the General Assembly*, 10th Sess, Supp No 19.

[81] See Mohamed Bedjaoui, 'Non-alignement et droit international' *Recueil des cours*, 151 (1976) 337, 349.

[82] See later chapters.

a suspension of ideological difference in favour of an attentiveness to the formalities of article 4 as the ICJ had dictated. If anything, it was the opposite. Growing numbers of States were gaining independence outside the UN fold. The spectre of rival organisations being established in the non-aligned world, which might marginalise the authority of the UN, was never far in the background.[83] In the end, the most powerful States (and those who held a veto at the UN), who each had sought to assert political control in the face of these changes, made a tacit deal to suspend a substantive assessment of the legal conditions and simply expand the membership of the UN.

Once the log-jam was unblocked, there was little appetite for a return to the old battleground. From that point on, as Grant notes, '[it] scarcely was asked again whether an applicant for admission was peace-loving; whether it had pledged to fulfil the obligations set out in the Charter; or whether it had the ability or willingness to fulfil them.'[84] In dispensing with the substantive terms of article 4, UN organs retreated to the somewhat narrower question as to whether the aspirant member was, or was not, a 'state'. Whilst this did not preclude ongoing arguments between East and West (e.g. in relation to China or the two Germanies, Vietnams and Koreas), the composition of the General Assembly began to slip out of the controlling hands of the Western powers, leading to a shift in the geopolitical orientation of political rivalry to that between North and South.

Indeed, from the time of the adoption of the Declaration on the Granting of Independence to Colonial Countries and Peoples (the 'Colonial Charter') in 1960[85] onwards, the key battleground was to become the principle of self-determination and rival conceptions over what 'self-rule' might imply, both in terms of membership and in terms of the rules that governed processes of national liberation.[86] But even though membership became increasingly automatic for those territories

[83] See, e.g., Trygve Lie, *In the Cause of Peace: Seven Years with the United Nations* (London: Macmillan, 1954) 252–73.

[84] Thomas Grant, *Admission to the United Nations: Charter Article 4 and the Rise of Universal Organization* (Leiden: Martinus Nijhoff, 2009) 145.

[85] UNGA Res 1514 (XV) (14 December 1960).

[86] See James Crawford, 'The Right of Self-Determination in International Law: Its Development and Future' in Philip Alston (ed.), *Peoples' Rights* (Oxford: Oxford University Press, 2001) 7–67; and in a different sense, John H Jackson, 'Sovereignty-Modern: A New Approach to an Outdated Concept' *American Journal of International Law*, 97(4) (2003) 782; Gerard Kreijen, *State Failure, Sovereignty and Effectiveness: Legal Lessons from the Decolonization of Sub-Saharan Africa* (Leiden: Martinus Nijhoff, 2004).

extracting themselves from colonial rule, this did not supplant or dispel Cold War ideological disputation. Instead, it shifted the terrain of battle away from the question of statehood or membership towards the more fundamental question of who might enjoy the right to govern and represent the State internationally. Was this a matter of domestic jurisdiction or one in which the wider interests of the international community were involved?

2.5 Which Government? The Problem of Representation and the Two Chinas

As we have seen, the terms of article 4 of the UN Charter appeared to sublimate a dispute over the preferred ideological orientation of governments into a debate over the formal meaning of the phrase 'sovereign statehood'. But there were also moments in which such disagreement arose quite independently of the issue of membership itself. After the Soviet intervention in Hungary in 1956, for example, Western States refused to accept the credentials offered by the Kadar government[87] on the grounds that it was a regime that had been 'imposed on the Hungarian people by the armed intervention of the Union of Soviet Socialist Republics'.[88] But in doing so, the sponsors refrained from demanding that the General Assembly take the matter any further, and the Hungarian government was able to continue to occupy the seat in the United Nations despite rejection of its credentials.[89] Indeed, it even participated in the General Assembly deliberations over its own credentials.[90]

87 UN Doc. A/3536 (1957), 11 UNGAOR, Annexes, A.I.3, 1. This position was continued until 1963. It is clear, however, that the US mission in the UN was sceptical as to the approach adopted by the US administration: 'Rejecting credentials in GA is at best ... questionable from a legal as well as a political standpoint. No one seriously questions that Hungarian credentials are technically and legally in order, and this is only ground on which, under present practice, UN considers question of credentials.' Telegram from the Mission at the United Nations to the Department of State, 10 February 1959, in *Foreign Relations of the United States, 1958–1960*, vol. II (Washington, DC: United States Government Printing Office, 1992).

88 UNGA Res 1133 (XI) (14 September 1957).

89 Article 29, Rules of Procedure of the United Nations General Assembly, UN Doc. A/520/Rev.17. Legal Council, 'Scope of "credentials" in rule 27 of the rules of procedure of the General Assembly' UN Doc. A/8160, 11 November 1970, 25 UN GAOR, Annexes A.i.3, p. 3.

90 See Report of the Special Committee on the Problem of Hungary, UN Doc. A_3592_EN, 1957.

Although the US had sponsored the adoption of the credential committee's recommendation in the Hungarian case, it was reluctant to take matters further because of two concerns. In the first place, no enforcement action had been taken against Hungary, no evidence had been adduced as to it persistently violating the terms of the Charter, and no recommendation had been made to that effect by the Security Council. So, in terms of legal process, to have insisted (as would later occur in case of South Africa)[91] on excluding the Hungarian representatives from participation in the UN would have been tantamount to suspending or expelling the State itself from the organisation outside the procedures elaborated in articles 5 and 6 of the Charter.[92]

A second, and more pressing reason, was that making an argument about the lack of representativeness on the part of the Hungarian government would have exposed the US to the charge of hypocrisy given its position in relation to China. This, by all accounts, was the more important issue because of China's privileged role in the Security Council. As in the case of Hungary, this also concerned the capacity of a government to represent the State, but unlike Hungary, this was a case in which there were two rival governments each claiming an identical right – the right to represent the State of China as a permanent member of the Security Council, enjoying, in the same measure, a right of veto. It was here that the issue of representation emerged most vividly, illustrating how Amero-Soviet ideological contestation operated in the interstices of Charter provisions.

At wartime meetings in Moscow and Tehran, the US had originally procured for China not only original membership in the UN but a permanent seat in the Security Council together with a power of veto.[93] Despite the protestations of Chou En-lai at the time of the San Francisco Conference,[94] the seat was initially occupied by the nationalist government of Chiang Kai-shek, leader of the Kuomintang. In 1949, after the communists defeated the Kuomintang on the mainland, the newly

[91] See Farrokh Jhabvala, 'The Credentials Approach to Representation Questions in the U.N.' *California Western International Law Journal*, 7(3) (1977) 615; Dan Ciobanu, 'Credentials of Delegations and Representation of Member States at the United Nations' *International and Comparative Law Quarterly*, 25 (1976) 351–81.

[92] UN Doc. A/8160 (1970), 25 UN GAOR, Annexes, A.I.3, 3.

[93] See generally, Evan Luard, *History of the United Nations: Vol 1, The Years of Western Domination, 1945–1955* (New York: St Martin's Press, 1982) chapter 2.

[94] Victor Docauer, 'Communist Chinese Attitudes toward United Nations Membership 1945–1971: An Essay' *Iustitia*, 2(2) (1974) 17–18.

established People's Republic of China (PRC) immediately requested that the UN deprive the Nationalist delegation 'of all rights to further represent the Chinese people in the United Nations'.[95] This was followed by an unsuccessful request by the Soviet Union to the Security Council 'not to recognize the credentials' of the representative of nationalist China 'and to exclude him from the Security Council'.[96] On being rebuffed, the Soviet delegate walked out of the Security Council[97] and initiated a seven-month boycott of UN organs. As it happens, this paved the way for the Security Council to avoid the possibility of a Soviet veto in its response to the Korean crisis. This in turn led to a war in which UN-authorised forces came into conflict with the forces of what was to become a permanent member of the Security Council (i.e. the PRC).

In the ensuing two decades, the campaign to change the representation of China at the UN proceeded unabated.[98] The Soviet States were joined by a shifting group of non-aligned States (Yugoslavia, India) in the search for change, whilst the US and the Chinese nationalist government were able to count on the, sometimes equivocal, support of a good number of States within the Western camp.[99] Various strategies were used by States opposed to the Chinese nationalist presence in the UN to dislodge the incumbent. India sought a General Assembly resolution affirming that Communist China be entitled to represent the Republic of China,[100] the Soviet Union sought to 'expel' the Nationalist Chinese delegation from both the Security Council and General Assembly[101] and the PRC itself submitted a complaint to the Security Council charging the United States with having invaded Taiwan.[102] Various strategies were also used to resist change – from demands that the PRC apply for membership in its own

[95] UN Doc. A/1123, GAOR (18 December 949).

[96] UN Doc. S/PV.458, VI SCOR, 458th mtg (13 January 1950).

[97] It followed a similar path in the Atomic Energy Commission, ECOSOC, UNICEF and the Trusteeship Council. Yearbook of United Nations (1950) 74–75, 415, 968. The PRC, for its part, seized the US diplomatic compounds in Peking and recognised the Ho Chi-Minh regime in Indochina in response. See Byron Weng, 'Communist China's Changing Attitudes towards the United Nations' *International Organisation*, 20(4) (1966) 680.

[98] *Yearbook of the United Nations* 1950, 968.

[99] On this question, divisions were to emerge between the US and the UK, the latter supporting the PRC's claim to represent China. It is notable that neither the PRC nor the ROC were invited to participate in the drafting of the treaty of peace with Japan in 1951 (the Treaty of San Francisco) as a consequence of that difference of opinion. The Soviet Union also denounced the treaty in part as a consequence of the absence of the PRC.

[100] UN Doc. A/1365, V GAOR (1950).

[101] UN Docs. A/1369 and A/1370, V GAOR (1950).

[102] UN Doc. S/1715, V SCOR (1950).

right, to the assertion that the question of Chinese representation was an 'important question' thus requiring a two-thirds vote in the General Assembly.[103]

The central legal difficulty on both sides was the 'intermediate' character of the question of representation. Most States agreed that the question of representation was categorically distinct from that of membership. Neither the supporters of the PRC nor those defending the right of occupancy on the part of the nationalist government questioned membership for a 'Chinese state' in the United Nations.[104] Certainly it was occasionally suggested that Chinese membership might be pluralised (the 'two Chinas' option)[105] but this still left up in the air the question as to which of them would assume the existing seat, and the prerogatives associated with it, in the Security Council and General Assembly. To demand, for example, that the PRC seek membership as a new State[106] ignored the simple fact that it controlled the entirety of mainland China and was not, in any case, prepared to cede the territory of Taiwan to another State. To demand, conversely, that the nationalist government renounce its seat would problematically have required its withdrawal or expulsion from the organisation.[107]

Whilst it could not be dealt with as a membership issue, the question of Chinese representation didn't appear to be a matter of credentials either. Although the General Assembly and the Security Council each had their own credentials committees, their respective rules of procedure made it clear that the role of such committees largely concerned the examination of the authenticity of the documents submitted to them, the

[103] UNSC Res 1668 XVI (15 December 15, 1961). Jerome Ahn Cohen, 'Chinese Participation in the United Nations: Changing Realities and the Imperatives of New Policy' *ASIL Proc.*, 65(4) (1971) 1–8.

[104] McDougal and Goodman presented this as one of three 'schools' of juridical analysis. Myres McDougal and Richard Goodman, 'Chinese Participation in the United Nations: The Legal Imperatives of a Negotiated Solution' *American Journal of International Law*, 60 (1966) 672–74. Rather than a school, it is probably better described as a juridical drift caused by the absence of standards or procedures governing the question of representation.

[105] On this, see Higgins, *The Development of International Law*, 266–67. For Chinese reaction see Hungdah Chiu and R. R. Edwards, 'Communist China's Attitude toward the United Nations: A Legal Analysis', *American Journal of International Law*, 62(1) (1968) 35.

[106] McDougal and Goodman, 'Chinese Participation in the United Nations', 673.

[107] See Charter of the United Nations (adopted 26 June 1945, entered into force 24 October 1945) 1 UNTS XVI, arts 4–5.

identity of delegates and the scope of powers conferred upon them.[108] Rule 27 of the General Assembly's rules of procedure, for example, merely states that credentials and names of delegates should be submitted to the Secretary-General not less than one week before the opening of session and that they be issued by either the 'Head of State or Government or by the Minister of Foreign Affairs'. In case of objection, a representative would be seated provisionally with the same rights as other representatives until the credentials committee had reported and the General Assembly had given its decision.[109] Absent any change made to the rules of procedure, there appeared to be little formal scope for enquiring as to whether the Head of State, for example, was the head of a government legitimately representing the State.[110]

If the issue of representation could be reduced neither to a question of membership nor one of credentials,[111] it was, nevertheless, a question that sat at the hinge-point of both. Just as State membership depended upon the existence of a government possessing effective control over the territory in question, so too credentials were to be issued by the relevant government of the State. But there was nothing in the Charter – no procedure, no committee, no substantive test – for determining that issue when there were two or more governments claiming to represent the same State.[112]

The real difficulty was the fact that the normal processes by which a government's claim might be assessed *inter se* were unavailable within the confines of the organisation. Outside the context of membership, States retained an almost unfettered discretion as to whether they would 'recognise' the government of another State, certainly as to whether to dispatch diplomatic representatives, establish embassies or enter into agreements with them.[113] They were also free to decide whether to

[108] Rules of Procedure of the General Assembly, UN Doc. A/520/Rev.19 (1984), r 27; Rules of Procedure of the Security Council, UN Doc. S/96/Rev.7 (1982), r 13.

[109] Rules of Procedure of the General Assembly, UN Doc. A/520/Rev.19 (1985), r 29; Rules of Procedure of the Security Council, UN Doc. S/96/Rev.7 (1983), r 16.

[110] This was not to stop the General Assembly or its Credentials Committee from doing precisely that, e.g., in relation to the Congo, Yemen and South Africa. See Ciobanu, 'Credentials of Delegations and Representation of Member States at the United Nations'.

[111] See, e.g., Herbert Briggs, 'Chinese Representation in the United Nations' *International Organization*, 6 (1952) 193–95.

[112] See Letter from India, UN Doc. S/1447 (1950) 2, 5 UN SCOR, Supp January–May 1950.

[113] See generally, Hersch Lauterpacht, *Recognition in International Law* (Cambridge: Cambridge University Press, 1947); Higgins, *The Development of International Law.*

accord such governments de jure, or merely de facto, recognition.[114] Needless to say, such freedom of action was not obviously available in the institutional context of membership where such matters were determined collectively and in which the terrain of institutional politics necessarily involved at least acknowledging the capacity of other governments to act competently within the institution.[115] This was particularly evident in the case of a government occupying the seat of a permanent member of the Security Council.

This was not, however, to prevent the question of recognition from entering into the debate over representation. The Soviet Union initially insisted that the exclusion of the 'Kuomintang group' from the Security Council had nothing to do with the recognition, or otherwise, of the Communist government.[116] On the other hand, the US and its allies insisted, in the early stages at least, that recognition counted, and literally so, for purposes of representation.[117] Whilst some States, such as India, Yugoslavia and the UK, had joined the Soviet bloc in recognising the new communist regime in China, the pattern of recognition at that time still largely favoured the former nationalist government, and for that reason it retained the primary rights of representation in the United Nations.[118]

A UN Secretariat memorandum of 1950[119] attempted to dispel this line of argument, asserting that representation and recognition were separate questions. It reasoned that decisions in the UN were collective not individual and that voting to accept a representative did not imply recognition of, or a readiness to assume diplomatic relations with, the government concerned and that therefore 'the principle of numerical

[114] The only caution being that an act of recognition might be regarded as tantamount to intervention if not justified on the basis of either the government's effective control of territory or the legitimacy of origins. The general trend in the twentieth century was largely held to be one in which the old nineteenth-century criteria of legitimacy had started to give way to an 'objective' criterion of effective control. See, e.g., Lauterpacht, *Recognition in International Law.*

[115] See Hans Kelsen, 'Recognition in International Law' *American Journal of International Law*, 35(4) (1941) 605–17.

[116] UN Doc. S/1443, 5 UN SCOR, 459th mtg.

[117] See, e.g., Letter from China, UN Doc. S/1470, 15 March 1950, 5 UN SCOR Supp (1950) 23.

[118] It is perhaps notable that the ICJ, following the views of most Western States, had specifically denied the relevance of recognition in decisions over admission. Those same States, however, insisted here that recognition was nevertheless important for purposes of determining who may represent that State.

[119] 'Legal Aspects of the Problems of Representation in the United Nations', UN Doc. S/1466, 5 UN SCOR Supp (1950) 18.

preponderance of recognition is inappropriate and legally incorrect'.[120] It went on to suggest that the determining consideration should be whether the government was capable of carrying out the obligations of membership and therefore 'whether the new government exercises effective authority within the territory of the State and is habitually obeyed by the bulk of the population'.[121]

The memorandum's emphasis on governmental effectiveness attempted to sever the question of representation from conflict over the political character of the government concerned (and for that reason might have given some support to the PRC's ambitions).[122] But by framing the matter in terms of a State's ability to fulfil the conditions for membership (article 4), it did little more than shift the terrain of argumentation. And so, rather than focusing on the question of recognition, per se, States simply turned their attention to the question of whether the communist regime was, indeed, peace-loving or able and willing to carry out the obligations in the Charter.[123] The involvement of 'volunteers' from the PRC in the Korean conflict, fighting against what were ostensibly UN forces, meant that they did not have to look too far for an answer. But that memorandum did set the stage for the ensuing debates. On one side were the Socialist States who largely wanted to reduce the question of representation to a bare decision over credentials premised upon the communist government's effective control over Chinese territory.[124] On the other side was an array of Western-allied powers that wanted to elevate the issue to one equivalent to membership, demanding that the government concerned show its ability and willingness to comply with the obligations of the Charter. Pre-revolutionary

[120] UN Doc. S/1466, 5 UN SCOR Supp (1950) 6. For the argument that this does, indeed, constitute a form of recognition, see Hans Martin Blix, 'Contemporary Aspects of Recognition' *Recueil des Cours*, 130 (1970) 693 ('By accepting treaties constituting international organizations' states 'must be deemed to have obliged themselves to accept the measures of relations which is necessary under these constitutions – but not more – with authorities which fulfil the international law criteria of governments of State members'.)

[121] UN Doc. S/1466, V SCOR (1950).

[122] Higgins was to note, however, that whilst 'most states concur in statements that these criteria [vis criteria for recognition] are irrelevant, they seem to be unable to resist using them in support of their own viewpoints'. Higgins, *The Development of International Law by the Political Organs of the United Nations*, 269.

[123] See, e.g., McDougal and Goodman, 'Chinese Participation in the United Nations'.

[124] Higgins, *The Development of International Law by the Political Organs of the United Nations*, 269.

Cuba pushed the argument further, suggesting that the requirements should also include the question of whether the government concerned enjoyed 'the general consent of the population' and demonstrated 'respect for human rights and fundamental freedoms'.[125] Each side emphasised one particular aspect of the memorandum (effective control or compliance with Charter obligations) and one particular locale for decision-making (whether that be the Credentials Committee or the General Assembly).

In the event, arguments over the question of representation came to be fielded in a variety of fora including a Security Council Committee of Experts,[126] an Ad Hoc Political Committee[127] and a General Assembly Sub-Committee,[128] before returning to the Assembly in plenary session leading to the adoption of Resolution 396(V) of 1950.[129] In that Resolution, the Assembly largely endorsed a US agenda (against, as it happens, the views of the UK)[130] – both symbolically to centralise decision-making in the hands of the General Assembly and to make it substantively contingent upon prospective compliance with the UN Charter. The Resolution declared that questions of representation should be 'considered' by the General Assembly 'in light of the Purposes and

[125] Cuban Proposal, UN Doc. A/AC.38/L.6 (7 October 1950). This was supplemented by a Chinese amendment adding the proviso that effective authority should be established 'without the intervention of any other State' and that it be achieved through 'freely conducted or internationally supervised or observed elections' UN Doc. A/AC.38/L.22 (1950). For a discussion, see Higgins, *The Development of International Law*; Yuen-Li Liang, 'Recognition by the United Nations of the Representation of a Member State: Criteria and Procedure'*American Journal of International Law*, 45 (1951) 689–707.

[126] UN Doc. S/1457 and Corr 1 (1950), 5 UN SCOR Supp (1950) 18.

[127] UN Docs. A/AC.38/SR.18–24, 57–60, V UNGA (1950).

[128] UN Doc. A/AC.38/L.45 (21 November 1950). The Sub-Committee had recommended that wherever more than one authority claims to be the government entitled to represent a Member State in the UN, it should be considered 'in the light of the purposes and principles of the Charter and the circumstances of each case'. It went on to suggest that three factors should be taken into consideration, including the extent to which the new authority exercises effective control over the territory 'and is generally accepted by the population; the willingness of the authority 'to accept responsibility for carrying out' obligations under the Charter'; and 'the extent to which that authority has been established through internal processes in the Member state'.

[129] The matter was also discussed in the ECOSOC (10th Session, 344th meeting), the Trusteeship Council (7th Session, 1st meeting), and the UNESCO, UN Doc. A/1344 (September 1950), 2.

[130] The UK had suggested that the determinant should be an 'objective' one, conditioned merely by reference to whether the government concerned exercised effective control over the majority of territory.

Principles of the Charter and the circumstances of each case', and that a State's 'attitude' should be taken into account by other organs of the United Nations and Specialised Agencies.[131] Whatever the relative merits of Resolution 396(V) in terms of laying down the criteria for representation,[132] and whether or not its competence in that regard was well founded,[133] what was to become ever more clear as time went on was that questions of substance were one thing, but what really counted was the votes.[134]

From 1951 to 1961, the matter of Chinese representation – which was routinely tabled first by the Soviet Union then by Albania – was continually 'postponed' by the General Assembly by way of simple majority vote. At the same time, US political influence within the Assembly was waning, so it sought to bolster its position by introducing a five-power draft resolution proclaiming the matter of Chinese representation to be an 'important question' within the terms of article 18. This meant a two-thirds majority vote was required for any subsequent resolution demanding the replacement of the nationalist delegation with that of the PRC. This was to remain the pattern for the next decade – the General Assembly reiterating, by majority vote, the 'important' nature of the question, then, having raised the bar, rejecting resolutions calling for the replacement of the Nationalist representatives.

What was to change were the circumstances surrounding the question of Chinese representation. Whilst many in the West had long been concerned to ensure that communist China should not be able to 'shoot its way' into the United Nations,[135] its estrangement from the organisation – coupled with a mounting number of resolutions critical of its activities in Korea, Tibet and Indochina – were causing it to revise its initial commitment to the UN Charter (as distinct from what it called the 'US dominated UN Charter') and leading it to agitate for the creation of a

[131] UNGA Res 396 (V) (14 December 1950).

[132] As Higgins noted, Resolution 396(V) 'can hardly be said to provide close guidance on the matter of the representation of a state', Higgins, *The Development of International Law*, 252.

[133] See Ciobanu, 'Credentials of Delegations and Representation of Member States at the United Nations', 366–68.

[134] For many commentators, tracking the successive vote counts in the General Assembly became a preoccupation, see, e.g., Winberg Chai, 'China and the United Nations: Problems of Representation and Alternatives' *Asian Survey*, 10 (1970) 401–2.

[135] Particular concern was about the PRC's involvement in the ongoing conflict in Vietnam and the ability of the UN to respond effectively to it, when one of the major parties involved was not a 'member' of the organisation. See, e.g., United Nations General Assembly, Twentieth Session, 1371st Plenary Meeting (New York, Tuesday 9 November 1965) A_PV-1371-EN.

revolutionary alternative. In 1965, following Indonesia's withdrawal from the UN in protest against Malaysia assuming a seat on the Security Council, the PRC took the opportunity of floating the establishment of a Conference of New Emerging Forces (CONEFO) together with Indonesia with a view to it becoming an anti-imperial forum for states disaffected by the UN.[136] When, in the late 1960s, the PRC began to signal an interest in participating in the UN again, the US seized the chance to exploit the emergent rift between the USSR and communist China and finally acceded to the latter's demands ('playing the China card' as Nixon put it). Ultimately, then, the question of Chinese representation came to be determined by General Assembly Resolution 2758 (XVI) of 26 October 1971, which decided that the Chinese seat would be offered to the delegates of the PRC. The effect of this was to exclude the Republic of China from participation in the organisation thereafter. This was followed by similar decisions in the WHO, the ICAO, the FAO, and subsequently by the IBRD, the IDA and IFC.[137]

Formally speaking, all that had changed as part of that decision was the willingness of the UN to accept the credentials of one rival government over those of another. No one, however, was in any doubt that it was far more momentous than that. On one side, a nuclear power that had, for many years, been marginalised from active involvement in the UN had been brought within the fold. On the other side, a largely self-governing territory with a population of some 14 million was permanently excluded from membership and, indeed, from any representation in the UN. The Chinese civil war, which had been initially frozen by Truman's decision to 'neutralise' the straits of Formosa in 1950,[138] was structurally embedded in the representative architecture of the UN. In terms of the UN Charter, the resolution of this situation could only ever be either a reconciliation between the rival authorities and their unification or a renunciation of their respective claims. But both these

[136] Weng, 'Communist China's Changing Attitudes towards the United Nations', 699; Docauer, 'Communist Chinese Attitudes toward United Nations Membership', 23.

[137] See Hungdah Chiu, 'The Right of the Republic of China and Its 21 Million Chinese People to Participate in the United Nations' *John Marshall Law Review*, 28 (1994) 252.

[138] The US had originally declared that it would not intervene in the Taiwan Strait disputes, but after the outbreak of the Korean War, President Truman resolved to 'neutralise' the Straits of Formosa and sent the US Navy's Seventh Fleet to prevent the outbreak of conflict. This was later bolstered by the conclusion of a Sino-American Mutual Defence Treaty in 1955. For discussion of the legal formalities of the intervention, see Edwin Hoyt, 'The United States Reaction to the Korean Attack: A Study of the Principles of the United Nations Charter as a Factor in American Policy-Making' *American Journal of International Law*, 55 (1961) 58–76.

options would require an unravelling of deeply embedded political and ideological differences.

The case of Chinese representation in the UN made apparent the way in which Cold War politics operated neither outside nor beyond the terms of the UN Charter, but inside it, within the gaps, spaces and equivocations that the text offered out. What was in dispute was neither an avowal nor disavowal of the principles of sovereignty, territorial integrity or of statehood, nor indeed of self-determination or the realisation of human rights and fundamental freedoms. All these things were points of departure common to the rival powers – they represented a shared language and shared vision of global ordering. Where they differed was in the way in which these ideas might be interpreted and the formative role that either socialism or liberal democracy might have in their realisation. It was in relation to this that the question of 'governments' became the most visible and vital point of antagonism.

Governments, as such, had no formal place in the Charter itself. They were merely the instrument through which states could speak, the intermediary locus of authority that linked the abstract 'State' to the 'delegates' representing it, on one side, and the general populace, on the other. Neither the UN Charter nor international law more generally was concerned with guaranteeing the endurance of governments. What mattered was States – their integrity and their survival – and it was precisely the necessity of distinguishing between the 'two bodies' of the State,[139] the actual and the metaphysical, the temporary and the permanent, that made the architecture of the Charter, and international law more generally, meaningful. For it was only by abstracting the State from the government – by associating the former with the people or the nation and the latter with the momentary occupants of the seat of rule – that enduring meaning could be given to the principles of consent, of *pacta sunt servanda*, or indeed of State responsibility.[140] All these ideas depended upon the permanence of the State.[141]

And yet, Cold War rivalry took the intermediate, transient entity – the government – as a focal point of hostilities. In this presumed order, it was

[139] Cf. Ernst Kantorowicz, *The King's Two Bodies: A Study in Medieval Political Theology* (Princeton: Princeton University Press, 2016).

[140] This also had implications for the ongoing existence of property rights putatively acquired during the colonial era. See Chapter 4.

[141] It was for this reason that a long-standing distinction was made between State and governmental succession. For a critique, see D. P. O'Connell, *The Law of State Succession* (Cambridge: Cambridge University Press, 2015).

an entity that was both central to the operations of international relations and yet both dispensable and replaceable. Not even an absence of government – in the sense of anyone having effective control over a territory or population – would be sufficient to dislodge faith in the new operative order of sovereignty.[142] It was this dissonance between the categories of sovereign statehood and governmental effectiveness that provided space not simply for rivalry over Chinese representation but for the division of Korea, Germany and Vietnam. In the latter cases, as much as the temporary order of governmental authority seemed to point to the existence of two Koreas, two Germanies and two Vietnams, it was precisely the persistence of the idea that these were single states or unitary territories[143] that gave rise both to the language of 'division' and to the rivalry between the governments on either side. In a certain way, as we shall see, the gap between statehood and government also made space for interventions, both covert and overt.

2.6 Intervention and Proxy Warfare

So far, we have been describing how the UN Charter provided the juridical scaffolding for a contest over the manner and form in which the peoples of the world might be 'represented' internationally. The staging of that rivalry was enabled, on the one hand, by the elaboration of a common vision about the legal form through which the political organisation of the world would take place, and, on the other, by the creation of the necessary space within that order for the pursuit of the rival projects of East and West. As we have seen, that 'space' was provided principally by the relative quiescence of the Charter on the question of governmental representation. But Amero-Soviet rivalry over the question of governmental representation was not limited to the relatively sanitised confines of organisational decision-making over questions of membership and credentials. Indeed, it was to find its most violent and spectacular expression, throughout the period of the Cold War, in the active policies of intervention and proxified warfare of the rival powers. Even as the authors of the UN Charter declared themselves

[142] This was particularly true in respect of the concepts of both 'belligerent occupation' and 'governments in exile' but also became an occasional feature of decolonisation itself as with the Congo in 1960. Crawford, *The Creation of States in International Law*, 56–58

[143] Cf. Crawford, *The Creation of States in International Law*, 449–78, who was uncertain as to the validity of the category of divided states.

determined 'to save succeeding generations from the scourge of war', they nevertheless inaugurated an era in which armed conflict between rival powers was re-scaled and re-calibrated – 'domesticated' in internal armed conflicts or conflicts elsewhere, described as having a 'non-international' character. The question of 'intervention' was thus to become central in the ensuing decades in all discussions on the use of force.[144]

In practice, the forms of third-party 'intervention' were various. Sometimes it took the form of direct military intervention (Czechoslovakia, Hungary, Dominican Republic, Grenada, Afghanistan) or direct or indirect military assistance such as the provision of arms and the training of proxy agents (Nicaragua, Laos, Cambodia, Angola, Mozambique). In other cases, intervention was broadly non-military, extending to everything from economic embargos and the offer of aid and assistance to the dissemination of propaganda or threats of non-recognition. Sometimes intervention would be publicly acknowledged (embodied, for example, in the various presidential 'doctrines' of Truman, Eisenhower, Brezhnev, Johnson and Nixon), at other times it would be covert (Iran, Guatemala, Chile) and organied by one of the many 'intelligence agencies' that had been established in the aftermath of the war. Sometimes it would be directed towards propping up beleaguered governments (Greece, Lebanon, Jordan), at others, their subversive overthrow (Iran, Cuba, Guatemala, Dominican Republic, Grenada).[145] In all, however, the one consistent theme was an evident determination to control the political complexion of the government in question and to bring, or keep, the 'State' within the orbit of the intervenor.[146]

At the time of the drafting of the UN Charter in San Francisco, a number of Latin American States had fought to include within it, a set of principles outlining the fundamental rights and duties of States.[147]

[144] See generally, Michael Poznansky, *In the Shadow of International Law: Secrecy and Regime Change in the Postwar World* (Oxford: Oxford University Press, 2020).

[145] J. E. S. Fawcett, 'Intervention In International Law: A Study Of Some Recent Cases' (Volume 103), in *The Hague Academy Collected Courses Online* (Leiden: Brill, 1961) 352–53.

[146] As Fawcett was to observe, 'Intervention generally takes place along the power frontiers of the world.' Fawcett, 'Intervention In International Law', 348.

[147] See, e.g., Mexican Proposal, Doc 2 G/7(c), 3 UNCIO 54; Brazil, Doc 2 G/7, 2 May 1945, 3 UNCIO 232; Chile, Doc 2 G/7(i), 3 UNCIO 282; Honduras, Doc 2 G/7(m), 3 UNCIO 349; Ecuador, Doc 2 G/7, 3 UNCIO 393; Cuba, Doc 2 G/14(g), 3 UNCIO 493; Dominican Republic, Doc 2 G/14(o), 3 UNCIO 562; Bolivia, Doc 2 G/14(r), 3 UNCIO 577; Colombia, Doc 2 G/14(s), 3 UNCIO 587; Panama, Doc 2 G/7(g), 3 UNCIO; Paraguay, Doc 2 G/7(l), 3 UNCIO.

Drawing upon their own long experience of Western intervention within the region (including for the recuperation of debts and the 'protection of nationals'),[148] they proposed the inclusion of two related principles. The first, was a duty of non-intervention in the internal and external affairs of other States; the second, a covalent duty on States to prevent the organisation of activities within its territory calculated to foment civil strife in neighbouring countries. These proposals were picked up in a high profile American–Canadian 'technical plan'[149] circulated at the San Francisco conference, whose authors included the chair, Manley Hudson, and a number of high-profile legal scholars in the United States including Hans Kelsen, Philip Jessup, Wilfred Jenks, Quincy Wright, Roscoe Pound and John Foster Dulles.

In the commentary to the plan, the first of these principles – the duty of non-intervention – was said to be a corollary 'of the general precept' that each State 'must be responsible for the conduct of its own household' and that 'in its internal affairs each State must be free from interference by other States acting on their own authority'.[150] The authors explained that

> Instances have not been rare in the past in which a powerful State has sought to impose its will on a less powerful State in the latter's disposition of its economy, and the fear engendered by such action has been a disturbing factor in relations between many States. Such interference became so frequent that efforts were made to justify it by tentatives of law permitting intervention, and these tentatives even derived a semblance of authority from an award of a tribunal of the Permanent Court of Arbitration in the *Venezuela Preferential Claims Case*.[151]

The technical plan went on to point out that American States had long urged the emphatic condemnation of such forms of intervention and had included within the Montevideo convention of 1933 and various

[148] Active US intervention in the region in the early twentieth century followed from the issuance of the Roosevelt Corollary to the Monroe doctrine in 1904–5 followed by the adoption of the Platt Amendment in relation to Cuba and the inclusion of a right of intervention in the Panamanian constitution. The Latin American response was initially formulated in terms of a set of 'doctrines' including the Drago, Calvo and Carranza doctrines. See Juan Scarfi, 'Mexican Revolutionary Constituencies and the Latin American Critique of US Intervention' in Kathryn Greenman, Anne Orford, Anna Saunders and Ntina Tzouvala (eds.), *Revolutions in International Law: The Legacies of 1917* (Cambridge: Cambridge University Press, 2021) 218.

[149] Hudson et al., 'The International Law of the Future'.

[150] Ibid., 76.

[151] Ibid.

subsequent instruments[152] a definitive statement to the effect that: 'no State has a right to intervene in the internal or external affairs of another State'.[153]

As regards the second principle – concerning the duty to prevent subversive activities in other states – the technical plan pointed out that 'each State' must 'be assured of its internal security, free from subversive influence due to non-official activities in other States'. 'Governments themselves', it argued, 'must refrain from participation in the internal political contests to which other Governments are subjected. But they should do more. They should see that activities are not organised within their territory which are calculated to foment civil strife in the territory of other States.'[154] Various examples of such a duty were to be found, amongst others, in the 1928 Havana Convention on Civil Strife[155] the US–USSR agreement of 1933[156] and the 1936 Geneva Convention on the Use of Broadcasting in the Cause of Peace.[157]

For all the undoubted influence of the authors of the plan, neither of these principles ultimately found their way directly into the terms of the Charter. In the end, the principles came to be folded into two separate clauses, neither of which entirely subsumed their latent content. On one side, the problem of intervention was wrapped into a debate over the

[152] Convention on the Rights and Duties of States, Montevideo, 26 December 1933; Additional Protocol Relative to Non-Intervention, Buenos Aires, 1936; Declaration of American Principles, Lima, 1938.

[153] Hudson et al., 'The International Law of the Future: Postulates, Principles and Proposals', 77. The one caveat here was that any such prohibition would not 'preclude action taken on behalf of the Community of States with the mandate of a competent agency' in case of threats to international peace and order.

[154] Hudson et al., 'The International Law of the Future: Postulates, Principles and Proposals', 78.

[155] Convention on the Duties and Rights of States in the Event of Civil Strife, Havana, 20 February 1928: 'to use all means at their disposal to prevent the inhabitants of their territory, national or aliens, from participating in, gathering elements, crossing the boundary or sailing from their territory for the purpose of starting or promoting civil strife'.

[156] Roosevelt–Litvinov Agreements, Washington, DC, 16 November 1933, in which each undertook 'not to permit the formation or residence on its territory of any organization or group . . . which has as its aim the overthrow or the preparation for the overthrow of, or bringing about by force of a change in the political or social order' of the other.

[157] That instrument obliged states to prohibit 'the broadcasting within their respective territories of any transmission which to the detriment of good international understanding is of such a character as to incite the population of any territory to acts incompatible with the internal order or the security of a territory' of another State, Convention on the Use of Broadcasting in the Cause of Peace, Geneva, 23 September 1936.

general prohibition on the use of force under article 2(4) of the UN Charter. Despite the efforts by Brazil to open this clause out to include broader forms of intervention such as economic coercion,[158] the final text merely provided that all members 'shall refrain in their international relations from the threat or use of force against the territorial integrity or political independence of any state, or in any other manner inconsistent with the Purposes of the United Nations'.[159] This was an obligation that was importantly qualified by the right of individual and collective self-defence in circumstances of an armed attack (article 51) and by the power of the Security Council to authorise the use of force under Chapter VII. On the other side, the question of intervention was subsumed within the debate over the content of article 2(7), which protected States against interference in their domestic jurisdiction (their 'reserved domain'). But here again, the question of intervention in the sense alluded to in the technical plan was excluded from the text on the basis that the Charter was principally concerned with the prerogatives of the organisation, not the rights and duties of States in their widest sense.[160] What it sought to protect, in other words, was States' right to determine their own economic, social and cultural policies free from interference by, for example, the newly formed Economic and Social Council (ECOSOC),[161] rather than from their hegemonic neighbours.

It was clear then, that articles 2(4) and 2(7) fell short of the kind of prohibition envisaged by the sponsors of the technical plan. Not only did the provisions leave untouched a swathe of non-forcible[162] forms of

158 See 6 UNCIO (San Francisco, 1945), 334–35.

159 Charter of the United Nations, 26 June 1945, Art. 2(4).

160 Supplement to Report of Rapporteur, Committee I/1 to Commission I, Doc 1070, I/1/34 (1)(d), VI UNCIO 486. ('It is evident that the subject we are dealing with is not the intervention of one State in matters which fall within the domestic jurisdiction of another, but that we are dealing with the relations of the Organization and its members with respect to domestic and international jurisdiction'.)

161 Report of Committee I/1, 6 UNCIO Docs, Doc 1070. Higgins comments that 'Throughout the stages of drafting there was a basic dichotomy between the desire to grant broad powers to the United Nations and the fear that these might impair the freedom of states in matters of domestic jurisdiction.' Higgins, *The Development of International Law*, 121.

162 Whether the term 'force' might extend to forms of economic and political coercion was widely debated and was to become a particular point of difference in the drafting of the Declaration on Friendly Relations. See Edward McWhinney, *The UN Declaration on Friendly Relations and the Systems of the Sources of International Law*, by Gaetano Angio-Ruiz, Noordhoof 1979' *American Journal of International Law*, 75(1) (1981) 29–31. More generally, see Hans Kelsen, *Collective Security under International Law*

'intervention' (however 'coercive' they might be in practice),[163] they left in the air the question of whether forms of armed intervention *not* directed against the territorial integrity or political independence of a State were also prohibited. Examples of this might include intervention to prop-up an existing government, or to support a people in the exercise of their self-determination or for the 'protection of nationals'. In the mix was also the question of collective self-defence and whether that might justify an intervention where a sitting government was facing an insurgency sponsored by non-State agents beyond its borders.

A profound irony, then, attached to the decision to exclude the principle of non-intervention from the Charter. Whilst the UN itself was, on the face of it, precluded from intervening in matters of domestic jurisdiction, no such explicit prohibition operated in case of intervention by member States except and insofar as it either involved the (uninvited) dispatch of troops across a border or threatened international peace and security as determined by the Security Council. Within the organisation, this meant that lengthy battles had to be fought in order to bring within the UN's purview matters that were argued to fall within States' domestic jurisdiction – including, but not limited to, the exercise of self-determination (e.g. in relation to Morocco, Tunisia, Algeria and Cyprus)[164] and policies of apartheid in Southern Rhodesia and South Africa.[165] On the flip side of this, it meant that for the rival Cold War powers, the Charter provided little restraint on the pursuit of active policies aimed at dictating or controlling the political profile of new or existing governments elsewhere in the world.

And so, in several senses, the UN Charter might be thought to have been uniquely designed for the pursuit, by remote means, of a thoroughly 'legitimate' ideological contest on the part of the Amero-Soviets. In the first place, it enabled both rival blocs to situate their messianic activities (as either the champions of liberal democracy or of democratic socialism) squarely within the terms of the Charter. Both framed these agendas in

(Washington, DC: United States Government Printing Office, 1954) 57; Ian Brownlie, *International Law and the Use of Force by States* (Oxford: Oxford University Press, 1963) 255; D. W. Bowett, *Self-Defence in International Law* (London: Praeger, 1958) 106–14.

163 Friedman was to point out that the (legitimate) economic embargo on Cuba was vastly more 'coercive' than the illegitimate overflight of Cuban territory by U2 spyplanes. Jeremy Friedman, *Shadow Cold War: The Sino-Soviet Competition for the Third World* (Chapel Hill: University of North Carolina Press, 2015).

164 Higgins, *The Development of International Law*, 158–75.

165 See generally, Higgins, *The Development of International Law*, 144–45.

Charter terms – as promoting self-determination and opposing acts of aggression or subversion (both direct and indirect). Both adhered to the language of democracy, self-government, freedom and human rights and claimed for themselves the right to intervene in territories abroad to secure those objectives.

In the second place, the Charter's distribution of legitimate coercion – regulating the 'international' use of force directed against the territorial integrity or political independence of States but silently standing by in case of warfare that was presumptively internal – meant that the Cold War powers were encouraged to domesticate their own rivalry in local competitions for power, within the framework of the sovereign State. Because the Charter was 'neutral' on the matter of revolution (revolution was often said to be a political not a legal concept), the two rivals had both opportunity and impetus to try to advance their respective causes through the medium of sponsored agents engaged in forms of ostensibly intra-state violence and to do so in the name of either the self-determining prerogatives of the people or the legitimacy of their governments. Cold War rivalry could thus assume, under the Charter, the form of a global civil war[166] in two different senses: on the one hand, as an internecine conflict fought between rival global 'religions'[167] and, on the other, as a war conducted principally inside the borders of existing, or would be States.[168]

In the third place, far from barring the practice of cross-border intervention, the Charter's recognition of the right of individual and collective self-defence served only to provide a fertile ground for legitimating such activities. Intervention at the request of a government resisting a local insurgency had become the object of widespread critical reflection in the interwar years[169] (as was evidenced in the adoption of the abortive

[166] Hoffman remarks, in that sense, that the Cold War was a form of international civil warfare in which domestic institutions were projected into world politics, and world-wide ideological clashes were injected into domestic affairs. Stanley Hoffmann, 'International Systems and International Law' *World Politics*, 14(1) (1961) 205–237.

[167] Hans Morgenthau, 'To Intervene or Not to Intervene' *Foreign Affairs*, 45(3) (1967) 429.

[168] It is perhaps notable on the occasion in which wars became visibly international (e.g. Korea and Vietnam) there was an ongoing debate over its characterisation as an international conflict.

[169] See generally, Ellery C. Stowell, *Intervention in International Law* (Washington, DC: John Byrne and Co, 1921); W. E. Hall, *International Law*, 7th ed., ed. A. Pierce Higgins (Oxford: Clarendon Press, 1924) ch. VIII.

policy of neutrality in relation to Spain in 1936).[170] But the Charter's recognition of a right of not just individual but collective self-defence largely reversed that critical trend. In the context of a form of global civil warfare conducted in part by the rival powers arming and equipping opposing forces, self-defence provided the generous mantle under which every intervention could be presented as a counter-intervention, or a counter-counter-intervention – and all in the name of securing the sovereignty and political independence of the State.[171] As Franck was to observe, there was little, if any, control over the determination as to whether 'an act of aggression' (or more precisely an 'armed attack') might be said to have occurred[172] (indeed, the definition of aggression was to be a point of contentious debate for at least two decades).[173] There was also the problem of determining whether 'the regime calling for help was, in fact, the legitimate government' or merely a 'puppet' propped up by hegemonic intervention.[174]

Finally, the Charter's apparent subsumption of the question of intervention within the terms of article 2(4) of the Charter[175] offered the possibility not just of supplying arms, equipment and support to governments on request but of using a range of ostensibly 'non-forcible' measures to control or influence either the policy direction of foreign governments or the outcome of local struggles for power. The range of levers available extended to everything from the dissemination of propaganda to financing opposition parties, granting or withholding

170 See Norman J. Padelford, 'The International Non-Intervention Agreement and the Spanish Civil War' *The American Journal of International Law*, 31(4) (1937) 578–603.

171 As Akehurst notes, article 51 was included in the Charter in part at least to placate the US and USSR's concerns that the requirement of prior Security Council authorisation of regional enforcement action (as provided by article 53) might preclude a right of action against external aggressors within their respective spheres of influence. See Michael Akehurst, 'Enforcement Action by Regional Agencies with Special Reference to the Organization of American States' *British Yearbook of International Law*, 42 (1967) 175–228.

172 Lauterpacht classically observed that in the appreciation of whether an act of self-defence was necessary, every State must be a judge in its own cause, Hersch Lauterpacht, *The Function of Law in the International Community* (Oxford: Oxford University Press, 1933) 179.

173 See generally, Julius Stone, *Aggression and World Order* (London: Stevens and Sons, 1958), chapter 1.

174 Thomas Franck, 'Who Killed Article 2(4) or: Changing Norms Governing the Use of Force by States' *American Journal of International Law*, 64 (1970) 818.

175 The classic definition offered by Lauterpacht in 1955, Lassa Oppenheim, *International Law*, 8th ed. (London: Longman, 1955) 305.

recognition of foreign governments, providing or withholding aid or instituting economic boycotts.

And so, from the time of the Soviet-inspired removal of the Beneš-Masaryk government in Czechoslovakia in 1948 and the British/American intervention in Greece in the same year, the tone was set.[176] From this point onwards, the rival powers would routinely invoke the spectre of 'indirect aggression' or external subversion to justify their respective armed interventions – as, for example, was the case in Korea (1950), Hungary (1956), Lebanon (1958), Jordan (1958), Vietnam (1961), Czechoslovakia (1968) and Afghanistan (1979). In nearly all cases, intervention was apparently 'requested' on the part of a (sometimes yet to be established) compliant government, and in nearly all cases, it was justified in the language of the Charter.[177] 'Self-defence' was thus to become the major theme in the practice of intervention and was the principal rationale given for the formation of both NATO and the Warsaw Pact. Both of these arrangements authorised participating States to 'provide assistance' to a State party subject to attack, independently of any approval by the Security Council.[178]

2.7 'Mere Interference' and the Defence of International Law

Direct military intervention, however, was only part of the story. Alongside the covert instigation of coups d'êtat, the Amero-Soviets routinely involved themselves in practices of what they called 'mere interference'. This included broadcasting propaganda, offering economic inducements by way of aid, trade agreements or withholding recognition. Most of these were, in the language of Sinclair, the normalised threats and inducements of everyday diplomatic practice that fell 'below the line' of Lauterpacht's classic definition of intervention as a 'dictatorial compulsion'.[179]

[176] John Lewis Gaddis, 'Was the Truman Doctrine a Real Turning Point? Reconsiderations' *Foreign Affairs*, 52 (1974) 386, 388.

[177] US Intervention was also regularly justified on the basis of the protection of nationals (e.g. Lebanon [1958], Dominican Republic [1965], Grenada [1983]). Jessup was to argue that the use of force for the protection of nationals 'may escape the prohibition of the first clause of Article 2 of the Charter'. It was nevertheless, in his view, 'inconsistent with the Purposes of the United Nations'. Philipp Jessup, 'Force under a Modern Law of Nations' *Foreign Affairs*, 25(1) (1946) 98.

[178] This would have been required had the organisations been established as 'regional security arrangements' under Chapter VIII of the Charter.

[179] Ian Sinclair, *The Vienna Convention on the Law of Treaties* (Manchester: Manchester University Press, 1984) 178–80.

One interpretation of this practice was that the Charter had been overtaken by events – that the 'Queensberry-like' practices of traditional warfare, as Franck put it, had been displaced by a new kind of antagonism, or warfare, that had simply 'by-passed' the already outdated terms of the Charter.[180] But as Henkin rightly observed, it was not the case that the two powers chose to set aside the Charter – indeed, they went to great lengths to justify their actions in Charter terms, seeking to reassure the rest of the international community (who, after all, were their audience) that they were each the upholder of a would-be virtuous international legal order.[181] So just as Truman premised his famous 'doctrine' upon the need to 'support free peoples who are resisting attempted subjugation by armed minorities or by outside pressures',[182] so too did Brezhnev seek to justify his own doctrine by the need to protect the sovereignty and independence of the peoples within the Soviet sphere and their right to self-determination.[183] Anything less would subvert the logic of their respective agendas, which, ultimately, was to be measured in terms of the degree of influence and control they exerted over the 'hearts and minds' of the peoples of the world.[184]

And so the Amero-Soviets sought to base their interventionist activity upon a defence of not just the rights to democracy and self-determination but a defence of international law itself. This had three particular consequences. In the first place, it rendered the problem of intervention an intractable one. This was so in the sense that the more vehemently each of them defended the principles of territorial integrity, political independence and self-determination, the more difficult it was for them, not simply to justify their own acts of intervention (on the grounds that communism or capitalism simply had to be stopped) but also to stand by in face of the surreptitious manipulation of democratic processes by the other power. They were either committed to the

180 Franck, 'Who Killed Article 2(4)', 812

181 Henkin, 'Force, Intervention and Neutrality', 150.

182 In Truman's terms, that was right of all nations to 'choose their own form of government by their own freely expressed choice'. Harry Truman, 'Address on Foreign Policy at the Navy Day Celebration in New York City', 27 October 1945.

183 Speech by First Secretary of the Soviet Union Leonid Brezhnev (13 November 1968).

184 This was a phrase of currency in counter-insurgency practice in the 1950s, often attributed to Sir Gerald Templer, the British High Commissioner in Malaya between 1952–54. Its origins, however, have been traced back to the colonial policies of Sir Robert Sandeman, governor general in Baluchistan in the 1880s. See Benjamin Hopkins, 'The Problem with "Hearts and Minds" in Afghanistan' *Middle East Report*, 255 (2010) 24–29.

principle of self-government or they were not, and so far as they were, no strict policy of non-intervention seemed to be sustainable.[185]

Secondly, because they associated their respective policies with a defence of (rival versions of) international law, there was no way to assume a position of 'neutrality' in relation to local struggles for political control. Just as the Charter narrowed the scope for an assertion of neutrality in relation to international armed conflicts (reintroducing, in Schmitt's terms, the logic of the just war), so too did it seem that the common commitment to sovereignty, self-determination and democracy (despite evident differences as to what those terms meant in practice), effectively ruled out neutrality in relation to non-international armed struggles. And so, although the Latin American Republics had fought to include within the Charter a principle of political neutrality, as far as the Amero-Soviets were concerned, the world was definitively bi-polar both politically and juridically. This indeed, seemed to be the logic of the Soviet commitment to 'peaceful coexistence'.[186]

Thirdly, a dissonance between ideological ends and legitimate means was hardwired into Amero-Soviet practice. A systematic division of labour was developed that discriminated between what might be disclosed and what was to be shrouded in secrecy.[187] Cold War intervention was thus marked, from the beginning, by the development or perfection of a new set of covert methods of combat – subversive propaganda, psychological warfare, covert operations, coups d'être, targeted assassinations – that were to assume prominence, in time, alongside the older 'diplomatic' arts of espionage, counter-espionage and surveillance.[188] Such methods, if they were to have any degree of success, either had to be kept out of the public eye or, at the very least, be subject to what the US dubbed the doctrine of 'plausible deniability', such that the hand of the hegemon could remain at one remove. If 'peace' was thus maintained in all formal, public senses between the rival powers, their mutual animosity would nevertheless come to be channelled through agents or 'proxies' operating, ostensibly, within a 'domestic' setting.

[185] Thomas Franck and Edward Weisband, 'The Johnson and Brezhnev Doctrines: The Law You Make May Be Your Own' *Stanford Law Review*, 22 (1970) 979–1012.

[186] This is something we take up further in Chapter 5.

[187] Melley notes that the 'Cold War not only divided the world into two "incompatible" worlds, but also divided the public sphere into overt and covert components'. Timothy Melley, *The Covert Sphere: Secrecy, Fiction and the National Security State* (Ithaca: Cornell University Press, 2012) 39.

[188] We take this up further in Chapters 5 and 7.

All of this was made explicit, on the part of the US at least, in the National Security Council directive 10/2 of 1948 in which the recently established CIA[189] was afforded a new public mandate: that of combating 'the vicious covert activities' of the USSR, its satellite countries and Communist groups that were working to 'discredit and defeat the aims and activities of the United States'.[190] And so alongside the conduct of espionage and counter-espionage operations abroad, from that point on, the CIA was authorised to engage in an open-ended range of covert operations that included 'propaganda; economic warfare; preventive direct action, including sabotage, anti-sabotage, demolition and evacuation measures; subversion against hostile states, including assistance to underground resistance movements, guerillas and refugee liberation groups, and support of indigenous anti-communist elements in threatened countries in the world'.[191] The two main constraints placed upon such operations were that they should not extend to 'armed conflict by recognized military forces' and were to be 'so planned and executed that any US government responsibility for them is not evident to unauthorised persons and that if uncovered the US Government can plausibly disclaim any responsibility for them'.[192] The NSC Directive thus had the effect of institutionalising both 'secret warfare' and 'public deception' as fundamental elements of US policy.[193] Both were to emerge, as practices, in large part as a consequence of the apparent negative effects of both domestic and international attribution, if not disclosure.[194] Certainly, this time, a form of political 'realism' had become

189 The CIA was established under the National Security Act of 1947, the main purpose of which would be to act as a clearing house for intelligence information gathered from a variety of sources. National Security Act of 1947, 61 Stat. 495 (1947).

190 National Security Council Directive on Office of Special Projects (NSC 10/2), 18 June 1948. In the earlier NSC 4-A, 9 December 1947, the CIA had been instructed to 'initiate and conduct . . . covert psychological operations designed to counteract Soviet and Soviet-inspired activities that constitute a threat to world peace and security'. See also NSC 5421/2, March 1954.

191 National Security Council Directive on Office of Special Projects (NSC 10/2), 18 June 1948, para. 5.

192 National Security Council Directive on Office of Special Projects (NSC 10/2), 18 June 1948.

193 Melley, *The Cover Sphere*, 3

194 Richard Falk, 'CIA Covert Action and International Law' *Society*, 12 (1975), 39–40. ('The international law case is, in a sense, self-evident and is partially conceded by the CIA's insistence upon secrecy and the related practice of defending itself against allegations by cover stories (i.e. lies). The secrecy/deception pattern arises in part because the behavior is inherently objectionable to a segment of domestic and, even more so, world public

the common ideological mantra on both sides of the Iron Curtain – with international law derided in some quarters either for its vapid 'moralism' or for its essentially 'class' character. And yet the Amero-Soviets also worked with a shared sense of the necessity of, at least, appearing to venerate the UN Charter and respect the sovereignty of other nations.

2.8 Resisting the Irresistible

As we have seen, the UN Charter seemed to provide the juridical structure for the pursuit of a Cold War rivalry that was to take place by changing the shape of contests for political power in other countries. This was a practice that would face growing opposition from a broad alliance of States in the South. Latin American attempts to incorporate a provision on non-intervention into the terms of the Charter had been rebuffed. They had persisted with their agenda in the early years of the United Nations, beginning with the attempt to persuade the newly formed International Law Commission to take up the matter in the form of a Declaration on the Rights and Duties of States. But that particular project was stymied by opposition from both the Soviet Union and the United States,[195] which left the declaration project dead in the water. By the late 1950s, however, the same initiative regained new impetus when the Latin American Republics were joined by a number of new member States from Africa and Asia. These were States who had recently obtained their independence from colonial rule, and who embraced the principle of non-intervention as a bulwark against colonial, neo-colonial and imperial[196] practices of interference. But whilst the

opinion. There is also an implicit awareness that CIA covert activities in foreign societies violate their fundamental international law rights as sovereign states.') Michael Reisman and James Baker, *Regulating Covert Action* (New Haven: Yale University Press, 1992) 13: 'The normative conclusion conveyed by the word *covert* is that the action per se and the way it has been accomplished are unlawful.'

195 The text of what was to remain a draft declaration incorporated a general prohibition on any 'intervention in the internal or external affairs of any other state' (article 3) coupled with a duty 'to refrain from fomenting civil strife in the territory of another state' (article 5) both the US and Soviet members of the Commission voted against its adoption. Various grounds were cited, ranging from its inclusion of references to human rights (Hudson) to it being a manifesto for world domination (Koretsky). Draft Declaration on the Rights and Duties of States, Yearbook of the International Law Commission (1949), vol. II, 286, 287 n 21; UN General Assembly Resolution 596(VI), 7 December 1951.

196 Kwame Nkrumah, *Neocolonialism: The Last Stage of Imperialism* (London: Thomas Nelson & Sons, 1965) 241.

Latin Americans saw the principle of non-intervention as a generalisation of their experience,[197] the Afro-Asian states sought to broaden its terms as a principle of geo-political independence, or non-alignment.

As the various declarations of Bandung (1955),[198] Belgrade (1961) and Cairo (1964) made clear, the principle of non-intervention had two aspects, one 'anti-colonial' the other 'anti-neo-colonial'. On one side, the declarations invoked a prohibition on any form of 'intimidation, interference or intervention' in the exercise of the right of self-determination,[199] affirming the right of peoples to resort to arms in self-defence, as well as asserting a commitment by the parties to render 'all necessary aid and support, whether moral, political or material' to peoples involved in such struggles. On the other side, the declarations attempted to prohibit 'neo-colonial' policies directed against newly independent states including acts of 'economic pressure and domination, interference, racial discrimination, subversion [and] intervention'.[200] In other words, a broad coalition of states sought to broaden the prohibition on intervention both by extending protection to pro-independence liberation movements and by including economic as well as political themes within it. At the same time, this coalition of states, as a matter of solidarity, committed to providing support to movements fighting for independence.[201]

In the aftermath of the Congo crisis from 1960 to 1965, the General Assembly itself picked up this project. The period leading up to the 1960s had been marked by a variety of disastrous interventions both overt and covert. This had led to the adoption of Resolution 2131(XX) on the Inadmissibility of Intervention in the Domestic Affairs of States and the Protection of their Independence and Sovereignty.[202] That Declaration was adopted in the face of significant disquiet on the part of a number of Western states (which, in a familiar strategy, sought to assert its 'political' and 'non-binding' character). But its main terms were later included in the 1970 Declaration on Friendly Relations, widely recognised as a definitive 're-statement' of Charter principles.[203]

197 Which they had generalised in the form in the Charter of the Organization of American States. Followed in this respect by the League of Arab States and the OAU.

198 Declaration on World Peace and Co-operation, Bandung Conference, 24 April 1955.

199 Belgrade Declaration, 2 June 1955.

200 Cairo Declaration, 27 November 1943, 5.

201 See Chapter 4 on the Algerian struggle.

202 GA Res 2131(XX), 21 December 1965. This was followed by the adoption of Resolution 2225(XXI) of 1966 calling upon all states to desist from acts of intervention.

203 From that time, the principle has been repeatedly reaffirmed with new emphases – in the first phase with the emphasis on economic intervention (see, e.g., Charter on Economic

The Declaration on Friendly Relations combined a general statement of the doctrine of political neutrality (every State 'has the inalienable right to choose its political, economic, social and cultural systems') with a broadly articulated prohibition on intervention. Armed intervention 'and all other forms of interference or attempted threats against the personality of the State or against its political, economic, and cultural elements' were, it stated, 'in violation of international law', and no State was entitled to 'use or encourage the use of economic, political or any other type of measures to coerce another State in order to obtain from it the subordination of the exercise of its sovereign rights and to secure from it, advantages of any kind'. The Declaration did add that 'no State shall organize, assist, foment, finance, incite or tolerate subversive, terrorist or armed activities directed towards the violent overthrow of the régime of another State, or interfere in civil strife in another State'. But it made clear that peoples exercising their right to self-determination were 'entitled to seek and to receive support in accordance with the purposes and principles of the Charter'.

In many respects, the provisions on non-intervention in the Friendly Relations Declaration represented a victory for the committed 'neutralists' seeking to resist the predatory impulses of the rival hegemons and to re-shape international law. The statement of political neutrality did not simply offer states a choice between two alternatives but asserted that the question itself was a matter inherently falling within their domestic jurisdiction. Both the Truman and Brezhnev doctrines were thus implicitly rejected. Similarly, the prohibition on intervention was not just confined to measures involving the use of armed force but was extended to the use of coercive economic or political measures.

At the same time, as befits a Declaration that received almost unanimous support in the General Assembly, there was also enough in it to engage the support of both the US and the Soviet Union in their symmetrical rivalry. For the Soviets, the Declaration interwove the principle of non-intervention with an affirmative expression of the right of all peoples to self-determination, including their right to 'seek and receive' support. This meant that the Soviet Union's long-standing commitment to providing military and other assistance to national liberation movements in the fight against colonial rule could continue. Similarly, for the US, the key point was the limitation of intervention to measures that were essentially of a 'coercive' nature. This meant that it could

Rights and Duties of States, GA Res 3281 (XXIX) (1974) and more recently with the emphasis upon election interference.

continue to provide military support on 'request' to existing governments, or to engage in a broad spectrum of 'suasive' enterprises – from trade deals or economic assistance to propaganda – on the basis that such activities fell short of 'coercion' and, indeed, formed part of the everyday practice of diplomacy.[204]

The Friendly Relations Declaration (and the Declaration on Non-Intervention before it) were to become key instruments in the International Court's subsequent condemnation of the US intervention in Nicaragua.[205] But these had little effect upon the wider practice of intervention. The involvement of China, the US, South Africa, Britain and France, the Soviet Union, Yugoslavia and Cuba in the Angolan wars of independence are evidence of that fact. More broadly, though, neither declaration could ever quite come to grips with the essential problematic, which concerned the way in which the Charter joined an emerging principle of self-determination together with a right of collective self-defence.

What the Declaration and debates around it exposed were the pathologies of an international legal order committed to the protection and promotion of sovereign statehood but in which governments were not protected, no matter how they came to power. This was particularly poignant in the case of recently independent states with governments chosen by the people. In other words, 'government' was simultaneously suppressed in international terms as putatively a matter of domestic jurisdiction but preserved as a site of legitimate contention in both legal and political terms. The question of who was to represent the state or the people and thereby gain the power to decide political and economic policy, to dispose of natural resources or (re)configure the terms of trade, was to become the central battleground of the Amero-Soviet Cold War configuration. What was produced was an ideological formation that relied upon a separation between the international and the non-international, as well as between the sovereign state (or the 'people') as bearer of international rights and obligations, and the government as the momentary occupant of the seat of office. At the same time, this ideological formation authorised violent interposition in the effort to make those conjoined categories meaningful. In the process, rival and

[204] See Robert Rosenstock, 'The Declaration of Principles of International Law Concerning Friendly Relations: A Survey' *American Journal of International Law*, 65 (1971) 726.

[205] Case Concerning Military and Paramilitary Activities in and Against Nicaragua (Nicaragua v USA) Merits, Judgment, ICJ Reports 1986, 14.

competing accounts as to what was rightly 'domestic' and what was properly 'international' were to become structural features of a 'juridified' Cold War violence throughout the period from Korea and Algeria to Vietnam and Angola.

2.9 Conclusion

In this chapter, we explored the role of the UN Charter in creating the formal conditions for the 'Cold War'. Although at its inception, the Charter's lawful world and the realm of ideological contestation between the former Allies seemed to be in opposition, they turned out to be part of the same world-making project. Intentionally or not, the Charter provided the legal architecture for the rivalry between the US and the USSR and its patterning into a broader 'Cold War'. What enabled this patterning were the ambiguities and silences within the legal forms the Charter engaged, created, protected and prescribed. These ambiguities enabled the rivals to both compete violently and claim to be lawful at the same time. The terrain included ideas of representation and intervention, evident in disputation around UN membership and credentials and the question of self-determination for non-self-governing territories. At the same time, as enabling and provoking formal contests, the Charter provided a negative space in which US–Soviet rivalry could be conducted covertly in and around the terms of the Charter itself. The Charter also inaugurated a particular vision for global order meditated through the legal form of the sovereign State. This prescribed the form through which decolonisation would take place. It did not prescribe its form of government but effectively assured the globalisation (or 'universalisation') of the nation-state form, and the stabilisation of forms of property ownership asserted as lawful during the imperial period.

But the Charter was inaugural and prefigurative rather than descriptive. This made it open to rival interpretations, from the Latin American states and from states in Africa and Asia as they won their independence. And so the Charter also created space for the articulation of a variety of political and juridical agendas. In later chapters, we will follow through this idea and track the plurality it enabled. But first, we turn in Chapter 3 to what we call the 'Amero-Soviet' project. This was a joint project of world-making conducted both through the UN Charter and around it, in jurisdictional projects of détente, peaceful coexistence, 'proxification' and spheres of influence. This project was divided by ideology but unified by the shared traditions of North Atlantic modernity and a singular European cosmology.

3

The Amero-Soviet Cold War

3.1 Introduction

When American President Harry Truman first articulated his famous 'doctrine' of containment (the 'Truman Doctrine') in 1947, he went to some pains to locate his strategy within the framework of the Charter of the United Nations:

> To ensure the peaceful development of nations, free from coercion, the United States has taken a leading part in establishing the United Nations. The United Nations is designed to make possible lasting freedom and independence for all its members. We shall not realize our objectives, however, unless we are willing to help free peoples to maintain their free institutions and their national integrity against aggressive movements that seek to impose upon them totalitarian regimes. This is no more than a frank recognition that totalitarian regimes imposed on free peoples, by direct or indirect aggression, undermine the foundations of international peace and hence the security of the United States ....
>
> The world is not static, and the status quo is not sacred. But we cannot allow changes in the status quo in violation of the Charter of the United Nations by such methods as coercion, or by such subterfuges as political infiltration. In helping free and independent nations to maintain their freedom, the United States will be giving effect to the principles of the Charter.[1]

On the face of it, Truman placed the need for a new set of policies and programmes for purposes of combating communist subterfuge and political infiltration within the existing framework of international law. As he sought to present it, the US was condemned to act in defence of the UN Charter – and its commitments to the principles of 'domestic

[1] Harry S. Truman, 'Special Message to the Congress on Greece and Turkey', 12 March 1947, Truman Library, www.trumanlibrary.gov/library/public-papers/56/special-message-congress-greece-and-turkey-truman-doctrine.

jurisdiction', 'territorial integrity' and 'self-determination' – by 'helping free and independent nations maintain their freedom'.

But the immediate difficulty was that for all the references to 'aggression' and 'coercion', and for all the efforts to situate US policy within the four corners of the UN Charter, it was clear that the threat to be countered was neither one that would fall squarely within the prohibition on the 'use of force' as articulated in article 2(4) of the UN Charter[2] nor one that could justify resort to a claim of collective self-defence.[3] Rather, the particular threat to which Truman averred concerned the more subtle, and difficult, problem of 'behind the scenes' subversion, political infiltration and agentic co-optation, which had characterised the Soviet Union's efforts in creating 'people's democracies' in Eastern Europe.[4] A similar pattern of subversion would in turn mark, as we have seen, the US interventions in Guatemala, Cuba, Laos and Iran.

The American diplomat George Kennan had already set out the nature of the perceived problem from the point of view of the United States in his notorious 'Long Telegram' of 1946.[5] In that telegram, he had observed that Moscow was likely to pursue a dual strategy for expanding Soviet influence.[6] He predicted that, on one hand, in all public and

[2] See Thomas Franck, 'Who Killed Article 2(4)? Or Changing Norms Governing the Use of Force by States' *American Journal of International Law*, 64 (1970) 809–37; Michael Reisman, 'Coercion and Self-Determination: Construing Charter Article 2(4)' *American Journal of International Law*, 78 (1984) 644. Describing instances in which a putsch is 'externally inspired, encouraged and/or financed' and in which 'the officers ... seek the support of an outside superpower', which then proceeds to offer military and administrative assistance, he observes that 'most of the sequences of this scenario are compatible with traditional international law and Article 2(4)'.

[3] Cf. US critique of the Soviet Union's intervention in Czechoslovakia. Herbert Reis, 'Legal Aspects of the Invasion and Occupation of Czechoslovakia' *Department of State Bulletin*, 59 (1968) 395.

[4] Norman Naimark, 'The Sovietization of Eastern Europe, 1944–53' in Melvyn Leffler and Odd Arne Westad (eds.), *The Cambridge History of the Cold War. Volume I, Origins, 1945–1962* (Cambridge: Cambridge University Press, 2010) 175. On the attempt by the General Assembly to outlaw such activities, see, e.g., Declaration on the Inadmissibility of Intervention in the Domestic Affairs of States and the Protection of their Independence and Sovereignty, UNGA Res 2131 (21 December 1965).

[5] George Kennan's 'Long Telegram', 22 February 1946, History and Public Policy Program Digital Archive, National Archives and Records Administration, Department of State Records (Record Group 59), Central Decimal File, 1945–1949, 861.00/2-2246; reprinted in US Department of State (ed.), *Foreign Relations of the United States*, 1946, vol. VI, Eastern Europe; The Soviet Union (Washington, DC: United States Government Printing Office, 1969), Doc. 475, pp. 696–709. See discussion in Preface.

[6] Ibid., Part 3, 701.

official senses, the Soviet Union would express its commitment to the United Nations and other international organisations. But for Kennan, this would be a purely instrumental commitment, subsisting only so long as it was seen to serve the Soviet Union's own interests: 'Moscow has no abstract devotion to UNO ideals', he argued, 'its attitude to that organization will remain essentially pragmatic and tactical'.[7] On the other hand, Kennan predicted that the Soviet Union would also pursue a range of activities on what he would call the 'subterranean plane'. On this plane, it would seek to spread its influence covertly through the 'conspiratorial' direction and control of communist parties and various other national and international associations in target countries. The associations he identified included everything from 'labour unions, youth leagues, women's organizations, racial societies, religious societies, social organizations, cultural groups, liberal magazines, publishing houses',[8] to the international labour movement, Pan-Slav movements and even the Russian Orthodox Church. The main objectives of such 'subterranean' activities, he maintained, would be to 'disrupt national self-confidence, to hamstring measures of national defence, to increase social and industrial unrest and stimulate all forms of disunity', to 'weaken the power and influence of Western Powers of [on] colonial backward, or dependent peoples', to remove from power those governments that stand in its way and to create dissension within and between Western powers. Thus 'in general' he concluded, 'all Soviet efforts on unofficial international plane will be negative and destructive in character, designed to tear down sources of strength beyond the reach of Soviet control'.[9]

Kennan's analysis of a Soviet Union adopting an opportunistic and instrumental approach to the precepts of the UN Charter was not unfair insofar as it reflected those elements of Soviet jurisprudence that were to view international law as intrinsically class-based. In that jurisprudence, international law was a transitional system of accommodation, bourgeois in form yet socialist in content,[10] acceptable only as far as it was 'compatible' with the interests of the Soviet State. But the charges of instrumentalism and opportunism were equally capable of being directed

[7] Ibid., Part 3(c), 702.
[8] Ibid., Part 4(3), 704.
[9] Ibid., Part 4(f), 705.
[10] See Evgeniĭ Bronislavovich, 'Pashukanis "International Law" (1925–1926)' in Piers Beirne and Robert Sharlot (eds.) *Pashukanis, Selected Writings on Marxism and Law* (London, Academic Press, 1980). Generally, John Hazard, 'Cleansing Soviet International Law of Anti-Marxist Theories' *American Journal of International Law*, 32 (1938) 244–52.

against the US itself.[11] Indeed in September 1946, the Soviet Ambassador in Washington, Nikolai Novikov, wrote his own equivalent of the Kennan telegram. In it he spelt out a contrasting account of 'the imperialist tendencies of American monopolistic capital': the way in which it was striving for 'world supremacy', turning the United Nations into an 'Anglo-American private domain', undermining the processes of democratisation fostered by the Soviet Union and creating conditions for the penetration of American capital into the economies of the world.[12]

Truman's announcement was significant in two respects. In the first place, it both inaugurated a condition of warlike enmity that characterised relations between the US and the Soviet Union over the following forty years and spelt out the terms under which that rivalry would be performed. This would be a largely subterranean contest fought out by third parties elsewhere. In the second place, it presaged the way the positions adopted by the US and the USSR would mirror one other, both strategically and rhetorically. If the threat perceived by Truman concerned itself with the surreptitious and subversive overthrow of democratic institutions by communist forces around the world, his answer was to commit the US to respond in kind, albeit (in his terms) in defence of the principles of the UN Charter and directed against the forces of totalitarianism. Precisely the same structure of ideas and actions permeated the cause of proletarian internationalism advanced by the Soviet Union. For it, the global struggle against monopoly capitalism and imperial intervention was equally pressing and equally aligned with the Charter's commitments to sovereign equality, self-determination and political independence. In each case, the rivals would accuse the other of precisely that which they intended to do themselves, and each waved the banner of legality in their own corner.

In Chapter 2, we showed how the UN Charter, designed by the great powers at Dumbarton Oaks, provided the framework for this Amero-Soviet contestation over the terms under which the world might be governed. As we saw, the UN Charter's commitments to sovereign statehood, territorial integrity, political independence and self-

[11] For the argument that the World Public Order method advanced by Lasswell, McDougal and Reisman was equally 'instrumental', see Iain Scobbie, 'Voyaging Towards Ithaca: Thinking about International Legal Theory' in Malcolm Evans (ed.), *International Law*, 6th ed. (Oxford: Oxford University Press, 2024).

[12] Telegram from Nikolae Novikov, Soviet Ambassador to the US, to the Soviet Leadership, 27 September 1946, History and Public Policy Program Digital Archive AVP SSSR, f. 06. Op. 8, 45; 759. See discussion in Preface.

determination provided not so much a restraint upon their rivalry as a common framework within which that rivalry might be performed. The focal point of that rivalry, we argued, was not to be the structures of the international order itself – indeed sovereign statehood and the principle of self-government were to be common points of departure (or better, common destinations) – but its operational content. The key question, and central point of contention, was who might be said to represent the nation-state or act in its name? Who, in other words, should have the right to govern?

In this chapter, we want to pick up that thread but develop it one step further. For as much as the UN Charter appeared to provide the stage for an East–West ideological contestation, we will argue here that Amero-Sovietism was a surprisingly collaborative project both within and outside the UN order. This was a project informed by a remarkably consistent set of ideas about the world and the terms under which it should be governed (through the medium of sovereign statehood), about the salient tasks to be performed (not just the preservation of peace but economic development and modernisation) and about the institutional structure through which that should be achieved (a United Nations and various specialised agencies under superintendence of the rival powers). Indeed, when seen from a certain vantage point, for all that the two powers were to foreground their mutual hostility, they also engaged with one another in a joint venture to exercise a controlling influence over the destiny of the globe, over the terms under which it might be ruled and the agendas that might be pursued.

Our term for this collaborative venture is 'Amero-Sovietism.' By this we mean a politics of bi-polarism that appeared, when looked at from the outside, as a conjunctive uni-polar order. This was an order born in the North with its zone of active operations in the South. It was an order that sought to encode all opposition to it in its own terms. Our readers will see that Amero-Sovietism would appear in various guises over the duration of the Cold War. It appeared at first in the guise of a co-imperium that was formalised in wartime plans for the disposition of the territories of the Axis powers in which the world was divided, at least provisionally, into various spheres of influence or interest. What were initially merely administrative demarcations – determining who might have responsibility for handling the terms of peace on behalf of the United Nations – were to become more enduring, ideological, frontiers dividing, in some cases, sovereign territory. Whilst the material effects of the wartime plans for co-imperium were to outlast the initially amicable relations upon which they were based, it would come to be superseded by another juridico-political framework of analysis – that of 'coexistence'. Whilst 'coexistence' was a language utilised for the most part by the Soviet Union, it served to give juridical expression to what the American government (but not the Soviets) called the 'Cold War' and was given formal expression in a range of (largely bilateral) instruments that sought to stabilise, or contain, Amero-Soviet competition. In the language of coexistence, the world was divided between the two rival social systems (in East and West) that remained in competitive isolation from one another but between whom a common set of legal principles governed their mutual relations. As we will see, though, the idea of coexistence was also to expose fractures within the Soviet bloc itself, particularly as regards its relationship to China and to anti-colonial movements elsewhere in the world. By the late 1960s, coexistence in turn gave way to a third idea – that of détente. During détente, the Amero-Soviets increasingly imagined themselves as partners in joint endeavours of a global character. Like coexistence (of which it was possibly a variant), the idea of détente came to be given formal expression in a number of legal instruments of the time. Where it differed was in its tendency to assume a multilateral, rather than a merely bilateral, form.

These three juridical/ diplomatic frames of reference – co-imperium, coexistence and détente – may be conceived as sequential historic phases in the arc of Cold War history. But they were also more than that, acting as three formulations of the idea of the Cold War itself in which notions of collaboration and competition came to be differentially articulated and expressed.[13] Their patterning became most evident in the legal instruments through which they were given expression – in the first, through the (imperial) arrangements for handling the conditions of peace; in the second, through the bilateral agreements between the rival powers establishing the conditions of their competition; in the third, through the crafting of new multilateral agreements through which they would conjointly lead the world into the future and secure their authority within it.

[13] For a discussion of the question around the 'cold warness' of international law and the 'international lawness' of the Cold War, see Matthew Craven, Sundhya Pahuja and Gerry Simpson (eds.), *International Law and the Cold War* (Cambridge: Cambridge University Press, 2019). For a standard approach, see Georg Schwarzenberger, 'The Impact of the East–West Rift on International Law' *Transactions of the Grotius Society* 36 (1950) 229–69.

For all of their differences, each of these three Amero-Soviet juridical/diplomatic enterprises had one thing in common: their tendency towards monopoly and the globalisation of Amero-Soviet Cold War thought and practice. At each moment, though, rival visions and accounts of global order were available, and forms of resistance to Amero-Soviet dominance were to emerge. Alternative orderings were both offered and sought, for example, in Korea in domestic opposition to Amero-Soviet trusteeship, in China in its resistance to Soviet imperialism or reformism, in the emergence of the Non-Aligned movement at the conferences in Bandung, Cairo and Belgrade and in Pan-Africanism. Amero-Sovietism, however, was consistent above all else in its hostility to such projects, or in its determination to ingest them within its own aleatory canals. Within the ideology of Amero-Soviet ideological dissensus, anti-imperialism was nothing other than anti-colonialism, anti-colonialism nothing other than national self-determination and national self-determination nothing other than choosing which side to join.

3.2 The Amero-Soviets

The Soviets and Americans reflected each other. Both States were born of revolution, and for each, revolution was not simply a birthright but a vocation.[14] Revolution was that which undergirded their own sense of collective identity and their claim to be the standard bearers of modernity but also that which they exported to the world in the name of its peoples. As Raymond Aron observed:

> American and Soviet ideologies are both revolutionary, directed against European domination of the peoples of Africa and Asia (a domination discredited by the word 'colonialism'), against the traditional caste systems and the inequitable distribution of wealth. Both ideologies promise happiness in this world by the application of science and technology to production, by the overthrow of despotic governments, by the liberation of peoples or masses or proletariats. Despite their rivalry (perhaps we should say *because* of it), they appear in the Near East and in Asia, it would seem, as two forms of the same Western industrial civilisation, which, although of European origin, is represented especially today by the two heir states.[15]

[14] In case of the US, see Claes Ryn, *The New Jacobinism: America as Revolutionary State* (National Humanities Institute, 1991).

[15] Raymond Aron, 'The Diffusion of Ideologies' *Confluence*, 2 (1953) 9.

Each possessed its own grandiose notion of political and economic life, and each sought to advance its own world-making project.[16] They were both committed to what Balibar called 'extensive universalities', that is, a universal code, which 'seeks to gather humanity ... together under a single authority, belief system or form of hope, if not indeed a shared "way of life"'.[17] They were also, as Scott Newton has suggested, 'weird sovereigns': hyper-legal, litigious, each modelling internally that which they imagined for the world – a multinational federal sovereignty.[18] And, finally, they were nuclear dark twins, each capable of destroying not only each other but the whole world.[19] Unusually, however, for two 'great powers', they had never been at war with each other (this remains the case, notwithstanding the face-off in Ukraine).

Despite their frequent claims to the contrary, there was a fundamental parallelism in the approach of both the Soviet Union and the US to international law. Both adopted a combination of self-conscious and performative law-abidingness and a willingness to think about international law in fundamentally strategic or instrumental ways.[20] If this posture was necessarily in-built in the case of the Soviet Union, which had grappled with the problematic legacies of the bourgeois international law of the nineteenth century,[21] it also came to mark US approaches to international law that sought to navigate between a Morgenthau-inspired political 'realism' and a Kelsenian scientific formalism.[22] In the case of

16 See Susan Buck-Morss, *Dreamworld and Catastrophe: The Passing of Mass Utopia in East and West* (Cambridge, MA: MIT Press, 2000).

17 Étienne Balibar, *Politics and the Other Scene* (London: Verso, 2002) 35.

18 Scott Newton, *Law and the Making of the Soviet World: The Red Demiurge* (Abingdon: Routledge, 2015) 2.

19 On 'dark twins', see Martin Sixsmith, *The War of Nerves: Inside the Cold War Mind*, Wellcome Collection (London: Profile Books 2021) 13. Walt Whitman in 1881 talked of Russia and the US as twins 'each with its own historic and divine mission' (Sixsmith, *The War of Nerves*, 9).

20 Charles Chaumont, *Nations Unies et Neutralité* (Leiden: A. W. Sitjthoff, 1956) 362. As Chaumont observed, both the realists of the Anglo-Saxon world and Marxist–Leninist analysts took the view that 'l'obligation juridique n'a pas de contenu normative autonome, mais ce contenu est le reflet d'une situation, qui s'exprime par des manifestations de volonté. Il ne s'agit pas d'une volonté diffuse, encore moins d'une volonté mondiale'.

21 See John Hazard, *Law and Social Change in the USSR* (London: Stevens and Sons, 1953) 275. Hans Kelsen attributed it to the inherently 'political' character of the Soviet theory of law. See Hans Kelsen, *The Communist Theory of Law* (New York: Frederick A Praeger, 1955) 193.

22 Martii Koskenniemi, *The Gentle Civiliser of Nations: The Rise and Fall of International Law, 1870–1960* (Cambridge: Cambridge University Press, 2002). See, too, Louis Henkin,

the US, the stance found its most prominent expression in a policy-inspired, process-driven account of international order that measured everything in terms of its contribution to the international 'values' most cherished by the US administration. For all its intellectual sophistication, the Yale policy school, as it became known, came suspiciously close, at times, to being merely a mouthpiece for US foreign policy.[23]

Despite the instrumental cast of their respective approaches to international law, each of the two rivals also thought of itself as unusually law-conforming. As far as the US was concerned, the opinions voiced by the likes of Truman and Kennan were generally shared within the American international legal academy in the post-war era. That literature was uniformly written against the background of a barely stated but nevertheless iron-clad, assumption that the United States was the law-abider, the Soviets the disregarder.[24] By 1951, this idea had taken such root in the *American Journal of International Law* that the Soviet jurist Korovin resigned from the American Society of International Law, accusing it of a 'slanderous misrepresentation' of the Soviet Union.[25]

On the Soviet side, we could find the same ideas represented in mirror image. Alongside routine denunciations of US imperialism and aggression, one encountered ardent defences of the Soviet Union's probity. Prior to his resignation from the American Society, for example, Korovin often extolled the Soviet Union's fidelity to treaty obligations. This was, he argued, not merely an age-old tradition of the Russian people but an innate characteristic of the Soviet Union itself. Flowing from the essentially democratic quality of Soviet diplomatic practice, and the 'monolithic nature of the Soviet society and state' characterised by 'the absence of antagonistic classes or groups',[26] 'no treaties in the world' he maintained 'are more stable than the treaty obligations of the USSR'.[27]

How Nations Behave: Law and Foreign Policy, 2nd ed. (New York: Columbia University Press, 1979).

23 See Richard Falk, 'Casting the Spell: The New Haven School of International Law' *The Yale Law Journal*, 104(7) (1995) 1991; Scobbie, 'Legal Theory as a Source of International Law'; David Kennedy, *International Legal Structures* (Baden-Baden: Nomos Verlagsgesellschaft, 1987).

24 See, e.g., Schwarzenberger 'The Impact of the East–West Rift on International Law', 268, who speaks of the 'cynical disregard by the Eastern States of established principles of international customary law, especially of the basic rule pacta sunt servanda'.

25 'The Society and the USSR' *American Journal of International Law*, 45 (1951) 780.

26 Eugene Korovin, 'The Second World War and International Law' *American Journal of International Law*, 40 (1946) 751–52.

27 Ibid.

And so, on both sides, the Soviet Union and the US each held onto the idea that they were unusually committed to honouring their treaty obligations and accused the other either of a straightforward lawlessness or a tendency to instrumentalise international law for political ends. Just as the US and its allies, for example, were to chastise the Soviet Union for its violation of the Protocol of Potsdam during the Berlin crisis of 1948,[28] or were to condemn its interventions in Hungary (1956) and Czechoslovakia (1968) as contrary to the terms of the UN Charter, so also was the USSR to counter that the US had engaged in illegal aggression in Taiwan, Vietnam, Laos and Cuba, or that it had engineered the division of Germany in violation of existing agreements. At various moments, each was to mimic the behaviour they denounced in the other. So, despite its condemnation of NATO as being fundamentally incompatible with the UN Charter, the Soviet Union constructed the Warsaw Pact on identical lines, and whilst the US denounced Soviet interventionist policy under the Brezhnev Doctrine, it would adopt a similar course in Guatemala and the Dominican Republic.[29]

To a certain extent, none of these claims were straightforward misrepresentations, but it would be equally wrong to imagine that law-abidingness was insincere. Of course, there were cynics among the international legal diplomatic corps and intelligentsia on both sides, but there was also a pervasive belief in international law and in the lawfulness of one's own State's activities.[30] As we have already seen, it was not the case that either the Soviet Union or the United States denounced the terms of the UN Charter or sought to claim that they were somehow excused from the obligations that it imposed upon them. Rather, they advanced the vision for the world imagined in the Charter – encouraging the dismantling of European colonial empires and the creation of a world of sovereign nation-states – whilst exploiting the gaps, silences and

[28] See Secretary of State for Foreign Affairs to Parliament, 'Germany: An Account of the Events leading up to a Reference of the Berlin Question to the United Nations', Cmd. 7534 (1948), 47

[29] See Franck, 'Who Killed Article 2(4)?'.

[30] A revealing example is the debate over a Hoover Institute study on 'The Soviet Government as a Treaty Partner, 1917' conducted by Jan Triska and Robert Slusser later published as Jan Triska, *The Theory, Law, and Policy of Soviet Treaties* (Stanford: Stanford University Press, 1962), which was subject of critique by Krylov. For a translation of Krylov's response in *Izvestiia*, see E. Finch, 'Shifting the Blame' *American Journal of International Law*, 51 (1957) 771–73.

ambiguities of the Charter to productive effect, utilising it as a strategic template for the conduct of their mutual antagonism.

In the rest of this chapter, we focus upon the mutual – sometimes conflictual, sometimes convivial – practices of the ideological rivals, on the way in which they conjointly crafted regimes for the delimitation of their respective spheres of interest and influence across the world and in which they translated their mutual rivalry into the language of peaceful coexistence and détente. If our end-point will be to turn to the mutual hostility of the Amero-Soviets towards antipathetic projects of world-making, our starting point is the more straightforward idea of an Amero-Soviet co-imperium through the creation of hegemonic spheres of influence. As we shall see, the creation of those spheres can be tracked back to the various allied conferences in Cairo, Moscow, Yalta and Potsdam, through which, we would argue, the Amero-Soviet Cold War was to be initially geographically instantiated.

3.3 Co-Imperium and Spheres of Influence

Only two years before his famous 'Iron Curtain' speech at Fulton, Missouri, Churchill had concluded a secret[31] 'informal' agreement with Stalin at the Fourth Moscow Conference. This became known as the 'percentages agreement'[32] that purported to delineate the 'spheres of influence' of each Allied power in South and Eastern Europe.[33] According to the document agreed upon in October 1944, 'Russia' was to have 90 per cent influence in Romania, 'the others' 10 per cent; Britain and the US were to have 90 per cent influence in Greece, and Russia 10 per cent. The shares in Yugoslavia and Hungary would be 50/50, and in Bulgaria, Russia would have 75 per cent, and the others a remaining 25 per cent. At a subsequent meeting between Molotov and Eden, the

[31] The content of the document became public in 1954 with the publication of Churchill's history of the Second World War. See Winston Churchill, *The Second World War: Triumph and Tragedy*, vol. 6 (London: Cassell and Co Ltd, 1954) 197–98.

[32] See Albert Resis, 'The Churchill–Stalin "Percentages" Agreement on the Balkans, Moscow, October 1944' *American Historical Review*, 82 (1978) 368–87. The immediate antecedent of the Percentages Agreement was the Anglo–Soviet London Treaty of 1942: Treaty for an Alliance in the War against Hitlerite Germany and Her Associates in Europe, London, 26 May 1942, Treaty Series No 2 1942 Cmd. 6376.

[33] See Winkler, *The Cold War*, 2. The Percentages Agreement was not quite a division but a more mathematical allocation of authority the implementation of which in terms of concrete policy was obscure.

'shares' allocated for Bulgaria and Hungary were altered, increasing the USSR's share to 80 per cent.[34] In Churchill's memoir, the agreement was sealed when Stalin appended a tick to the page of figures drafted by Churchill. The document was then left in Churchill's safekeeping with instructions that it be retained rather than 'burned'.[35]

Whilst the commanding significance of Churchill's self-styled 'naughty document' may well be doubted[36] (not least because it was concluded without the knowledge or participation of the US nor with any attendant instruction as to how it might be implemented), it was nevertheless profoundly illustrative. Not only did it evince a shared imperial mindset that would be carried through into post-war deliberations over the future of Eastern Europe, Germany and Japan and into the architecture of the UN itself, but it also illustrated the emergence of a bipolar (or, sometimes tripolar) zonal demarcation.[37] If not specifically proposing the creation of

[34] Eden remarks that 'Stalin had admitted that Greece was primarily a British concern, but Molotov showed a disposition to haggle over the percentages for other countries. Finally I told him that I was not interested in figures. All I wanted was to be sure that we had more voice in Bulgaria and Hungary than we had accepted in Roumania.' Athony Eden, *The Reckoning: The Eden Memoirs* (London: Cassell, 1965) 559. The record of the meeting, however, shows that Eden was more than willing to engage in a discussion of percentages. See Record of Meeting at the Kremlin, Moscow on 10 October 1944, 7 pm, Wilson Centre Digital Archive doc/123187.

[35] Churchill, *Triumph and Tragedy*, 198. Churchill claimed to have said: 'Might it not be thought rather cynical if it seemed we had disposed of these issues, so fateful to millions of people, in such an offhand manner? Let us burn the paper' to which Stalin apparently responded 'No, you keep it'.

[36] Aside from Churchill's own claim that it was a short-term arrangement (Churchill, *Triumph and Tragedy*, 197), it is commonly pointed out that the Soviet Union appeared to honour the agreement during the Greek crisis in 1945 but less evidently so in Romania and Hungary. For a critical analysis, see Panos Tsakaloyannis, 'The Moscow Puzzle' *Journal of Contemporary History*, 21 (1986) 37–55; Mark Percival, 'Churchill and Romania: The Myth of the October 1944 "Betrayal"' *Contemporary British History*, 12 (1998) 41–61; Warren F. Kimball, 'Naked Reverse Right: Roosevelt, Churchill and Eastern Europe from TOLSTOY to Yalta and a Little Beyond' *Diplomatic History*, 9 (1985) 1–24; P. G. H. Holdich, 'A Policy of Percentages? British Policy and the Balkans After the Moscow Conference of October 1944' *The International History Review*, 9 (1987) 28–47; Gavin Scrase, 'The Balkans and International Politics in the 1940s: On the Eden-Gusev Pre-Percentages Agreement' *Journal of Southern Europe and the Balkans*, 2 (2000) 163–76.

[37] Such thinking had circulated widely in both the Soviet and US foreign policy establishments. In the case of the Soviet Union, see M. M. Litvinov, *The Bolshevik Revolution: Its Rise and Meaning* (London: British Socialist Party, 1918). And generally, Geoffrey Roberts, 'Ideology, Calculation, and Improvisation: Spheres of Influence and Soviet Foreign Policy 1939–1945' *Review of International Studies*, 25 (1999) 655–73. In the case

'spheres of influence' (that language was deliberately avoided),[38] the agreement certainly sought to establish something analogous. Of significance, however, was not simply the idea that the Americans and the Soviets might divide the world between them (as Nixon once intimated to Kissinger)[39] but that those delineations spoke to a Cold War divide – both an 'Iron curtain', to use Churchill's evocative phrase, and a 'frontier zone' within which their mutual enmity might be played out.

3.3.1 *Division by Armistice*

Whatever the fate of the percentages agreement itself, it was already obvious by the time of the Moscow Conference in 1944 that the three allies were committed to two apparently contradictory objectives. One of these was to build an international organisation for securing global peace premised upon the territorial integrity and political independence of its members. The other was to enable the three powers (in the guise of the United Nations) to preside over that same world, securing their paramount interests within specified zones. If all had in mind the necessity of stabilising political borders (rolling back the clock sometimes to 1939 sometimes to 1941), all were equally clear that, in practice, the political orientation of the States to emerge out of the conflict would largely be dependent upon who would handle the terms of surrender.

The immediate manifestation of the resulting divisions could be found in the armistice agreements (or their functional equivalents) that were concluded in latter stages of the war.[40] Armistice agreements had long been the instrument of choice for bringing about a cessation of hostilities in international conflicts pending the conclusion of a treaty of peace.[41]

of the US, see Walter Lippmann, *US War Aims* (Boston: Little Brown & Co, 1944) and Sumner Welles, *The Time for Decision* (New York: Harper & Brothers, 1944).

[38] Resis, 'The Churchill–Stalin "Percentages" Agreement on the Balkans, Moscow, October 1944', 372. Resis points out, however, that 'the British and the Russians went through an elaborate pretense that their informal understanding was not a division of southeastern Europe into spheres of interest, while they were making just such a division' (ibid., 384).

[39] Sixsmith, *The War of Nerves*, 487.

[40] Neither the Japanese nor the German agreements were, strictly speaking, armistice agreements. See Karl Zemanek, 'Unconditional Surrender and International Law' *The Annual, Journal of the AAA*, 26 (1956) 29–37.

[41] For the 1918 armistice agreements, see Frederick Maurice, *The Armistices of 1918* (Oxford: Oxford University Press, 1943). In the interwar years, an armistice agreement was concluded to halt the Sino-Japanese conflict in 1932 and another in the conflict between Bolivia and Paraguay over the Gran Chaco in 1935. On armistice agreements

But in 1944 it was already apparent that the modalities by which such agreements were to be concluded would not only have a pre-figurative effect on the terms of any subsequent treaty of peace but would have more lasting effects upon the global distribution of purported authority amongst and between the Allied powers themselves. As such, the three Allied powers spent considerable time debating the terms under which the cessation of hostilities with Axis powers or their allies would be handled. And the terms of the agreements themselves largely determined the political 'destiny' of the territories in question (at least in the short term).

Whilst the Soviet Union had little involvement in the negotiation of the armistice agreement with Italy in 1943;[42] in the cases of both Romania (12 September 1944)[43] and Finland (19 September 1944),[44] it was agreed that the Soviet High Command of the Allied Forces should conclude the agreements 'on behalf of' the United Nations. Each of these agreements provided, amongst other things, for handing over to Soviet authorities the control of military materiel, the disarming of German forces, the repatriation of Allied prisoners of war and return of allied property, the payment of reparations to the Soviet Union[45] and sundry border adjustments.[46] In both cases, the agreement was to be superintended by an Allied Control Commission consisting of the Soviet High Command 'acting on behalf of the Allied Powers'.[47] Although in both cases the armistice agreement was merely an act prefatory to the

generally, see Howard S. Levi, 'The Nature and Scope of the Armistice Agreement' *American Journal of International Law*, 50 (1956) 880–906.

42 Armistice of Cassibile, 3 September 1943. This was later supplemented by the Instrument of Surrender, Malta, 29 September 1943, 61 Stat. 2742.

43 'United States – Great Briain – Soviet Union Armistice with Rumania' *American Journal of International Law Supplement*, 39 (1945) 88–108.

44 'Finland – Soviet Union: Armistice' *American Journal of International Law Supplement*, 39 (1945) 85–88.

45 In both cases, the indemnification was fixed at $300 million (art 11). In the case of Romania, this was paid 'over six years in commodities (oil products, grain, timber, seagoing and river craft, sundry machinery, et cetera)' and would be supplemented later by compensation for losses caused to other Allied powers.

46 In the case of Finland, this entailed the 'return' of the Oblast of Petsamo (Pechenga) to the Soviet Union and the restoration of the Aaland Islands agreement (arts 7 and 9). In the case of Romania, the restoration of the Soviet–Romanian state frontier and the return of the greater part of Transylvania to Romania (arts 4 and 19).

47 Romania, article 18; Finland, article 22.

conclusion of a later treaty of peace,[48] it was readily recognised that the composition of the Allied Control Commission would have a bearing on the political orientation of the local government that emerged. And whilst Finland was later to engineer for itself a path towards a sort of non-alignment,[49] Romania became firmly ensconced within the Soviet bloc. An almost identical armistice agreement was concluded with Hungary in January 1945,[50] following the agreement of a somewhat more nuanced one with Bulgaria in the previous year.[51]

These arrangements set the scene for the establishment of a number of satellite States in the European East under guise of 'people's democracies' (that ultimately included not just Romania, Hungary and Bulgaria but Poland,[52] Ukraine, Byelorussia, and Albania). But they were also evidently part of a broader bargain that included British and American freedom of action in Greece and Turkey, American control over the future of Japan and territories in the Pacific and joint post-war administration in the cases of Germany, Austria and Korea.

48 Treaty of Peace with Romania, London, 10 February 1947; 'Treaty of Peace with Finland, 1947' *American Journal of International Law Supplement*, 42 (1948) 203–23.

49 Finland refused Marshall aid and sought to develop economic relations with both the West and the Soviet Union. It was pressured into concluding an Agreement of Friendship, Cooperation and Mutual Assistance with the USSR on 6 April 1948, which committed it to 'fight to repel' any attack by Germany 'or any state allied with the latter' upon Finland or the Soviet union through Finnish territory (article 1) and to abstain from joining any alliance or coalition directed against the other High Contracting Party (article 4). In turn, the parties pledged themselves 'to observe the principle of mutual respect of sovereignty and integrity and that of non-interference in the internal affairs of the other state' (article 6).

50 Hungarian Armistice Agreement, Moscow, 20 January 1945, 59 Stat. 1321.

51 Armistice Agreement with Bulgaria, Moscow, 28 October 1944, article 18. In this case, as per the terms of the percentages deal, the armistice agreement provided that the Allied Control Commission would operate 'under the chairmanship' of the representative of the Soviet High Command and with the 'participation' of representatives of the United States and the United Kingdom. See Resis, 'The Churchill–Stalin "Percentages" Agreement on the Balkans, Moscow, October 1944', 376–77 who points out that the reason for more 'balanced' control was that, at the time in which the agreement was drafted, Bulgaria was not currently occupied by any of the allied powers (ibid., 379).

52 Poland became something of a cause célèbre in the West having been 'abandoned' by the allies at Yalta in 1945 in which it was agreed not only that the Soviet-installed Provisional Government should form the basis for the new Polish Government of National Unity but that the Eastern frontier should follow the Curzon line (which effectively transferred Lwow and Wilno into Soviet hands). See Protocol of Proceedings of the Yalta Conference (4–11 February 1945), VII.

3.3.2 *Japan and the 'Far East'*

The future of Japan and the 'Far East' was initially the subject of discussion at the Cairo Conference in 1943. At that conference, the US, Britain and China agreed that Japan should be 'stripped' of the islands in the Pacific, which she had 'seized or occupied' since 1914. These included the Carolines, Marshalls and Marianas, which Japan had been allowed to retain in 1919 and included also the territories 'stolen from the Chinese' such as Manchuria, Formosa and The Pescadores, which would be 'restored to the Republic of China'.[53] Japan would also be ousted from 'all other territories she has taken by violence and greed', which included presumptively Indo-China, Thailand, Burma, Malaya, the Philippines, the Dutch East Indies and Korea (which, it was said, would become independent 'in due course'). As Lippman put it, for the delegates in Cairo, Japan was 'to be an island nation near a continent where she has no foothold, and in an ocean which others command'.[54] It would experience a retrocession, in other words, to the territorial status it possessed in 1868.

The Soviet Union was not in attendance at Cairo and did not, at the time, formally align itself with the commitments spelt out there.[55] But the agreement was later referenced in the Potsdam Declaration of 1945. Paragraph 8 stated that 'the terms of the Cairo Declaration shall be carried out and Japanese sovereignty shall be limited to the islands of Honshu, Hokkaio, Kyushu, Shikoku and such minor islands as we determine'. In turn, the Potsdam Declaration set the stage for the subsequent occupation of Japan by US forces and would become a key reference point in the Japanese Instrument of Surrender,[56] which was 'accepted' by the Supreme Commander for the Allied Powers, General

[53] Cairo Declaration, Cairo, 26 November 1943. The agreement caused a certain amount of discontent in Australia and New Zealand who had anticipated that they would be consulted over future plans for the Pacific. See Herbert V Evatt, 'Risks of a Big-Power Peace' *Foreign Affairs*, 24 (1946) 197.

[54] Lippmann, *US War Aims*, 101.

[55] It is evident that the terms of the Cairo declaration were subject to discussion at the following meeting between Churchill, Stalin and Roosevelt in Teheran, albeit the joint declaration from that conference makes no mention of the fact. See, e.g., Keith Sainsbury, *The Turning Point: Roosevelt, Stalin, Churchill, and Chiang-Kai-Shek, 1943: The Moscow, Cairo and Teheran Conferences* (Oxford: Oxford University Press, 1985) 307–8. One of the obstacles facing the Soviet Union was the fact that it had signed a Neutrality Pact with Japan on 13 April 1941.

[56] Instrument of Surrender, Tokyo Bay, 2 September 1945, EAS No. 493.

MacArthur, on behalf of 'the United States, Republic of China, United Kingdom and the Union of Soviet Socialist Republics'. From that time onwards, the US largely had a free hand in the exercise of military government over Japan.[57] The various territorial concessions outlined in Cairo were also later formalised in the Japanese Peace Treaty (the Treaty of San Francisco) of 1951 in which Japan formally 'renounced' all right, title or claim to Korea, Formosa and the Pescadores, the Kurile, Spratly and Paracel Islands, the Antarctic area and the Mandate system.[58] Notably, however, with the exception of those territories that were to be 'returned to China' under the Cairo Declaration,[59] no specific mention was made as to the future of such territories, some of which became the subject of separate arrangements.[60]

One significant feature of the arrangements made in relation to the Far East was the conclusion between US and the Soviet Union (with the subsequent concurrence of the UK)[61] of a secret protocol appended to the Yalta agreement in which it was agreed that the Soviet Union would acquire sovereignty over part of Sakhalin and the Kurile Islands, a lease over Port Arthur for a Soviet Naval base, the internationalisation of the port of Dairen, a share in the operation of the Manchurian Railways and the 'preservation of the status quo' in Outer Mongolia. Ostensibly, the agreement had been reached in order to secure Soviet participation in the war on Japan, which took place two days after the atomic bombing of Hiroshima. The various terms of the Yalta protocol that related to China were then formalised in the Sino–Soviet Treaty of Friendship and Alliance of 14 August 1945, the terms of which had largely been dictated by the entry of Soviet troops into Manchuria.[62]

[57] See generally, Leslie C. Green, 'Law and Administration in Present-Day Japan' *Current Legal Problems*, 1 (1948) 118–205.

[58] Treaty of Peace with Japan, San Francisco, 8 September 1951, 1832 UNTS 46, Article 2.

[59] For a review of the arguments relating to Formosa, see D. P. O'Connell, 'The Status of Formosa and the Chinese Recognition Problem' *American Journal of International Law*, 50 (1956) 405–16.

[60] The US assumed responsibility for the Trust Territories of the Pacific Islands pursuant to SC Resn. 21 (2 April 1947).

[61] See Churchill, *Triumph and Tragedy*, 342, in which he comments: '[T]hough on behalf of Great Britain, I joined in the agreement neither I nor Eden took any part in making it. It was regarded as an American affair'.

[62] 'China, Soviet Union: Treaty of Friendship and Alliance' *American Journal of International Law Supplement*, 40 (1946) 51–63. The 'treaty' consisted, in fact, of a series of treaties that included, in addition to the main Treaty on Friendship and Alliance, an Agreement concerning Darien together with an appended Protocol, an Agreement on Port Arthur together with a signed Appendix, an Agreement relating to the entry of

The secret Yalta protocol spoke to the imperial ambitions of the wartime allies in their plans for the post-war world, but its shortcomings quickly became visible. Shortly after the founding of the PRC in 1949 following the ousting of the Kuomintang from mainland China, the USSR was forced to resile from the advantages it had obtained for itself at Yalta. Having recognised the PRC two days after its formation, it was induced to conclude a new Sino–Soviet Treaty of Friendship, Alliance and Mutual Assistance in 1950 (this time with the PRC rather than the ROC). In that treaty, the Soviet Union relinquished its claims in relation to the Manchurian railways, Dairen and Port Arthur.[63] On one hand, this appeared to be a necessary concomitant of securing Chairman Mao's commitment to 'lean towards' the Soviet Union. On the other hand, it exposed the tangible contradictions that underlay the emergent Amero-Soviet order, in which their commitment to the principles of self-determination and political independence that had been written into the Charter of the United Nations ran counter to a concurrent imperative to secure a controlling influence over the post-war world for the 'Great Powers' in their respective zones of interest.[64] As much as both the US and the USSR sought to burnish their anti-imperial credentials, they were also, as it transpired, imperial anti-imperialists. The resulting contradictions were to become ever more evident in those sites in which the Allies were to work most closely together – in Germany, Korea and, to a lesser extent, Austria.[65]

3.3.2.1 Austria

On 1 November 1943 in Moscow, the US, Britain and the Soviet Union had agreed that Austria, 'the first free country to fall a victim to Hitlerite aggression, shall be liberated from German domination'.[66] They declared the annexation imposed upon Austria by Germany to be 'null and void', and they committed themselves to the re-establishment of a 'free and

Soviet troops into the three eastern provinces and an Agreement concerning the Chinese Changchun Railway.

63 See generally, Austin Jersild, *The Sino–Soviet Alliance: An International History* (Chapel Hill: University of North Carolina, 2014); Bruce Elleman, *International Rivalry and Secret Diplomacy in East Asia 1896–1950* (Abingdon: Routledge, 2019).

64 See Chaumont, *Nations*, 350–53.

65 See generally, Günter Bischof, *Austria in the First Cold War, 1945–55: The Leverage of the Weak* (London: Palgrave Macmillan, 1999).

66 In a Tripartite Declaration at the Moscow Conference, see Tripartite Declaration on Austria, Moscow, 1 November 1943.

independent Austria' with the caveat that 'she has a responsibility which she cannot evade for participation in the war on the side of Hitlerite Germany'.[67]

Following the invasion and occupation of Vienna by Soviet Forces (one day after the Americans themselves had entered Austria), a provisional government was established by the former chancellor Karl Renner on 27 April 1945. Renner proclaimed the re-establishment of Austria as a democratic republic. Although the Western Allies were initially reluctant to recognise the Renner government, all four powers nevertheless agreed over the following months to divide Austria into four zones of occupation[68] and establish an Allied Council that, pending the establishment of a 'freely elected Austrian Government', would exercise supreme authority within Austria.[69] The Allied Council was composed of military commissioners drawn from each of the four powers. Their mandate was to exercise joint authority in relation to matters affecting Austria as a whole, but otherwise each could exercise supreme authority in the zone occupied by their respective forces.[70]

Despite the growing enmity between the rival powers in the following years, they nevertheless proceeded to follow through with the original plans for Austria, if on a delayed schedule. Two factors were influential. In the first place, the Renner government managed to obtain recognition from the Western powers following elections in December 1945 and could then claim to represent the interests of the Austrian people as a whole.[71] Secondly, the general perception that Austria was neither an

67 Ibid. See further Austrian State Treaty (Vienna, 15 May 1955) 6 UST 2369 (in force 27 July 1955); TIAS 3298.

68 Agreements concerning Control Machinery and Zones of Occupation in Austria and the Administration of the City of Vienna, London, 9 July 1945, Cmd 6958. The city of Vienna was divided into five 'parts' subject to the administrative authority of an 'inter-Allied Governing Authority (Komendatura)'.

69 Agreement on Control Machinery in Austria, London, 4 July 1945, Cmd 6958.

70 These agreements were supplemented three weeks later by a Protocol of the Potsdam Conference in which it was agreed that a Soviet proposal to provide for the extension of the authority of the Austrian Provisional Government to all of Austria would be examined after the entry of the British and American forces into Vienna. Potsdam Agreement, Protocol of the Proceedings, Potsdam, 1 August 1945, VII.

71 Agreements concerning Control Machinery and Zones of Occupation in Austria and the Administration of the City of Vienna, Vienna, 28 June 1946, Cmd 6958 (authority of Austrian government to extend fully throughout Austria subject to supervisory role of Allied Commission for Austria and Allied Council). From March 1946, the Austrian government had been permitted to exchange diplomatic representatives with all countries except Germany and Japan.

'ex-enemy state' nor to be burdened by reparations[72] meant that obstacles experienced in Austria were not of the same order as those found in Germany. There were certainly complications, which became evident in ensuing negotiations over the text of a State Treaty.[73] But the deadlock was ultimately broken by the conclusion of a Soviet–Austria agreement in 1955 in which Austria committed itself inter alia to a condition of permanent neutrality 'of the type maintained by Switzerland'[74] with provisions made for compensation of the Soviet Union.[75] On 15 May 1955, the Austrian State Treaty[76] was signed by the four occupying powers. This treaty recognised the re-establishment of Austria as a sovereign, independent and democratic State within the borders existing on 1 January 1938 and committed the four powers to respect Austria's independence and territorial integrity and to withdraw their forces. This was followed by Austria's admission to the United Nations and by four power recognition of Austrian neutrality.[77]

That a 'State Treaty' was deemed necessary to provide for Austrian independence once a freely elected government had been elected and recognised by all was by no means obvious. As was clear, however, the main consideration was the need for the Allied powers to agree between themselves the place that Austria would assume in the new European order. Eventually a functional compromise was reached in which Austria was allowed to engage in 'Westwards' facing activities (involvement in the Marshall aid programme as part of the OEEC, participation in the

[72] Potsdam Agreement, Protocol of the Proceedings, Potsdam, 1 August 1945. One of the main causes of delay over the conclusion of a Treaty in relation to Austria to bring about the end of occupation, however, concerned the identification of German assets in Austria itself. See Ernest Bevin, HC Deb. (5th ser), cols. 1738–39 (15 May 1947).

[73] The Council of Foreign Ministers of the four powers met in Moscow and London (1947), Paris (1949) and Berlin (1954) to work on the details during which time they met some 260 times. See generally, Gerald Stourzh and Wolfgang Mueller, *A Cold War over Austria: The Struggle for the State Treaty, Neutrality and the End of East–West Occupation, 1945–1955* (Lanham: Lexington Books, 2018) – in which debate over the recovery of 'German assets' in eastern Austria and Yugoslav territorial claims were central.

[74] See generally, Alfred Verdross, 'Austria's Permanent Neutrality and the United Nations Organization' *American Journal of International Law*, 50 (1956) 61–68.

[75] By the time of this agreement, Austria had already agreed to participate in the Marshall plan (2 July 1948), which provided the basis for the payments to be made to the Soviet Union. It received, in total, $962 million under that programme.

[76] State Treaty for the Re-establishment of an Independent and Democratic Austria, 15 May 1955, 277 UNTS 222.

[77] Which was confirmed by exchange of notes. For the text of the US note, see *Department of State Bulletin*, 33 (1955) 1011–12.

Council of Europe and EFTA and by its eventual conclusion of a free trade agreement with the EEC in 1972) on condition that it assume a posture of permanent neutrality, the conditions of which were to be constitutionally inscribed.[78]

Austrian neutrality, as was more than evident, was not a neutrality conceived in its traditional sense. It did not involve a generic posture of independence in relation to any present or future armed conflict, but rather a neutrality between East and West, and one which was imposed upon it, rather than freely chosen. This was expressed not only in a commitment not to adhere to any military alliance, and not to accept any military base on its territory, but also in the injunction that it engage between the powers in an 'even handed way'.[79] That it posed theoretical problems for the system of collective security there was no doubt,[80] but since the conflicts in contemplation under the terms of the Charter were not those that were to involve the rival powers themselves, there was little prospect that its neutrality would be seriously put to the test. Either way, however, Austria became a paradigmatic site for the re-coding of the concepts of both neutrality and political independence and an early example of Amero-Soviet coexistence.[81]

3.3.2.2 Germany

The situation in the case of Germany shared certain features with the post-war occupation of Austria but was in many respects very different. Here there was no 'government in waiting', no absence of resolve to impose punitive measures, no prospect of neutrality as a salve. In 1943, at the tripartite Conference in Moscow,[82] the foreign ministers of Britain, the US and USSR (Edan, Hull and Molotov) had agreed to establish a European Advisory Commission to study post-war political problems in Europe and to make recommendations to the three governments on matters relating to the surrender of enemy States and the machinery necessary for their fulfilment. The Advisory Commission held meetings in London throughout 1944 and produced a series of recommendations

[78] *Neutrality Act*, 26 October 1955.

[79] Wolfgang Mueller, *A Good Example of Peaceful Coexistence? The Soviet Union, Austria, and Neutrality, 1955–1991* (Vienna: Verlag der Österreichischen Akademie der Wissenschaften, 2011).

[80] On which, see Chaumont, *Nations*, 27–31.

[81] See Mueller, *A Good Example*.

[82] 'Tripartite Conference in Moscow' *American Journal of International Law Supplement*, 38 (1944) 3–8.

for the treatment of Germany post-surrender including a Protocol on the Occupation Zones in Germany[83] and an Agreement on Control Machinery.[84] These agreements were to form the background for the broader decisions made by the Powers in Yalta (4–11 February 1945) and Potsdam (17 July–2 August 1945) about the terms of German surrender and the post-war arrangements to ensure a lasting peace.

The agreed plan, as described in the Yalta Report of 1945, was that after the unconditional surrender of Nazi Germany, 'the forces of the Three Powers will each occupy a separate zone of Germany' and that 'coordinated administration and control' would be provided by a 'central Control Commission consisting of the Supreme Commanders of the Three Powers with headquarters in Berlin'.[85] Separate arrangements were made for the 'special Berlin area'[86] (which would be administered by an Inter-Allied Governing Authority [Kommandatura]) and for French participation in the occupation regime.[87] As was made confirmed at Yalta and reiterated in Potsdam,[88] 'supreme authority' was to be exercised by the Commanders-in-Chief of the armed forces of the four powers 'each in his own zone of occupation' and as members of the Control Council. The main object of occupation would be the pursuit of a series of 'D's': disarmament, demilitarisation, de-Nazification, democratisation and decentralisation.[89]

In the early stages, all three of the Allied leaders – Roosevelt, Churchill[90] and Stalin[91] – had embraced the idea of German

[83] Protocol on Zones of Occupation in Germany, London, 12 September 1944, 227 UNTS 279. The terms of this agreement were amended by Agreement on 14 November 1944.

[84] Agreement on Control Machinery in Germany, London, 14 November 1944, 5 UST 2062; TIAS 3070.

[85] Crimea (Yalta) Conference, 1945. Report signed at Yalta, 11 February 1945, 45 Foreign Relations 968. II

[86] Protocol on Zones of Occupation in Germany and the Administration of 'Greater Berlin', 1944, 227 UNTS 279.

[87] Agreement of 26 July 261945, amending Protocol between the Allies on the Occupation Zones in Germany London, 12 September 1944 5 UST 2087; TIAS 3071; Agreement of 1 May 1945 amending Agreement on Control Machinery in Germany, London, 14 November 1944, 5 UST 2072; TIAS 3070.

[88] Potsdam Agreement, Protocol of the Proceedings, Potsdam, 1 August 1945, IIA1.

[89] See Potsdam Agreement, 1945.

[90] See Keith Sainsbury, 'British Policy and German Unity at the End of the Second World War'*Historical Review*, 94 (1979) 786–804.

[91] Benn Steil, *The Marshall Plan: Dawn of the Cold War* (Oxford: Oxford University Press, 2018) 79. Maisky had set out Soviet postwar aims in relation to Germany in a memo of 11 January 1944, AVPRF, f.6, op.6, d. 147, II.14, 1–40.

dismemberment, and a plan was formulated by Morgenthau by which Germany was to be partitioned and 'pastoralised'.[92] Enthusiasm for that objective waned, however, as the Allies came to consider its ongoing economic costs.[93] Dismemberment was certainly mentioned as a possible outcome at Yalta[94] and a Committee on the Dismemberment of Germany was set up as a consequence, but all references to dismemberment were omitted from the Potsdam Protocol, 1 August 1945.[95] And in the Declaration of Berlin on 5 June 1945, the 'Allied Representatives' declared that whilst they assumed 'supreme authority with respect to Germany, including all the powers possessed by the German Government, the High Command, and any state, municipal, or local government or authority',[96] this was not to constitute the 'annexation' of Germany (albeit the case that they reserved the right to 'determine the boundaries of Germany or any part thereof and the status of Germany or of any area at present being part of German territory').

[92] Amongst his recommendations were the suggestions that Germany should be divided into two autonomous States in the South and North, that the Ruhr be 'internationalised' under UN control and that it should be stripped of its industrial capacity through the removal of industries vital to military strength that would be re-located to other countries as a form of restitution. See Henry Morgenthau, 'Suggested Post-Surrender Program for Germany' 5 September 1944, Quebec; Henry Morgenthau, *Germany Is Our Problem* (New York: Harper 1945). See also Welles, *The Time for Decision*.

[93] See generally, Philip E. Mosely, 'Dismemberment of Germany: The Allied Negotiations from Yalta to Potsdam' *Foreign Affairs*, 28 (1950) 487–98; Warren F. Kimball, *Swords or Ploughshares? The Morgenthau Plan for Defeated Nazi* Germany, *1943–1946* (Philadelphia: Lippinncott, 1976); Frank King, 'Allied Negotiations and the Dismemberment of Germany' *Journal of Contemporary History*, 16 (1981) 585–95. For a more recent take, see Steil, *Marshall Plan*.

[94] Protocol of Proceedings, 11 February 1945, s III.

[95] Whilst the US, UK and USSR all eventually abandoned their plans for dismemberment, France remained a vocal advocate until 1947. In that guise, it sought the transformation of the Saar and Western Rhineland into autonomous political entities, the international isation of the Ruhr and the creation of a large number of small, autonomous German States. See Hans-Peter Schwarz, 'The Division of Germany, 1945–1949' in Melvyn Leffler and Odd Arne Westad (eds.), *The Cambridge History of the Cold War* (Cambridge: Cambridge University Press, 2019) 144.

[96] 'Declaration Regarding the Defeat of Germany and the Assumption of Supreme Authority with Respect to Germany by the Governments of the United Kingdom, the United States of America and the Union of Soviet Socialist Republics, and the Provisional Government of the French Republic', Berlin, 5 June 1945, Cmd. 6648. The Declaration noted that 'there is no central Government or authority in Germany capable of accepting responsibility for the maintenance of order, the administration of the country and compliance with the requirements of the victorious Powers'.

Despite this, many speculated that Germany had, indeed, ceased to exist. Even before the end of the war, for instance, Hans Kelsen had already predicted that since the conclusion of a peace treaty with the Nazi government appeared impossible,[97] and since the regime of belligerent occupation precluded its partition or reconstruction, the only viable option was to extinguish the State of Germany by conquest and re-found it afresh.[98] Whilst the formal extinguishment of the State of Germany was to be a foundational jurisdictional necessity for the Nuremberg Tribunal (whose creation, it was claimed, was based upon a 'sovereign legislative power' that the Allied powers had somehow acquired),[99] other commentators were more willing to take at face value the allied powers' declaration of non-annexation. In the process, though, they were forced into convoluted explanations as to the character of the occupation. A variety of rubrics were at play. For some it was best described as a 'government in commission',[100] for others, a 'condominium',[101] a 'co-imperium',[102] a 'trusteeship'[103] or an 'international administration'.[104] What all had in common, however, was the idea that 'Germany' as such continued to exist, even if only in virtual or anticipatory form, and that the Allied powers exercised the requisite authority to determine its present and future.

[97] The Doenitz government having been displaced by the occupying authorities and several of its members put on trial.

[98] Hans Kelsen, 'The International Legal Status of Germany to Be Established Immediately upon the Termination of the War' *American Journal of International Law*, 38 (1944) 689–94; Hans Kelsen, 'The Legal Status of Germany according to the Declaration of Berlin' *American Journal of International Law*, 39 (1945) 519.

[99] See International Military Tribunal (Nuremberg) Judgment 'The making of the Charter was the exercise of the sovereign legislative power by the countries to which the German Reich unconditionally surrendered; and the undoubted right of these countries to legislate for the occupied territories had been recognized by the civilized world', 216. For commentary, see Quincy Wright, 'The Law of the Nuremberg Trial' *American Journal of International Law*, 41 (1947) 50–51.

[100] R. Y. Jennings, 'Government in Commission' *British Yearbook of International Law*, 23 (1946) 123.

[101] Kelsen, 'The Legal Status of Germany according to the Declaration of Berlin', 519; Schwarzenberger, 'East–West Rift', 17.

[102] F. A. Mann, 'The Present Legal Status of Germany' *Problems of Public and Private International Law*, 33 (1947) 119–45.

[103] Max Rheinstein, 'The Legal Status of Occupied Germany' *Michigan Law Review*, 47 (1948) 24.

[104] Michel Virally, *L'Administration Internationale de l'Allemagne: Du 8 Mai 1945 au 24 Avril 1947* (Paris: Pedone, 1948).

The terms of the agreed settlement became a regime of co-imperium premised upon the conjoint authority of the allied powers in place of an otherwise absent German government. They were neither mere occupants of German territory, nor did they exercise sovereignty over it in their own right. Rather, they enjoyed the power, both individually within their own designated zones and collectively, on behalf of Germany as a whole, to act *as if* they were the government of Germany.[105] This created a structural dynamic through which a formally unitary German State was effectively divided along ideological lines.[106] And so what was, in one sense, an act preserving the integrity of Germany – holding in place the promise offered in Potsdam for the 'eventual reconstruction of German political life'[107] – was in another sense the medium through which the Amero-Soviet Cold War would come to be spatially configured by way of its reproduction along divisional lines.

But the roots of the ensuing divisions that were to secure the effective partition of Germany until its 'reunification' in 1990 could all be traced back to the contradictions that were set in place in the text of the Potsdam declaration. Potsdam envisaged not merely the de-nazification and de-militarisation of Germany but its political and economic 'decentralisation', enabling each of the occupying powers to extract reparations (primarily by way of the removal of industrial plant) in their respective zones.[108] At the same time, though, the Potsdam agreement

[105] James Crawford, *The Creation of States in International Law*, 2nd ed. (Oxford: Oxford University Press, 2007) 453.

[106] The decision had already been taken at Potsdam that, 'pending a final determination', the City of Königsberg and surrounding area would be 'placed under the administration' of the Soviet Union and that the territory West of the Oder-Neisse line should be administered by Poland (and, for such purposes, 'should not be considered as part of the Soviet zone of occupation in Germany'). So, by the end of 1945, Germany had already been divided into seven separate areas: the four zones of occupation, the 'special Berlin area', Königsberg, and the territory granted to Poland. Greater Berlin itself was subdivided into four sectors (British, French, US and USSR); and, in the following year, France was to carve out a Saar protectorate from the Allied zones of occupation. In total, then, there appeared eleven discrete 'provisional' demarcations that would serve as the initial topography for the spatial instantiation of the cold war in Germany.

[107] Potsdam Agreement, Protocol of the Proceedings, Potsdam, 1 August 1945, IIA1, article 3(iv), which described one of the purposes of the occupation of Germany to be 'to prepare for the eventual reconstruction of German political life on a democratic basis and for eventual peaceful cooperation in international life by Germany'.

[108] The formula for reparations was, in fact, somewhat more complex. Whilst the Allied powers contented themselves with reparations from Western Zones and from 'appropriate German external assets', the USSR was to receive, in addition, 10 per cent of industrial capital equipment from the Western Zones without payment and a further

insisted that Germany 'shall be treated as a single economic unit' and common policies be developed in relation to a range of issues including mining, industrial production, agriculture, wages, prices, import and export programmes, currency, banking, transport and communications.[109] It also proposed that the Control Council should ensure 'the equitable distribution of essential commodities between the several zones so as to produce a balanced economy throughout Germany and reduce the need for imports'.[110] Reparations, furthermore, were to leave 'enough resources to enable the German people to subsist without external assistance',[111] whilst ensuring that German living standards should not exceed 'the average of the standards of living of European countries'.[112]

It became immediately apparent that a central tension in the Potsdam agreement was its commitment to both political and economic decentralisation and at the same time as the maintenance of a central coordinating function on the part of the occupying powers in the name of Germany as a whole. A great deal depended, therefore, upon the willingness of the occupying powers themselves to coordinate and align their respective administrative policies with one another. As it transpired, though, any such coordination was to last less than a year.

The original US occupation policy (JCS 1067 of April 1945)[113] had largely oriented itself towards the imposition of a Morgenthau-style 'hard peace'. This changed in September 1946 when US Secretary of State Byrnes issued his 'Restatement of US Policy on Germany' (known also as his 'Speech of Hope').[114] In that restatement, he argued that the economically independent Germany that had been imagined in the Potsdam Agreement[115] had been fatally undermined by the failure of

15 per cent in exchange for food, coal, potash, zinc, timber, clay products, petroleum products and any other commodities 'as may be agreed upon'. Potsdam Agreement, Protocol of Porceedings, 1 August 1945, Section III.

109 Ibid., Section II.B.14

110 Ibid., Section II.B.15.(c).

111 Ibid., Section II.B.19

112 Ibid., Section II.B.15.(b).

113 'Directive to the Commander in Chief of the United States Forces of Occupation' *Department of State Bulletin*, 13 (1945) 596. Its first objective, it was stated, should be to bring home to the German people that 'Germany's ruthless warfare and the fanatical Nazi resistance have destroyed the German economy and made chaos and suffering inevitable' and that they 'cannot escape responsibility for what they have brought upon themselves'.

114 James F. Byrnes, 'Restatement of Policy on Germany' *Department of State Bulletin*, 15 (1946) 496.

115 See Potsdam Protocol, II, B, 14.

the Allied Control Council to take the necessary measures[116] and by the Soviet Union's actions in taking reparations from current production (rather than by removing industrial plants or sequestering foreign assets). He proposed as an alternative that the US zone be economically and politically unified 'with any or all of the other zones willing to participate in the unification'.[117] Within a year, the US zone was merged with the British zone,[118] and within another year, the French zone.[119] Although these mergers took place in accordance with the devolved powers accorded to the occupying authorities under the Protocols, the process was roundly denounced by the Soviet Union for effecting 'the political and economic splitting and dismemberment of Germany'[120] violating the terms of the Potsdam agreement. The repercussions were to be long-lasting. The Soviet representative, Marshal Vasily Sokolovsky, walked out of the Allied Control Council for Germany, never to return.[121] This brought the Control Council to an end as an effective instrumentality of government.[122] This was followed by the Soviets refusing to participate in the Berlin Kommandatura and imposing restrictions on allied road and rail traffic between the Western Zones and Berlin leading ultimately to the institution of a full blockade of Berlin on the 24 June 1948.

On both sides of the ideological divide there was a startling parallelism in their respective positions on Germany. The Western Allies simultaneously pushed for the economic unification of Germany and its political 'decentralisation'. Stymied in their efforts to secure common economic policies for Germany as a whole (including, for example, decartelisation and monetary reform) they pushed for the integration of the (West) German economy into a broader European economic alliance through the medium first of the Marshall Plan and then the Schuman plan. They

[116] Byrnes, 'Restatement', 498: 'So far as many vital questions are concerned, the Control Council is neither governing Germany nor allowing Germany to govern itself.'

[117] Byrnes, 'Restatement', 498, and if economic unification of German as a whole was not possible, it sought to 'do everything in its power to secure the maximum possible unification'.

[118] Agreement between the Governments of the United Kingdom and the United States on the Economic Fusion of their Respective Zones, New York, 2 December 1946.

[119] In the process, it formed what became known as 'Tri-Zone' or 'Trizonia'. See Schwarz, 'The Division of Germany', 144.

[120] See Declaration of the Warsaw Conference of Foreign Ministers, Warsaw, 24 June 1948.

[121] The Allied Control Council did meet once again in 1971 to conclude the Four Power Agreement on Berlin.

[122] This was followed, in June, by the Soviet representative walking out of the Kommandatura.

believed that in order to reduce the ongoing costs of occupation and stave off the prospect of communist encirclement, they needed to merge the Western economies placing the industrial might of West Germany at the heart. On the other hand, they actively promoted the creation of a decentralised Federal political system – re-creating the Länder and empowering local political constituencies. The Soviet Union, by contrast, held out for the political unification of Germany as a whole – supposing, it seemed, that a united Germany could be brought under Soviet influence and 'indirect rule'.[123] Accordingly, it actively centralised political authority in the East (rejecting, as Schwarz puts it, 'Western pluralism').[124] Economically, on the other hand, Stalin opposed the 'unification' of Germany along the lines proposed by the Western Allies. He insisted, instead, upon the Soviet Union's right to extract reparations from the East-German economy and to maintain Soviet control over the economy in the process. What all this meant was that if Germany was visibly being split in two in a popular sense, it was also being 'doubled' in much in the same way as China was 'doubled' during the period between 1948 and 1971. The difference was, though, that in China, the rival governments pitched themselves in permanent opposition to one another, whereas in Germany the doubling took on a decidedly provisional cast.

One of the extant causes of the Berlin crisis of 1948 had been the convening of the Six Power London Conference in February 1948 to which the Soviet Union was not invited,[125] and which had led to a series of measures designed to establish a constitutional German government in the Western Zones.[126] A Parliamentary Council was formed to draft a 'basic law'[127] alongside arrangements for of the organisation of

[123] Vladimir O. Pechatnov, 'The Soviet Union and the World' in Melvyn Leffler and Odd Arne Westad (eds.), *The Cambridge History of the Cold War* (Cambridge: Cambridge University Press, 2019) 103.

[124] Schwarz, 'The Division of Germany, 1945–1949', 148.

[125] The convening of the conference was treated, by the Soviet Union, as a 'violation of the Potsdam Agreement and of other decisions . . . in accordance with which responsibility for the administration of Germany and for the determination of policy with respect to Germany is borne jointly by the occupying Powers, which is incompatible with separate activities'. The Soviet Ambassaor (Panyushkin) to the Acting Secretary of State (Lovett), 13 February 1948, in Foreign Relations of the United States, 1948, Germany and Austria, vol. II, Doc. 229, 338.

[126] See Foreign Relations of the United States, 1948, Germany and Austria, vol. II, Docs. 1–251.

[127] The 'Basic Law (Grundgesetz) of the Federal Republic of Germany' on 8 May 1949.

elections.[128] This was followed in 1949 by the adoption of an 'Occupation Statute', which gave the Federal Republic full legislative and judicial powers.[129] Ultimate authority, however, was retained by the Western Allies. An Allied High Commission was constituted to assume the powers vested in the three Commanders-in-Chief of the three Western Allies ('from whatever source') to exercise control over the Federal Government and the Governments of the constituent Lander.[130] It was also decided[131] that the FRG would join the Convention for European Economic Cooperation[132] that had been established to give effect to the Marshall Plan. In a manner redolent, as we shall see, of its policy in Korea, the Soviet Union simultaneously protested against the formation of the FRG and proceeded to set up a parallel government – the German Democratic Republic – in the East (7 October 1949). In each instance, the occupying authorities concerned used their individual authority under the zonal arrangements to delegate governmental responsibly to the respective governments.[133]

In face of the establishment of a rival German government in the East, the Western Allies issued a Declaration in the following year asserting that the government of the FRG was 'the only German Government freely and legitimately constituted and therefore entitled to speak for the German people in international affairs'.[134] This position was subsequently re-affirmed in the Tripartite Convention on Relations of 26 May 1952, which terminated the occupation regime and declared, in article 1(2), that the FRG had 'the full authority of a sovereign State over

[128] Ferenc Vali, 'Legal Constitutional Doctrines on Germany's Post-World War II Status' *North Dakota Law Review*, 42 (1965) 25.

[129] The 'Occupation Statute' of 17 April 1949, Official Gazette of the Allied High Commission for Germany, 23 October 1949. This was followed by the holding of elections on 7 August 1949 and the establishment of the Allied High Commission in Germany on 7 September 1949. The occupation statute entered into force on 21 September 1949. See Declaration Concerning the Entry into Force of the Occupation Statute, Bonn, 21 September 1949.

[130] Charter of the Allied High Commission for Germany, Paris, 20 June 1949.

[131] Memorandum on the Powers and Responsibilities of France, United Kingdom and United States Following the Establishment of the FRG, Washington, DC, 8 April 1949.

[132] Convention for European Economic Cooperation, Paris, 16 April 1948.

[133] See Crawford, *The Creation of States*, chapter 10, albeit the case that in both instances the 'sponsoring authorities' went someway beyond the confines of a mere delegation of powers.

[134] 'Communiqué on Germany', 19 September 1950, Foreign Relations of the United States, 1950, Western Europe, vol. III, Docs. 589, 1296.

its internal and external affairs'.[135] This was followed once again by a parallel initiative in the east in which the Soviet Union and the GDR concluded a bilateral agreement in 1955, which formally recognised the GDR and accorded it general freedom of action in relation to its domestic and foreign policy.[136]

Whilst the Soviet Union recognised the FRG on 13 September 1955 (retroactive to 1949), Western States withheld their recognition of the GDR for nearly two decades.[137] The rationale variously provided was that it was not independent from the USSR, that there were no free elections, or that it violated the German population's right of self-determination.[138] Indeed, this became a policy most vigorously pursued by the FRG itself in the guise of the 'Hallstein doctrine',[139] one of the aims of which, according to Kissinger, was to preclude German unification becoming a matter of bilateral negotiation between the two States.[140] It was only following the conclusion of a treaty in 1970 between the USSR and the FRG that declared the frontiers of all States 'inviolable' (including that between Poland and the FRG and GDR),[141] and another in 1972 between the two German republics recognising the limits of their respective authority,[142] that an accommodation was reached that ultimately led to the admission of the two States to membership in the United Nations on 18 September 1973 by way of a 'dual' resolution.[143]

[135] Convention between the United Kingdom of Great Britain and Northern Ireland, the United States of America, France and the Federal Republic of Germany on Relations between the Three Powers and the Federal Republic of Germany (with Annex) (signed 26 May 1952, entered into force 5 May 1955) 331 UNTS 328.

[136] Treaty concerning Relations between the USSR and the GDR, Moscow, 20 September 1955, 226 UNTS 201. As Kissinger pointed out, the recognition given to the GDR effectively removed the issue of German unification from the international agenda – consigning it, essentially, to negotiations between the two German States. Kissinger, *Diplomacy*, 520.

[137] See generally, William Gray, *Germany's Cold War: The Global Campaign to Isolate East Germany 1949–1969* (Chapel Hill: University of North Carolina Press, 2003)

[138] Crawford, *The Creation of States*, 456–57.

[139] See generally, Gray, *Germany*, 81–87; Thomas Grant, 'Hallstein Revisited: Unilateral Enforcement of Regimes of Nonrecognition Since the Two Germanies' *Stanford Journal of International Law*, 36 (2000) 223–30.

[140] See Kissinger, *Diplomacy*, 572.

[141] Moscow Agreement, Moscow, 12 August 1970, article 3.

[142] Treaty on the Basis of Intra-German Relations, East Berlin, 21 December 1972: 'The Federal Republic of Germany and the German Democratic Republic proceed on the assumption that neither of the two States can represent the other in the international sphere or act on its behalf.'

[143] UNGA Res 3050 (XXVIII)(18 September 1973); UNSC Res 355 (22 June 1973).

The new territorial settlement that appeared around the time of the constitution of the new German republics had two particular features. First, it worked on the basis of a differentiation being held in place between the spatial order of the FRG and GDR as sovereign States and that of the (pre-1945 and, ultimately, post-1989) unified Germany of which they were a vestigial part. As Crawford observed, 'prior to 1990 there were not one but three German States'[144] since, in addition to the FRG and GDR, the 'quadripartite government of Germany retained functional and territorial authority with respect to "Germany as a whole"', including, in particular, Greater Berlin, and in that capacity was 'formally independent of both the FRG and GDR'.[145] If the resulting multiplication of German statehood ran counter to the theoretical purity of the Charter vision of the unitary nation-state, it was nevertheless one that gave visible expression to the basic contradictions of a Cold War international law: a law that sought to formalise, and in the same measure freeze, a political contestation over the future of Germany and the terms under which the German people might govern themselves. If Amero-Soviet nuclear rivalry threatened the destruction of Germany, and Europe alongside it, the most appropriate response, as Kennedy acknowledged, was to maintain 'the state of political suspension'.[146] Even if, as he put it, the building of the Berlin wall was 'not a very nice solution', it was, nevertheless, 'a hell of a lot better than a war'.[147]

Secondly, the status of Berlin was central to this imaginary in both a material and symbolic sense. As the former capital of the pre-1945 German State, it came to stand – at least in the West – as a symbol both of the vestigial aspiration of a united Germany and more broadly of hopes for global peace in a post–Cold War world.[148] Following the collapse of the system of quadripartite occupation envisaged for Berlin on 1 July 1948 (when the Soviet Union withdrew from the joint administration), and following the subsequent blockade of West Berlin by the Soviets, an agreement was reached between the Four Powers on

[144] Crawford, *The Creation of States*, 465.

[145] Ibid.

[146] Quoted in Jeremy Suri, *Power and Protest: Global Revolution and the Rise of Détente* (Cambridge, MA: Harvard University Press, 2003) 23.

[147] Ibid.

[148] This was nowhere more keenly felt than in the FRG itself, which, in its Declaration on Aid to Berlin, Bonn, 26 May 1952, it emphasised both 'the special role which Berlin has played' and which it 'is destined to play in the future for the self-preservation of the free world'.

4 May 1949, the effect of which consolidated 'the new actual and legal situation which had arisen in the two parts of Berlin'.[149] From that time onwards, although the German city administration was divided into the Western and Eastern sectors of Greater Berlin – demarcated after 1961 by wire and walls – it remained stubbornly subject to quadripartite authority. Despite their many differences,[150] the Western Allies resisted any attempt by the GDR to incorporate East Berlin within its exclusive jurisdiction as its capital,[151] and all four powers equally refused to contemplate West Berlin becoming subject to the jurisdiction of the FRG.[152] Berlin remained, as such, the material representation of a juridically, and politically, divided Cold War world and remained the focal point of discussions as to the future of Germany and ultimately Europe with it.

If the case of Germany was unique, it was also deeply emblematic of how the practice of the emergent Cold War would shape itself around the formal agreements concluded at Yalta and Potsdam. For whilst the terms of those agreements were by no means fully implemented at the time – in the sense of leading the way to the 'eventual reconstruction of German political life on a democratic basis' and for the 'eventual peaceful cooperation in international life by Germany'[153] – they nevertheless provided the grounds upon which the ideological division of Germany would be performed. Yalta and Potsdam provided both the structural conditions and raw materials for an improvised political settlement – not by way of the occlusion of German sovereignty, or by its permanent division, but through its duplication on either side of the line in which the two nascent representatives of the German 'whole' could be formed and enveloped within strategic blocs in which the promises of the two Charters (Atlantic and UN alike) (and their respective interpretations) could be held in place.

3.2.2.3 Korea

Whilst the division of Germany was shaped by the way the Allied conjoint powers' plans for the imposition of a 'hard peace' upon a former

[149] Adam D. Rotfeld, 'Legal Foundations of the West Berlin Status' *Polish Yearbook of International Law*, 6 (1974) 103.
[150] See generally, Kissinger, *Diplomacy*, 568–93.
[151] This was the central issue in the abortive Soviet proposals of 1959 for a German peace treaty between the two German States incorporating a 'Free city of West Berlin'.
[152] Rotfeld, 'Legal Foundations', 98.
[153] Potsdam Protocol IIA3(iii).

Axis power unravelled, that of Korea followed a rather different path. In this case, the division resulted initially from both occupying powers being unwilling to permit the self-determination of a people whom they claimed to have 'liberated'. This was a division that became provisionally formalised through warfare and subsequently reaffirmed as permanent at the 'end' of the Cold War. But although the trajectories diverge, they are resonant of the overall character of Amero-Sovietism. The fate of Germany in the North appears to serve as a material representation of a dominant narrative of the Cold War's rise and fall: Germany's unification putatively erasing the ideological battlelines that had divided the State of Germany for half a century. On the other hand, the story of Korea in the South is about the subversion of an anti-colonial struggle, a not-so-cold warfare by proxy and the ultimately permanent division of a territory in the name of its liberation.

On 1 December 1943, the United States, China and Great Britain all agreed, in the Joint Declaration of Cairo, to liquidate the Japanese protectorate over Korea. They expressed their determination that 'in due course Korea shall become free and independent'.[154] That declaration was reaffirmed on 26 July 1945 in the Potsdam Declaration with the concurrence of the Soviet Union.[155] The possibility of Korea regaining its independence after thirty-five years of colonial rule appeared to be on offer. But the phrase 'in due course' was a laden one. It spoke not only of the fact that Korea would have first to be occupied before becoming independent but also that its independence was likely to be preceded by the establishment of a trusteeship.[156]

As in case of much of Eastern Europe, the terms of the enemy surrender were of decisive importance. It had been (secretly) agreed that Japanese forces north of the 38th parallel would surrender to Soviet

[154] 'Conference of President Roosevelt, Generalissimo Chiang Kai-Shek, and Prime Minister Churchill in North Africa' *American Journal of International Law Supplement*, 38 (1944) 8.

[155] Proclamation for Defining Terms of Japanese Surrender' *Department of State Bulletin*, 13 (1945) 137–38.

[156] The initial suggestion was that China, the US and the USSR would act as trustees. Britain was later included in proposals for a quadripartite trusteeship. See William Stueck, *The Korean War: An International History* (Princeton: Princeton University Press, 2001) 268. Sumner Welles had earlier asserted that 'with the restoration of Korean independence, one of the great crimes of the twentieth century will have been rectified'. Sumner Welles, 'Preface', in Robert Oliver, *Korea: Forgotten Nation* (Washington, DC: American Council on Public Affairs, 1944).

forces, and those to the south, to the United States forces.[157] Soviet forces then entered north Korea on the 10 August 1945 to receive the surrender of Japanese troops. The US followed suit in the South a month later. It was generally understood that following the disarmament of Japanese forces, Korea would be reunited under a government of its own choice. As it was to transpire, there was considerably less agreement about how this might take place. Whilst the Soviet Union, for its part, began by organising a 'People's Committee' in the northern zone under leadership of Kim il Sung, in the South, General MacArthur quickly established military government,[158] sidelining in the process the government of the 'Peoples Republic of Korea' that had established itself prior to the arrival of US troops.

Since early relations between military commanders proved less than fruitful, in December 1945, the question of 'unification' was placed on the agenda of the Council of Foreign Ministers at a meeting in Moscow. A Tripartite Agreement was ultimately concluded in which the powers agreed to implement the Cairo Declaration's objective of forming a free and independent Korea 'in due course' (27 December 1945).[159] This was to be achieved through the formation of a 'provisional Korean democratic government' under the guidance of a Joint Commission whose task it was to prepare for 'the re-establishment of Korea as an independent state'. The role of the Joint Commission was to develop a set of proposals for the governments of the USSR, US, China and Britain to work through. One of the objectives would be 'working out of an agreement concerning a four-power trusteeship of Korea for a period of up to five years'.[160]

[157] United States Department of State Historical Office, *The Record on Korean Unification 1943–1960: Narrative Summary with Principal Documents* (1960) 44. This division was both revealed and operationalised in General MacArthur's General Order No. 1 governing the conditions of Japanese surrender. See further Robert Oliver, *Why War Came in Korea* (New York: Fordham University Press, 1950) 117.

[158] General Order No. 1 of 7 September 1945, Foreign Relations of the United States, Diplomatic Papers, 1945, The British Commonwealth, the Far East, vol. VI, Docs. 776, 1043.

[159] In the joint communique, it was agreed that 'with the view to the re-establishment of Korea as an independent State … there shall be set up a provisional Korean democratic government' and that a joint commission should be established to 'assist the formation' of such a government. Foreign Relations of the United States, Diplomatic Papers, 1945, The British Commonwealth, the Far East, vol. VI, Docs. 845, 1150.

[160] Ibid., 1151.

In fact, the trusteeship idea had been circulating since the conference at Yalta.[161] But it became a central point of tension in the work of the Joint Commission. Many Koreans viewed the 'trusteeship' idea as equivalent to the Japanese protectorate that had been established in 1910[162] and, for that reason, actively opposed the Moscow agreement. But by 1947, differences between the two occupying powers over how new 'consultations' should be organised in light of such opposition had brought effective cooperation to an end.[163] At this point, the US changed track and unilaterally referred the matter to the newly formed General Assembly, introducing a resolution calling for the creation of an all-Korean government elected throughout the country under UN observation.[164]

The Soviet Union vigorously opposed the idea that the United Nations might stand as the 'impartial' arbiter[165] between the increasingly rivalrous occupying powers. The USSR read the US-proposed resolution to be a violation of the agreement reached in Moscow.[166] It nevertheless proposed that both American and Soviet forces be withdrawn by the beginning of 1948 in order to enable the Korean people to choose their own government and that representatives of the Korean people be invited to the General Assembly to 'take part in the discussion of the question'. Neither of the Soviet proposals on this score was approved: Western powers, fearing that the early withdrawal of troops would facilitate communist infiltration and control, decided instead to recommend that

[161] The possible creation of a 'trusteeship' for Korea had been mooted in a briefing paper for President Roosevelt at the Yalta Conference. See Leland Goodrich, *Korea: A Study of US Policy in the United Nations* (New York: Council on Foreign Relations, 1956) 10–11; Cordell Hull, *The Memoirs of Cordell Hull*, vol. II (New York: Macmillan Company, 1948) 1596.

[162] Michael Seth, *A Concise History of Modern Korea: From the Late Nineteenth Century to the Present* (Lanham: Rowman & Littlefield, 2016) 101; Goodrich, *Korea*, 19.

[163] The main point of dispute concerned the USSR's policy that all Koreans who opposed the Moscow agreement (i.e. trusteeship) should be excluded from the consultation process. Goodrich, *Korea*, 23–25; Oliver, *Why War Came*, 119.

[164] Goodrich, *Korea*, 29 noting that the US effectively 'discarded the idea of a four-power trusteeship, substituting for it such United Nations assistance as the General Assembly might see fit to recommend'.

[165] George Marshall, 'Address by the Chief of the US Delegation to the General Assembly' *Department of State Bulletin*, 17 (1947) 620. In his address to the General Assembly, Marshall suggested that 'although we shall be prepared to submit suggestions as to how the early attainment of Korean independence might be effected, we believe that this is a matter which now requires the impartial judgment of other members'.

[166] Goodrich, *Korea*, 30.

elections be held in North and South under the supervision of a temporary commission.

Accordingly, on 14 November 1947, the General Assembly (then Western dominated) adopted resolution 112(II) establishing a temporary Commission on Korea (UNTCOK)[167] instructed with the task of supervising free and open elections on a zonal basis before 31 March 1948 in order to provide a popular basis for the establishment of a National Government for Korea. It was envisaged that the National Government would ultimately take over the functions of government from the military commands and facilitate the withdrawal of occupying forces.[168] But the Soviets were not assuaged. The fact that the General Assembly had broadly endorsed the proposals of the US (whilst rejecting those of the Soviet Union), confirmed Soviet suspicions that the Assembly was acting as an arm of US foreign policy.[169] And to the extent that the active cooperation of both powers was necessary for the elections to take place along the lines proposed, this did not augur well for the formation of a National Government.

In the end, under instructions from Moscow, the Soviet military command in the Northern Zone indicated to UNTCOK that it wasn't prepared to allow it to operate within the north. The Temporary Commission was initially unclear what to do about this and opinion within South Korea itself was sharply divided.[170] Whilst a majority of the Temporary Commission[171] concluded that the formation of a sovereign government in the South would neither be conducive to the achievement of Korean national independence nor the withdrawal of occupying forces,[172] it was decided, nonetheless, that some measure of progress

167 The members of UNTCOK were Australia, Canada, China, El Salvador, France, India, the Philippines, Syria and Ukraine.

168 UNGA Res 112(II) A & B (14 November 1947), in which it referred to the belief 'that the national independence of Korea should be re-established'.

169 Goodrich, *Korea*, 39 who contrasts the approach adopted with that of Palestine.

170 Whilst the chairman of the National Association for the Rapid Realization of Korean Independence, Dr Syngman Rhee, favoured forging ahead with elections in the South alone, many other parties were opposed, both on grounds that continued occupation was not conducive to the holding of free elections, and because of the threat they might pose to Korean unity. See Oliver, *Why War Came*, 125.

171 See UNGA Report of KPS Menon, (1948) UN Doc. A/AC.18/28.

172 The 'split' within the Temporary Commission did not break down along 'expected' lines. The delegates of Canada, Australia, India and Syria were all doubtful as to the merits of proceeding with elections, whilst El Salvador, the Philippines, the Republic of China and, to a lesser extent France, were all in favour.

might be achieved by allowing supervised elections to proceed in the South not least so as to allow the appointment of representatives who could be consulted by the General Assembly.[173] In face of opposition from both Canada and Australia[174] (both members of UNTCOK) who were concerned that the UN was effectively sanctioning a division of Korea,[175] the General Assembly interim committee[176] endorsed the proposal instructing the Temporary Commission to continue to implement the programme 'in such parts of Korea as are accessible' to it.[177]

The US Commanding Officer announced that elections would be held on 10 May 1948. The Temporary Commission 'observed' the elections and subsequently confirmed that the elections represented 'a valid expression of the free will of the electorate in those parts of Korea which were accessible to the Commission'.[178] On 31 May 1948, and in accordance with a proclamation issued by General Hodge, the elected representatives in the South constituted themselves as the Korean National Assembly with Syngman Rhee as its President. In the meantime, authorities in the North had proceeded to conduct their own elections to a new Supreme People's Assembly with representatives from both the South and the North, which, on 9 September 1948, established itself as the Democratic People's Republic of Korea.

When the matter came back to the General Assembly the following December, the UN General Assembly received and approved the report of UNTCOK in a resolution drafted by the United States.[179] The Soviet Union objected but the UNGA ploughed on, noting that whilst the

[173] Goodrich, *Korea*, 44.

[174] See Frederic Soward, *Canada and the United Nations* (New York: Manhattan Publishing Group, 1956) 124.

[175] Philip Jessup, *The Birth of Nations* (New York: Columbia University Press, 1974) 34.

[176] UNGA Resn. 111(II) (13 November. 1947). See Jessup, *The Birth of Nations*, 32–33. The formation of the interim committee met with strong opposition from the Soviet bloc on the grounds that it would encroach on the powers of the Security Council. See Yuen-li Liang, 'Notes on Legal Questions Concerning the United Nations' *American Journal of International* Law, 42 AJIL (1948) 435–39.

[177] UN Doc. A/583, GAOR 3rd Sess. Supp. No. 10 (1948), 20.

[178] Report of the UN Temporary Commission on Korea, UN Doc. A/575, UN GAOR, 3rd Sess., Supp. No. 9 (1948) Part 1, p. 47.

[179] Goodrich, *Korea*, 67.

'unification of Korea has not yet been achieved', it could declare not only that the Republic of Korea had been lawfully established 'having effective control and jurisdiction' over that part of Korea 'in which the great majority of the people of all Korea reside' but that it represented the 'only such government in Korea.'[180] US Secretary of State John Foster Dulles claimed that the language chosen had been 'carefully worded' so as to avoid the assumption that 'the present government was in fact the government of all Korea or deny that another regime existed in certain parts of Korea'.[181] But it was language that clearly pointed in that direction.

And so, in the short space of time between 1945 and 1948, and like the case of Germany, the effective bifurcation of Korea happened by way of a series of subtle transpositions in the relationship between North and South in which the status of the 38th parallel became emblematic. The 38th parallel began life as a (secret, and entirely arbitrary)[182] military/administrative demarcation for purpose of 'accepting the surrender of Japanese forces' but become, in short order, a demarcation line between two zones of occupation. Those occupation zones then, in turn, became cemented as a political demarcation with governments elected in both South and North, each of which claimed to represent the populace of the entirety of the Korean peninsula,[183] and each of which garnered recognition from powers on either side of the divide.[184] In the process, it came to represent both a political and an ideological frontier – in which each party sought to keep the other 'from bringing all Korea within its zone of influence'.[185] The juridical status of the frontier would ultimately remain obscure not least because it was a frontier brought into being by two occupying powers that possessed no formal 'sovereign' authority and because it effectively divided a people in the guise of securing their

[180] UNGA Res 195 (III) (12 December 1948) para. 2.

[181] UNGAOR, 3rd Sess., Pt I, First Committee, 1023.

[182] As a contemporary commentator noted, 'The 38th Parallel [made] no political, topographical, geographic, economic, of military sense. It cut right through whole towns, and even, in one case, separated one wing of a factory from another.' John Gunther, *The Riddle of MacArthur: Japan, Korea and the Far East* (New York: Harper, 1951) 163.

[183] See, e.g., article 3 Constitution of the Republic of Korea, 12 July 1948; the Constitution of the DPRK, in a similar vein, spoke of Seoul as being its capital.

[184] The DPRK by the Soviet Union, Ukraine and the PRC, the ROK by nationalist China, the US and Britain.

[185] Goodrich, *Korea*, 15.

'liberation'. Perhaps unsurprisingly, the applications of both the ROK[186] and DPRK[187] for membership in the UN were rejected.[188]

The subsequent 'invasion' of South Korea by North Korean forces on 25 June 1950 posed a challenge both to the provisional political settlement that seemed to have emerged and to the authority of the United Nations itself. On the same day, the United States referred the matter to the Security Council which proceeded to adopt three resolutions in quick succession. The first resolution of 25 June (SC Resn. 82) declared the 'armed attack' on the Republic of Korea constituted a 'breach of the peace' and called upon 'the authorities of North Korea' to withdraw their forces to the 38th parallel.[189] The second (Resn. 83) recommended that UN members assist the Republic of Korea to repel the armed attack and restore international peace and security in the area.[190] The Third (Resolution 84 of 7 July 1950) welcomed the assistance offered to the Republic of Korea and recommended that such forces be made 'available to a unified command under the United States' (which was authorised to use the UN flag).[191] Almost every aspect of the arrangements put in place by the Security Council were subject to contestation. At centre stage was the fact that the decisions had all been made in absence of the Soviet Union, which had absented itself from the Security Council in protest at the continued occupancy of the seat of China by the Nationalists.[192] But

[186] Letter of 19 January 1949, UN Doc. S/1238. Letter Dated 19 January 1949 From the Acting Foreign Minister of the Republic of Korea to the Secretary-General Concerning the Application of the Republic of Korea for Admission to Membership in the United Nations and a Declaration Accepting Obligations Under the Charter, 19 January 1949, UN Doc. S/1238.

[187] Letter of 11 February 1949, UN Doc. S/1256. Letter Dated 11 February 1949 from the Representative of the Union of Soviet Socialist Republics Addressed to the President of the Security Council Concerning the Application of the Democratic People's Republic of Korea for Admission in the United Nations, 11 February 1949, UN Doc. S/1256.

[188] See, UNSC Official Records, Fourth Year No.13, (1949) UN Doc. S/PV 410, 14–15. UN Doc. S/PV 410, 16 February 1949, pp. 14–15. UNSC Official Records, Fourth Year: Meeting 423, (1949) UN Doc. S/PV 423. 423rd mtg, 8 April 1948.

[189] SC Resn 82 (1950), 25 June 1950.

[190] Ibid.

[191] Ibid. This was followed by a fourth Resolution (Resn. 85 [1950], 31 July 1950) calling upon the Unified Command to make arrangements for the relief and support of the civilian population.

[192] The UN Legal Department was later asked for advice on the issue and concluded that the occupation of the Chinese seat was an internal matter for the Security Council itself and that the absence of the Soviet Union did not have the effect of vetoing resolutions but was in the nature of an abstention. See Trygve Lie, *In the Cause of Peace: Seven Years with the United Nations* (New York: Macmillan, 1954) 335.

there was, in addition, a pervasive lack of clarity as to the character of the conflict itself and the terms under which the Security Council might exercise its powers.

The initial response of the UN seemed to hinge upon the thoroughly ambiguous status of the 38th parallel variously understood as a quasi-sovereign demarcation between putatively sovereign States, as an international frontier between rival ideological blocs and as an internal governmental division of an otherwise unitary 'State to be'. As the conflict developed, the points of doubt and confusion would only multiply. Was this a case of Chapter VII enforcement action or one of collective self-defence?[193] Was this an international or internal armed conflict? Was it the integrity of the UN, or that of the ROK, that was at stake?[194] Was the ultimate objective the repulsion of the attack, and the restoration of the integrity of the 38th parallel, or the securing of a lasting peace through a process of (enforced) unification?[195]

Throughout the whole conflict, the US/UN was faced with the task of creatively redefining the purpose and nature of the collective security system to take account of the novelties it encountered, setting what were later to be described by Western commentators as important 'precedents'. These included the UN's right to authorise coercive action in case of internal conflicts that threaten international peace and security, the Security Council's ability to authorise enforcement action in absence of a permanent member, the Security Council's power to 'delegate' the exercise of enforcement measures to member States, the General Assembly's residual power to recommend collective measures in cases where the Security Council was unable to exercise its 'primary responsibility for the maintenance of international peace and security'[196] and the power of the

[193] See Hans Kelsen, *The Law of the United Nations* (London: Stevens & Sons, 1951) 928–30.

[194] For Western Allies, the challenge represented by the North Korean 'invasion' was one that struck to the heart of the UN itself – drawing parallels, in the minds of many, with the League's failures in Manchuria in 1931. See, e.g., Goodrich, *Korea*, 132

[195] In the midst of the war, the General Assembly recommended the establishment of a seven-Power Commission for the Unification and Rehabilitation of Korea that gave tacit support for the decision of UN forces to cross the 38th parallel: UNGA Res 376 (V) (7 October 1950). The British foreign minister, Ernest Bevin, was very explicit in his support for the (enforced) re-unification of Korea, see 'Bevin Would Eradicate 38th Parallel, Unify Country as Solution for Korea' *New York Herald Tribune*, 30 September 1950.

[196] Uniting for Peace Resolution, UNGA Res 377(V) (3 November 1950). See also UNGA Res 498(V) (1 February 1951) condemning Chinese aggression and calling upon 'all

UN to authorise enforcement measures (if that is what they were) against non-member States.[197] If the response of the Soviet Union was to regard all such 'developments' as basic violations of the terms of the Charter, in the West it was a question of the UN having to adjust itself to the new conditions of its existence.

The Korean conflict was ultimately concluded with an Armistice Agreement signed at Panmunjom on 27 July 1953. The terms of that agreement visibly exemplified the contingent legalities of the emergent Cold War international law.[198] The agreement itself was signed by delegates from the KPA and PVA, on one side, and the UN Command, on the other (without the involvement, in other words, of the ROK itself) and sought to secure a lasting ceasefire by fixing a demarcation line and demilitarised 'buffer' zone along the 38th parallel. It also provided for the exchange of prisoners of war and initiated a process that might lead to the eventual establishment of 'a unified, independent and democratic Korea'.[199] As in case of Germany, all the agreement secured in reality was a return to the status quo ante, but this time under the formalities of an armistice agreement that both kept alive the idea that Korea existed in a state of suspended warfare (the exemplar, par excellence, of the existence of a Cold War) and the idea that its continued division was only ever provisional. And so it remained, trapped in the countercurrents of ideological division, on the one hand, and anti-colonial/anti-imperial self-determination, on the other. Any attempt to resolve the issue one way or the other was destined to fail so long as it remained within the spatial ambit of the Amero-Soviet co-imperium. It was for that reason, and in contrast to the position of the two Germanys, that subsequent attempts to admit North and South Korea to membership in the United Nations were routinely rejected until their joint admission in 1991 as separate States. Whilst the belated admission of the two Koreas to the United Nations heralded, as many saw it, the end of the Amero-Soviet

States and authorities to continue to lend every assistance to the United Nations action in Korea'; and UNGA Res 500(V) (18 May 1951) imposing an embargo on war materials against both the PRC and the North Korean authorities.

197 See Dana Constantine 'Korean War (1950–53)' *Max Planck Encyclopaedia of International Law* (2015)

198 See Dino Kritsiotis, 'The Elusive Peace of Panmunjum' in Matthew Craven, Sundhya Pahuja and Gerry Simpson (eds.), *International Law and the Cold War* (Cambridge: Cambridge University Press, 2019).

199 As declared at The Geneva Conference of Foreign Ministers on Korea and Indo-China, 27 April–15 June 1954, Geneva.

Cold War, it also, ironically enough, inscribed that very contestation into the architecture of the post–Cold War world.[200] What was provisional during the Cold War became permanent after it's 'end'.

In Korea, Germany and Austria, we have three different ways in which the Amero-Soviet project of provisional co-imperium would leave its mark on both the Cold War and post–Cold War worlds: in Austria, by the imposition of an imposed condition of neutrality; in Germany, by the formalisation of a 1949 stalemate between Allied powers acting in the name of the German government; and in Korea, by the division of a State emerging from colonial rule in the name of its liberation.[201] In both Germany and Korea, the divisions marked, not so much the partition of a unitary territory, as its duplication – mirroring the case of China – in which rival accounts as to which government might properly be seen to be representative of the whole came to be instantiated through a formal, but nevertheless explicitly provisional, demarcation as to the space within which each might operate. In both cases, the divisions bore the marks of their wartime origins – military demarcations born of instruments of armistice or surrender – whose continued efficacy spoke only of the latent enmity that underpinned the conditions of peace.[202] They also spoke, however, of the implicit contradictions that lay at the heart of the Amero-Soviet co-imperium – in which an ostensible desire to promote

[200] The DPRK, however, was admitted to the WHO in 1973 and was given observer status in the UN the same year. See generally, Crawford, *The Creation of States*, 471.

[201] Mention might also be made, here, of the parallel case of Vietnam, which was also 'divided' like Korea and Germany, but whose division was not the product of a project of co-imperium so much as the waging of an anti-anti-colonial war. The DRV had been initially established in 1945 followed shortly thereafter by the establishment of the RVN with French support. Each claimed jurisdiction over the entirety of the territory of the former colony, and each was recognised by States on either side of the cold war divide. Following the French debacle at Dien Bien Phu, the Geneva Accords of 1954 established a provisional military (but not political) demarcation line between the rival powers on the 17th parallel. The subsequent involvement of the US in the conflict in Vietnam between 1954 and 1973 was premised upon the idea, however, that there were, indeed, two Vietnamese States – a view that gained some measure of support in the Paris Peace Agreement of 1973. In the aftermath of the 'third' Vietnamese war, the government of the RVN collapsed on 30 April 1975, leading to the unification of North and South Vietnam under a single government. The Socialist Republic of Vietnam was admitted as a member State of the UN in 1977. See generally, Crawford, *The Creation of States*, 472–77; Richard Falk (ed.), *The Vietnam War and International Law*, 4 vols. (Princeton: Princeton University Press, 1968–76); John Norton Moore, *Law and the Indochina War* (Princeton: Princeton University Press, 1972).

[202] As Jeremy Suri puts it, from Washington's perspective 'nuclear weapons made stable walls preferable to open frontiers'. Suri, *Power and Protest*, 25.

the principle of self-rule and national self-determination (or, in case of Germany, its 'reconstruction') was undercut by their common determination to exercise an ongoing controlling influence over that process.

3.3.3 Hemispheric International Law

We have seen, thus far, how the initial idea of a collaborative, but distinctly provisional, Amero-Soviet co-imperium became a semi-permanent feature of the divided Cold War world. In this section, we suggest that it emerged, in part at least, as a consequence of a fundamental contradiction that lay at the heart of the UN project itself, which turned upon the question of 'regionalism' in the new global order. Before 1945, the one part of the globe to have most visibly encouraged and promoted the idea of regionalism was Latin America.[203] Certainly nineteenth-century Europeans had increasingly come to understand their own cultures and traditions in regional terms, but for them those ideas and values were meant to be projected outwards and universalised as part of a civilising mission.[204] That projection, indeed, was reflected in the canon of positivist international law that emerged at the time, which positioned Europe at the centre of a putatively global legal order.

Latin American regionalism had been given incipient form in the Monroe Doctrine of 1823 but had developed over the course of the nineteenth century with Latin American republics increasingly seeking to distance themselves from the practice of European diplomacy and law, articulating in the process a vision of a distinct regional order.[205] As a 'regional understanding', the Monroe Doctrine itself was given specific recognition in article 21 of the Covenant of the League despite widespread concern that it represented little more than a 'unilateral political doctrine'.[206] However, by 1930, the regional ethos to which it gave rise

[203] See, e.g., John Spencer, 'The Monroe Doctrine and the League Covenant' *American Journal of International Law*, 30 (1936) 413.

[204] Smaller scale European regionalisms were to emerge, however, such as in the Locarno agreements, the Little Entente, the Balkans Entente and the Baltic Union. Briand had advanced proposals for a European Union, but these had made little progress. Documents Relating to the Organization of a System of European Federal Union, LN Doc. VII, 4 (1930).

[205] See, e.g., Alejandro Alvarez, *Monroe Doctrine: Its Importance in the International Life of the States of the New World* (New York: Carnegie Endowment for International Peace and Oxford University Press, 1924).

[206] See, e.g., Elihu Root, 'The Real Monroe Doctrine' *American Journal of International Law*, 8 (1914) 431; A. Pearce Higgins, 'The Monroe Doctrine' *British Yearbook of*

had developed two contrasting strands. On one side, and in the US itself, the region was understood in terms of an exclusive sphere of interest of the US government, which had arrogated to itself (under the Roosevelt corollary) the right to intervene to protect the markets, 'investments', and other 'vital interests' in the region.[207] On the other side, and in a reactive sense, American regionalism also gave expression to the common values and interests of the various American Republics that sought for themselves not just immunity from the predations of imperial powers (the US included) but to advance a distinctive, regional brand of international law: American international law.[208] The first strand of thought found intellectual support in the emergent tradition of 'geopolitics' (in the work, for example, of Mahan, Kjellen, Mackinder, Spykman and Strausz-Hupé). The second strand of thought was developed, in particular, by the diplomats and jurists of the Latin American sub-continent (Drago, Calvo, Bello, Alvarez and Barbosa). These two strands ultimately came together when, at the time of the Seventh Pan-American Conference in 1933, Roosevelt appeared to renounce US hegemonic pretentions in the region emphasising, in its place, the principle of 'good neighbourliness'.[209]

Needless to say, when discussions began around the shape of the new institutions of global order during the 1940s, both accounts of regionalism – as a geopolitical sphere of interest and as system of regional solidarity – were in play. In the US and UK, the geopolitical account of regionalism assumed a particular prominence in discussions about the post-war order[210] with prominent advocates in both the US

International Law, 5 (1924) 103, 113; Spencer, 'The Monroe Doctrine and the League Covenant'.

207 Theodore Roosevelt's Annual Message to Congress for 1904, House Records HR 58A-K2.

208 Alejandro Álvarez, *Le Droit International Américain: Son Fondement, Sa Nature* (Paris: A Pendon 1910). See generally, Liliana Obragon, 'Noted for Dissent: The International Life of Alejandro Álvarez' *Leiden Journal of International Law*, 19 (2006) 983–1016; Juan Pablo Scarfi, *The Hidden History of International Law in the Americas: Empire and Legal Networks* (New York: Oxford University Press 2017) 59–86.

209 Franklin Roosevelt, *The Public Papers and Addresses of Franklin D Roosevelt: Volume 2 The Year of Crisis 1933* (New York: Random House, 1938) 129–33.

210 See, e.g., Nichola Spykman, *America's Strategy in World Politics: The United States and the Balance of Power* (New York: Harcourt, Brace and Company, 1942) and *The Geography of the Peace* (New York: Harcourt, Brace and Company, 1944); Robert Strausz-Hupé, *Geopolitics: The Struggle for Space and Power* (New York, G. P. Putnam's Sons, 1942) and *The Balance of Tomorrow: Power and Foreign Policy in the United States* (New York: G. P. Putnam's Sons, 1945); William Fox, *The Superpowers:*

(Welles)[211] and in the UK (Toynbee, Jebb and Churchill).[212] But as many saw it, if the US necessarily had to retain its overall ascendance across the Americas, they were equally cognisant of the apparent necessity of allowing the Soviet Union the same within its own 'sphere'. As the prominent American journalist Walter Lippmann observed in 1944:

> The crucial question of how long and how confident can be the peace after this war will be determined by the maintenance of the substance of the alliance between the Russian Orbit and the Atlantic Community. Whether there is to be a third World War in the twentieth century depends upon whether the Russians come to rest within their orbit, the Atlantic States in theirs . . .. I do not say that such a concert of power with the Russian Orbit is a world order of peace. But I do contend that such a concert must be achieved in order to found a world order . . .. It is also necessary if there is to be any prospect of order and good relations with the emergent peoples of Asia and Africa.[213]

Lippman gave expression, here, to what became a vital structural contradiction that ran, like a red thread, through discussions as to the shape and functions of the prospective UN order: how might such an institution guarantee international peace and security across the globe without acknowledging the vital role that the great powers would necessarily have in securing that objective? How might they, at the same time, promote the values that they purported to share and promote – namely, the rights to self-determination, sovereign equality and political independence?[214]

In the original Dumbarton Oaks proposals, an Anglo-American 'compromise' of sorts was found. The text sought to balance Senator Hull's dream of a centralised security system in which, as he put it, there would

The United States, Britain and the Soviet Union – Their Responsibility for Peace (New York: Harcourt, Brace and Company, 1944); Arnold Wolfers, 'Anglo-American Postwar Cooperation and the Interests of Europe' *American Political Science Review*, 36 (1942) 663; Walter Lippmann, *US Foreign Policy: Shield of the Republic* (Little, Brown & Co, 1943); and Lippman, *US War Aims.*

211 Welles, *Time for Decision.*

212 Winston Churchill, *The Second World War, Vol IV: The Hinge of Fate* (London: George Philip & Son, 1956) 717–21.

213 Lippman, *US War Aims*, 91.

214 John Lewis Gaddis, *We Know Now: Rethinking Cold War History* (Oxford: Oxford University Press, 1998) 16. The Soviets, in apparent allusion to the obvious contradictions, had said of the Atlantic Charter that 'practical application of these principles will necessarily adapt itself to the circumstances, needs, and historical peculiarities of particular countries', in Lloyd Gardner, *Spheres of Influence: The Great Powers Partition Europe, From Munish to Yalta* (Lanham: Ivan R. Dee Publishers, 1993) 203.

be no more need for 'spheres of influence, for alliances, for balance, or any other arrangements',[215] with Churchill's contrasting vision of a security system that would operate largely through the medium of four regional councils, each under the superintendence of one or more Great Powers.[216] The text itself gave priority to the creation of a UN 'Security Council' with enforcement powers to maintain and secure international peace and security. But it also envisaged the 'existence of regional arrangements or agencies for dealing with such matters relating to international peace and security as are appropriate for regional action'.[217] The regional arrangements, though, were constrained to operate in accordance with the purposes and principles of the Organisation, and such agencies could not take enforcement action in absence of Security Council authorisation. The Security Council would be the centrepiece of the envisaged juridico-political architecture of security whose operative conditions would ultimately be dependent upon continued cooperation between the four (or five) 'permanent members'.

In the aftermath of the Dumbarton Oaks conference, the Soviets took up a posture somewhat adjacent to that of the US and the UK. Shortly after the conference a certain 'Malinin' (suspected of being pseudonym of Litvinov, the People's Commissar for Foreign Affairs in the 1930s)[218] wrote an influential editorial in the December 1944 issue of *War and the Working Class*, which was then dispatched to the US by Litvinov himself. In that editorial, he argued that the proposal relating to 'regional agreements' was fundamentally dangerous and equivalent to the creation of 'spheres of influence' or 'blocs'. Blocs (such as the Triple Alliance, the Triple Entente or Hitler's Axis) did nothing for peace but merely invited warfare pitching one against another. Similarly, 'nothing alluring' was found 'in the so-called spheres of influence', which differed only in respect of their form and undermined the basic principle of sovereign equality.[219] But while it opposed a Churchillian regionalism, the article

[215] Documents on Foreign Relations 1943–44, 13, 14. Cordell Hull, *The Memoirs of Cordell Hull*, vol. 2 (Hodder & Stoughton, 1948) 1647–48.

[216] Churchill, *The Hinge of Fate*, 717–21.

[217] 'Proposals for the Establishment o a General International Organisation' (7 October 1944, Dumbarton Oaks), Section C, 1.

[218] See Vojtech Mastny, *Russia's Road to the Cold War: Diplomacy, Warfare and the Politics of Communism, 1941–1945* (New York: Columbia University Press, 1979) 231.

[219] Charles Prince, 'Current Views of the Soviet Union of the International Organization of Security, Economic Cooperation and International Law: A Summary' *American Journal of International Law*, 39 (1945) 455.

nevertheless proposed that the Charter should make reference to 'security zones.' The frontiers of such zones would be delimited by agreement between the 'leading states of a given continent' and would provide security whilst protecting the independence of the States within each zone. As a complement to this, he proposed that the General Assembly itself be divided into four 'sections' – European, American, Asiatic-Pacific and African – which would be incorporated as subdivisions of the main organisation. For 'Malinin', the advantage of this arrangement was that the subdivisions would be part of the whole and would reinforce the authority of the United Nations rather than undermine it. The response of the United States to all this was equivocal. Whilst it agreed that regional 'blocs' or 'spheres of influence' were undesirable, it nevertheless expressed doubts about the proposals for the recognition of security zones or for the division of the General Assembly.[220]

In several respects, the debate over regionalism wasn't what it seemed. Both the US and the Soviet Union openly opposed the creation of blocs or spheres of influence, and both also committed themselves to the principle of sovereign equality. Neither doubted, however, the necessity for the self-described great powers to have a controlling interest in the architecture of security that was be devised, nor that they might have specific regional interests to be advanced either within the organisation or outside. What the debate mainly concerned, then, was whether the great powers would have more or less independence in their actions within their regional locales and the extent to which that authority would be formally recognised within the UN Charter itself. So, when Republican Senator Arthur Vandenberg observed that the Monroe Doctrine could only be protected 'if we kick the daylights out of the world organization',[221] he was only partly right.

What was entirely absent from the Allied discussions over post-war plans was the kind of regionalism that had been promoted by Álvarez and the American international law movement. But in the pause between Dumbarton Oaks and the San Francisco Conference, a variety of forms of counter-hegemonic regionalism was to emerge. In Europe, the 'Oslo Group' was formed to promote the economic and security interests of

[220] Acting Secretary of State Grew, Telegram to the Ambassador in the Soviet Union (Harriman), 27 January 1945, Foreign Relations of the United States, Diplomatic Papers, 1945, General: The United Nations, vol. 1, Doc. 8, 34–35.

[221] Arthur Vandenberg, *The Private Papers of Senator Vandenberg* (Boston: Houghton Mifflin, 1952) 188.

the smaller nations. Two members of that group, Paul-Henry Spaak and Paul Van Zeeland, devised the formation, by the exiled governments of Belgium, the Netherlands and Luxembourg, of the Benelux customs agreement. In the Middle East, the leaders of Egypt, Saudi Arabia, Iraq, Transjordan, Lebanon, Syria and Yemen signed up to the terms of the Alexandria Protocol, forming, in the process, a League of Arab States on 22 March 22 1945.[222] And in the Americas, nineteen Latin American republics (excluding Argentina) organised a special Inter-American Conference on Problems of War and Peace together with the US in February and March 1945. This latter initiative resulted in the adoption of the Act of Chapultepec, which institutionalised a system of collective self-defence within the region.[223] Both the Act of Chapultepec and the Alexandria Protocol sought to provide for systems of regional security quite independently of any hegemonic oversight. Whilst opposing the idea that global security should be the exclusive domain of the self-styled great powers, they also showed their determination to pre-empt discussions that were yet to take place in San Francisco. In case of the Arab League, for example, it was declared that the Council would determine 'the means whereby the League will collaborate with the international organizations which may be created in the future to guarantee peace and security and organise economic and social relations'.[224] In a similar vein, the Act of Chapultepec determined that the Declaration constituted a 'regional arrangement for dealing with such matters relating to the maintenance of international peace and security as are appropriate for regional action in this Hemisphere' and that it '*shall be* consistent with the purposes and principles of the general international organization, *when established*'. What those purposes and principles might be, of course, was a matter yet to be formally determined.

[222] As Gyallay-Pap notes, 'Though informed by western international law, the treaty was written in Arabic (dated the eighth day of Rabi' II, 1364) and conceived in the spirit of Arab cultural unity.' Peter Gyallay-Pap, *Regionalism and the Allied Debate on Postwar World and European Organization, 1940–1945* (PhD Thesis, London School of Economics, 1990) 223–24.

[223] Inter-American Reciprocal Assistance and Solidarity (Act of Chapultepec), 6 March 1945, 60 Stat. 1831. Article 3 of the Act stated that 'every attack of a State against the integrity or the inviolability of the territory, or against the sovereignty or political independence of an American State, shall ... hereof be considered an act of aggression against the other States which sign this act'.

[224] Act of Chapultepec, Article 3.

At the San Francisco Conference in 1945, and largely as a consequence of the efforts of the Latin American States to make acceptance of the terms of the Act of Chapultepec a condition of their participation, regionalism became a central point of debate.[225] The difficulty, as Vandenberg noted at the time, was how they might 'find a rule which protects legitimate existing groups (like Pan-Am) without opening up the opportunity for regional balance-of-power groups'.[226] One avenue, proposed by Egypt (and which, incidentally, made no mention of States at all) had been to introduce a definition of regionalism that emphasised the 'proximity, community of interests or cultural, linguistic, historical or spiritual affinities' of the countries concerned.[227] Another had been to introduce limited exceptions to the Dumbarton Oaks formula – such as the Soviet and French proposals in relation to 'enemy states'.[228] But the main 'solution' that emerged came in the form of an entirely new article on the right of self-defence.

What was to become article 51 UN Charter[229] left intact the idea that the UN would retain its general monopoly over the use of coercion and the idea that the enforcement power of regional agencies would be subject to the authority of the Security Council. But it opened up a new space for 'regional action' by postulating a novel formula for self-defence that was independent of the sanctioning authority of the Security Council. Drawing upon the terms of the Act of Chapultepec, the

[225] See James Green, *Collective Self-Defence in International Law* (Cambridge: Cambridge University Press, 2024) 85.

[226] Vandenburg, *Private Papers*, 190.

[227] The text reads: 'There shall be considered as regional arrangements organizations of a permanent nature, grouping in a given geographical area several countries which, by reason of their proximity, community of interests or cultural, linguistic, historical or spiritual affinities, make themselves jointly responsible for the peaceful settlement of disputes which may arise between them and for the maintenance of peace and security in their region, as well as the safeguarding of their interests and the development of their economic and cultural relations.' 12 UNCIO, Doc. WD 70, III/4/A/11, 2 June 1945, p. 857.

[228] See 3 UNCIO, Doc. 2, G/7(o)(2), 6 May 1945, 392 (France); Doc. 2, G/14(w)(1), 8 May 1945, 601 (USSR).

[229] Which reads, 'Nothing in the present Charter shall impair the inherent right of individual or collective self-defence if an armed attack occurs against a Member of the United Nations, until the Security Council has taken measures necessary to maintain international peace and security. Measures taken by Members in the exercise of this right of self-defence shall be immediately reported to the Security Council and shall not in any way affect the authority and responsibility of the Security Council under the present Charter to take at any time such action as it deems necessary in order to maintain or restore international peace and security.'

Charter formalised the idea that States enjoyed an 'inherent' right of both individual and collective self-defence, conjoining, in the process, the defensive measures that might be taken by an individual State that has experienced an armed attack, with those of other States that might intervene to assist it. All such action was subsumed under the same right. When seen through the lens of individual States' rights and obligations, 'collective' self-defence was always something of a misnomer in the sense that it conflated the rights and interests of the State seeking to defend itself with those coming to assist it.[230] But when viewed within the context of a burgeoning regionalism, the idea of a 'one and all' solidarity undoubtedly made more sense.

As the Cold War gathered pace, though, the problem with the 'solution' would become evident. Regionalism, as we have seen, always had two faces. So, while, on one hand, it could indicate an anti-hegemonic solidarity associated with engendering cultural, political, economic and social bonds across the hemisphere (the Act of Chapultepec), on the other, it could be an imperial imaginary that made space for the establishment of hegemonic spheres of interest or influence. And as much as regionalism could be premised on the bonds of friendship, amicable relations, etc., there was always the danger that they might nevertheless be pressed into the service of the latter.

Not long after the adoption of the UN Charter, article 51 would become the explicit basis for a series of regional security pacts that delineated the territorial parameters of the emergent Cold War. In 1947, as anticipated by the Act of Chapultepec, the Inter-American Treaty of Reciprocal Assistance was signed at Rio de Janeiro[231] (later to become a core component of the OAS) followed by the Brussels Treaty on Economic, Social and Cultural Collaboration and Collective Self-Defence of 17 March 1948[232] and the Washington Treaty forming the

[230] For a general discussion, see Green, *Collective Self-Defence*, 23–65. Bowett's somewhat singular view was that 'the term "collective self-defence", as used in the Charter, does no more than recognize that members may exercise collectively what is their individual right; it does not create new rights, nor, by permitting the use of a legal fiction, convert action unauthorized by a competent organ of the United Nations into action in the exercise of the right of collective self-defence'. Derek Bowett, *Self-Defense in International Law* (Westport: Fredrick A. Praeger, 1958) 216.

[231] Inter-American Treaty of Reciprocal Assistance, Rio de Janeiro, 2 September 1947, 21 UNTS 324.

[232] Brussels Treaty on Economic, Social and Cultural Collaboration and Collective Self-Defence, Brussels, 17 March 1948, 19 UNTS 304.

NATO Alliance on 4 April 1949.[233] All were viewed with considerable dismay by the Soviet Union. The Soviet Union was in no doubt that all three were directed against it and its allies and that, despite their overtly 'defensive' cast, the Soviets conceived them as acts of aggression. This view was only reinforced by the subsequent conclusion of the Manila Treaty of 1 September 1954 establishing SEATO[234] and the Baghdad Pact of 4 February 1955 for Mutual Cooperation between Iraq, Turkey, the UK and Iran.[235]

Following a predictably abortive attempt to persuade NATO powers to allow the Soviet Union to join the alliance (as part of a broader strategy to wrest control of European defence arrangements away from the US), the Soviet Union itself responded in kind by forming its own defensive military alliance. The Treaty of Friendship, Co-operation and Mutual Assistance of 14 May 1955 creating the Warsaw Pact[236] was largely modelled upon that of NATO incorporating many of the same terms, including reference to article 51 UN Charter. But for its proponents, it differed fundamentally. As then Prime Minister of the Soviet Union, Nikolai Bulganin put it, where 'blocs created by imperialist States [such as NATO] are based on the principles of domination and subordination' and serve, in the same measure, the interests of the 'big imperialist Powers', the Warsaw Pact 'proceeds from the principle of respect for the national sovereignty, and non-interference in the internal affairs of others' and thus 'fully accords with the objects and principles of the United Nations Charter.'[237] Whether this was entirely convincing given the Soviet intervention in Hungary the year before, is an open question.

233 North Atlantic Treaty, Washington, DC, 4 April 1949, 34 UNTS 541. The formation of NATO was followed by the signature of the Treaty of Paris in 1952 that proposed the formation of a European Defense Community that would include West Germany alongside France, the Netherlands, Italy, Belgium and Luxembourg. For an early account, see Robert Osgood, *NATO: The Entangling Alliance* (Chicago: University of Chicago Press, 1962).

234 Pacific Charter and Manilla Pact 209 UNTS 2819.

235 233 UNTS 199. In a somewhat different context, the Arab League followed suit, in adopting the Joint Defence and Economic Co-operation between States of the Arab League, Cairo, 13 April 1950, see *American Journal of International Law Supplement*, 49 (1955) 51.

236 Treaty of Friendship, Co-operation and Mutual Assistance (signed 14 May 1955, entered into force 6 June 1955) 219 UNTS 3 (Warsaw Pact). A host of other bilateral and trilateral mutual defence treaties or assistance pacts were concluded alongside the multilateral agreements. For a list, see Ian Brownlie, *International Law and the Use of Force by States* (Oxford: Clarendon Press, 1963) 127–29. Other multilateral agreements include the Organisation of Eastern Caribbean States of 1981.

237 Bulganin, in Report of the Special Committee (1957) 50 (316).

In formal terms, these were all simply mutual defence agreements directed against unspecified 'aggressors'. But in most cases, it was all too clear who the enemy was deemed to be. That became more apparent as time went by.[238] In case of the OAS, for example, the US secured a resolution at the Ninth International Conference of American States in Bogotá in 1948 declaring that 'by its anti-democratic nature and its interventionist tendency, the political activity of international communism or any totalitarian doctrine is incompatible with the concept of American freedom'.[239] This was later put into effect, in 1954, in response to a series of political reforms that were being introduced by the Árbenz government in Guatemala. Having secured another resolution from the OAS to the effect that the introduction of communism within the region 'would constitute a threat to the sovereignty and political independence of the American states, endangering the peace of America' and calling for 'appropriate action',[240] the US proceeded to initiate a covert insurgency campaign directed against the Árbenz government (Operation PBSUCCESS), funding and supporting insurgent forces in both Honduras and Nicaragua. Following a violent interlude during which the Árbenz government vainly appealed to the UN Security Council,[241] it was eventually forced to step down on 27 June 1954.

[238] See, e.g., Chester J. Pach, 'The Containment of US Military Aid to Latin America 1944–49' *Diplomatic History*, 6 (1982) 232–34; Melvyn Leffler and David Painter, *The Origins of the Cold War: An International History*, 2nd ed. (New York: Routledge, 2005) 22.

[239] Secretary of State to Diplomatic Representatives in the American Republics, (810.00B/6-2148, Secret Dispatch of 21 June 1948) in Foreign Relations of the United States, 1948: vol. IX (1972).

[240] Resolution 93. 'Declaration of Solidarity for the Preservation of the Political Integrity of the American States against the Intervention of International Communism' *American Journal of International Law Supplement*, 48 (1954) 123–24. For general discussion, see Gordon Connell-Smith, *Pattern of the Post War World* (London: Penguin 1957) 229–40; Liliana Obregón 'Latin America During the Bandung Era: Anti-Imperialist Movements vs Communist States' in Luis Eslava, Michael Fakhri and Vasuki Nesiah (eds.), *Bandung, Global History and International Law: Critical Pasts and Pending Futures* (New York: Cambridge University Press, 2017) 239.

[241] The US argued that the matter was merely a 'local dispute' and subject to the jurisdiction of the OAS and not the UN. Claude observed, in that respect, that 'the transfer of the case from the Security Council to the OAS was not simply a matter of having the latter substitute for the former as a peaceful settlement mechanism, but a device for reversing the terms of the case. The OAS was prepared to treat Guatemala as the defendant, not the plaintiff'. Inis Claude, 'The OAS, the UN, and the United States' *International Conciliation*, 547 (1964) 30.

This set a pattern in following years in which the US drew alternately upon the 'external' threat posed by Communism (supposedly 'alien' to the American continent) or the offer of development loans and assistance to assert its control over the OAS agenda. In 1962, it secured Cuba's expulsion from the organisation, followed by the imposition of an arms embargo and naval blockade upon it at the height of the Cuban Missile Crisis. In the following years, it garnered OAS support for its intervention in the Dominican Republic in 1965 (through the medium of an Inter-American Force) and general OAS quiescence in the US-supported coups in Argentina, Bolivia, Chile and Brazil. In the case of Nicaragua, the US ultimately sought to justify its intervention on the grounds of Nicaragua's breach of alleged pledges made by the government to the OAS in 1979.[242] Only in case of Grenada, in which the US intervened following a purported 'request' by the Organisation of Eastern Caribbean States (Blum calls this a fundamental falsehood),[243] would a majority in the OAS condemn the intervention.[244]

And so, even if the foundation of the Inter-American system had been broadly informed by the principle of regional solidarity, it increasingly became a vehicle for the reassertion of US hegemony, forcing many Latin American States themselves to turn to the UN rather than the OAS to combat its influence.[245] This influence indeed became increasingly explicit. So, in 1960, when responding to Khrushchev's claim that the Monroe Doctrine was 'dead and should be buried',[246] the State Department brazenly responded that 'the principles of the Monroe Doctrine are as valid today as they were in 1823 when the Doctrine was proclaimed' and that it continued to be 'supported by the Inter-American security system through the Organization of American States'.[247]

But if the US was reasserting its historic sphere of influence over the Americas through the medium of the OAS and in Europe through the establishment of NATO, very much the same was occurring in Soviet-

[242] See *Military and Paramilitary Activities in and against Nicaragua (Nicaragua v United States)* (Merits) (1986) ICJ Rep 14, 257–64.

[243] William Blum, *Killing Hope: A Forgotten History of the CIA* (London: Bloomsbury, 2022) 306.

[244] See Ved Nanda, 'The United States Armed Intervention in Grenada – Impact on World Order' *California Western International Law Journal*, 14 (1984) 395–424.

[245] Gordon Connell-Smith, *The Inter-American System* (Oxford: Oxford University Press, 1966) 315.

[246] *New York Times*, Int. ed., 14 July 1960.

[247] DSB xliii/1101 (1960), 170.

controlled Eastern Europe under guise of the Warsaw Pact. Whilst the terms of the Warsaw Pact suggested that it was both open to all European States and premised upon the independence and sovereignty of its members,[248] its effective purpose would become clear soon after its adoption. In 1956, the communist government in Hungary embraced a set of liberal and democratic reforms, taking seriously their formal status as a sovereign, independent State. Soviet troops invaded, entering the territory in order to 'help the Hungarian People's Army and the Hungarian authorities to establish order in the city'.[249] The Soviet government argued that the Hungarian government had requested the help of Soviet military units stationed there 'under the terms of the Warsaw Treaty' and referred specifically to the terms of article 5 of the Warsaw Pact that provided for 'concerted action' by contracting parties 'necessary to reinforce their defensive strength, in order to defend the peaceful labour of their people, guarantee the inviolability of their frontiers and territories and afford protection against possible aggression'.[250] That they had, in the process, displaced the Nagy government from power (which, incidentally, had initiated Hungary's withdrawal from the Warsaw Pact) and installed in its place a sympathetic Kádár government confirmed that the essential function of the Pact, despite Bulganin's protestations otherwise, would be to assure Soviet political control within the region. In face of appeals from the Nagy government to the UN and sharp criticism from the UN General Assembly, the Soviet Union vetoed any measures being adopted by the Security Council.[251]

Twelve years later, the USSR was to reprise the strategy it had pursued in Hungary, but this time in Czechoslovakia in response to the political reforms that had been initiated by the Dubček government as part the 'Prague Spring'. In this case, no 'invitation' had been received, and the intervention itself was collective – involving not just forces of the Soviet Union but those of Poland, Bulgaria and Hungary.[252] The Prague Spring, however, as we shall see, was to open up cracks in the Warsaw Pact.

[248] This was one of the grounds upon which the Soviets claimed.
[249] Declaration of the Government of the USSR, 31 October 311956, Report of the Special Committee on the Problem of Hungary 11 GAOR, Supp. No. 18 (A/3592), 1957, 14 (104).
[250] Memorandum of 4 February 1956. Report of Special Committee, p. 51, para. 320.
[251] UNGA Res 1131 (XI) (12 December 1956) which accused the Soviet Union of 'violating the political independence of Hungary' and with it, the Charter of the United Nations.
[252] Albania and Romania both refused to participate.

And so there was a marked parallelism in both attitude and approach, between the US and the Soviet Union in relation to the question of regional security. Both publicly decried the formation of regional blocs or spheres of influence and supported the centralisation of enforcement powers in the UN, yet both also made use of the liberating language of article 51 of the Charter to secure what Julius Stone called 'the clandestine distribution of the Cold War military status quo'.[253] Both drew upon political doctrines inflected with a regionalist sensibility, but in which regionalism was essentially construed in oppositional and hegemonic terms: it was not about what tied peoples and communities together but about what had to be kept out; not about a solidarity of equals but about ensuring the dominion of the one power that mattered. Through the regional compacts, both found a way of fighting the Cold War without confronting one another. In these battles the targets were various – students, trades unions, democracy movements, radical leaders and non-compliant governments – but, above all else, the central target was the threat of non-conformism or the emergence of an anti-bloc mentality.

Both the Western and Eastern hemispheric blocs, thus, were organised not around the dangerous notions of non-intervention and political independence that were to be found in the UN Charter but instead on an Amero-Soviet Cold War international law that prioritised the integrity of spheres of influence. Such spheres were not just background geostrategic divisions or matters of political 'context' but were themselves a law of the Cold War. Putin's invasion of Ukraine in February 2022, indeed, can be thought of as a continuation of these assumptions – assumptions that also underlay Kennedy's threat to destroy Cuba if Soviet nuclear weapons were placed (or remained) on Cuban soil. What they gave expression to was the idea that the world is (both factually and normatively) divided, sometimes implicitly but sometimes explicitly too, into mini-worlds of Great Power prerogative.[254]

3.4 Peaceful Coexistence

The concept of co-imperium captures the spirit of the Amero-Soviet plans outlined in Moscow, Cairo, Yalta and Potsdam for the creation

[253] Julius Stone, *Aggression and World Order: A Critique of United Nations Theories of Aggression* (Berkeley: University of California Press, 1958)

[254] For a defence of America's intervention in Vietnam in international legal terms, see Moore, *Law and the Indo-China War*. See, for different views, Falk, *The Vietnam War and International Law*.

and maintenance of their respective zones of influence and interest in territories formerly occupied by enemy powers. But by the time Khrushchev came into power in the Soviet Union, a new, and more official, concept had come into prominence: peaceful coexistence.[255] From that time onwards, the practice of Amero-Sovietism as a conjoint political and juridical project not only came to be formulated in the language of coexistence, but coexistence provided its animus and its operational rationality.[256] Coexistence was what the Amero-Soviet Cold War was about.

In McWhinney's 1964 book on the subject of Soviet–Western international law, the word 'coexistence' is placed in quotation marks. In his view, its origins were plausibly diffuse (was it Lenin's idea? Molotov's? Khrushchev's?), and its range, meaning, and status were all up for debate.[257] Yet, the idea of coexistence was vitally important to Cold War international law.[258] Coexistence was not merely an empty phrase with a thousand meaningless synonyms ('friendly relations and cooperation among states', 'peace among nations') but an organising principle of Amero-Soviet international law. It was an idea that signified both the existence of a state of enmity between rival powers and their determination not just to refrain from direct hostilities with one another but to acknowledge the existential imperative of their lawful 'coexistence'. It found its expression formally, if sometimes implicitly, in a range of instruments such as the *Partial Test Ban Treaty*, the *Outer Space Treaty* of 1967 the *Nuclear Non-Proliferation Treaty* of 1968. It was evidenced

[255] See *American Society of International Law Proceedings* (1963); *International Law Association Proceedings* (1962).

[256] For a general introduction to Soviet approaches, see Ebrahim Afsah, 'Cold War (1947–91)' in *Max Planck Encyclopedia of Public International Law* (Oxford: Oxford University Press, 2009).

[257] Edward McWhinney, *'Peaceful Co-existence' and Soviet-Western International Law* (Leiden: A. W. Sythoff, 1964). Its official origins are usually traced to Khruschev in the post–Cuban Missile Crisis period or earlier to the ILA Meeting in Dubrovnik in 1956 (the Soviet establishment was very keen not to accord the Yugoslavs any credit for the idea). Kennan observed that 'no term has been used more loosely, and at times unscrupulously, than the word "coexistence"'. George Kennan, 'Peaceful Coexistence: A Western View' *Foreign Affairs*, 38 (1960) 171.

[258] Edward McWhinney, 'Soviet and Western International Law and the Cold War in the Era of Bipolarity: Inter-Block Law in a Nuclear Age' *Canadian Year Book of International Law*, 1 (1963) 40–81. For a more contemporary perspective, see Janne Nijman, 'Cold War Bi-Polarity: ILP Hanging in the Balance' in *The Concept of International Legal Personality: An Inquiry into the History and Theory of International Law* (The Hague: T. M. C. Asser Press, 2004) 245–344.

too in the practice of diplomacy in which the formalities of bipolar negotiations over arms control or nuclear proliferation were supplemented by presidential correspondence, State visits and the creation of 'hot lines'. Sometimes, indeed, it even provided the impetus for proposals for a more explicit and substantive alliance (Bulganin's proposals for joint Soviet–American action after the Anglo–French intrusion in Suez being a case in point).

Coexistence had its roots in a long trajectory of Soviet thought from revolutionary opposition to accommodationist rule, from nihilism to formalism. Internally, the Soviets had long developed a particular penchant for legalism,[259] and its approach to what the Americans called the 'Cold War' was no exception.[260] Scott Newton, in his *Red Demiurge*, describes the Soviet Union, itself, as a 'gargantuan legal artefact', despite the flirtations with legal nihilism during the Stalinist purges. [261] This was, at the very least, rule by law with a blanket of enabling rules, command and control norms and social entitlements directing (and dictating) the lives of Soviet citizens. This might account for Stalin's enthusiasm for Allied cooperation at Nuremberg where he was happy enough with the idea of a courtroom reckoning for the leading Nazis and in which the Soviet Union participated in what might be called 'good-bad faith'.

How this legalism was to relate to the development of peaceful coexistence and international law is worth telling in detail. By the late 1930s, and under influence of Stalin's conception of 'socialism in one country', Soviet jurists had abandoned both the idea of international law as a 'temporary compromise' or 'transitional arrangement' and the idea that a separate field of Soviet International Law might exist.[262] Instead, it had

[259] See Judith Shklar, *Legalism: Law, Morals, and Political Trials* (Cambridge, MA: Harvard University Press, 1964). On Soviet legalism see, Richard Erickson, *International Law and the Revolutionary State: A Case Study of the Soviet Union and Customary International Law* (Washington, DC: Oceana, 1972) 162. See, too, Tatiana Borisova and William B Simons (eds.), *The Legal Dimension in Cold War Interactions: Some Notes from the Field* (Leiden: Martinus Nijhoff, 2012).

[260] For a discussion of the more familiar American approaches, see Nijman, '*Cold War Bi-Polarity*', 245–344.

[261] Newton, *Red Demiurge*, 2.

[262] John Hazard, 'Communist States and International Law' *Problems of Communism*, 24 (1975) 41; Lauri Malksoo, 'The Soviet Approach to the Right of Peoples to Self-Determination: Russia's Farewell to *jus publicum europaeum*' *Journal of the History of International Law*, 19 (2017) 200, 204. Tunkin categorically dismissed that idea: 'In fact there are not two international laws, there is only one international law, obligatory for all States. There are two opposite policies: on the one hand, the policy of the countries of the democratic camp which is in agreement with international law, the norms of which are

increasingly sought to occupy the centre-ground arguing not only that international law was unitary – consisting, in the words of Krylov, as the 'sum of all norms regulating the relationships between States in the course of their competition, their struggle, and their cooperation'[263] – but that the validity of those norms was dependent upon their consistency with the precepts of the (inevitable) transition to socialism.[264] By the time of Khrushchev's ascendence to power in 1958, the idea that ideological rivalry would find expression *within* international law had acquired a new form in the principle of 'peaceful coexistence'.[265]

Of course, there was internal dissension, as we shall see later, but by the end of the 1940s the Soviets, having lurched back and forth between the different formalisms of international legal exactitude and Marxist–Leninist dogma[266] were now entering a pragmatic phase in which the Soviet jurists (and diplomats) Grigory Tunkin and Evgeny Korovin dominated the scene.[267] As far as the emergent Soviet tradition was concerned, the doctrine of peaceful coexistence, which could be linked to the work of both Lenin[268] and

strictly observed, and, on the other hand, the policy of the countries of the imperialist camp which systematically violates even the most elementary norms of international law.' Tunkin cited in RS 'Soviet Theories of International Law' *Soviet Studies*, 4 (1953) 335.

263 Serge Krylov, 'Les notions principals du droit des gens (La doctrine soviétique du droit international)' *Recueil des cours*, 70 (1947) 417.

264 In practice this meant placing greatest emphasis upon treaty law supplemented by customary international law insofar as the latter had been assented to by Soviet States.

265 See, e.g., UNGA, 'Declaration concerning the peaceful coexistence of States' Twelfth Session, Agenda Item 66 UN Doc. A/3673, (20 September 1957).

266 On legal formalism, see Jean d'Aspremont, *Formalism and the Sources of International Law: A Theory of the Ascertainment of Legal Rules* (Oxford: Oxford University Press, 2011). On Soviet doctrine and the question of formalism, see Anna Isaeva, 'History of Soviet Legal Doctrine' (PhD thesis, University of Florence, 2016).

267 The Pashukanian idea of class struggle (adapted for post-WWII era by the likes of Kozhevnikov) had given way to the 'objective facts of co-existence' (Erickson, *International Law and the Revolutionary State*, 11) and a move to practical medium-termism with the likes of Krylov and Tunkin not interested in solving 'theoretical problems' or reverting to revolutionary justice. Grigory Tunkin, *Co-Existence and International Law* (Leiden: Martinus Nijhoff, 1958); Grigory Tunkin, *Politics, Law and Force in the Interstate System* (Leiden: Martinus Nijhoff, 1989); Edward McWhinney, 'Contemporary Soviet General Theory of International Law: Reflections on the Tunkin Era' *Canadian Yearbook of International Law*, 25 (1987) 187–217.

268 See Ivo Lapenna, 'Legal Aspects and Political Significance of the Soviet Concept of Co-existence' *International and Comparative Law Quarterly*, 12 (1963) 743.

Stalin[269] in the 1920s,[270] had been given its first systematic expression in Krylov's lectures to the Hague Academy in 1947.[271] It was thereafter to become, as McWhinney put it, the leitmotiv of Soviet foreign policy over the next few decades and was formally embraced as an expression of Soviet foreign policy in 1961.[272] Peaceful coexistence was also the central concept around which Soviet jurists, predominant among them Grigory Tunkin, would subsequently arrange their accounts of international law.[273] It was also ultimately to find its way, under Soviet sponsorship, into the work of both the International Law Association[274] and the International Law Commission[275] and would be one of the defining marks of Amero-Soviet agreements during the period of détente.

Resort to the language of 'peaceful coexistence' was, by no means, however, a strictly Soviet initiative. Indeed, despite attempts to locate the idea in a Soviet tradition that tracked it back in time to the work of Lenin,

269 J Stalin, Report to the Fourteenth Congress of the Communist Party, 18 December 1925 (in which he spoke of a 'temporary equilibrium of forces' that had ushered in a 'period of "peaceful coexistence" between the Soviet state and the capitalist states'. J Stalin, *Works* (1954) vol. 7, 2934. An important precursor to this was his famous 'two camps' thesis ('The world has definitively and irrevocably split into two camps: the camp of imperialism and the camp of socialism .... The struggle between these two camps constitutes the hub of present-day affairs, determines the whole substance of the present home and foreign policies of the leaders of the old and the new worlds'). Ibid., vol. 4, 240, 244.

270 Lapenna notes that the term was first used in a diplomatic context by G. V. Chicherin in 1920 speaking about the Peace Treaty with Estonia. Lapenna, 'Legal Aspects', 744.

271 Krylov, 'Les notions principals du droit des gens' *Recueil des cours*, 70 (1947) 407. Khrushchev had maintained that the doctrine of peaceful coexistence had been a central plank of Soviet policy since the revolution in 1917. See Nikita Khrushchev, 'On Peaceful Coexistence' *Foreign Affairs*, 38 (1959) 3. For a discussion, see Warren Lerner, 'The Historical Origins of the Soviet Doctrine of Peaceful Coexistence' *Law and Contemporary Problems*, 29 (1964) 865–70.

272 1961 Programme of the Communist Party of the Soviet Union, chap. VIII, Peaceful Coexistence and the Struggle for World Peace, in Jan Triska (ed.), *Soviet Communism: Programs and Rules: Official Texts of 1919, 1952 (1956), 1961* (San Francisco: Chandler, 1962) 637.

273 See, e.g., Grigory Tunkin, 'Coexistence and International Law' *Hague Recueil* 95 (1958) 1–79; Edward McWhinney, "Peaceful Coexistence" and Soviet-Western International Law' *American Journal of International Law*, 56 (1962) 951–70. For later commentary, see Edward McWhinney, 'International Law Making in Times of Competing Ideologies or Clashing Civilizations: Peaceful Coexistence and Soviet–Western Legal Dialogue in the Cold War Era' *Canadian Yearbook of International Law*, 44 (2007) 421–36.

274 The ILA embarked on a programme of study initiated by Tunkin in 1956 initially under the auspices of the Committee on Juridical Aspects of Peaceful Coexistence. This work continued at the conferences in New York (1958), Hamburg (1960) and Brussels (1962).

275 Edward McWhinney, 'The Renewed Vitality of the Five Principles of Peaceful Coexistence' *Chinese Journal of International Law*, 3 (2004) 3823.

it was Indonesian President Sukarno who had first given it international visibility in his 'Pancasila' (or 'Pansheel') speech of 1945, with concrete recognition following in the Indonesian Constitution of the same year. The five principles of the Pansheel were thereafter to be given explicit recognition in the 1954 Sino–Indian Treaty relating to Tibet[276] and in a host of joint statements, communiqués and declarations in subsequent years,[277] including, if more equivocally, in the Bandung conference in 1955.[278] Later initiatives adopted by the Non-Aligned movement, such as the Charter of Economic Rights and Duties of States[279] and New International Economic Order,[280] would also be informed by its core precepts. And in all of these contexts, the Non-Aligned concept of peaceful coexistence arguably took on a somewhat different valence to that adopted in Soviet (or indeed Chinese) thought – emphasising 'neutralism', 'non-commitment' and 'non-alignment'[281] – rather than the centrality of mutual antagonism or competition.[282]

As with its Asian counterpart, the Soviet 'principle' of peaceful coexistence gave particular prominence to five key principles: (a) mutual respect for territorial integrity and sovereignty, (b) mutual non-aggression, (c) mutual non-intervention in internal affairs, (d) equality and mutual benefit and (e) peaceful coexistence. Quite apart from the somewhat awkward nesting of principles within principles, the default reaction of many Western jurists was that the principle of coexistence was either

[276] Agreement on Trade and Intercourse between Tibet Region of China and India, Beijing, 29 April 1954.

[277] For a list, see Brownlie, *International Law*, 123–26.

[278] Whilst the Bandung Communiqué extended the five principles to ten, it was also to replace the phrase 'peaceful co-existence' by 'live together in peace'. This formulation was, in fact, proposed by Chou En-Lai himself who had urged the Conference to embrace the five principles as the starting point of their discussions. See Russell Fifield, 'The Five Principles of Peaceful Co-existence' *American Journal of International Law*, 52 (1958) 507.

[279] UNGA Res 3281 (XXIX) (12 December 1974).

[280] UNGA/Res 3201 (S-VI), 'Declaration on the Establishment of a New International Economic Order' (1 May 1974)

[281] See V. P. Gupta, 'The Asian Concept of "Peaceful Coexistence"' *Philippines Law Journal*, 45 (1970) 623–33. In the case of the Bandung Communiqué, this was expressed through the commitment to abstain 'from the use of arrangements of collective defense to serve the particular interests of any of the big powers' (principle 6A).

[282] Fifield observes that 'within its Communist framework peaceful coexistence by no means implies an end to the strife between the Communist states lead by the Soviet Union and the Western alignment led by the United States. The class struggle applied to world politics is fundamental.' Fifield, 'Five Principles', 508.

merely a 'political slogan' or a somewhat banal recitation of norms that were already well recognised in international law and more specifically in the UN Charter itself.[283] As Cabot Lodge put it in 1957: '[T]hese principles, stated in another way, are what we are all committed to by our adherence to the Charter of the United Nations.'[284]

As far as Soviet scholars were concerned, however, what it sought to give expression to was not simply the idea that the two ideological blocs should seek to 'coexist' with one another in a condition of mutual tolerance (or indeed peaceful enmity) but that the conditions of such peaceful coexistence would frame the operating code of international law itself. 'Peaceful coexistence' was, in that sense, not so much a principle as an 'environmental condition' – rather like 'global warming' or the 'balance of power' – that would operate as a meta-level ordering concept for the purposes of organising international legal relations between the antagonistic blocs.[285]

As Tunkin put it, 'the problem of the co-relation of peaceful coexistence and international law' gave recognition to the fact that the 'coexistence and struggle of two systems' was a necessary feature of 'the

[283] But insofar as the content of the principle of peaceful coexistence seemed merely to re-affirm many of the existing principles and precepts of international law, it was equally as vulnerable to being dismissed as a superficial ideological gloss. See, e.g., Wolfgang Friedmann, *The Changing Structure of International Law* (New York: Columbia University Press, 1964) 331: 'It is evident that all these principles are, in essence, somewhat platitudinous restatements of elementary principles of international law, as accepted by all other members of the family of nations', as it was venerated as a key explanatory doctrine. What its detractors saw as its fundamental weakness, its proponents saw as its strength (some Western writers much preferred Tunkin's more congenial legal politics with its promotion of harmonious relations between East and West and its rejection of 'weasel word exceptions' (like 'imperialism' and 'colonialism') to the rules of international law. McWhinney, *'Peaceful Co-existence'*, 89.

[284] Cabot Lodge, *Department of State Bulletin*, 37 (1957) 693. It was not the case that Soviet scholars disagreed with this assertion. Indeed, many were to argue that the UN Charter did indeed give expression to the principle of peaceful coexistence. See, e.g., Victor Karpov, 'The Soviet Concept of Peaceful Coexistence and its Implications for International Law' *Law and Contemporary Problems*, 29 (1964) 861; G. Tunkin, 'Co-existence and International Law' *Recueil des cours*, 95 (1958) 77 (the five principles of peaceful coexistence 'constitute nothing more than principles already contained in the Charter, but given more precise formulation').

[285] As Karpov put it 'we cannot even discuss this principle in terms whether we should "accept" or "reject" it. The point is that today peaceful coexistence is *an indisputable fact* of international life and not someone's suggestion. Peaceful coexistence is an objective necessity stemming from the contemporary stage of the development of human society.' Karpov, 'Soviet Concept of Peaceful Coexistence and its Implications for International Law' *Law and Contemporary Problems*, 29 (1964) 858.

transition period from capitalism to socialism' and that the 'entire world situation is determined by the struggle between the Soviet republics and the imperialist states standing against them'.[286] Coexistence was not, thus, just a principle *of* international law but a principle upon which international law was ultimately dependent:

> The very possibility of peaceful coexistence of the socialist and capitalist states immediately conditions the possibility of the existence of general international law, since the basic contradiction of contemporary international relations lies in the relations between states of the two systems.[287]

So far, according to Tunkin, as international law necessarily reflected the terms of that struggle, it differed from 'traditional' international law but not to the extent that nothing remained of the 'old'.[288] The new international law was not born, like a deus ex machina, out of the October Revolution, but emerged as a consequence of the 'resolute struggle of socialism and progress against the forces of reaction and war' and came subsequently to be validated in the concordant wills of States in the international community.[289] International law as it emerged during the Cold War was by necessity a law of coexistence insofar as it gave expression to the dualistic character of the economic structure of international society at the time, pivoting on the competition between 'two diametrically different economic systems'.[290]

Even though it generally endorsed the principles to which it gave expression, the US was, for a long time, reluctant to embrace the language of peaceful coexistence. Mostly, US objections turned upon the Soviet Union's habit of associating the principle of peaceful coexistence with the 'revolutionary struggle against imperialism'[291] and the advancement of proletarian internationalism (particularly its support for national liberation struggles). The US preferred to use the apparently more 'neutral' language of 'peaceful' and 'friendly relations' and of 'cooperation' – a compromise formula that ultimately found its way into the General Assembly Declaration on Friendly Relations of 1974. But in

[286] Tunkin, 'Co-existence and International Law', 21 (quoting Fedoseev).
[287] Ibid., 235.
[288] Ibid., 2523.
[289] Ibid., 253.
[290] Ibid., 47.
[291] Andrei Gromyko, 'Open Letter of the Central Committee of the Communist Party', cited in Bernard Ramundo, *Peaceful Coexistence; International Law in the Building of Communism* (Baltimore: John Hopkins Press, 1967) 113.

many respects, this was a relatively superficial objection, particularly in light of US endorsement of the five principles. And so, in the midst of détente, when the Amero-Soviets set out to make the terms of their mutual relations explicit in the 1972 agreement on Basic Principles of Relations between the United States and the Union of Soviet Socialist Republics,[292] coexistence was central to the juridical framework.[293] The first paragraph declared that the agreement proceeded 'from the common determination that in the nuclear age there is no alternative to conducting their mutual relations on the basis of peaceful coexistence'. It went on to say that 'differences in ideology and in the social systems of the USA and the USSR are not obstacles to the bilateral development of normal relations based on principles of sovereignty, equality, non-interference in internal affairs and mutual advantage'.[294]

So, the idea of coexistence appeared to be fundamental to the juridical ordering of the Amero-Soviet Cold War. It had two features that are worth drawing out. First, the idea of peaceful coexistence was not simply descriptive of the 'state of play' of international law at that time but also described the key means by which the struggle between the social systems could, and should, be conducted. Above all else, as the diplomat Victor Karpov noted, was its emphasis on peace and the avoidance of nuclear warfare:

> It is not war that should settle the controversy between the two systems. In the final analysis, it will not be the system which produces the greatest quantity of means of destruction that will triumph, but the system which produces the most of material and spiritual values, which provides man with a better life. We are absolutely sure that one cannot drive people to paradise with a club, or drive them to communism by means of war.
>
> Communists do not conceal from anyone their desire to attract all people of the world to the side of socialism. This is regarded by them as their prime international task. But the question is: by what means is that cause to be advanced? We are not going to attain it by unleashing wars, nor by forcing our way of life on other nations. It is through creative labour, through the great constructive force of the liberated peoples, through the

[292] 'Basic Principles of Relations between the United States of American and the Union of Soviet Socialist Republics' *American Journal of International Law*, 66 (1972) 920–22.

[293] In Tunkin's work, the 'Cold War' is a descriptor for US foreign policy and is always referred to in inverted commas. See, e.g., 'Co-existence and International Law', 75 ('The "position of strength" policy and the "cold war" which is the outcome of that policy, have undoubtedly diminished the role of international law in international relations since the end of the Second World War').

[294] Ibid., para. 1.

> revolutionary energy of the working people, that we are going to raise the prestige of socialism and to win it more and more support on the part of various nations.[295]

Much the same could be said of US liberal internationalism in its efforts to promote freedom, democracy and liberal institutions worldwide.

Peaceful coexistence, in that sense, committed the Amero-Soviets to a project of peaceful change, to the avoidance of conflict, to disarmament (where possible) and the reduction of tensions that might lead to war between the nuclear powers. In contrast, it also committed them to a struggle – of seeking to win a competition for the hearts and minds of the peoples of the world by peaceful means, to promote self-determination and ward off interference in that process. If avoiding nuclear warfare was its precondition, self-determination was its objective and principal site of contestation.

In the second place, if the idea of peaceful coexistence inscribed at the centre of international law the contestation between capitalism and communism that marked relations between the Americans and the Soviets, it did so by generalising that contestation across the globe and generalising also its productive conditions (i.e. sovereign statehood).[296] It was not just a regional[297] or 'interbloc' law[298] but a mode of social and legal relations that engaged the entirely of the globe, giving expression to the (momentary) common interests of the antagonists on either side. In this guise, peaceful coexistence became a medium through which the Cold War might represent itself as thoroughly global – this was a conflict that engaged the entirety of international society; there was no 'outside'. That process of globalisation was carried forward in the form of both threat and hope: both in the threat of global nuclear annihilation and the hope that adhesion to the principle of peaceful coexistence might allow the iron 'laws of historical development' or of 'progress' to resolve the existing conflict by peaceful means.[299]

295 Karpov, 'Soviet Concept', 859.

296 Tunkin ('Co-existence and International Law', 51), who observes that whilst 'the State is a form of organisation existing only during a certain stage of development of human society' also notes that 'the existence of sovereign States' was a necessary feature of 'the development of society in our epoch'. Ibid., 50.

297 Ibid., 55–58.

298 See Ibid., 46: 'One must keep in mind that the question is not one of "interbloc" law, which is nonexistent . . . but of general international law.'

299 Tunkin argued, for example, that 'history shows that in the long run the progressive forces have always been victorious and assured the progressive development of human

The key markers of the principle of coexistence as a diplomatic and juridical style were thus twofold. On one side was a commitment to peace – to the introduction of principles and norms 'aimed at reducing armaments, banning the tests, use and manufacture of nuclear weapons, prohibiting war propaganda, [and] defining aggression'.[300] On the other side was a similar commitment to self-determination[301] – to the ending of colonial rule, to the advancement to independence of non-self-governing territories, to the elimination of unwarranted external intervention and coercion in the exercise of self-rule, to territorial integrity and political independence. But in the case of both, as was implied by the idea of *co*existence, there was an essential element of reciprocity at work.[302] In the case of arms negotiations, the principle to be obtained was not so much total disarmament as one of balance. This meant ensuring, on one side, a proportionate distribution of threat and risk between the powers (as set out in quantified terms in the ABM Treaty of 1972, SALT I and II) and, on the other, ensuring that any such balance would not be upset by 'third' powers acquiring the same annihilatory capacity (NPT, 1968). Whilst such agreements were, by no means, exclusively bilateral, they nevertheless assumed that practical form, albeit the case that they were uniformly concluded in the 'interests' of the world.[303] The Limited Test Ban Treaty of 1963 spoke, for example, of the desire 'to put an end to the contamination of man's environment by radioactive substances', and the ABM treaty of 1972 referred to the 'premise that nuclear war would have devastating consequences for all

society'. Even if one might demonstrate there were occasional moments of regression, these 'do not set aside the basic laws of the development of society which ultimately prevail'. Grigory Tunkin, 'The Legal Nature of the United Nations' *Recueil des cours*, 119 (1966) 17

300 Tunkin, 'Co-existence and International Law', 78.

301 See Johannes Socher, *Russia and the Right to Self-Determination in the Post-Soviet Space* (Oxford: Oxford University Press, 2021) chapter 1.

302 'Both sides recognize that efforts to obtain unilateral advantage at the expense of the other, directly or indirectly, are inconsistent with [the objective of peaceful coexistence]'. Agreement on Basic Principles of Relations between the United States and the Soviet Union (Moscow, 29 May 1972), para. 2.

303 The Basic Principles not only reaffirmed the Amero-Soviet's 'special responsibility' in ensuring that 'conflicts or situations will not arise which would serve to increase international tension' (para. 3) but of their intention to 'widen the juridical basis of their mutual relations' to ensure that both bilateral and 'multilateral treaties and agreements to which they are jointly parties are faithfully implemented'. Ibid., para. 4.

mankind'.[304] All were concluded, furthermore, with the accompanying promise that, at some stage in future, a 'general and complete disarmament' would be forthcoming. A form of 'global bilateralism', understood in the language of peaceful coexistence, would therefore become one of the key features of the juridical Cold War.[305]

In the case of self-determination, as we have already seen, the commitment on both sides was both reciprocal and conditional – dependent ultimately upon the extent to which the populace concerned might have been swayed by the 'interventionist' activities of the rival power. That reciprocity was formalised in doctrines on either side – in the Truman Doctrine in case of the United States and the Brezhnev Doctrine in case of the Soviet Union. Each of these doctrines, in their own way, sought to bring together the principle of self-determination with a right of intervention, whilst opposing, in the same measure, the idea of 'exporting revolution' to other States.[306] Whatever the evident contradictions in their mutual position here, the resonant parallelism gave expression, once again, to the idea of a global bilateralism found in the security pacts and economic institutions on either side.

Coexistence then was a bipolar arrangement with global implications. It organised a form of mixed friend-enemy relationship between the two superpowers while at the same time acting as a mode of organisation imposed jointly by those same powers on the rest of the world. If it was a law of the Cold War, it was also a law of war. And when it came to the question of war, like the Cold War in general when viewed from the North, coexistence was thought of as an 'intermediate state' between war

304 The same terminology was to be found in the Intermediate-Range Nuclear Forces Treaty (INF Treaty), Washington, DC, 8 December 1987.

305 This is discernible in the formally redundant, but politically prescient, denial in the eleventh paragraph of the Basic Principles in which it was stated that 'the development of US-Soviet relations is not directed against third countries and their interests'. Why else, one could ask, might one believe that such a clause was necessary? On this theme generally, however, see Chapters 7 and 8.

306 It was on this ground that Mao criticised Khrushchev's concept of 'the general line of peaceful coexistence'. For Mao, Khrushchev had abandoned the principle of proletarian internationalism that was destined to govern relations between socialist States inter se and between socialist States and the peoples living under colonial. Coexistence, for him, could only subsist as a governing principle as between socialist and capitalist/imperial States. See Mao Tse-tung, 'Peaceful Coexistence – Two Diametrically Opposed Policies. Comment on the Open Letter of the Central Committee of the CPSU (VI)' 12 December 1963,

and peace, disrupting the classical categories of international law itself.[307] There was indeed a renunciation of war (inside the Amero-Soviet bloc between the Americans and Soviets), a commitment to non-proliferation (except in the US and Soviet Union, and to an extent their blocs), and a rule against 'volunteers' (i.e. the arming of insurgents in the blocs [e.g. Hungary]), that each largely adhered to. This was, for McWhinney, a 'new jus gentium' based on 'observation of actual norms'.[308] But a peaceful 'peaceful coexistence' was, ultimately, only possible *between* the US and Soviets.[309] There were no aspirations for it to be applicable as a *pacific* global order. Indeed, all bets were off in the Global South where other people's wars could happily be fought, or among socialist States where the principles of territorial inviolability were subordinated to the defence of socialist internationalism,[310] or in the American sphere of influence where violent coup, counter-coup and intervention were the orders of the day.[311]

3.5 Détente

Coexistence quickly became the dominant juridical framework of the Amero-Soviet Cold War but by the end of the 1960s had acquired a different valence. At that time, détente, a new term, and a new conceptual frame for Amero-Soviet diplomatic thought and practice, emerged. Whether détente represented a radical break from the politics of coexistence or its continuation in a new guise was never entirely clear. It did

[307] Philip Jessup, 'Should International Law Recognize an Intermediate Status between Peace and War?' *American Journal of International Law*, 48 (1954) 98–103. See also Myres McDougal, 'Peace and War: Factual Continuum with Multiple Legal Consequences' *American Journal of International Law*, 49 (1955) 63–68. Interestingly, Tunkin rejected this idea calling it 'Cold War' thinking and contrasting it with peaceful coexistence (for him, not 'Cold War'). See Tunkin 'Co-existence and International Law' *Recueil des cours*, 95 (1958) 60.

[308] McWhinney, *'Peaceful Co-existence'*, 125.

[309] It was this idea that underpinned both Austrian 'neutrality' and its subsequent pursuit of a diplomacy of 'peaceful coexistence' with the Soviet Union. See Mueller, *A Good Example*.

[310] Erickson, *Law and the Revolutionary State*, 47.

[311] The Soviets were enthusiastic about sovereign equality but at the same time the Brezhnev Doctrine insisted that governments harmful to Soviet interests would not be permitted in the Eastern bloc (Erickson, *Law and the Revolutionary State*, 53). For an overview of Soviet approaches, see latter half of Ebrahim Afsah, '"Cold War" (1947–91)' in *Max Planck Encyclopaedia of Public International Law* (Oxford: Oxford University Press, 2009).

signify – and signal – an explicit suspension of relations of enmity in favour of a (hesitant) collaboration, but even in the darkest of Cold War times collaborative acts of bargaining and compromise were never entirely absent (as the unfolding of the Cuban Missile Crisis would appear to evidence). On the flip side, détente did not mean a complete renunciation of the conflictual terms of their relationship with one another either.

Perhaps what détente did describe was not simply an atmospheric change in Amero-Soviet relations – a 'thawing' of their relations as was often remarked, marked by the conclusion of a series of agreements on matters that had visibly divided them (the limited test ban treaty, the NPT, ABM Agreement and SALT I) – but a new mode of coexistence. As we have seen, coexistence found its principal expression in an ethos of (global) bilateralism that pervaded negotiations on disarmament, on the future of Germany and on nuclear testing. Détente appeared to give expression to an alternative imaginary: one in which the two powers would rule together, not through the divisible architecture of a co-imperium, or in the establishment of spheres of interest/ influence, but in the form of a unitary, collaborative, authority exercised in the name of international society as a whole. The juridical model for détente was thus to be multilateral not bilateral, collaborative not competitive, peaceful not warlike. It would bring into play a new imaginative landscape – of humanity, the environment and the preservation of global interests – but one in which no one was left in any doubt as to the primacy of Amero-Soviet interests.

The politics of détente as Suri and others have suggested was given significant impetus in the late 1960s in the wake of a series of 'internal' disruptions within the American and Soviet blocs – the Prague Spring, the Paris Uprisings, the Cultural Revolution, student riots, the anti-Vietnam War protests. On both sides, these events provoked efforts to pacify the respective domestic constituencies through a de-radicalised foreign policy.[312] Tensions had certainly arisen within each bloc. The US had to contend not only with a Gaullist France, which had long sought to assert its independence from a US-dominated Western alliance (defecting from the command structures of NATO in 1966 and calling for the withdrawal of NATO troops from French territory) but also with both West Germany and Austria, each of which had begun to seek the

[312] Suri, *Power and Protest.*

'normalisation' of their relations with the Soviet Union (the former in the language of Ostpolitik,[313] the latter in the language of peaceful coexistence).[314] The 1967 military coup in Greece further fractured the Western alliance, with Norway, Denmark and the Netherlands instituting novel inter-State proceedings against it before the Council of Europe's European Commission on Human Rights.[315]

For its part, the Soviet Union's relations with China had disintegrated (to the point of outright conflict in 1969) as had those with Albania (which withdrew from the Warsaw Pact in the aftermath of the Prague Spring). Hungary and Poland both embarked upon ambitious new economic programmes (the latter eventually seeking loans from both the US and West Germany), and Romania, for its part, pursued an increasingly independent course, refusing to abandon its industrialisation and refusing also to embrace Brezhnev's re-casting of the Warsaw Pact. What had been a fairly monolithic bloc was becoming increasingly plural.

Political 'normalisation' appeared as the central theme of détente. For a while, it also seemed to represent, as Brezhnev put it, a way of 'overcoming the cold war',[316] or at least of palliating its effects. Ultimately it did not secure that end. The Amero-Soviets returned to conflictual relations at the end of the 1970s, marked on one side by the Soviet invasion of Afghanistan and, on the other, by the election of President Reagan in the US on an 'anti-détente platform'. In his view, the Soviets couldn't be trusted on détente.[317]

[313] See William Griffith, *The Ostpolitik of the Federal Republic of* Germany (Cambridge, MA: MIT Press, 1978); Julia von Dannenberg, *The Foundations of Ostpolitik: The Making of the Moscow Treaty between West Germany and the* USSR (Oxford: Oxford University Press, 2008); Benedikt Schoenborn, *Reconciliation Road: Willy Brandt, Ostpolitik and the Quest for European Peace* (Oxford and New York: Berghahn Books, 2020). This, perhaps, understates the extent to which the French and Germans were also committed to détente but, for the Germans at least, Ostpolitik was a more visionary effort to bring East and West together in a new settlement as opposed to a stabilisation of great power relations and consolidation of the Yaltan territorial settlements (see Suri, *Power and Protest*, 2–6, 29).

[314] Mueller, *A Good Example*.

[315] See generally, Antonis Klapsis et al. (eds.), *The Greek Junta and the International System* (London: Routledge, 2020).

[316] Leonid Brezhnev, *Moscow News*, June 1979.

[317] This reflected a powerful lobby agitating against détente. For a description of those powerful interests, for example, the Committee on the Present Danger, who wanted to abandon détente and return to the Cold War, see, e.g., Simon Dalby, *Creating the Second Cold War: The Discourse of Politics* (London: Bloomsbury, 1990).

In the meantime, though, the politics of détente became visible in several discrete juridical settings.[318] In the first place, as we have already mentioned, it underpinned the series of arms control agreements that were thrashed out during that time – including the Hot Line Agreement and the Limited Test Ban Treaty of 1963, the NPT of 1968, the ABM treaty of 1972 and SALT I of the same year, running through to the unratified SALT II of 1979.[319] The largely bilateral or plurilateral character of such agreements, however, did not distinguish them, in any radical sense, from the politics of coexistence. Here, indeed, coexistence was very literally what was in question – not merely a 'living alongsideness', or a willingness to cooperate, but the need for co*existence* and what the Soviets described as the 'objective interest' in preventing thermonuclear war.[320]

In the second place, détente appeared to mark, or be marked by, a reassertion of the values of the UN Charter and its commitment to multilateral diplomacy. A series of long-standing membership issues were resolved – with agreement being reached to allow the PRC to assume the seat of China in the UN in 1971 and the two Germanies being admitted to membership in 1973. The working languages of the UN were expanded by the inclusion of both Arabic and Chinese and the appointment of Kurt Waldheim as Secretary General from 'neutral' Austria all seemed to point to a new role being assumed by the UN. At the same time, the UN General Assembly finally managed to conclude its work on the Declaration on Friendly Relations with support on all sides. That declaration reanimated faith in the terms of the UN Charter by heralding its commitment to the prohibition on the use of force, the stability of borders, non-intervention and decolonisation (self-determination).

The commitment to multilateralism was given particular expression in the Amero-Soviet agreement on 'Basic Principles of Mutual Relations' mentioned above, which recognised, inter alia, that they 'make no claim for themselves and would not recognise the claims of anyone else to any

[318] See Edward McWhinney, *The International Law of Detente: Arms Control, European Security and East–West Cooperation* (Alphen aan den Rijn: Sijthoff & Noordhoff International, 1978).

[319] The INF Treaty of 1987 has been described as an outcome of 'détente from below'. See Luc André Brunet and Eirini Karamouzi, 'Introduction: Globalising the History of the Anti-nuclear Activism' in Luc André Brunet and Eirini Karamouzi (eds.), *Beyond the Euromissile Crisis: Global Histories of Anti-Nuclear Activism in the Cold* War (Oxford: Berghahn Books, 2025) 10.

[320] Dimitri Tomashevsky, *On the Peaceful Co-Existence of States* (Moscow: Novosti Press Agency, 1973).

special rights or advantages in world affairs'.[321] The commitment here to 'the sovereign equality of all states' was unremarkable given the presence of that language in the UN Charter itself, but its implications were nonetheless evident. What it appeared to represent was a renunciation of the privileges the Amero-Soviets had claimed for themselves within their own blocs, a renunciation, in particular, of the Brezhnev and Monroe doctrines.[322] Whether or not that would be evidenced in practice (and many commentators were deeply sceptical),[323] it nevertheless reflected a shift in the language and outlook of the Amero-Soviets and signalled their willingness to set themselves alongside (as opposed to above) other members of the international community.

In the third place, détente was evidenced very explicitly at the (long-anticipated) Conference on Security and Cooperation in Europe between 1973–75. The resulting Helsinki Final Act of 1975 spoke of the desire to 'make *détente* both a continuing and an increasingly viable and comprehensive process, universal in scope' and did so by seeking to broaden the common ground shared between the powers (in the spirit of 'better and closer relations' or 'better mutual understanding'). Many of the terms of the Final Act followed the language of the Friendly Relations declaration before it – including extensive references to sovereign equality, non-intervention, the non-use of force – but it also included, notably, a section on respect for human rights and fundamental freedoms.

As part of the overall aim of seeking to temper political relations between the two blocs in Europe, the Final Act was directed towards two ends. The first of these – flowing from the otherwise unobjectionable clauses securing the 'inviolability of frontiers' and 'territorial integrity' – froze the territorial status quo within Europe. In a positive sense, this obviously precluded any further coercive changes to the territorial frontiers in Europe. The aim of stabilising the existing distribution of political power also led to formal recognition of a 'right to neutrality'.[324] More problematic, however, was that it further cemented the existing division of Germany (a partition that, by that stage, had already been 'formalised' through the admission of the two Germanies to the United Nations) and also gave legitimacy to all the contested territorial changes that preceded

[321] Basic Principles on Mutual Relations, para. 11.

[322] Stephen M. Schwebel, 'The Brezhnev Doctrine Repealed and Peaceful-Coexistence Enacted' *American Journal of International Law*, 66 (1972) 818.

[323] Ibid., 816.

[324] For further discussion of neutrality, see Chapter 4.

it – including acceptance of the Oder-Neisse line as the presumptive border between Germany and Poland and of Soviet claims in respect of the Baltic Republics.

The other apparent 'end' to which Helsinki was directed was a smothering of internal dissent.[325] If, as Suri has pointed out, détente was a policy response to the various dissident movements within the respective blocs, then Helsinki was arguably the policy-instrument par excellence for doing so. On one side, it sought to cut off all external sources of subversion – no more interventions, propaganda campaigns, hostile activities across the line – no more externally sponsored political change.[326] On the other side, it also sought to 'normalise' dissent itself, embedding it in a progressive language of human rights and fundamental freedoms to which all States committed themselves. Peaceful, democratic, change was, thus, the order of the day[327] even if, as later became apparent, the invocation of human rights and fundamental freedoms would have much greater, and more far-reaching, effects with respect to vernaculars of solidarity in Eastern Europe.[328]

The final context in which détente came to be performatively disclosed to the world was in the Apollo–Soyuz space initiative that followed the conclusion of an agreement between the US and the Soviet Union (the Moscow Agreement of 24 May 1971) to develop cooperation in the fields of space meteorology, the study of the natural environment, the exploration of near space and in space biology and medicine. In the 'Apollo-Soyez Test Project', as it was called by the US, the two powers agreed to develop compatible rendezvous and docking systems of 'Soviet-American' manned spacecraft and stations and to conduct an experimental flight in which two space craft would come together allowing 'cosmo-astronauts' to engage in mutual visits.[329] This was accomplished on 17 July 1975, and the spirit of détente that it presented to the world

325 See Suri, *Power and Protest*, 5; meanwhile, 'Nuclear weapons stabilised the international system.' Ibid., 11.

326 See Ralph B. Levering, *The Cold War: A Post-Cold War History*, 3rd ed. (West Sussex: Wiley Blackwell, 2016) 154–213.

327 See Suri, *Power and Protest*, 5.

328 See Florian Hoffman, 'Human Rights and the Cold War' in Matthew Craven, Sundhya Pahuja and Gerry Simpson (eds.), *Cambridge History of International Law, Vol XI: International Law during the Cold War (1945–1990)* (Cambridge: Cambridge University Press, forthcoming).

329 See generally, Committee on Aeronautical and Space Sciences, *Soviet Space Programs, 1971–75* (Washington, DC: US Government Printers Office, 1976).

was famously sealed by the televised handshake between astronaut Thomas Stafford and cosmonaut Aleksei Leonov.

In a way, the scientific and technical collaboration instanced in the Apollo–Soyuz project represented the high point of the emergent détente between the rival powers (albeit in face of escalating conflict in Vietnam). Its origins, however, could be traced back somewhat earlier to the parallel, and largely competitive, 'scientific' activities that took place in 1957–8 under title of the International Geophysical Year, which provided the setting for the launch of Sputnik (4 October 1957) and for the establishment of a series of scientific research posts in Antarctica under the guidance of the International Council of Scientific Unions.[330] Both of these initiatives led to the conclusion of subsequent international agreements in which the Soviet Union and the US had a decisive common input. These included two agreements related to Antarctica and Outer Space, respectively, which were jurisdictionally delimited as domains of peaceful scientific activity free from any claim to sovereignty, free also from the presence of nuclear weaponry. In both such cases, Amero-Soviet rivalry was suspended, alongside any claim to sovereignty, in the 'interest of science and the progress of all mankind'.[331]

The Outer Space Treaty, in particular, served as the generative model for a politics of détente in two different ways. In the first place, it sought to confine the ambit of nuclear competition between the powers by prohibiting nuclear weapons from being placed in orbit. In that respect, it foreshadowed the other arms control agreements that were to be concluded between the USSR and the US in subsequent years. But in the second place, it achieved that end by crafting a new jurisdictional order, not just for the globe but for the cosmos, in the name of 'all mankind'. Despite their effective monopoly in the 'use' of outer space (only one other power had successfully launched an orbital space craft by

[330] Extensive collaboration between the Soviet Union and the US in the field of science included the 1962 Dryden–Blagonoravov Agreement providing for collaboration in relation to (1) the exchange of weather data and the coordination of the launch of meterological satellites, (2) a joint effort to map the magnetic field of the earth by coordinated launch of geomagnetic satellites and (3) cooperation in the experimental relay of communications via the Echo satellite. See Memorandum from the Under Secretary of State (Ball) to President Kennedy, Washington, DC, 5 July 1962, in Foreign Relations of the United States, 1961–1963, vol. XXV, Organization of Foreign policy; Information Policy; United Nations; Scientific Matters, Doc. 392, 893–94. In 1972, the US and USSR concluded an Agreement on Cooperation in Environmental Protection, 852 UNTS 106.

[331] Antarctic Treaty, 1 December 1959, 402 UNTS 71.

1965), the terms under which any future use might occur were effectively legislated into place by the Amero-Soviets in the form of a multilateral agreement (the ratification of which by other powers was largely incidental). This, indeed, was to be a model that would continue through the period of détente from the ratification of the NPT in 1968 through to that of ENMOD in 1977.

And so détente was double-edged. On the one side, it admitted the possibility of a plural global political order – embracing multilateralism and the principle of sovereign equality, admitting the possibility of neutrality between the blocs, renouncing the desire for territorial change. But on the other side, it was also deeply conservative, marked by the desire to procure universal acceptance of the status quo including to the technological, military, political and economic dominance of the Amero-Soviets in global affairs. For skeptical audiences, détente – understood as the 'the policy of the two biggest states' –merely offered the Amero-Soviets the power 'to carve out spheres of influence under new conditions'.[332] It remained, from this perspective, a form of 'bipolarized politics' and was even described at one point as 'American-Soviet *détente*', a form of bloc exclusivity, much of it accomplished through legal instruments.[333]

3.6 Collaboration and Competition

Throughout the three periods we have been describing, the willingness of the Amero-Soviets to act conjunctively was most transparent when they jointly crafted agreements that served to both limit and legitimise their activities in a particular space. The Outer Space Agreement is one example. But this by no means exhausted the variety of different rhetorical, ideological, moral, (sometimes strategic) projects in which they participated conjointly. Indeed, the presence of an ideational Amero-Sovietism may be found in an array of different initiatives from their mutual support for self-determination (resistance to anti-anti-colonialism at Suez being the apogee of this shared attitude), to treaties that sought to administer the Amero-Soviet relationship and maintain their shared privileges (the NPT, the ABM Treaty), to juridical arrangements that afforded the two protagonists special prerogatives in zones of

[332] Radovan Vukadinovic, *Non-Aligned Countries and Détente* (Beograd: Jugoslovenska Stvarnost, 1979) 12–14.

[333] Ibid., 18.

interest (the Warsaw Pact and NATO) and diplomatic protocols that resulted in juridified division spaces (in Germany and Korea). It was also found in a shared distaste for the active neutralisms of the Global South and the 'proxification' of endogenous and indigenous politics around the globe. Much of this, and the resulting push and pull, is the subject of the chapters to follow. Sometimes Amero-Soviet initiatives were carried through conventional legal forms (for example, *The Partial Test Ban Treaty*), at other times they deployed less familiar but still recognisably lawful *techne* (e.g. *The Helsinki Accords*). But very often these projects took the form of sub-legal orderings where the juridical aspect of the world being made has, in commentary, subsequently been glossed over or obscured by a tendency to mark the activities as economic or informal ('coexistence') or political ('spheres of interest').[334]

It was, of course, not the case that the Amero-Soviets saw themselves as collaborators – or, at least, did so only on occasion. And each placed a heavy emphasis upon the belligerent, warlike, nature of their relationship with one another. The Cold War remained, in many respects, a rivalry between two hegemons. Our argument, though, is that the rivalry is best understood as an 'internal' or 'sibling' rivalry – one very similar to the rivalries that divided European powers in the nineteenth century in their competition for colonies, protectorates or spheres of influence in the non-European world. And as with that earlier time, the sibling rivalry developed – and developed within – a common juridical frame that counterposed itself against (and, indeed, obliterated) rival 'laws of encounter' that it met around the world.[335] Here again, in the context of the Cold War, were two European rivals seeking to export their rivalry across the globe in the form of common sets of ideas – political, economic, social, cultural and juridical – and once again, the opposition it encountered was either neutered or translated into the language of the Cold War itself. For one of the products of the Cold War – evidenced most concretely in the way in which the 'Cold War' has come to be used as a shorthand expression for a period of global history – was its ability to totalise itself and envelop everything within its own account of the world. This is its historiographical effect.

334 This mirrors a comment of Kennan's that Soviet action always took place on two planes: 'a subterranean plane and an official plane'. David Featherstone, *Solidarity: Hidden Histories and Geographies of* Internationalism (London: Zed Books, 2012) 69.

335 Sundhya Pahuja, 'Laws of Encounter: A Jurisdictional Reading of International Law' *London Review of International Law*, 1(1) (2013) 63–98.

3.7 Proxification and 'Opposition to Blocs'

One key way in which the Amero-Soviets subordinated alternative political programmes or national projects – and the way these programmes and projects were classed in the North Atlantic – was through the language and techniques of proxification. "Proxification" is both a contemporaneous geo-strategic technique and a historiographical gloss through which rival politics were/are excluded or sublimated into the Atlantic Cold War.[336] As we shall see in a later chapter, even the possibility of neutrality was given a bad name (when it wasn't being reinvented). By 1948, Judge Krylov was already stating, in the *Membership* case, that Eire and Portugal could not be 'peace-loving' because they had been neutral during the war.[337] This anti-neutrality position was then repurposed and became a determination to ensure that there was no place on earth in which the Cold War did not happen.[338] And to the extent that neutrality or neutralism were permissible, these were understood not as exceptions to the Cold War but as extensions of its governing norms (as was to become apparent in the case of Austria). Decolonisation, meanwhile, became for the Amero-Soviet a project of constraint and limit, a battle against plural conceptions of self-determination, economic independence and the formation of anything resembling indigenous foreign policies. As McWhinney put it 'Soviet-Western differences had found their physical outlets in widely scatted geographical locales'.[339] The violence of hot war in the Global South was vital to the Cold War, not so much an expression of ideological differences or conflicting approaches to decolonisation but as a necessary

[336] There are debates about the extent to which proxification was the key to understanding these Cold War moments. See, for example, the removal of Mosaddeq with some writers emphasising the external aspects of his overthrow (Ali Rahnema, *Behind The 1953 Coup in Iran: Thugs, Turncoats, Soldiers and Spooks* (Cambridge: Cambridge University Press, 2015)) and others laying much more stress on local actors and levers of power (Darioush Bayandor, *Iran and the CIA: The Fall of Mosaddeq Revisited* (London: Palgrave MacMillan, 2010)).

[337] Dissenting Opinion of Judge Krylov, Admission of a State to the United Nations (Charter, Art. 4), Advisory Opinion, ICJ Rep 1948, 107, 112.

[338] Cf. Adlai Stevenson's speech at the UN on Cuban missiles, www.britishpathe.com/asset/98254/. See Sara Kendall on the idea that even exoticising certain places was a Cold War trope, 'Postcolonial Hauntings and Cold War Continuities: Congolese Sovereignty and the Murder of Patrice Lumumba' in Craven, Pahuja and Simpson, *International Law and the Cold War*. See further the novels of Grahame Greene and John Le Carre here.

[339] McWhinney, *'Peaceful Co-existence'*, 19.

adjunct to the repressed North Atlantic peace; the Global South became a place where warfare could safely go.

But in late decolonisation, peaceful coexistence and détente had perverse effects on national liberation struggles. The official line of the Soviets involved support for national liberation movements and an opposition to 'unequal treaties' but this waxed and waned depending on the state of US–Soviet (and indeed Sino–Soviet) relations. So, from a certain perspective, coexistence began to look like a project of joint pacification of a Global South always threatening to disrupt the architecture of Amero-Soviet relations. At least one story of the great Bandung/AAPSO[340] moments in Cairo 1957 and Conakry in 1960 featured a Soviet Union committed to peaceful coexistence[341] but fearful also of the revolutionary declarations being made at these gatherings and by everything from Indo-Egyptian 'neutrality' to Chinese revolutionism. In those moments, the approach of the Soviet Union, whose suspicion towards the League of Nations (shared by the Americans) continued into its attitudes towards the United Nations, was to calibrate its response to the early Afro-Asian conferences by emphasising coexistence and disarmament over radical anti-colonialism and anti-neo-colonialism.

Zhu Ziqi, the Chinese member of the AAPSO Secretariat, brought this out in his suggestion that the Soviets were not interested in national liberation at all and that delegates should therefore begin 'conspiring to boost the policy of so-called opposition to blocs'.[342] The Chinese were, in a way, mobilising against the Cold War and against (Soviet) coexistence here, worrying justifiably that the achievement of global communism was being compromised by Amero-Sovietism.[343] In a similar way, many national liberation movements from Algeria through to the Congo sought to steer a course away from any involvement by the Amero-Soviets, relying instead upon support from other indigenous movements in the South.

[340] See further Chapters 4 and 6.

[341] Jeremy Friedman, *Shadow Cold War: The Sino–Soviet Competition for the Third World* (Chapel Hill: University of North Carolina Press, 2018) 200.

[342] On Chinese frustrations with peaceful coexistence, see Friedman, *Shadow Cold War*, 193–97.

[343] Before the Havana Conference in 1966 Brezhnev offered a strategic response to this kind of thinking in *Pravda* where he argued that coexistence as necessary to the revolution: 'The arms race, international tensions ... violations of state sovereignty ... all of these interfere with the unity of anti-imperialist forces'. Friedman, *Shadow Cold War*, 209.

In Havana, the USSR signed the final communiqué calling for violent revolution but didn't mean it, reassuring the Chileans, for example, that they were committed to peaceful coexistence and non-interference.[344] The USSR was in an awkward spot. It was in the position of offering 'a firm rebuff to imperialism' by supporting national liberation movements, while also promoting an idea of peaceful coexistence among States with different systems.[345] The Cubans, meanwhile, after the Missile Crisis, believed their needs had been subordinated to US–Soviet relations with Cuba no longer the (final) battleground of a great ideological war but the victim of an Amero-Soviet diplomatic coup.[346]

The Amero-Soviet spheres of influence did not extend to the South and this meant that there was always the question about what to do with countries 'not firmly allocated to one bloc rather than the other'.[347] Here, according to one prominent international lawyer, there was 'a mutual interest in assuming joint responsibility for economic and social development aid projects in the "new countries" of SE Asia and Africa'.[348] It could hardly be made more explicit.

And so it is not so difficult to think of the Amero-Soviets as themselves imperial powers. The USSR insisted on military prerogatives in Czechoslovakia and Hungary, territorial dominion in Ukraine and Georgia and spheres of influence in Asia. The United States maintained Monroe Doctrine privileges in Central America, engaged in a form of archipelagic expansion in the Azores and Diego Garcia and inherited colonial 'rights' from the French in Indo-China.[349] With one or two exceptions, neither side seemed capable of viewing liberation struggles or trans-continentalism in the South as anything but cynical or

344 Ibid., 212.

345 Dimitri Tomashevsky, *On the Peaceful Co-Existence of States* (Moscow: Novosti Press Agency, 1973), 5.

346 See for example, Preface and Chapter 8.

347 McWhinney, *'Peaceful Co-existence'*, 93.

348 Ibid., 113.

349 This is something accepted even by John Lewis Gaddis (Gaddis, *We Know Now*, 284–85) though he is at pains to distinguish the benevolence of US empire and the evil of Soviet expansion using a comparison between conditions in West and East Germany to make his point (rather than in say Allende's and Pinochet's Chile) to make his point. Not that the Europeans themselves had quietly departed the scene. When Hassan II attacked Algeria there were still 80,000 French troops stationed there after decolonisation. In Cuba, meanwhile, Kennedy was authorising terrorism 'against refineries, storage facilities, ships'. Piero Gleijeses, *Conflicting Missions: Havana, Washington, and Africa 1959–1976* (Chapel Hill: University of North Carolina Press, 2002) 25.

opportunistic Cold War manoeuvring. The Americans could not comprehend, for example, why Algerians would want to ally with Cubans given the economic cost of pulling away from the US. The USSR's more natural affinity for national liberation or revolutionary change, meanwhile, was undercut by a certain cautious Amero-Sovietism. We could read Soviet passivity in southern Africa as resulting from a desire to prop up détente (not to mention a concern about the reliability of Castro).[350] At the same time, the Americans were expressing *sotto voce* a 'basic sympathy with the White Rhodesians'.[351] Anti-imperialist credentials were, thus, being burnished in public but undercut in private.[352] There continued to be a great deal of talk about countries or indeed whole continents being 'lost'.[353]

Many of these imperial reflexes constituted a sort of shadow or deep structural law (of spheres of influence, of forward projection, of base maintenance), existing alongside (or under) the UN Charter's commitment to 'territorial integrity' or 'peaceful resolution of disputes' or self-defence. To take just one instance, Ben Bella, before being deposed as president of Algeria, was berated for receiving Cuban aid after the Moroccan invasion of his country, as if the deep norms of the Cold War had rendered recourse to UN Charter principles of self-defence illegitimate.

Perhaps then in this period there operated what Joyce, following Schmitt, called a 'Katechon': a single (split) project blocking the realisation of a supreme world order – as well as foreshadowing the new order and joint administration to come – that also sought to prevent the emergence of a plurality of world orders.[354] All of this was underscored by an international law that coexisted with, and set the parameters of, these two-power arrangements.[355]

350 Gleijeses, *Conflicting Missions*, 371.

351 Ibid., 390.

352 On white internationalism, see Christopher Gevers, '"News from Pan-Africa": Black Internationalism, Literature & International Law, 1900–1963' (PhD Thesis, Melbourne Law School 2024). Meanwhile, Cubans were delivering a vaccine programme in The Congo in 1966–67 (Gleijeses, *Conflicting Missions*, 153) or preventing a coup in Congo with the loss of one Congolese soldier (Jorge Risquet Expedition).

353 Gleijeses, *Conflicting Missions*, 69.

354 Richard Joyce, 'International Law and the Cold War: Reflections on the Concept of History' in Craven, Pahuja and Simpson, *International Law and the Cold War*, 27–48.

355 Schwarzenberger, 'East–West Rift'. See, too, Kurt Wilk, 'International Law and Ideological Realignment: Universality Reexamined' *New York University Journal of International Law and Politics*, 10 (1978) 463–90; Kurt Wilk 'International Law and

3.8 Conclusion: 'The Last Constraint'

Amero-Sovietism was a collaboration – often implicit or unconscious – in many places and around many things. Our focus in this chapter has been on the way in which this collaboration was realised through forms of collective lawmaking, secretive regime maintenance, spatial division, international administration and a juridified diplomacy. In one sense, the Amero-Soviet Cold War was a global project to distribute and redistribute war and peace, one in which there was a public international law operating at the surface of certain legal texts and practices while a private or informal juridical project of reordering either undercut the permissions and prohibitions embedded in that first order or forced other actors to read those textual assertions (like territorial integrity) and practices differently – even perversely.[356] It was this sense of a double international law that led Che Guevara to say of Patrice Lumumba that he had been a victim of his own mistakes: 'he had trusted international law' as Guevara put it.[357] Perhaps Lumumba had invested too much faith in international law's self-pronounced standards and desiderata and had misunderstood the underlying distributional rules of the game.[358] Over-reliance on the formal texts of international law was a special kind of mistake in the midst of an order that was founded on a series of 'division spaces'.[359] While textbooks were full of forensic examinations of the rules of the UN Charter or the dicta of the ICJ in the Nicaragua case, the superpowers were, in John Lewis Gaddis's words, 'Dividing the World'.

A symptom of this order was the idea of a world split between different 'worlds': a West, an East, a First, a Second, and a Third World, or a developed and underdeveloped (or developing) World. To re-read the Amero-Soviet Cold War in the way we have proposed in this chapter, however, is to emphasise its parochial character. And that, in turn, moves us to consider the way it encounters other world-making projects that were circulating at the time. Such a reading also directs our attention to a different axial split – that between North and South.

Global Ideological Conflict: Reflections on the Universality of International Law' *American Journal of International Law*, 45 (1951) 648–70.

356 Andrew Rubin, *Archives of Authority: Empire, Culture, and the Cold War* (Princeton: Princeton University Press, 2012).

357 Gleijeses, *Conflicting Missions*, 77.

358 Raoul Peck, *Lumumba: Death of the Prophet* (Velvet Film, 1992).

359 Scott Newton, 'Parallel Worlds: Cold War Division Space' in Craven, Pahuja and Simpson, *International Law and the Cold War.*

In subsequent chapters, we take up some of the forms of alternative international laws that coexisted with (and contested) either the official UN Charter Law that lived on the surface of the Cold War or the world-ordering infrastructures that constituted it. The majority of these emanated directly from the Global South. But it is clear that within the United States and the Soviet Union, the idea of 'coexistence', for example, was not universally welcomed. Most obviously, there was a mismatch between the idea of US–Soviet harmony, on one hand, and the requirements of Soviet revolutionary legalism, on the other. 'Marxist–Leninist' international law was repressed during much of the mid-to-late Cold War. Experimental forms of international law were sidelined while officially the 'theoretical' questions around (i.e. revolutionary potential of) the relationship between international law and Marxist doctrine were set aside. In the United Kingdom, meanwhile, radical projects of resistance at Greenham Common or in the Campaign for Nuclear Disarmament (or in the Labour Party itself) were widely regarded as politically immature and incompatible with the politics of deterrence and détente. And in the United States, the visions of Cold War international law that might have been teased out of Black Panther activism or the agitations of the radical left Weathermen, or in the Labor movement barely merited consideration in the official organs of Cold War international law such as the American Society of International Law or the Council for Foreign Relations. That resistance – and the solidarity it engendered - both cut across and was, at times, a rejoinder to, or destabilisation of, the global diplomatic geographies of the Amero-Soviet Cold War.

In the three chapters that follow this one, the Cold War is re-imagined as a form of world-making emerging from the South not as a variant on Cold War international law nor parasitic on it, nor as a regional off-shoot of a core tradition developed in western Europe in the sixteenth century, nor as a colourful historical addendum to a completed project. Instead, we read it as a set of cross-cutting and plural re-engagements with the possibilities of international law and revolutionary global justice. In this account, bipolarity and the practices of Amero-Sovietism are each challenged by a plurality of alternative world-making projects subsequently elided by most retrospective histories of the Cold War. We offer an account of some of these projects. We also describe sites of resistance to dominant Euro-American law. In both cases, these are sometimes European and American sites, but most often emerge from the Global South. Our readers could no doubt think of, or discover, many more. We argue that these are projects to be understood as lawful and independent of the Atlantic Cold War – not proxy struggles and not something exhausted by decolonisation but a series of juridical programmes sustained in different genres. Although these programmes are rarely consummated fully, we retrieve these laws as part of an effort to find the resources to put into question, or defamiliarise, existing arrangements.[360]

However, we argue that these rivalries produced two contradictory effects. On one hand, Amero-Sovietism placed limits on the self-realisation of political communities in the Third World. Even when the American and Soviets were not acting together, their competition created a global condition in which both the form of legal and political community and the legal and political content of these communities were deeply constrained, and in which an array of other possibilities (Pan-Africanism, indigenous nationalism) were not simply treated with suspicion but actively quashed. Indeed, one of the Amero-Soviet Cold War's most lasting effects has been to stamp its name upon an era of global history producing the enduring image of an all-enveloping conflict in relation to which there was/is no 'outside'. The more one thinks in those terms, the more evident the parallels seem between the nineteenth and twentieth centuries, between the forms of law and legal experimentation that were associated with the formation of European empires, and those associated with the Cold War. On this reading, the Cold War emerges, not as a point of discontinuity but of continuity: both periods were equally competitive, both were founded upon the export of European ideas and institutions to the rest of the world, both were equally hegemonic. Indeed, in both, one can find parallel strategies and institutions – administrative trusteeship, condominia, spheres of influence, interventionist policies and the crafting of global spaces in the interest of those best equipped to exploit them.

On the other hand, where they may have differed is that, for all its hegemonic ambitions, its destructive war-making and its cynicism, the Cold War also encouraged and produced a form of interstitial manoeuvring, economic experimentalism and heterodox collective aspiration elsewhere. Contestation at the heart of European modernity allowed for forms of plausible opposition to it from the outside that were not reducible to the terms of that rivalry itself but sought to articulate a distinctive world-view.

360 See, e.g., David Estlund, *Utopophobia: on the Limits (if Any) of Political Philosophy* (Princeton: Princeton University Press, 2019); Fredric Jameson, *Archaeologies of the Future: The Desire Called Utopia and Other Science Fictions* (London: Verso, 2005).

4

Practices of Diplomacy or International Law and Being Neutral

4.1 Introduction

This chapter is about practices of diplomacy during the Cold War and, in particular, the ways in which the Cold War reshaped the shared terrain of diplomacy and international law. Our intention is to direct our readers' thought away from the image of the Cold War as a diplomatic struggle and towards the idea that the period involved a more fundamental struggle over diplomacy itself, a contest over what it was, and what various roles international law plays, or could and should play in the life of diplomacy. These questions overlapped too with the way different groups of States related to the emergent international institutions. But familiar groupings of States and how they overlapped with certain ideas were not always stable. So, whilst Western scholars were keen to view the UN Charter as a nascent constitution of the new global order, Soviet scholars repeatedly stressed its purely 'contractual' character as an *inter partes* agreement whose terms should be narrowly construed. On the other hand, the Soviet Union was also more likely than the West to treat the UN as a performative stage from which it could join the denunciations of colonialism. Third Worldists, meanwhile, tended to regard the UN as a slightly different kind of stage – perhaps an Agora, or stage for and of encounter, rather than a spectator sport. We begin the chapter with a consideration of the sometimes obscure relations between diplomacy and international law. We then track three battles over diplomacy during the Cold War. The first bears upon the relationship between openness and secrecy. The second relates to diplomacy as theatre; and the third to neutrality and neutralism.

It has now become a commonplace that diplomatic life and treaty negotiation are worlds in which secrecy is paramount. Yet the Cold War followed a period in global politics when the idea of a clandestine diplomacy had been renounced as a European disease to be eradicated. By the time of the inter-war period, the assumption was that clandestine diplomacy would be replaced by covenants 'openly arrived at' and transparent institutional arrangements. But this changed with the Amero-Soviet Cold War, and here we trace a return to secrecy through the legal forms that facilitated it and depended on it. What was novel about the diplomacy of the Amero-Soviet Cold War was the particular ways the formal activities of public diplomacy were interwoven with the activities of intelligence and covert operations, conducted through protean modes of publicity and secrecy and all framed by legal forms.

In a second innovation, there is a move in the opposite direction, away from secrecy and towards diplomacy as performance. To a certain extent these elements are reflected in the pivot towards the General Assembly of the United Nations and the increasing sense that world affairs were being conducted through extravagant forms of oratory from a diplomatic pulpit at the UN. Third Worldism was the main carrier and exponent of this form, which began in the anti-colonial struggle and was manifested in 1955 at Bandung and the conferences that were to follow. In a way, this is a return to the open diplomacy of the concert.[1] But where concert was the province of the great, the conference was a festival of the (geo-politically) weak, actors united in struggle and seeking solidarity rather than security and the (re)distribution of power. At least in its early incarnations, this form of diplomacy was as much about the cultural performance of friendship, openness and strategic co-operation, as it was about pronouncing new laws or generating treaties. But the ideological rivalry between the 'greats' and emerging technologies of translation and news dissemination gave such festivals of justice more persuasive force than has ever been the case since. We pair this turn with the response it engendered from the powerful States, a response we call 'anti-diplomacy'. The practices we describe on this score are refusals of the diplomatic invitations and overtures offered by the Third World. The contrast between the dignified and optimistic invitations to meet lawfully and the way the West, in particular, responded is marked and worth remembering.

The third involved a contest over the meaning of 'neutrality' and its peculiar place in the world of Cold War diplomacy. In a sense this was a manifestation of the diplomatic encounter between the rival projects of world-making themselves. It was an argument conducted around three positions. European, or 'classical' international law was committed to the

[1] Gerry Simpson, *Great Powers and Outlaw States: Unequal Sovereigns in the International Legal Order* (Cambridge: Cambridge University Press, 2004) chapter 4.

protection of neutrality as a way of limiting the spread and extent of warfare. The Amero-Soviets, on the other hand, disparaged neutrality – particularly in the Third World – as a failure in a moment of existential conflict to make the required moral and political commitments.[2] Among the anti-colonial peoples of the South there was an embrace of an active neutralism or non-alignment that refused both the Cold War in toto and the depiction of non-alignment itself as 'neutrality'.

4.2 Diplomacy and International Law

Most contemporary definitions of diplomacy emphasise the idea of (peaceful) public relations between States or the conduct of these relations by accredited officials of States.[3] Sometimes this is narrowly conceived as being the conduct of those relations by a diplomatic caste, or in terms of a diplomatic style (as in Sir Ernest Satow's famous definition of diplomacy as the 'application of tact and intelligence to the conduct of international relations').[4] Much of this diplomatic practice has been historically about trade, but an important strand relates to war.[5] Indeed, many accounts give the impression of diplomacy as a counterpoint to war or a negotiated means of preventing it. It is here that military, diplomatic and intelligence practices converge. The highly rational, dispassionate business of advancing one's State's objective interests with skill and tact has always been coupled with an intelligence gathering function. Diplomats have long been in the business of keeping their eyes open in order to report on local conditions or military capabilities. The military attaché, for example, was a figure poised between diplomat and spy; one might say he was an emblematic figure of the Cold War. And the Cold War – to the extent that it was 'cold' – was a war conducted through diplomacy. But if it was a diplomatic war, it was also a war over diplomacy and its relationship to both lawfulness and plurality.

[2] While at the same time deploying it in Austria and Switzerland as an organising principle of intra-European affairs.

[3] Hedley Bull, *The Anarchical Society: A Study of Order in World Politics*, 2nd ed. (London: Macmillan, 1995) 162.

[4] Ernest Satow, A Guide to Diplomatic Practice, 4th ed. (London: Longmans, 1954) 1; François de Callières, *On the Manner of Negotiating with Princes* (Notre Dame: University of Notre Dame Press, 1963) 9.

[5] Barkawi has described the various ways in which war and diplomacy are intertwined. Tarak Barkawi, *Soldiers of Empire: Indian and British Armies in World War II* (Cambridge: Cambridge University Press, 2017).

Historically, diplomacy was not limited to emissaries of States and tended to be performed in a ritualistic mode, with symbols, artefacts, theatre, gifts and even magic playing a large part (the herald with his coat of arms, the message stick, the delivery of a rhinoceros, tennis balls, etc). These rituals provided protocols of encounter. The gatherings were rarely governed by one law but were more often sites of lawful encounter, where those gathered understood that no singular account of law transcended those who met. For Walter Benjamin, indeed, (true) diplomacy was 'beyond all legal systems' and therefore beyond violence.[6] But it might be more accurate to say that historically, each polity or association drew on their own legal traditions to govern the lawful modes by which they encountered others.[7] Sometimes there was a struggle over whose legal traditions would prevail.[8] But by the beginning of the nineteenth century, diplomacy had become increasingly professionalised and bureaucratised and – at least superficially – captured by State actors. With the positivist turn in international law, this practice was asserted more and more often, as belonging to a rubric of 'international law', rather than the law of nations, and was becoming steadily more rule-bound.[9] Indeed, a positive law of diplomacy came into existence around the inviolability of resident embassies, the immunity of diplomatic representatives and the taboo on visiting or resident diplomats involving themselves in local politics.[10]

[6] Walter Benjamin, 'Critique of Violence' in Peter Demetz (ed.), *Reflections: Essays, Aphorisms, Autobiographical Writings* (New York: Schocken Books, 1978) 247.

[7] See Lauren Benton, *A Search for Sovereignty: Law and Geography in European Empires 1400–1900* (Cambridge: Cambridge University Press, 2009); Shaunnagh Dorsett and Shaun McVeigh, *Jurisdiction* (Abingdon: Routledge, 2011); C. H. Alexandrowitz, *The Law of Nations in Global History*, David Armitage and Jennifer Pitts (eds.) (Oxford: Oxford University Press, 2017). See further Shaunnagh Dorsett and Shaun McVeigh, 'Conduct of Laws: Native Title, Responsibility, and Some Limits of Jurisdictional Thinking' *Melbourne University Law Review*, 36(2) (2012) 470–93; Lauren Benton, *Law and Colonial Cultures: Legal Regimes in World History, 1400–1900* (Cambridge: Cambridge University Press, 2002); C. H. Alexandrowicz, *An Introduction to the History of the Law of Nations in the East Indies (16th, 17th and 18th Centuries)* (Oxford: Clarendon Press, 1967).

[8] James Hevia, *Cherishing Men from Afar: Qing Guest Ritual and the Macartney Embassy of 1793* (Durham: Duke University Press, 1995); Robert Bickers, *Ritual and Diplomacy: The Macartney Mission to China (1792–1794)* (London: Wellsweep Press, 1993).

[9] See Alexandrowitz, *The Law of Nations in Global History*; Alexandrowicz, *An Introduction to the History of the Law of Nations in the East Indies.*

[10] See generally, Biswanath Sen, *A Diplomat's Handbook of International Law and Practice*, 1st ed. (The Hague: Martinus Nijhoff, 1965).

The effect of Amero-Sovietism as a world-making project gave the relationship between international law and diplomacy a double inflection. First was the effect of epistemic similarity – the joint inheritance of a European cosmology and the consolidation of statehood as the dominant legal form of association. Second was the effect of difference – the ideological divide between them often meant a turn to procedure when agreement could not be found in substance (think of the law of State responsibility). This trend culminated in the *Vienna Convention on Diplomatic Relations* in 1961. In contrast, the diplomatic activities of the Third World emphasised both plurality and substance and were often conducted in a juristic idiom, taking up international law not as proceduralism under a universal law but as protocols and procedures engaging international law as a way of resisting old and making new, lawful worlds. As we shall see, the response to this from Western States was often conduct that was both undiplomatic and illegal.

4.3 Openness and Secrecy

In the immediate aftermath of the 1914–18 war,[11] the newly formed Bolshevik government publicly denounced a series of 'secret' imperial alliances in which the former Czarist regime had participated (such as the Sykes–Picot pact of 1916). This denunciation fed into a wider debate concerning the practice of secret diplomacy and whether it had contributed to the scale of warfare that had broken out in 1914 (e.g the Treaty of London of 1915 and the Ottoman–German alliance of 1914). US President Woodrow Wilson championed the new agenda, promoting in the process a new practice of diplomatic transparency. His formula – 'that there should be no private international understandings of any kind' and that 'diplomacy shall proceed always frankly and in the public view'[12] – ultimately fed through into the design of the League of

[11] The critique of secret treaties focused, in one direction, upon the discovery of the 'secret' agreements between the Allied powers and Italy and Japan that had conditioned the latter's involvement in the recent war and, in another direction, the publication by the Bolsheviks, of a range of secret treaties concluded by the Tsar such as the Sykes–Picot Agreement of 1916 (all of which it immediately denounced). See generally, Richard Caddell, 'Secret Treaties', *Max Planck Encyclopaedia of International Law* (2006) 1, 2–3.

[12] Woodrow Wilson, 'Fourteen Points as set forth in an address made before the joint session of Congress, January 8th 1918', point 1: 'Open covenants of peace openly arrived at, after which there shall be no private international understandings of any kind, but diplomacy shall proceed always frankly and in the public view.'

Nations. Embodied in the League, the creation of a public assembly for the collective discussion of matters of international concern was accompanied by a requirement that all treaties should be made public (even if not concluded in public forums).[13] The former was partially realised through the creation of the League Assembly. The latter was achieved by way of the inclusion of article 18 in the Covenant of the League of Nations,[14] which conditioned the validity of treaties upon their registration.

Despite the evident failure of the League of Nations, the ideal of creating an institutional architecture for a new form of public diplomacy was in play again at the San Francisco conference in 1945, just as it had been at Versailles in 1919. On this occasion, from the perspective of the Great Powers at least, the evident deficiencies of the League were fixed – no more consensual decision-making, recognition of the key role of the great powers, distinguishing between the appropriate competences of the Assembly and the Council and so on. Article 102 of the UN Charter also replicated the terms of article 18 of the League providing that unregistered agreements would be subject to the 'ambiguous sanction'[15] of not being invocable before organs of the United Nations.

But it was not long before these designs and ambitions were thwarted in the emergent Cold War. The General Assembly – the gestational public assembly of the new global, and still imperial, order – was quickly beset even in the non-colonial world, by disputation over questions of membership, credentials and voting rights and the powers of the organisation itself. Because they stressed the contractual character of the Charter, Soviet scholars refused to treat the practices of the UN General Assembly as lawmaking. So when the powers of the UN organs came into question – such as the powers of the General Assembly operating under the Uniting for Peace Resolution in 1950 – the Soviet response was almost consistently negative, denying the lawmaking character of UNGA Resolutions, opposing a 'gap filling' role for the Assembly as keeper of the peace and stressing the superordinating role of the principle of 'peaceful coexistence'.[16]

[13] See, e.g., Paul S. Reinsch, *Secret Diplomacy: How Far Can It Be Eliminated?* (New York: Harcourt, Brace and Company, 1922); Manley Hudson, 'The Registration and Publication of Treaties' *American Journal of International Law*, 19 (1925) 273–92.

[14] Covenant of the League of Nations, art. 18.

[15] Richard Caddell, 'Secret Treaties', *Max Planck Encyclopaedia of International Law* (2006) 1.

[16] See Edward McWhinney, *The International Court of Justice and the Western Tradition of International Law* (Berlin: Grutyer, 1987) 196.

And so the UN General Assembly's potential to be a forum within which a new form of public diplomacy might emerge was challenged from the start.[17] And it was just as clear that the old practice of concluding agreements in secret was not going to disappear despite the general commitment to the public registration of treaties.[18] The secrecy surrounding the conclusion of the Yalta Protocols of 1945 had set the tone. Given the potentially embarrassing concessions that had been made to the Soviet Union in return for its support in the war against Japan (for example, the transfer of southern Sakhalin and the Kuriles to the Soviet Union), it was decided at Yalta that those clauses would be contained within a separate Protocol. This Protocol was kept out of the public eye for at least a year on the grounds that the agreements were principally military or strategic in nature.[19] As Donaldson points out, in face of the demand for publicity, this introduced a practice in which secrecy was channelled in new directions: by the use of executive agreements,[20] or agreements subject only to signature,[21] by encouraging ambiguity as to the legal status of texts (e.g. in relation to 'inter-agency' or 'inter-departmental agreements') and by severing secret protocols, annexes or 'administrative arrangements' from the public version of agreements.[22] As the US and USSR quickly learned from the Yalta protocols, absolute secrecy in relation to a formal agreement was rarely to be guaranteed. Secrecy was much more likely if the details of what was meant to remain hidden were contained in a confidential letter, exchange of notes or agreed minute. Fealty to publicity could be maintained if what was secret was

[17] For a critique of the legalism of the 'new diplomacy of the United Nations', see Hans Morgenthau, 'Diplomacy' *Yale Law Journal*, 55 (1945–46) 1067–80; Hans Morgenthau, *Politics among Nations: The Struggle for Power and Peace* (Chicago: University of Chicago Press, 1949), chapters XXVIII and XXIX.

[18] See further GA Resn. 97/1, 14 December 1946.

[19] For a scathing review of the terms of the Far East Protocol and its conclusion, see Herbert Briggs, 'The Leaders' Agreement of Yalta' *American Journal of International Law*, 40 (1946) 376–83.

[20] See United States Department of State, Circular No. 175 (13 December 1955) para 3, *American Journal of International Law*, 50 (1956) 784.

[21] Megan Donaldson, 'The Survival of the Secret Treaty: Publicity, Secrecy, and Legality in the International Order' *American Journal of International Law*, 111 (2017) 575–627; Ashley Deeks, 'A (Qualified) Defense of Secret Agreements' *Arizona State Law Journal*, 49 (2017) 713, 723.

[22] Megan Donaldson, 'The Survival of the Secret Treaty: Publicity, Secrecy, and Legality in the International Order' *American Journal of International Law*, 111 (2017) 609.

simply hived off as an administrative annex, a supplement to the formal agreement[23] or if it was treated as an entirely distinct class of agreement.

And so the post-1945 era was marked by a paradoxical commitment to publicity coupled with 'a gradual systematization of secrecy' in relation to treaty making.[24] But this was not because the agreements in question contemplated acts that were, as Donaldson puts it, 'radically irregular'. Some agreements certainly were: One example being the Protocol of Sèvres of 1956 setting out the detailed arrangements and timetable for the invasion of the Suez Canal zone by France, Britain and Israel on 30 October in the same year.[25] But many agreements were also broadly consistent with Charter principles concerning the containment of aggression, the right of self-defence and the promotion of human rights.[26] Agreements on intelligence cooperation, on the stationing of military forces and cooperation in relation to atomic energy, for example, were, more often than not, concluded under veil of secrecy, not out of fear of illegality but out of fear that public disclosure would undermine the very objective they sought to enable. Intelligence sharing agreements, for example, were particularly sensitive on this score insofar as it was generally feared that publicity would potentially expose the nature and source of the information being shared or indeed the modalities through which that information had been gathered.

But as Deeks notes, secrecy was not confined to the conspiratorial relationship between 'allies' but extended also to agreements concluded between the Amero-Soviets themselves.[27] So, for example, the US and USSR were to enter into a series of disarmament protocols in the 1970s under cover of the SALT and ABM agreements[28] in which the detailed

[23] In 1972, the United States enacted the Case–Zablocki Act, requiring all executive agreements to be transmitted to Congress. Section 112b provided, however, that agreements 'prejudicial to the national security of the United States' could instead be submitted to the Senate Committee on Foreign Relations 'under an appropriate injunction of secrecy': Case–Zablocki Act of 1972, 1 U.S.C. § 112b (as amended). See also Deeks, 'A (Qualified) Defense of Secret Agreements', 723.

[24] Donaldson, 'The Survival of the Secret Treaty', 615.

[25] Within days, the text of the agreement had been 'leaked', much to the chagrin of the British Prime Minister who had, by that stage, already denied its existence. See generally, Charlotte Peevers, *The Politics of Justifying Force: The Suez Crisis, the Iraq War, and International Law* (Oxford: Oxford University Press, 2013) 66–127.

[26] Deeks, 'A (Qualified) Defense of Secret Agreements'.

[27] Ibid., 748–49.

[28] SALT and ABM refer to the Strategic Arms Litigation Talks and the Anti-Ballistic Missile Treaty.

measures to be taken were kept out of public view. This may have been in part out of a concern that the general public would not be sympathetic to the apparent concessions that were being granted – that the waging of the Cold War was not being pursued vigorously enough. But in a way, this was a symptom of the paradox of Amero-Soviet world ordering, coexisting with the ideological dispute between them and the propagandistic elements of this dispute, mobilised by so many people, for so many reasons. What emerged was a refined practice of secret diplomacy that followed the protocols of formal treaty negotiation, but which secreted itself in the margins of public diplomacy as a political practice. The apparent motivations for this contortion were both to avoid public embarrassment and to protect the sources of secret information.

4.3.1 Intelligence and Diplomacy

The interplay between publicity and secrecy in the conduct of diplomacy has a long lineage. What was novel about the diplomacy of the Cold War, however, was the way the formal activities of public diplomacy were supplemented by, and partially overlapped with, the subterranean activities of of the myriad of intelligence agencies that had been created in the years after 1945. The existence of these agencies fostered the appearance of a functional separation between diplomacy and intelligence. With this separation, the promotion of a public, transparent and lawful style of diplomacy could be advanced by hiving off to another 'sphere' those activities that needed to be kept out of public sight. But this could only partly be sustained.

As far as public diplomacy was concerned, the Vienna Convention on Diplomatic Relations of 1961[29] drew an implicit line between the covert intelligence collection activities of States and their publicly acceptable diplomatic analogues. The Convention recognised that one of the functions of a diplomatic mission was to ascertain 'conditions and developments in the receiving State'. But it nevertheless provided in article 3(d) that such activities could only be undertaken by 'lawful means'. Article 41 underscored that all those enjoying privileges and immunities as diplomatic staff were under an obligation to abide by local laws and refrain from interfering 'in the internal affairs of that State'. To that end, the main sanction recognised in the Convention for those abusing their

[29] Vienna Convention on Diplomatic Relations (opened for signature 18 April 1961, entered into force 24 April 1964) 500 UNTS 95.

diplomatic privileges was a power on the part of the receiving State to declare, without explanation, any member of the diplomatic staff to be persona non grata (article 9).[30]

But this regime of lawful, public diplomacy was simultaneously undercut by a series of provisions that both envisaged and sought to protect channels of secret communication between the diplomatic mission and the sending State.[31] The premises of the mission itself, its archives (article 24) and all its communications (article 27) were declared to be inviolable, and the mission was entitled to 'employ all appropriate means' for communication, including the sending of messages in 'code and cipher'. The diplomatic bag was not to be 'opened or detained', and the person of the courier would be immune from arrest or detention. Indeed, as the ILC noted, the very rationale for the grant of privileges and immunities to administrative and technical staff in the mission (in addition to those enjoyed by diplomatic agents) was the preservation of secrecy and confidentiality. Administrative and technical staff would often 'perform confidential tasks which, for the purposes of the mission's function, maybe even more important than the tasks entrusted to some members of the diplomatic staff'.[32] An ambassador's secretary or an archivist could, it was said, be 'as much the repository of secret or confidential knowledge as members of the diplomatic staff'.[33]

And so even while it purported to limit the intelligence gathering activities of accredited diplomats, by maintaining the absolute secrecy of channels of communication, and immunising accredited members of the diplomatic corps from civil and criminal jurisdiction,[34] the Vienna Convention created an enabling environment in which active espionage

[30] This was stated by the ICJ to be a sufficient sanction. See *United States Diplomatic and Consular Staff in Tehran (United States of America v Iran)* [1980] ICJ Rep 3, 38: 'The Vienna Conventions of 1961 and 1963 contain express provisions to meet the case when members of an embassy staff, under the cover of diplomatic privileges and immunities, engage in such abuses of their functions as espionage or interference in the international affairs of the receiving State.'

[31] See generally, Sanderijn Duquet and Jan Wouters, 'Diplomacy, Secrecy, and the Law' in Claudio Barbieri and Christoph Friedrich (eds.), *Secret Diplomacy: Concepts, Contexts and Cases* (London and New York: Routledge, 2016) 85.

[32] One should note, here, the weight placed upon the 'extension' of diplomatic privileges to associated staff by the Soviet Union. G. I. Tunkin, *Theory of International Law* (Cambridge, MA: Harvard University Press, 2013) chapter 11.

[33] International Law Commission, *Draft Articles on the Law of Treaties* (1958) 2 YBILC 101, 102.

[34] Vienna Convention on the Law of Treaties, opened for signature 23 May 1969, 1155 UNTS 331 (entered into force 27 January 1980).

was not merely envisaged but would visibly flourish. By the simple ruse of accrediting members of their intelligence agencies as 'military attachés' with diplomatic cover, States could wilfully engage in (illicit) acts of espionage behind a façade of diplomatic immunity. The main sanction for breach would not be the application of any local laws governing espionage but simply the possibility that the agent concerned would be declared persona non grata if their less than lawful activities were to be uncovered. The possibility that a request might be made for the agent concerned to be 'recalled' (in the anodyne diplomatic language that was often employed), whilst inconvenient, was hardly a danger either to the agents themselves or to the security interests of the sending State. Given this configuration of the Cold War around the accumulation of secret knowledge, it is perhaps not surprising that the regular expulsion of diplomats as personae non grata was a far more common feature of the diplomatic intercourse between East and West[35] than the trial of spies. Indeed, the latter sanction was largely confined to those, like the Rosenbergs, Fuchs, Hiss or Tolkachev, who were conceived to have 'betrayed' their own country,[36] rather than foreign agents operating without any diplomatic cover. Only very rarely were so-called 'illegals' put on trial and subject to imprisonment;[37] more often than not, they were simply deported[38] or, like Rudolf Abel and Gary Powers, 'exchanged' between the powers.

4.3.2 Clandestine Diplomacy

If the practice of regular diplomacy appeared to secrete the activities of intelligence agencies behind the formalities of immunity, the agencies

[35] Eileen Denza, *Diplomatic Law: Commentary on the Vienna Convention on Diplomatic Relations*, 4th ed. (Oxford: Oxford University Press, 2016) 65. Noting that in 1971, for example, the British government declared 105 members of the Soviet diplomatic and trade establishments in London to be persona non grata, and in the following year Bolivia expelled 119.

[36] See generally, John Haynes and Harvey Klehr, *Early Cold War Spies: The Espionage Trials That Shaped American Politics* (Cambridge: Cambridge University Press, 2006).

[37] For some exceptions, see United States v Coplon, 84 F Supp 472 (SDNY 1949); Abel v United States, 362 US 217, 80 S Ct 683 (1960); United States v Melekh, 190 F Supp 67 (SDNY 1960); United States v Egorov, 292 F Supp 106 (EDNY 1963); United States v Valdik Aleksandrovich Enger and Rudolf Petrovich Chernyayev, 472 F Supp 490 (DJN 1978).

[38] E.g. Gubitchev who had been convicted together with Judith Coplon, but whose sentence was suspended on condition that he leave the country and never return. See John Earl Haynes and Harvey Klehr, *Early Cold War Spies: The Espionage Trials That Shaped American Politics* (Cambridge: Cambridge University Press, 2006) chapter 6, 'Judith Coplon: The Spy Who Got Away with It'.

responsible for intelligence gathering, in turn, engaged in their own diplomatic activity. In what might be termed a form of 'clandestine diplomacy', intelligence agencies acted in parallel to their public counterparts engaging in practices of diplomatic communication, negotiation and policy formation – sometimes apparently even without the full knowledge of their political superiors.[39] KGB or CIA operatives, for example, frequently became the preferred channel of communications between friendly or rival powers[40] and often involved themselves in the forging of agreements with both State and non-State actors. To the extent that such agreements occasionally mimicked their formal diplomatic counterparts, they also seemed to bring into view a separate world of secret international law. Perhaps the most significant example was the conclusion in 1946 of a (secret) British–US Communication Intelligence Agreement[41] – which became known as the 'Five Eyes Agreement' – that set out, in formal terms, the protocols governing the acquisition, retention and use of secret intelligence.[42] As an inter-agency agreement (it was concluded between the US Communications Intelligence Board and the London Signal Intelligence Board), it eluded both the demands on registration imposed by article 102 UN Charter[43] and the respective domestic scrutiny that was associated with treaty making more generally. It remained, indeed, an entirely confidential agreement that was only brought to public attention in 2005.[44] Throughout the Cold War, then, and more or less inspired by it, diplomacy and intelligence were conducted through protean modes of publicity and secrecy, in each case organised and articulated – or at least framed – by legal forms.

39 See, e.g., L. Scott, 'Secret Intelligence, Covert Action and Clandestine Diplomacy' *Intelligence and National Security*, 19(2) (2004) 322–41.

40 See, e.g., the role of intelligence agents in the Cuban Missile Crisis. For an overview, see Scott, 330–34.

41 Later renamed the United Kingdom–United States Communication Intelligence Agreement in 1955.

42 The UKUSA Agreement of 1948 refined the terms of the earlier British–United States Communications Intelligence Agreement (BRUSA) of 1946 that, itself, renewed an earlier 1943 agreement between the powers to cooperate in the field of communications intelligence.

43 Donaldson, 'The Survival of the Secret Treaty', 612.

44 Five years later, certain documents were de-classified. See National Security Agency/Central Intelligence Agency, 'Press Release: Declassified UKUSA Signals Intelligence Agreement Documents Available' (24 June 2010), www.nsa.gov/Press-Room/Press-Releases-Statements/Press-Release-View/Article/1629812/declassified-ukusa-signals-intelligence-agreement-documents-available/.

4.4 Theatrical Diplomacy

In contrast to the contortions around publicness and secrecy of Amero-Soviet diplomacy, the diplomatic style of anti-colonial internationalism celebrated openness and solidarity. This project took up a tradition in which diplomatic encounters were conceived as lawful but not law-bound.[45] Positivist traditions elevate one international law to the status of the 'universal' and either proceduralise diplomacy through specific rules or expel it to the realm of politics, or at least non-law. In contrast, traditions of diplomacy that emphasise lawful meetings between organised groups enact a plural vision of international law as itself a law of meeting, or of encounter.[46] In the mid-twentieth-century context, these traditions were to understand the new international institutions as meeting places rather than managed bureaucracies. And it is in observing this contrast that the Cold War struggle over the meaning of diplomacy itself becomes most apparent. The theatrical style of 'diplomacy-as-encounter' may have been the diplomacy of the weak, but it was weakness often combined with moral strength. This played upon the possibilities offered by the performative rivalries of the US–Soviet ideological divide and the ambition of each super-power to claim moral (as well as military) leadership. As C. L. R. James put it, the 'cold war offered unprecedented opportunities to colonial peoples'[47] through what Rogers has called 'the creative exploitation of rivalries'.[48] We will gain further insight into these possibilities in Chapter 5. But as we have noticed in other contexts, these

[45] On International Law as diplomacy and lawful encounters with strangers, see Anne Orford, 'Ritual, Mediation and the International Laws of the South' *Griffith Law Review*, 16 (2007) 353–74.

[46] The conversations conducted as part of the conference 'Taking up a Training in Conducting Lawful Encounters' (21–23 August 2019, Melbourne Law School) and the broader project 'Offices of the Southern Jurist-Diplomat' led by Adil Hasan Khan provide examples. See https://law.unimelb.edu.au/centres/iilah/research/projects/offices-of-the-southern-jurist-diplomat/taking-up-a-training-in-conducting-lawful-encounters. See further Sundhya Pahuja, 'Letters from Bandung: Encounters with Another International Law' in Luis Eslava, Michael Fakhri and Vasuki Nesiah (eds.), *Bandung, Global History and International Law: Critical Pasts and Pending Futures* (Cambridge: Cambridge University Press, 2017).

[47] Peter Kalliney, *The Aesthetic Cold War: Decolonization and Global Literature* (Princeton: Princeton University Press, 2022) 208.

[48] Asha Rogers, 'Peter J. Kalliney. *The Aesthetic Cold War: Decolonization and Global Literature*' *The Review of English Studies*, 74 (2023) 772.

possibilities were most potent when Amero-Soviet relations were under strain and least effective during periods of détente.[49]

The tradition of anti-colonial meetings was long. Whether we start with the first Pan African Conference in Westminster in 1900,[50] the First Congress of the Peoples of the East in Baku in 1920 or the first conference of the League against Imperialism in Brussels in 1927, solidarity and symbolism were elements in the repertoire of anti-colonial diplomacy and its place in the wider struggle against imperial rulers. Many of these early meetings were assisted if not sponsored by the Soviets whose ideological commitments included anti-imperialism and self-determination (the latter even extending to a nominal right to secede from the Soviet Union).[51]

The 'League Against Imperialism' was so called as a direct reference to the nomenclature of the League of Nations. It was grounded in a particular reading of Woodrow Wilson's Fourteen Points, even though the US did not join the League. The League of Nations was itself strongly imperialist, creating the mandate system and forestalling anti-colonial struggle through the civilisational 'not yet'.[52] Indeed, the Covenant of the League explicitly described colonised peoples as those 'not yet able to stand by themselves'. Whatever was to follow later, during the 1920s and '30s, the contrast between Wilson and Lenin's conceptions of self-determination and the dignity, autonomy and practical support accorded

49 See Jeremy Suri, *Power and Protest: Global Revolution and the Rise of Détente* (Cambridge, MA: Harvard University Press, 2005).

50 See Christopher Gevers, 'To Seek with Beauty to Set the World Right: Cold War International Law and the Radical "Imaginative Geography" of Pan-Africanism' in Matthew Craven, Sundhya Pahuja and Gerry Simpson (eds.), *International Law and the Cold War* (Cambridge: Cambridge University Press, 2019).

51 See 'The Strategy and Tactics of the Communist International in the Struggle for the Proletarian Dictatorship' in the *Programme of the Communist International Adopted at its Sixth Congress, 1 September 1928*, Section VI. Lenin's account in *The Right to Self-Determination* (*Prosveshcheniye*, 1914) is markedly different to Wilson's Fourteen Points in his address to Congress on 8 January, www.archives.gov/milestone-documents/president-wo.

52 Antony Anghie, *Imperialism, Sovereignty and the Making of International Law* (Cambridge: Cambridge University Press, 2005); Partha Chatterjee, *Nationalist Thought and the Colonial World: A Derivative Discourse?* (London: Zed Books for the United Nations University, 1986). On the idea of 'the waiting room of history', see Dipesh Chakrabarty, *Provincialising Europe: Postcolonial Thought and Historical Difference* (Princeton: Princeton University Press, 2000), introduction.

to the 'darker nations' is clear.[53] Both the tradition and the nascent organisational activities were somewhat interrupted by the war and by the large number of independence leaders who were imprisoned for their activities during the 1930s and '40s. But by the early 1950s, efforts were redoubled to foster diplomatic practices of anti-colonial solidarity and to link them to strategies involving the new international institutions.[54]

The Bandung Conference is perhaps the most widely celebrated – and mythologised –[55] instance of Third World international diplomacy during the Cold War. The conference – more formally known as the African-Asian Conference – was held from 18 to 24 April 1955 in Bandung, Indonesia. Much has been written about the conference, though the style and tone of writing about it has changed over time. And yet right through from contemporaneous reports, to post-1989 dismissals, to revived accounts written as the archives have opened up,[56] a certain consistency of interpretation and representation has endured around its significance as a symbolic moment in international diplomacy.[57] The diplomatic style it embodies expresses a political imaginary distinct from a friend/enemy style of play. It is almost

[53] See Vijay Prashad, *The Darker Nations: A People's History of the Third World* (New Delhi: LeftWord Books, 2007); and Siba N'Zatioula Grovogui, *Sovereigns, Quasi Sovereigns and Africans: Race and Self-Determination in International Law* (Minneapolis: University of Minnesota Press, 1996) 116. See further Upendra Baxi, '"The Dust of Empire": The Dialectic of Self-Determination and Re-colonisation in the First Phase of the Cold War' in Matthew Craven, Sundhya Pahuja and Gerry Simpson (eds.), *International Law and the Cold War* (Cambridge: Cambridge University Press, 2019); Loqman Radpey, 'Self-Determination during the Cold War' in Matthew Craven, Sundhya Pahuja and Gerry Simpson (eds.), *Cambridge History of International Law, Vol XI: International Law during the Cold War (1945–1990)* (Cambridge: Cambridge University Press, forthcoming).

[54] See the distinct accounts of Massimiliano Tomba, *Insurgent Universality: An Alternative Legacy of Modernity* (Oxford: Oxford University Press, 2019); and Siba N'Zatioula Grovogui, *Beyond Eurocentrism and Anarchy: Memories of International Order and Institutions* (London: Palgrave Macmillan, 2006).

[55] Robert Vitalis, 'The Midnight Ride of Kwame Nkrumah and Other Fables of Bandung (Ban-doong)' *Humanity*, 4(2) (2013) 261–88.

[56] Shimazu makes this observation. See Naoko Shimazu, 'Diplomacy as Theatre: Staging the Bandung Conference of 1955' *Modern Asian Studies*, 48(1) (2013) 225–52. See further Derek McDougall and Antonia Finnane (eds.), *Bandung 1955: Little Histories* (Melbourne: Monash University Press, 2010); Christopher Lee (ed.), *Making a World after Empire: The Bandung Moment and Its Political Afterlives* (Athens: Ohio University Press, 2019); Luis Eslava, Michael Fakhri and Vasuki Nesiah (eds.), *Bandung, Global History and International Law: Critical Pasts and Pending Futures* (Cambridge: Cambridge University Press, 2017)

[57] Shimazu, 'Diplomacy as Theatre'.

unimaginably far away from today's securitised and heavily guarded diplomatic events. The conference was highly staged, its choreography participatory and inclusive. No motorcades of black limousines prowled the perimeter of a cyclone-fenced fortress. Instead, leaders were required to walk each morning from their hotels along the renamed 'Jalan Africa-Asia' to the conference venue at Merdeka ('Freedom') House.[58] Leaders understood the importance of this performance. They stopped to wave, talk, smile and greet people. Pedestrians could enter the zone, and approached delegates with a fervour we reserve today for celebrities, asking for autographs and having photographs taken. Sirens were sounded as delegations passed to call people out of businesses and restaurants nearby, and waiting areas were created to allow the public to wait to meet delegates in person.[59] As Shimazu describes it, the conference was a week-long street theatre performance, with an atmosphere of celebration.[60] Watching the newsreel footage of this event reveals huge differences between then and now, in how relations between leaders and led were imagined, in the absence of fear between 'elites' and those who are marked by identity, racialisation or poverty and in the nature of the relationship between democratic participation and legitimacy for States still in the making.[61]

The diplomacy had both an internal and external – or national and international – aspect. The staging of the Bandung conference drew the people of the emerging Third World into these events and interpellated them into both their respective nations and a relation with each other as 'world' in a way that offered dignity and the promise of participation. This stood in contrast to the humiliations of the racialised hierarchies of colonialism, which, in 1955, were still strongly in play. The message was clear to observers from the West, as well as to those engaged in struggles for independence, that colonised peoples would no longer sit patiently

[58] The topography of the city was changed to facilitate the Conference. Streets and buildings were renamed and new paths made.

[59] As Shimazu observes, this was not the only event that did this; the Asian Relations Conference in Delhi in 1947 also included huge numbers of the public in the ceremonial events of the conference, accommodating people in huge marquees. Shimazu, 'Diplomacy as Theatre', 238.

[60] This account is drawn gratefully from Shimazu, 'Diplomacy as Theatre' and the references therein.

[61] A recent documentary film by Johan Jimonprez, *Soundtrack to a Coup d'Etat*, also contains a great deal of footage from UN meetings of the period. Johan Grimonprez, *Soundtrack to a Coup d'État* (docu-essay, 150 min, France/Belgium/Netherlands, 2024).

in the waiting room of history. The double-edged character of the internal/external nature of postcolonial statehood has become manifest in particular ways since that euphoric moment.[62] But there is no need for nostalgia to notice that the relation between leaders that led and world was imagined in quite a different way then as compared to now.

Pan African conferences took up the performance, and every independence day in the succession of African countries becoming independent became another symbolic message of anti-colonialism. In the independence ceremony of the Congo on 30 June 1960, King Baudouin of Belgium gave a speech extolling the greatness of King Leopold. The tone was meant to be one of grateful concordance with Belgium. But Patrice Lumumba took the microphone unannounced and made a searing speech.

> For though this independence of the Congo is today being proclaimed in a spirit of accord with Belgium ... no Congolese worthy of the name can ever forget that we fought to win it, a fight waged each and every day ... in which there was ... not one drop of blood that we ever spared ourselves .... [This was] an indispensable struggle if we were to put an end to the humiliating slavery that had been forced upon us. The wounds that are the evidence of the fate we endured for eighty years under a colonialist regime are still too fresh and painful for us to be able to erase them from our memory.[63]

The Belgian king was apoplectic. Gerit writes that Baudouin had to be persuaded by the Prime Minister not to walk out of the ceremony.[64] In her recent book describing CIA interventions in the Congo, and in Africa more generally during the era of formal decolonisation, Williams describes the independence day of Ghana and the clothing of Prime Minister Kwame Nkrumah. Along with a smock made of the Kente cloth from the north of Ghana, he wore what she describes as a Gandhi-type prison cap, marked with the initials 'PG' standing for 'prison graduate', a

[62] For the point, see Sundhya Pahuja 'Laws of Encounter: A Jurisdictional Account of International Law' *London Review of International Law*, 1 (2013) 63–98, especially 80–81. For a subtle and persuasively elaborated account of the way in which the 'national' is 'international' in the Global South, see Luis Eslava, *Local Space, Global Life: The Everyday Operation of International Law and Development* (Cambridge: Cambridge University Press, 2015).

[63] Patrice Lumumba, 'Speech at Proclamation of Independence' (30 June 1960) Columbia University, www.columbia.edu/itc/history/mann/w3005/lumumba.html.

[64] Frank Gerits, '"When the Bull Elephants Fight": Kwame Nkrumah, Non-Alignment, and Pan-Africanism as an Interventionist Ideology in the Global Cold War (1957–66)' *International History Review*, 37(5) (2015) 958.

badge worn by many Ghanaians in their struggle. Gerit describes, too, Ghana's campaign of public diplomacy of African integration. This included the establishment of Radio Ghana and the transmission of the 'Voice of Africa' designed to attract African leaders to Nkrumah's position on continental integration.[65]

The concerted diplomacy of anti-colonialism made extensive use of the UN. This became more true after the large-scale admission of new States in 1955 and 1960 meant that the non-aligned States, or Third World countries, had a majority. They made use of this majority at the end of 1960 when the General Assembly adopted a declaration condemning colonialism. Krushchev had proposed a declaration on the granting of independence to colonial countries for inclusion on the agenda of the UNGA in September of that year. But in addition to the draft Declaration submitted by the USSR,[66] the General Assembly also had another draft submitted, on 28 November, by Cambodia on behalf of twenty-six Asian and African countries. The topic was discussed in the General Assembly from 28 November to 7 December 1960 and from 13 December to 14 December 1960.[67] The latter draft was eventually sponsored by forty-three delegations[68] and was adopted without change by the General Assembly in resolution 1514 (XV) 'Declaration on the Granting of Independence to Colonial Countries and Peoples'.[69] The records of proceedings are more moving than one might imagine. We can read the speeches given as text of course, but the old footage of the speeches is revealing, both for the rivalry between anti-colonial and colonial world-making projects and for their respective diplomatic styles.[70] The phlegmatic Australian, Mr Plimsoll, warns that 'we have heard in this debate at various stages, fanciful phrases about the lash of the overseer and the crimes of the colonialist', but we are assured that . . . 'they are certainly not true of any territory administered by Australia'.

65 Gerits, 'When the Bull Elephants Fight', 955.

66 Nikita Sergeyevich Khrushchev, *Declaration on the Granting of Independence to Colonial Countries and Peoples* (UN Doc. A/4502, 23 September 1960).

67 UNGA A/PV.925–939 and A/PV.944–947.

68 UNGA Draft Resolution A/L.323 and Addenda 1 to 6.

69 UNGA Res 1514 (XV) (14 December 1960), 'Declaration on the Granting of Independence to Colonial Countries and Peoples', adopted without change by a vote of 89 to 0, with 9 abstentions (Australia, Belgium, Dominican Republic, France, Portugal, Spain, Union of South Africa, United Kingdom and United States).

70 United Nations, Audiovisual Library of International Law, 'Declaration on the Granting of Independence to Colonial Countries and Peoples', https://legal.un.org/avl/ha/dicc/dicc.html.

The leader of the Indonesian delegation, Mr Wirjopranoto, notes that 'this is the first time that the United Nations is considering the entire question of colonialism.' The Nepali delegate, Mr Saha, is frank. 'My delegation', he says,

> welcomes the initiative of the delegation of the USSR in sponsoring the item entitled "Declaration on the granting of independence to colonial countries and peoples". We feel that the time has come for the United Nations to pronounce itself clearly and unequivocally on the necessity and urgency of unconditionally ending colonialism in all its forms and manifestations . . . no matter what justification the colonial Powers themselves may have for their own policies and actions . . . it is true that some countries have a better colonial record than others, but this alone does not entitle those countries with a more favourable record to seek justification for the pursuit of their colonial policy in the changed circumstances of the present-day world. We might have some reservations of our own with regard to the form of the Soviet declaration on the granting of independence to colonial countries and peoples, but it cannot be denied that the Soviet declaration brings this idea of the ending of colonialism into a sharp focus. Every Member should realise the importance and seriousness of this matter that is presently being debated and should direct all its efforts and attention towards enabling the peoples still under colonial domination in the world to realise their aspirations for freedom and independence in the immediate future.

He goes on to warn of the danger that the question will be proxified.

> We are afraid of one thing, and this is that . . . it might also be treated by certain interested parties as an item for Cold War propaganda. But to us, in Asia and Africa, who have experienced colonial domination in the past and are even now seeing the true picture of colonialism with its grim consequences to the people under its yoke, this is a matter of freedom which should not be treated lightly and must not be allowed to be given the Cold War treatment in this debate. To us it is something which is vital to the evolution of a new world order based on freedom, justice and equality for all men, irrespective of their colour or the region to which they belong. This is the kind of world order which is envisaged in the Charter of the United Nations itself.[71]

Ghana too avers to the potential derailment of the struggle,

> this is not a document that should give rise to any partisan rancour. We are here dealing with the hopes and aspirations of millions of

[71] UNGA A/PV.935 (5 December 1960, 3 pm plenary meeting), https://legal.un.org/avl/pdf/ha/dicc/A%20PV%20935.pdf.

> people . . . who look to the United Nations to help them in their long and arduous march towards freedom and independence. Indeed, we would be failing in our duty if we were to forget these peoples and allow this debate to degenerate into one more fruitless exercise in the so-called cold war. History . . . will not forgive us if we allow our endeavours here to be bedevilled by irrelevant ideological wranglings.[72]

The new institutions were imagined by the Third World to be an Agora rather than a governance body, and the style of diplomacy enacted at these events gave expression to, not only plural traditions of diplomacy, but plural international laws. Even from within the confines of the State form, those at Bandung did not believe that European 'International Law' was the only law through which one could conduct relations between nations. At that conference – and in the Afro-Asian Legal Consultative Committee that came out of it – the Third World imagined and asserted its own version of international law.[73] In this, the 'Third World' was not only a political and economic project but also a juridical one.[74] The States of the Third World and their diplomats adopted doctrinal, rhetorical and institutional strategies that served to articulate the contest between their experience of a multiplicity of laws in the world, with the ostensibly 'universal' jurisdictional forms being asserted and actualised on the international plane[75] even as struggles for decolonisation were being waged and won. The opening of archives has enabled the production of revived and vibrant accounts of what the Bandung conference was and what it stood for.[76] We recall it here

[72] Mr Quaison-Sackey (Ghana), UNGA Fifteenth Session, Plenary Meeting (29 November 1960, 10:30 am, New York), Agenda Item 87, A/PV/927, 1012. Thanks to Chris Gevers for this reference.

[73] For some of AALCO's early work, see Asian-African Legal Consultative Organization (AALCO), *Principles Concerning Admission and Treatment of Aliens*, 25 February 1961, www.refworld.org/legal/resolution/aalco/1961/en/21817; Asian-African Legal Consultative Organization (AALCO), *Addendum to the Principles Concerning Treatment of Refugees*, 27 January 1970, www.refworld.org/legal/resolution/aalco/1970/en/91416.

[74] Others have shown us that the 'Third' World was a project of world-making rather than a place. We know it to be a political, and political-economic, assertion. See Prashad, *The Darker Nations*.

[75] Shaunnagh Dorsett and Shaun McVeigh, *Jurisdiction* (Abingdon: Routledge-Cavendish, 2012).

[76] See Eslava, Fakhri and Nesiah, *Bandung, Global History and International Law*; Frank Gerits, *The Ideological Scramble for Africa: How the Pursuit of Anticolonial Modernity Shaped a Postcolonial Order, 1945–1966* (Ithaca: Cornell University Press; 2023); Lee, *Making a World after Empire*; Christopher Lee, 'Afro-Asia as Method: Bandung, the

because it offers a powerful account of a rival world, of an international domain and a rival international law deeply at odds with the versions of these things coming from the respective empires. It brought together plural legal traditions and significant strands of thought in which rival modes of existence, rival laws and even rival cosmologies coexist,[77] but in which it is not necessary to give up an idea of lawfulness in the interactions between people with rival or different accounts of the world. This was a vision of international law signalled earlier by Pan-Africanists for one, taken up at Bandung and carried forward at the Asian Socialist Conferences by the Belgrade–Brioni Group and in the vernaculars of neutralism we explicate below.

4.4.1 Anti-diplomacy

In large measure, States in the West met such diplomatic practices with a combination of contempt, condescension, racism and paranoia. As Nehru observed on his return from Bandung,

> none of us who went to Bandung are quite the same now. [But if] you have read any of the criticisms in some foreign newspapers, and which I have been reading since I came back, mostly they are angry criticisms: "What business have these people to meet without their elders and mentors." "Oh! They are going to meet like children away from their teacher, they want to play about and misbehave."[78]

The West fought symbolism with propaganda and assertions of autonomy with intervention. Attending to these aspects of the period turns on its head any image of the lawful North and the lawless South. It is worth remembering too that independence in African States was occurring when segregation was alive and well in the United States. The literature is full of ironic – and potent – instances of black dignitaries experiencing segregation in the US and black Americans in Africa experiencing 'rights'

Production of Postcolonial Space and the Cruel Optimism of the 1960s' *The Global Sixties*, 15(1–2) (2022) 134–49.

77 We take up the idea of thinking in terms of cosmologies from Christine Black, *The Land Is the Source of the Law: A Dialogic Encounter with Indigenous Jurisprudence* (Abingdon: Routledge, 2011).

78 Jawaharlal Nehru, 'Recollections of the Conference', speech given at a closed-door meeting of members of the Congress Parliamentary Party, New Delhi, 3 May 1955, reproduced in Sarvepalli Gopal (ed.), *Selected Works of Jawaharlal Nehru – Second Series: Volume 28: 1 February–31 May 1955* (New Delhi: Jawaharlal Nehru Memorial Fund, 1995).

unavailable to them at home.[79] Many States and leaders in the Third World were involved in the movement around civil rights,[80] offering harbour and support in solidarity with the struggle.[81] Williams describes one incident at the independence celebrations of Ghana in Accra, when Richard Nixon congratulated a black man, asking him, 'what's it like to be free?' He replied, 'I don't know sir, I'm from Alabama'.[82]

The clandestine diplomacy of the Amero-Soviets as between themselves produced interventionism in the Third World, overwhelmingly by the United States and its allies. This intervention turned putatively on an axis of 'intelligence' but often more predictably on paranoia, misinformation and various forms of corporate predation.[83] This was where the world-making project of anti-anti-colonialism met the Cold War. The European empires were waging violent wars of counterinsurgency against independence movements in Vietnam, Algeria, Kenya, Angola, Mozambique, Indonesia and Malaysia and covert operations against those asserting economic sovereignty inimical to Western interests in Iran, Egypt, Iraq, Ghana and the Congo. At the same time, Europeans were working hard to distinguish the moral and political force of their resistance to Axis rule in Europe from the justifications being made for the manner and fact of often violent domination in their unwilling colonies and protectorates. Generating overblown intelligence about Soviet influence for an American audience and emphasising the threat to American corporate interest was the strategy most often used to draw the US into these wars on the wrong side of history. The Anglo–Iranian Oil Company affair, discussed in Chapter 5, is a good example of this. The British government's intelligence strategy in that instance was

[79] Williams describes an incident in which Gbedemah, the finance minister of Ghana, was refused entry to a roadside restaurant in Delaware on the basis that 'coloured people are not allowed to eat here'. Eisenhower issued a formal apology and invited him to dine at the White House. Susan Williams, *White Malice: The CIA and the Covert Recolonisation of Africa* (New York: PublicAffairs, 2021).

[80] Elaine Mokhtefi, *Algiers, Third World Capital: Freedom Fighters, Revolutionaries, Black Panthers* (London: Verso, 2018); Robeson Taj Frazier, *The East Is Black: Cold War China in the Black Radical Imagination* (Durham: Duke University Press 2015). See also *Soundtrack to a Coup d'État*; Mary Dudziak, *Cold War Civil Rights: Race and the Image of American Democracy* (Princeton: Princeton University Press, 2000) 14.

[81] Mokhtefi, *Algiers, Third World Capital*; Mélanie Torrent, *Algerian Independence and the British Left: Solidarities and Resistance in a Decolonising World* (London: Bloomsbury Academic, 2024); Tomba, *Insurgent Universality.*

[82] Williams, *White Malice*, 14.

[83] Andrew Rubin, *Archives of Authority: Empire, Culture, and the Cold War* (Princeton: Princeton University Press, 2012).

shaped by the idea that the Americans would be more likely to work with it in overthrowing Mossadegh 'if it saw the problem as one of containing communism than restoring the position' of a British oil company.[84] Indeed, if Walter Benjamin was right about the 'forms and virtues' of the diplomat and their historical role of securing 'nonviolent agreement',[85] the combination of the anti-anti colonial struggle and Amero-Soviet rivalry over the South produced an anti-diplomatic mode in which North encountered South. This anti-diplomacy had three aspects.

4.4.1.1 One World, One International Law

First, the diplomatic performance and prefiguration by the Third World of a new, or alternative, international law was represented by prominent Western commentators as a challenge to the claimed universality of existing 'International Law'. This representation has two parts worth noticing. One is the idea that the non-West was being disruptive of law, the other is the assumption that there was a pre-existing system of law that could be 'disrupted'. As we will explore further in Chapter 5, this 'existing' international law of Europe was itself largely a prefiguration, representing as solid and systemic an international law the West was seeking to bring into being. In relation to the first idea – of disruption – whether they explained it explicitly through positivism and the test of legality, or implicitly by racist understandings expressed as developmentalist stage theory, Western commentators would not read what was being put forward as a different tradition.[86] Because one European 'International Law' was understood by Western States as the only 'proper' inter-national law, the challenge from the Third World could not be understood in terms of a meeting between different laws nor even between different versions of inter-national law, which could be engaged with as such.[87] This was a syncretic tradition certainly, not hermetically

[84] Rubin, *Archives of Authority*, 34.

[85] Walter Benjamin, 'Critique of Violence' in *Reflections: Essays, Aphorisms, Autobiographical Writings*, trans. Edmund Jephcott (New York: Schocken Books, 2007) 247.

[86] James Brierly, *The Law of Nations: An Introduction to the International Law of Peace*, 6th ed. (Oxford: Clarendon Press, 1963) 43, quoted in J. J. G. Syatauw, 'The Relationship between the Newness of States and their Practices of International Law' in R. P. Anand (ed.), *Asian States and the Development of Universal International Law* (New Delhi: Vikas, 1972).

[87] Racism was obviously at work here too in the failure of imagination in the West. It could scarcely be imagined that the 'natives' could have their own international law. For a

sealed and 'authentic' to pre-colonial difference, but it was a rival account of 'international law' nonetheless. The fact, then, that African and Asian States were taking up some elements of a European international law and adapting them to different legal traditions was perceived as a 'crisis' for the system. British jurist, J. L. Brierly, for example, dismissed Third World challenges as illegitimate and capricious: 'some of these nations are at least inclined to look on international law as an alien system which the Western nations, whose moral or intellectual leadership they no longer recognise, are trying to impose on them, and in effect they have begun to claim the right to select from among the rules only those which suit their interests or which arise out of agreements to which they have themselves been parties'.[88]

Diplomatic conferences like Bandung, or later UNCTAD, were interpreted by the West as a demonstration that an existing 'International Law' was expanding – from being the law of the 'small family of nations' amongst which it arose, into one that was worldwide and now 'claiming the allegiance' of new nations. This fed into the European[89] idea that there was a pre-existing 'world' governed by law, into which nations gained 'entry' through the assumption of State form. But Western States were worried that the 'pre-existing' law was not understood nor ever really known by these new members. They were fearful that these African and Asian nations might not accept the fundamental beliefs and sentiments on which 'international law' was 'originally' founded.[90]

The multiplicity of laws that existed during the colonial period is not often understood as having endured as law during and after the struggles for independence, and which lived on at the time of the Bandung conference.[91] But that multiplicity was the lived experience of both

detailed account of the derision with which the Bandung Conference was treated by the West, see Pahuja, 'Letters from Bandung'.

88 Brierly, *The Law of Nations*, 43.

89 We are including the US and the USSR here as rival heirs to the European tradition.

90 Syatauw, 'The Relationship between the Newness of States and their Practices of International Law', 11–12.

91 Scores of books have been written about the rival forms of law that existed in colonial spaces during the colonial period. For just two examples, see Peter Fitzpatrick, *Law as Resistance: Modernism, Imperialism, Legalism* (Aldershot: Ashgate, 2008); and Ian Duncanson, *Historiography, Empire, and the Rule of Law: Imagined Constitutions, Remembered Legalities* (Abingdon and New York: Routledge, 2012). The imperial posture invariably involved creating some kind of hierarchy between laws, downgrading the laws of the colonised to 'custom' and/or 'tradition' vis-à-vis 'proper' (imperial) Law, or inventing fictions about authority having been delegated to local leaders and/or practices.

leaders and (international) lawyers of the South. The Third World leader and Third World international lawyer had no choice but to take up the practice of international law in a syncretic and sometimes contradictory way. But through its practice, the Third World was describing not only a different international law but a different world, one that was not yet made but that had to be remade through lawful encounters. The struggle outlived the Cold War, of course. As Zapatista leader Subcomandante Marcos said some years later when asked if he would come to the negotiating table with the president of Mexico, 'there is no table at which to sit in dialogue . . .. We have to construct it'.[92] In other words, there was not yet an international law equal to the task of making a world after empire. And so not only did the Third 'World' have to be made,[93] it would have to be a juridical project as well as a geopolitical, imaginative and economic one.

4.4.1.2 Relegation

The second aspect of the North's anti-diplomacy in relation to the Third World was the question of how to live together after the end of empire. At the end of the Second World War, the formal British Empire was at its apogee.[94] For the Third World, it was self-evident that imperialism should not be forgotten. It insisted on the importance of remembering, weaving this into its diplomatic practice in a style we describe above as historiographical diplomacy. In the face of this, the North performed a diplomacy of forgetfulness, involving the rhetorical erasure of colonialism and the repeated inauguration of the world. Remember the opening to Harry Truman's inaugural address? 'For the first time in human history . . ..'[95] These gestures licensed a world-making project that bracketed colonialism, denied the necessity of reparations of any kind

It was so clear that a rivalry of laws existed during the colonial period, that it seems extraordinary that we imagine today that as soon as decolonisation happened, a 'system' of post-European laws automatically came into being with the adoption of the state form, united by International Law.

92 Gabriel García Márquez and Roberto Pombo, 'Subcomandante Marcos: The Punch Card and the Hourglass' *New Left Review*, 9 (2001).

93 Rather than a place, as Prashad has suggested, see Prashad, *The Darker Nations*.

94 This is partly because of the way the Mandate system had been developing. See Anghie, *Imperialism, Sovereignty and the Making of International Law*, chapter 3; Cait Storr, 'Mandates in International Law' Oxford Bibliographies (2020), DOI: 10.1093/obo/9780199796953-0203.

95 Harry S. Truman, 'Inaugural Address', 20 January 1949, www.trumanlibrary.gov/library/public-papers/19/inaugural-address. See further Jennifer Beard, *The Political Economy of*

and in characterising most of the world as simply 'lacking', blamed the South for its own poverty. Once the causes of poverty were understood as primordial rather than historical, the political-economy of imperialism could continue and be repackaged as development.[96] This was a direct counter to the organised moves towards establishing a 'New International Economic Order' after empire.[97] The agitation for the latter was so effective it ignited a rearguard action by the West, launched secretly at the Rambouillet meetings described in Chapter 5, which blossomed into the G7 and the Washington consensus.[98]

Developmental diplomacy was also a mode of relegation. Most diplomatic responses by North to South redescribed the encounter between them in terms of development and in developmental terms favourable to the North. Several States in the North interpreted the Bandung conference as a call for more development aid.[99] But the response to the New International Economic Order is particularly telling. That endeavour was a classic diplomatic assertion: relations of trade between States had (along with war and peace) been one of the traditional matters of diplomatic

Desire: International Law, Development, and the Nation-State (Abingdon: Routledge, 2007), chapter 1; Pahuja, *Decolonising International Law.*

96 See Sundhya Pahuja, *Decolonising International Law: Development, Economic Growth and the Politics of Universality* (Cambridge: Cambridge University Press, 2011); Luis Eslava, 'Development, International Law and the Cold War: A Long History of Disembedding' in Matthew Craven, Sundhya Pahuja and Gerry Simpson (eds.), *The Cambridge History of International Law, Vol XI: International Law During the Cold War (1945–1990)* (Cambridge: Cambridge University Press, forthcoming).

97 Pahuja, *Decolonising International Law*; Arturo Escobar, *Encountering Development: The Making and Unmaking of the Third World* (Princeton: Princeton University Press 1995); Gilbert Rist, *The History of Development: From Western Origins to Global Faith*, trans. Patrick Camiller, 3rd ed. (London: Bloomsbury, 2008); Wolfgang Sachs (ed.), *The Development Dictionary: A Guide to Knowledge as Power*, 2nd ed. (London: Zed Books, 2010).

98 See generally, Jessica Whyte, *The Moral of the Market: Human Rights and the Rise of Neoliberalism* (London: Verso, 2019); Quinn Slobodian, *The Globalists: The End of Empire and the Birth of Neoliberalism* (Cambridge, MA: Harvard University Press, 2020); Anne Orford, 'Beyond Harmonization: Trade, Human Rights and the Economy of Sacrifice' *Leiden Journal of International Law*, 18 (2005) 179–213; Kerry Rittich, 'Transformed Pursuits: The Quest for Equality in Globalized Markets' *Harvard Human Rights Journal* 13 (2000) 231–61. See also 'Address by President Nixon to the United Nations General Assembly', New York, 23 October 23 1970, Office of the Historian, https://history.state.gov/historicaldocuments/frus1969–76v01/d78.

99 Frank Gerits, *The Ideological Scramble for Africa: How the Pursuit of Anticolonial Modernity Shaped a Postcolonial Order, 1945–1966* (Ithaca: Cornell University Press, 2023), for instance, offers an account of how the West interpreted Bandung as a call for more development aid.

endeavour for centuries. The response of the North, however, was to refuse the questions as matters for diplomatic negotiation and to send them instead to the realm of development. This was a sphere in which authority remained institutionally and epistemically with the North, and where relations were hierarchically structured between 'developed' and 'developing'.

Kissinger's speech at the UN in response to the NIEO, in 1973[100] (discussed in Chapter 5) prefigures the institutionalisation of this strategy. Indeed, what followed soon after the NIEO took flight included the inauguration in 1978 of the *World Bank Development Report.*[101] Its contemporaneity with the demand for an economic reckoning with the legacies of empire is not a coincidence. Sridath Ramphal, then Secretary General of the Commonwealth, made the point in an interview in 1978 in the *Third World Quarterly.* Ramphal, legally trained and a respected statesman, was being interviewed by Altaf Gauhar, editor of the journal. The interview was the first in a new section in the journal called 'North–South Dialogue' intended to provide 'eminent statesmen and scholars involved in North-South issues' a forum to express their views. The subject of the interview was precisely the World Bank Development Report. They didn't know then that it was to be the first report in what would become an annual occurrence for the Bank. It's worth quoting Ramphal at length:

> I think the World Development Report is a compound of many elements and some are contradictory. The Report has caused me a great deal of anguish and I feel it can be quite dangerous in the way it will turn out however well-intentioned it might be. It is a good example of what Third World people have been saying for a long time; how easy it is for the North and the South to see the world through opposite ends of the telescope. This Report projects the world essentially from the Northern end of the telescope. The North sees a world which the South does not recognise; it does not recognise it because it isn't the world that people in the South live in.[102]

[100] Daniel Moynihan (United States of America), 'Address Delivered at 2327th Plenary Meeting' *Official Records of the United Nations General Assembly*, 1 September 1975, New York.

[101] World Bank, *World Development Report 1978* (Washington, DC: World Bank 1978); Shahid Yusuf et al., *Development Economics through the Decades: A Critical Look at 30 Years of the World Development Report* (Washington, DC: World Bank Publications 2008).

[102] Shridath Ramphal, 'Not by Unity Alone: The Case for Third World Organisation' *Third World Quarterly*, 1(3) (1979) 43–52.

He links this clash of perspectives – and of worlds – to the demands for a New International Economic Order, and North-led ideas of development as the response:

> The North would have us believe that a major effort, supportive of development, has been under way during the last twenty five years or so. So, they have, in some way, to convince themselves that it has been a success story . . .. Now that is a very dangerous presentation, because the truth of the matter is that what needs to be done should be qualitatively different from what has been done so far . . .. The necessity for qualitative change arises from the fact that what has been done up to now has contributed little or nothing to the alleviation of the basic poverty in the world. It is of fundamental importance that this difference should be clearly understood. If you are trying to do more of the same then you have to justify what you have done before as being essentially right, but not perhaps enough. But if what went before was not right in coping with the problem, then what you need is not more of the same, but something different, and that is the heart of the matter between North and South today. The New International Economic Order (NIEO) is something different; it aims at structural change, not more of the same. The World Development Report is a projection of more of the same.[103]

As Ramphal points out later, the South had been 'trying to convert Northern governments through dialogue' between governments. Instead, questions of political economy were 'relegated' (a diplomatic term for banishment or removal to a different, lower level) through being re-cast as matters of development. They no longer fell within the realm of government-to-government dialogue and diplomacy but were re-assigned into the hands of Northern (or Northern trained) 'experts'.

The practice of relegation instanced here extended more broadly to non-European and non-State forms of law that were likewise relegated to a sphere other than that of law. From the Bandung Conference, it is clear that for those gathered there, the main challenge was to work out a way to allow for the ongoing existence of a multiplicity of laws in the world precisely without them being relegated to a non-legal domain.[104] The fear was that such laws would be relegated to the realm of culture read as 'tradition', the realm of 'religion' set up as separate to secular law[105] or

[103] Ramphal, 'Not by Unity Alone'.

[104] The reference here to 'most people' echoes Chatterjee; see Partha Chatterjee, *The Politics of the Governed: Reflections on Popular Politics in Most of the World* (New York: Columbia University Press, 2004).

[105] See generally, Brent Nongbri, *Before Religion: A History of a Modern Concept* (New Haven and London: Yale University Press, 2013). Also on this point, see the argument

simply to realms on a continuum with 'law' but lower down the hierarchy, because they were 'primitive', 'uncivilised', 'backward', 'underdeveloped' or, euphemistically, 'developing'. Those at Bandung tried to refuse these registers of relegation, whilst holding onto an account of multiple forms of lawful conduct. But looking back and understanding their actions in this way seems to have become more difficult today than at other times. The horizons of the possible imaginaries of lawful life seem to have closed in, and we have come too readily to accept the idea that there is no longer anything 'outside' Europe[106] and the world of its making. This is particularly true of Africa. As Gerits observes, in the international relations literature, Sub-Saharan Africa is still approached as a 'politically empty space'.[107] The same is true for most literature generated in international law.[108] And even now, rather than rethinking the question of African agency and placing it at the centre of international thought (even when it comes to questions about Africa), we move too quickly to think of inclusion and its corollary – diversity – as the most appropriate gestures towards the non-European other.

4.4.1.3 Self-Determination and Political Dependence

The third form of anti-diplomacy is perhaps the most tragic. This was where the clandestine diplomacy of the United States, the State-based world of the Amero-Soviets and the juridical diplomacy of the Third World came together. This was a form of anti-diplomacy in which statehood was putatively 'respected', whilst governments were toppled. Propaganda, which bypassed political structures to reach directly into the 'hearts and minds' of peoples, was a complementary practice to this style

made by Bandhyopadhyay in 1920 about the way that rules of interstatal relations underpinned by Dharma were disqualified from consideration as 'international law' according to a definition too greatly influenced by Austin: 'Followers of Austin have denied the title International Law to rules based on religious sanction. They put their case too high'. Pramathanath Bandyopadhyay, *International Law and Custom in Ancient India* (Calcutta: Calcutta University Press, 1920) 7–8.

[106] See generally, Michael Hardt and Antonio Negri, *Empire* (Cambridge, MA: Harvard University Press, 2000). We don't mean the 'constitutive outside', our critical sensitivity to which is arguably part of the problem of the forgetting about the outside.

[107] Frank Gerits, 'When the Bull Elephants Fight', 964 (quoting Hans J. Morgenthau, *Politics Among Nations: The Struggle for Peace and Power* (New York: Alfred A Knopf, 1985), 369).

[108] Cf. Christopher Gevers, 'Literal Decolonization: Re-reading African International Legal Scholarship through the African Novel' in Jochen von Bernstoff and Philipp Dann (eds.), *The Battle for International Law: South–North Perspectives on the Decolonization Era* (Oxford: Oxford University Press, 2019).

of anti-diplomacy.[109] A different way of saying this was that formal independence could be upheld even as substantive independence, or autonomy, was disregarded. We saw the way the Charter of the United Nations made this possible in Chapter 2. As a question of (anti)diplomacy, it is visible also in the US denial of its own involvement in so many interventions.[110]

This form of anti-diplomacy culminated at the end of the Cold War in the emergence of the discourse of 'failed States'. 'Failed States' was a term first used in the early 1990s, by some commentators in relation to the former Soviet Union.[111] But it was a language forcefully taken up by the US Foreign Policy establishment to describe the political crises that emerged at the end of the Cold War, in Somalia, Bosnia, Liberia and Afghanistan. A 'State Failure Task Force' was established in 1994 in response to a request from then US Vice-President Al Gore to design and carry out 'a data-driven study on the correlates of State failure'.[112] In 1998, the US National Security Strategy was then revised to describe 'Failed States' as a significant threat to US security.[113] By 2005, a 'Failed States Index' had emerged, compiled by the journal *Foreign Policy* and an American think tank, the Fund for Peace.[114] Much could be said about

[109] See Rubin, *Archives of Authority*; Frances Stonor Saunders, *Who Paid the Piper? The CIA and the Cultural Cold War* (London: Granta Books, 1999).

[110] This was common in the media of the time. Alan Dulles, head of the CIA, once said, 'to my knowledge, we never intervened', the recording of which is reproduced in Jimonprez, *Soundtrack to a Coup d'Etat.*

[111] On a search of university library catalogues, no results for 'failed States' appear before 1992, but 18 results appear between 1992 and 1994.

[112] Jack Goldstone et al., 'The State Failure Project: Early Warning Research for U.S. Foreign Policy Planning' in John L. Davies and Ted Robert Gurr (eds.), *Preventive Measures: Building Risk Assessment and Crisis Early Warning Systems* (Lanham: Rowman & Littlefield, 1998).

[113] As early as page 7, it reads, 'Failed states: We can expect that, despite international prevention efforts, some states will be unable to provide basic governance, services and opportunities for their populations, potentially generating internal conflict, humanitarian crises or regional instability. As governments lose their ability to provide for the welfare of their citizens, mass migration, civil unrest, famine, mass killings, environmental disasters and aggression against neighbouring states or ethnic groups can threaten U.S. interests and citizens.' See US, 'National Security Strategy for a New Century' (1998), https://history.defense.gov/Historical-Sources/National-Security-Strategy.

[114] Foreign Policy and Fund for Peace, *Failed States Index 2005* (Foreign Policy, July/August 2005). See further David Corn, 'Public Interest Power Games: Turf Wars at the Fund for Peace' *The Nation*, 250(10) (12 March 1990) 342.

the terminology of 'failed States', the development of the index, and the doctrine of 'humanitarian' intervention that emerged alongside it around the same time.[115] What is instructive about the emergence of this discourse from the perspective of the arguments being offered in this book is the way official accounts and those close to them erased the relationship between the Amero-Soviet project and the generalisation of the State form, both in terms of the formal spread of the legal form of the nation-state and in terms of the types of statehood being supported.[116] It is telling that the Congo (strategically crucial for the uranium necessary for the production of nuclear weapons) recurs in all stories, from the assassination of Lumumba to taking second place in the first Index of 'failure'. An early commentator in the debate was David Kay, Secretary General of the Uranium Institute.[117] The idea of failed States was to describe the situation in which a local people failed to reach the level of development required by the State form, which itself was taken for granted as universal. There was never any genuine enquiry into whether the external imposition of the State form itself might be the problem. What this historical forgetfulness licensed was an external stabilisation of the State form – holding the State together from the outside – and the corollary ability to assert (if not always defend) property rights and the 'rights' acquired by foreign investors (particularly in minerals).

4.5 Neutralist Diplomacy: Neutrality, Neutralism and Non-Alignment

The third struggle over diplomacy concerned the possibility of being neutral during the Cold War and what that might mean. It was an argument conducted around three different positions. European, or 'classical', international law was committed to the protection of the principle of neutrality as a way of limiting the spread and extent of warfare. The Amero-Soviets, on the other hand, disparaged neutrality,

[115] Anne Orford, *Reading Humanitarian Intervention: Human Rights and the Use of Force in International Law* (Cambridge: Cambridge University Press, 2003).

[116] See, for example, Jeffrey Herbst, 'Responding to State Failure in Africa', *International Security*, 21 (3) (1996/97) 120–44.

[117] See David A. Kay et al., 'Letters' *Foreign Policy*, 90 (1993) 169.

or the 'neutralism' of the Third World, as a failure to make the required moral and political commitments in a moment of existential conflict.[118] Among the anti-colonial peoples of the South, there was an embrace of an active neutralism or non-alignment that refused both the Cold War in toto and the depiction of non-alignment itself as old-school 'neutrality'. In a sense, this contest was a manifestation of the diplomatic encounter between the rival projects of world-making themselves.

4.5.1 *The 'Law of Neutrality'*

In nineteenth- or early twentieth-century textbooks on international law, 'the law of neutrality' typically absorbs a sizeable chunk of the table of contents. A State was at war or at peace, or it was juggling the politics and law of trying to remain halfway between the two in exercise of its neutral rights and in conformity with its duties as a neutral.[119] Certainly, the rules governing the rights and duties of non-belligerents occupied a large part of the international law imaginary of the time.[120] Article 17 of the Fifth Hague Convention of 1907, for example, defines neutrality in terms of the adoption of a posture of impartiality and abstention in relation to powers involved in an ongoing conflict.[121] Neutrality, in that context, did

[118] While at the same time deploying it in Austria and Switzerland as an organising principle of intra-European affairs.

[119] For overviews, see Stephen Neff, 'A Three-Fold Struggle over Neutrality: The American Experience in the 1930s' in P. Lottaz and H. R. Reginbogin (eds.), *Notions of Neutralities* (Lanham: Lexington Books, 2018); J. H. W. Verzijl, *International Law in Historical Perspective: The Law of Neutrality* (Leiden: Brill Nijhoff, 1979); Constantine Antonopoulos, *Non-Participation in Armed Conflict: Continuity and Modern Challenges to the Law of Neutrality* (Cambridge: Cambridge University Press, 2022). See generally, Francis Deák and Philip Jessup (eds.), *A Collection of Neutrality Laws, Regulations, and Treaties of Various Countries* (Washington, DC: Carnegie Endowment for International Peace; Columbia University Press, 1939); Alfred Rubin, 'The Concept of Neutrality in International Law' *Denver Journal of International Law and Policy*, 16 (1988) 353–75.

[120] The Alabama Claims, arising out of Anglo-American relations during the American Civil War, and subsequent codification efforts throughout the nineteenth century culminated in the articulation of the rights of neutral powers in the Fifth Hague Convention (1907) concerning land warfare, as well as the Thirteenth Hague Convention (1907) on the rights and duties of neutral powers in sea warfare. These were complemented by the London Declaration of 1909 on the laws of naval warfare. A notable antecedent is the Declaration of Paris (1856), 46 BFSP 137.

[121] See Dietrich Schindler and Jiri Toman (eds.), *The Laws of Armed Conflicts: A Collection of Conventions, Resolutions, and Other Documents* (Leiden: Martinus Nijhoff, 1973) 228. The territory of a neutral power is inviolable (article 1) and cannot be used, nor shall the neutral power allow it to be used (articles 4 & 5), by belligerents. Its nationals are neutral

not simply describe a policy of 'non-participation' but also a status defined in contradistinction to that of belligerency. One was either a belligerent or a neutral, there was no space between.[122] States not participating in warfare were bound to apply the rules of neutrality; States engaged in conflict with one another were obliged to respect the rights of neutrals.

These legal texts did not exhaust the diplomatic practice of neutrality. As a matter of law and diplomacy, 'neutrality' came in other forms. Alongside the 'Hague' rules on neutrality (to be applied only in armed conflict and defining the rights and obligations of the belligerents and non-belligerents vis-à-vis each other),[123] there was also the neutralisation of States through Great Power accord (Austria during the Cold War, Belgium and Switzerland in the nineteenth century). Alongside these forms was another diplomatic – perhaps even popular – usage of 'neutrality' that described a posture of indifference or disinterestedness (two different things) adopted by States in relation to a conflict or alignment of forces in the international order. As we shall see, the Cold War seemed at once both to threaten the existence of this latter form of neutrality (how was it possible to be neutral in a world divided between two monsters?) and to affirm its necessity (how could one be anything but neutral when confronted with the need to choose between monsters?).

According to Carl Schmitt, neutrality had been in recession since the Great War. On 2 April 1917, one year after he affirmed the United States' position as an impartial bystander ('we must remain neutral in thought and action'), Woodrow Wilson had announced the end of the era of neutrality.[124] Later, in 1935, the Greek diplomat and professor of international law Nicolas Politis, commenting on efforts to outlaw certain kinds of aggressive war (in the League of Nations Covenant and the

(article 16), and whilst it is entitled to defend its own neutrality (article 10), a neutral power cannot, without losing said status, commit hostile acts against a belligerent or acts in favour of a belligerent.

[122] Schindle and Toman, *The Laws of Armed Conflict*, 230.

[123] See variously, Hersch Lauterpacht, *Oppenheim's International Law, Vol II, Disputes, War and Neutrality*, 7th ed. (London: Longmans, Green & Co, 1952) 666–67; Nicolas Politis, *Neutrality and Peace* (Washington, DC: Carnegie Endowment for International Peace, 1935); J. H. W. Verzijl, *The Law of Neutrality* (Leiden: Brill, 1979) 4. It is not quite correct to say then that 'it is impossible for neutrality to exist without war'. See Antonopolous, *Non-Participation in Armed Conflict*, 144.

[124] Carl Schmitt, *The Nomos of the Earth in the International Law of the Jus Publicum Europaeum* (New York: Telos Press, 2003) 296–97: The US returned to neutrality in 1939 promising to deal with all the parties 'on terms of friendship'.

Kellogg Briand Pact), called neutrality an "anachronism ... irrevocably doomed".[125] But by the early 1940s, the Americans were worried again about their duties under the law of neutrality (the use of the word itself in fact peaks in 1939–40).[126] Robert Jackson, at the time US attorney general, sought the support of Hersch Lauterpacht, who reassured him that the Pact of Paris (1928), prohibiting 'recourse to war' in foreign relations, had 'destroyed the historical and juridical foundations of the doctrine of neutrality'. If aggressive war was unlawful, how could one be neutral between aggressor and victim? Or, to put it more bluntly, how could any State remain neutral as between Nazis and defenders of civilisation?

Schmitt believed this attitude and the decline of neutrality spelt disaster. He regarded neutrality as one of the signal achievements of European nineteenth-century international law: a 'natural institution' in the context of the system of equilibrium that characterised the balance of power. And it was in that context that the doctrine of permanent neutrality emerged

[125] See Maria Gavouneli, 'Neutrality: A Survivor?' *European Journal of International Law*, 23 (2012) 267. The seat of the League was nevertheless in Geneva. For similar views, post-1945, see Charles Fenwick, *International Law*, 4th ed. (New York: Appleton-Century-Crofts, 1965) 727; Charles Fenwick, 'The Old Order Changeth, Yielding Place to the New' *American Journal of International Law*, 47 (1953) 84–87. Chaumont: 'The concerted action that characterizes the notion of collective security is opposed to the individual, and even individualistic, action of traditional warfare, where international law did not use the notion of aggression and did not distinguish between aggressor of his victim. It therefore seems to be opposed at the same time to what, in this individualist perspective, is the natural complement of the competence of war: the competence for peace which constitutes the regime of neutrality.' Charles Chaumont, *Nations Unies et neutralité: cours à l'Académie de la Haye, juillet 1956*, in *Recueil des cours* (Collected Courses of the Hague Academy of International Law), vol. 89 (The Hague: Nijhoff /Brill, 1956) 5. The position adopted post-1945 was that the concept of neutrality had essentially been repudiated, e.g., Hans Kelsen, *The Law of the United Nations: A Critical Analysis of Its Fundamental Problems* (New York: F. A. Praeger, 1951) 91–94; Charles Rousseau, *Droit International Public* (Paris: Recueil Sirey, 1953) 676–77.

[126] Some believed neutrality retained its validity (Guggenheim, Verdross, Stone, von Glahn). Others avoid the topic or speak of the 'chaotic' nature of the law of neutrality (Kunz). Still others believed the lines had become exceedingly blurred: it is a context dependent idea, no longer 'crystalline'. 'Experience shows that belligerent and neutral states are satisfied with approximate neutralities, the content of which is determined by the margin, the moving border which separates the non-belligerent state from full participation in hostilities, a margin which is fixed in each case by the historical contingencies which allow or do not allow a State to escape from war'. Thus, States were able to declare war without taking part in hostilities during the war of 1914 and 1939 or favour one of the belligerents without declaring war or being considered as belligerents. Chaumont, *Nations Unies et neutralité*, 11.

so as to prevent territories of strategic importance from being absorbed by one or other of the great powers (hence the neutralisation of Switzerland in 1815 'in the true interests of the policy of the whole of Europe' as well as the protected status of Belgium in 1839 and Luxemburg in 1867).

European war, meanwhile, was a contest between two equally situated sovereigns, neither of whom could claim to be acting in the name of anything but their own sovereign desire. In this image of nineteenth-century intra-European conflict, there were no lawful sovereigns, no aggressive monsters. Or, to put this another way, all were lawful sovereigns and/or aggressive monsters. There was no United Nations Charter–style international legal norm capable of apportioning liability between the parties. And yet the behaviour of third States was governed by the law of neutrality with its insistence on a position of impartiality and abstention.

The move to collective security in the twentieth century changed all this. This was a matter of enormous regret for Schmitt. It transposed the hierarchical structure of colonial war beyond 'the Amity Line' (civilised/barbarian) to the European theatre and upended decades of limited warfare. It replaced warring sovereigns and 'non-discriminatory war' with an existential struggle between law and lawlessness (the inter-war years), police and criminal (the text of Chapter VII of the UN Charter) and ultimately humanity and its enemies (the post–Cold War period).[127] War was no longer bracketed off, juridically or geographically. In this sense, law lost its own 'neutrality', its long-standing refusal to adjudicate between humanitarian war and aggressive war. Although Schmitt did not express it as such, this was a reflection of the ongoing struggle between those who understood international law as a law of encounter, which patterned relations between groups and plural laws but was normatively neutral, to a law of inclusion, which asserted a normativity, if not norm, above particular, plural laws. At the same time as this shift was occurring, States were in danger of losing their entitlements to neutral status. The United Nations, purporting to represent 'humanity', could be understood as incompatible with neutrality. At the first Committee meeting of the San Francisco conference, a French amendment to the Charter proposed the inclusion of the phrase 'without a State being able ... to invoke a

[127] Schmitt, *The Nomos of the Earth in the International Law of the Jus Publicum Europaeum*, 246.

status of neutrality'.[128] It was 'understood' that the status of perpetual neutrality was incompatible with article 2(5) insofar as no State could avoid the obligations of the Charter. In the world of good and evil, or law and lawlessness, a State could hardly adopt a posture of neutrality in relation to the Devil. That would be taking agnosticism too far, surely?

So, by the early Cold War period, we can say that neutrality was being threatened from three different directions, which were in some ways contradictory. First, the UN Charter transformed war into a policing matter. This seemed to render a *law* of neutrality defunct. A bystander might be loyal to the police (urging them on as the criminals are apprehended) or hostile to them (condemning overzealous enforcement or taking the side of the criminals) but the position of the bystander in law was already settled, she was under an obligation to support (or at least not impede the work of) the police.[129]

Second, across this constitutional structure of the UN, the Cold War had laid a system of ideological enmity that made political neutrality both vulnerable to accusations of betrayal and susceptible to subversion. It was vitally important to take sides in order to survive the confrontation of great powers. The Cold War – understood here as a Manichean confrontation between the two superpowers armed to the teeth and advancing mutually exclusionary ideological world-views – seemed to render the space for neutrality vanishingly small. And this receding horizon included the neutrality of international law itself. It is significant that the Americans and Soviets both shared an antipathy to forms of compulsory (or even optional) judicial dispute settlement because neither really believed in the idea of a neutral legal space.[130]

[128] But the establishment for Austria of a condition of permanent neutrality at the moment of its admission to the UN seemed to render this proposal simultaneously obsolete. See the *Moscow Memorandum*, 15 April 1955. The General Assembly admitted Austria to UN on 14 December 1955 by 59 votes to 0 two months after the adoption by the Austrian parliament of the constitutional law proclaiming the perpetual neutrality of Austria as a constitutional feature of the new Austrian State.

[129] One scholar argues that neutrality is 'not totally excluded by the Charter' (Antonopoulos, *Non-Participation in Armed Conflict*, 60–64) and that when collective security arrangements fail, then States may plead neutrality or adopt a position of qualified neutrality in relation to the victim of unlawful force. Even when they do not, the US Department of Defense in 1992 noted that States retained their rights to neutrality providing such exercise did not impede the military operations under Chapter VII. See too Andrew Clapham, *War* (Oxford: Clarendon Press, 2021) 53.

[130] Schindler's six conditions for the emergence of the doctrine of neutrality: (a) the balance of power; (b) the legitimacy of warfare; (c) the limited character of war (war as duel); (d) economic liberalism (separation between public and private spheres); (e) global power of

Third, it was becoming apparent that the Americans and Soviets were increasingly uniting around the idea of a system in which the stability of the order was assured by a form of explicit joint administration or implicit geo-political division. This shared rule-ship was incompatible with the idea of a Third Way, an alternative diplomacy that refused the injunction to take sides in the Amero-Soviet bi-ordering of the world. In 1922, speaking on the subject of international courts, Maxim Litvinov (later to become the USSR Peoples Commissar for Foreign Affairs) said: 'Only an angel would be capable of the necessary impartiality', before adding even more starkly: 'It was necessary to face the fact that there was not one world but two, a Soviet world and a non-Soviet world . . . because there was no Third World to arbitrate'.[131] And just as there was no 'third world' of impartial judicial officers, there was no third *world*, itself capable of autonomous action and free of the manipulations of Amero-Soviet Cold War thought and practice.[132] All of this meant that, some exceptions apart, the legal rules of neutrality were in trouble.[133]

4.5.2 Neutralism and Non-Alignment

Neutralism was another matter altogether. 'Neutralism' was a neologism coined at the end of the Second World War. According to Peter Lyon, a scholar writing in 1963 almost contemporaneously with its emergence, it was centrally concerned with practices of 'dissociation from the Cold

neutrals (esp US); (f) emergence of humanitarian and pacifist currents were all missing or compromised by the beginning of the twentieth century when instead we had the emergence of total warfare underpinned by both technology and ideology (war as crusade) and a system of collective security.

131 Kazimierz Grzybowski, *Soviet Public International Law: Doctrines and Diplomatic Practice* (Leiden: A. W. Sijthoff; Durham: Rule of Law Press, 1970) 473.

132 See Norman Frucher and Stuart Hall, 'Notes on the Cuban Dilemma' *New Left Review* May/June (1961) 2–12.

133 For example, it continued to be positively recognised in legal texts (the Geneva Conventions, which not only recognise the institution of neutrality but entrust to neutral States certain protective functions) and by legal institutions (the UN appealed to neutral States to collaborate in the application of the armistice in Korea in 1953 neutral commissions in Korea). Five neutral States were invited to be part of the neutral commission for the repatriation of prisoners of war. Two were proposed by the UN (Sweden and Switzerland) were deemed to be mandatories of the UN, two neutrals proposed on the communist side (Poland and Czechoslovakia) were seen as proxies of the communist camp, whilst India would act as an arbiter between the groups. 'Thus, not only the belligerents, but the neutrals themselves were divided into blocs.' See Schindler, 'L'interdépendance des conventions' *Recueil des cours*, 121 (1967) 225.

War'.[134] For Mohammad Bedjaoui, it was the 'phenomenon' of non-alignment that emerged in the 1950s that gave rise to neutralism as a new concept in international relations. In his view, neutralism was distinct from the received categories of ordinary and permanent neutrality insofar as non-alignment did not simply connote an unwillingness to engage in the passive warfare of the Cold War powers, nor a neutralisation imposed from above, but instead involved an active engagement in the promotion of international peace and cooperation on the basis of sovereign equality. Neutralism was an active, or positive neutrality.[135] As he explained:

> Une telle politique de non-engagement n'implique pas seulement de demeurer à équidistance des grandes puissances et de leurs allies, mais bien de se déterminer concrètement, à l'occasion de chaque conflit ou de chaque situation, en fonction d'une appréciation libérée de toute attache politique ou idéologique à l'égard d'un bloc quelconque.[136]

According to Bedjaoui, the non-aligned movement opposed bipolarity (and the associated concentration of economic, political and military power in a small number of decision-making centres) and countered it with multi-polarism and the democratisation of international relations.[137] It sought to replace an 'international law of confiscation' with an 'international law of participation' that used the power of 'raw material diplomacy'.[138] Bandung's 'Pancha Shila' represented, for Bedjaoui, a 'charter of neutrals': 'for neutrality, which until now had no end other than independence, could adorn itself with the moral ideal which it had

[134] Peter Lyon, 'Neutrality and the Emergence of the Concept of Neutralism' *Review of Politics*, 22(2) (1960) 255–68.

[135] Louis Henkin remarked that 'Neutralism might be the better term for this thirdness. It is a political not a legal term'. Louis Henkin, 'Force, Intervention, and Neutrality in Contemporary International Law' *Proceedings of the American Society of International Law at Its Annual Neeting*, 57 (1963) 162. For Henkin, this was a good thing if it promoted order by urging the UN to intervene and exclude 'big-Power intervention' (e.g. Congo) but it was less attractive when it afforded smaller nations 'a kind of immunity to censure'. Ibid.

[136] Mohammed Bedjaoui, 'Non-Alignment and International Law' *Recueil des cours*, 151 (1976) 349–467. Our translation: 'Such a policy of non-engagement does not only imply remaining equidistant from the great powers and their allies, but also making a concrete decision, as each conflict or each situation arises based on an assessment free from any political or ideological attachment to any bloc.'

[137] Bedjaoui, 'Non-Alignment and International Law', 354.

[138] Ibid.

lacked: that of working towards the establishment of a new and better world from which war would be banished'.[139]

The key to Bedjaoui's conception of non-alignment was that of 'national independence' with its five accompanying key principles: an independent politics of peaceful coexistence, support for movements of national liberation, non-membership in collective military pact, non-participation in bilateral alliances with the great powers and refusal to grant foreign military bases.[140] In general, it was opposed to the 'oligarchic system' and the more or less 'amicable' partition of the world into zones of influence and different economic well-being, 'falsely' referred to as 'peaceful coexistence'.[141] Bedjaoui even tried for a definition: 'For us, the main dividing line in today's world passes not between the "big" and the "small", the "rich" and the "poor", but between the forces of socialism, progress and peace and those of the imperialism, colonialism and the reaction to them.'[142]

The Non-Aligned Movement was, of course, itself full of non-alignments and misalignments. Its membership was rarely either stable or defined. At the Belgrade meeting, North Korea, North Vietnam, Panama and the PLO were present; Mozambique, Sao Tome and Principe were there by virtue of their status as members of the OAU; El Salvador and Grenada were admitted as observers; and Sweden, Austria, Finland, Romania, Australia, Portugal and Honduras were 'invitees'. This was, on the face of it, both more and less than the 'Third World'. And at the AAPSO, the Algerians and Moroccans created a third neutral bloc in the context of a split in the NAM itself.[143] But regardless of its stripe, it was certainly the case that to be 'neutral' was to find oneself in opposition to the regionally dominant and proximate superpower. The price paid was often a violent coup d'état (Chile's experiment in social democracy, Mossadegh in Iran), endless, debilitating, war (Ho Chi Minh's Vietnamese nationalism) or decades of insecurity (Yugoslavia).

Salvador Allende was an intriguing figure in all this. For different reasons, he was a thorn in the side of both the Soviets and the United

[139] Ibid., 360.
[140] Ibid., 364–66.
[141] Ibid., 377.
[142] Ibid., 380.
[143] Blanca Mar León, 'Revolutionary Diplomacy and the Third World' in Tanya Harmer and Alberto Alvarez (eds.), *Towards a Global History of Latin America's Revolutionary Left* (London: Routledge, 2021) 80.

States, in part because of his commitment to democracy and what his policy and politics showed up about each of them. Remember that in the General Election of 1970, Salvador Allende was elected president by a majority of the Chilean electorate. But the Soviets (never that enamoured of parliamentary elections) had in any case internalised the South American cone as a US sphere of influence and were wary of becoming embroiled in another Cuba. They were also deeply uncertain about Allende's credentials. In Moscow's eyes, he was a socialist committed to forms of parliamentary democracy rather than a reliable communist ally. Meanwhile, Washington's assault on Chilean democracy, culminating in the violent and repressive 1973 coup, was prompted by a counter-intuitive fear that Allende might lose an election and respect the result. The concern was that he 'would *not* turn Chile into a Cuban-style Soviet satellite' (our emphasis).[144] To the United States and the USSR, the likes of Castro and de Gaulle were, respectively, obvious and known 'enemies'. Allende was something much worse, he was, from the perspective of their unified bipolarity, dangerously 'neutral'.

Later, the proximate aim of the Chicago Boys would be to remove Allende and 'defeat communism' but the deeper imperative was to destroy the prospect of a welfare State in Latin America.[145] What the Americans feared was not Castroism but welfarism.[146] And Allende's 'third way' politics threatened to undermine 'Kissinger's effort to divide the world into two stable spheres of influence',[147] Kissinger's real fear, it seems, was not that Allende would refuse to be voted out but that he would be voted out and relinquish power through a democratic process.[148] Allende had, after all, introduced workplace safety, land reform and pre-natal care for women. He had become a hero to the Global South – his reception at the UN in 1972 was rapturous. His was the dreaded path of peaceful resistance – the refusal of global civil war or accommodation: a social democracy distinguishable from North American anti-social democracies and a socialist internationalism separable from parallel Soviet efforts. This was all too much for Nixon and so

144 See Greg Grandin, *The Last Colonial Massacre: Latin America in the Cold War* (Chicago: University of Chicago Press, 2004) 175.

145 Greg Grandin, 'Don't Do What Allende Did' *London Review of Books*, 34(14) (19 July 2012) 3–4.

146 Grandin, *The Last Colonial Massacre*, 6.

147 Ibid.

148 According to Seymour Hersch's interview with an NSC Staffer, see Grandin, *The Last Colonial Massacre*, 175.

the death squads were funded, with black ops and destablisation campaigns soon underway.[149]

Indeed, in more general terms, and viewed from a certain perspective, it was precisely neutralism that the Amero-Soviets feared most. The Amero-Soviets were, after all, constructing a division space without any space outside it.[150] The enemy was known and could be faced. But the figure who rejected the Cold War altogether was a danger to the system itself. Indeed, Kennedy wanted to secure an Amero-Soviet peace before the 'struggle for the uncommitted nations' began.[151] Tunkin called this third way 'the peace camp',[152] a camp that came to encompass presumably everything that was not the Cold War.[153] John Foster Dulles, meanwhile, on the other side, had called neutralism a 'sin'[154] – a view that found echoes in Stalin's famous hatred of Tito, the leader of Yugoslavia.[155]

In a way, they were right. There was something real to be afraid of, for although the non-aligned movement was trying to stay out of the Cold War, it was far from neutral. Its 'neutrality' was largely describable as such only from the vantage of the North where the primacy of bipolarity was a fixed point of reference. The NAM's internationalist visions, its political commitments from the anti-apartheid struggle to the NIEO to the Common Heritage of Mankind, its anti-nuclearism, its decolonising energy, its roots in negritude or worker's rights or pan-Africanism, its

[149] By this time there had already been military coups in twelve South and Central American States (e.g. Cuba in 1952, Paraguay in 1954, Peru in 1962 and Brazil in 1964).

[150] On 'division space', see Scott Newton, 'Parallel Worlds: Cold War Division Space' in Craven, Pahuja and Simpson, *International Law and the Cold War*.

[151] The Soviets and the West agree on one thing, the Third World was 'underdeveloped'. See Frucher and Hall, 'The Cuban Dilemma', 2.

[152] Even when Tunkin conceded that there was a third camp (a departure from his 'one system, two camps' mentality) even this 'peace camp', he claimed, was slowly becoming integrated into the bicameral system. See Kazimierz Grzybowski, *Soviet International Law and the World Economic Order* (Durham: Duke University Press, 1987) 9–10.

[153] There is a certain similarity to contemporary British politics where the war camp with its two nominally rivalrous factions (the Tories and Keir Starmer's Labour Party) is opposed by a peace camp (largely Labour supporters and including a former leader of the party, all threatened with disciplinary action by the Party).

[154] See Frucher and Hall, 'The Cuban Dilemma'.

[155] Though non-alignment aligned with more advanced conceptions of Soviet international law too. For Korovin, there is not one international law but many international laws – European, American, Colonial, Socialist, Transitional (where there is the possibility of cooperation on technical, conceptual and economic matters). See Richard J. Erickson, *International Law and the Revolutionary State* (New York: Oceana, 1972), xi, 4.

opposition to a five-hundred-year-old global order founded on white supremacy and empire make it an unlikely candidate for 'neutralism'. This was not the equidistance of the 'uncommitted Third'. These commitments took a number of different forms. By 1960, many Third World leaders saw non-alignment not as a way of abstaining from the Cold War but rather a way of waging it.[156]

4.6 Conclusion

From the post-triumphalist perspective of the present, we may tend to regard the First, Second and Third Worlds as both hierarchical designations and places on a map. But in the imaginative contestation of the second half of the twentieth century, each designation stood not for a place within one world but a project to assert another whole world. The Third World was also a juridical project as much as a geopolitical one, and – like the other two – imagined its own international law. The four rival practices of world-making we are drawing out in this book, all at play during the Cold War, had different diplomatic styles and practices attached to them. At the same time, rival styles emerged as the projects encountered each other. The Bandung conference provides just one example of the diplomatic projection of that world and the iteration of its laws; but to see that projection clearly, we need to interrupt the assumption common to three of the four rival world-making projects described in this book, that European International Law has no rivals.

Whilst the Cold War might have been a period of time in which secrecy (and its correlate, espionage) became a significant feature in the practice of diplomacy on the part of the rival powers, it was neither an entirely new formation nor the only way of conducting diplomatic relations during the period of the Cold War. But in the historiography of the post–Cold War, the projects are recast as political rather than juridical projects. The story also makes both the Global South and the former Soviet Union seem to be devoid of law. The consequence of this is that we have an impoverished retrospective understanding of Cold War diplomacy and the international legalisms that went with it. Indeed, once the period of lawful rivalries was over, the internationalist imaginaries we have described here – and others we have not – were discredited and deemed to have 'failed'. The political economy of the Cold War and the

[156] Jeffrey Byrne, *Mecca of Revolution: Algeria, Decolonization, and the Third World Order* (Oxford: Oxford University Press, 2016) 86–87.

end of empire brought debt crisis,[157] and the debt crisis brought austerity.[158] Debt conditionality radically reshaped universities in Africa and the Global South more generally.[159] The radical intellectual centres of Makerere, Dar es Salaam and others – the schools of plural worlds – are literally dismantled. Neither the Bandung spirit nor the anti-colonial world-making project die, but there is a shift in location of (elite) intellectual energy from southern States, as their children travel to the North and take up their inheritance in universities in the Global North. Here they produce diasporic internationalisms. The consequence for disciplinary scholarship is that these extraordinary attempts to remake the world after empire become 'theoretical approaches' rather than remaining concrete institutional projects. Third Worldism becomes Third World Approaches to International Law, Socialist International Law becomes 'Marxist approaches to international law'.[160] But before all that happens – or maybe while it's happening – the struggle continues for at least two decades. In Chapters 5 and 6, we reconsider particular ways in which the Third World attempted to reconfigure global politics and international law after empire and the relationship between these struggles and the Amero-Soviet Cold War. In Chapter 5, we describe three particular examples of the strategic use of international law by the Third World in the domains of war, resources and foreign corporations and what happened to them. In Chapter 6, we reconsider wholesale rival internationalisms and their expression in which new forms of national assertion, spatial re-configuration and revolutionary (socialist) struggle emerged.

[157] Michael de Groot, *Disruption: The Global Economic Shocks and the End of the Cold War* (Ithaca: Cornell University Press, 2024); Eslava, 'A Long History of Disembedding'.

[158] Eslava, 'A Long History of Disembedding'; de Groot, *Disruption*.

[159] Mahmood Mamdani, 'University Crisis and Reform: A Reflection on the African Experience' *Review of African Political Economy*, 20(58) (1993) 7–19.

[160] This is also noted in Chapter 6.

5

International Legal Experimentalism

Anti-anti-colonialism and Third World Legalities

5.1 Introduction

The story we have been telling so far has invited us to consider the 'Cold War' as a particular form of international relations imagined and projected from a certain place. In this chapter, we continue to parochialise the dominant North Atlantic version of the story by describing quite familiar forms of international law practiced by the Global South: making treaties, arguing at the International Court of Justice and establishing UN institutions. There are so many instances we could have described, but we have chosen three exemplary vignettes. Together they show that far from being a settled 'system', international law was instead a terrain of struggle between rival projects of world-making when the Cold War began. Each example highlights a particular aspect of a more general contest over how international laws should be understood, whose interests they might advance and what worlds they do and should seek to produce and reproduce. This is not the familiar story of the 'reformation' of a pre-existing international law[1] to account for 'new States' but a more radical account of the Third World's engagement and role in the creation of a general international law per se.

We begin the chapter with Algeria's war for independence. In this example, the nascent Algerian State sought to use the terms of the Geneva Conventions to mobilise support for its cause both within the

[1] Among others, see F. Northrop, 'Naturalistic and Cultural Foundations for a More Effective International Law' *Yale Law Journal*, 59 (1950) 1430–50; Daniel Patrick O'Connell, 'Recent Problems of State Succession in Relation to New States' *Recueil des Cours*, 130 (1970) 95–206; Quincy Wright, 'The Strengthening of International Law' *Recueil des Cours*, 98 (1959) 1–296; Wolfgang Friedmann, *The Changing Structures of International* Law (Calcutta: The World Press Ltd, 1960) 317–24; Richard Falk and Saul Mendlovitz, 'Some Criticisms of Wilfred Jenks' Approach to International Law' *Rutgers Law Review*, 14(1) (1959) 4–16.

United Nations and elsewhere. Its objective was to strategically 'internationalise' its armed struggle against France and thereby re-shape the legal landscape of anti-colonial struggle. For Algeria's battle was not just against the anti-anti-colonial forces in France but against the generic description of anti-colonial warfare as presumptively 'internal' to empire. In describing these practices of strategic internationalism, we want to correct both the romanticised impression of the Third World as naïve and idealistic about international law in the aftermath of Empire, and the cynical impression of it as consisting of autarkic and sovereigntist States who rejected international law in favour of a raw, or 'primitive', politics. In our story, Algeria both advances a jurisprudential counter-project (so not 'against' law) and advances its diplomatic interests strategically (so not naïvely idealistic). Describing Algerian strategic internationalism in this way also has the effect of detaching the story of national liberation from the proxification effect of the Cold War, then and now. Here was a proto-State in an existential struggle not over socialism or liberalism or capitalism or communism but over its own survival. Its adversary was an exhausted but violent European power whose high-minded (imperial) internationalism had mutated into a vindictive anti-anti-colonialism in the face of struggles for independence.[2]

Second, we describe the Anglo–Iranian Oil case at the International Court of Justice. This case exemplifies our argument that North–South relations were not defined simply by an acceptance or rejection of existing international law (and along with it, the jurisdiction of the International Court of Justice) but represented a contest over the very terms of international law and institutional authority at the moment of their creation. As in the *Corfu Channel* case and the later *South-West Africa* cases, it represented a struggle over the role and authority of judicial institutions in the burgeoning global legal order, and one that engaged the capacity and prerogative to speak the language of international law. In the process, the case challenges the post–Cold War myth-making around a lawful North/West and a lawless South/East. It also makes visible a rival imaginary about the relationship between

[2] Franz Fanon asserted that 'the Third World must start over a new history of man'. Frantz Fanon, *The Wretched of the Earth*, trans. Richard Philcox (New York: Grove Press, 2004; originally 1963) 238. Homi K. Bhabha asks in respect of this: Is this 'merely a vain hope? Does such a lofty ideal represent anything more than the lost rhetorical baggage of that daunting quest for a non-aligned postcolonial world inaugurated at the Bandung Conference in 1955. Who can claim that dream now?' Bhabha, 'Foreword: Framing Fanon' in Fanon, *The Wretched of the Earth*, ix.

public authority and corporate power that was being configured in this moment of jurisdictional flux.

Our third example is the particular dispute about public authority and corporate power that played out in the battle to establish a Commission on Transnational Corporations at the United Nations. This was a moment of North Atlantic *disunity* and of an alliance between the Third World and the Soviet Union who shared a very different idea to the US about corporate power, as well as whether rights and protections were to be subject to international or domestic jurisdiction. In this instance, US legal policy was both allied with the interests of the colonial powers and was, at the same time, part of an effort to universalise existing elements of imperial and inter-imperial law. This final example importantly illustrates the way in which particular projects flourished and/or were closed off both during the Cold War and after and offers a space in which to think about what has now become unthinkable: the global regulation of transnational corporations through a *public* international law.

When read together, these examples bring out the contrasting topographies of the Third World's engagement with international law and with the Cold War itself and the divergent range of issues and strategic standpoints adopted. To these examples could be added many other diplomatic, institutional and juridical engagements that might further diversify the account. What they have in common, however, is a resistance to the idea that there was, at the time, a settled corpus of 'universal' international law to which all were beholden. Whether one looks at human rights law, humanitarian law, the law of foreign investment or of the law of the sea, what jurists and diplomats saw in front of them was an array of (historic) materials and argumentative strategies that were capable of being put to work in the crafting of rival versions of international law and rival internationalisms. The examples here show that the Third World neither accepted the idea nor behaved as though European 'International Law' was the *only* inter-national law[3] at large in the world as the Cold War began. If this stance was manifest – and the plurality most visible – during colonial times, it also continued afterwards, through the period of decolonisation and Cold War from the late

[3] Sundhya Pahuja, 'Laws of Encounter: A Jurisdictional Account of International Law' *London Review of International Law*, 1 (2013) 63–98. Or to use Benton and Clulow's phrase, 'interpolity law'. Lauren Benton and Adam Clulow, 'Interpolity Law and Jurisdictional Politics' *Law and History Review*, 42 (2024) 197–209.

1940s onwards. Retrospective projections of the Cold War era have flattened out much of that history.

5.2 Anti-anti-colonialism, the Laws of War and the Algerian War of Independence

Many anti-colonial nationalists quickly understood that the nature of the superpower rivalry meant that internationalisation could be a useful element in the struggle for decolonisation. This strategy was not based on a naïve faith in those laws and institutions but was strategically grounded. Internationalising an anti-colonial war was useful for two reasons. First, it supported the argument that the peoples fighting back against imperial powers should be understood juridically as nations subject to hostile occupation and not 'overseas territories' subject to the metropole's law. The second reason was that it made clear the fact that the European powers needed the help of the professedly anti-colonial United States to maintain colonial rule in the face of independence movements. This strategy was available because of the 'resources of ambiguity' available in the international legal space and the public dimensions of the ideological rivalry that made powerful States vulnerable to moral argumentation in ways that have since largely been lost.

European States, on the other hand, had their own strategies of anti-internationalisation. These centred on redescribing anti-colonial struggles either as internal matters (Portugal, for example, in Angola, Mozambique and East Timor) or as the proxy machinations of the Soviet Union (the UK in Iran, France in Vietnam).[4] The enunciative 'proxification' of anti-colonial struggle was, ostensibly enough, a technique by which the colonial powers would seek support from the US by characterising the matter in question as one concerned with the containment of communism rather than the exercise of self-determination.

Since the time of Wilson, the US had been a somewhat inconsistent advocate of self-determination.[5] It had long championed the cause of dismantling European empires, but its support for self-determination

[4] On Britain's strategy of labelling Iran's Mohammed Mossadeq government as 'an emerging communist threat to Anglo-American dominance', see Andrew N. Rubin, *Archives of Authority: Empire, Culture, and the Cold War* (Princeton: Princeton University Press, 2012) 34. Sometimes this redescription took the form of producing false intelligence.

[5] Michla Pomerance, 'The United States and Self-determination: Perspectives on the Wilsonian Conception' *American Journal of International Law*, 70 (1976) 1–27.

was also frequently to fall foul of a more general fear of the contagious possibilities of communist subversion. And so, at times, the US would join the Soviet Union in its promotion of an attenuated form of self-determination (even to the point of partitioning States – East and West Germany, North and South Korea). At other times, it would actively oppose it (in Cuba or Vietnam). For the anti-colonial movements themselves – who could nearly always count on the support of the Soviet Union – the posture of the US was not necessarily determinative. Indeed, in time of détente, the prospective gains from the absence of US opposition were often counterweighed by the more muted support of the Soviet Union and by the foreclosure of the horizons of difference within which the struggle might be located.[6] At other moments, by contrast, and the case of Algeria is exemplary, the liberation movement was able to exploit the space between the various powers to promote its strategy of inter nationalisation.[7] The legacies of this strategy, and this war, are to be found in the text of the *UN Declaration on the Granting of Independence to Colonial Countries and Peoples*[8] and the First Additional Protocol to the 1949 Geneva Conventions (1977).

The Algerian war began in 1954,[9] the same year as the decisive Viet Minh victory over the French in Dien Bien Phu. It was not the first war of national liberation after 1945 (see, for example, the Mayalan Emergency of 1948–60, the Mau Mau rebellion of 1952–60 and the Indonesian national revolution of 1945–49),[10] but it can be read as presaging the

[6] See Jeremy Suri, *Power and Protest: Global Revolution and the Rise of Détente* (Cambridge, MA: Harvard University Press, 2003); Matthew Connelly, *A Diplomatic Revolution: Algeria's Fight for Independence and the Origins of the Post-Cold War Era* (Oxford: Oxford University Press, 2002).

[7] See Nathaniel Berman, 'In the Wake of Empire' *American University International Law Review*, 14 (1998–99) 1521, 1535.

[8] UNGA Res 1514 (XV) (14 December 1960).

[9] The French conquest of Algeria began in the year 1830. See James McDougall, *A History of Algeria* (Cambridge: Cambridge University Press, 2017); Gary Wilder, *Freedom Time: Negritude, Decolonization, and the Future of the World* (Durham: Duke University Press, 2015); Jennifer E. Sessions, *By Sword and Plow: France and the Conquest of Algeria* (Ithaca: Cornell University Press, 2015); Martin Evans, *Algeria: France's Undeclared War* (New York: Oxford University Press, 2012); Todd Shepard, *The Invention of Decolonization: The Algerian War and the Remaking of France* (Ithaca: Cornell University Press, 2006); Connelly, *A Diplomatic Revolution*; Terrence G. Peterson, *Revolutionary Warfare: How the Algerian War Made Modern Counterinsurgency* (Ithaca: Cornell University Press, 2024).

[10] David Van Reybrouck, *Revolusi: Indonesia and the Birth of the Modern World* (London: Bodley Head, 2025).

break-up of the French empire.[11] And, for France at least, Algeria was part of France, a case distinct from the the position of its other 'saltwater colonies'. The war began with a series of coordinated attacks organised in the Constantine and Aurès regions of northern Algeria by the newly formed Front de Libération Nationale (FLN). In response, France dropped leaflets from the air throughout that region, which read as follows:

> Agitators, among the strangers, have brought bloody strife to our country and have, in particular, established themselves in your area. They have been followed by the misguided few whose notion is to start a civil war.
>
> Moslems: you will not follow them but will assemble immediately and not later than November 21 at 6pm in the security zones with your families and goods . . .. Those of you who have enlisted without thinking, if you have no crime on your conscience, proceed immediately to the security zones with your arms and no harm will come to you.
>
> Soon a terrifying calamity will overtake the rebels, after which French peace will reign again.[12]

Apart from the latent symbolism of its medium of delivery, the message itself bought into sharp focus the French government's attitude and intentions in relation to the 'bloody strife' with which it was engaged. In contrast to the anti-colonial rallying cries of the FLN, the attacks were presented by the French government as a 'civil disturbance' taking place on French soil ('our country').[13] It implicitly invoked the fact that according to the French Constitution, Algeria was an integral 'department' within the Fourth Republic, a historic home to the wartime French Committee of National Liberation and some 1 million immigrant *Français d'Algérie* ('*pieds-noirs*'). Even whilst describing it as constitutionally 'internal', the French State also cast the conflict in racial and religious, even civilisational, terms. Despite a series of reforms made in

[11] Talks with Tunisia and Morocco were given impetus during this time. Sylvie Thénault, 'The End of Empire in the Maghreb: The Common Heritage and Distinct Destinies of Morocco, Algeria, and Tunisia' in Martin Thomas and Andrew S Thompson (eds.), *The Oxford Handbook of the Ends of Empire* (Oxford: Oxford University Press, 2018) 299–316.

[12] Quoted in Arnold Fraleigh, 'The Algerian War of Independence' *Proceedings of the American Society of International Law at Its Annual Meeting*, 61 (1967) 7.

[13] Evans notes, nevertheless, that 'in legal terms this remained an undeclared war because Algeria was an integral part of France. France was not fighting a separate nation-state but preserving internal sovereignty and on these grounds the word war was banned from the official lexicon.' Evans, *Algeria*, 118.

the inter-war years (including the abolition of the infamous *code d'indigénant*),[14] French law and administration in Algeria continued to differentiate systematically between French citizens and native subjects. Here, that same differentiation was deployed to mark those who were suspected of involvement in agitation and those who were not. It was to 'Muslims' that the address was made, not to the French-speaking, predominantly Catholic, immigrant community. The government's response, then, was both to criminalise and suppress – no quarter would be afforded to 'combatants' (who would be both cast as 'terrorists'[15] and subject to the full weight of the criminal law), and the 'suspect' native population was to become the object of quarantine and pacification. Nevertheless, the predicted 'terrifying calamity' foreshadowed the French government's decision to proclaim a state of emergency[16] and subdue the uprising by use of military force.

Immediately, then, an open paradox in the French government's response became apparent: whilst Algeria was held in French law to be part of France, the majority of the Algerian population was also held either to be engaged in outright conflict with it, or under suspicion of nurturing such conflict. And whilst the acts of resistant violence were held to be crimes, and subject to suppression by the police, it was to the French armed forces that the government turned in response. It was in the gaps that opened out, here, between the French State and its bifurcated society – an Algeria of French citizens and of Muslim colonial subjects – and between a policing action and open warfare between military forces, that the analytical space for the development of a strategy of anti-colonial resistance, in which international law and institutions were to prove central, would emerge. This strategy would ultimately shape the contours of the theory and practice of decolonisation not just in Algeria, but more generally, and would provide the active template not only for the development of the right of self-determination within the United Nations but also for the creative re-description of anti-colonial warfare in the Additional Protocols of 1977.[17]

[14] See Fabian Klose, *Human Rights in the Shadow of Colonial Violence: The Wars of Independence in Kenya and Algeria* (Philadelphia: University of Pennsylvania Press, 2013) 23.

[15] Klose, *Human Rights in the Shadow of Colonial Violence*, 124–25.

[16] Law no 55-385 of 3 April 1955. Emergency legislation was adopted on 3 April 1955 authorising the army to take action against the FLN.

[17] Protocol Additional to the Geneva Conventions of 12 August 1949 and Relating to the Protection of Victims of International Armed Conflicts (Protocol I), Geneva, 8 June 1977,

From almost the first moment, the FLN looked to the UN Charter in framing its anti-colonial liberation struggle. It did not seek a pan-Arab confederation, nor a return to the complex political geographies of the pre-colonial political era.[18] Still less did it seek to align itself with the kind of liberation offered by the Soviet Union. What was being sought was both independence from France and the creation of a free and independent State of Algeria.[19] To achieve that end, however, two things were required – one was a State-like infrastructure within the territory (and particularly a government capable of speaking in the name of the Algerian people), the second was international recognition by other States and ultimately the admission of Algeria to the United Nations.[20]

If the formation of the FLN and the pursuit of armed struggle through the medium of its Armée de Liberation Nationale (ALN) provided a hesitant pathway for the first,[21] the second was somewhat more challenging. Because of the claim by the French government that Algeria was constitutionally part of France, any third State choosing to recognise the independence of Algeria would face the charge that it had engaged in an illegitimate act of intervention and had threatened the territorial integrity of France. For all the parallels with the situation in Indochina, both in timing and symbolic effect, this was no far-flung colony that the French government was seeking to 're-colonise' but a territory some 400 miles from mainland France that formed not just part of France

1125 UNTS 3; Protocol Additional to the Geneva Conventions of 12 August 1949, and Relating to the Protection of Victims of Non-International Armed Conflicts (Protocol II), Geneva, 8 June 1977, 1125 UNTS 609.

18 Even though, for rhetorical purposes, the re-establishment of the *dawla* had long been a dream of generations of Algerian nationalists. Bedjaoui was to argue that Algeria had been a sovereign State in 1930 and that the French Royal Ordinance of July 1834 purporting to annex Algeria was invalid. Mohammed Bedjaoui, *Law and the Algerian Revolution* (Brussels: International Association of Democratic Lawyers, 1961) 17–37.

19 This was made explicit in the Declaration of the FLN issued on 1 November 1954. See Evans, *Algeria*, 116.

20 This was the central objective of the FLNs plan to 'internationalise' the struggle. See generally Martin Thomas 'France Accused: French North Africa before the United Nations, 1952–62' *Contemporary European History*, 10 (2001) 91; Connelly, *A Diplomatic Revolution*; Boyd van Dijk, *Preparing for War: The Making of the 1949 Geneva Conventions* (Oxford: Oxford University Press, 2022); Evans, *Algeria*.

21 For an account of the various factions and struggles within the FLN and its relationship to other independence movements, see Evans, *Algeria*.

constitutionally but part of the spatial ambit of NATO[22] and (after 1957) of the European Economic Community.[23]

In any case, the resources provided by the UN Charter to the Algerian anti-colonialists were profoundly ambiguous. Algeria could plausibly invoke the principle of self-determination in articles 55 and 56 of the Charter and could also claim to be a 'non-self-governing territory' entitled to benefit from the principle of 'self-government' (article 73), but on neither score was the case for independence an indisputable one. Not only was it unclear whether self-determination was something that gave rise to a right of independence on the part of colonial peoples (as opposed to merely some measure of self-government),[24] but the position of territories administered as an integral part of the mother country was even more uncertain.[25] France had signally refused even to recognise Algeria as a non-self-governing territory (in sharp contrast to its position in relation to Tunisia, Morocco, Indochina and French equatorial Africa).[26] In so doing, it claimed that the decision about whether a territory was, or was not, non-self-governing for the purposes of article 73 was a matter of 'national competence'[27] and, in accordance with the terms of article 2(7) of the Charter, was not something that could be examined or questioned within the United Nations.

But in truth, the French claims about international law were no more 'obvious' than those being made by the FLN. If article 2(7) did purport to protect the domestic jurisdiction of States, it was already well-established that the determination of what was, or was not, purely 'domestic' was not a matter of pure self-judgment and depended upon the terms of any relevant international law.[28] What's more, the General Assembly possessed the competence, under Article 10, to discuss and make recommendations on any matter within the scope of the Charter (which included, presumably, the promotion of self-determination under articles

[22] The transfer of NATO troops from Europe to Algeria was justified on grounds that France was facing a proxy war sponsored by the Soviets. Evans, *Algeria*, 160

[23] This is linked to the development of the idea of 'Eurafrica' in 1957 – integrating Algeria into the EEC with France as the pivot between Europe and Africa. Evans, *Algeria*, 194–95.

[24] Josef L. Kunz,'Chapter XI of the United Nations Charter in Action' *American Journal of International Law*, 48 (1954) 105.

[25] Alf Ross, *Constitution of the United Nations: Analysis of Structure and Function* (New York: Rinehart, 1950) 180.

[26] See UNGA Res 66(I) (14 December 1946).

[27] UN Doc. A/74.

[28] *Nationality Decrees Issued in Tunis and Morocco (French Zone) on November 8th, 1921* (Advisory Opinion) (7 February 1923) PCIJ (ser. B) No. 4.

55 and 56). So, the existence of article 2(7) did not automatically preclude the UNGA from considering Algerian matters nor prevent it from exercising its interpretive powers to extend the principle of self-determination to all colonial territories. Whether metropolitan powers were entitled to decide themselves which territories were, or were not, non-self-governing was an undoubtedly contestable assumption given the principle of international accountability that underpins Chapter XI[29] and the reality of widespread anti-colonial struggle. What was brought into play, therefore, were rival accounts of the vision of peace and order provided within the terms of the Charter and rival accounts as to how best to make sense of its interpretive ambiguities.[30]

As Connelly explains, the Algerian strategy, as it was to develop, largely hinged upon three axes of internationalisation.[31] The first was to secure within the United Nations recognition of its right to self-determination. This depended upon the willingness of friendly governments within the UN to sponsor its struggle and of UN organs to interpret Charter provisions constructively in its favour. Secondly, and from 1958 onwards, the newly formed Provisional Government of the Algerian Republic (GPRA) sought to gain recognition by friendly powers in order to sustain the claim that it already enjoyed a right to independence and self-determination and to short-circuit the idea that this right might be granted to it by the French State only after negotiations. The third strategy, and in a sense an intermediary one, was to seek recognition of its status as a belligerent authority, invoking the terms of the recently adopted Geneva Conventions (1949) in order to advance the argument that the revolution was not a conflict internal to France but an international struggle between a colonising power, on the one hand, and, on the other, a people (like the French themselves only ten years earlier) engaged in a war for their own liberation. Belligerent recognition would also have the added benefit of legitimising the assistance provided to the ALN by its North African neighbours (Tunisia, Egypt and Morocco) without which it had little hope of making much military headway.

The first of these objectives was achieved in October 1955. In face of opposition from a coalition of Western powers (Belgium, the

[29] See, for example, Leland M. Goodrich and Edvard Hambro, *Charter of the United Nations: Commentary and Documents* (Boston: World Peace Foundation, 1948) 11.

[30] See James Crawford, *The Creation of States in International Law*, 1st ed. (Oxford: Clarendon Press, 1979) 359.

[31] Connelly, *A Diplomatic Revolution*, 237–38.

Netherlands, US, UK and Norway) who disputed the General Assembly's competence to consider the question of Algeria given the terms of article 2(7), fourteen Afro-Asian States, buoyed by the support given the Algerian cause at the Bandung Conference in April, managed to convince the Assembly, by the narrowest of margins (28:27, 5ab) to inscribe the Algerian question onto its agenda for the first time. The conflict had initially been brought to the attention of the Security Council by Saudi Arabia in January 1955, but in the face of the French argument that the matter fell within its domestic jurisdiction, the Saudis were unable to secure agreement for it to be placed on the Council's agenda. In contrast, by the time the matter was bought before the General Assembly in October of the same year, twenty-four Afro-Asian States had already publicly declared their support for the right of the people of Algeria to 'self-determination and independence' at the Bandung Conference, and these States worked together to put pressure upon the General Assembly to place Algeria on its agenda for discussion.

The French reaction was twofold. On the one hand, and in the immediate aftermath of the vote, the French Foreign Minister, M. Pinay, declared that France would consider as 'null and void' any recommendation made by the Assembly in connection with Algeria and immediately departed the Assembly Hall together with his delegation thereby initiating a momentary 'boycott' of the General Assembly. On the other hand, however, France moved rapidly to begin independence negotiations with both Tunisia and Morocco in order to head off accusations that it was dragging its feet on the question of decolonisation. These French initiatives meant that further debate on the Algeria situation was foreclosed and the matter was taken off the agenda.[32]

Over the following few years, the FLN campaigned to internationalise the conflict within the United Nations with France holding firm to the idea of an *Algérie Française*. Whilst each could rely upon support from certain quarters (Germany, Britain and several Francophone African countries in the case of France; and Tunisia, Morocco and Egypt in the case of Algeria), the two Cold War powers themselves remained equivocal – neither wanting to associate themselves with a colonial power, nor keen to entirely alienate France.[33] While the Soviet Union supported the FLN in votes within the United Nations, it held off recognising the Provisional Government (GPRA) until 1960 after the abortive conference

[32] UNGA Res 909(X) (25 November 1955).
[33] Connelly, *A Diplomatic Revolution*, 230.

on Berlin had exposed East–West divisions once more. The FLN/GPRA, for its part, sought to exploit potential divisions both within and between the Eastern and Western blocs, threatening both France's Western allies and the Soviet Union with the possibility of seeking Chinese support for its independence movement, whilst encouraging the US to distance itself from France.

In September 1958, the FLN took matters into its own hands and announced the formation of the GPRA with Ferhat Abbas as president. Morocco and Tunisia immediately extended their diplomatic recognition, and they were joined by all the other Arab States (with the exception of Lebanon), as well as by China (PRC), North Vietnam, North Korea and Indonesia.[34] Such recognition, of course, did not reflect matters on the ground, coming, as it did, merely one year after the 'battle of Algiers', but it did signal the growing strength of international support for the Algerian cause. Its effect, as Connelly suggests, was to constitute the GPRA 'like a state turned inside out'.[35]

Over the next several years, various attempts were made to bring the matter before both the Assembly and the Council. In each instance, the bodies were divided between a cohort of Western States that supported the French contention that the matter was essentially a domestic one governed by the terms of article 2(7) and an uneasy alliance of Afro-Asian, Latin American and Soviet States that argued that it was a matter of international concern and of legitimate interest to the United Nations. In the ensuing debates, the general contours of the legal battleground were to emerge. On one side was the argument that the core principle of domestic jurisdiction was in no way modified by the Charter's reference to self-determination. As the delegate of the UK argued, since no legal right of self-determination existed in the wording of the Charter 'or in the spirit . . . or circumstances in which the Charter came to be signed', there was no basis on which to disregard the 'fundamental' provisions of article 2(7).[36] This was bolstered by the argument that the Algerian situation was fundamentally different from that of other non-self-governing territories because of its deep connections to metropolitan France.[37] Here, France was to exploit the famous 'Belgian

[34] Ibid., 232.
[35] Ibid.
[36] 2 UN Review (1955) 65, 66.
[37] Article 74 of the UN Charter itself made a distinction between the 'territories to which this Chapter applies' and 'metropolitan areas'.

thesis'[38] that sought to render the problem of self-determination intractable by associating it with every racial or national 'minority' across the globe. France built on this thesis by arguing that if the UN were to intervene whenever a racial, religious or linguistic minority existed within a State, it would 'end the security of the many and the independence of the weakest'.[39]

On the other side, the arguments ranged from accepting France's claim that Algeria was part of French territory but insisting that discussion and debate did not constitute 'intervention' in the sense of article 2(7)[40] to rejecting outright French claims to sovereignty over Algerian territory.[41] In between these two poles were those who supported the right of the Algerian people to determine their own political future in line with the principle of self-determination and saw the struggle to be emblematic of a wider battle that needed to be fought against those colonial powers determined to hold on to their possessions. Spain and Portugal, for instance, had similarly declined to accept the separate status of their colonial holdings and continued to resist involvement by the General Assembly in overseeing the implementation of the obligations found in Chapter XI relating to non-self-governing territories. The case of Algeria was something of a test case in that respect, and particularly for other instances such as that of Angola, Mozambique and Spanish Sahara, in which colonial powers continued to repudiate both decolonisation and UN involvement in their 'colonial affairs'.

In 1957, the Assembly adopted a muted resolution expressing its hope that 'in a spirit of co-operation, a peaceful, democratic and just solution' would be found.[42] A similar resolution was adopted in the following year, in which it took note of the offer of good offices made by Morocco and Tunisia and expressed its wish that '*pourparlers* will be entered into ... with a view to a solution, in conformity with the purposes and principles of the Charter of the United nations'.[43] And yet change could

[38] Memorandum of the Belgian Government Relative to Non-Self-Governing Territories, in Replies of Governments Indicating their Views on the Factors to be Taken into Account in Deciding whether a Territory is or is not a Territory whose People have not yet attained a Full Measure of Self-Government, Ad Hoc Committee on Factors, 8 May 1953, UN Doc. A/AC.67/2 and Corr 1 and 2, 3 and 23.

[39] 2 UN Review (1955) 65.

[40] Ibid., 65, 66.

[41] Ibid.

[42] UNGA Res 1012 (XI) (15 February 1957).

[43] UNGA Res 1184 (XII) (10 December 1957).

incrementally be observed through the voting patterns within the UN[44] as support for France began to wane in the aftermath of the Suez crisis and following its abortive attempts to derail the process of independence in Guinea. On 16 September 1959, the newly installed de Gaulle delivered a speech promising the Algerian people 'a free choice' over their political future 'at the latest four years after the actual restoration of peace'.[45] He made clear, nevertheless, that if 'secession' was chosen, such a choice would be accompanied by partition in which Saharan oil reserves would remain in French hands as part of a Saharan enclave.[46] He laid three choices before the Algerian people – secession, 'francisation' or federation within a Franco-African community.[47] Despite the limited repertoire of freedom on offer, once the proposal for a referendum was announced (albeit with the proviso that it would only happen sometime after 'pacification'),[48] any further objection to the application of the principle of self-determination to the Algerian situation seemed to fall away. In the following year, the General Assembly recognised the right of the Algerian people to 'self-determination and independence', calling for 'adequate and effective guarantees to ensure the successful and just implementation of the right to self-determination on the basis of respect for the unity and territorial integrity of Algeria' and recognising also the legitimate role of the United Nations itself in that process.[49]

In many respects, that resolution, 1573(XV) of 1960, represented the culmination of a successful diplomatic campaign – and strategy of inter nationalisation – waged by Algeria, one that exploited divisions both within and between the Cold War blocs, enabling the FLN/GPRA to marginalise France in its attempts to keep the matter off the UN agenda. In the process, France was abandoned by some of its closest supporters (including both the US and Britain) and became exposed to the criticisms of an increasingly determined Soviet and Afro-Asian bloc keen to bring

44 See Mohamed Alwan, *Algeria before the United Nations* (New York: Robert Speller & Sons, 1959) 67.

45 Evans, *Algeria*, 261–62.

46 Ibid., 263.

47 See Elizabeth Schmidt, *Cold War and Decolonization in Guinea, 1946–1958* (Athens: Ohio University Press, 2007) 168–77.

48 General de Gaulle's Statement on Algeria (16 September 1959).

49 UNGA Res 1573 (XV) (19 December 1960). In 1960, whilst the GPRA's efforts to secure a favourable resolution were to fail by only a single vote, by a majority of 63:8, the General Assembly demanded guarantees for self-determination for the whole of Algeria, insisting also on a role for the UN.

decolonisation to the forefront of UN activities. But the campaign also left its marks on the international legal terrain, which was both the subject of, and the field within which, that diplomacy took place. And it was of no small consequence that the Algerian resolution was adopted within days of the, soon to be famous, 'colonial declaration' – Resolution 1514(XV) – the terms of which were, without doubt, significantly informed by the preceding debates over the situation in Algeria.

5.2.1 *The Colonial Declaration of 1960*

Almost every paragraph of the Colonial Declaration spoke to events in Algeria.[50] The Declaration expressed a desire to re-shape the juridico-political landscape within which both colonialism and self-determination were to be conceived within the United Nations. And if many of the colonial powers – including both Britain and France – had acceded to the idea that the principles of trusteeship found in Chapters XI and XII of the Charter imposed upon them an obligation to advance their colonial possessions towards independence at some appropriate stage in the future, the declaration sought not only to dispose of the conditional character of that commitment but to re-cast it entirely.

Its first, and ultimately defining paragraph, was to condemn colonialism[51] as 'a denial of fundamental human rights ... [as] contrary to the Charter of the United Nations and ... [and as] an impediment to the promotion of world peace and co-operation'. This declaratory condemnation of colonialism 'in all its manifestations' was to have the effect of ascribing to all colonial peoples a subjectivity that was otherwise unavailable to them in the prevailing language of Trusteeship. In political terms, the declaration adhered to a sociology that understood the onwards march of decolonisation to be both inevitable and a product, not of the benevolent concessions of the colonial powers but of the radical agency of the colonial peoples themselves. Independence, in other words, was not something granted but seized. The peoples of the world, it declared, had a 'yearning for freedom' that could not be stymied.

[50] The Algerian conflict was specifically raised as an issue by various delegations in the General Assembly including Quaison-Sackey (Ghana). UNGA A/PV/927 (29 November 1960) 1011, [55]–[56].

[51] UNGA Declaration on the Granting of Independence to Colonial Countries and Peoples. UNGA Res 1514(XV) (12 December 1960) (It described colonialism as 'the subjection of peoples to alien subjugation, domination and exploitation').

The immediate effect of the declaration, thus, was to put paid to French claims that matters Algerian were essentially internal and beyond the formal competence of the United Nations. Not only was self-determination stated to be an essential pre-requisite for the enjoyment of all human rights and fundamental freedoms (in line with the earlier decision to include an article on self-determination in the draft UN Covenant on Human Rights), but its ongoing denial was held out to be a threat to international peace and security. It was not just that, in many cases, claims to independence had been accompanied by anti-colonial violence – as was evident in Vietnam, Indonesia, Kenya and Algeria – but that such violence was integral to the maintenance of the colonial system itself. The problem, as the representative of Ghana observed, was not that the Algerian people sought their independence, or felt the necessity of doing so by resort to arms, but that the French government had decided to 'intervene' militarily to suppress that natural urge.

If the colonial declaration was to identify the end of colonial rule as the main focus of the self-determination agenda, the influence of the Algerian conflict was felt in the way the declaration both avoided confining the incidence of colonial rule to trust territories, or territories described as non-self-governing, and associated the ensuing conflicts with its attempted suppression. As the declaration went on to point out (with South Africa and Palestine in the background), self-determination was particularly relevant in the context of regimes of Apartheid and racial discrimination. So, rather than being restricted to territories described as 'non-self-governing' as the French had maintained, it was a right that also applied 'to all other territories which have not yet attained independence'. But if, in scope, the colonial declaration sought to circumvent the kinds of arguments that had been put forward by France to deny the Algerian people themselves a right of self-determination, the content of the right was even more evocative. Independence was 'nowhere to be delayed', 'all armed action and repressive measures directed against dependent peoples [were to] cease', and all powers were to be transferred 'to the peoples of those territories, without any conditions or reservations'. Aside from implicitly condemning the French military efforts to suppress the revolution, it also pointed towards the terms under which independence should be conceded – no *pourparlers* (talks) were necessary, no conditional negotiation or compromise required. In this respect it was, perhaps, starker than the even GPRA itself might have hoped.

One final clause, however, stood out. In paragraph 6, the General Assembly proclaimed that 'any attempt at the partial or total disruption of the national unity and the territorial integrity of a country is incompatible with the purposes and principles of the Charter of the United Nations'. Whilst the genesis of this clause was to be found in a Guatemalan proposal, for most delegates the prime example was that of Algeria. For it was the disquiet that had been fomented by de Gaulle's intimation that Algeria might be partitioned – with an oil rich Saharan Algeria remaining in French hands and an impoverished coastal Algeria becoming independent – that provided the key impetus for the text, bringing together the demand for political independence with a concern to ensure that it did not come at a cost of economic subjugation.

In truth though, it was a clause liable to be read in a number of different ways. Many saw it as an attempt to forestall secessionist enterprises and curtail the application of self-determination beyond the confines of colonial rule.[52] Here the case of Katanga was fresh in everyone's mind. But the paragraph's Algerian roots, traceable in the language of 'countries' rather than 'States', lends it a very different meaning. Here, it performed the function of severing the legal identity of colonial territories from that of the metropole, vesting the former with rights normally only associated with States – territorial integrity and national unity – and paving the way, indeed, not just for recognition for a people's 'permanent sovereignty over natural resources'[53] but for anti-colonial struggles everywhere to be conceived as having an essentially international character. On this ground, wars of national liberation could be represented as struggles of self-defence aimed against an external aggressor in the name of a national liberation that has already been given an independent legal identity. Henceforth, there was simply no room for treating colonial dependencies as part of the metropole, for imagining conflicts within them to be policing actions or for bartering away 'valuable' territory in the interests of a vested colonial elite. International law, at this moment, was being decisively (re)shaped.

5.2.2 *The Laws of War*

If the Algerian conflict and the strategy of internationalisation adopted by its proponents transformed international laws on colonialism and self-determination, the strategy of internationalisation also reshaped the laws of war. In the background of the conflict were the rules of humanitarian

[52] UNGA Doc. A/PV/947 (14 December 1960).
[53] UNGA Res 1803 (XVII) (14 December 1962).

law that had been adopted in Geneva in 1949. One of the most striking features of the new Conventions was the inclusion of (Common) Article 3, which provided a (minimal) set of guarantees for those involved in warfare of a 'non-international character'. Drafted at a time in which many of the colonial powers were actively involved in counter-insurgency warfare in their various colonies (France in Indochina, Britain in Malaya, the Netherlands in Indonesia), and in which the US had become embroiled in suppressing communist rebels in the Greek civil war, its adoption was regarded as something of a diplomatic triumph, not least for the Soviet Union whose voice had been influential throughout the negotiations.[54] This was particularly so given the opposition from a number of Western powers to the prospect of effectively 'internationalising' colonial warfare. In broad terms, the Western bloc maintained that colonial warfare was a purely internal matter in which the government concerned was entitled to employ all necessary means to suppress revolt through the exercise of emergency powers and the application of its criminal laws. And it was only after concerted pressure on the part of a coalition of Afro-Asian, Latin American and Soviet States (with active support from the ICRC itself) that a French compromise proposal to incorporate a minimum humanitarian guarantee in case of 'armed conflict not of an international character' came to be accepted.

But as much as the text of Common Article 3 seemed to put to bed the idea that colonial counter-insurgency operations fell outside the framework of the Geneva Conventions, the formulation chosen merely shifted the terrain of debate from the identity of the combatants themselves (which was key to describing conflict as either internal/civil or international) to the existence or otherwise of an armed conflict. Mere 'riots' and 'sporadic acts of violence' were not to be governed by the guarantees in article 3, only those that rose to the threshold of an 'armed conflict' the determination of which lay in the hands of those involved (even if the ICRC claimed for itself the right to offer an independent view). Article 3 also did not address a key point of contestation between Algeria and France – namely, the applicability or otherwise of French criminal law.

[54] See generally, Boyd van Dijk, '"The Great Humanitarian": The Soviet Union, the International Committee of the Red Cross, and the Geneva Conventions of 1949', *Law and History Review*, 37 (2019) 209–35; Giovanni Mantilla, 'Frum Isolation: Social Opprobrium and the Origins of the International Law of Internal Conflict' *International Organization*, 72 (2018) 317–49; Fabian Klose, 'The Colonial Testing Ground: The International Committee of the Red Cross and the Violent End of Empire' *Humanity*, 2 (2011) 107–26.

For all its humanitarian promises, insurgents still remained liable to prosecution (and, in all probability, execution) for their participation in hostilities. This meant that from the Algerian perspective, the application of French criminal law was merely one more technique of warfare. As Perret and Bugnion put it: 'The insurgents, who no longer recognise the jurisdiction of the courts or the legal system of the State against which they are fighting, will consider each conviction in the courts as a new injustice and every execution as an assassination.'[55]

Despite its reliance upon military forces to quash the insurgency, the French government initially denied the existence of an armed conflict, claiming instead that it was simply dealing – by use of police resources and the application of the criminal law – with certain 'événements'.[56] The postulated divide between the national and international was thus recalibrated through the medium of a power of sociological description the effect of which was to ensure that the policing prerogative remained *outside* international law in relation to the colonised. And in that sense, it recalled the operations of the nineteenth-century 'standard of civilisation' that had accompanied the establishment of colonial rule in the first place.[57] In that context, as Abi-Saab puts it:

> the relations between what had become the 'centre' of the world and its 'periphery', which were formerly recognized in diplomatic and treaty practice as being of an international character, were *internalized*, in the sense of being taken out of the ambit of international law, as a prelude to direct domination.[58]

The result of this, as Lorimer had asserted in 1883, was 'the conquest of Algeria by France was not ... [to be considered] a violation of international law. It was an act of discipline which the bystander was entitled to exercise in the absence of police.'[59]

55 François Perret and François Bugnion, 'Between Insurgents and Government: The International Committee of the Red Cross's Action in the Algerian War (1954–1962)' *International Review of the Red Cross*, 93 (2011) 717.

56 Klose, 'The Colonial Testing Ground', 110.

57 Antony Anghie, *Imperialism. Sovereignty and the Making of International Law* (Cambridge: Cambridge University Press, 2005); Siba Grovogui, *Sovereigns, Quasi-Sovereigns, and Africans: Race and Self-Determination in International Law* (Minneapolis: University of Minnesota Press, 1996).

58 Georges Abi-Saab, 'Wars of National Liberation in the Geneva Conventions and Protocols' *Recueil des cours*, 165 (1979) 367.

59 James Lorimer, *The Institutes of the Law of Nations: A Treatise of the Jural Relations of Separate Political Communities* (Edinburgh and London: William Blackwood and Sons,

In the event, it took eighteen months and the extension of the conflict across Algeria before the French government would admit to the existence of a non-international armed conflict to which Common Article 3 applied.[60] In face of mounting pressure, both domestically and internationally, the French Prime Minister Guy Mollet finally recognised the applicability of Common Article 3 to the Algerian situation on 23 June 1956. On 19 March 1958, General Salan, commander-in-chief of French forces in Algeria, ordered the creation of special camps for ALN fighters who were captured whilst bearing arms openly. Although the circular stated that they should not be treated as POWs, there was tacit admission that such a regime would be applied in practice.[61] This was informed less by any humanitarian concern than by the fear of radicalising the opposition. But it did echo an ICRC memorandum of 28 May 1958 in which it was asserted that Common Article 3 should apply and that those members of armed forces who were captured should not be prosecuted 'for the mere fact of having participated in the conflict'.[62]

Having obtained recognition from France that the conflict should be governed *de minimis* by the terms of Common Article 3 of the Geneva Conventions, the GPRA was to raise the stakes even higher in its quest to use the laws of war as a way to cement its claim to independent statehood. On 23 February 1956, the Algerian delegation in Cairo sent a letter to the International Committee of the Red Cross (ICRC), signed by both Mohamed Khider of the FLN and Ahmed Ben Bella of the ALN. The letter indicated their willingness to implement the provisions of the Geneva Conventions concerning all French prisoners of war taken by the ALN, 'subject to reciprocity on the part of the Government of the French Republic'.[63] They also sought recognition from the ICRC of the Algerian Red Crescent. In 1958, the ICRC was allowed access to prisoners held by the ALN in an effort to demonstrate its willingness to abide by the terms of the Geneva Conventions and in order to demand the same from the

1883) 161, quoted in Ram Prakash Anand, 'The Formation of International Organizations and India: A Historical Study' *Leiden Journal of International Law*, 23 (2010) 6.

60 Perret and Bugnion, 'Between Insurgents and Government'.

61 Ibid., 720.

62 Ibid., 741–72 (appendix 4).

63 ICRC Archives, B AG 200 (12), Letter from the Algerian Delegation in Cairo to David de Traz, 23 February 1956, in Perret and Bugnion, 'Between Insurgents and Government', 716.

French.[64] Further, on 11 April 1960, Ferhat Abbas officially signed the GPRA's instruments of accession to the Geneva Conventions of 12 August 1949,[65] which were communicated to the Swiss Federal Council on 20 June in the same year. As was subsequently to become clear, the rationale for this move rested on the proposition that Algeria was already a sovereign State (having been one in 1830 prior to its unlawful annexation by France in 1834) and that the ALN itself was, if not a 'regular, national and belligerent army in law' (as Bedjaoui maintained),[66] then an 'organised resistance movement' constituted in accordance with the terms of article 4 of the Third Geneva Convention.[67] This, indeed, was the basis on which the GPRA justified its accession in its *White Paper on the Application of the Geneva Conventions of 1949 to the French-Algerian Conflict* of 1960.

But if doubts persisted about the extent to which the GPRA/ALN was either willing or capable of comporting itself entirely in accordance with the Geneva Conventions (given, on the one hand, its resort to guerrilla warfare, and, on the other, its limited capacity to accord prisoner of war treatment to its captives),[68] the main formal obstacle was the extent to which the Geneva Conventions were premised upon the High Contracting Parties being 'States'.[69] This was also the main cause for accession. So in seeking adhesion to the Conventions, the GPRA not only sought to draw attention to the catalogue of abuses that had attended the French counter-insurgency initiatives – and, as Kinsella argues, to appropriate and invert the discourse of 'civilised warfare' to its own ends[70] – but also to establish, by way of its application to accede, the very right to do so.[71]

64 Perret and Bugnion, 'Between Insurgents and Government', 725.
65 Eldon Greenberg, 'Law and the Conduct of the Algerian Revolution' *Harvard International Law Journal*, 11 (1970) 37, 64; Perret and Bugnion, 'Between Insurgents and Government', 729.
66 Bedjaoui, *Law and the Algerian Revolution*, 53.
67 See Greenberg, 'Law and the Conduct of the Algerian Revolution', 42–43.
68 Ibid., 60.
69 International Committee of the Red Cross, *Convention (I) for the Amelioration of the Condition of the Wounded and Sick in Armed Forces in the Field, Geneva, 12 August 1949: Commentary of 1952* (Geneva: International Committee of the Red Cross, 1952); Commentary to Article 1: Respect for the Convention.
70 Helen M. Kinsella, *The Image before the Weapon: A Critical History of the Distinction between Combatant and Civilian* (Ithaca and London: Cornell University Press, 2011) 19.
71 Raphaëlle Branche, 'The French Army and the Geneva Conventions during the Algerian War of Independence and After' in Matthew Evangelista and Nina Tannenwald (eds.), *Do the Geneva Conventions Matter?* (New York: Oxford University Press, 2017) 161–73.

The Swiss Federal Council, acting as depositary to the Geneva Conventions, proceeded to declare in a public note of 20 July that the GPRA could not use its adhesion to the Conventions as indication that it was a State, and that for States that had not recognised Algeria, adhesion was 'without juridical relevance' (sans portée juridique).[72] This much was, perhaps, only to be expected, although by the expiry of the six-month accession period, only France and Switzerland amongst the other High Contracting Parties had issued formal reservations. As a result, even two years before its independence, Algeria had managed to obtain widespread recognition, as a national liberation movement, of its right to be regarded as party to the Geneva Conventions and in the same measure assume some of the prerogatives of an independent State. On one account, this may be attributed to its apparent willingness to embrace the humanitarian ethos that pervaded the Conventions and prove itself, as Kinsella argues, 'competent, rational, and most importantly civilised enough to demand and deserve self-rule'.[73] On another, it may signal something more disturbing: that the clearest measure by which statehood was to be obtained, was by demonstration of a willingness to fight like one and renounce in the process the forms of guerrilla or partisan warfare that were ultimately most threatening to that order.

5.2.3 The Aftermath – the Additional Protocols

As we have seen, almost from the outset, the FLN had understood – and represented – its struggle to be more than a merely local affair affecting the Algerian population and their relations with the French government. It also exemplified a global movement amongst populations of the colonial world to the cause of anti-colonial struggle. By seeking the inte rnationalisation of their own struggle – inscribing it in the language of a putatively universal international law – the Algerians simultaneously wrested the legal and political agenda from the hands of the French government and connected it to like struggles elsewhere across the globe. In that respect, the GPRA saw itself as the vanguard of a broader, global, anti-colonial movement stretching not only from the Mediterranean to sub-Saharan Africa but across the Atlantic to Cuba and across Asia to Indochina. Eschewing alignment with both Cold War blocs, the

[72] Maurice Flory, 'Algérie algérienne de Droit international' *Annuaire frančais de droit international*, 6 (1960) 973, 988.

[73] Kinsella, *The Image before the Weapon*, 131.

government of the newly independent Algeria was to situate its capital as a meeting place for a coterie of anti-colonial dissidents (Fanon, Cesaire, Castro, etc.) and actively involved itself in the various South-South/non-aligned initiatives that were developing at the time.[74]

The FLN's internationalisation agenda asserted or reshaped three strands of international law, the laws of statehood, self-determination and armed conflict in a mutually reinforcing campaign to garner recognition of its latent legal agency as a 'would-be' State prior to its actual independence. In this, it contributed to shaping (or re-shaping) an emergent law of self-determination in a way that accorded all colonial territories, and territories under 'alien' rule, the prerogatives of statehood (i.e. territorial integrity and a right to independence), even pending the termination of relations of colonialism. The full implications of the reasoning here (which could be seen alternatively as the novation of a pre-colonial status, or as a prescriptive invalidation of the acts by which colonial powers sought to establish their sovereignty over colonial territories) were not, however, fully worked through in case of the law of armed conflict itself. Unlike the Charter, these existing laws were not amenable to creative re-description through the work of the General Assembly alone. Whilst the General Assembly did, indeed, adopt a series of resolutions proclaiming, amongst other things, that wars of national liberation were akin to international armed conflicts, and that the full range of the Geneva Conventions should be applied to them[75] (a view widely shared in relation to the subsequent conflicts in Mozambique, Guinea Bissau, Sao Tomé, Namibia and Southern Rhodesia), the experience of Algeria had already shown the limits of that strategy.

It was not until a series of Diplomatic Conferences convened by the Swiss Federal Government between 1974 and 1977 that parties to the Geneva Conventions were enjoined to reconsider the law of armed conflict in light of the practice of anti-colonial, guerilla, and counter-insurgency warfare that had marked many of the conflicts in the aftermath of the Algerian revolution and, in so doing, give operational force to the re-modelled concept of self-determination that had been developed by the General Assembly in the meantime.

[74] Mokhtar Mokhtefi, *I Was a French Muslim: Memories of an Algerian Freedom Fighter*, trans. Elaine Mokhtefi (New York: Other Press, 2021; originally 2016).

[75] For example, UNGA Res 2674 (XXV) (9 December 1970), which affirmed that participants in national liberation struggles 'should be treated, in case of their arrest, as prisoners of war'.

As we have seen, an early key moment had been the recognition, by the General Assembly in the Colonial Declaration, of the independent status of all non-self-governing territories (understood in its broadest sense). This had been followed, in 1970, by the adoption of the Declaration on Friendly Relations, which included several provisions that had bearing upon national liberation struggles such as that fought by the Algerian nationalists. There it was stated that:

> Every State has the duty to refrain from any forcible action which deprives peoples referred to above in the elaboration of the principle of equal rights and self-determination of their right to self-determination and freedom and independence.

And that:

> In their actions against, and resistance to, such forcible action in pursuit of the exercise of their right to self-determination, such peoples are entitled to seek and to receive support in accordance with the purposes and principles of the Charter.

Building upon the 'separate status' idea found in the earlier Colonial Declaration, the Friendly Relations Declaration appeared to extend its logic to the law governing the use of force[76] – States were under an obligation not only to refrain from the use of force as against the territorial or political independence of other States (as spelt out in article 2(4) UN Charter) but also from the use of force against peoples struggling for self-determination. In the same measure, (armed) resistance to the forcible denial of self-determination was not just legitimate (equivalent to an act of self-defence perhaps) but also justified third-State intervention and support. It also implied, albeit not explicitly, that the armed conflicts arising from such struggles assumed an international character and that they were subject to application of 'the international *jus in bello* in its entirety'.[77]

In the ensuing three years, the General Assembly was to reaffirm many of these conclusions. In Resolution 2787(XXVI) of 1971, for example, it spoke of the 'legality' of the people's struggle for self-determination and liberation from 'colonial and foreign domination and alien subjugation' citing specifically the case of South Africa and 'that of the peoples of Zimbabwe, Namibia, Angola, Mozambique and Guinea (Bissau) as well

[76] Abi-Saab, 'Wars of National Liberation', 371–72.
[77] Ibid., 372.

as the Palestinian people'. And in Resolution 3103(XXVIII) of 12 December 1973 it was to state explicitly that:

> The armed conflicts involving the struggle of peoples against colonial and alien domination and racist régimes are to be regarded as international armed conflicts in the sense of the 1949 Geneva Conventions and the legal status envisaged to apply to the combatants in the 1949 Geneva Conventions and other international instruments are to apply to the persons engaged in armed struggle against colonial and alien domination and racist régimes.

If the General Assembly was clear that wars of national liberation were, in view of the separate status accorded to those peoples enjoying a right of self-determination, essentially international armed conflicts to which the entirety of the Geneva Conventions of 1949 applied, it was also clear that this issue was going to be one of the key battlegrounds at the Conferences organised by the Swiss government for purposes of the revision of the laws of war.

Unlike the Diplomatic Conference of 1949 that gave birth to the Geneva Conventions, the conferences of 1974–77 included representatives from an array of newly independent States (there were 150 States in total) as well as eleven national liberation movements (including those from Mozambique, South Africa and Palestine). Taking their lead from the strategic initiatives of the Algerians some twenty years earlier, these new States and movements were to advocate two main changes to the existing terms of the Geneva Conventions: one of which involved the 'internationalisation' of wars of national liberation, the other a loosening of the criteria by which those engaged in armed conflict might legitimately claim combatant status and hence both immunity from criminal prosecution and entitlement to protection as prisoners of war.

Both of these issues proved to be points of significant contention in the Diplomatic Conferences in which proposals advanced by a coalition of Asian and African States (together with active support of the Soviet bloc and more equivocal support from Latin America) were strenuously opposed by a caucus of Western States including the US, Britain, France, Belgium and the FRG.[78] On the first issue, a fifteen-power amendment[79] was proposed to include within the definition of an

[78] See generally, Giovanni Mantilla, *International Humanitarian Law and Internal Armed Conflict* (New York: Cornell University Press, 2020) chapter 5.

[79] See CDDH/I/11 (8 March 1974) in *Official Records of the Diplomatic Conference on the Reaffirmation and Development of International Humanitarian Law Applicable in Armed Conflicts*, vol III (Geneva, 1974–77).

international armed conflict a clause specifying that it extended also to 'armed struggles waged by peoples in the exercise of their right of self-determination'. Whilst a revised version of this amendment was to be adopted as article 1(4) of Additional Protocol 1, opposition to it focused, in particular, upon the instability of the category of self-determination struggles and its apparent re-invocation of the doctrine of just warfare.[80] As US President Reagan later put it, in his letter to the US Senate:

> Protocol I is fundamentally and irreconcilably flawed .... One of its provisions, for example, would automatically treat as an international conflict any so-called 'war of national liberation'.[81]

In his view, whether such wars are international or non-international should turn exclusively on objective reality, not on one's view of the moral qualities of each conflict. To rest on such subjective distinctions based on a war's alleged purpose would politicise humanitarian law and eliminate the distinction between international and non-international armed conflicts. It would give special status to

> 'wars of national liberation,' an ill-defined concept expressed in vague, subjective, politicized terminology .... [W]e must not, and need not, give recognition and protection to terrorist groups as a price for progress in humanitarian law.[82]

Tapping into the long tradition of Western commentary on the principle of self-determination, which – in line with the 'Belgian thesis' – was to render invisible the practice of colonial rule by proffering self-determination as a universal, yet unrealisable, ethical ideal for all communities, the US, alongside its other Western counterparts, was rehearsing here a theme that was to become a prevalent one in later years: namely, that the distinction between national liberation struggles and other acts of mere 'terrorism' was a matter of subjective appreciation – a question of morality or politics, rather than one of law or of 'objective reality'. To introduce such matters into the laws of war, the argument went, represented a dangerous reinvocation of the 'just war' tradition.[83]

[80] On the objections generally, see Abi-Saab, 'Wars of National Liberation', 376–84. On the just war, see Kinsella, *The Image before the Weapon*, 137–38.

[81] President Ronald Reagan, 'Message to the Senate Transmitting a Protocol to the 1949 Geneva Conventions' (Washington, DC, 29 January 1987).

[82] Reagan, 'Message to the Senate Transmitting a Protocol to the 1949 Geneva Conventions'.

[83] Jessica Whyte, 'The "Dangerous Concept of Just War": Decolonization, Wars of National Liberation, and the Additional Protocols to the Geneva Convention' *Humanity*, 9 (2018) 326–29.

The starting point of much of the Western criticism, however, and one that had been a visible point of contention in Algeria and elsewhere, was the idea that such conflicts were presumptively 'internal'. To speak about the ' internationalisation ' of an anti-colonial conflict meant treating it, by default, as one that fell within the domestic jurisdiction of the colonial power concerned. And this, as we have seen, was a contention that the General Assembly had sought to displace since its colonial declaration of 1960. What the debate over article 1(4) really brought into view, therefore, was the existence of two rival juridico-political imaginaries and two different ways of conceptualising global political space: one of which rested upon the historical residue of empire, emphasising the intrinsic legitimacy of colonial holdings (even if only as matters of 'fact'), and which thereby proceeded to characterise all efforts to break its shackles as being of an 'adverse' character; while the other began with the presumptive illegitimacy of all colonial holdings and understood violent conflict in such spaces to be, by definition, international, and the overthrow of colonial regimes to be a vindication of the precepts of the Charter.

But beyond seeking to unpick the logic of the 'separate status' of colonial territories, what the US and its allies also introduced was a relatively new discourse – a discourse in which 'terrorism' would gain ground as a way of re-modelling the juridico-political relations between the West and the peoples of the former colonial world. Here, the 'one man's freedom fighter' logic (a formulation originally introduced by Seymour in *Harry's Game* in 1974) was to re-cast the very distinction between national liberation, on the one hand, and mere criminal violence, on the other, through the introduction of a third term – terrorism – that sat at the unstable interstices of the two. Terrorism was a phenomenon conceived as being both national and international, both a crime and an act of political violence, both defined by its means (unlawful violence) and its ends (political change). It was, however, to become the global countermand to anti-colonial national liberation seeking to destabilise the cause of self-determination by rendering its evaluation either entirely subjective or by invalidating the mode of conflict with which it was associated.

This was to become particularly clear in relation to the second point of contestation – namely, the conditions under which those engaged in anti-colonial struggles might rightfully claim the privileges of combatants (POW status). As had become apparent in the Algerian conflict, the modus operandi of the ALN, as with many other liberation movements, had been to resort to a mode of guerilla (or partisan)[84] warfare that challenged the postulates of 'conventional warfare' written into the terms of the Hague and Geneva Conventions. If the latter had been modelled, as Abi-Saab put it, on a form of warfare where 'regular armies – composed of military personnel clearly distinguishable from civilian populations – confront each other along an equally distinguishable front line',[85] anti-colonial guerilla warfare largely shunned these forms of warfare in favour of one that prioritised mobility, surprise and dissimulation, and in which those engaged in combat sought to secrete themselves amongst the general population.

The rules of combatant status in the Hague and Geneva Conventions (e.g. Articles 13/13/4A of Conventions I–III)) had provided that the 'status of privileged combatants' extended not merely to members of the armed forces of a party to the conflict but to those members of militias or other volunteer forces so long as they fulfilled certain conditions, including being under responsible command, carrying a fixed distinctive sign, carrying arms openly and conducting their operations in accordance with the laws and customs of war.[86] Whilst it was reasoned that only by insisting that combatants distinguish themselves from the civilian population might the latter be effectively protected from the enemy, it was also evident, by the time of the Diplomatic Conference, that even these conditions were barely being met in the case of anti-colonial struggles akin to Algeria's.

At the Diplomatic Conference itself, the ICRC itself had initially taken the lead in presenting a proposal that considerably loosened the terms of Common Article 13/4A and that was deemed to apply, according to a footnote, to 'cases of armed struggle where peoples exercise their right to self-determination'. Its main innovation was to simplify the test of visibility and limit it to the duration of military operations. After

[84] See Carl Schmitt, *Theory of the Partisan: Intermediate Commentary on the Concept of the Political*, trans. G. L. Ulmen (New York: Telos Press, 2007).

[85] Abi-Saab, 'Wars of national liberation', 416.

[86] Paragraph 6 was to include a somewhat more relaxed requirement for those who 'spontaneously take up arms to resist the invading forces' of a would-be occupying army, so long as they 'carry arms openly and respect the laws and customs of war'. See Convention for the Amelioration of the Condition of the Wounded and Sick in Armed Forces in the Field, Geneva, 12 August 1949, 75 UNTS 31; Convention for the Amelioration of the Condition of Wounded, Sick and Shipwrecked Members of Armed Forces at Sea, Geneva, 12 August 1949, 75 UNTS 85; Convention Relative to the Treatment of Prisoners of War, Geneva, 12 August 1949, 75 UNTS 135.

extensive and at times acrimonious discussion, the Conference adopted what was to become article 44 of Protocol I modelled on the ICRC draft, which provided a de minimis requirement of carrying arms openly during each military engagement (and prior deployment) and specified that even in cases in which a combatant failed to meet the requirement of privileged combatancy, they would nevertheless be entitled to be given 'protections equivalent in all respects to those accorded to prisoners of war'.

Once again, opposition from the Western cohort was fierce. Here, however, the US (for whom the question of POW status had become a burning issue during the war in Vietnam) was unexpectedly to align itself with the Soviet Union around the text, on the grounds that there was sufficient slippage in the terminology used to allay concerns that it might simply legitimise guerrilla warfare.[87] Once the US was on board, the other Western States fell into line for fear of being politically exposed. This was not, however, to completely assuage the residual concerns in the West about the implications for future warfare and its burgeoning concerns to address the phenomenon of 'terrorism'. And as a marker, President Reagan would make direct reference to article 44 in his explanation for the US subsequent refusal to ratify the agreement. As he put it, the provision 'would grant combatant status to irregular forces even if they do not satisfy the traditional requirements to distinguish themselves from the civilian population and otherwise comply with the laws of war. This would endanger civilians among whom terrorists and other irregulars attempt to conceal themselves.'[88] What was left unspoken, of course, was the conditions under which the US and its allies might end up meeting such 'irregular' forces or the blunt absurdity of privileging combatancy in the name of humanity.

5.3 Anglo-Iranian Oil and the Jurisdiction of the International Court of Justice

Whilst the Algerian conflict brought into prominence the generative role that anti-colonial movements from the South played in the shaping

[87] Mantilla, *International Humanitarian Law*, 158–63. The US had advanced an interpretive statement to the effect that the word 'deployment' should be read in extremely broad terms and that 'equivalent' treatment would not necessarily mean immunity from prosecution.

[88] Reagan, 'Message to the Senate Transmitting a Protocol to the 1949 Geneva Conventions'.

humanitarian law and law of self-determination, elsewhere international institutions themselves became spaces in which rival accounts as to what they were for and what they could and should do, were brought into play. This rivalry had roots long before the 'Cold War' in its most familiar periodisation. But one example from the Cold War era itself is provided by the Anglo–Iranian Oil case.[89]

The Anglo–Iranian Oil case is particularly interesting for two reasons. In the first place, beneath the surface of what has often been read to be a purely procedural matter was a much more profound quarrel over the putative role of judicial settlement in international relations. When we look 'slant'[90] at the judgment, we can see the long roots of Cold War disputes, as well as a range of disputed visions of what the role of the International Court of Justice might, could and should be at a crucial moment in the Court's formation.

In the second place, it also brings into visibility the way in which, in contrast to a familiar post–Cold War story about a lawless South and a lawful North, Iran sought to conduct itself in a lawful way, whereas Britain, with the support of the United States, did not. This is a familiar pattern in the Cold War period in which the active Cold War powers themselves often viewed international law in instrumental terms treating compliance as a strategic choice. Britain's response to the decision of the ICJ (supporting Iran's position that the Court did not have jurisdiction to deal with the merits of the case) was to resort to force to 'repossess' Iranian oil and to orchestrate a coup with the assistance of the United States to depose the parliamentary nationalist Mohammad Mossadeq.[91] The consequences of British and American actions in Iran in the 1950s

[89] This section draws heavily on Sundhya Pahuja and Cait Storr, 'Rethinking Iran and International Law: The Anglo-Iranian Oil Company Case Revisited' in James Crawford, Abdul G. Koroma, Said Mahmoudi and Alain Pellet (eds.), *The International Legal Order: Current Needs and Possible Responses, Essays in Honour of Djamchid Momtaz* (Leiden and Boston: Brill, 2017) 53–74.

[90] We refer here to the poem by Emily Dickinson, 'Tell All the Truth but Tell It Slant'.

[91] The CIA officially admitted its role in the 1953 coup in 2013. See Malcolm Byrne, 'CIA Admits It Was Behind Iran's Coup' *Foreign Policy*, 19 August 2013, http://foreignpolicy.com/2013/08/19/cia-admits-it-was-behind-irans-coup/. The UK Government has yet to do so. For just one detailed account of this story by an eminent historian who revisited the story in 2004 and 2006, drawing on newly available documents and discussions and correspondence with four former British Officials involved with the events of 1951–53, see William Roger Louis, 'Mussadiq, Oil and the Dilemmas of British Imperialism' in *The Ends of British Imperialism: The Scramble for Empire, Suez and Decolonization* (London: Tauris, 2006) 727–88. This chapter was originally published as William Roger Louis, 'Britain and the Overthrow of the Mosaddeq Government' in Mark J. Gasiorowski and

have cast long shadows, not only in Iranian political history but also in the structuring of the international investment regime and the militarisation of resource disputes in the Middle East. But like so many stories in this book, revisiting the incident also challenges the post–Cold War myth-making around the enduring commitment of Western powers to the international rule of law (or what, today, is termed the 'global rules based international order').

5.3.1 *The Background*

The background to the case is a struggle for meaningful independence in the face of imperial entitlement and commercial vested interests. At the turn of the twentieth century, the Persian Empire was a socio-political entity with a history of over two millennia, although its status in the European law of nations was unclear. European companies had been formed to exploit Persian oil deposits from the mid-nineteenth century,[92] putatively authorised by the legal device of the 'concession'.[93] Most notorious of these was the extensive and enormous concession granted in 1901 to English mining entrepreneur William Knox D'Arcy by the

Malcolm Byrne (eds.), *Mohammad Mosaddeq and the 1953 Coup in Iran* (New York: Syracuse University Press, 2004) 126–77.

[92] Ronald W. Ferrier, *The History of the British Petroleum Company, Volume 1: The Developing Years, 1901–1932* (Cambridge: Cambridge University Press, 2009) 24–27. This is the authorised history of the Company and is read as such.

[93] The precise nature of the 'concession' in international law remains unclear and highly contested. It usually denotes a contract between a ruler or public authority with a foreign company or State to exercise both commercial and 'public' functions in a given area, often enormous. It was a favoured colonial instrument for two centuries and taken up by the petroleum industry in the early twentieth century. It is a term that fell out of favour in the era of decolonisation. Matthew Craven, 'Colonial Fragments: Decolonization, Concessions, and Acquired Rights' in Jochen von Bernstorff and Philipp Dann (eds.), *The Battle for International Law: South-North Perspectives on the Decolonization Era* (Oxford: Oxford University Press, 2019) 101–23. For a statement as to the conceptual difficulties of defining the concession in international law, see *Saudi Arabia v Arabian American Oil Company* (Aramco) (Award) (1963) 27 ILR 117. For an overview and account of contests over the meaning and legality of concessions, see Muthucumaraswamy Sornarajah, *The International Law on Foreign Investment*, 3rd ed. (Cambridge: Cambridge University Press, 2010) 38–41. For an account of the terminology used today to apportion rights in functional modes not dissimilar to the older concession agreement (such as production sharing agreements, joint ventures, public-private partnerships, service contracts and so on), see Christoph Ohler, 'Concessions' in *Max Planck Encyclopedia of Public International Law* (Oxford: Oxford University Press, 2013).

Persian government of Amin al-Sultan under the auspices of Qajar ruler, Muzzafer al-Din Shah.[94] The granting of the D'Arcy Concession is often cited as a contributing factor in what has subsequently become known as the Iranian Constitutional Revolution of 1905. This was a movement that disputed the authority of those who had signed the concession – the Qajar Shahs – to represent Persia in agreements and to create and grant rights such as those contained in it.[95] The Constitutional Revolution resulted in the formation of the *Majlis*, the Iranian parliament.[96] The D'Arcy Concession, however, remained on foot.

In 1907, in the Anglo-Russian Entente, Britain and Russia agreed, without the involvement of the Shah or the *Majlis*, to divide Iranian territory into respective spheres of influence. The Anglo–Persian Oil Company was incorporated in London in 1909 with close involvement of the British imperial Government after the discovery of commercial quantities of oil.[97] Anglo–Persian became the first large-scale oil operation in the Middle East.[98] In 1921, the Qajar dynasty was overthrown,

[94] It was certainly notable for its sheer scale. D'Arcy was granted the 'special and exclusive privilege to search for and obtain, exploit, develop, render suitable for trade, carry away and sell' oil and gas 'throughout the whole extent of the Persian Empire for a term of sixty years', in exchange for a lump sum of sterling, paid-up shares to the value of £20,000 in the company formed to exercise the concession and royalty payments of 16 per cent of annual profits. Sornarajah, *The International Law on Foreign Investment*, 42. Despite the phrasing of the Concession, the arrangement was understood by both parties to exclude the five northern provinces, the traditional areas of Russian influence. See also Alan W. Ford, *The Anglo-Iranian Oil Dispute of 1951–1952: A Study of the Role of Law in the Relations of States* (Berkeley and Los Angeles: University of California Press, 1954) 15.

[95] Nikkie Keddie and Mehrdad Amanat, 'Iran under the Later Qājārs, 1848–1922' in Peter Avery, Gavin Hambly and Charles Melville (eds.), *The Cambridge History of Iran, Volume 7: From Nadir Shah to the Islamic Republic* (Cambridge: Cambridge University Press, 1991) 202–3. See also Ervand Abrahamian, *Iran between Two Revolutions* (New Jersey: Princeton University Press, 1982) 74ff. Other unpopular and potentially unauthorised economic policies pursued by Muzaffer al-Din Shah reportedly included granting road tolls to the Imperial Bank of Britain and the assumption of several loans including borrowing money from French companies to buy arms, from Russia to replay previous loans and from Britain to finance personal ('medical') travel to Europe.

[96] Ronald W. Ferrier, *The History of the British Petroleum Company, Volume 1: The Developing Years, 1901–1932* (Cambridge: Cambridge University Press, 2009) 203. For detail on the composition of the parliament, see Abrahamian, *Iran between Two Revolutions*, 86–92.

[97] Peter J. Beck, 'The Anglo-Persian Oil Dispute 1932–33' *Journal of Contemporary History*, 9 (1974) 124. On the Anglo–Russian Entente of 1907, see Maysam Behravesh, 'The Formative Years of Anglo–Iranian Relations (1907–1953): Colonial Scramble for Iran and Its Political Legacy' *Digest of Middle East Studies*, 21 (2012) 388–89.

[98] Ferrier, *The History of the British Petroleum Company*, 107.

preventing the ratification of the 1919 Anglo–Iranian Treaty that would have rendered Persia a British protectorate; and Reza Khan became the first shah of the Pahlavi dynasty in 1925.[99]

The relationship between the Anglo–Persian and the British Government was symbiotic from the time of its formation.[100] The Company involved itself both overtly and covertly in Iranian politics. It sought to monopolise both the oil industry and Iran's foreign relations in the South against Russian attempts to do the same in the North.[101] Domestic political movements in the first half of the twentieth century sought to build a modern Iranian State that would shift the weight of sovereignty away from the Persian Shahs and towards a democratically constituted *Majlis*. At the same time, the Anglo–Persian sought to use its position to secure political outcomes that would favour its profit margin and the interests of its majority shareholder, the British government.[102] Supporters of the Company maintained that those interests were consistent with the interests of the Iranian people: royalty payments from the Company's operations were the government's main source of revenue, and the Company developed the industrial infrastructure of significant regions of the country.[103] Yet within Persia, critics of the Company maintained that in the exploitation of Persian oil, the interests of the Iranian people and of the fledgling Iranian State were chronically subordinated to the interests of the Company and of the British Empire.[104]

A key critic of the Company was Mohammad Mossadeq[105] (later Iran's first prime minister) who had called for the abolition of the

99 Behravesh, 'The Formative Years of Anglo–Iranian Relations', 391.

100 In 1914, the Company secured a contract to supply fuel oil to the Royal Navy at a fixed below-market price, and the British Government acquired a majority shareholding. Ronald W. Ferrier, 'The Iranian Oil Industry' in Peter Avery, Gavin Hambly and Charles Melville (eds.), *The Cambridge History of Iran, Volume 7: From Nadir Shah to the Islamic Republic* (Cambridge: Cambridge University Press, 1991) 642.

101 Behravesh, 'The Formative Years of Anglo–Iranian Relations', 391–92; Abrahamian, *Iran between Two Revolutions*, 110.

102 Neveen Abdelrehim, 'Rethinking "Oil Nationalism": The Case of the Anglo–Iranian Oil Company' *International Journal of Signs and Semiotic Systems*, 4 (2015) 33–49.

103 See, for example, Laurence Lockhart, 'The Causes of the Anglo-Persian Oil Dispute' *Journal of the Royal Central Asian Society*, 40 (1953) 134–50.

104 N. Keddie and M. Amanat, 'Iran under the Later Qājārs, 1848–1922' in P. Avery, G. R. G. Hambly and C. Melville (eds.), *The Cambridge History of Iran, Volume 7: From Nadir Shah to the Islamic Republic* (Cambridge: Cambridge University Press, 1991) 174–212. Abrahamian, *Iran between Two Revolutions*, 143–44.

105 Mossadeq was a legal academic elected to the first *Majlis* who advocated a constitutionally grounded Iranian nationalism. Thought to be the first Iranian to receive a doctorate

capitulation treaties in order to strengthen Persia's territorial sovereignty.[106] In 1928, Shah Reza Khan abolished the British capitulation treaties and made a formal request to the Company to renegotiate the terms of the D'Arcy Concession[107] on the grounds that it was manifestly unfair.[108] As protracted negotiations took place between the Iranian Government and the Company over the terms of the Concession, in September 1932, the *Majlis* and Senate ratified the Government's 1930 Declaration accepting the jurisdiction of the Permanent Court of International Justice (PCIJ) in disputes arising 'with regard to situations or facts relating directly or indirectly to the application of treaties or conventions accepted by Persia and subsequent to the ratification of this declaration'.[109] The Declaration also excluded, inter alia, any 'dispute with regard to questions which, by international law, fall exclusively within the jurisdiction of Persia'.[110]

In November 1932, the D'Arcy Concession was cancelled by the Iranian Government at the direction of the Shah.[111] The British appealed

in law from a European university, Mossadeq studied at Sciences Po in Paris and Neuchâtel in Switzerland. James A. Bill and William Roger Louis, 'Introduction' in James A. Bill and William Roger Louis Tauris (eds.), *Musaddiq, Iranian Nationalism and Oil* (London: Tauris, 1988) 3.

106 In 1914, Mossadeq had written and self-published a monograph calling for the abolition of the capitulation treaties in Persia in order to strengthen Persia's territorial sovereignty. Roy Mottahedeh, *The Mantle of the Prophet: Religion and Politics in Iran* (New York: Simon and Schuster, 1985); Ali Pirzadeh, *Iran Revisited: Exploring the Historical Roots of Culture, Economics, and Society* (Cham: Springer, 2016) 208. For an analysis of the function of capitulation treaties in the Ottoman context, see Umut Özsu, 'Ottoman Empire' in Anne Peters and Bardo Fassbender (eds.), *The Oxford Handbook of the History of International Law* (Oxford: Oxford University Press, 2012) 429–448; and generally, Matthew Craven, 'What Happened to Unequal Treaties? The Continuities of Informal Empire' *Nordic Journal of International Law*, 74 (2005) 335–82.

107 Keddie and Amanat, 'Iran under the Later Qājārs', 174–212; Behravesh, 'The Formative Years of Anglo-Iranian Relations', 392.

108 Added to these formal iniquities, the Company was using accounting practices that limited its on-paper profit in order to reduce the sum of royalties it owed to Iran. James Bamberg, *The History of The British Petroleum Company, Volume 2: The Anglo-Iranian Years, 1928–1954* (Cambridge: Cambridge University Press, 1994) 22–26. The price at which the oil was being sold to the British government (its majority shareholder) was also very low, further reducing profits and royalties to Iran.

109 The text of the Declaration, written in French, is provided in English translation in the ICJ's judgment of 22 July 1952. *Anglo-Iranian Oil Company Case (United Kingdom v. Iran)* (Preliminary Objection) (1952) ICJ Rep 93, at 103.

110 *Anglo-Iranian Oil Company Case (United Kingdom v. Iran)* (Preliminary Objection) (1952) ICJ Rep 93, at 103.

111 Bamberg, *The History of The British Petroleum Company*, 33.

initially to the Council of the League of Nations asserting a right of diplomatic protection[112] but negotiations between the Company and the Iranian Government continued, and by October, a new (but ultimately provisional) settlement was reached in the form of a new Concession.[113]

Although relations with Britain were formally restored following entry into the 1933 Concession, the Shah worked to develop international relationships with 'third powers' as both a bulwark against the imperial interests of the United Kingdom and the Soviet Union in Iranian territory and a means of building international recognition of Iran as an independent nation.[114] The Shah's attempt to manoeuvre in European 'balance of power' politics was thwarted when Germany invaded the Soviet Union in June 1941. In the resulting Soviet–British alliance, Iran was occupied by Soviet armed forces in the north, and British armed forces in the south, essentially along the lines drawn by the Anglo–Russian Entente of 1907, while both imperial powers officially committed themselves to 'respect the sovereignty and territorial integrity' of Iran.[115] The invasion ruptured Reza Khan's autocratic hold on political power, and in September 1941, he was forced to abdicate.[116] Reza Khan's son Muhammad Reza Pahlavi was crowned as Shah.

The new Shah was supported by conservatives in the *Majlis* but faced opposition from the growing nationalist movement, organised from 1949 as the National Front of Iran.[117] This domestic instability was exploited by both the British and the Soviet governments. Whilst the Russians/Soviets and the British had originally worked in tandem through the delineation of their respective spheres of interest in Iran, their rivalry was to intensify in the early years of the Cold War. The British sought to bolster pro-British sentiment within the conservative opposition to the nationalist movement, whilst the Soviet Union sought to foster pro-Soviet agitation within the banned Iranian communist movement, incorporated during the war into the Hezb-e Tudeh-ye Iran

[112] Ibid.

[113] *Anglo-Iranian Oil Company Case (United Kingdom v. Iran)* (Preliminary Objection) (1952) ICJ Rep 93, at 111.

[114] Amin Saikal, 'Iranian Foreign Policy, 1929–1971' in Peter Avery, Gavin Hambly and Charles Melville (eds.), *The Cambridge History of Iran, Volume 7: From Nadir Shah to the Islamic Republic* (Cambridge: Cambridge University Press, 1991) 433–34.

[115] Saikal, 'Iranian Foreign Policy, 1929–1971', 434–36.

[116] Abrahamian, *Iran between Two Revolutions*, 163–65.

[117] Ibid., 252.

(Tudeh) party.[118] By the late 1940s, the various political movements in Iran had adopted incommensurable positions on the continued economic dominance of the Anglo-Iranian Oil Company. While the Shah and conservative supporters under General Ali Razmara advocated for the dedication of oil revenues to agricultural and industrial development, the National Front under Mossadeq campaigned for nationalisation of the oil industry.[119] Political instability intensified on the election of Razmara, a conservative, as Prime Minister in 1950. In March 1951, he was assassinated, and the *Majlis* and Senate passed the *Oil Nationalisation Acts*. The *Acts* approved the principle of nationalisation of oil resources and provided that all of the Company's rights in Iranian oil and related infrastructure would pass to a newly created National Iranian Oil Company for compensation at market rates.[120] In April 1951, Mossadeq was elected Prime Minister[121] and, in May, formally advised the Company of the Government's intention to implement the nationalisation policy.[122] As had been the case in 1932, the United Kingdom immediately initiated international legal action on the Company's behalf (which, by this point, had been re-named 'the Anglo-Iranian Oil Company'), and an action was commenced in the new International Court of Justice on 26 May 1951.

5.3.2 The Case

Against this backdrop, the primary argument of the United Kingdom was quite simple in form. In its *Application Instituting Proceedings* lodged on 26 May 1951, the UK submitted that the *Nationalisation Acts* constituted

118 Saikal, 'Iranian Foreign Policy, 1929–1971', 434–36. Abrahamian considers the social history the Tudeh movement at length; see Abrahamian, *Iran between Two Revolutions*, 281–318.

119 On the National Front, see Homa Katouzian, 'Mosaddeq's Government in Iranian History: Arbitrary Rule, Democracy and the 1953 Coup' in Mark J. Gasiorowski and Malcolm Byrne (eds.), *Mohammad Mosaddeq and the 1953 Coup in Iran* (New York: Syracuse University Press 2004) 1–6.

120 James Bamberg, *The History of The British Petroleum Company, Volume 2: The Anglo-Iranian Years, 1928–1954* (Cambridge: Cambridge University Press, 1994) 418–19; Samuel Nakasian, 'The Anglo-Iranian Oil Case: A Problem in International Judicial Process' *Georgetown Law Journal*, 41 (1953) 467–68.

121 Hussein Ala served as Prime Minister immediately after the assasination of Razmara, but only for 51 days as he could not garner the co-operation of parliament. Ford, *The Anglo-Iranian Oil Dispute of 1951–1952*, 52; Abrahamian, *Iran between Two Revolutions*, 266–67.

122 Bamberg, *The History of The British Petroleum Company*, 420.

a 'unilateral annulment' of the 1933 Agreement between the Imperial Government of Persia and the Anglo–Persian Oil Company and that Iran had failed to respond to the Company's attempts to resolve the matter both under the good faith and arbitration clauses of the 1933 Agreement and through diplomatic means via the United Kingdom.[123] As in the 1930s, the UK's standing to bring the application in the ICJ on behalf of the Company was again asserted on the basis of the right of diplomatic protection.[124] According to the Application, Iran had 'treated a British national in a manner not in accordance with the principles of international law and [had], in consequence, committed an international wrong against the Government of the United Kingdom'.[125] The UK argued that because Iran had, in September 1932, accepted the jurisdiction of the PCIJ in relation to treaties after 1932, the matter was within the jurisdiction of the ICJ.[126] The UK also ran a series of alternative arguments.[127] Most relevant here was the argument that Iran's conduct constituted a breach of Article 36(3) of the new Charter of the United Nations, pursuant to which legal disputes between member States should be referred to the ICJ.[128]

The Mossadeq government's response to the ICJ proceeding was to continue with the implementation of the *Nationalisation Acts*.[129] Prime Minister Mossadeq and his ministers asserted in writing to the Company, and in diplomatic engagements with the UK and the United States, that nationalisation was a sovereign act entirely within Iran's domestic jurisdiction and was not limited by private agreements.[130] The head of the

[123] *Anglo-Iranian Oil Company Case (United Kingdom v. Iran)* (Pleadings) (1951) ICJ Rep 8, at 10.

[124] On the historical use of diplomatic protection in international investment law, see generally Muthucumaraswamy Sornarajah, 'The Shaping Factors' in *The International Law on Foreign Investment*, 42–109, especially 37–38.

[125] 'Application Instituting Proceedings', *Anglo-Iranian Oil Company Case (United Kingdom v. Iran)* (Pleadings) (1951) ICJ Rep 8, at 12.

[126] That is, with respect to all situations or facts that dealt directly or indirectly with the application of treaties and conventions entered into after that date, and the Application concerned the 1933 Agreement. *Anglo-Iranian Oil Company Case (United Kingdom v. Iran)* (Pleadings) (1951) ICJ Rep 8, at 13.

[127] *Anglo-Iranian Oil Company Case (United Kingdom v. Iran)* (Pleadings) (1951) ICJ Rep 8, at 14–17.

[128] The third was that Iran's conduct breached general principles of customary international law, although this argument was left undeveloped. *Anglo-Iranian Oil Company Case (United Kingdom v. Iran)* (Pleadings) (1951) ICJ Rep 8, 17.

[129] Bamberg, *The History of The British Petroleum Company*, 430–36.

[130] *Anglo-Iranian Oil Company Case (United Kingdom v. Iran)* (Other Documents Submitted to the Court) (1951) ICJ Rep 672, at 684–97, especially 693.

Iranian Mixed Parliamentary Oil Commission appointed to oversee the nationalisation process made public statements assuring 'the West' of an uninterrupted oil supply under the new National Iranian Oil Company.[131]

In response to the Iranian Government's actions, on 22 June 1951, the UK sought an order for a series of measures[132] that would prevent Iran from implementing the nationalisation process until the merits of the case could be decided upon by the Court.[133] A week later, on 29 June 1951, Iranian Minister for Foreign Affairs Baqer Kazemi sent a letter to the ICJ containing a 'statement which the Imperial Government of Iran has prepared rejecting the petition submitted by the British Government'.[134] In stark contrast to the UK's highly technical submissions to the Court, the Kazemi letter is an elegiac appraisal of the failings of the international order and the history of British intervention in Iran. Adopting an epistolary mode of engagement with the Court,[135] the letter opens with a passage of bold rhetoric:

> [T]he question is often asked by many nations, how is it that with the existence of the United Nations Organization, the Security Council and the International Court of Justice, the foundations of world peace are still shaky and insecure? . . . If we view this question impartially, it will become clear to us that greed and selfishness on the part of the strong to procure illicit advantages from the weak nations are to be regarded as the main causes of this instability and the insecurity which prevails at the present; and for so long as fair play and justice are not governing the relations of

[131] *Anglo-Iranian Oil Company Case*, 688–90.

[132] Which States that the Court has power to indicate 'any provisional measures which ought to be taken to preserve the respective rights of either party'. Statute of the International Court of Justice, 26 June 1945, XV UNCIO 355, Art. 41 (adapted from Article 41 of the Statute of the Permanent Court of International Justice).

[133] *Anglo-Iranian Oil Company Case (United Kingdom v. Iran)* (Request for the Indication of Interim Measures of Protection) (1951) ICJ Rep 45. The grounds of the request were stated to be 'actions involving or threatening to involve the loss of skilled personnel, interference with management or the disruption of the integrated enterprise operated by the Anglo-Iranian Oil Company', on the one hand, and 'inflammatory speeches, broadcasts and articles', on the other.

[134] *Anglo-Iranian Oil Company Case (United Kingdom v. Iran)* (Other Documents Submitted to the Court) (1951) ICJ Rep 672, 672.

[135] For two meditations on epistolary form and court judgment, see Ben Kunbor, 'Epistolary Jurisdiction of the Indian Courts and Fundamental Human Rights in Ghana's 1992 Constitution: Some Jurisprudential Lessons' *Law, Social Justice and Global Development*, 2 (2001) 1–30, www2.warwick.ac.uk/fac/soc/law/elj/lgd/2001_2/kunbor/#a2; Peter Goodrich; 'Epistolary Justice: The Love Letter as Law' *Yale Journal of Law and the Humanities*, 9 (1997) 245–95.

> the strong and the weak, there can be no hope of bringing about world stability and achieving a lasting peace.[136]

The letter goes on to explain in substantive terms the bases of Iran's argument against the UK's original Application: that Iran's acceptance of the jurisdiction of the ICJ in 1932 applied prospectively only and excluded any matters bearing on Iran's national sovereignty,[137] that its treaties of friendship with the UK predated Iran's acceptance of ICJ jurisdiction, that the 1933 Agreement between Persia and the Company was invalid and that even if it was valid, the 1933 Agreement was between Iran and a private company and therefore not within jurisdiction.[138] Regarding the UK's Request for Interim Measures, the letter states that

> the respite given us by the Court is so short that one could not even procure the necessary visa for passports. Hence the Iranian government owing to the short respite, curtails its arguments; but earnestly hopes that the Court will not spare a moment to declare the case beyond its jurisdiction, as otherwise it would bring disappointment to the weaker nations as far as international justice and good-will are concerned.[139]

The ICJ chose not to recognise the Kazemi letter as a submission to the Court in the nature of a preliminary objection to its jurisdiction.[140] An *ex parte* hearing on the UK's Request for Interim Measures was held the following day on 30 June. On 5 July 1951, the ICJ issued an Order declaring that it had the necessary competence to issue interim measures[141] and that neither party should undertake any action that would prejudice the rights of the other or 'aggravate or extend the dispute'.[142]

In keeping with its position that the ICJ had no power to issue interim orders, the Mossadeq Government continued to implement the

[136] *Anglo-Iranian Oil Company Case (United Kingdom v. Iran)* (Other Documents Submitted to the Court) (1951) ICJ Rep 672, 672–73.

[137] See, Article 36 of the ICJ Statute.

[138] *Anglo-Iranian Oil Company Case* (Other Documents), 674–78.

[139] Ibid., 678.

[140] Despite the fact that the Court had been in existence for only a short time and that the Iranian team could not even get the necessary visas in time.

[141] The Court stated that the matter 'could not be regarded *a priori* to fall completely outside the bounds of international jurisdiction', which 'suffice(d) to empower the Court to entertain the Request for interim measures of protection', and that 'the indication of such measures in no way prejudges the question of the jurisdiction of the Court to deal with the merits of the case and leaves unaffected the right of the Respondent to submit arguments against such jurisdiction'. *Anglo-Iranian Oil Company Case (United Kingdom v. Iran)* (Order of 5 July 1951) (1951) ICJ Rep 89, at 93.

[142] *Anglo-Iranian Oil Company Case* (Order of 5 July 1951), 93–94.

Nationalisation Acts. In September 1951, the UK sought to have the Security Council enforce the ICJ's Order in accordance with Article 94 (2) of the UN Charter.[143] In October 1951, Prime Minister Mossadeq appeared at the United Nations to present Iran's case to the Security Council.[144] Mossadeq began his address by stating that the Iranian population had one of the 'lowest standards of living in the world' and that under British control the oil industry had 'contributed practically nothing to the people's well-being, or to the technical progress or industrial development of the country'.[145] He then reiterated Iran's position that the ICJ had no competence to hear the original Application and therefore no competence to issue provisional orders.[146] The Security Council, unable to reach agreement on the question of the ICJ's jurisdiction in either the principal or the interim matter, resolved to adjourn the debate until the Court had ruled on its own competence.[147]

On 22 July 1952, the ICJ delivered its judgment on the merits, holding that the Court had no jurisdiction to deal with the original Application submitted by the UK.[148] In its reasons, the Court held that it had jurisdiction over Iran only by virtue of Iran's Declaration made under Article 36(2) of its Statute, which applied only to disputes relating to the application of treaties or conventions entered into by Iran after in September 1932 when the Declaration was ratified.[149] Rejecting the UK's submission that the 1933 Agreement between Persia and the Company was of 'a double character', being both a concessionary contract with the Company and a treaty with the UK, the ICJ held that the

[143] Article 94(2), Charter of the United Nations 1945 UNTS XVI, provides as follows: '(I)f any party to a case fails to perform the obligations incumbent upon it under a judgment rendered by the Court, the other party may have recourse to the Security Council, which may, if it deems necessary, make recommendations or decide upon measures to be taken to give effect to the judgment.'

[144] Report of the United Nations Security Council to the United Nations General Assembly covering the period from 16 July 1951 to 15 July 1952 UN Doc. A/2167 (1952), 17–24.

[145] Report of the Security Council to the General Assembly covering the period from 16 July 1951 to 15 July 1952, UN Doc. A/2167 (1952), 20.

[146] Ibid.

[147] Ibid., 24. Nakasian offers an analysis of the Security Council debate in Samuel Nakasian, 'The Anglo-Iranian Oil Case: A Problem in International Judicial Process' *Georgetown Law Journal*, 41 (1953) 475–80.

[148] *Anglo-Iranian Oil Company Case (United Kingdom v. Iran)* (Judgment of 22 July 1952) (1952) ICJ Rep 93, at 115 (nine judges to five; Alvarez, Hackworth, Read, and Levi Carneiro JJ dissenting; separate opinion by McNair J).

[149] *Anglo-Iranian Oil Company Case (United Kingdom v. Iran)* (Judgment of 22 July 1952) (1952) ICJ Rep 93, 107.

Agreement was a private contract and thus not within the jurisdiction accepted by Iran in 1932.[150] The majority decision is silent on the matter of whether Iran's nationalisation of its oil industry was a sovereign act and thus beyond the jurisdiction of the Court.[151]

5.3.3 *Another International Law*

Familiar legal accounts of the *Anglo-Iranian Oil Company Case* typically end with the Court's decision of 22 July 1952. The case has been incorporated into the jurisprudence of both procedural international law and international investment law.[152] Such accounts, however,[153] typically rely upon a 'snapshot methodology'[154] that de-historicises the case and encourages the belief that authority – and legal forms – exist in the world as stable formations, rather than being produced through contested practices of authorisation that require ongoing stabilisation. Such a 'snapshot methodology' with its understanding of power to be extrinsic, rather than intrinsic, to law and the exercise of legal authority was a methodology that was largely developed within the West during the Cold War – consonant, as it was, with 'realist' approaches to international relations in which 'law' becomes the object of strategies of power, rather than its medium. Separating law from the world in this particular instance has had the effect of distorting the historical record – encouraging the view that it was Iran

150 Ibid., 112. The Court also rejected the UK's argument that treaties of friendship completed with Denmark, Switzerland and Turkey subsequent to Iran's acceptance of ICJ jurisdiction were sufficient to bring Iran's earlier treaties promising the UK most favoured nation status within its jurisdiction. *Anglo-Iranian Oil Company Case (United Kingdom v. Iran)* (Judgment of 22 July 1952) (1952) ICJ Rep 93, 113.

151 In his Dissenting Opinion, under a subheading 'Iran's nationalization of the oil industry and the "reserved domain" of that State', Judge Alvarez describes a shift from 'classical international law', under which a State could freely exercise sovereign rights within its 'reserved domain', and the 'new international law', in which 'the reserved domain of States has been modified and considerably reduced'. *Anglo-Iranian Oil Company Case (United Kingdom v. Iran)* (Dissenting Opinion of Judge Alvarez) (1952) ICJ Rep 124, 127–29.

152 Alexander Orakhelashvili, 'Anglo-Iranian Oil Company Case' in *Max Planck Encyclopedia of Public International Law* (Oxford: Oxford University Press, 2007).

153 See, for example, James Crawford, *Brownlie's Principles of Public International Law*, 8th ed. (Oxford: Oxford University Press, 2012) 630–31. Sornarajah's account of the case is a notable exception to this tendency toward dehistorication. See Sornarajah, *The International Law on Foreign Investment*, 36.

154 Julio Faundez, *Democratization, Development and Legality: Chile, 1831–1973* (New York: Palgrave Macmillan, 2007) 9.

who had somehow 'violated' international law and that Britain, by contrast, had merely sought vindication of its legitimate rights. It is an instance, in that respect, of a broader thesis that was developed during this period that sought to put in question the attempted assertions of 'economic sovereignty' by decolonising States.[155]

Britain's response to the decision of the ICJ was to resort to extralegal force, both overt and covert. Prior to the Court's decision, Britain had imposed economic sanctions upon Iran. The Company withdrew all British workers from the Abadan oilfields, and Iran was blocked from accessing its assets held in British banks.[156] Mossadeq entreated other States with whom Iran had diplomatic ties to provide technical support to the new National Iranian Oil Company during the transition to national control. The United States, Sweden, Belgium, the Netherlands, Pakistan and West Germany all refused. Only Italy agreed. In July 1952, a British RAF plane forced an Italian-chartered tanker carrying Iranian oil into the waters of the British protectorate of Aden and issued an action claiming the Italians were in unlawful possession of British property.[157] A month later, US President Truman and British Prime Minister Churchill issued a joint communiqué calling for the compensation to the Company to be arbitrated. Mossadeq responded by demanding 49 million pounds in compensation from the Company for intentional underpayment under the 1932 Concession.[158]

By February 1953, an anti-Mossadeq collaboration had formed between the United Kingdom, the United States and the conservative movement in Iran, that together sought to strengthen the position of the

[155] For an indicative account of the belief that Britain and the US were adhering to law whilst Iran was departing from it, even as the coup was being planned, see the postscript to the book by Alan Ford written in 1954, which announces 'the overthrow of Mossadeeq's Government' in an 'army coup led by General Fazollah Zahedi' and ends with the conviction that 'the British and American Governments will try to extend a helping hand as quickly and tactfully as possible'. Ford, *The Anglo-Iranian Oil Dispute of 1951–1952*, 231–32.

[156] James Bamberg, *The History of the British Petroleum Company, Volume 2: The Anglo-Iranian Years, 1928–1954* (Cambridge: Cambridge University Press, 1994) 457–58.

[157] The Supreme Court of Colony of Aden gave a decision in favour of the Company in *Anglo-Iranian Oil Company Ltd v. Jaffrate* [1953] 1 W.L.R. 246, which dismissed the ship master's testimony that the action was invalid as the ship entered the jurisdiction under duress with the following statement: 'No reasonable person could think it likely that H.M. Government in the year 1952 would try to resolve a commercial dispute by what would be little short of an act of war'. William W. Bishop Jr, 'Anglo-Iranian Oil Co. v. Jaffrate et al.' *American Journal of International Law*, 47 (1953) 326.

[158] Bamberg, *The History of the British Petroleum Company*, 473–76.

Shah against the National Front.[159] By April 1953, a joint operation of the CIA and MI6 was underway to further destabilise Mossadeq, accelerating the political disintegration of the structure of the Iranian Government.[160] Entering into a strategic alliance in the *Majlis* with the Tudeh party, the Mossadeq Government moved in 1953 to strip the Shah of his official powers and forbade contact between the Shah and foreign officials.[161] In June 1953, the US State Department approved a CIA-led coup, dubbed Operation Ajax.[162] After an initial failed attempt accompanied by increasing volatility in the State, on 19 August 1953, Operation Ajax succeeded. Following a nine-hour siege on Mossadeq's house that split the Iranian military, Mossadeq was arrested and charged with treason, and Muhammad Reza Shah Pahlavi was reinstated to political power in Iran with US and British support.[163] The historical consequences of foreign sponsorship of the Shah's prolonged rule in Iran are far more widely known than the story of oil nationalisation under Mossadeq precipitating that sponsorship. Twenty-five years later, the movement toward Iranian independence away from dynastic rule and foreign interference first formalised in the Constitutional Revolution of 1905 came to be reframed within the Islamist discourse of the Ayatollahs[164] – itself the subject of a further case before the International Court of Justice.[165]

As well as playing into a prevailing atmospherics of a law-abiding 'West' and recalcitrant Iran (if not a law-breaking 'rest'), recounting the

159 For a detailed account of this alignment against Mosaddeq, see Fakhreddin Azimi, 'Unseating Mosaddeq: The Configuration and Role of Domestic Forces' in Mark J. Gasiorowski and Malcolm Byrne (eds.), *Mohammad Mosaddeq and the 1953 Coup in Iran* (New York: Syracuse University Press, 2004) 27–101.

160 As Louis points out, in 1952 British diplomats were expelled from Iran, and MI6 had handed over control of its intelligence network to the CIA. Louis, 'Britain and the Overthrow of the Mosaddeq Government'.

161 Abrahamian, *Iran between Two Revolutions*, 271–73.

162 In 2000, the *New York Times* published the CIA's internal report on Operation Ajax. Donald N. Wilber, 'Overthrow of Premier Mossadeq of Iran: November 1952–August 1953' (Central Intelligence Agency, March 1954), https://nsarchive2.gwu.edu/NSAEBB/NSAEBB435/. For a popular history of the operation by a *New York Times* journalist, see Stephen Kinzer, *All the Shah's Men: An American Coup and the Roots of Middle East Terror* (New York: Wiley and Sons, 2003).

163 See Mark J. Gasiorowski, 'The 1953 Coup d'Etat against Mosaddeq' in Mark J. Gasiorowski and Malcolm Byrne (eds.), *Mohammad Mosaddeq and the 1953 Coup in Iran*, (New York: Syracuse University Press, 2004) 256–58.

164 Abrahamian, *Iran between Two Revolutions*, 530–37.

165 *United States Diplomatic and Consular Staff in Tehran (United States of America v. Iran)* (Merits) (1980) ICJ Rep 3.

Anglo-Iranian Oil Company Case without an attention to its historical context smooths over the variety of views that were in play at the time about what an international court of justice should be and what it should do in the world at a crucial moment in both the ICJ's formation and in the transition from an imperial to a putatively decolonising world. Such differences inhered amongst States of all kinds[166] but were particularly potent as 'new' States 'entered' a juridical world not of their own design and sought to engage with it in more or less syncretic ways.[167] Indeed, what looks from the vantage point of today like a routine procedural dispute about interim measures and jurisdiction, warranting only a footnote in most texts, looks from the historical milieu of the case itself like a battle about the proper role and function of the international court in a radically changing world.[168]

For the Iran of Mosaddeq at least, the *Anglo-Iranian Oil Company Case* was the stage upon which its sovereignty would be performed, in the space between technical legal doctrine and political struggle. It was an age when young Iranian international lawyers thought that decolonisation no doubt meant something. What was at issue was not simply a point of procedural jurisdiction but the power to define what sovereignty would mean for decolonising States and the relationship of that concept to the question of international adjudication. As both the content and form of the letter from Kazemi to the Court make clear, from Iran's perspective a dispute between a private company and the Government was a matter for domestic resolution. Compensation was envisaged as a way of settling with the Company, but the right of a State to determine who had control of its most significant resources was understood as falling squarely within the purview of sovereign decision-making. The idea that this new

166 For an exemplary document that gives some sense of the range of views of those behind the establishment of the court, see generally the report of the Commission headed by William Malkin, *Report of the Informal Inter-Allied Committee on the Future of the Permanent Court of International Justice*, reproduced in *American Journal of International Law*, 39 (1945) 1–56. See also James Headlam-Morley, *Studies in Diplomatic History* (New York: Alfred H. King, 1930), especially chapter 2.

167 On the question of syncretism and international law in the context of decolonisation, see Pahuja, 'Laws of Encounter'. For a survey of 'new' States and their attitude to the ICJ, see Ibrahim F. I. Shihata, 'The Attitude of New States toward the International Court of Justice' *International Organization*, 19 (1965) 203–22.

168 On the project of trying to reconstruct in detail a historical milieu in order to understand the concerns animating the actors at the time, particularly in the context of understanding struggles over decolonisation, see David Scott, 'The Temporality of Generations: Dialogue, Tradition, Criticism' *New Literary History*, 45 (2014) 157–81.

international law might not only support the international adjudication of such a dispute, but could potentially prevent the nationalisation of natural resources from happening at all even before the Court had established its jurisdiction,[169] was a grave disappointment to those who hoped that 'fair play and justice [might] govern the relations of the strong and the weak'.[170]

It is more than ironic then, that sovereign statehood was the only legal form by which a socio-political entity could enter the world and take up a lawful place in it, and yet even as non-European States took it up, the invocation of 'sovereignty' itself was decried as being *against* the (international) law of which it is a key jurisdictional form.[171] Accounts that treat disputes over the ICJ's jurisdiction during this crucial moment as purely technical questions miss the texture of what were jurisprudential struggles over the kind of worlds being authored and authorised through international law and risk participating in the rituals of contemporary international law, which imply that there is nothing outside Europe and the world of its making.[172]

[169] Iran was of course not alone in arguing against the ICJ's jurisdiction to 'indicate provisional measures' under Article 41 of the Statute where its jurisdiction to hear the merits was in doubt. There was contemporaneous debate about whether the Court's interim decision was good law. See Charles G. Fenwick, 'The Order of the International Court of Justice in the Anglo-Iranian Oil Company Case' *American Journal of International Law*, 45 (1951) 723–27; Brendan F. Brown, 'The Juridical Implications of the Anglo-Iranian Oil Company Case', *Washington University Law Quarterly*, (1952) 384–97; Ford, *The Anglo-Iranian Oil Dispute of 1951–1952*, 90. The legal threshold for jurisdiction to indicate interim measures is still not settled; it remains unclear whether the ICJ has to satisfy itself that the primary case does not a priori fall outside its jurisdiction, as held in *Anglo-Iranian Oil Company Case (United Kingdom v. Iran)* (Judgment of 22 July 1952) (1952) ICJ Rep 93, or whether it has to satisfy itself that it prima facie has jurisdiction to hear the primary case, as held in *Legality of Use of Force (Yugoslavia v. Belgium)* (Order of 2 June 1999) (1999) ICJ Rep 124 and *Armed Activities on the Territory of the Congo (New Application: 2002) (Democratic Republic of the Congo v. Rwanda)* (Order of 10 July 2002) (2002) ICJ Rep 219.

[170] *Anglo-Iranian Oil Company Case* (Other Documents), 672.

[171] On sovereignty as a 'jurisdictional form' of European international law, see Shaun McVeigh and Sundhya Pahuja, 'Rival Jurisdictions: The Promise and Loss of Sovereignty' in Charles Barbour and George Pavlich (eds.), *After Sovereignty: On the Question of Political Beginnings* (London: Routledge, 2009) 97–114.

[172] For the seminal critique of Eurocentric diffusionism, or the idea that Europeans are 'the makers of history' and that cultural processes tend to flow out of the European sector and toward the non-European sector over the course of history, see James M. Blaut, *The Colonizer's Model of the World: Geographical Diffusionism and Eurocentric History* (New York: Guilford Press, 1993). For an account of international law that describes the way in which administrative arrangements and legal forms moved from 'periphery' to 'centre'

The case offers a compelling illustration of the way a juridicalised legal order can work against equitable distribution and peaceful relations. Here, the Cold War context enhanced that danger. One of the key features of the Iranian Oil Company case was the way in which the British government actively misrepresented the actions of Mossadeq (and the Tudeh party with whom he formed a loose relation at particular times) as Soviet-influenced in order to draw the Americans into his covert overthrow. This was not the first time, nor would it be the last. The British government made similar misrepresentations in relation to Malaya, describing the anti-imperial/anti-British agitation as 'communist'.[173] It seems also that the perceived 'success' of the covert operation in Iran had its effects: encouraging Britain to invade Egypt after the nationalisation of the Suez Canal and the US to carry out a covert 'regime change' operation in Guatemala. Indeed, the practice of fomenting a coup to protect 'assets' acquired by Western corporations under conditions of colonial or semi-colonial coercion became widespread globally.

5.4 The UN Commission on Transnational Corporations and the Formation of the G7

5.4.1 The Initiative from the Third World

Our third story concerns the struggle to establish a Commission on Transnational Corporations at the United Nations. This was a moment of alliance between the Third World and the Soviet Union, who shared with each other a different idea to the United States about the distribution of authority between the national and the international with respect to transnational (or multinational) corporations. Specifically, the Third World and the Soviet Union shared a view on both the nature of sovereign rights and on which rights and protections were subject to international jurisdiction and which were subject to domestic jurisdiction. In this example, the United States' legal policy was allied with the interests of the colonial powers and marked an implicit effort to extend existing elements of imperial and inter-imperial law beyond imperial borders. This example also illustrates the way in which particular projects

rather than the other way around, see Cait Storr, *International Status in the Shadow of Empire: Nauru and the Histories of International Law* (Cambridge: Cambridge University Press, 2020).

173 See Rubin, *Archives of Authority*.

that flourished during the Cold War were closed off retrospectively. Here, that project was the global regulation of transnational corporations though a *public* international law.[174]

In 1972, at the Third Session of the newly formed United Nations Conference on Trade and Development (UNCTAD) being held in Santiago, Chile,[175] Salvador Allende gave the opening speech.[176] In it, he argued that the purpose of the Third Session was to continue the work begun during decolonisation to reform international economic structures (beginning with the creation of UNCTAD itself) and to transform the 'outdated and essentially unjust economic and trade order'.[177] Allende understood that poverty is not a natural phenomenon but is produced by economic arrangements.[178] The generation of wealth and the production of poverty exist in 'a clear-cut dialectical relationship': 'imperialism exists because under-development exists; under-development exists because imperialism exists'.[179] For Allende, transnational corporations were central to the problem. In his account, if corporations were to continue to expand, it would be fatal to the new worlds being made through Third

[174] This section draws on Sundhya Pahuja and Anna Saunders, 'Rival Worlds and the Place of the Corporation in International Law' in Jochen von Bernstorff and Philip Dann (eds.), *The Battle for International Law: South–North Perspectives on the Decolonization Era* (Oxford University Press, 2019); and André Dao, Caitlin Murphy and Sundhya Pahuja, 'Bad States, Good Corporations? The Intersecting Histories of Business and Human Rights and International Investment Law' in Jochen von Bernstoff, Phillip Dann and Surabhi Ranganathan (eds.), *The Battle for International Law in the Neoliberal Era (1975–2000)* (Oxford: Oxford University Press, 2026).

[175] Diego Cordovez, 'The Making of UNCTAD: Institutional Background and Legislative History', *Journal of World Trade Law*, 1 (1967) 272.

[176] 'Address Delivered by Mr. Salvador Allende Gossens, President of Chile at the Inaugural Ceremony on 13 April 1972', Proceedings of the United Nations Conference on Trade and Development (1972) UN Doc. TD/80 Annex VIII A); 'Address by Mr. Salvador Allende, President of the Republic of Chile', Official Records of the twenty-seventh session of the United Nations General Assembly, UN Doc. A/PV.2096 (4 December 1972).

[177] Salvador Allende (Republic of Chile), 'Address Delivered at the Inaugural Ceremony', Proceedings of the United Nations Conference on Trade and Development (13 April 1972, Santiago, Chile), at [9].

[178] Many people understood this. See Fanon, *The Wretched of the Earth*. See, too, Sundhya Pahuja, 'Corporations, Universalism, and the Domestication of Race in International Law' in Duncan Bell (ed.), *Empire, Race and Global Justice* (Cambridge: Cambridge University Press, 2019) 74–93.

[179] 'Address by Mr. Salvador Allende, President of the Republic of Chile', Official Records of the United Nations General Assembly (1972) UN Doc. A/PV.2096, at [65].

World solidarity (at the Bandung Conference in 1955,[180] in the 'non-aligned' movement[181] and in calls for a New International Economic Order).[182]

The speech is often remembered for its strong critique of the interference by corporations in the political and economic sovereignty of Chile. Just a year later, the companies Allende accused of being intent on destabilising the elected government because it pursued a socialist agenda (including nationalising the copper and telecommunications industries), had – with CIA assistance – fomented the coup that toppled that government, led to Allende's death and installed General Augusto Pinochet as president of Chile.[183]

But Allende was concerned not just with the question of the present interference in Chile's sovereignty. Instead, he drew a longer historical arc, referring back to colonialism as well as to the Monroe Doctrine of 1823[184] and the Roosevelt Corollary of 1904 (each of which ostensibly protected Latin America from recolonisation by European States but also asserted a US right to intervene in the continent to prevent 'flagrant and

[180] Luis Eslava, Vasuki Nesiah and Michael Fakhri (eds.), *Bandung, Global History, and International Law: Critical Pasts and Pending Futures* (Cambridge: Cambridge University Press, 2017).

[181] Natasa Miskovic, Harald Fischer-Tiné and Nada Boskovska (eds.), *The Non-Aligned Movement and the Cold War: Delhi – Bandung – Belgrade* (New York: Routledge, 2014); Hani Sayed, 'The Humanization of the Third World' in Eslava, Nesiah and Fakhri, *Bandung, Global History, and International Law*, 431–49; William Roger Louis and Ronald Robinson, 'The Imperialism of Decolonization' in James Le Sueur (ed.), *The Decolonization Reader* (London: Routledge, 2003) 49–79.

[182] Jennifer Bair, 'Taking Aim at the New International Economic Order' in Philip Mirowski and Dieter Plehwe (eds.), *The Road from Mont Pèlerin: The Making of the Neoliberal Thought Collective* (Cambridge, MA: Harvard University Press, 2009), 347–85; Mohammed Bedjaoui, *Towards a New International Economic Order* (New York: Holmes and Meier, 1979).

[183] Anthony Sampson, *The Sovereign State: The Secret History of International Telephone and Telegraph* (London: Hodder and Stoughton, 1973); United States Senate, 'Hearings before the Select Committee to Study Governmental Operations with Respect to Intelligence Activities, 4 and 5 December 1975', Volume 7, First Session, Ninety Fourth Congress 1975, www.intelligence.senate.gov/resources/intelligence-related-commissions.

[184] Mark Gilderhus, 'The Monroe Doctrine: Meanings and implications' *Presidential Studies Quarterly*, 36 (2006) 5–16; Juan Pablo Scarfi, 'In the Name of the Americas: The Pan-American Redefinition of the Monroe Doctrine and the Emerging Language of American International Law in the Western Hemisphere, 1898–1922' *Diplomatic History*, 40 (2016) 189–218.

chronic wrongdoing by a Latin American Nation').[185] The gesture towards the history of imperialism in the Americas was a retort to a habit on the part of Western States of repeatedly inaugurating the world anew, by describing the decolonised nations as 'new', or 'emerging' States, 'entering' the world for the first time (for example, through their 'membership' in the United Nations).[186] Third World figures like Allende, in contrast, conceived of the present as historical, linked to what had gone before through the legacies of empire and in emergent neo-imperialisms.[187] For them, diplomacy after empire was in large part an historiographical enterprise, involving a need to assert a continuity between pre- and postcolonial civilisations in the non-West and to reclaim a 'rightful place' in history for those civilisations.[188]

As well as making a historiographical assertion, Allende was also concerned with how to understand the modern corporation in its historical context. In his account, that entity too was historically grounded, existing on a continuum with colonial companies. Unlike the 'private' entities they were said to be in US jurisprudence,[189] he thought transnational corporations were better understood as political entities

[185] There is a version of this doctrine on the website of the Office of the Historian of the United States: Office of the Historian, 'New Policies for Latin American, Asia', https://history.state.gov/departmenthistory/short-history/newpolicies. For an analysis, see Mark Gilderhus, 'The Monroe Doctrine: Meanings and Implications' *Presidential Studies Quarterly*, 36 (2006) 5–16.

[186] Sundhya Pahuja, 'Letters from Bandung: Encounters with Another International Law' in Eslava, Fakhri and Nesiah, *Bandung, Global History, and International Law*, 552–73.

[187] On the 'durability' of imperial modes of thought and a challenge to the idea of the 'post' colonial, see generally, Ann Laura Stoler, *Duress: Imperial Durabilities in Our Times* (Durham: Duke University Press, 2016).

[188] For one example of this gesture at the level of the State, see Jawaharlal Nehru, 'Meeting Ground of East and West' (Speech given in the Constituent Assembly (Legislative) of India, 8 March 1949, New Delhi, India). Reproduced in Ministry of Information and Broadcasting, *Jawaharlal Nehru's Speeches, Volume One: September 1946–May 1949* (Coimbatore: Government of India Press 1967) 232–49. See also Upendra Baxi, 'Some Remarks on Eurocentrism and the Law of Nations' in Ram Prakash Anand (ed.), *Asian States and the Development of Universal International Law* (New Delhi: Vikas, 1972) 3–9.

[189] Terence Gourvish and Nick Tiratsoo (eds.), *Missionaries and Managers: American Influences on European Management Education, 1945–60* (Manchester: Manchester University Press, 1998) 3; Paddy Ireland, 'Defending the Rentier: Corporate Theory and the Reprivatization of the Public Company' in John Parkinson, Gavin Kelly and Andrew Gamble (eds.), *The Political Economy of the Company* (Oxford: Hart, 2001) 141–74.

exercising public authority.[190] For Allende, this experience produced two axes of concern. The first was how to manage the conduct and activities of transnational corporations (the conduct question); the second was the question of how corporations came to acquire assets and how those assets were protected (the property question). Each of these questions was marked by political fault-lines that could be mapped by reference to the distribution of authority between the national and the international.

In terms of the conduct question, Allende was concerned to ensure that all States should have the ability to assess for themselves whether transnational corporations doing business in their territories were making a contribution to the economic development of the country as a whole. Like many in the Second and Third Worlds, Allende understood that the devil of 'foreign investment' was – and remains – in the details.[191] In terms of the 'property' question, Allende was mindful of how companies had acquired investments and how these investments were protected. During the nineteenth century, the major European powers had 'propagate[d] Western standards of individual ownership around the world and secure[d] these standards' in the face of rival laws and rival forms of life in order to facilitate the security of foreign investment.[192] In the process, they displaced or radically transformed collective forms of ownership and systems of use rights (or confined them to 'native' sectors of dual economies) and created regimes of private property as part of a politically guaranteed 'order' for European States, doing this through a variety of means 'ranging from [direct] colonialism to extraterritorial laws to informal commercial empire'.[193] Although the language of law was used by some to justify these actions, these practices were highly contested and not accepted at the time as anything like the

[190] Bedjaoui, *Towards a New International Economic Order*, 36–37: 'The present situation, with the multinational companies, is even more alienating for the under-developed countries than it was in the colonization period with the chartered companies.'

[191] This included the density of linkages between the company's operations and the local economy and society as a whole, the extent of the repatriation of profits, the use of 'restrictive business practices', such as invoking intellectual property regimes to prevent technology transfer to the State 'hosting' the investment, the issue of environmental degradation and the conditions of work promoted by the corporation. David Fieldhouse, *The West and the Third World: Trade, Colonialism, Dependence and Development* (Oxford: Blackwell, 1999) 254–86.

[192] Charles Lipson, *Standing Guard: Protecting Foreign Capital in the Nineteenth and Twentieth Centuries* (Berkeley and Los Angeles: University of California Press, 1985) 20.

[193] Lipson, *Standing Guard*, 21.

'international legal order' they are now often retrospectively described as having become.

From the perspective of the West, this 'order' was asserted as something like an 'international law governing expropriation of foreign investments', imposing strict 'minimum standards' on all States and requiring full compensation in case of expropriation.[194] In keeping with the assertion of legality, these particular values were cast as universal, and enforcement of this 'standard' was closely intertwined with empire and intervention. As Detlev Vagts put it, 'at the high tide of this version of international law, breaches by host countries might be avenged by any number of plagues ranging from gunboats to arbitration'.[195] But even from the inside of this imperial international law, there was uncertainty over the status of 'foreign property'. The force of the Russian Revolution and Mexican nationalisations of the early twentieth century meant that there was no legal or institutional resolution at the League of Nations over the question of whether foreign-owned private property should be granted international protection.[196]

But as the post-war period went on and agitation for decolonisation increased, tremors began to shake the 'system'. The most notable example is the nationalisation of the Anglo–Iranian Oil company discussed above.[197] As decolonisation proceeded, the quakes became more frequent, as both the substance of the asserted 'rules' protecting foreign-owned private property and the preferred modes of 'enforcement' were subject to radical challenge. From the perspective of the West, this was perceived as a crisis of 'legitimacy'.[198] But from the perspective of the Second and Third Worlds, it represented the beginning of another struggle, this time to remake the international economic order after empire and to offer a wholesale challenge to the political-economic legacies of colonialism.

The response of the West in the face of this challenge was to experiment with a new mode of postcolonial enforcement to protect foreign-owned private property: intervention by the CIA with the aim of underpinning corporate/State alliances (e.g. the coup in Guatemala in 1954 to

194 Ibid., 24.
195 Detlev Vagts, 'The Global Corporation and International Law' *Journal of International Law and Economics*, 6 (1972) 254.
196 Arghyrios Fatouros, 'An International Code to Protect Private Investment: Proposals and Perspectives' *University of Toronto Law Journal*, 14 (1961) 79.
197 See generally, Pahuja and Storr, 'Rethinking Iran and International Law'.
198 See generally, Lipson, *Standing Guard*.

protect the interests of United Fruit).[199] Such activity was not the sole province of the United States. Cold War paranoia was actively mobilised by weakened imperial powers, such as Britain, to persuade the United States to help protect the property of their investors.[200] But as this new mode of protecting foreign property began to surface, in Chile certainly, and people suspected even then in Iran, the 'legitimacy' of the imperial regime was eroded further still, and resistance to it, even from inside the United States, increased.[201] This erosion of legitimacy, combining the Sino-Soviet critique of capitalism[202] with Third World solidarity, created space for the assertion of the Third World as a *juridical*, and not simply political, project. The particular terms of the juridical assertion now being forcefully made related to the distribution of legal authority. Specifically, the Third World asserted that the conduct of foreign corporations should be regulated by international law and that the authority to admit, restrict or expropriate foreign investment should rest with the nation-state. International coordination was needed to address the conduct question because of the collective action problem engendered by the mobility of the elements of production, while national authority was needed over the foreign ownership of property as a response to imperialism.

5.4.2 *The US Response*

Meanwhile, shortly after the first session of the newly established UN Commission on Transnational Corporations (UNCTC), the General Assembly of the UN held a Special Session on Development and Economic Co-operation on 1 September 1975. The session was planned as part of the ongoing institutional efforts to establish the principles of a New International Economic Order.[203] And although the question of a binding treaty to hold transnational corporations to international legal

199 For a list of instances, see William Blum, *Killing Hope: U.S. Military and C.I.A. Interventions Since World War II* (Monroe: Common Courage Press, 1995).

200 This was done through the Information Research Division, a secret division of the British Foreign Office. Rubin, *Archives of Authority*, 20, 34.

201 United States Senate, 'Hearings before the Select Committee to Study Governmental Operations with Respect to Intelligence Activities, 4 and 5 December 1975', Volume 7, First Session, Ninety Fourth Congress, 1975, www.intelligence.senate.gov/resources/intelligence-related-commissions.

202 See Jeremy Friedman, *Shadow Cold War: The Sino-Soviet Competition for the Third World* (Chapel Hill: University of North Carolina Press, 2015).

203 This was in the wake of the Declaration establishing a New International Economic Order at the UN General Assembly in 1974: UNGA Res 3201 (S-VI) (1 May 1974).

standards of behaviour had already fallen off the new UNCTC's programme of work (and despite Allende's death during the Chilean coup on 11 September 1973), the question of the corporation was very much alive at the General Assembly session.

The purpose of the gathering was to consider 'new concepts and options with a view to promoting effectively the solution of world economic problems, especially those of developing countries'.[204] At the forefront of the session was the United States.[205] Then US Secretary of State Henry Kissinger was due to deliver a speech at the beginning of the proceedings. As it turned out, he was drawn away,[206] and his speech was read in his absence by Daniel Moynihan, US Ambassador to the UN. The speech, called 'Global Consensus and Economic Development', announced the moment as 'an opportunity to improve the condition of mankind'. The United States, Kissinger declared, was committed to 'a programme of practical steps' to address the concerns of the developing world.[207] For Kissinger, the technical means now available engendered a positive duty to bring about 'the ancient dream of mankind – a world without poverty'. Like Truman before him, he argued that the way to fulfil that duty was not to transfer money or material resources but to share American knowledge.[208] For Truman in 1949, and Kissinger in 1973, the existence of human suffering, and superior technical know-how, authorised, as Siba Grovogui put it, 'a Western [and here, specifically American] claim to moral authority as a provider of rules and

[204] Azeredo Da Silverira (Brazil), 'Address Delivered at 2327th Plenary Meeting', *Official Records of the United Nations General Assembly* (1 September 1975, New York) [3], citing UNGA Res 3172 (XXVIII) (17 December 1963).

[205] Daniel Moynihan (United States of America), 'Address Delivered at 2327th Plenary Meeting', *Official Records of the United Nations General Assembly*, UN Doc. A/PV.2327 (1 September 1975) [33]–[203].

[206] By the conclusion of the Sinai Pact between Egypt and Israel. Bernard Gwertzman, 'Kissinger Seeks Approval Today of Mideast Pact', *The New York Times*, 1 September 1975, www.nytimes.com/1975/09/01/archives/kissinger-seeks-approval-today-of-mideast-pact-works-with-israelis.html.

[207] Daniel Moynihan (United States of America), 'Address Delivered at 2327th Plenary Meeting', *Official Records of the United Nations General Assembly*, UN Doc. A/PV.2327 (1 September 1975) [35]–[36]. Kissinger served as US Secretary of State from 1973 to 1977.

[208] Harry Truman, 'Truman's Inaugural Address', *Harry S. Truman Presidential Library and Museum*, 20 January 1949, www.trumanlibrary.org/whistlestop/50yr_archive/inagural20jan1949.html.

models to the rest'.[209] In contrast to the Third World's insistence on the continued presence of history, and the impoverishment by the West of the rest, Kissinger conceived the moment in which he spoke as ruptural, a radical break with the past: the 'global order of colonial power that lasted through centuries has now disappeared'.[210] The present was so new for Kissinger that, by 1972, even 'the cold war division of the world into two rigid blocs ha[d] now also broken down', and there remained, he said, only States united in the common endeavour of development.[211] But because of its obvious under-development, action taken by the Third World at the international institutional level could not be read as the assertion of a different account of (international) law. Instead, Third World solidarity was positioned in opposition to the inauguration of what Kissinger asserted could be a new era of 'human progress'. The threat lay in the formation of the Non-Aligned Movement, a 'new bloc' that was counterproductive to this endeavour, engaging 'in a kind of solidarity that often clearly sacrifices practical interests'.[212] What was required to address the economic problems faced by all States was not division, said Kissinger, but 'consensus, first and foremost, on the principle that our common development goals can be achieved only by co-operation, not by the politics of confrontation'.[213]

The 'transnational enterprise' was amongst the most contentious of these lines of 'political division'. The ongoing 'controversy over their role and conduct', which had continued in various forms and fora since Allende's speech, was 'itself an obstacle to economic development'. In his view, 'if the world community [was] committed to economic development, it [could] not afford to treat transnational enterprises as objects of economic warfare'.[214] Nevertheless, Kissinger conceded that 'the time [had] come for the international community to articulate standards of conduct' for corporations and acknowledged that the UNCTC 'had begun such an effort'. But for Kissinger, 'transnational

[209] Siba Grovogui, 'Come to Africa: A Hermeneutics of Race in International Theory' *Alternatives: Global, Local, Political*, 26 (2001) 427.
[210] Daniel Moynihan (United States of America), 'Address Delivered at 2327th Plenary Meeting', *Official Records of the United Nations General Assembly*, UN Doc. A/PV.2327 (1 September 1975) [38].
[211] Moynihan 'Address Delivered at 2327th Plenary Meeting', [38].
[212] Ibid., [44].
[213] Ibid., [47].
[214] Ibid., [105], [119].

enterprises ha[d] been powerful instruments of modernization' and 'one of the most effective engines of development'. As Allende had foreshadowed, 'foreign investment' was imputed with a tutelary dimension and tied closely to the salvific project of developing the under-developed. As Kissinger argued, only 'transnational enterprises' and the private capital they provided could facilitate the solution to the problem of under-development. Standards should therefore be formulated that applied both to the behaviour of corporations *and* to the governments that hosted them.[215]

The principles that Kissinger laid out contained two key elements. First was an insistence that corporate conduct should be governed by local, not international law. Transnational corporations were of course 'obliged to obey local law', 'refrain from unlawful interference in the domestic affairs of the host country' and 'respect local customs and employ qualified local personnel'. But second, in return, those corporations were to receive a stable, apolitical environment in which to operate, characterised by equitable and non-discriminatory treatment and subject to the protection of '*international law*'.[216] In Kissinger's account, these protections would be supported by a suite of international endeavours, including the harmonisation of tax treatment, the promotion of arbitral procedures for the settlement of investment disputes, the reduction of restrictive business practices and the multilateralisation of the insurance of foreign investment.[217] These would be underpinned by the 'development of agricultural technologies' for food production, 'assistance to improve productivity and competitiveness' in relation to non-agricultural food production and future access to 'borrowing in the [international] capital market' (something which was already relied upon heavily in the Latin American countries). In essence, what Kissinger was mapping out was a different kind of 'new international economic order' based on the idea of 'development' and the needs of the poorest 'one billion people', but which located authority in the First World, precisely contradicting in its every element the other 'New International Economic Order' being proposed by the Global South at the same moment.[218]

[215] Moynihan, 'Address Delivered at 2327th Plenary Meeting', [103], [108].
[216] Ibid., [110]–[111] (emphasis added).
[217] Ibid., [112], [118].
[218] Ibid., [84], [165].

5.4.3 *The Rest of the First World Joins In: The Establishment of the G7*

In his fateful Speech, Kissinger called for 'industrial nations' to 'work together more effectively to restore and maintain their non-inflationary expansion'. Indeed, he acknowledged that this work had already begun. 'In a new departure this past year', he said, 'the leaders of the United States and its major trading partners have begun closer co-ordination of their national economic policies'. According to Kissinger, this had a benevolent, even altruistic aim: '[S]ince the economic health of the industrial countries is central to the health of the global economy, their efforts to avoid the extremes of recession and inflation become an international, as well as a national, responsibility.' Kissinger exhorted the Third World to desist from its confrontational stance. The US, he said, was ready to meet in a spirit of mutual co-operation.

The records of the meetings between the rich nations immediately following Kissinger's speech show that this co-operation can be understood as a coordinated effort to defend the existing international order from challenge and to maintain its existing distributional patterns. This is encapsulated by an article written in 1975 by Moynihan in which he described the New International Economic Order as coming 'ominously close to looting'. As Jessica Whyte explains:

> [Moynihan] laid out an oppositional strategy with two key 'points of systematic attack' the first world should employ. The first was to defend liberal institutions (including the multinational corporation). The second was to challenge the idea that there was any sort of crisis in the Third World, and to assert instead that the Third World was to blame for its own predicament.[219]

As Moynihan put it: 'These economies do less well than they ought: ... the difference is of their own making and no one else's, and no claim on anyone else arises in consequence.'[220]

In November 1975, against the backdrop of co-ordinated Third World action, the activities of the Non-Aligned Movement and the successful agitation for a New International Economic Order, a portentous meeting

[219] Jessica Whyte, *The Morals of the Market: Human Rights and the Rise of Neoliberalism* (New York: Verso, 2019) 136 (emphasis added).

[220] Daniel Moynihan, 'The United States in Opposition' *Law, Government and Society* (March 1975).

took place. In a discrete chateau outside Paris,[221] the leaders of France, Germany, Italy, Japan, the United States and the United Kingdom quietly met.[222] The declassified records kept by the UK Government reveal that those present expressed growing concern about the changing international order.[223] They were particularly exercised by the proposals and actions from the Third World directed towards challenging, reforming and remaking existing international economic structures and relationships after Empire. Harold Wilson, then (Labour) Prime Minister of the UK, advised the meeting that the States assembled needed to stick together, in order to resist attempts at division by the group of newly independent States known as G-77.[224] Wilson warned the heads of State assembled that they 'should not underestimate the developing countries' speed of learning' because the 'OPEC syndrome was catching on'.[225] This meeting was the start of things to come, and once Canada had joined the following year, the assembly became the Group of 7.[226]

[221] Chateau de Rambouillet was the summer residence of the presidents of France until 2009.

[222] See The United Kingdom, 'Note of the First Session of the Conference of Heads of Government of France, Germany, Italy, Japan, the United Kingdom and the United States at the Chateau de Rambouillet on Saturday, 15 November 1975 at 6.00 pm' (The National Archives PREM 16/838), via the Margaret Thatcher Foundation, 'The G7 Summits', www.margaretthatcher.org/archive/G7. Multiple secret or confidential records reveal the seriousness with which leaders approached this emerging collective effort. The majority of these documents were declassified in 2006 through The National Archives of the UK or the Ford Library for relevant US records and published in a celebratory way by the Margaret Thatcher Foundation.

[223] The United Kingdom, 'Note of the First Session'.

[224] The United Kingdom, 'Note of the Third Session of the Heads of Government Conference at the Chateau de Rambouillet on Sunday 16 November 1975 at 4.15 pm', (The National Archives PREM 16/838), via the Margaret Thatcher Foundation, 'The G7 Summit', www.margaretthatcher.org/archive/G7.

[225] The United Kingdom, 'Note of the Third Session'. The Organisation of Petroleum Exporting Countries originally founded by Iran, Iraq, Kuwait, Saudi Arabia and Venezuela in 1960 had gained more members and more political power in the 1970s both by raising the price of oil and by an oil embargo following the 1973 Arab-Israeli conflict. For more detail see Christopher Dietrich, *Oil Revolution: Anticolonial Elites, Sovereign Rights, and the Economic Culture of Decolonization* (Cambridge: Cambridge University Press, 2017).

[226] The United States, 'Memorandum of Conversation: Dorado Beach, Puerto Rico, June 27 1976', Ford Library: National Security Adviser (International Economic Affairs Staff Files, Box 4), via the Margaret Thatcher Foundation, 'The G7 Summit', www.margaretthatcher.org/archive/G7; The United States, 'Memorandum of Conversation: Dorado Beach, Puerto Rico, June 28 1976', Ford Library: National Security Adviser (International Economic Affairs Staff Files, Box 4), via the Margaret Thatcher Foundation, 'The G7 Summit', www.margaretthatcher.org/archive/G7.

The meeting was sympathetic to Wilson's proposals.[227] Specifically, the leaders gathered at Rambouillet expressed a commitment to a unified strategy of multilateral trade liberalisation to prevent further 'disruption' from the G-77 with its advocacy for an NIEO. In strategic terms, Wilson advocated for unity amongst the nascent (then) G6 at UNCTAD IV.[228] In his account, there was a window of opportunity, as the Third World was 'realising confrontation was not getting them far'.[229] Helmut Schmidt, then Chancellor of Germany, thought that an important element of the West's strategy should be to 'educate' 'the developing countries to understand and think and operate in terms of a market economy'.[230] Schmidt thought that 'they [the South] should understand that no country could spend more than it earned' and that 'it was psychologically wrong' for the Third World to continue its 'dependence on gifts from the industrialised countries'.[231]

For Schmidt, the 'solution' was for States in the South to earn more 'by their own work'.[232] Wilson believed meanwhile that the NIEO would mean an end to the market order and to the Bretton Woods system set up after WWII. Much was at stake.[233] But, Wilson noted, 'he had succeeded at [the recent Commonwealth meeting in] Kingston in doing some education of the Commonwealth in explaining that these radical policies would set back progress for the developing countries by five to ten years'.[234] Records from the inaugural meeting of the then G6 at Rambouillet, and the subsequent annual summits of the nascent G7 at Puerto Rico in 1976 and London in 1977, reveal that the leaders were developing a three-pronged strategy to maintain 'world equilibrium'.[235]

[227] The United Kingdom, 'Note of the Third Session'

[228] Ibid. 'UNCTAD IV' refers to the fourth meeting of the United Nations Conference on Trade and Development held in Nairobi in 1976. For more detail on this meeting, see UNCTAD, 'Proceedings of the United Nations Conference on Trade and Development: Fourth Session' (1977) UN Doc. TD/281, https://unctad.org/meeting/fourth-session-united-nations-conference-trade-and-development-unctad-iv.

[229] The United Kingdom, 'Note of the Third Session'.

[230] Ibid.

[231] Ibid.

[232] Ibid.

[233] For an account of how US diplomats positioned the NIEO as a 'danger to Western civilisation', see Quinn Slobodian, *Globalists: The End of Empire and the Birth of Neoliberalism* (Cambridge, MA: Harvard University Press, 2018) 221 and surrounding chapter.

[234] The United Kingdom, 'Note of the Third Session'.

[235] In d'Estaing's words. Ibid.

First, at Rambouillet, Kissinger proposed exploiting the division emerging between and within oil-exporting and oil-importing States in the South.[236] This was the most explicitly coercive strategy of the three. It was also to become an element of the turbulent and unequal consequences of the debt crises in the 1980s and subsequent structural adjustment interventions by international financial institutions that eviscerated the public sectors of many States in the South. But at Rambouillet and Puerto Rico, the meeting notes record Kissinger saying that while 'military action would of course be inappropriate', the G7 could 'develop the idea that increasing the price of oil wasn't "free" economically or politically'.[237] He proposed that 'the West' should threaten to 'extract a price from both OPEC and the LDCs if their cooperation was not forthcoming or was inadequate'.[238] He hoped that 'no one thought this might be confrontation', but the States assembled should 'not enter consumer-producer dialogue without a strategy'.[239] This strategy and the G7's 'ability to affect the price' of oil would be possible 'only if the West backed the US' and 'if it took a strong stand, cooperating to separate moderate and radical OPEC' States and to stop 'more "pecs" from forming in primary producers'.[240]

The second strategy, as became clear at the Puerto Rico summit, was to encourage the internationalisation of private investment. The heads of State assembled knew this became more plausible as a foreign policy objective if corporations could be made (as Miki, the Japanese Prime Minister, put it) 'to curb their illegal activities'.[241] The years before the meeting would have provided many examples of such activities.[242] In light of this, the rich States believed they had to make a gesture towards regulating companies. Indeed, just days before the Puerto Rico summit, a

236 Ibid.

237 Ibid.

238 Ibid.

239 Ibid.

240 Ibid.

241 The United Kingdom, 'Note of the Second Session of the International Conference at Puerto Rico on Monday 28 June 1976 at 0900' (The National Archives PREM 16/821), via the Margaret Thatcher Foundation, 'The G7 Summit', www.margaretthatcher.org/archive/G7.

242 See in particular chapters 9 and 34 in Blum, *Killing Hope*. See further recently declassified documents on Kissinger's involvement in a failed CIA plan to support a Chilean military coup to stop Allende taking power found at the National Security Archives, https://nsarchive.gwu.edu/briefing-book/chile/2023-08-08/chiles-coup-50-kissinger-briefed-nixon-failed-1970-cia-plot-block.

wider grouping of wealthy nations, the OECD, had taken precisely this approach by adopting a 'Declaration on International Investment and Multinational Enterprises'.[243] On the one hand, the Declaration promoted the benefits of foreign private investment by including the principle of 'national treatment'. According to this principle, international law would require that States treat foreign-controlled enterprises in the same way – 'no less favourably' – as local, home-grown enterprises. Given the colonial context from which States were gaining independence, this expectation was, in itself, extraordinary. On the other hand, a set of voluntary Guidelines for Multinational Enterprises, annexed to the Declaration, purported to address the capacity of multinationals to 'abuse ... concentrations of economic power and to conflict [it] with national policy objectives'.[244] The OECD Declaration and Guidelines ostensibly represented, thus, the 'balanced' and 'fair' approach prefigured by Kissinger. They were both a concession to Third World and (First World) union pressure to rein in the conduct of TNCs and a marker of how far a united Western world was willing to go in the imminent negotiations on a UN Code of Conduct.[245] Finally, throughout the series of summits and in particular in London in 1977, multiple State leaders agreed that, in order to prevent people from voting for communist and socialist parties that might cause further disruption, the G7 would need to give some minimum level of aid to what its leaders refer to as the 'least developed countries'.[246]

[243] See OECD, 'The OECD Declaration on International Investment and Multinational Enterprises: Promoting Responsible Government and Responsible Business', https://web-archive.oecd.org/2012-06-14/82005-theoecddeclarationoninternationalinvestmentandmultinationalenterprisespromotingresponsiblegovernmentandresponsiblebusiness.htm. See also Karl Sauvant, 'Negotiations of the United Nations Code of Conduct on Transnational Corporations: Experience and Lessons Learned' *Journal of World Investment & Trade*, 16 (2015) 11–87; John Ruggie and Tamaryn Nelson, 'Human Rights and the OECD Guidelines for Multinational Enterprises: Normative Innovations and Implementation Challenges' *The Brown Journal of World Affairs*, 22 (2015) 101. This was an extraordinary erasure of the manner and mode of colonial exploitation.

[244] See OECD, 'OECD Guidelines for Multinational Enterprises' (2011, OECD), http://dx.doi.org/10.1787/9789264115415-en.

[245] See Sauvant, 'Negotiations of the United Nations Code of Conduct on Transnational Corporations' for an account of how the OECD guidelines came on the eve of UNCTC negotiations. We could note as well that for the US, the OECD was the most favourable forum to set ground rules for TNCs.

[246] Jeremy Friedman, *Ripe for Revolution: Building Socialism in the Third World* (Cambridge, MA: Harvard University Press, 2022).

The third strategy centred on offering aid to a Third World government in return for that government reorienting the State's economy towards a market-based one. This strategy was suggested by the French President, Giscard d'Estaing, who agreed with the G7 proposal to reject debt relief but suggested that Western States should consider increasing assistance and to ask for something in return. The quid pro quo would be that the States with economic policies (and ideologies) that more strongly tended towards a market economy would be rewarded. In a similar vein, Schmidt was unwilling to entertain any action to stabilise commodity prices and said that the G7 must 'help the developing countries, rather than please them'.[247] These three strategies found their thin edge in the debt crisis of the 1980s.[248]

As we know now, Kissinger's map in 1975 was prefigurative. What looked like a victory of sorts in the creation of the UNCTC failed to produce the collective State action sought by the Third World to regulate the conduct of multinational corporations. The UNCTC was quietly put to rest in 1993, folded into the United Nations Development Programme (UNDP) as part of the 'Division on Investment and Enterprise'. The UNCTC had failed, but Kissinger's detailed plan foreshadowed the eventual inversion of what was being attempted by the Third World and precluded the exercise by the Third World of juridical authority. Today, that particular attempt to establish a conversation at the United Nations about multinational corporations is almost invariably forgotten.[249] When it is remembered at all, it is usually characterised as an ill-fated attempt to assert a Third World sovereign jurisdiction against an international jurisdiction, with all the hierarchies of value that characterisation implies. The story is now largely retold (for better or worse) as 'sovereignty' versus international 'community'.

But slowing the story down reveals that what was being asserted was not the simple 'domestic' versus 'international' story but the authority to decide which matters should be put into the basket of 'domestic' and which should be 'international' and with what consequences. As it emerged from formal empire, the Third World sought to assert authority over private property in the national realm as a way to address the

[247] The United Kingdom, 'Note of the Third Session'.

[248] See generally, Jérôme Sgard, *The Debt Crisis of the 1980s: Law and Political Economy* (UK: Edward Elgar, 2023).

[249] For one notable exception to this, see Jennifer Bair, 'Corporations at the United Nations: Echoes of the New International Economic Order' *Humanity*, 6 (2015) 159–71.

economic legacies of imperialism and to internationalise the capacity to regulate corporate conduct as a response to the essential rootlessness of the multinational corporation. This has commonalities with both the Algerian and Iranian stories in terms of a struggle over what is to count as international in the first place.

Ultimately, what we see during the period from the end of the Cold War to the present is the *internationalisation* of the protection of private property through an emerging regime of 'international investment law'[250] and the relegation to the national sphere of the regulation over corporate conduct, along with the vulnerabilities and collective action problems that brings. This has been accompanied by a turn to 'business and human rights', which pushes responsibility for enforcing the standards downwards into the (Third World) nation-state but invests authority over setting the standards themselves upwards, into the international community through its jurisdiction over the universal 'human'.[251]

5.5 Conclusion: Decolonisation and the Making of International Law

'International Law' was a term invented by Jeremy Bentham around the end of the eighteenth century[252] to describe a law of encounter being asserted by Imperial Britain, which it imagined would best serve its interests.[253] This terminology gained currency and eventually displaced the 'law of nations' during the late nineteenth century. After the Second World War, many continued to use the name 'international law' to describe lawful relations between States. Grewe has argued that the use

250 Sundhya Pahuja, 'Part 3: Contemporary Patterns of Ordering: Business and Human Rights and International Investment Law' *Hersch Lauterpacht Memorial Lectures*, University of Cambridge, March 2018, www.lcil.cam.ac.uk/hersch-lauterpacht-memorial-lectures. See Muthucumaraswamy Sornarajah, 'The Myth of International Contract Law' *Journal of World Trade Law*, 15 (1981) 187–217. On the 'levitation' out of the sphere of domestic law into that of international law, see Muthucumaraswamy Sornarajah, *Law of International Joint Ventures* (Singapore: Longman, 1992) 298.

251 United Nations Human Rights Office of the High Commissioner, Guiding Principles on Business and Human Rights: Implementing the United Nations 'Protect, Respect and Remedy' Framework (Geneva: United Nations, 2011); Erika George, 'Incorporating Rights: Empire, Global Enterprise and Global Justice' *University of St. Thomas Law Journal*, 10 (2013) 917–59.

252 David Armitage, 'Globalizing Jeremy Bentham' *History of Political Thought*, 32 (2011) 63–82.

253 Lauren Benton and Adam Clulow, 'Interpolity Law and Jurisdictional Politics' *Law and History Review*, 42 (2024) 197–209.

of that same name – 'international law' – at that point is misleading because 'the system' changed irrevocably after the end of World War II.[254] It is true that the continuity of name is misleading. But for us, the reason it is misleading is because 'the system' that assumed the mantle was largely an illusion we see only when we look backwards with one eye closed. What did carry over from nineteenth century international law to Cold War international law were practices that authorised and stabilised statehood as the only way to claim legal personality. This was both cause and effect of the success of anti-colonial nationalism as the form of decolonisation that won the day. And as we saw in Chapter 2, the continuity of the State form was a key aspect of the Amero-Soviet Cold War project, embedded in the United Nations.

But the generalisation of the State as legal subject can trick us into seeing both a continuation of a nineteenth-century international legal order into the twentieth, and a universal 'system' in the mid-twentieth century where none existed. For what becomes clear from the story told in this chapter, and, more broadly, when we slow down our account of the mid-twentieth century, is that there was no single international law in existence and there was little agreement about substantive, procedural or adjudicative rules. In this chapter, we have described several examples of the state of flux that 'international law' was in during the Cold War period, including foundational disagreements about where authority lay between the national and international spheres and between institutional and judicial actors in a broad and substantive, rather than a narrowly technical, sense. This mirrors the struggle over diplomacy we described in Chapter 4. The point is not to say there was nothing, or no 'law' there in the space where organised groups, peoples and nations met. Instead, international law is revealed to be less a 'system' and more a resource of ambiguity, one that allowed different kinds of claims to be made about substance and form of legal rules.

Much of this has been forgotten because of three retrospective assumptions that erase these struggles and the profoundly legal character of Third World efforts to remake the world after empire. The first assumption is that the Global South is less law-full, and less law-abiding than the Global North. The second is that nothing much happened in international law during the Cold War. The third is that a liberal(ish)

[254] Wilhelm Grewe, *The Epochs of International Law*, trans. and rev. Michael Byers (Berlin: Walter de Gruyter, 2000) 29.

international law was imagined and institutionalised in 1945 but was suspended by the Cold War. None of these three things is true.

These assumptions have been encouraged by the dominant historiography of the Amero-Soviet Cold War and the new origin story it led to. As Beaulac has shown, the idea that 1648 was the origin of International Law and the 'Westphalian System' was a narrative invented in the middle of the nineteenth century.[255] The work of this myth of origin was to authorise the particular account of international law being asserted in the nineteenth century by groups of powerful actors. Arguably, 1945 performs the same mythic function vis-à-vis a twenty-first-century international law.[256] For what turned out to be a brief moment between 1989 and 2001, history was said to have ended and the liberal promise fulfilled. The dystopic first decades of the twenty-first century put paid to that idea, but it did not stop people – international lawyers, in particular – repeating that some 'thing' was inaugurated in 1945, which was completed at the end of the Cold War – the fulfilment of an originary promise.

But what our account reveals is that the Cold War was a time of great and consequential rivalry between worlds, laws, horizons, ideals and ideologies. The Third World debt crisis starting around 1984 followed by the 'end' of the Cold War in 1989 allowed the United States and its then allies to push to one side those rival practices of world-making that had been at large on the international plane from at least 1945. The international law that came to be asserted by the US and its allies in 1989 was in a sense then the same Cold War international law that those actors had been advancing and disseminating since 1945. But by 1989, their main rivals had been defeated or weakened and the dreams of a plural and lawful world after empire largely displaced.

[255] Stéphane Beaulac, 'The Westphalian Model in Defining International Law: Challenging the Myth' *Australian Journal of Legal History*, 8(2) (2004) 181. See also, Benno Teschke, *The Myth of 1648: Class, Geopolitics, and the Making of Modern International Relations* (London: Verso, 2009).

[256] We discuss this "historiography of hiatus" in the opening chapter of *International Law and the Cold War* volume. Matthew Craven, Sundhya Pahuja and Gerry Simpson, 'Reading and Unreading a Historiography of Hiatus' in Matthew Craven, Sundhya Pahuja and Gerry Simpson (eds.), *International Law and the Cold War* (Cambridge: Cambridge University Press, 2019) 1–24.

6

Disrupting The Cold War

Revolutionary Internationalism in the Global South

6.1 Introduction

> What the peoples have most in common to unite the people of three continents and of all the world today is the struggle against imperialism (applause); the struggle against colonialism and neocolonialism, the struggle against racism and, in short, all the phenomena which are the contemporary expression we call imperialism, whose center, axis, and principal support of Yankee imperialism.
>
> —Fidel Castro[1]

Havana, 15 January 1966. Fidel Castro ended his speech to the Tri-Continental Meeting with a rousing call to anti-imperialist world-making. He called this an 'internationalist duty'. 'The world is big', he said 'and for the Cuban revolutionaries the field of battle against imperialism takes in the whole world'.[2] Although this announcement was expressed as a call to arms, it might be better understood as the high point of a period of intense, plural and revolutionary world-making through violence, law and diplomacy. It is a phase that has been remembered by some as romantic, for it seemed to hold out the possibility of emancipation and autonomy after the end of formal imperialism.[3] But

[1] Fidel Castro, 'At the Closing Session of the Tricontinental Conference', Tricontinental Conference, Havana, 15 January 1966, www.marxists.org/history/cuba/archive/castro/1966/01/15.htm.

[2] Ibid. Following the Tricontinental Conference in 1966, the Organization of Solidarity with the People of Asia, Africa and Latin America (OSPAAAL) was founded in Havana. Okoth notes that OSPAAAL was 'the most explicitly leftist organisation that grew out of the Bandung moment' and it was aimed to give institutional form to what Fidel Castro described as 'a great feast of international solidarity'. Kevin Ochieng Okoth, *Red Africa: Reclaiming Revolutionary Black Politics* (London: Verso, 2023) chapter 1.

[3] Jeffrey James Byrne, 'The Romance of Revolutionary Transatlanticism: Cuban–Algerian Relations and the Diverging Trends within Third World Internationalism' in R. Joseph

retrospectively, the year 1966 was also to mark a split between the Algerians and Cubans over their position vis-à-vis the established hegemonic structures of global order.[4] The split was, perhaps, an early casualty of the assault on rival internationalisms by the US in which the entrenchment of projects of modernisation, nationalism and State-building were accompanied by the often violent removal of internationalist leaders in Africa and Asia.[5] Respected, popular, charismatic and intellectually compelling postcolonial leaders were removed, murdered or neutered, then replaced by more biddable figures. This was the Amero-Soviet international 'law' of intervention – the story of which more properly occupies the genre of tragedy rather than that of romance.[6]

This chapter turns to those projects of revolutionary world-making and locates them in relation to the Soviet Union's radical challenge to the international order and its own self-recasting as global. We begin the chapter with that challenge, though it is not the beginning of the story as such. Retrospective accounts, whether implicitly or explicitly, often describe Third World Internationalisms, including Pan-Africanism and Pan-Asianism, as derivative of Marxist internationalism. This description is a symptom of the historiographical effects of Amero-Sovietism and its cosmological Eurocentricity.[7] We suggest, instead, that the Soviet challenge to the capitalist and imperial order interacted with already existing anti-colonial and anti-racist projects emerging from Africa, China and Latin America. So, while the Soviet challenge – and its material support

Parrott and Mark Atwood Lawrence (eds.), *The Tricontinental Revolution: Third World Radicalism and the Cold War* (Cambridge: Cambridge University Press, 2022) 169.

4 As Byrne describes it, whilst the Algerians invested efforts in using existing structures to adjust the shape of global order, the Cubans pursued a militant revolutionary path. Byrne, 'The Romance of Revolutionary Transatlanticism'.

5 In the Republic of Guinea French intervention, 1959–60 was designed to destabilise the new State under Toure through economic and military sabotage. In the DRC there was the Katangan secession – Lumumba's assassination prompted by Cold War fears that the Shinkolobwe Uranium mine couldn't get into Soviet hands. Kevin Okoth, 'Poison Is Better' *London Review of Books*, 45 (2023) 27–29.

6 David Scott, *Conscripts of Modernity: The Tragedy of Colonial Enlightenment* (Durham: Duke University Press, 2004) 209–12. Scott built the book on the observation that the genre of C. L. R. James' preface to *The Black Jacobins* changed between its first (1938) and second (1963) editions, from 'romance' to 'tragedy', not because the story of Toussaint L'Ouverture had changed but because the promise of decolonisation which comprised James' own context had been reinflected.

7 On cosmology, see Christine Black, *The Land Is the Source of the Law: A Dialogic Encounter with Indigenous Jurisprudence* (Abingdon: Routledge, 2011).

for anti-colonialism – were crucial, it would be more accurate to say it created a space for, rather than started, a tradition. The projects they enabled embodied a series of different and plural juridical styles and political goals. Pan-Arabists, Asians and Africanists were motivated partly by a desire to substitute different juridical-territorial imaginaries for the alienated politics of the more limited forms of decolonisation on offer. But these projects also had to be worked within the legal forms of the Amero-Soviet world in the making. (Legal) sovereignty, for instance, had to be repurposed to serve various programmes of Third World assertion and what was to become 'national liberation'.

A sharp point of distinction between socialist and liberal internationalisms lay in where they each located the authority to assert independence and their respective accounts as to who could enforce the associated rights and how. Global revolutionary socialism insisted on a right to arm and support anti-colonial forces and the connection of those rights to the principle of self-determination. This placed authority with the colonised and held out the possibility of legitimate – and lawful – revolutionary violence. As we shall see, this stood in sharp contrast to the liberal version in which self-determination was to be 'granted' rather than seized. This latter is the version that has retrospectively come to hold sway through post–Cold War conceptualisations of 'self-determination.' The ascendancy of this tradition has deradicalised the principle, negating the right to resist by shifting the focus instead towards the rights and duties of other States in guaranteeing its 'protection'.[8] And so, although we saw in Chapter 5 that non-alignment itself was a project both inaudible and unsettling for the Amero-Soviets, in many cases, various anti-imperial projects of the South were recast in relation to projects of Soviet anti-imperialist internationalism for strategic and tactical reasons. These projects of recasting, hybridisation and adaptation included the pluralistic socialism of Nyerere, Cuban interventionism in Africa, North Vietnamese national self-determination, some versions of Africanism (Nkrumah) and pan-Africanism (Senghor, Césaire), in revolutionary socialism, in alternative visions of the international political economy (Allende, Tito, NIEO) and in the various prospects for an actionable global revolution.

[8] Palestine has recently at times been caught in this trap at the ICJ in the Advisory Opinion proceedings (*Request For an Advisory Opinion by the United Nations General Assembly in Resolution 77/247 of 30th December 2022 pertaining to the question of Palestine*).

6.2 Revolutionary Socialism: Soviet Roots

As Scott Newton has pointed out, the spatial dynamics of the Cold War were represented in practices of partition and duplication in the production of what he has called 'division space': two Germanies, two Koreas, two Vietnams and two Chinas, each existing in parallel, but in which sovereign claims were often 'cross-hatched'[9] rather than independent of one another.[10] But the pattern of those divisions had been prefigured some thirty years earlier in the aftermath of the October Revolution in 1917. From its early days, the new Soviet Republic had become embroiled in a wide-ranging struggle with a range of Western powers. Alongside its military engagements with the intervening Western powers in its battles against White Russian forces, the Soviets launched a legal and diplomatic offensive, the target of which was the received framework of international relations forged by the Czarist regime before its overthrow. Not only did the Russian Soviet Federal Republic (as it was then known) declare its unwillingness to honour the debts of its predecessor,[11] it publicly disavowed all 'imperialist' treaties to which the (former) Russian State was party.[12] Indeed, it was this disavowal that brought to light the secret Sykes–Picot agreement of 1917. The RSFR also embarked on a programme of nationalisation that had led, in some cases, to the compulsory purchase of foreign-owned undertakings.[13] In response, many Western States refused to recognise the legitimacy of the new Soviet government[14] and sought to challenge Bolshevism through the sponsorship of White

[9] This allusion was drawn from the vivid representation of parallel worlds in China Mieville's *The City and the City* (New York: Macmillan, 2009).

[10] Scott Newton, 'Parallel Worlds: Cold War Division Space' in Matthew Craven, Sundhya Pahuja and Gerry Simpson (eds.), *International Law and the Cold War* (Cambridge: Cambridge University Press, 2019) 117–36.

[11] Decree of 28 January 1918, RSFSR Laws 1917–18, No. 27, Article 353.

[12] See ILC, 'Memorandum on the Soviet doctrine and practice with respect to the law of treaties, prepared by the Secretariat' (21 November 1950) UN Doc. A/CN.4/37, 26. Further, Eugene A. Korovin, 'Soviet Treaties and International Law' *American Journal of International Law*, 22 (1928) 762.

[13] See, e.g., *Luther v Sagor* [1921] 3 KB 532.

[14] Britain, France, Mexico and Denmark formally recognised de jure the government of the USSR in 1924. Diplomatic relations with the US were established following the Litvinov Assignment of 1933. See generally, Eugene A. Korovin, 'The Problems of the International Recognition of the Union of Socialist Soviet Republics in Practice' *Iowa Law Review*, 19 (1934) 259–71; Jonathan L. Adler, 'The Unrecognized Government in the Courts of the United States' *Virginia Journal of International Law*, 5 (1964) 36–52. Diplomatic relations with the UK were severed on 26 May 1927, with China on 6 April 1927.

Russian forces and the dissemination of anti-communist propaganda. By the 1930s, relations between the Soviet Union and the West were gradually 'normalised', culminating in the Litvinov assignment of 1933.[15] But doubts remained in both camps as to whether the protagonists might settle upon a common understanding of the rules of international law that were to govern their mutual relations. As we saw in Chapter 3, Litvinov offered a kind of prototype for the forms of Amero-Sovietism that flourished in the Cold War, but during the early phases of Bolshevism the very 'unity' of (European) international law seemed to be threatened by the incipient ideological divide. This was a divide that expressed itself in rival approaches to international law and that left space for plural forms of inter-State ordering. It is this distinctive, novel and revolutionary prospect that provided one point of connection between revolutionary socialism and the radicalism of the Global South's juridical world-making in the Cold War – a connection that was later to be partly smothered by the collaborative aspects of US–Soviet relations and the softening of Soviet internationalism.

From the time of the formation of the USSR in 1922, Soviet jurists sought to develop a distinctive Marxist theory of international law,[16] the central concern of which was how to bring to an analysis of international law the Marxist–Leninist intuition that all law was, in essence, a class tool.[17] Whilst early Soviet practice had been marked by its rejection of

[15] The Litivinov assignment was a financial agreement concluded between the Soviet Union and the United States settling outstanding debts in return for the US recognition of the Soviet government. See 'Exchange of Communications between the President of the United States and Maxim Litvinov of the Union of Soviet Socialist Republics, November 16, 1933' in *Public Papers and Addresses of Franklin D. Roosevelt. Volume 2* (New York: Random House, 1933) 471–86.

[16] On the development of Soviet law generally, see Michael Head, *Evgeny Pashukanis: A Critical Reappraisal* (Abingdon: Routledge-Cavendish, 2007). On international law more specifically, see John N. Hazard, 'The Soviet Union and international law' *Soviet Studies*, 1 (1950) 189–99; Edward McWhinney, 'Changing International Law Method and Objectives in the Era of the Soviet–Western Detente' *American Journal of International Law*, 59 (1965) 1–15; Edward McWhinney, 'The New Thinking in Soviet International Law: Soviet Doctrines and Practice in the Post-Tunkin Era' *Canadian Yearbook of International Law*, 28 (1990) 309–37; John Quigley, 'The Soviet New Thinking in International Law: An Opening to End the Cold War' *Wisconsin International Law Journal*, 9 (1989) 97–122; Lauri Mälksoo, *Russia, the Soviet Union, and Imperial Continuity in International Law* (Oxford: Oxford University Press, 2025)

[17] This Marxist theory of international law has been deemed relatively unsophisticated and uninteresting by writers like China Mieville, 'Commodity-Form Theory of International Law: An Introduction' *Leiden Journal of International Law*, 17 (2004) 271–302. But see

various facets of the existing, 'bourgeois', international law, it was far from consistently in opposition.[18] This led scholars such as Korovin and Pashukanis to speculate about the theoretical grounds under which the Soviet Union might engage with the Western world and the forms of law it might adduce to those ends. Both Korovin and Pashukanis appreciated that the *telos* of Marxist orthodoxy – the withering away of the State – would ultimately leave no place for law, let alone international law.[19] Both also appreciated, however, that whilst relations within the Soviet orbit could readily be organised along the lines of Marxist thought, the contemporary conditions of communist encirclement meant that the Soviet Union would be forced into some kind of rapprochement with the capitalist West. This would require an engagement with the legal forms of what they saw to be the 'bourgeois' tradition of international law.[20] Each responded in different ways to the challenge.

For Korovin,[21] the answer (at least for a while) was to be found in the postulates of legal plurality. The central message of Korovin's thesis was that international law was a temporary compromise between the Soviet

too, Scott Newton, *Law and the Making of the Soviet World: The Red Demiurge* (Abingdon: Routledge, 2014). Obviously, Marxist international law has undergone a renaissance in which much more theoretically complicated Marxisms have emerged. See Rob Knox, 'Marxism, International Law, and Political Strategy' *Leiden Journal of International Law*, 22 (2009) 413–36; Susan Marks (ed.), *International Law on the Left: Re-examining Marxist Legacies* (Cambridge: Cambridge University Press, 2008), B. S. Chimni, *International Law and World Order: A Critique of Contemporary Approaches*, 2nd ed. (Cambridge: Cambridge University Press, 2017).

18 E.g. its application of the Hague Conventions. John Hazard, 'The Soviet Union and international law' *Illinois Law Review*, 43 (1948) 591–607; Zofia Maclure, 'Soviet International Legal Theory: Past and Present' *The Fletcher Forum*, 5 (1981) 51–52.

19 Bill Bowring, 'Yevgeniy Pashukanis, His *Law and Marxism: A General Theory*, and the 1922 Treaty of Rapallo between Soviet Russia and Germany' *Journal of the History of International Law*, 19 (2017) 274–95.

20 Boris N. Mamyluk and Ugo Mattei, 'Comparative International Law' *Brooklyn Journal of International Law*, 19 (2011) 399. See, too, Gleb Bogush, 'Aron Trainin: The Legal Mind Behind a Soviet International Criminal Law Project' in Frédéric Mégret and Immi Tallgren (eds.), *The Dawn of a Discipline: International Criminal Justice and Its Early Exponents* (Cambridge: Cambridge University Press, 2020) 260–79.

21 E. Korovin, *Mezhdunarodnoe pravo perekhodnogo vremeni* [*International Law of the Transitional Period*] (Moscow/Petrograd: Gosudarstvennoe Izdatel'stvo 1923); E. Korovin, *Sovremennoe Mezhdunarodnoe Publichnoe Pravo* [*Contemporary International Public Law*] (Moscow: Gosudarstvennoe izdatel'stvo 1926). By 1935, Korovin had abandoned many of the 'unorthodox' aspects of his earlier work. See Earl A. Snyder and Hans Werner Bracht, 'Coexistence and International Law' *The International and Comparative Law Quarterly*, 7 (1958) 54, 61–62.

Union and the bourgeois West.[22] Starting with the idea that, for the duration of its encirclement by capitalist States, the Soviet Union was forced to 'remain in legal "isolation"',[23] Korovin was to bring into view a distinctive Soviet International Law the content of which would be determined by the dictates of the proletarian revolution and the interests of the USSR as its principal agent.[24] Three distinct fields of international law could thereby be discerned: international law as applied between capitalist States, international law as would operate between socialist States and finally the international law that governed the relations between the two social orders. The latter - which he called the 'international law of the transition period' - operated as a mediating device that governed, temporarily at least, the relations between the two opposed, and occasionally antagonistic, social systems.[25] In that context, traditional, bourgeois, international law was not to be revered for its own sake - indeed, many of its central practices were deemed incompatible with the precepts of Marxist–Leninism - and priority was thus given to treaty law[26] built upon the rock of State sovereignty. [27]

Pashukanis, by contrast, and following the earlier critiques by Sabanin and Hrabar,[28] doubted Korovin's claim that a new international law was emerging. Rather, he suggested, modern international law remained 'the legal form of the struggle of the capitalist States among themselves for

[22] For Korovin, international law was merely the totality of rules governing and established by 'the ruling classes in their capacity as participants in international relations'. Korovin, *Sovremennoe Mezhdunarodnoe Publichnoe Pravo*, 5.

[23] Korovin, *Mezhdunarodnoe pravo perekhodnogo vremeni*, 44, cited in Mamyluk and Mattei, 'Comparative International Law', 401.

[24] This gave rise in the end to the idea of the Eastern Bloc as a concrete regional order, universalistic in its credo, regional and local in its material conditions.

[25] Korovin ultimately imagined that an inter-soviet law would become the successor to the contemporary international law. See generally, Earl A. Snyder and Hans Werner Bracht, 'Coexistence and International Law' *International & Comparative Law Quarterly*, 7 (1958) 58.

[26] Korovin, 'Soviet Treaties and International Law'. An important exception concerned the principle of *rebus sic stantibus*, which was invoked by the USSR in its renunciation of the former treaties concluded by the Czarist regime, but whose field of operation was limited to the specific context of 'social revolution'.

[27] W. E. Butler, 'Soviet Law and the Cold War' *Journal of Comparative Law*, 7 (2012) 334–41.

[28] V. E. Hrabar, 'Das heutige Völkerrecht vom Standpunkte eines Sowjetjuristen' *Zeitschrift für Völkerrecht*, XIV (1928) 188–214. Snyder and Bracht, 'Coexistence and International Law', 59–60; Zofia Maclure, 'Soviet International Legal Theory: Past and Present' *The Fletcher Forum*, 5 (1981) 49–73.

domination over the rest of the world'.[29] 'International law', he explained, 'owes its existence to the fact that the bourgeoisie exercises its domination over the proletariat and over the colonial countries',[30] its spread, furthermore, 'occurred on the basis of the spread and development of the capitalist mode of production'.[31] Nevertheless, he noted,

> With the emergence of Soviet states in the historical arena, international law assumes a different significance. It becomes the form of a temporary compromise between two antagonistic class systems ... [where] ... one system (the bourgeois) is already unable to ensure its exclusive domination, and the other (proletarian and socialist) has not yet won it .... The significance of this transitional period consists in the fact that open struggle for destruction (intervention, blockade, non-recognition) is replaced by struggle within the limits of normal diplomatic relations and contractual exchange. International law becomes inter-class law, and its adaptation to this new function inevitably occurs in the form of a series of conflicts and crises.[32]

Pashukanis' account, here, of international law operating as a 'temporary compromise' between two antagonistic class systems[33] differed from that of Korovin insofar as he refused Korovin's insistence upon the plurality of international laws. By positioning international law as a law that governed relations of class warfare (inter-class law), however, he not only appeared to distance himself from the idea that there might exist a distinctive 'Soviet international law' applicable between the 'proletarian States'[34] but appeared also to endorse the view that international law itself somehow transcended those class divisions.[35] It possessed, he

[29] Piers Beirne and Robert Sharlet (eds.), *Pashukanis: Selected Writing on Marxism and Law*, trans. Peter B. Maggs (Cambridge, MA: Academic Press 1980) 169.

[30] Beirne and Sharlet, *Pashukanis*, 172.

[31] Ibid.

[32] Ibid., 172–73.

[33] Korovin's version of this was to describe international law as being a law of the 'transitional period'. See Korovin, *Mezhdunarodnoe pravo perekhodnogo vremeni.*

[34] Pashukanis was to suggest that 'international law assumes an entirely different meaning as the inter-State law of the Soviet states. It now ceases to be a form of temporary compromise behind which an intensified struggle for existence is hidden. Because of this the very opposition between international law and the state, so characteristic of the preceding period, disappears. The proletarian states, not having merged formally into one federation or union, must present in their mutual relationships an image of such a close economic, political and military unity, that the measure of "modern" international law becomes inapplicable to them.'

[35] See John N. Hazard, 'Cleansing Soviet International Law of Anti-Marxist Theories' *The American Journal of International Law*, 32 (1937) 247.

seemed to suggest, a certain formal neutrality[36] such as to allow the dialectical relations between classes to be pursued within its substantive terms.

Whilst Pashukanis would later be denounced (and, indeed, 'liquidated') for his 'anti-Marxist theories',[37] the problematic with which both he and Korovin engaged was a persistent one: how to square the precepts of Marxist–Leninism with the apparent need of the Soviet Union to utilise (existing) international law as an instrument of foreign policy? To posit the existence of a 'Soviet international law' as a juridical rival to the traditional bourgeois international law of the West was to encounter two obvious criticisms. First, that the USSR still gave recognition (by necessity or otherwise) to the familiar institutions of the latter – to the sanctity of treaties, to the principle of State sovereignty and self-determination, to general principles of law. Secondly, that as a 'rival' to the bourgeois international law of the West, some account had to be provided of the way in which the two traditions, or 'world outlooks',[38] would relate to one another – what forms would it take? To posit in response that international law was essentially bourgeois in form yet open to being infused with socialist content was to encounter the objection that such a position would invert the Marxist axiom that social consciousness determined the juridical and political superstructure and not the other way round. The closest one might come to that position would be to have said that the norms of international law were an ongoing 'site of struggle and contestation'.[39]

But there was disagreement too within Marxist–Leninism about the status and content of revolutionary socialism. Of course, Marx was committed to proletarian resistance inside States as a way of moving towards a revolutionary international. But this hardly resolved the problem of nationalism or national self-determination. A number of Left polemicists after the Bolshevik Revolution were deeply concerned that organising politics around the 'nation' or 'ethnie' would fragment and undercut revolutionary possibilities in general or that a focus on secession or separatism would inhibit the prospects of an (intermediate) State-

36 The characteristic phraseology of law being 'bourgeois in form, yet socialist in content'.

37 Hazard, 'The Soviet Union and International Law'.

38 G. I. Tunkin, *Theory of International Law*, trans. W. E. Butler (Cambridge, MA: Harvard University Press, 1974) xiv.

39 These questions were, to some extent, set aside between 1937 and 1953 when Vishinsky's intellectually vapid and ad hominem Stalinism (see his notorious appearance at Nuremberg) came to dominate.

wide proletarian uprising. Others, like Pashukanis, seemed to think either that self-determination was of negligible importance in the context of East–West enmity and the prospects for revolution and/or that it was a formal right of an international law in thrall to its own externalised commodity form.[40]

Lenin, though, put the official position in stark terms: 'We demand freedom of [*sic*] self-determination . . . because we want large states and the closer unity and even fusion of nations.'[41] This became Soviet policy during the Cold War when the USSR devoted significant resources (both in diplomatic circles at the UN and elsewhere and in terms of military and logistical support) to promoting national liberation through independent statehood in the Third World.[42]

Marx and Lenin offered resources to those forms of resistance and reimagination that did not rely on, or refused to be constrained by, existing models of self-determination that imagined it merely as an avenue to sovereign statehood. As international legal practice began to narrow permissible resistance to a non-violent transition to a territorial sovereignty within a pre-formed colonial cartography, revolutionary practice in the Third World held on to the idea of legitimate – and lawful – violent resistance to colonial rule and imaginative resistance to the postcolonial territorial settlement.[43] To a certain extent, these too were offered space in a legal idiom by a Marxist inheritance.[44] Certainly, Marx and Lenin were not squeamish about violence, seeing it as a necessary adjunct to the task of responding to the systemic violence of capitalist relations themselves (a tradition continued, amongst others, by Mao). At the same time, Marxism was a universalist belief system committed to a literal and expressive idea of the 'international'. To think with Marx is to think beyond national boundaries, and beyond

[40] Bill Bowring, 'Positivism versus Self-determination: The Contradictions of Soviet International Law' in Susan Marks (ed.), *International Law on the Left: Re-examining Marxist Legacies* (Cambridge: Cambridge University Press, 2008) 133–68.

[41] V. I. Lenin, 'The Revolutionary Proletariat and the Right of Nations to Self-determination' in Julius Katzer (ed.), *Lenin Collected Works*, vol. 21 (Moscow: Progress, 1964) 407, cited in Bowring, 'Positivism versus Self-determination', 143.

[42] See Galia Golan, *The Soviet Union and National Liberation Movements in the Third World* (Abingdon: Routledge 1988).

[43] Frantz Fanon, *The Wretched of the Earth*, trans. Richard Philcox (New York: Grove Press, 2004; originally 1963) chapter 1, 'On violence'.

[44] Andrée Blouin, *My Country, Africa: Autobiography of the Black Pasionaria* (London: Verso, 2005; originally 1983); Okoth, *Red Africa*; Vijay Prashad, *Red Star over the Third World* (New Delhi: LeftWord Books, 2017).

Empire, and it is this tradition within Marxist thought that made space for revolutionary leaders and writers to draw on their own rival traditions and to imagine political orders tied neither to international legal sovereignty nor rehashed forms of colonial and neo-colonial internationalism.

6.3 Inheriting, Adapting, Disrupting

Alongside participating in these theoretical debates within Marxism, leaders and thinkers in the Third World also had to grapple with a Soviet foreign policy that oscillated between traditions of coexistence and revolutionism. Throughout the Cold War, Soviet foreign policy moved back and forth between a foreign relations strategy that favoured support for revolutionary governments and a Brezhnevian diplomacy embodied in Amero-Sovietism that emphasised gradualism and coexistence. It was sometimes willing to sacrifice liberationist allies in the Third World to the dictates of superpower spheres of influence.[45] At other times, coexistence seemed to have an affinity with the richer notions of encounter finding expression in the idioms and practices of the non-aligned movement. But it was stronger, less strategic, forms of socialist revolutionism that had also been, and continued to be, an important inspiration for many of those seeking freedom from centuries of colonial rule. Because of the intimate association between anti-imperialism and Leninist thought, movements agitating for national self-determination not only looked to the Soviet Union as an ally but regarded the *Critique of Imperialism*, itself, as a central text.[46] The Soviets became increasingly responsive to this in the period between Stalin's Mother Russia nationalism and the pacified international diplomacy of the Brezhnev era. In Telepneva's book, *Cold War Liberation: The Soviet Union and the Collapse of the Portuguese Empire in Africa*, she writes at one point: 'The main thrust of Khrushchev's policy in the Third World was to revive Soviet socialism based on an idealised notion of "Leninist principles."' In Telepneva's account, this meant that the Soviet *nomenklatura*

[45] Jeffrey James Byrne, *Mecca of Revolution: Algeria, Decolonization, and the Third World Order* (Oxford: Oxford University Press, 2016) 180. See, too, Johannes Socher, 'Lenin, (Just) Wars of National Liberation, and the Soviet Doctrine on the Use of Force' *Journal of the History of International Law*, 19 (2017) 219–45. See Edward McWhinney, 'Contemporary Soviet General Theory of International Law: Reflections on the Tunkin Era' *Canadian Yearbook of International Law*, 25 (1987) 187–217.

[46] Vladimir Lenin, *Imperialism, the Highest Stage of Capitalism: A Popular Outline* (New York: International Publishers, 2013, originally 1917).

regained its ideological confidence and revived its Africa-facing governmental and educational institutions (a great deal of socialist internationalism involved providing tertiary education to future Third World leaders).[47] Meanwhile, those in the Global South who were more aware of the limits of statist solutions to the problem of empire and who were at the vanguard of what was cast as a global revolutionary struggle, drew on Marxist–Leninism in its more disruptive variants. These chimed with experimental non-Westphalian modes of political reorganisation (e.g. Pan-Africanism) or forms of revolutionary class struggle. These influences of Marx in the Global South were consonant with international Marxism, of course, with its multiple shades of opinion.[48]

At the same time, at the height of decolonisation, the United States was now being treated with deep suspicion.[49] *Its* anti-imperial credentials had been seriously tarnished by its support for French colonialism in Indochina and then, later, by its involvement in, often sponsorship of, multiple violent coups against African and Asian postcolonial governments, its rather qualified support for a UN based on the formal sovereign statehood of emerging States ('a fortuitous collection of social entities', as George Kennan put it) and its commitment to a basal imperialism of its own, organised around enclaval territorialism combined with clientelism.[50] So, by the time decolonisation was in full swing, Soviet Marxist–Leninism (with its emphasis on a revolutionary struggle that promised an end to exploitative labour and class relations, its theorised practices of guerrilla and cell warfare, its textual anti-imperialism and its anti-racist credentials) was an obvious and more promising resource for Third World States and national liberation

[47] E.g. the 1958 Conference of African and Asian Writers, which featured Portuguese Marxists and W. E. B. Du Bois. See Okoth, 'Poison Is Better', 27–29.

[48] And after all, the First International, founded in 1864, itself was an agglomeration of utopian Socialists, anarchists, trade unionists, Bakunians and so on, see Werner Blumenberg, *Karl Marx: An Illustrated Biography*, trans. Douglas Scott (London: New Left Books, 1972) 147–49.

[49] Susan Williams, *White Malice: The CIA and the Covert Recolonization of Africa* (New York City: PublicAffairs Press, 2021).

[50] Dean Rusk had given a speech with a revealing pun as its title, 'The Bases of United States Foreign Policy' *Proceedings of the Academy of Political Science*, 27 (1962) 98–110. Keenan, 'United Nations' (14 November 1949) in Anna Kasten Nelson (ed.), *The State Department Policy Planning Staff Papers 1949* (New York: Garland, 1983) 187–98, quoted in Mark Mazower, *Governing the World: The History of an Idea* (London: The Penguin Press, 2012) 258.

movements who sought to use it and radicalise it.[51] But this came with a lot of baggage: its association with a failing, increasingly exhausted authoritarian patron, a certain unsuitedness to conditions on the ground, a tendency to sometimes underplay the role of imperialism in capitalism's developmental logics and an ideological reliance on the prospect of an industrial proletariat that did not speak directly to the Global South's peasant masses. At various points in the period of decolonisation, it did not seem to offer the right path for African and Asian revolutionaries.[52]

Some national liberation movements and theorists in the Global South, meanwhile, were trying to work out how to reconcile radical internationalism with the need for coexistence (Marx and Grotius), or the relations between national self-determination and international socialism (perhaps, Marx and Mazzini)[53] or weigh up the differing appeal of Maoism and Marxism for the purposes of engaging in the sphere of the international.[54] The two strains of Soviet thought discussed earlier were also in competition. One strain believed that coexistence might be an interim or even medium-term solution to the problems of global relations. The other held on to the view that coexistence was too passive and had led to the abandonment by the USSR of 'revolutionary internationalism' and its replacement by a disappointing fetish for sovereignty, a form of imperial rule in Eastern Europe, Great-Power accommodationism and, ultimately, a prioritisation of Amero-Sovietism. This more revolutionary tradition,

[51] There were, of course, a variety of views. See, for example, Padmore's doubts about Sovietism in Padmore, *Pan-Africanism or Communism*; C. L. R. James' enthusiastic deployments of Trotskyism in *World Revolution, 1917–1936: The Rise and Fall of the Communist International* (London: Secker & Warburg, 1937); and Nyerere's softer African socialism. See, too, China Mieville, *Between Equal Rights: A Marxist Theory of International Law* (Leiden: Brill, 2005); Anne Peters, 'Introduction – A Century after the Russian Revolution: Its Legacy in International Law' *Journal of the History of International Law*, 19 (2017) 133–46.

[52] See, e.g., George Padmore's lengthy excoriation of communist meddling, racism and opportunism in his essay, Padmore, *Pan-Africanism or Communism*; Boris N. Mamlyuk, 'Decolonization as a Cold War Imperative: Bandung and the Soviets' in Luis Eslava, Michael Fakhri and Vasuki Nesiah (eds.), *Bandung, Global History, and International Law: Critical Pasts and Pending Futures* (Cambridge: Cambridge University Press, 2017) 196–214. For a longer durée, see Walter Rodney's lectures delivered at the University of Dar es Salaam in the 1970s, *The Russian Revolution: A View from the Third World* (London: Verso, 2018) and Enzo Traverso's *Revolution: An Intellectual History* (London: Verso, 2021).

[53] Mazower, *Governing the World*, 248.

[54] By the late '40s, Mao had transformed China from a defeated Japanese vassal into one of the world's great revolutionary States. See Paul Thomas Chamberlain, *The Cold War's Killing Fields: Rethinking the Long Peace* (New York: HarperCollins, 2018) 9.

in turn, took the view that international law was ultimately imperial and had to be resisted.[55] In the end, then, we can perhaps see that many National Liberation Movements adopted Marxism in an improvisational mode, using what they felt was relevant and useful, discarding that which was not (heavy industrial bases, a dynamic proletarian class). In the end, as the saying went, 'the revolution makes itself'[56] and what was undoubtedly created out of these forms of engagement with Marxist Internationalism, and many, many other resources, was an original, *sui generis* Third World /Anti-Imperial Project:[57] a radical re-envisioning of global legal politics through, respectively, a comprehensively anti-colonial vision of national self-determination, the spatial disruptions of pan-Africanism/pan-Arabism, the specificity of Cuban Internationalism and the promise or spectre of world revolution.[58] We discuss each of these below.

6.4 National Self-Determination

The most comprehensive, successful and dramatic reorganisation of the map of global politics in history resulted in the world we now inhabit in which more than two hundred States form the structuring ecology of global relations. For better or worse, during the Cold War, sovereign statehood under international law became the default objective of

[55] One commissar had written, 'the so-called states of high culture . . . defied their mandate rights by force of arms and mercilessly enslave the peoples under their tutelage'. John Quigley, *Soviet Legal Innovations and the Law of the Western World* (Cambridge: Cambridge University Press, 2007) 141. This position was more representative of a Soviet Union that had declined capitulatory rights in Asia and called for an immediate end to colonialism. Ibid., 138. Mazower, perhaps, gives too much weight to the dissolution of Commintern. Mazower, *Governing the World*, 245.

[56] See Norman Fruchter and Stuart Hall, 'Notes on the Cuban Revolution' *New Left Review*, I/9 (May/June 1961) 2–11.

[57] Vijay Prashad, *The Darker Nations: A People's History of the Third World* (New York: The New Press, 2008); Robert Vitalis, 'The Midnight Ride of Kwame Nkrumah and Other Fables of Bandung (Ban-doong)' *Humanity*, 4 (2013) 261–88.

[58] For the Soviet role and position on all this, see Natalia Telepneva, *Cold War Liberation: The Soviet Union and the Collapse of Portuguese Empire in Africa, 1961–1975* (Chapel Hill: University of North Carolina, 2021) esp. 14–16. These were not, of course, the only arrangements that rivalled Amero-Soviet 'coexistence'. Any list of these would have to include various other competing cross-hemispheric configurations (the Anglo–French–Israeli bloc at Suez, Czech or Norwegian Third World engagements, the international Vietnam War movements or forms of neutrality (Djilas and the Third Way in Belgrade, the muscular non-alignment of the Swedes).

movements for national self-determination and decolonisation.[59] With that, the subject of the revolutionary project had in a sense split into two streams. In one stream, the revolutionary subject was 'the people', broadly understood and capable of encompassing the population of the Global South as a single entity (the Third World, the non-aligned movement). In another stream, 'the nation' was to be led from colonial rule to freedom in the form of a territorially demarcated self-expression.[60] Even for some 'Marxist' leaders like Fidel Castro, for all its theoretical impurity, this latter, national self-determination remained important.[61]

There has been an understandable tendency to think retrospectively of these national projects as disappointingly modest, defeatist or subject to capture by Western-trained elites.[62] And indeed, many new States – often formed in the crucible of revolutionary struggle – eventually devolved into combinations of formal independence and substantive dependency (often described in the language of 'neo-colonialism').[63] The legal form of

[59] Excluding, of course, all sorts of selves. See, e.g., Upendra Baxi, '"The Dust of Empire": The Dialectic of Self-determination and Re-colonisation in the First Phase of the Cold War' in Matthew Craven, Sundhya Pahuja and Gerry Simpson (eds.), *International Law and the Cold War* (Cambridge: Cambridge University Press 2019) 397–413; Natália Medina Araújo, Tatiana Cardoso Squeff and Bianca Guimarães Silva, 'What about the Fourth World Self?' *Cadernos do Programa de Pós-Graduação*, 17 (2022) 87–105. On the point about decolonisation and statehood, see Sundhya Pahuja, *Decolonising International Law: Development, Economic Growth and the Politics of Universality* (Cambridge: Cambridge University Press, 2011).

[60] Charles McKelvey, 'Reflections on the Communist Manifesto from Third World socialism' *Sociological Review*, 52 (2018) 527.

[61] On Castro's communist credentials, see generally, Charles McKelvey, 'Reflections on the Communist Manifesto from Third World Socialism' *Sociological Review*, 52 (2018) 523–41.

[62] There is a vast literature: Makau wa Mutua, 'Why Redraw the Map of Africa: A Moral and Legal Inquiry' *Michigan Journal of International Law*, 16 (1995) 1113–76; W. Ofuatey-Kodjoe, *The Principle of Self-Determination in International Law* (Cambridge, MA: Nellen, 1977); M. G. Kaladharan Nayar, 'Self-Determination beyond the Colonial Context: Biafra in Retrospect' *Texas International Law Journal*, 10 (1975) 321–46; Nathaniel Berman, 'Sovereignty in Abeyance' *Wisconsin International Law Journal*, 7 (1988) 51–105 (demonstrating the internal tensions in theories and applications of self-determination in mainly judicial materials); Philip Allott, 'The Nation as Mind Politic' *New York Journal of International Law and Politics*, 24 (1992) 1361–98 (mixing Hegel and poetry); Edward M. Morgan, 'The Imagery and Meaning of Self-determination' *New York University Journal of International Law and Politics*, 20 (1988) 355–404 (exploring the literary meaning of self-determination).

[63] Kwame Nkrumah, *Neocolonialism: The Last Stage of Imperialism* (New York: International Publishers, 1965).

the nation-state as the outcome of decolonisation facilitated this by allowing the United States in particular, formally to respect the 'independence' of the nation-state whilst substantively disrespecting (displacing, overthrowing) governments and binding economies into relationships of dependence. Western scholars were on hand to redescribe and naturalise this split between the formal and the substantive by drawing on nineteenth-century distinctions between colonised and coloniser or between civilised and uncivilised States but now often in a more sanitised register, usually in terms of development.[64] And so in a way, many suspected even then that 'Peoples' had become sovereign in name only. The levers of power were, it was argued, pulled elsewhere (by former colonial powers or international financial institutions or multinational corporations). What was left was a kind of international legal 'nearly State', a State that was not quite sovereign in the 'original' European sense or sovereign in a mythic or promised sense.[65]

National self-determination thus became both a legal imperative and a political impossibility. While the UN was announcing the end of colonialism and the rights of peoples to choose their own destiny, destiny itself turned out to be vulnerable to capture. The repertoire of choices of self-determination proved to be increasingly attenuated. Future leaders with independent ideas were either assassinated (Lumumba, Ben Barka, Guevara, Cabral), deposed (Allende, Sukarno, Nkrumah, Mossadeq), imprisoned or were reshaped as biddable violent autocrats (Mobutu) or as dictators (the Mugabe syndrome).[66] In its broadly re-distributive,

[64] See John Rawls, 'The Law of Peoples' *Critical Inquiry*, 20 (1993) 36–68 repeating the distinctions found in James Lorimer's *The Institutes of the Law of Nations: A Treatise of the Jural Relations of Separate Political Communities* (Edinburgh: William Blackwood & Sons, 1883).

[65] See Siba N'Zatioula Grovogui, *Sovereigns, Quasi Sovereigns and Africans: Race and Self-Determination in International Law* (Minneapolis: University of Minnesota Press, 1996). See Robert H. Jackson, *Quasi States: Sovereignty, International Relations and the Third World* (Cambridge: Cambridge University Press, 1993); Jennifer Beard, *The Political Economy of Desire: International Law, Development and the Nation State* (Abingdon: Routledge, 2007).

[66] This story or at least a version of it with the various sub-narratives in play is recounted in Peter Abrahams' *A Wreath for Udomo* (London: Faber & Faber, 2022; originally 1956), in which Udomo begins his career as an ardent if clear-eyed follower to a generation of idealistic future African leaders before taking up power in 'Pluralia' where he is confronted by the possibility of economic crisis, by an increasingly dissatisfied population and by foreign financial blackmail. He betrays his comrades and many of his own principles to save the State and ends up being assassinated by internal enemies. Interestingly, in the translator's preface to the new edition of the book, the failure of

progressive variants, self-determination was often also undermined by interests external to the State and by competition from within. In a few cases, from the Dergue in Ethiopia to the Khmer Rouge in Phnom Penh, revolutionary States descended into grotesque forms of violent rule: in the former case, partly as a result of the effects of the global oil crisis and the rise of a Soviet-influenced military cadre; in the latter case, as a result of the Nixon–Kissinger secret bombing campaign in which the country was traumatised from the air.[67] In hindsight, this generalised experience was to be narrated in terms of disappointment: as one of tragedy or even comedy.[68] State-building forms of self-determination, initially experienced as moments of liberation, became increasingly written off as the road that ought not have been taken, the wrong choice, a missed opportunity: a disappointingly Westphalian anti-climax to a centuries' long struggle to be free from European rule and thought.[69]

Yet this retrospective depiction of national self-determination misses the revolutionary spirit that animated a number of liberation leaders, many of whom were both nationalists and

the revolution is attributed to Udomo's personal 'flaws': (at viii). We thank Christopher Gevers for bringing this book to our attention. See Gevers, '"Land[s] beyond the White World": (Re)imagining the International through Fiction' *Law & Literature*, 36 (2023) 241–64.

[67] This was hardly unique to 'Marxist' States. Violent (sometimes genocidal) dysfunction was the order of the day in a Central America, in thrall to American Cold War paranoia (Guatemala, El Salvador, Honduras) and interference.

[68] See variously, Scott, *Conscripts of Modernity*; William Boyd, *A Good Man in Africa* (London: Hamish Hamilton, 1981); Giles Foden, *Last King of Scotland* (London: Faber & Faber, 1998); Slavoj Žižek, *First as Tragedy, Then as Farce* (London: Verso, 2009).

[69] See Michelle D. Paranzino, '"Two, Three, Many Vietnams": Che Guevara's Tricontinental Revolutionary Vision' in R. Joseph Parrott and Mark Atwood Lawrence (eds.), *The Tricontinental Revolution: Third World Radicalism and the Cold War* (Cambridge: Cambridge University Press, 2022) 279–303 (arguing that the NIEO and Che's Tricontinental envisions fell victim to the 'appeal of nationalism' [at 303] and that Che had failed to understand the continuing appeal of nationalism in the Global South [at 278]); Cheikh Anta Diop, *Black Africa: The Economic and Cultural Basis for a Federated State* (Chicago: Lawrence Hill, 1978), arguing that even Pan-Africanism tended to fall at the hurdle of 'general interests that make people cling to the established frontiers' (quoted in Kehinde Andrews, 'Beyond Pan-Africanism: Garveyism, Malcolm X and the End of the Colonial Nation State' *Third World Quarterly*, 38 (2017) 2506). This struggle between an apologetic statism and a global revolutionism again repeats the kind of debates we see in the mid-nineteenth century when Bakunin's visionary socialism came into conflict with Marx's early statist pragmatism (the State would wither but only at the end of the revolutionary struggle; it was not a precondition).

internationalists.[70] From the post-triumphalist perspective of the present, we may tend to regard the First, Second and Third Worlds as hierarchical designations for places on a map. But in the second half of the twentieth century, each designation stood not for a place within one world but a project to assert another whole world. Self-determination was, in a way, a road both taken and not taken (or better, a road that was opened, and then closed off, to African and Asian peoples). It was taken in the obvious sense that numerous new sovereign States emerged in the postcolonial moment, usually after a violent struggle with colonial administrations and their enforcers. It was this that was envisaged by the 89 States who voted at the UN General Assembly in favour of the UN *The Declaration on the Granting of Independence to Colonial Countries and Peoples* in 1960, which called for an immediate end to the great evil of colonialism and the reconstruction of post-imperial space around the sovereign State. But as some African States, in particular, struggled with economic decline and/or civil war, it is important not to forget the achievements of an independence that was not just 'formal'. African diplomats had achieved a major textual breakthrough and had, in effect, re-written the UN Charter. This had effects on the ground in many places too, where guerrilla leaders began to think of themselves as 'soldiers for the United Nations' fighting for international legal ideals and in the equivocal struggles pursued through the judicial machinery.[71] What happened afterwards is a mixed picture, but the moment itself has been described by Getachew as 'an effort to break with a world order that was built on racial slavery'.[72]

On the other hand, self-determination's lost future haunts Cold War history. This lost version of self-determination might have been constituted – and to some extent was being crafted – by a powerful combination of an independent foreign policy, a deep engagement with regional

[70] See various speeches by Julius K. Nyerere in *Freedom and Socialism/Uhuru na Ujamaa: A Selection from Writings and Speeches 1965–1967* (Oxford: Oxford University Press, 1968).

[71] Amilcar Cabral, 'Anonymous Soldiers for the United Nations' in *Revolution in Guinea: An African People's Struggle* (London: Love & Malcomson, 1969) chapter 3, quoted in Adom Getachew, *Worldmaking after Empire: The Rise and Fall of Self-Determination* (Princeton: Princeton University Press 2019) 73; *South West Africa cases (Ethiopia v. South Africa; Liberia v. South Africa)* (Prelimiary Objections) (1962) ICJ Rep 319; and *South West Africa cases (Ethiopia v. South Africa; Liberia v. South Africa)* (Second Phase) (1966) ICJ Rep 6; Ntina Tzouvala, *Capitalism as Civilisation: A History of International Law* (Cambridge: Cambridge University Press, 2020) chapter 4.

[72] Getachew, *Worldmaking after Empire*, 79.

and African, Asian or Latin American collective self-governance, a distinctive culture of authority and government derived from local circumstances and forms of economic autonomy as came to be articulated in the language of 'permanent sovereignty over natural wealth and resources'.[73] Such a vision might seem utopian today, but this mixture represented the declared policy of a cadre of African and Asian leaders whose governments were very often undermined by external agitation (especially CIA coups and assassinations) or co-opted by the large corporate interests embedded through colonial laws and left behind by the colonists or disciplined by international financial institutions or simply brought into line by the operations of international capital.

This self-determination was, as Getachew has argued, a form of worldmaking with internationalism at its heart, one whose reverse mirror-image was the world made by empire, not a series of disconnected European conquests but a global mode of domination that 'exceeded the bilateral relations of colonizer and colonised'.[74] What was being enacted was not the extension or gift of Westphalian sovereignty (a gift that would inevitably lead to forms of 'unequal integration' internal to the State system) but its rejection.[75] What was both required and envisaged then was a similarly global form of resistance and redistribution in which an egalitarian national self-determination was an opening move to be followed by projects of economic renewal. The enunciation of a 'New International Economic Order'[76] alongside the 'Charter on the Economic Rights and Duties of States' were plausibly exemplary in that respect, enacting a kind of class struggle writ large. But the same spirit was also to be observed in the 'the partial exit' of experimental federation (see Section 6.5) and a 'welfare world' of revolutionary and socialist (or at least Fabian) internationalism.[77]

6.5 Pan-Africa

If many Third World intellectuals and leaders were committed to adopting the State from as part of the decolonisation of Africa and

[73] UNGA Res 1803 (XVII) (14 December 1962).
[74] Getachew, *Worldmaking after Empire*, 11.
[75] Ibid. See, too, Antony Anghie, *Imperialism, Sovereignty, and the Making of International Law* (Cambridge: Cambridge University Press, 2005).
[76] UNGA Res 3201 (S-VI) (1 May 1974).
[77] Getachew, *Worldmaking after Empire*, 24.

Arabia, others tried to revolutionise global politics by directing their energies towards supra-territorial forms of world-making. Thus far, we have traced a number of what we might think of as counter-revolutionary projects of juridical internationalism, for example, national self-determination in its dependent variants, international legalism and Amero-Sovietism, each of which supported, or became resigned to, familiarly, pseudo-European forms of State sovereignty. Looked at from the position of the post–Cold War world, this outcome appears almost inevitable. But at the time, the prospects were more varied and open. As Gevers puts it (drawing on Fanon), these were projects that rejected (white) International Law's 'underlying geographic imaginary'.[78] At least one – quite different – imaginary envisaged arrangements of trans-national – even inter-continental – political organisation.

These ideas preceded the Cold War period, even if we stretch it back to the 1917 revolution itself. Some scholars have traced them back to Marcus Garvey's Black Zionism of the 1920s[79] (including the ill-fated attempt to privately settle large tracts of Liberia) and du Bois' Pan-Africanism – expressed through five Pan-African Congresses between 1919 and 1945 and one that, according to Padmore, might have devolved into 'a Pan-African Federation of United States'.[80] Christopher Gevers traces them back further still, to 1900 at least, and the first Pan African Conference held in Westminster Town Hall. According to Gevers, the historiographical move that locates the 'origins' of Pan-Africanism in 1919 is itself symptomatic of a gendered Eurocentrism in the sense that it renders Pan-Africanism coincidental with the nascent internationalism of Versailles.[81] His detailed archival research shows that the 1900

[78] Christopher Gevers, 'To Seek with Beauty to Set the World Right: Cold War International Law and the Radical "Imaginative Geography" of Pan-Africanism' in Matthew Craven, Sundhya Pahuja and Gerry Simpson (eds.), *International Law and the Cold War* (Cambridge: Cambridge University Press, 2019) 402–509.

[79] See Andrews, 'Beyond Pan-Africanism', 2502.

[80] Padmore, *Pan-Africanism or Communism*, 118. See Adom Getachew and Jennifer Pitts, *W E B Du Bois: International Thought* (Cambridge: Cambridge University Press, 2022); and Christopher Gevers, '"Land[s] beyond the White World": (Re)imagining the International through Fiction' *Law & Literature*, 36 (2023) 241–64.

[81] Christopher Gevers' work as a whole is directed towards correcting the historiographical and epistemic practices of international legal scholars (and others), which locate Black Internationalism as emanating from the 'minds of white men' (including Marx). See, among others, Christopher Gevers, '"Unwhitening the World": Rethinking Race and International Law' *UCLA Law Review*, 67 (2020–21) 1652–85; Christopher Gevers, 'Refiguring Slavery through International Law: The 1926 Slavery Convention, the "Native Labor Code" and Racial Capitalism' *Journal of International Economic Law*, 25

conference – precipitated by a pamphlet written by a black South African woman, Alice Kinloch, about the conditions of colonial subjects – would be a better starting point, if not the 'origin' per se. At that conference, a resolution was passed, appealing '*To the Nations of the World*', which anticipated many of the struggles to come and provided the later generations of anti-colonial revolutionaries with a political idiom.[82] This is not to undermine the importance of those ideas – or those men – but to show that a black internationalism was at large long before Versailles and not derivative of the European project. As Gevers puts it, 'the work of the 1900 Conference was carried forward by DuBois'[83] in the Pan African congresses in 1919, 1921, 1923 and 1927 and then by others still.

A defining feature of many of such projects was their invocation of a world beyond, or perhaps other than, nation-states. As Siba Grovogui puts it, '[the] radical Pan-Africanists suspected that political independence under the circumstances described [in nationalist post-colonial plans, whatever their provenance] would amount to little change.'[84] Accordingly, the 1945 Congress in Manchester, for example, was opposed to national self-determination along colonial lines, denouncing 'the artificial divisions and territorial boundaries created by imperialist powers . . . to obstruct the political unity of the West African peoples'.[85] This, in turn, restated an earlier rejection of international legal territorialism in 'The Atlantic Charter and British West Africa', a wartime expression of the aspirations of West Africans demanding a self-determination not under Western eyes.[86]

These were all, in a way, announcements of, and invitations to, an alternative international law that stands in contrast to that announced in the UN Charter of 1945. When read through such declarations, the UN Charter becomes a prescription for colonial consolidation masquerading as a manifesto for emancipation,[87] a set of humanitarian *desiderata* built

(2022) 312–33; Christopher Gevers, '"News from Pan-Africa": Black Internationalism, Literature & International Law', 1900–1963' (PhD Thesis, Melbourne Law School, 2024).

82 Gevers, '"News from Pan-Africa"'.

83 Ibid., 16.

84 Grovogui, *Sovereigns, Quasi Sovereigns and Africans*, 198.

85 The Fifth Pan-African Congress Report (Manchester, 15–21 October 1945) 164. Later Michael Manley at the LSE (and influenced by Harold Laski there) was agitating in favour of the idea of a West Indian Federation: Getachew, *Worldmaking after Empire*, 8.

86 Padmore, *Pan-Africanism or Communism*, 152–53.

87 See also Mark M. Mazower, *No Enchanted Palace: The End of Empire and the Ideological Origins of the United Nations* (Princeton: Princeton University Press, 2009).

on the foundations of continuing, often brutal and *wholly lawful*, practices of colonial oppression.[88] The delegates in Manchester, like many Third World leaders to come, knew that the dream of a post-war decolonisation would not be delivered from above. Early initiatives after the signing of the Atlantic Charter had revealed as much when the efforts of nationalist leaders to apply the pronouncements on self-determination to themselves were rebuffed.[89] After all, in the words of a British civil servant of the Raj, 'the maxims of international law' only applied to 'the relations of independent and co-equal European States'.[90] And so, by the time decolonisation was taking hold, it became associated, in most international legal minds, with the achievement of national sovereignty.

For others though, proposed supra-nationalist, federal and regional arrangements were viewed as a natural extension of self-determination.[91] These ranged from Nkrumah's Union of African States to the West Indian Federation and later the United Arab Republic.[92] In his book, *Freedom Time*, Gary Wilder recovers the possibilities of the transnational formations in the thinking and writing of Aimé Césaire and Leopold Senghor, Africans who wanted to turn imperialism against itself by reconstituting France *and* its colonies as a revolutionary, plural,

[88] This is true in at least two senses. First, and most obviously, the drafters of the Charter at Dumbarton Oaks certainly did not think of it as offering a mandate for decolonisation. How could they? Two of them remained unapologetically colonial powers (the UK and France). It's no surprise then that the Charter mentions nowhere the word 'decolonisation' or, indeed, imperialism. Second, though, the Charter even interpreted in its renewed, more anti-colonial, variant from 1960 (with the 1960 Declaration understood, say, as a constitutional amendment continues to insist on the sanctity of colonial borders).

[89] See Cemil Aydin, *The Politics of Anti-Westernism in Asia: Visions of World Order in Pan-Islamic and Pan-Asian Thought* (New York: Columbia University Press, 2007); See, too, generally Elizabeth Borgwardt, *A New Deal for the World: America's Vision for Human Rights* (Cambridge, MA: Harvard University Press, 2005).

[90] See Mark Mazower, *Hitler's Empire: How the Nazis Ruled Europe* (London: Penguin, 2008) 587. Delegations of African and Asian leader had visited the UK with a view to persuading the British to make the Charter applicable to the colonised. One of those disaffected African visitors to wartime Britain was Nigerian then-newspaper editor Nnamdi Azikiwe, a friend of Nkrumah's who had written *Liberia in World Politics* (Luton: Arthur H. Stockwell, 1934).

[91] UNGA Res 1514 (XV) (14 December 1960) envisaged independence. On the same/next day, UN Res 1541 (XV) (15 December 1960) offered up a choice between independence, free association and integration but this integration was with the former colonial power. Federalism was off the table as an institutional choice.

[92] See Getachew, *Worldmaking after Empire*, 109–41. Andrews, 'Beyond Pan-Africanism', 2507 (describing Nkrumah's vision of pan-Africanism as one of the few that survived the transition to decolonisation).

pan-African, pan European, quasi-federal arrangement. They imagined in that respect an emancipatory scheme far removed from the narrow self-actualisations envisaged in the UN Charter and the various UN declarations on self-determination – what Césaire called in relation to Martinique and Haiti 'the autonomy of poverty'.[93] As Wilder argues, these post-war intellectuals and artists perceived national or local forms of freedom as self-limiting. Instead, they were engaged in an effort to remake the world and redeem humanity by abolishing the inside-outside antinomies of European and international legalism.[94]

This kind of redemptive thought had its roots in international socialism, too. Senghor had been a member of the Senegalese socialist party and had subsequently formed his own BDS (Seneghalese Democratic Bloc) around a familiar set of Left aspirations and the desire to transcend territorialisation. Senghor's Marxism was less emphatic about class struggle or economic determinants but instead sought to work towards a system of unalienated labour and a self-realised life through a transformed world politics. For him, revolution would be 'nothing other than the permanent transformation of the world by and for man'.[95] This was a conjoined art-culture-economy.[96] Yugoslav models of workers management jostled with producers' cooperatives, local assemblies, agricultural communes and forms of sometimes federalised trans-territorialism: a self-determination in the absence of sovereignty.[97] Only in this way, could the 'Cold War' be overcome. Césaire and Senghor, then, had a distinctive political vision for postcolonial Africa.[98] In a sense it combined three different legal forms – the nation-state, the trans-sovereign

[93] Gary Wilder, *Freedom Time: Negritude, Decolonization, and the Future of the World* (Durham: Duke University Press, 2015). This particular approach to decentering the nation-state has not met with approval in all quarters. See Musab Younis, 'Against Independence' *London Review of Books*, 39 (2017). It is an unusual and provocative rethinking with its descriptions of Martinique and Senegal as '"European" places and integral parts of "France"'. Wilder, *Freedom Time*, 10. The idea, though, was that Africans decolonise France. Ibid., 214.

[94] Wilder, *Freedom Time*, 8. Not the 'exclusive preserve' as he puts it of the Amero-Soviets, the Europeans or 'international lawyers'.

[95] Wilder, *Freedom Time*, 212.

[96] See Musab Younis, 'Against Independence' *London Review of Books*, 39 (2017). Some of this veered into spiritualism and might have been regarded by Marx himself as a form of mysticism, but some of it was the product of serious engagement – while he was president, he translated T. S. Eliot and W. B. Yeats into French.

[97] Wilder, *Freedom Time*, 215.

[98] Aimé Césaire, *Discourse on Colonialism* (first published 1955 in French as *Discours sur le colonialisme*, trans. Robin D. G. Kelley (New York: Monthly Review Press, 2000).

political association and post-imperial archipelago. African colonies would have autonomy but within a structure of quasi-integration with fellow postcolonial sovereigns and as part of a structure within which the former metropolitan power would be centrally located.

It was not uncontroversial to call for forms of amalgamation. In General Assembly Resolution 1541 passed in the same month as the Colonial Declaration,[99] the UN made it clear that colonised territories had a choice between independence, integration (with the coloniser) or free association (an interim arrangement). But it was equally clear that the UN machinery was mobilising in favour of independence and looked upon integration with suspicion (perhaps as a form of colonialism in a different guise).[100] Senghor himself initially preferred that Senegal be tied to a federal structure of West African States but with France as the anchor, holding to this position even as other colonies were asserting their independence (Algeria, Ghana and Tunisia, for example). Such an arrangement went from being politically impossible at the time in which the French political class took the view that empire was non-negotiable (the period of the French Union from 1948 to 1956), to deeply regressive by the time when decolonisation was in full swing. This (Francophone) pan Africanism, thus, was never realised.[101] The 1959 agreement at Bamako to create a federal African State composed of Senegal, Sudan, Dahomey and Upper Volta[102] was undercut by rapid defections (the Mali Federation composed of the two remaining entities dissolved shortly afterwards).[103] The territorialists (Houphouet-Boigny in Cote d'Ivoire), territorialism (the UN Charter, formal decolonisation) and what Senghor called 'balkanisation' (and what Wilder calls the 'nationalist vector of decolonisation') had won the day.[104]

But Senghor was by no means alone. Even those leaders styled as decolonising nationalists at least gestured towards a cross-border

[99] UNGA Res 1541(XV) (15 December 1960).

[100] Curiously, Martinique, the birthplace of both Fanon and Césaire chose to remain a French overseas department in this period.

[101] See too Frederick Cooper, *Citizenship between Empire and Nation: Remaking France and French Africa, 1945–1960* (Princeton: Princeton University Press, 2014).

[102] See, Constitution de la Féderation du Mali 1959 (Mali).

[103] See, Rosalyn Cohen, 'Legal Problems Arising from the Dissolution of the Mali Federation' *British Yearbook of International Law*, 36 (1960) 375–84.

[104] Senghor eventually undermined his own position by supporting a *Communitae Francais* in which the metropole would have extensive and centralised powers over defence, foreign relations and other international matters. Wilder, *Freedom Time*, 219–20.

coalition of States (e.g. Nyerere's references to East African 'unity' or Nkrumah's 'African personality' and continental unity).[105] In 1958 in Accra, the All-African Peoples Conference had even passed a resolution on 'Frontiers, Boundaries and Federations' in which they stated that 'artificial barriers and frontiers drawn by imperialists to divide African peoples operate to the detriment of Africans and should therefore be abolished, or adjusted'.[106] Senghor and others had understood something important about an international law wedded as it was to 'independence as a form not a reality'.[107] And similar ideas were to find favour elsewhere, such as in the formation of the (similarly short-lived) Federation of the West Indies in 1958.[108] In the end, though, his model of democratic communitarian socialism with fully realised humans at its heart was entirely sidelined and erased. New forms of political organisation – even boundary changes – were off the table; a thin form of national self-determination – with a besieged sovereignty as the final goal of political struggle – had prevailed. And this was formally confirmed at the first 'ordinary' session of the OAU Assembly of Heads of State and Government in 1964 at which all member States pledged themselves 'to respect the borders existing on their achievement of national independence'.[109]

6.6 Cuban International Law (Havana–Algiers–Luanda)

> I don't know whether Fidel is a communist but I am a Fidelista.
>
> —Nikita Khrushchev on returning from the UN[110]

[105] See generally, speeches found in Julius K. Nyerere, *Freedom and Socialism/Uhuru na Ujamaa: A Selection from Writings and Speeches 1965–1967* (Oxford: Oxford University Press, 1968); Kwame Nkruma's speech at the Conference of Independent African States and the All-African Peoples Conference in Accra, 1958; Byrne, *Mecca of Revolution*, 69–70.

[106] 'Current Documents: Resolution on Frontiers, Boundaries and Federations' *Current History*, 37 (1959) 41–46.

[107] Wilder, *Freedom Time*, 224, quoting Léopold Sédar Senghor 'Rapport sur la doctrine et la politique générale; ou, Socialisme, unité africaine, construction nationale' (Union Progressiste Sénégalaise, Dakar 1962). Original in French – a copy can be accessed here: www.jstor.org/stable/44824251.

[108] British Caribbean Federation Act 1956. See generally, C. B. Bourne, 'The Federation of the West Indies' *University of Toronto Law Journal*, 13 (1960) 135–65.

[109] Organization of African Unity, 'Border Disputes Among African States', Res 16(1) (17–21 July 1964).

[110] See Fruchter and Hall, NLR May/June 1961, 9

What would happen if we looked at the international law of the Cold War not from the Quai d'Orsay or Whitehall but from Havana or Algiers? More specifically, were there forms of internationalism available to the Third World within territorial boundaries bequeathed by empire? In *The Black Jacobins*, C. L. R. James offers up the possibility of Castro as a latter-day Bolivar, someone who brings something 'new to the world'.[111] Cuba's international legal diplomacy and its military and medical internationalism in Africa was a joint anti-colonial project and an East–West relation of the South. It was a form of revolutionary internationalism (maybe even globalism) for those who seriously envisaged and worked towards an international law of independent nations advancing in the cause of the proletarian internationalism envisaged by Marx and Engels (workers of all lands uniting in global revolutionary struggle).

At first, Cuba's radical and cross-cutting international legal politics worked a rather familiar diplomatic seam through its engagement with the AAPSO (the Afro-Asian People's Solidarity Organisation) at its five meetings (in Cairo, Conakry, Moshi and Winneba ending with the Tricontinental Conference) and then with the NAM. But, as Blanca Mar León notes, Cuban socialists were initially divided about how to advance socialism.[112] Two of the three major political groupings after the January 1959 overthrow of the Cuban dictator and kleptocrat, Batista (the July 26 Movement and the March 13 Students Directorate) were in favour of (permanent) armed struggle, believing it as 'both necessary and possible to subvert the entire world'. The Popular Socialist Party by contrast adopted the language and praxis of peaceful coexistence.[113] The Tricontinental itself – both the 1966 conference and the Group that emerged[114] – was organised along representative and democratic lines,

[111] See James, *The Black Jacobins*, 321.

[112] See, for a discussion of Cuban–Chilean diplomacy not involving armed struggle, Tanya Harmer, *Allende's Chile and the Inter-American Cold War* (Chapel Hill: University of North Carolina Press, 2011) 3 and *passim*.

[113] Blanca Mar León, 'Revolutionary Diplomacy and the Third World: Historicizing the Tricontinental Conference from the Cuban Ministry of Foreign Affairs' in Tanya Harmer and Alberto Alvarez (eds.), *Towards a Global History of Latin America's Revolutionary Left* (Gainesville: University Press of Florida, 2021) 75–76. The 26 July Movement was famous for having kidnapped Juan Manuel Fangio, the Formula One world champion, from his hotel in Havana just before a Grand Prix organised to support the Batista regime. He was released within a day.

[114] OSPAAL – The Organisation of Solidarity with the People of Asian, African and Latin America.

and this intra-Cuban split reflected a broader tension within the Tricontinental Group between those who placed anti-imperial revolutionary violence at the heart of the struggle and those who favoured mass mobilisation and political reform.

Castro's own communist credentials were not especially secure in the early days of the Cuban Revolution (Che had said once that he was 'an authentic leader of the leftist bourgeoisie').[115] His fidelity – so to speak – to Sovietism was qualified by an insistence that Cuba's development be independent of some of the strictures of the European planned economy. The Cuban missile crisis intensified this sense of independence in two ways. On one hand, Castro was further radicalised by the seriousness of Washington's threat to the survival of the Cuban Revolution; on the other hand, he had lost a certain amount of faith in Soviet incrementalism after the disappointment of the Kennedy–Khrushchev agreement over the missiles. The result was a different kind of Cuban internationalism, one less reliant on (and displaying less deference to) the Soviets and committed to a stronger global revolutionary programme that would protect and advance anti-imperialist States everywhere. Castro advanced what has been called a 'reverse doctrine of intervention', an international legal norm existing outside the UN Charter that would permit, oblige even, anti-imperialist States to defend countries threatened by 'Yankee imperialism'.[116] The focus, for Castro, was to be Africa with its (shared) history of slavery and its distance from the United States.[117]

At first, this began with the adoption of the *foco* model of armed resistance, which involved sending sometimes tiny numbers of guerrillas to precipitate the conditions for broader revolutionary struggle, for instance in the Congo and Bolivia, as well as an episode of cross-hemispheric South–South friendship between Algeria and Cuba. But Cuban militant internationalism intensified with the overthrow in Portugal, of the Salazarist regime and its president, Marcelo Caetano, in what become known as the Carnation Revolution.[118] In a sense, this itself was a mini–world revolution. The coup in Lisbon set off a chain of

[115] Carlos Franqui, 'Che Guevara to Daniel [René Ramos Latour], 14 December 1957' in *Diary of the Cuban Revolution* (New York: The Viking Press, 1980) 269.

[116] Arne Westadt, *The Global Cold War: Third World Interventions and the Making of Our Times* (Cambridge: Cambridge University Press, 2007) 176–77.

[117] On the deployment of narratives of slavery, see generally, Yogita Goyal, *Runaway Genres: The Global Afterlives of Slavery* (New York: New York University Press, 2019) esp. 29–32.

[118] On the *foco* model, see Chamberlain, *The Cold War's Killing Fields*, 11.

events in Angola, Mozambique, Guinea Bissau and East Timor in which revolutionary socialism was taken up by liberation movements within the settings of postcolonial conflict.

In Angola, the three principal factions were the FLN (an American-Zairean outfit led by the cynical and insubstantial Holden Roberto and supported by white mercenaries), UNITA (based largely in the South and centred around the personality of Jonah Savimbi) and the MPLA (a Marxist–Leninist party supported by the Soviets). With some justification, the forces arrayed against the MPLA were described by the Soviet Solidarity Committee as part of a 'serious international imperialist conspiracy';[119] after all, the Belgians, South Africans and Americans had already assassinated Lumumba in Zaire and now the same forces were moving against Neto's MPLA in Luanda. The Soviets remained cautious, fearful and diffident and though they supported Neto's MPLA in Angola, his organisation failed to build relations with Moscow's advisers in the country. And so the Angolans at first turned to Tito whose non-aligned status was enormously attractive to them (both Tito and Neto had condemned the invasion of Czechoslovakia in 1968) and then to the Cubans who represented another kind of third force.[120]

By October 1975, the South African Defence Force had begun a full-scale invasion of Angola proceeding quickly with rapid advances up the coast. But on 2 November 1975, a South African armoured column was ambushed by the MPLA and forty Cuban advisers. Emboldened by this success and the Soviet decision to recognise Angola as an independent State with the MPLA in Luanda as its legitimate government, the Cubans then sent regular troops to Angola in November 1974 to defend the new State and government.[121] The Cubans continued to support armed struggle (in Syria, in the Horn, in Angola) as well enacting a form of humanitarian internationalism[122] throughout this period and remained both non-aligned and very much part of the Soviet bloc, a position requiring a certain amount of 'finesse'.[123] In the aftermath of Angola and decolonisation, the Cubans continued to export their medico-educational expertise with mass literacy programmes built around the

[119] Okoth, 'Poison Is Better', 183.
[120] Okoth, 'Poison Is Better', 27–29.
[121] The Cubans had 50,000 troops in Angola at one point.
[122] Byrne, *Mecca of Revolution*, 175.
[123] Ibid., 168. Westadt, *The Global Cold War*, 172 (on Cuba's uptake of Soviet theory and practice).

Cuban model of 'Yo Si Puedo' endorsed by UNESCO and trialled also in Timor, Tanzania (1971–83), Mozambique (1978–79), Kerala (1986), Australia and Nicaragua (1980).[124] All of this occurred despite opposition from Western States who claimed that these programmes were politicising pupils. And perhaps, in a sense, they were, as 'people discovered that they were part of a wider adult literacy movement among "people of colour" in countries of the Global South'.[125] In Cuba, itself, the revolution had begun in this pedagogical mode with the thirty rebel army schools established in the mountains by Che Guevara.[126] If this was an international socialism, it emphasised housing, education and medical care over industrial development and accumulation.[127]

This has been necessarily a brief sketch, but it suggests that the Cubans enacted, for some time, a different kind of internationalism – perhaps we can call this a responsibility to protect (unrecognisable as such because emerging from the South). It was founded on the potency of revolutionary ideas and the need for (an expanded notion of) self-defence, projected through insurrectionist warfare and outright intervention and continued in later forms of medical and educational interventionism.[128] Havana developed what in effect was a(nother) rival 'Cold War international law' and accomplished this in the face of Amero-Soviet opposition (a United States that was committed to removing the Castroists from power in Cuba, a Soviet Union careful not to antagonise the Americans in their own backyard and very keen to build trading relations with some of the governments that the Cubans were trying to overthrow).[129] It had many distinct phases – national self-determination, anti-Yankeeism, world revolution, *foco* guerilla-rebellion, foreign intervention – but the essence of Cuban internationalism was perhaps mapped out most emblematically during its romantic alliance with the FLN when the shared internationalism and fierce nationalism of the two

[124] Bob Broughton, Donna Ah Chee, Jack Beetson, Deborah Durnan and Jose Le Blanch, 'An Aboriginal Adult Literacy Campaign Pilot Study in Australia Using Yes I Can' *Literacy and Numeracy Studies*, 21 (2013) 9.

[125] Ibid., 27. See, of course, Paulo Freire, *Pedagogy of the Oppressed* (New York: Penguin, 1972).

[126] Leo Huberman and Paul Sweezy, *Cuba: Anatomy of a Revolution* (New York: Monthly Review Press, 1960).

[127] See Fruchter and Hall, 'Notes on the Cuban Dilemma', *passim*.

[128] Byrne, *Mecca of Revolution*, 175; Piero Gleijeses, 'We Wrapped the Guns in Plastic Bags' *London Review of Books*, 39 (2017) 184–87.

[129] Gleijeses, 'We Wrapped the Guns in Plastic Bags'.

revolutionary cadres produced a counter-imperial fraternalism grounded in 'natural amity', a commitment to economic and political freedom, an acceptance of violence as a form of revolutionary practice (overlaid with what Byrnes calls 'guerrilla chic') and an avant-gardism in cultural and political matters. This mix was all underpinned by a belief in the desirability of humanist socialism through global revolution.[130]

6.7 World Revolution and Its (international) Law: Disrupting the North–South Axis

> The laws of Marxism are present in the events of the Cuban Revolution, independently of what its leaders ... know of these laws from a theoretical point of view.[131]

On 29 December 1917, at a meeting of the Russian-Socialist-Democratic Labour Party, the Party had called for a cessation of 'all diplomatic relations with ... the diploma'd highwaymen of all countries'.[132] At the same time, Trotsky himself had wondered if legal-diplomatic work would be necessary after the Bolshevik ascendancy, warning that he would make some 'revolutionary sounding speeches' and then 'close the shop'. By the late 1930s, a figure like C. L. R. James, disgusted by the League's failure to protect Ethiopia from the predations of a European (fascist) army, took a Trotskyite turn away from gradualism and from international institutions and called for a world revolution, which would 'turn the imperialist war into a civil war'.[133] But what was 'world revolution' during the Cold War? And what did it imply for international law? This final section takes up the question of revolutionary socialism as a moment of Cold War world-making (if necessary through international civil war) and as a demand for a transformed 'law' of international politics.[134]

130 See generally, Byrne, *Mecca of Revolution*, 73–79.

131 Guevara, 'Notes for the Study of the Ideology of the Cuban Revolution' October 8, 1960, in David Deutschmann (ed.), *Che Guevara Reader: Writings by Ernesto Che Guevara on Guerilla Strategy, Politics and Revolution* (Melbourne: Ocean Press, 1997) Pt. 2.

132 Dmitry G. Tomashevsky, *On the Peaceful Co-Existence of States* (Moscow: Novosti Press Agency Publishing House, 1973).

133 C. L. R. James, *World Revolution, 1917–1936: The Rise and Fall of the Communist International* (North Carolina: Duke University Press, 2017; originally 1937) 421.

134 Amidst its struggles with other Cold Wars (and especially with softer, more quietist forms of coexistence); by the early 1960s, Soviet policy was increasingly committed to peaceful coexistence, and this more ambivalent Soviet State diplomacy was at odds with

By the 1950s at least, for the Global South – the historic locale for capitalist expansion and colonial conquest – the idea of a socialist world revolution posed several thorny questions. One concerned the relationship between the anticipated worker's revolt in the industrialised North and the often agrarian, peasant rebellions in the South. This was, we might say, 'the Chinese question'. National liberation movements also had to work out how exactly various forms of decolonisation squared with the idea of a world revolution (necessary to Marxist internationalism) and to what extent the Soviet Union – given its periodic rapprochements with the imperialist powers and its own variable ideological commitments – was committed to either violent revolution on a global scale or self-determination as an end in itself. Soviet orthodoxy, after all, was certainly suspicious of anything that smacked of a Third Way or bourgeois nationalism *within* States.[135]

In the end, a certain form of highly protean Marxist–Leninism held sway in some of the anti-colonial movements (e.g. Cuba, North Korea, East Timor, Vietnam, Angola, Mozambique). Lenin had adapted Marx for national liberation with his re-descriptions of imperial accumulation as a kind of encore to the final stage of human development in markets and capital, and it was this anti-imperialism that became a loose blueprint for some revolutionary aspiration in the postcolonial world. Though the politics of anti-metropolitan uprisings were, naturally, very mixed, the shared experience of a particular form of European racial domination lay at the heart of Third World self-assertion. In many cases, this was wedded to a belief in modernisation and industrialisation (in both its Soviet and Western variants) and State-building. But there was also a powerful tendency that reflected a more radical view of the possibilities of hemispheric re-ordering. This was revolutionary socialism: the realisation of the Korovinian *telos* of a world united (under

the radical core of Marxist–Leninist thought taken up in parts of the Global South by Maoist and other more radical anti-colonialists in the Global South who were less concerned with offending the Americans and more inclined to engage in violent armed struggle. For a history of Russian and Soviet international law, see V. E. Grabar, *The History of International Law in Russia 1647–1917: A Bio-Bibliographical Study*, trans. W. E. Butler (Oxford: Clarendon Press, 1990; first published 1958 in Russian); Lauri Mälksoo, *Russian Approaches to International Law* (Oxford: Oxford University Press, 2015) 36–66. Tomashevsky, *On the Peaceful Co-Existence of States*, 15.

135 'We are not importing a foreign ideology into Tanzania.' Julius K Nyerere, *Freedom and Socialism/Uhuru na Ujamaa: A Selection from Writings and Speeches 1965–1967* (Oxford: Oxford University Press, 1968) 2.

communism).[136] For all his tentativeness, Khrushchev too believed, at times, that national liberation might revive 'the forgotten dream of revolution'.[137] Soviet foreign policy adapted accordingly with a whole bureaucracy (e.g. 'International Development', 'The Communist Institute of the Toilers of the East') created to advance Soviet interests and Marxist principles in the Third World. And, as Telepneva notes, the policy-making branch was full of people who had experienced revolution themselves and supported its export to Asia, Latin America and Africa.[138]

In the Global South itself, new leaders were embracing forms of revolutionary socialism.[139] At times there were latent references to Marx, whether it was Julius Nyerere calling for a 'a socialist society consist[ing] of workers and only of workers'[140] or the 5th Congress declaring: 'Today there is only one road to effective action – the organisation of the masses.'[141] But Nyerere's own plan emphasised the many paths to socialism, describing it broadly as the application of equality to the organisation of human relations within society and the ending of relations of exploitative production (and cataloguing its many variations).[142] If national liberation in the Global South sometimes lacked ideological inflection, then this was understood as an advantage

[136] Ibid. See also Tomashevsky, *On the Peaceful Co-Existence of States*, 15. Tomashevsky, for example, points out that early Soviet foreign policy faced a puzzle – namely, how to have a foreign policy at all when there was socialism in only one country, i.e., in the absence of world revolution. The Soviets had disliked McDougal–Lasswell precisely because of their over-emphasis on the idea of a 'unified world community'. Hans Morgenthau had by then already described the UN as a grand alliance against the Soviet Union. Compare Justin Rosenberg, arguing that sovereignty was capitalism's (commodity) form: Justin Rosenberg, *The Empire of Civil Society: A Critique of the Realist Theory of International Relations* (London: Verso, 1994). The Third World States were later using the General Assembly to move against South Africa and to adopt anti-colonial declarations. Alexander Dallin, 'The Soviet View of the United Nations' *International Organization*, 16 (1962) 39.

[137] Quoted in Telepneva, *Cold War Liberation*, 18.

[138] Telepneva, *Cold War Liberation.*

[139] 'Nkrumah's Ghana', according to Leslie James, 'allowed African nationalist groups to avoid metropolitan institutions and instead look to locales with similar historical experiences in order to think through 'political alternatives' for their postcolonial futures'. Okoth, 'Poison Is Better', 27–29.

[140] Nyerere, *Freedom and Socialism/Uhuru na Ujamaa*, 5 Though this was to include *all* workers, including 'women who look after small children'. Ibid., 6.

[141] Nyerere, *Freedom and Socialism/Uhuru na Ujamaa*, 178.

[142] Ibid., 2, 3, 103.

and often served to 'maintain unity among the anti-colonialist forces'.[143] Sometimes these were adaptations of what might be called a humanist socialism. This humanist socialism seemed more obviously sentimental than Marxism itself or emphasised the question of alienation more than that of exploitation. In some respects, it was just as concerned about the trivialisation of life and about the deformities of a consumerist society than it was about relations of production *stricto sensu.*[144] These sentiments are powerfully expressed in Nkrumah's 'Motion of Destiny' speech to the Legislative Assembly of the Gold Coast on 10 July 1953, where he quotes Burke: 'Our business carefully to cultivate our minds . . . to rear every sort of generous and honest feeling . . . to bring the dispositions that are lovely' and commits Ghana to freedom and development and raised standards (but not at the cost of what he called 'fundamental happiness').[145] There was a more tough-minded psychological aspect to this for Nkrumah who knew that decolonisation required a change of mind, a revolutionary order in which relations of dependence would be erased.[146] Cedric Robinson described this aspect of decolonisation in Fanon's *White Masks* as a form of 'disalienation'.[147]

Many of these ideas were expressed through forms of State-building. But alongside this national orientation, there remained, in large parts of the Third World – in Vietnam, in Cuba, in Algeria, in Rhodesia – a belief in the existence of a new global revolutionary subject composed not of an industrial proletariat but made up instead of a diverse collection of peasants, students, the unemployed, the intellectuals and indigenous people. This revolutionary creed was both critical of international law's conservatism and yet at the same time willing to mobilise it in struggle often through forms of international socialism.[148] Two aspects of an international law of global revolution are present here.[149] The first is

[143] Ibid., 28.

[144] This found expression in the cultural gatherings that were a mark of the period (e.g. Fesman, the Senegalese Festival in 1966, see Sean Jacobs, 'Chop-Chop Spirit' *London Review of Books*, 46 (2024) 9–14.)

[145] Kwame Nkrumah speech before the House of Commons, London, United Kingdom (10 July 1953). Kwame Nkrumah, *Africa Must Unite* (New York: Frederick A. Praeger, 1963) 2, 10.

[146] Nkrumah, *Africa Must Unite*, 50.

[147] Cedric Robinson, 'The Appropriation of Frantz Fanon' *Race & Class*, 35 (1993) 79–91.

[148] Harmer, *Allende's Chile*, 260.

[149] See, generally, Hannah Arendt, *On Revolution* (New York: Penguin, 1963); George Lawson, *Anatomies of Revolution* (Cambridge: Cambridge University Press, 2019). On the idea that the global evolutions traced here are now passé, see Chantal Mouffe

the project to valorise – perhaps even legalise – revolutionary violence, claimed as a right under international law. The second is found in the idea of 'the global' as a site for transformation.[150] The revolutions of the national liberation movements tend to be remembered as moments of national consolidation. But this misses the very real sense in which they saw themselves as part of a collective project: a new, different, upended international legal order.[151]

6.7.1 Revolutionary War

As part of this project, Third World leaders and intellectuals grappled with the question of violent struggle (and, in particular, guerrilla warfare) in the face of efforts to exclude it as a legitimate form of political activism and in light of the existence of an international legal regime that seemed committed to promoting 'peace'.[152] No such discussion seemed to take place in relation to counter-revolutionary violence, which proceeded apace,[153] albeit that the Friendly Relations Declaration prohibited any 'forcible action which deprives people ... of their right to self-determination and freedom and independence'.[154] The question of

and Ernesto Laclau, *Hegemony and Socialist Strategy: Towards a Radical Democratic Politics* (London: Verso, 1985). David Graeber, *Debt: The First 5,000 Years* (Brooklyn: Melville House, 2011).

150 See, e.g., description of the Organisation of Afro-American Unity with its aim 'to build a Black nation from the ground up ... rather than from the top down based on colonial nation state borders'. Andrews, 'Beyond Pan-Africanism', 2512.

151 See elsewhere in this chapter but also, e.g., on the cosmopolitan character of Frelimo, see Jason Sumich, '"Just Another African country": Socialism, Capitalism and Temporality in Mozambique' *Third World Quarterly*, 42 (2021) 588.

152 Sometimes resistance to the idea of violence was itself implacable. See George Padmore on the congressional approach of the Pan-Africanism and the 'road of non-violent revolution instead of Mau Mauism'. Padmore, *Pan-Africanism or Communism*, 185. In Nyerere's August 1968 introduction, he emphasises a preference for non-violent transition but does not rule out violence altogether. Benita Parry, on the other hand, has referred to Fanon's 'paradigm of the colonial condition as one of implacable enmity between native and invader, making armed opposition both a cathartic and a pragmatic necessity.' Quoted in Cedric Robinson, 'The Appropriation of Frantz Fanon' *Race & Class*, 35 (1993) 85. In any event, violence was sometimes not necessary as colonial regimes collapsed without a shot being fired. See Gabriel Kolko, *Century of War: Politics, Conflict and Society Since 1914* (New York: The New Press, 1994) 346–50 (on the Communist take-over in Vietnam immediately after the war).

153 See Greg Grandin, *Empire's Workshop: Latin America, the United States, and the Rise of the New Imperialism* (New York: Holt Paperbacks, 2006) for Latin American variations.

154 UNGA Res 2625 (XXV) (24 October 1970).

violence divided the postcolonial leaders with a split emerging between the softer moderate (and often sovereigntist) wing and a group devoted to armed struggle and transnational anti-imperialism.[155] By the late 1950s, this second group seemed to be in the ascendance with the delegates at the APCC, inspired by the Algerians and by Fanon's advocacy, agreeing on the legitimacy of armed violence.[156] By the end of Nkrumah's conference in Accra, the delegates had made their view known in a resolution declaring support for 'all fighters of freedom in Africa . . . who are compelled to retaliate against violence to attain national independence'.[157] For some this even extended to forms of outright terror. Guevara in *Guerrilla Warfare* argued that: 'We must carry the war into every corner the enemy happens to carry it: to his home, to his centres of entertainment; a total war.'[158] Revolutionary violence came to be understood then as a primary means by which global revolution would be 'summoned'.[159]

But violent subversion and insurgency was a problem for Third World insurrectionists and freedom fighters because defeating colonial or Western armies in the field became an impossibility after the first, and perhaps last, defeat of a European power in open battle at Dien Bien Phu. The huge disparities in technological, military and material resources meant that wars of national resistance were inevitably conducted using methods whose 'legality' under the assumed standards of the laws of war was at least questionable. But the presumed illegalities of insurgency had several particular contextual features.

In the first place, the development of the laws of war (with a civilian/combatant distinction at its core) was to emerge precisely at the moment in which the colonial era was coming to an end, and at the point of time in which the blurring of that distinction was a necessary element of

155 Byrne, *Mecca of Revolution*, 70, discusses the way this played out in relations between the FLN and Ghana at the Accra Conferences in 1958.

156 *The Wretched of the Earth* was published two years later in 1961 at the same time as the founding of the NAM. Byrne, *Mecca of Revolution*, 70. See, on Guevara's belief in the legitimacy of violence, David Priestland, *The Red Flag: A History of Communism* (New York: Grove Press, 2009) 370.

157 *All African Peoples' Conference Resolution on Imperialism and Colonialism* (Accra, 5–13 December 1958).

158 Che Guevara, *Guerrilla Warfare* (Lincoln: Bison Books, 1998; originally 1961) 173.

159 See Che Guevara, 'Message to the Tricontinental', Organization of Solidarity with the People of Asia, Africa and Latin America, Havana, 16 April 1967, www.marxists.org/archive/guevara/1967/04/16.htm. On 'summoning', see Paranzino, 'Two, Three, Many Vietnams', 285.

anti-colonial struggle. As we have already seen in Chapter 4, what was to become known as 'humanitarian law' was itself to become a battleground in which anti-colonial resistance had to fight for its own legitimacy. In the second place, the reliance by the colonial powers on weapons of mass destruction precisely obliterated the very distinction that they sought to apply to Third World 'resistance'. If Guevara's 'total warfare' was to be disparaged, no such condemnation was offered in relation to the total warfare on offer under the policy of deterrence (Chapter 7). So, as much as anti-colonial struggle had established a new international legal *grundnorm* in 1960, it did so in a context in which one of its primary methods was simultaneously being described as illegal. And this was to culminate, ultimately, in the invocation in the 1970s and '80s of 'terrorism' as a generic descriptive alternative to the phrase, 'struggles of national liberation'[160] rather than, and more obviously, a description of the generalised threat offered by nuclear weapons globally.

This final development gave rise to the contemporary anxiety about 'terrorism'. In this sense, the Cold War can be understood both as origin and counterpoint to our own present. It was a period in which revolutionary violence moved from being authorised or at least acknowledged as possessing some legitimacy, to becoming illicit or subject to procedural norms. To reverse a phrase used by Adam Shatz, there is a move, here, from nouns to verbs.[161] Instead of asking questions about the substantive politics of a revolutionary movement (anti-apartheid, say) or the alignment of its goals with international legal norms (decolonisation), by the end of the Cold War, violence was to become evaluated in procedural terms (are the methods employed 'proportionate' and 'discriminate'?).[162]

160 See Thomas Meaney, 'The Winning Side' *New Left Review: Sidecar*, 10 May 2024, https://newleftreview.org/sidecar/posts/the-winning-side; Christopher Goscha, *The Road to Dien Bien Phu: A History of the First War for Vietnam* (Princeton: Princeton University Press, 2022). Ho's policy of land reform had been a successful prelude to peasant-class consciousness and the establishment of a war economy. On the invention of anti-terrorism, see Conor Gearty, *Homeland Insecurity: The Rise and Rise of Global Anti-Terrorism Law* (Oxford: Polity Press, 2024).

161 Adam Shatz, *Writers and Missionaries: Essays on the Radical Imagination* (London: Verso, 2023) 316.

162 When it comes to such questions, of course, nouns do matter a great deal. When it comes to States, proportionality and discrimination become a kind of argumentative terrain, a set of debates about 'the lesser evil'. For two different views, see Gabby Blum and Philip B. Heymann, *Laws, Outlaws, and Terrorists: Lessons from the War on Terrorism* (Cambridge, MA: MIT Press, 2010); Eyal Weizman, *The Least of All Possible Evils: Humanitarian Violence from Arendt to Gaza* (London: Verso, 2011).

At the height of the anti-colonial struggle, some international lawyers pointed to the ambiguous phrasing found in the great instruments of decolonisation where, implicit in the text, was a right to resist (by all means), colonial occupation.[163] To take an example, General Assembly Resolution 2138 called upon States 'to extend all moral and material support to the people of Zimbabwe in their legitimate struggle to overthrow the illegal, racist regime'.[164] Describing that struggle as 'legitimate', and the regime itself as 'illegal', seemed to bring into view, not just a right to receive support from outside but a lawful right to engage in violent resistance (akin, one might think, to a State's right to use force in self-defence). This claim, however, was often only partly audible.[165] As many were to note, a right to armed insurrection or rebellion had never been prohibited under international law, even if it might be criminalised by the State itself. This was a purely 'internal' matter notwithstanding the illegalities associated with the regime itself. At best, it seemed, there might be a right to remedial secession available for peoples living under oppressive States or in unendurable conditions as suggested in the preamble to the Universal Declaration of Human Rights.[166]

But, however equivocal the recognition given to the right to resist, by the 1970s and '80s, this kind of thinking had been entirely sidelined by anti-terrorist discourses.[167] As Joey Slaughter points out, throughout the 'heady days of decolonisation', terrorism was a term used, most frequently, to describe 'those acts and policies of Governments which were designed to spread terror among a population for the purpose of ensuring its submission to and conformity with the will of those

The killing of civilians in any circumstances by non-State actors is almost always understood as 'terrorism'.

163 See, e.g., Georges Abi-Saab, 'Wars of National Liberation in the Geneva Conventions and Protocols' *Recueil des cours*, 165 (2007) 1979. The Cold War, of course, was extremely violent. Three 'My Lais' occurred every day, the equivalent of 1,200 people dying in conflict on every single say of what has been termed a 'long peace'. See Chamberlain, *The Cold War's Killing Fields*, 19.

164 UNGA Res 2138 (XXI) (22 October 1966), para 10. Similar sentiments are found in UNGA Res 2625 (XXV) (22 October 1975).

165 See, e.g., John Dugard, 'Towards the Definition of International Terrorism' *American Society of International Law Proceedings*, 67 (1973) 97.

166 The UDHR even begins with a preamble in which it is said to be 'essential, if man is not to be compelled to have recourse, as a last resort, to rebellion against tyranny and oppression, that human rights should be protected by the rule of law'.

167 Joseph R. Slaughter, 'Hijacking Human Rights: Neoliberalism, the New Historiography, and the End of the Third World' *Human Rights Quarterly*, 40 (2018) 735–75.

Governments'[168] and extended also to the practices of 'racist, colonial, and alien regimes'.[169] This was to shift decisively in two ways: on one side, governmental repression lost any association with 'terrorism' and became associated instead with violations of human rights and fundamental freedoms;[170] on the other side, terrorism was individualised (associated with specific criminal acts such as kidnapping,[171] hostage taking[172] or hijacking)[173] and stripped, in the process, of any political connotations.[174] If a majority in the South continued to resist any association of national liberation movements with terrorism simpliciter, that position was increasingly undercut by the gradual erosion of the space within which any form of (violent) revolutionary conduct might legally operate. And the lasting legacy of that evolving movement has been the almost complete erasure of the 'national liberation movement' as a legal or political category with any meaning, such that even relatively mild statements of support for, say, Palestinian resistance have become subject to administrative sanction in British and American universities. Alongside it, terrorism has displaced enmity as the dominant motif even in inter-State conflict (e.g. Russian 'terror' attacks on Ukrainian cities, Ukrainian 'terrorist' incursions into Kursk).

[168] UNGA, 'Measures to Prevent International Terrorism, Study prepared by the Secretariat' (2 November 1972) UN Doc. A/C.6/418, 6.

[169] Slaughter, 'Hijacking Human Rights', 762–63. See, e.g., UNGA Res 3034 (XXVII) (18 December 1972) para 4 (which 'Condemns the continuation of repressive and terrorist ats by colonial, racist and alien regimes in denying people their legitimate right to self-determination and independence'). Historically, it extended also to the spreading of terror in other States, see Convention for the Prevention and Punishment of Terrorism, Geneva, 16 November 1937, 10 League of Nations – Official Journal (January 1938) 23.

[170] Slaughter, 'Hijacking Human Rights', 763.

[171] Convention to Prevent and Punish the Acts of Terrorism Taking the Forms of Crimes Against Persons and Related Extortion That Are of International Significance, Washington, DC, 2 February 1971, OAS TS No. 37.

[172] International Convention against the Taking of Hostages, New York, 17 December 1979, 1316 UNTS 205; UNGA Res 146 (XXXIV) (17 December 1979).

[173] Convention for the Suppression of Unlawful Seizure of Aircraft, The Hague, 14 October 1971, 860 UNTS 105; Convention for the Unification of Certain Rules for International Carriage by Air, Montreal, 28 May 1999, 2242 UNTS 309. Notably, however, neither of these conventions, nor UNGA resolutions associated with them, actually mentioned the word 'terrorism'.

[174] See, e.g., European Convention on the Suppression of Terrorism, Strasbourg, 10 November 1976, 15 ILM 1272.

6.7.2 *Global Revolution (Solidarity?)*

Alongside the debate about whether armed violence constituted a legitimate form of resistance, there was also the question of where revolutionary struggle might be understood to take place or find succour. There were certainly many vibrant trans-nationalisms between African and Asian diasporas, Western mass movements and States in the Global South. From the overtures made to African Americans by African leaders (and vice versa) in 1965 after the Watts Riots, to Stokely Carmichael's visit to Cuba, to the links made by the Cubans themselves between slave trade and colonialism when building solidarity with African States,[175] to the ways in which Black African resistance in Soweto referred back to Vietnam, Mozambique and Angola,[176] to Malcolm X's calls for a war against a common enemy 'in Alabama and in Zaire alike',[177] Amero-Soviet internationalism was being undercut by these collaborations across worlds that performed the disruption of the North–South categorisation itself.[178] These movements and dissenting traditions were organised around combinations and re-combinations of at least three anti-capitalisms – the revolutionary urban and peasant organisations in the South, the Soviet bloc's anti-imperialism and the working class and radical student movements in the West. Each of these, to an extent, disrupted and undid the spatialised legalities of the Cold War.

As we have seen in previous chapters, the question of international law 'itself' was also in play.[179] The new forces of anti-colonialism very often refused the language of law to describe the colonial administration of large parts of the globe by the elite. When Ben Bella addressed the United Nations in 1962, he called on nations of the Third World to tear up 'the

[175] Piero Gleijeses, *Conflicting Missions: Havana, Washington, and Africa, 1959–1976* (Chapel Hill: University of North Carolina Press, 2002) 200.

[176] Gleijeses, *Conflicting Missions*, 341; Carlos Martinez, *The East Is Still Red – Chinese Socialism in the 21st Century* (Glasgow: Praxis Press, 2023); Massimiliano Tomba, *Insurgent Universality: An Alternative Legacy of Modernity* (Oxford: Oxford University Press, 2019).

[177] Gleijeses, *Conflicting Missions*, 131. The Black Panthers were a violent insurrectionist nationalist movement but also an anti-imperialist network with the aim of achieving a reformulation of international law along liberationist lines.

[178] We have already seen an example of this in the way in which the Yugoslav–India–Ghana axis breaks both with the North–South categorisation of global relations and, at the same time, rejects both the East–West split and, in the case of Yugoslavia, the norms of Amero-Sovietism.

[179] Gleijeses, *Conflicting Missions*, 77 (on Che's famous comment that Lumumba had placed too much trust in international law).

gentleman's agreements' that constituted the new UN order. This is vitally important because it suggests that the law of refusal (or the refusal of law) worked both ways. The North believed that the practices of Third World resistance were either non-law (i.e. violence or politics) or of marginal legality (i.e. soft law, or neutralism).[180] But Ben Bella turned this gesture on its head and asserted his own 'diplomacy of revolutionary internationalism'.[181] The stage was set for what the Tri-Continental preparatory committee called 'the two currents of world revolution . . . the socialist revolution of October and that of national liberation revolution'.[182]

Che Guevara had famously called for radicals around the globe to create 'one, two, three Vietnams'; the revolutions taking place in the South could, he believed, succeed best if they were accompanied by world-making projects in the North. 'Instead of invading Vietnam with generosity, let Vietnam invade us', as the film-maker Jean-Luc Godard said.[183] So, in the United States, the old civil rights organisations were being out-manoeuvred by newer and more aggressive movements like the SDS (Students for a Democratic Society) and the African American RAM (Revolutionary Action Movement). African American organisers were trying to think their way out of the confines of a counter-revolutionary international law that understood its claims as 'minority rights' or 'self-determination'. Instead, at the core of their politics was a new international law, a world-making in which freedom was achieved through a self-determination that was a beginning and not an end to global revolution. The categories of international law were repurposed to re-animate and re-read the circumstances of African Americans (as a colonised people) and the nature of the American polity (seen as a form of internal colonisation).[184] More to the point for our purposes, the plight of African Americans and the Vietnamese was thought of as the

180 R. Jospeh Parrott, 'Introduction: Tricontinentalism and the Anti-imperial Project' in R. Joseph Parrott and Mark Atwood Lawrence (eds.), *The Tricontinental Revolution: Third World Radicalism and the Cold War* (Cambridge: Cambridge University Press, 2022) 1–2.

181 Byrne, 'The Romance of Revolutionary Transatlanticism', 177.

182 International Preparatory Committee of the First Solidarity Conference of the peoples of Africa, Asia and Latin America, *Towards the First Tricontinental Conference* (Havana, 1966).

183 Salar Mohandesi, *Red Internationalism: Anti-Imperialism and Human Rights in the Global Sixties and Seventies* (Cambridge: Cambridge University Press, 2023) 113.

184 Ibid., 114.

same: each was subjected to violence by a colonising regime (in fact, in this case, the same one) and the appropriate response was violent revolution.[185] So, this was primarily a 'revolution of the hungry countries'[186] but also a revolution in which the revolutionary subject was the Third World in the Global South and the Global West, a subject constituted, according to Che, by a sense that it had been subject to 'the deceit of racial inferiority'.[187] This revolutionism was also a new way of doing international law: an international law of regular 'conferencing' (the Tricontinentals, the Bandungs).[188]

This North–South unity (also found among French radicals) was mirrored by South–South collaborations between, for example, the Latin Americans and the Vietnamese (at the OLAS meeting in Havana in the summer of 1967) with the Vietnamese subsequently shifting from a national strategy to a commitment to the overthrow of imperialism throughout the globe.[189] These organisations made it clear that they were not pacifists. In some respects, they were not opposed to the 'American War' (as the Vietnamese called it). What they wanted was the comprehensive defeat of US imperialism *through* war. In France, the Latin Quarter was occupied, its streets renamed; and the offices of US businesses were bombed. There was talk of France descending or ascending into revolution. But all the while, the international, global and violent revolutionary nature of this struggle was being emphasised.[190] Workers, meanwhile, were laying down tools and demonstrating in French factories through 1967 and 1968. These strikes, including the National Strike of 1968, were partly about local grievance and national politics. But mostly, they were inspired by an internationalist solidarity, an international 'law' at one level removed from that of bourgeois diplomacy.

[185] On Fanon's competing idea of reparation, see Harmer, *Allende's Chile*, 263.

[186] Fruchter and Hall, 'Notes on the Cuban Dilemma'.

[187] See Anne Garland Maher, *From the Tricontinental to the Global South: Race, Radicalism, and Transnational Solidarity* (Durham: Duke University Press, 2018). This might have encompassed at various junctures, the anti-colonial intellectual elites in the West. See Rafael Rojas, *Fighting Over Fidel: The New York Intellectuals and the Cuban Revolution* (Princeton: Princeton University Press, 2016). See Paranzino, 'Two, Three, Many Vietnams', 284.

[188] Byrne, 'The Romance of Revolutionary Transatlanticism', 166.

[189] Note here the central role of Beijing in training and educating a generation of insurgents (Algerians, Palestinians, Vietnamese). See Chamberlain, *The Cold War's Killing Fields*, 13.

[190] See Paranzino, 'Two, Three, Many Vietnams', 282 on Che's call for a triangulated violent strategy after the fall of Arbenz in 1954.

When we see these movements not as political dissidence but as internationalist world-making, both they, and international law itself, begin to look quite different. In *Red Internationalism*, Mohandesi notes that, 'In the face of the mounting carnage [a million tons of bombs had been dropped in Vietnam by the end of 1967], radicals began to argue that the kind of intellectual condemnation exemplified by the International War Crimes Tribunal was inadequate.'[191] It's worth remembering that this world-making imagined not just a new State but a new man to be created through both a change of mentality and structure.[192] At the Pan African Congress, this lost language of redemptive humanity is articulated in the starkest possible terms when the participants call for rights to 'express our thoughts and emotions, to adopt and create forms of beauty'.[193] Nyerere speaks fondly at one point of his love of books and the way that reading can offer a resource for national revival. As he announces, in a speech in the United Arab Republic: 'socialism is a state of mind' (this does not mean he is not also committed to nationalisation and a suspicion of private property).[194] But, as Jason Sumich puts it: 'Socialism was not restricted solely to technologies of rule; it was principally a moral claim: the promise of justice and a better world.'[195] The revolutionary anti-colonialism of the Cold War moment was the expression of a radically different, and, what is now, to most of us, a radically unfamiliar, politics of emancipation: a stark contrast to the bland, complicit internationalism that seems to populate official discourse today. This was an international law of carnival, pedagogy, informality and battle dress.[196] To read back into this thinking is to discover an attention to languages of love and friendship (Nyerere, Bandung) and 'moral incentive' (Guevara), a powerfully oppositional political economy of decolonisation, a refusal to exclude (and an agonising debate about) revolutionary violence as a means of struggle. It also demonstrated an enthusiasm for the reconstitution of sovereignty (sometimes as pan-federal arrangements, sometimes through an expansive vision of 'sovereign equality', sometimes as 'Cuban–Algerian

[191] Mohandesi, *Red Internationalism*, 121.

[192] See Priya Lal, *African Socialism in Tanzania: Between the Village and the World* (Cambridge: Cambridge University Press, 2015).

[193] The fifth Pan-African Congress, 'The Challenge to the Colonial Powers' (Manchester, 1945).

[194] Nyerere, *Freedom and Socialism/Uhuru na Ujamaa*, 309.

[195] Sumich, 'Just Another African Country', 595.

[196] See Fruchter and Hall, 'Notes on the Cuban Dilemma', 16.

Transatlanticism'), a humanist ambition expressed through global class consciousness and a self-determination with internationalist, world-conceiving ambition.[197]

6.8 Conclusion: Revolution to Approach

> At one point, during Polo II, Henry Kissinger received a (counter) draft joint statement from Chou. He responded by saying: 'We can't have an American President sign a document which says … "the people's revolutionary struggles are just"!'[198]

In *Sambizanga*, Sarah Maldoror's 1972 film set in the pre-independence Cold War Angola of the early '60s, the main character, Maria, sets out on a journey to find her husband, Domingos Xavier. Earlier, Xavier had been taken from their family hut by a group of (Angolan) policemen in a white Land Rover. In the early scenes, Maldoror depicts the arduous work of African contract labourers as they break up large stones for use by the Portuguese colonial regime, the impoverished but communitarian lives of the workers and their families and the love shared between Maria, Domingos and their baby boy. The bulk of the film, though, is devoted to Maria's search for Domingos. She looks to law for some kind of answer: visiting jailhouses, speaking to smoothly technocratic legal officers and sympathetic indigenous policemen. The law promises so much but it is, she discovers, a highly ordered system of bureaucratic control in which she possesses 'rights' – including the right to see the tortured body of her dead husband. Her fateful quest is juxtaposed throughout by the machinations of an embryonic independence movement as its members meet in secret places. Some of the members are trying to gain access to Xavier by seeking to work out how to parse and mobilise the existing legal system, while others teach the rudiments of Marx's theory of surplus labour and revolutionary struggle to sceptical auditors (some of whom

[197] See, e.g., Donald C. Hodges, *The Intellectual Foundations of the Nicaraguan Revolution* (Austin: University of Texas Press, 1986). On Che, see Helen Yaffe, *Che Guevara: The Economics of Revolution* (London: Palgrave Macmillan, 2009) 41. On Cuban–Algerian Transatlanticism, see Byrne, 'The Romance of Revolutionary Transatlanticism', 166.

[198] See Richard Nixon, *The Memoirs of Richard Nixon* (London: Arrow Books, 1978) 555. POLO was the code name for the preparatory meetings Kissinger held in the PRC.

believe that the rich must be rich in order that the poor may live).[199] There is little to indicate at this point that Angola is about to be the site of one of the great Cold War struggles for national liberation, one that would involve not only the superpowers but also a regime continuing to practice a form of apartheid (South Africa) and a revolutionary State located in another hemisphere altogether (Cuba).

The plurality of actors engaged in the Angolan struggle for national liberation gives expression to a key theme that we have been developing in this chapter and in the book more generally – namely, that the era of the Cold War may best be understood, not just as one marked by a bipolararity of a global character but as a period in which a rich and diverse range of rival forms of world-making and revolutionary activism came together. That much of this diversity and pluralism has been lost to history is a consequence, as much as anything else, of a historiographical choice: a choice in which the simplified rubric of an Amero-Soviet rivalry has been deployed to enable the erasure of anything that might challenge it or question its aftermath. As a result, we now find ourselves in the midst of a politics in which communism is invoked not as an alternative to, but as a limit on, the possible range of distributional choices in political discourse, and the (memory of) 'the Cold War' determines the permissible range of diplomatic manoeuvre.[200] Once the period of explicit lawful rivalries was over, the imaginaries we describe here were either discredited or deemed to have 'failed'.

In re-invoking the rich tapestry of revolutionary world-making during this time, we seek to break with a historiographical tradition that habitually recasts such projects as political rather than juridical. In challenging that assumption, we seek to unsettle both the idea that there was a singular, overarching and uncontested international law within which communist revolutionaries or national liberation movements, for example, sought to locate their struggles and the associated idea of a 'lawful' North and an 'unlawful' South. In North and South alike, there were both varying forms of world-making on offer and varying forms of

[199] See the film *Sambizanga* (1972) directed by Sarah Maldoror (screened at The Garden Cinema, London, 17 June 2024). For further discussion of the film and Maldoror's work, see Jeremy Harding, 'I Am Only Interested in Women Who Struggle' *London Review of Books*, 46 (2024).

[200] It is this Cold War Jodi Dean refers to when she remarks: 'One would think the Cold War never ended'. Jodi Dean, *The Communist Horizon* (London: Verso, 2012) 40.

(international) law to which they sought to give expression. These were more complex, and often more syncretic, than might be captured in the usual tripartite division between First-, Second-, and Third-World approaches to international law. The 'approachification' of international law, indeed, would appear to be just one more symptom of a dominant 'Cold War thought' that reduces all forms of political contestation to questions of 'interpretation' of an otherwise stable canon and whose ultimate heir would be 'proved' by history.

Trotsky once asked if revolutions had their own laws.[201] The lost revolutionary projects we have described here represent an alternative Cold War international law history: a history with the dead awakened. This history is a response to those retrospectives, or memories of the Cold War, that have become a constituent element of – and are vital to – the apologetic politics of the present. Those memories of the Cold War are memories of a defeated totalitarian State that has come to represent – indeed exhaust the representation of – communism and revolutionary socialism in the world. Jodi Dean (writing from the US) has pointed out that a qualification for participating in political life today is that one declares that one is not a communist – or at the very least that any invocation of communism or revolution comes with a set of qualifiers and apologies for its (necessary) excesses.[202] The Cold War (and its popular histories) re-produce a version of communism that is highly particular and strongly associated with Stalin, the camps and the persecutions (which peaked during the warmest period of US–Soviet relations).[203] As Brown and Martin have said: 'The Communist icon of the Cold war is now the negative ideal type.'[204] So, for Dean, the only and best response to all of this is to 'shatter the chain; communism-Soviet Union-Stalinism-collapse, and make a new one out of the rich variety of movements and struggles'.[205] This, for Dean, is an important corrective to the idea that 1991 represents a break, 'a temporal horizon separating the validity of Soviet experiment from the capitalist … present'.[206] But

201 Enzo Traverso, *Revolution: An Intellectual History* (London: Verso, 2021).

202 Dean, *The Communist Horizon*, 8–11; Frederic Jameson, *Archaeologies of the Future: The Desire Called Utopia and Other Science Fictions* (London: Verso, 2005).

203 Dean, *The Communist Horizon*, 31.

204 Michael E. Brown and Randy Martin, 'Left Futures' *Socialism and Democracy*, 9 (1995) 80.

205 Dean, *The Communist Horizon*, 38.

206 Ibid.

where Dean sees the loss of 'communist' variety, we attend to a wider range of revolutionary and plural possibilities, many of which could be read as communist, but some of which involve re-alignments of political space (Pan-Africanism or the promise of genuine 'national' liberation), the retrieval of social democratic practices (Chile), the reconfigurations of global political space, and the assertion of rival forms of law.

7

Secrets and Spies

Espionage, Surveillance and the Covert Cold War

7.1 Introduction

On 1 May 1960, a Lockheed U-2 aircraft flown by a CIA operative, Francis Gary Powers, took off from a US military airbase in Peshawar, Pakistan. His instructions were to traverse the Soviet Union to identify and photograph military installations in Tyura-Tam and Plesetsk. The flight was part of a programme devised by the CIA in 1956[1] to improve US intelligence on Soviet military capabilities[2] and verify the size of the vaunted 'missile gap' that US strategists feared had opened out.[3] Flying as part of the Second Weather Observational Squadron (Detachment 10-10) at a height of around 68,000 ft (high enough in theory to avoid Soviet air-defences), Gary Powers was shot down over Sverdlovsk by a surface-to-air missile. This was not entirely unexpected.[4] But instead of activating the aircraft's self-destruct mechanism, Powers parachuted to the ground. He was then immediately captured and transferred to Lubyanka Prison

[1] The CIA ran 51 overflights of the Soviet Bloc, the majority of which were over Russia and China, between 20 June 1956 and 1 May 1960. Allen Dulles, 'U-2 Overflights of Soviet Bloc', Central Intelligence Agency CHAL 1138–60, 18 August 1960.

[2] The U-2 programme was the continuation of an earlier programme that had begun in 1952. For an overview, see R. Cargill Hall, 'The Truth about Overflights' *Quarterly Journal of Military History*, 9 (1997) 24–39.

[3] For an interesting reflection on the 'missile gap', see David Runciman, 'The Great Political Films: Dr Strangelove & Fail Safe with Jill Lepore', Past Present Future Podcast, 3 November 2024, https://podcasts.apple.com/ee/podcast/the-great-political-films-dr-strangelove-fail-safe-w/id1682047968?i=1000675489492.

[4] It was evident from discussions in the White House in April 1960 that continuing the U-2 programme was a risk given evidence that the Soviets had a missile capable of homing in on a target flying at 80,000 ft. See Leonard Mosely, *Dulles: A Biography of Eleanor, Allen and John Foster Dulles and Their Family Network* (London: Hodder and Stoughton, 1978) 453; William E. Burrows, *Deep Black: Space Espionage and National Security* (New York: Berkley Books, 1988).

in Moscow where he was interrogated by the KGB over the next two months and subsequently put on trial.

The incident had immediate political repercussions.[5] The US State Department initially claimed that the U2 was a meteorological observation aircraft belonging to NASA that had experienced difficulties with oxygen equipment and had 'accidentally violated Soviet airspace'.[6] But it was forced to amend its account when President Khrushchev revealed that both the pilot and his equipment had been captured intact. The US then asserted that the plane was 'probably' an 'unarmed civilian U-2' dispatched in order 'to obtain information now concealed behind the iron curtain' but without explicit Presidential authorisation.[7] A third version came to light when Eisenhower himself admitted knowledge of the mission. Soviet objections were not muted. The flight constituted a 'treacherous incursion' into Soviet airspace, 'an aggressive' and 'provocative' act, an act of 'espionage and sabotage' that violated Soviet sovereignty and territorial integrity.[8] No public apology from the US to the USSR was forthcoming, and the US would not give an assurance that the flights would be terminated and those responsible for the flight punished.[9] In response, Khrushchev offered Eisenhower a stinging rebuke, not least for the public lies that had been disseminated by the US administration, and walked out of the Four Power Summit Conference in Paris.

Ultimately the US defence was not to dispute the illegality of the incursion (nor indeed to protest the later trial and conviction of Gary Powers)[10] but to claim that it was forced into such operations as a consequence of excessive Soviet secrecy and the corresponding need to

5 See generally, Michael R. Beschloss, *Mayday: Eisenhower, Khrushchev, and the U-2 Affair* (New York: Harper & Row, 1988).

6 See NASA Press Release, 5 May 1960, Christian Herter Papers, Box 20, U-2 (1); NAID #12009392. Generally, Stephen Kinzer, *The Brothers: John Foster Dulles, Allen Dulles and Their Secret World War* (New York: Times Books, 2013) 256.

7 Quincy Wright, 'Legal Aspects of the U-2 Incident' *American Journal of International Law*, 54 (1960) 838.

8 See remarks by Krushchev in the 'Proceedings of the Summit Conference and Bilateral and Tripartite Discussions, 16–20 May 1960' in *Foreign Relations of the United States, 1958–1960*, vol. IX (Washington, DC: United States Government Printing Office, 1993) doc. 168, 439.

9 These demands were initially set out in a meeting between Khrushchev and De Gaulle, *Foreign Relations of the United States, 1958–1960*, vol. IX (Washington, DC: United States Government Printing Office, 1993) doc. 160, 416.

10 Oliver J. Lissitzyn, 'Some Legal Implications of the U-2 and RB-47 Incidents' *American Journal of International Law*, 56 (1962) 136.

guard against aggression. In a private meeting with de Gaulle and Macmillan just before the summit, Eisenhower expressed his frustration at the reaction of the Soviets. He said that whilst it was difficult to justify espionage either legally or morally (it was, as he put it, both 'distasteful and disagreeable'), it was nevertheless a practice in which all engaged, and for good reason. 'We had to have information' he asserted 'in order to defend the free world and ourselves against surprise attack'.[11] 'He was damned', however, 'if he was going to be the only one at the conference to raise his hand and promise never to do again something that everybody else was doing'.[12] He was only 'prepared to say that spying was illegal, distasteful and wrong if all said it'.[13]

In the end, Eisenhower was more circumspect. At the meeting the next day, he merely reiterated the 'distasteful necessity of espionage activities' and the lack of 'aggressive intent'[14] on the part of the US. He affirmed that the U-2 programme had already been suspended 'not to be resumed'.[15] But this was not enough to tempt Khrushchev back into the Conference Hall. Soviet Foreign Minister Gromyko presented a draft resolution to the Security Council condemning the 'aggressive acts' of the air force of the United States as violations of the sovereignty of the Soviet Union and as 'incompatible with the principles and purposes of the Charter of the United Nations'.[16] In response to Gromyko's complaints that the U2 operation was, amongst other things, 'perfidious',

[11] *Foreign Relations of the United States, 1958–1960*, vol. IX (Washington, DC: United States Government Printing Office, 1993) doc. 165, 427.

[12] Ibid.

[13] Ibid. It is perhaps revealing that Allen Dulles, former head of the CIA, was later to turn this observation on its head in remarking that espionage 'is not tainted with any "legality"'. Allen W. Dulles, *The Craft of Intelligence: America's Legendary Spy Master on the Fundamentals of Intelligence Gathering for a Free World* (London: Weidenfeld and Nicolson, 1963) 182.

[14] *Foreign Relations of the United States, 1958–1960*, vol. IX (Washington, DC: United States Government Printing Office, 1993) doc. 168, 444. Macmillan followed this by stating that 'espionage is a disagreeable fact of life' even if 'most forms of espionage involve violation of national sovereignty' (445). De Gaulle dismissed Khrushchev's concerns stating that 'the concept of these overflights is bound to change and they are bound to become a natural phenomenon' (446). There was, he noted, already a 'Soviet satellite which is going through the skies around the world and it crosses through French skies 18 times a day'.

[15] It was clear, by that stage, that the US had already started to run satellite reconnaissance missions under the name of CORONA.

[16] See, Gromyko's statement in UN Doc. S/PV.857 (23 May 1960) 4–19; Wright, 'Legal Aspects of the U-2 Incident', 841.

'provocative', and 'piratical',[17] Cabot Lodge Jr (the US Ambassador to the UN) simply reasserted the US position: the real problem was not the fact of espionage (as the unmasking of numerous spies in the US attested) but rather the Soviet Union's secrecy. 'When such a government insists on secrecy', he suggested, 'it is in effect also insisting on preserving its ability to make surprise attacks on humanity'.[18] In other words, it was secrecy that justified the acts of surveillance, never mind that the surveillance itself could only be effected by way of an equal measure of secrecy.[19]

The immediate consequences of the U-2 debacle were significant. It spelled the end of the incipient détente upon which both Eisenhower and Khrushchev had pinned significant hopes for a public normalisation of US–USSR relations. This particularly affected the ongoing discussions about the future of Berlin. Eisenhower's reputation at home was in tatters because he had lied openly to the public. Khrushchev fared little better with the incident, which fomented discontent within the party over his foreign policy vis-à-vis both the US and China.[20] Because the plane had been launched from Peshawar in Pakistan, it also had consequences for the relationship between intelligence activities and Cold War diplomacy in South Asia.[21]

But beyond the immediacies of the political aftermath, the incident brought two things into prominence. The first was the centrality of both secrecy and surveillance to relations between the rival superpowers. The second was the way in which espionage and other related covert activities were structured by the Amero-Soviets in and through international law. Both were to have lasting consequences.

[17] Wright, 'Legal Aspects of the U-2 Incident', 841.

[18] See, Lodge's statement in UN Doc. S/PV.857 (23 May 1960) 21.

[19] Thomas M. Franck and Edward Wiesband, *Secrecy and Foreign Policy* (Oxford: Oxford University Press, 1974) xv: 'In a curious way, claims by government for secrecy involve two conflicting sub-claims: the right of government to know more about everybody, and the refusal by government to allow anyone to know much about it.'

[20] William Taubman, *Khrushchev: The Man and His Era* (New York: W. W. Norton & Company, 2003); Vladislav M. Zubok and Constantine Pleshakov, *Inside the Kremlin's Cold War: From Stalin to Khrushchev* (Cambridge, MA: Harvard University Press, 1997) 205.

[21] Paul M. McGarr, 'Tinker, Tailor, Soldier, Subversive: India, Pakistan and the Politics of Cold War Intelligence' in Leslie James and Elisabeth Leake (eds.), *Decolonization and the Cold War: Negotiating Independence* (London: Bloomsbury Academic, 2015) 285–302. See generally, Paul McGarr, *The Cold War in South Asia: Britain, the United States and the Indian Sub-continent, 1945–1965* (Cambridge: Cambridge University Press, 2013).

In the course of this chapter, we will explore these two ideas. We turn first to the creation of what might be called an 'international intelligence community'. This was a community of newly minted intelligence agencies engaged in competitive, and sometime collaborative, ventures. Their main focus was the preservation of something the US was calling 'National Security'. Through the example of the US, we will show how 'National Security' became a capacious notion, capable of providing the rationale for the pursuit of unlimited practices of surveillance. The emerging notion of 'National Security' would also provide the justification for waging a putatively 'defensive' form of covert warfare across a broad front, not just political or military but social, economic and cultural – and not just in East and West but across the globe. The practice of intelligence would also become a routinised part of the security apparatus of many newly independent States. In the process, the operational patterns of what became known as the 'securitised State'[22] would become lodged within the patterns of governmentality as they were to be disseminated around the world along with the State form, 'securing' such States from both without and within.

From there, we turn to two related dimensions of the practice of intelligence: secrecy and espionage. First in relation to the question of secrecy, we make the argument that a central paradox of Cold War ideological rivalry was that it depended upon both an unprecedented broadening of the field of secret knowledge and a parallel commitment to publicising the fact of secrecy itself. The inevitable porosity of secrecy about activities being conducted away from home encouraged the development of two associated strategies of deferral: one being ideological disavowal, the other plausible deniability.[23] Each of these had particular resonance in legal debates over the legitimacy of forms of covert warfare and were ultimately aimed at avoiding the attribution of responsibility. It was not until the *Nicaragua Case* that such practices came under judicial scrutiny, and the ICJ was forced to navigate around the epistemic problems that this formation produced. Whilst the court did categorically denounce the practice of covert warfare as an illegitimate act of

[22] Cf. Barry Buzan and Ole Wæver, *Regions and Powers: The Structure of International Security* (Cambridge: Cambridge University Press, 2003). Itty Abraham makes this point. Itty Abraham, *The Making of the Indian Atomic Bomb: Science, Secrecy and the Postcolonial State* (London: Zed Books, 1998).

[23] Timothy Melley, *The Covert Sphere: Secrecy, Fiction, and the National Security State* (Ithaca: Cornell University Press, 2012).

intervention, it nevertheless re-affirmed the intrinsic logic of the practice of secrecy and the idea that the only knowledge that could be fully trusted was the revealed secret.

Finally, we turn to the question of espionage. This was an idea framed by reference to legal texts – both national and international – that sought, on the one hand, to proscribe espionage and render it punishable (sometimes on pain of death), whilst, on the other hand, to legitimate it as practice intrinsic to warfare. It operated through a series of distinctions - between war and peace, the overt and the covert, the combatant and the non-combatant – all of which produced a certain vacillation as to the legality of the practice even in time of war.

But it was in the context of air rights that the problem of peacetime espionage became most acute. The formulas adopted in Paris and Chicago affirming sovereign rights over airspace were largely informed by the idea that airspace sovereignty was essential for purposes of security and, in particular, defence against the possibility of espionage. A further phase of the same debate opened out in the aftermath of the Sputnik launch in 1957. Here our argument is that the rival Cold War powers were effectively collaborating with one another to produce a new legal domain: 'Outer Space'. The domain was an effect wrought by a concern to legitimise their respective satellite reconnaissance programmes, and remove, in the process, the problem of territorial intrusion that had marked the U-2 debacle. This new legal (or jurisdictional) space provided one of the conditions for the production of a new global imaginary – one imprinted with the logics and pathologies of the Cold War.

7.2 Intelligence Agencies

The emergence of an Amero-Soviet 'Cold War' in the late 1940s was marked institutionally by the formation of a panoply of intelligence agencies throughout the West and the Soviet States in the aftermath of the Second World War. For the most part, such organisations found their origins in a varied cluster of wartime military intelligence services some of which dated back to the late nineteenth century. Their existence was often simultaneously both a secret and a matter of public knowledge.[24]

[24] The existence of MI5 and MI6 was only publicly acknowledged in the Intelligence Services Act 1994, which proclaimed that 'there shall continue to be a Secret Intelligence Service'.

The decision taken by many around 1945, not only to retain the services of such agencies in 'peacetime' but to give them permanency was an institutional marker not only of the emergent enmity between the erstwhile allies in the aftermath of war but of the specific ways in which they would elect to perform and enact that ideological rivalry.

The agencies established included the CIA and NSA in the US (1947), MI5, MI6 (1909) and GCHQ (1946) in the UK; the SDECE in France (1946); the StB in Czechslovakia (1945); the Stasi in East Germany (1950) and the BND in West Germany (1956); the UB in Poland (1945); and the GRU (1942), MVD, MGB (1946) and KGB (1954) in the Soviet Union. Many such agencies operated nationally as part of an institutional network with functional divisions between intelligence gathering and analysis, counter-intelligence and between foreign and domestic affairs. They were often also networked internationally with information being shared between agencies on either side of the divide, often under the guise of formal cooperation and collaboration agreements.[25] Collectively, the creation of such agencies marked the emergence of what might be called an 'international intelligence community' broadly united by reference to their objectives (the securing of 'State' or 'national security') and by their means and methods of operation (surveillance, intelligence, counter-intelligence, etc.), while necessarily separated by their mutual enmity.

Most such agencies were established by way of military, administrative or political fiat, and their operational mandates remained obscure for a considerable time. The one notable exception to this was the Central Intelligence Agency in the United States, which was created under the terms of the National Security Act of 1947. It was notable not only because an institution dedicated to the secret gathering of (secret) information as well as to a variety of other forms of covert international activity was publicly legislated into being but also because only a quarter of a century earlier, the US had championed the cause of public diplomacy. But its creation was a marker of the opening of a Cold War whose operational terrain would be marked by secrecy, as well as of the fact that secrecy itself would become a matter of public knowledge and debate and a key means by which that 'covert warfare' would be waged.

[25] Most prominently in the West was the 'five eyes' agreement concluded between the UK, US, Canada, Australia and New Zealand. The UKUSA Agreement of 1948 had its origins in the earlier British–United States Communications Intelligence Agreement (BRUSA) of 1946 that, itself, renewed an earlier 1943 agreement between the powers to cooperate in the field of communications intelligence.

Ostensibly, the purpose of the National Security Act was to 'promote national security' by coordinating the disparate activities of the various branches of the military and placing them under central 'civilian control'. Alongside creating a 'Defense Department' and the institution of the 'Joint Chiefs of Staff', the Act created a National Security Council tasked with advising the US President on the 'integration of domestic, foreign, and military policies relating to national security'[26] and a Central Intelligence Agency tasked with correlating and evaluating intelligence 'relating to national security' for the 'appropriate dissemination of such intelligence within the Government'.[27] Importantly, the CIA was also tasked with performing such other 'functions and duties related to intelligence affecting the national security as the National Security Council may from time to time direct'[28] – a clause that was to prove vital in the subsequent development of both its clandestine intelligence collection activities and covert operations.[29]

None of this was immediately apparent in the terms of the NSA itself. The Act contained no specific definition of intelligence[30] nor any specific description as to how it might be gathered. If, as Sheldon Kent was to describe it, intelligence seemed to concern itself with 'the kind of knowledge' that a State must possess 'regarding other states in order to assure itself that its cause will not suffer nor its undertakings fail because its statesmen and soldiers plan and act in ignorance',[31] the question remained as to what *kind* of intelligence might be required for such purposes. What forms of knowledge were necessary for the preservation

[26] National Security Act of 1947, s 101.

[27] Ibid., s 102(d)(3). The CIA replaced the non-statutory Central Intelligence Group, which, since January 1946, had been formed as a successor to the wartime Office of Strategic Services (OSS).

[28] Ibid., s 102(d)(5).

[29] Dulles, *The Craft of Intelligence*, 45.

[30] A definition of 'intelligence' was only added in 1992 in the Intelligence Organization Act, which defined it as consisting of two kinds – foreign intelligence and counterintelligence. The former was defined as meaning 'information relating to the capabilities, intentions, or activities of foreign governments or elements thereof, foreign organizations, or foreign persons'. Intelligence Organization Act, 106 Stat. 3188 (1992).

[31] Sherman Kent, *Strategic Intelligence for American World Policy* (Princeton: Princeton University Press, 1966) 3. See also George S. Pettee, *The Future of American Secret Intelligence* (Washington, DC: Infantry Journal Press, 1946); William L. Langer, 'Scholarship and the Intelligence Problem' *Proceedings of the American Philosophical Society*, 92 (1948) 43; Roger Hilsman, *Strategic Intelligence and National Decisions* (Glencoe: The Free Press, 1956); Washington Platt, *Strategic Intelligence Production* (New York: Frederick A Praeger, 1957).

of 'national security' in the context of a burgeoning Cold War? What had to be known?

The first clue could be found in the concept of 'national security' itself. As Neocleous points out,[32] the term 'national security' was something of a neologism at the time[33] and had been used in preference to the older, and somewhat more narrowly conceived, idea of 'national defence'.[34] What this new concept of national security introduced was a much broader array of concerns, it stitched together the age-old question of political security with ideas of 'economic security' and 'social security' that had been key ideological terms underpinning Roosevelt's New Deal legislation.[35] This more expansive conception of national security, Neocleous argues, was to inform US foreign policy in the early years of the Cold War, providing the backdrop for a 're-ordering of global capital' through, amongst other things, the Marshall Plan, the formation of the International Monetary Fund and the GATT (1947) and the Brussels Pact of 1948.[36] 'The key institutions of "international order" in this period' he writes 'invoked a particular vision of order with a view to reshaping global capital as a means of bringing "security" – political, social and economic – from the communist threat.'[37]

This idea of 'security' provided a framework that brought together diverse strands of US foreign policy – economic, political, military and social – and was consonant with the broad terms of the ideological

[32] Mark Neocleous, *A Critique of Security* (Edinburgh: Edinburgh University Press, 2012). Preston suggests that the concept of national defence was exemplified by Secretary of State Daniel Webster's advocacy of a narrow conception of self-defence in the Caroline Case. Andrew Preston, 'Monsters Everywhere: A Genealogy of National Security', *Diplomatic History*, 38 (2014) 477–500, 483.

[33] He draws, here, upon Schurmann who argued that 'a new ideology, different from both nationalism and internationalism, forged the basis on which bipartisanship could be created. The key word and concept in that new ideology was *security*'. Franz Schurmann, *The Logic of World Power* (New York: Pantheon Books, 1974) 65. See further, Dexter Fergie, 'Geopolitics Turned Inwards: The Princeton Military Studies Group and the National Security Imagination' *Diplomatic History*, 43 (2019) 644–70; David Ekbladh, 'The Interwar Foundations of Security Studies: Edward Mead Earle, the Carnegie Corporation and the Depression-Era Origins of a Field' *Global Society*, 28 (2014) 40–53.

[34] Mark Neocleous, *A Critique of Security* (Edinburgh: Edinburgh University Press, 2012) 76–77. Anderson adds that 'this became the key slogan linking internal atmospherics and external operations into a single front, and assuring passage from the New Deal to the Truman Doctrine.' Perry Anderson, 'Imperium' *New Left Review*, 83 (2013) 5, 29.

[35] Neocleous, *A Critique of Security*, 81–92.

[36] Ibid., 97.

[37] Ibid.

conflict in which members of the Amero-Soviet foreign policy establishment saw themselves engaged.[38] Defending Western, or indeed Socialist values (the 'containment' of communism or capitalism, respectively) depended upon bringing into play all kinds of resources – not just military, but economic, social and cultural – in order to win the battle for hearts and minds and not just locally, or regionally, but globally. This 'total Cold War', as Eisenhower later described it, carried the language of warfare across the military/civilian divide, conscripting society as a whole – commercial enterprises, education institutions, trades unions, charitable bodies and even families – into the field of combat. It also generalised that warfare globally. For as Alan Dulles, the Director of the CIA from 1953 to 1961, put it, it had become 'impossible to predict where the next danger spot may develop. It [was] the duty of intelligence to forewarn of such dangers, so that the government [could] take action. No longer [could] the search for information be limited to a few countries. The whole world is the arena of our conflict.'[39] There was scarcely a place on earth, nor a community nor resource within it, that was not capable of being brought within the impressive spread of this ideological contestation, barely a form of knowledge or instrumental technique that was beyond its compass. And as part of that, the functions to be served by the nascent CIA, as with its institutional equivalents elsewhere, were as potentially capacious as they were ill-defined.

Much of this may be discerned in Kent's account of the core descriptive elements of intelligence required for the effective formulation of foreign policy. According to Kent, such knowledge included information on the characteristics of the military, core descriptions of the 'physiques of these countries' (their natural topography and environment, including their cities, transport networks, agriculture and industry), their people (how settled, how occupied), the 'status of their arts, sciences and technologies' and 'the character of their political systems, their economies, their social groupings, their codes of morality, and the dynamic interrelations which prevail among all these'.[40] The task of accumulating such knowledge required not just sophisticated techniques of data gathering and processing (including, importantly, computational resources) but

[38] Preston remarks that 'Americans . . . pursued the Cold War under the aegis of "national security" [understood] as the pursuit of total security . . .. In the Cold War, it seemed that Americans were finding monsters everywhere.' Preston, 'Monsters Everywhere', 499.

[39] Dulles, *The Craft of Intelligence*, 51–52.

[40] Kent, *Strategic Intelligence for American World Policy*, 6.

teams of researchers with a wide variety of skills. Alongside the political scientists would sit geographers, anthropologists, linguists, sociologists, cryptologists, mathematicians and data analysts. 'Area studies' would be born as part and parcel of the desire to 'know' the enemy, to predict their decisions, to estimate their capabilities and plan a strategy of countermeasures.[41]

Some of the activities of those agencies involved gathering information that was publicly available (for example, by diplomatic agent),[42] without any intrusion in either the territory of the States subject to surveillance nor by way of interception of their systems of privileged communication (e.g. diplomatic cables). Such activities didn't trouble the legal advisors to the State Department or their overseas equivalent. But, of course, as intimated by Eisenhower in the context of the U2 incident, intelligence requirements would seldom be limited to such knowledge.[43] And the more closely guarded the 'secrets of State', the more surreptitious the means had to be by which they might be gathered. And it was in devising technologies and techniques to discover what was being kept out of public view that States invariably involved themselves in measures the legality of which were to be the subject of ongoing dispute.

The idea that States might legally engage in intrusive and surreptitious measures of surveillance during wartime had been given formal recognition in the late nineteenth and early twentieth century in the various codes on the laws of war. As Oppenheim put it in 1912:

> War cannot be waged without all kinds of information about the forces and the intentions of the enemy and about the character of the country within the zone of military operations. To obtain the necessary information, it has always been considered lawful to employ spies, and on the other hand, to make use of the treason of enemy soldiers or private enemy subjects, whether they were bribed or offered the information voluntarily and gratuitously.[44]

[41] Bruce Cummings, *Parallax Visions: Making Sense of American–East Asian Relations at the End of the Century* (Durham: Duke University Press, 1999) 179–91.

[42] Kent, *Strategic Intelligence for American World Policy*, 9–10 (who notes that 'the foreign service officer, although not specifically trained as an intelligence man, is by virtue of his location and talent often a valuable and effective purveyor of intelligence').

[43] Not least because it was in the nature of such agencies that, as gatherers of information, they were equally enjoined to a practice of secrecy. Kent, *Strategic Intelligence for American World Policy*, 190. 'The grand strategist – military or civilian – whose exact intentions and capabilities are known by the party of the second part finds himself without a strategy.'

[44] Lassa Oppenheim, *International Law: A Treatise, Vol. II: War and Neutrality*, 2nd ed. (London: Longmans, Green and Co., 1912) 411.

This 'old customary rule', as Oppenheim put it, was reflected in Article 24 of the Hague Regulations of 1907, which provided that 'the employment of measures necessary for obtaining information about the enemy and the country are considered permissible',[45] albeit that the same regulations went on to specify the conditions under which a person might be considered a spy and punished accordingly.[46]

The key question, of course, was whether such acts were legitimate in peacetime. And it was here that invocation of the language of a Cold 'War' was to have particular valence, suggesting an enduring condition of hostilities in time of peace. This was not lost on Allan Dulles, who could see no legitimacy in spying on 'our friends and allies' in time of peace, but for whom 'the answer to the question of the need for intelligence particularly on the Communist bloc, is that we are not really "at peace" with them, and we have not been since Communism declared its own war on our system of government and life'.[47] In other words, the language of the Cold 'War' specifically brought into play the technologies of enmity authorised under the existing laws of war, particularly those that did not involve the deployment of armed forces in the field of battle.

As the Hague Regulations themselves were to indicate, what was being contemplated in this non-war warfare was not simply acts of espionage but also a variety of other measures of deception that went under the heading '*ruses de guerre*'. Such 'ugly acts', as Oppenheim called them, went beyond the standard forms of military deception, such as the use of camouflage, false flags, decoys or feints, but extended also to the broadcast of hostile or revolutionary propaganda,[48] to the 'bribery of enemy

[45] Convention (IV) respecting the Laws and Customs of War on Land and its annex: Regulations concerning the Laws and Customs of War on Land, The Hague, 18 October 1907, Regulations: article 24. See also Protocol Additional to the Geneva Conventions of 12 August 1949 and Relating to the Protection of Victims of International Armed Conflicts (Protocol I), Geneva, 8 June 1977, 1125 UNTS 3, article 37(2) which reaffirms that '[r]uses of war are not prohibited. Such ruses are acts which are intended to mislead an adversary or to induce him to act recklessly but which infringe no rule of international law applicable in armed conflict and which are not perfidious because they do not invite the confidence of an adversary with respect to protection under that law. The following are examples of such ruses: the use of camouflage, decoys, mock operations and misinformation.'

[46] Ibid., articles 29–31.

[47] Dulles, *The Craft of Intelligence*, 55.

[48] See Hersch Lauterpacht, 'Revolutionary Propaganda by Governments' *Transactions of the Grotius Society*, 13 (1927) 152–53, where he notes that whilst many 'modern writers' were 'apt to condemn revolutionary propaganda as a means of warfare' such 'disapprobation cannot . . . be supported by reference to the practice of states'.

commanders and officials in high position and [the] secret seduction of enemy soldiers to desertion and of enemy subjects to insurrection'.[49] The one main restraint – about which there continued to be much anxious debate – concerned the 'perfidious' use of protected symbols (e.g. the red cross).[50] But all else was plausibly permissible.

So, if the 'Cold War' as a name was doing any legal work or having any concrete effects beyond being a mobilising slogan of ideological alignment, it was to be found, here, in a claim to the legitimacy if not legality of covert acts of intelligence, infiltration, deception, manipulation and subversion. In the absence of direct hostilities between the rival powers, however, such a claim had to be stood on its own head. These were not simply methods of combat incidental to armed conflict, they were a form of combat in their own right and could justify countermeasures of similar kind. As Dulles explained:

> As long as Khrushchev or his successors use their subversive assets to promote 'wars of liberation' – which means to them any overt or covert action calculated to bring down a non-Communist regime – the West should be prepared to meet the threat. We can either organize to meet the Communist program of subversion and vigorously oppose it as it insinuates itself into the governments and free institutions of countries unable to meet the danger alone, or we can supinely stand aside and say this is the affair of each imperiled country to deal with itself.[51]

This was not simply a form of *tu quoque* reasoning but a position informed by the idea that the covert action employed by the US was both necessary and legitimate. In that sense, it appeared to borrow from the observations made by Lauterpacht in his account of the legality of revolutionary propaganda back in 1926. There, Lauterpacht had suggested that '[W]hen resorted to apart from an actual state of belligerency (in which case no illegality attaches to it) it [revolutionary propaganda] inevitably tends to obliterate the border-line between a state of peace and the state of war'.[52] Lauterpacht's point was not that disseminating revolutionary propaganda was a 'belligerent measure' undermining a condition of peace (to be regarded, therefore, as straightforwardly unlawful)

[49] Oppenheim, *International Law*, 165. Note that there is a change in the Oppenheim editions and the term 'ugly acts' is not in his second edition of 1912.

[50] See Protocol Additional to the Geneva Conventions of 12 August 1949 and Relating to the Protection of Victims of International Armed Conflicts (Protocol I), 8 June 1977, 1125 UNTS 3, article 38.

[51] Dulles, *The Craft of Intelligence*, 216.

[52] Lauterpacht, 'Revolutionary Propaganda by Governments', 155.

but that the pursuit of such measures might appear to demonstrate the existence of a belligerency in its own right. By performatively 'blurring' the categories of peace and war, so also did it 'blur' the possibility of judgement. Seen in that light, the new practice of intelligence – understood in its various guises – could be seen in a continuum with the *ruses de guerre* of old. In effect, intelligence was – and is – a practice that provided the grounds for its own legitimacy. Constituting itself as a legitimate form of non-war warfare it avoided the prohibitions of the UN Charter so long as it fell short of an actual 'use of force'. But because of the perception that it was ultimately necessary for 'national security', it also dodged the opprobrium that might be attached to it in time of outright peace.

Whether or not the logic of this reasoning was ever made entirely explicit, the terms of this emergent form of covert warfare were spelled out, clearly enough, in National Security Council Directive 10(2). This Directive authorised the use of propaganda, economic warfare, sabotage, demolition, subversion and the provision of support for anti-communist 'elements' around the world.[53] The Truman and Eisenhower Doctrines suggested that the Directive extended to providing aid and assistance to governments imperiled by the threat of communism (as in Greece and Lebanon). In the view of Dulles and those like him, it also legitimately extended to providing support to 'anti-communist elements' in places such as Iran and Guatemala where the government appeared to be veering towards communism (and in which, as he put it, the danger was ultimately 'successfully met').[54] This was matched, of course, by a parallel policy pursued by the Soviet Union and its allies in the support it provided to communist revolutionaries, trade unionists and national liberation movements of various kinds, as well as to established, or nascent, governments in the 'Soviet sphere'.

Many States in the South waged a campaign to have all such covert practices condemned as forms of unlawful intervention. But that did not extend, per se, to the practice of intelligence itself. And just as the subterranean Cold War would shift its point of focus from the 1950s onwards from North to South – from Europe to battlegrounds in Africa, Asia or Latin America – the practice of intelligence would move alongside it, lodging itself within the governmental rationalities of the (newly) independent States of the South. For incoming elites, the security and

[53] See Chapter 2.
[54] Dulles, *The Craft of Intelligence*, 208.

intelligence apparatus provided by the former colonial powers[55] offered both opportunity and danger.[56] On one side, they were openly derided as forms of neo-colonialism, the evidence for which was amply demonstrated in the Congo events of 1960. On the other side, however, they often provided a means by which the newly installed government could maintain a hold over the exercise of sovereign authority through the surveillance and suppression of subversive groups. And so just as decolonisation seemed to mean sovereign statehood, so too did the exercise of sovereignty seem to require the establishment of (predominantly secret or extra-constitutional) security and intelligence agencies for purposes of defending the new State from internal and external threats.

This patterning – of the exercise of sovereignty with the practices of intelligence – meant that the emergent art of government would be fractured from the start, and at the heart, between the overt and the covert: between the lawful exercise of constitutional authority and the extra-legal practices of surveillance, deception and manipulation. The respective intelligence services came to be engaged, in the meantime, in a parallel system of international relations structured around the distinction between lawful and unlawful means, between what could be 'known' and what had to be kept under wraps. And international law, ultimately, was to provide the architectural scaffolding for that practice, delineating both its objectives (the defence of sovereignty, territorial integrity, self-determination, or the creation of a world in which freedom would flourish) and modulating its means, (whether they be overt or, by necessity, covert).

7.3 The Secret

As much as the Cold War was shrouded in secrecy, it was not the case that secrecy itself was a secret. Indeed, far from it. Celebrated culturally in the literature of Fleming, Le Carré, Greene, Forsythe, Gulyashki, Semyonov and Ludlum, or in the films in the same genre – *Secret Agent, The Spy who Came in from the Cold, Encounter at the Elbe, The*

[55] Philip Murphy, 'Creating a Commonwealth Intelligence Culture: The View from Central Africa 1945–1965' *Intelligence and National Security*, 17 (2002) 131.

[56] See generally, McGarr, 'Tinker, Tailor, Soldier, Subversive'; Sandy Africa, *Changing Intelligence Dynamics in Africa* (Birmingham: GFN-SSR, 2009); Roy Pateman, 'Intelligence Agencies in Africa: A Preliminary Assessment' *Journal of Modern African Studies*, 30 (1992) 569; Ryan Shaffer, *African Intelligence Services: Early Postcolonial and Contemporary Challenges* (Lanham: Rowman & Littlefield, 2021).

Ipcress File, The Manchurian Candidate, The Secret Mission, The Mackintosh Man, Torn Curtain – the secret Cold War was publicly consumed on both sides of the Iron Curtain.[57] As a war conducted in cinemas and bookstores, in television and on the radio, the activities of the newly established 'intelligence agencies' were made most visible in virtual, or fictional, form. In this war, secrecy was transparent – to be both celebrated and reviled in equal measure – but in which the conditions of knowledge, or knowingness, were to come under its spell. 'Never before', as Shils put it, had 'the existence of life-controlling secrets been given so much publicity . . . [yet] never before [had] such exertions been made for the safeguarding of secrets'.[58]

For all the attention given to it in the post-war period, the practice of State secrecy itself was by no means an invention of the Cold War. It had long been regarded in Europe as a necessary adjunct to the stabilisation of domestic authority and its complement – espionage – an activity necessary for purposes of prizing open the secrets of the 'enemy'. Most accounts, however, point to an important transition that occurred in the late eighteenth century in which the practice of State secrecy met the emergent enlightenment ideals of democracy, transparency and public accountability.[59] In his classic study on the sociology of secrecy published in 1906,[60] Georg Simmel observed that:

[57] For an account of Soviet Cold War Spy Fiction, see Erik Jens, 'Cold War Spy Fiction in Russian Popular Culture: From Suspicion to Acceptance via *Seventeen Moments of Spring*' *Studies in Intelligence*, 16 (2017) 31–41; Viktoria A. Sukovataya, 'Spy and Counterspy as a "Cultural Hero" in the Soviet Cinema of the Cold War' *Diacronie*, 302 (2017) 1–18.

[58] Edward Albert Shils, *The Torment of Secrecy: The Background and Consequences of American Security Policies* (Glencoe: The Free Press, 1956) 36. The first book on the CIA was published as early as 1953. See Gordon Stewart, *The Cloak and Dollar War* (London: Lawrence and Wishart, 1953).

[59] See, e.g., Jurgen Habermas, *Structural Transformation of the Public Sphere* (Cambridge, MA: MIT Press, 1989) 53–54. As Foucault was to express it: 'A fear haunted the latter half of the eighteenth century: the fear of darkened spaces, of the pall of gloom which prevents the full visibility of things, men and truths. It sought to break up the patches of darkness that blocked the light, eliminate the shadowy areas of society, demolish the unlit chambers where arbitrary political acts, monarchical caprice, religious superstitions, tyrannical and priestly plots, epidemics and the illusions of ignorance were formented.' Michael Foucault, 'The Eye of Power: A Conversation with Jean-Pierre Barou and Michelle Perrot' in Colin Gordon (ed.), *Power/Knowledge: Selected Interviews and Other Writings 1972–1977* (Hampshire: Harvester Press, 1980) 153.

[60] Georg Simmel, 'The Sociology of Secrecy and of Secret Societies' *American Journal of Sociology*, 11 (1906) 441.

> As late as the seventeenth and eighteenth centuries, governments most anxiously covered up the amounts of public debts, the conditions of taxation, and the size of their armies. In consequence of this, ambassadors often had nothing better to do than to act as informers, to get possession of the contents of letters, and to prevail upon persons who were acquainted with valuable facts, even down to servants, to tattle their secrets. In the nineteenth century, however, publicity takes possession of national affairs to such an extent that the governments themselves publish the official data without concealing, which no government would earlier have thought possible. Accordingly, politics, administration, justice, have lost their secrecy and inaccessibility in precisely the degree in which the individual has gained possibility of more complete privacy.[61]

Aside from pointing out how the 'privilege of secrecy' had undergone a transition – moving, in a sense, from State to individual – Simmel shows the way in which State secrecy was no longer conceived as a field of arcane knowledge (the *arcana imperii*) that was to be treasured and secured at all costs (in which even the possession of secret knowledge itself was to be kept secret)[62] but as knowledge that constituted a limited exception to the principle of public, transparent government,[63] and

[61] Ibid., 468–69.

[62] See generally, Jon R. Snyder, *Dissimulation and the Culture of Secrecy in Early Modern Europe* (Oakland: University of California Press, 2009); Alain Dewerpe, *Espion: Une Anthropologie Historique du Secret d'État Contemporain* (Paris: Gallimard, 1994); Stéphane Levebvre, 'A Brief Genealogy of State Secrecy' *Windsor Yearbook of Access to Justice*, 31 (2013) 95–114. Eva Horn, *The Secret War: Treason, Espionage and Modern Fiction* (Evanston: Northwestern University Press, 2013) 84–85: Historically, the *arcana imperii* were the 'unspoken basis for the preservation of power' – that which 'precedes the decision between truth and falsehood or justice and injustice' and which opens up a 'discretionary space for actions that do not have to be accounted for, that will not have to stand the trial of legitimization, that will not have to be justified – since, ideally, they will never be known or discussed'. Shils refers to the 'arcana imperium' as the 'private, unshared knowledge of the art and practice of ruling' that was 'both symbolically and factually important for the distribution of power and dignity in the *ancient régime* all over Europe'. Shils, *The Torment of Secrecy*, 23.

[63] Transparency, indeed, was an idea that was also embraced for the conduct of international affairs. In 1913, Wilson wrote: 'Government ought to be all outside and no inside. I, for my part, believe there ought to be no place where anything can be done that everybody does not know about .... Secrecy means impropriety.' Woodrow Wilson, 'Let There Be Light' in Woodrow Wilson, *The New Freedom: A Call for the Emancipation of the Generous Energies of a People* (New York: Doubleday, Page & Company, 1913) 70. Point One of his Fourteen Points: 'Open covenants of peace, openly arrived at, after which there shall be no private international undertakings of any kind but diplomacy shall proceed always frankly and in the public view.' See Wilson's Fourteen Points (8 January 1918).

which had actively to be justified by reference to public ends (security, administrative efficiency, privacy, candidness, etc.). The State secret thus differed from the medieval *arcana imperii* in three main ways. First, it was constituted as a form of secret knowledge the possession of which was not, itself, secret. The fact of secrecy was to become itself a matter of public knowledge and debate.[64] Secondly, it brought into play a public discourse and practice of administrative compartmentalisation,[65] separating those who could be trusted to have access to secret knowledge from those from whom such knowledge should be withheld. This practice came to be operationalised in the bureaucracies of the West as a mode of technical administration.[66] New procedures were put in place for purposes of the classification of State knowledge ('restricted', 'secret', 'top secret', etc.),[67] the modulation of access to it (vetting procedures, 'clearance', 'indoctrination' etc.) and for the punishment of unauthorised disclosures. Espionage statutes were widely adopted for the first time, delineating 'espionage' as a criminal offence, distinct and separable from the older crimes of treason and sedition.[68] In the third place, State secrecy differed from older notions of *arcana imperii* by bringing the practice of secrecy into relation with two other ideas – public transparency and privacy – that were ultimately to become, as Dean puts it, 'the matrix through which we think about democracy' today.[69]

As much as a differentiation was frequently posited between the 'open societies' of the West and the 'closed societies' of the Communist

[64] Michael Taussig, *Defacement: Public Secrecy and the Labor of the Negative* (Redwood City: Stanford University Press, 1999) 50–51; Anthony Glees, 'Open Secrecy' in Corneliu Bjola and Stuart Murray (eds.), *Secret Diplomacy* (London: Routledge, 2016) 108–31.

[65] Compartmentalisation was a technique employed, in particular, in the Manhattan project under supervision of General Groves. See Leslie Groves, *Now It Can Be Told: The Story of the Manhattan Project* (New York: Harper, 1962) 138–39. 'Each man should know everything he needed to know to do his job and nothing else.'

[66] Max Weber, *Political Writings* (Cambridge: Cambridge University Press, 1994) 179. 'Officialdom's most important instrument of power is the transformation of official information into secret information by means of the infamous concept of "official secrecy", which ultimately is merely a device to protect the administration from control.'

[67] The US classification system (Top Secret, Secret, Confidential) was created by Presidential Executive Order 10290 (24 September 1951). See Sam Lebovic, 'The Historical Presidency: Rethinking the Origins of National Security Classification' *Presidential Studies Quarterly*, 54 (2024) 259–70.

[68] See Peter Galison, 'Secrecy in three Acts' *Social Research*, 77 (2010) 941–74.

[69] Jodi Dean, *Publicity's Secret* (New York: Cornell University Press, 2002) 4 (she refers more specifically to 'publicity and secrecy').

world[70] (providing justification, as we have seen, for the US reconnaissance programmes over the Soviet Union), it was never really the case that this meant a straightforward choice between secrecy and transparency. Openness, after all, had its limits. As Derrida pointed out, democracy's aspiration to be 'public and phenomenal through and through'[71] – to the elimination of any kind of secret in social life – seemed to be just as totalitarian as its denial, eliding any space for individuality, for privacy or authorised life outside that of the community.[72] This was precisely the lesson learnt by those facing interrogation by the House Committee on Unamerican Activities (HUAC) in the 1950s, for whom no aspect of private life was safe from investigation for purposes of exposing, or rooting out, potential subversive sympathies.[73] This passion for publicity, for seeking out of the 'enemy within' and uncovering the activities of the subversive 'fifth-column', demanded the employment of secretive methods of surveillance. As Shils pointed out, this combined both a 'relentless publicity and a degree of secrecy even greater than the subversives themselves would employ'.[74] The 'obsessive fear of conspiratorial secrecy' thus gave rise to a 'secretiveness' without object – that was to be 'enjoyed and reveled in for its own sake'.[75]

[70] The differentiation between 'open' and 'closed' societies is usually attributed to Henri Bergson who differentiated between two sources of morality and religion, one of which is closed or static and directs itself towards social cohesion and ultimately war, the other, which is open and dynamic and directs itself to creativity, progress and ultimately peace. Henri Bergson, *The Two Sources of Morality and Religion*, trans. R. Ashley Audra and Cloudesley Brereton (South Bend: University of Notre Dame Press, 1935). The distinction was picked up and used for very different purposes by Karl Popper in *The Open Society and Its Enemies* (London: Routledge, 1945). Arendt was also to associate secrecy with totalitarian movements, speaking of such movements as 'secret societies established in broad daylight', Hannah Arendt, *The Origins of Totalitarianism* (New York: Harcourt, Brace and Company, 1951) 376–88. For its relevance in relation to the treatment of complex evidential problems, see Schwebel, dissenting opinion, *Military and Paramilitary Activities in and against Nicaragua (Nicaragua v USA)* (1986) ICJ Rep 14, 314 para 139.

[71] Jacques Derrida, *Rogues: Two Essays on Reason* (Redwood City: Stanford University Press, 2005) 65.

[72] As Shils was to put it: 'The need to dissolve other people's secrets arises from the need to be surrounded by like-mindedness... The demand for extreme solidarity is the product of fear of betrayal ... [and] culminates in the denial of the right of private difference.' Shils, *The Torment of Secrecy*, 34.

[73] On HUAC, see Renee DiResta, 'Process as Punishment: An American History of Political Spectacle' Lawfare, 14 April 2025, www.lawfaremedia.org/article/process-as-punishment-an-american-history-of-political-spectacle.

[74] Shils, *The Torment of Secrecy*, 34.

[75] Ibid.

The way the Cold War was experienced on both sides of the ideological divide gave impetus to this obsession with secrecy. For what was perceived to be at stake, as Kennan and Novikov made clear, were the relative merits of rival systems of knowledge and belief and, in turn, the ideological fealty or loyalty on the part of individuals and populations to one cause or the other. What the Amero-Soviets had in common was a commitment to sovereignty and self-determination. Where they differed were the terms under which a people might be governed internally and represented internationally.[76] And insofar as it was a battle to be fought in those terms, it was not to be won with 'guns, tanks and atom bombs' but with 'words and ideas'[77] and through the medium of a seductive pedagogy – through the arts of public relations[78] and 'propaganda',[79] the promotion of cultural and educational exchange, the publication, translation and distribution of books, the production of films and posters, the granting of aid and educational scholarships and the development of forms of camouflaged 'psychological warfare' that employed independent news media, non-governmental organisations and individuals as 'surrogate communicators for conveying propaganda messages'.[80]

But the key to such warfare was secrecy. By its very nature, propaganda obviated methods of communication that were blatant or direct and

[76] This is an idea taken up in other parts of this book, including Chapter 2.

[77] Kenneth Osgood, *Total Cold War: Eisenhower's Secret Propaganda Battle at Home and Abroad* (Lawrence: University Press of Kansas, 2006) 2.

[78] A key early text is Edward Bernays, *Crystallizing Public Opinion* (New York: Liveright, 1923). See also Edward Bernays, *Propaganda* (New York: Liveright, 1928).

[79] Propaganda became a particular matter of intellectual study and debate in the aftermath of WWI but gained heightened traction during the Cold War as a form of psychological warfare. Harold Lasswell, later to be associated with the Yale school World Public Order project, was an influential figure in early studies on propaganda alongside figures such as Walter Lippman. See, e.g., Harold D. Lasswell, 'The Theory of Political Propaganda' *American Political Science Review*, 21 (1927) 627–31 and Harold D. Lasswell, *Propaganda Technique in the World War* (New York: Peter Smith, 1927); Walter Lippman, *Public Opinion* (New Brunswick: Transaction Publishers, 1922). The key theorists in the period of the Cold War itself include: Jacques Ellul, *Propaganda: The Formation of Men's Attitudes* (New York: Vintage Books, 1962); Terence H. Qualter, *Propaganda and Psychological Warfare* (New York: Random House, 1962); Lindley Fraser, *Propaganda* (Oxford: Oxford University Press, 1957); and Edward S. Herman and Noam Chomsky, *Manufacturing Consent: The Political Economy of the Mass Media* (London: The Bodley Head, 1988). See generally, Christopher Simpson, *Science of Coercion: Communication Research & Psychological Warfare, 1945–1960* (New York: Open Road, 1994).

[80] Kenneth Osgood, *Total Cold War: Eisenhower's Secret Propaganda Battle at Home and Abroad* (Lawrence: University Press of Kansas, 2006) 5.

embraced techniques of psychological manipulation in their place.[81] The effectiveness of these techniques were, in part at least, premised upon the masking of intentions and, at times, the dissemination of claims known to be false.[82] This gave rise to distinctions between 'white', 'black' and 'grey' psychological operations. And so even if the dissemination of 'revolutionary propaganda' was in some cases deemed to constitute an 'international delinquency',[83] the art of propaganda was always more subtle than this. The 'propagandist', as Ellul claimed,

> will not accuse the enemy of just any misdeed; he will accuse him of the very intention that he himself has and of trying to commit the very crime that he himself is about to commit. He who wants to provoke a war not only proclaims his own peaceful intentions but also accuses the other party of provocation.[84]

So just as the active participants in the Cold War routinely denounced the 'propaganda' disseminated by the 'enemy', the very claim to enjoy the power to speak or reveal the 'truth' was part of the same ideological battleground the Cold War was to be inserted into. That ground was not merely the consciousness but the sub-consciousness of the peoples of the world. The agents of both ideological blocs saw themselves in a secret battle for 'hearts and minds'.[85] But they had to remain vigilant within (in

[81] Ellul, *Propaganda*, 27. 'To be effective, propaganda must constantly short-circuit all thought and decision. It must operate on the individual at the level of the unconscious. He must not know that he is being shaped by outside forces . . . but some central core in him must be reached in order to release the mechanism in the unconscious which will provide the appropriate – and expected – action.' Lippman was to make a similar point in Walter Lippman, *Public Opinion*: 'Without some form of censorship, propaganda in the strict sense of the word is impossible. In order to conduct a propaganda, there must be some barrier between the public and the event.' Bernays was to conclude that propagandists were thereby the 'invisible rulers who control the destinies of millions'. Bernays, *Propaganda*, 35.

[82] Ellul, *Propaganda*, 58–61. 'One cannot make propaganda in pretended good faith. Propaganda reveals our hoaxes even as it encloses and hardens us into this system of hoaxes from which we can no longer escape.'

[83] Lauterpacht, 'Revolutionary Propaganda by Governments', 146. See also UNGA Res 290 (IV) (1 December 1949) and UNGA Res 381(V) (17 November 1950). John B. Whitton and Arthur Larson, *Propaganda: Towards Disarmament in the War of Words* (New York: Oceana, 1964) who cite, as illegal, warmongering, subversive and defamatory propaganda.

[84] Ellul, *Propaganda*, 58.

[85] This was a term coined, apparently, by General Templer in relation to the British counter-insurgency campaign in Malaya (1948–60). See Paul Dixon, '"Hearts and Minds"? British Counter-insurgency from Malaya to Iraq' *Journal of Strategic Studies*, 32 (2009) 353–81.

respect of their own populations) as well as without – and to seek out, expose and condemn those found within to have 'sympathies' antagonistic to the cause. High-profile public trials of spies, defectors or others suspected of subversion or treason (Fuchs, the Rosenbergs, Powers) were thus to become the public face, on both sides, of a Cold War fought by way of the mass conscription of the Amero-Soviet populace to ideological conformity, in which the encouragement of sentiments of paranoia and eternal vigilance were necessary supplements.

Paradoxically then, as much as the ideological Cold War was fought in secret, it was nevertheless an open, or 'public', secret.[86] If secrets were to remain secret, secretiveness was not. Far from being a matter kept entirely out of the public eye, secrecy was not merely openly recognised and discussed (hidden, like Poe's purloined letter, in plain sight) but became, in the West at least, a public obsession. The periodic disclosures and revelations of the activities of the security services at home and abroad – such as the Rockerfeller Commission,[87] the Church Commission[88] and the Pentagon Papers[89] – made all too clear that the practice of secrecy was not only 'widespread' but largely 'official'. And the more open and more official it became, the more concerned observers would become about the 'secret cult'[90] or 'invisible government'[91] that had somehow come into existence, emptying out democracy from within.

But just as much as secrecy gave rise to a climate of fear and anxiety, it was sustained as a practice, as Melley argues, by a 'cultural imaginary' that both shaped and was shaped by the 'secret work of the state'.[92] This 'covert sphere', as he describes it, was not merely an accidental supplement to the emergence of the covert State but a vital, necessary element

[86] Taussig, *Defacement*.

[87] See Report to the President by the Commission on CIA Activities within the United States (Washington, DC, June 1975).

[88] See Report of the Senate Select Committee to Study Governmental Operations with Respect to Intelligence Activities (Washington, DC, 29 April 1976).

[89] See Report commissioned by Secretary of Defense Robert S. McNamara entitled 'United States – Vietnam Relations, 1945–1967', also known as the Pentagon Papers. The final report was submitted to Robert S. McNamara's successor Clark M. Clifford on 15 January 1969.

[90] See, e.g., Victor Marchetti and John D. Marks, *The CIA and the Cult of Intelligence* (New York: Dell, 1974).

[91] David Wise and Thomas B. Ross, *The Invisible Government* (London: Jonathan Cape, 1964).

[92] Timothy Melley, *The Covert Sphere: Secrecy, Fiction and the National Security State* (New York: Cornell University Press, 2012) 5.

of it. For it was not merely necessary for the covert State to engage in the production of falsehoods – the dissemination of the 'necessary lie' as George Kennan put it [93]– but it had to secure the support of 'a public that *thinks* it has a general knowledge of such work but *does not* and *cannot* know in detail'.[94] Vital support for the covert State arrived in the form of the production (officially and otherwise) of fictive accounts of its activities that avoided the perils of disclosing sensitive, or secret, information but nevertheless alluded to the necessity of engaging in that kind of activity. Such accounts offered representations of State secrecy that institutionalised the half-truth (through partial public disclosure and the com partmentalisation of knowledge), traded in 'strategic fictions' (elaborate simulations and invented plots, propaganda, psychological operations and public deception)[95] and relied upon two epistemic operations: 'ideological disavowal' (public cynicism) and 'plausible deniability' (lack of 'proof').[96]

The practice of ideological disavowal was exemplified particularly well in the U-2 incident we discussed earlier in this chapter. Eisenhower's open acknowledgement of the undesirability, and potential illegality, of espionage and surveillance operations was accompanied by a determined unwillingness either to act upon those intuitions or publicly condemn the practice. The 'disavowal' thus operated at two different levels. At one level, it operated as a disavowal of any *belief* in the legal or moral wrongfulness of espionage itself, exemplified by Eisenhower's unwillingness to confirm that opinion publicly. Here the desirability of any conformity to the dictates of international law or morality was simply 'outweighed', as per the standard realist analytic,[97] by the interest in securing vital knowledge of the Soviet Union. This kind of reasoning – which might be referred to as a form of 'strategic' disavowal – was to subordinate the place of international law in strategic reasoning but had the obvious disadvantage of undercutting public faith, both national and international, in the legal values that the US was keen to advance.[98]

[93] Frances Stonor Saunders, *Who Paid the Piper? The CIA and the Cultural Cold War* (London: Granta Books, 2000) 38.

[94] Timothy Melley, *The Covert Sphere: Secrecy, Fiction and the National Security State* (New York: Cornell University Press, 2012) 9.

[95] Ibid., 29.

[96] Ibid., 1–31.

[97] Cf. Hans Morgenthau, *Politics Among Nations: The Struggle for Power and Peace* (New York: Alfred A Knopf, 1949).

[98] Thomas Franck and Edward Weisband, 'The Johnson and Brezhnev Doctrines: The Law You make May Be Your Own' *Stanford Law Review*, 22 (1970) 979–1014.

In another sense, however, a different form of disavowal was also at play in Eisenhower's reluctance to condemn the *practice* of espionage despite his acknowledgement of its legal and moral shortcomings. Here, the disavowal was not so much of the values as such but of a requirement to bring practice into to conformity with them. The disavowal in this second case was, thus, by no means a straightforward case of ideological 'false consciousness' in its typically Marxist sense – there was no obvious dissonance here between action and knowledge, no naïve misrecognition of the conditions of social reality. Rather it assumed the form of what Žižek calls an 'ideological fantasy'[99] in which a certain knowledge or belief about the world (here, a belief in the 'wrongfulness' of espionage or other forms of covert intervention) is consciously suspended in practice, such that the practice itself becomes guided by an 'illusion' or a 'fetishistic inversion'. Žižek's formula – 'they know very well how things really are, but still they do it as if they did not know'[100] – was one in which the illusion was not on the side of knowledge but in the 'reality of doing itself', in which agents of the State were to act *as if*[101] they were unconscious of the dissonance between what they professed to believe (i.e. that espionage was immoral or illegal) and what they were prepared to do.

This form of ideological disavowal – of cynical dissociation from avowed norms[102] – was not necessarily limited to the practice of espionage but was equally evident in other forms of covert warfare, particularly those that involved the subversion of democratic processes. In Iran and Guatemala, in Czechoslovakia and Hungary, a critical distance had to be maintained between the overt commitment to democracy, sovereignty and non-intervention and a practice that tended towards their denial.

This was of no small concern to international lawyers at the time. In 1974, shortly after the publication of Marchetti and Marks' influential

99 Slavoj Žižek, *The Sublime Object of Ideology* (London: Verso 1989) 27–30.

100 Ibid., 30.

101 The philosophy of the 'as if' may be traced to the work of Hans Vaihinger. See Hans Vaihinger, *The Philosophy of 'As If': A System of the Theoretical, Practical and Religious Fictions of Mankind*, trans. C. K. Ogden, 2nd ed. (London: Kegan Paul, Trench, Trubner and Co., 1935; originally 1925).

102 Falk, in his analysis of the legalities of covert operations was to comment that 'CIA enthusiasts ... do not doubt that covert operations may, on occasion, be "illegal" or involve "immoral" practices, but accept their occurrence as essential to the furtherance of national purpose' which, in his account, included the promotion of the legal and moral norms that it violated. Richard A. Falk, 'CIA Covert Operations and International Law', 12 September 1974, www.cia.gov/readingroom/docs/CIA-RDP88-01315R000200030001-2.pdf.

(if heavily redacted) account of the work of the CIA[103] (which came, itself, in the aftermath of the Pentagon Papers[104] and Watergate[105] scandals), a panel discussion was convened at the American Society of International Law on the question of covert intervention. On that panel, a series of speakers addressed the apparent conundrum associated with the fact that whilst the US, for all public purposes, had maintained its commitment to international law and the UN Charter, it had nevertheless engaged itself in a series of covert operations that appeared to violate the very principles of sovereignty, territorial integrity and non-intervention that lay at the Charter's core.[106] In his intervention, Richard Falk argued that the point was not really whether one could justify intervention legally – there were remarkably few arguments available to that end – nor whether it was consistent with the 'values the United States professes to hold in the domain of foreign affairs' (vis. human rights, civil liberties, self-determination). The main concern, rather, was the 'discrepancy between professed values and actual practice', which

> allows and encourages our officials to proclaim one set of objectives in public discourse, and to pursue a completely different course of action through secret foreign policymaking .... The CIA and its covert operations allow us to have our cake and eat it too. We can be both liberal constitutionalists, in public arenas and for the sake of our own society, and we can also play the game of nations the tough way it is played in the 'jungle'.[107]

Falk proposed thus that the US should practice what it preached and 'internalize the norms of international law and automatically adhere to

[103] Marchetti and Marks, *The CIA and the Cult of Intelligence*. As was pointed out by Lewis in the preface to the 1983 version of the book, nearly one-fifth of the book was initially marked, by the CIA, to be redacted in interests of security. Anthony Lewis, 'Introduction' in Marchetti and Marks, *The CIA and the Cult of Intelligence*, xi.

[104] Final Report of the Office of the Secretary of Defense Vietnam Task Force, Washinton, DC, 15 January 1969.

[105] Richard Nixon Presidential Library and Museum, 'Watergate Exhibit Evidence' (National Archive) www.nixonlibrary.gov/watergate-exhibit-evidence.

[106] See Arghyrios Faturos, 'Remarks by the Chairman' *Proceedings of the American Society of International Law Annual Meeting*, 69 (1975) 192–95; Richard Falk, 'An Alternative to Covert Intervention' *Proceedings of the American Society of International Law Annual Meeting*, 69 (1975) 195; David S. Stern, Robert Borosage and Tom Farer, 'Covert Intervention and the Third World' *Proceedings of the American Society of International Law Annual Meeting*, 69 (1975) 200–16; Robert Borosage, 'Comments' *Proceedings of the American Society of International Law Annual Meeting*, 69 (1975) 203–6.

[107] Falk, 'An Alternative to Covert Intervention', 198.

them as a matter of national policy'.[108] This, he argued, would not only lead to more consistency but would also have the added benefit of allowing the US administration to 'reveal to the American people the real methods and objectives we have been pursuing in the world'.[109] Legal conformity, he deduced, would eliminate the necessity of secrecy and deception.

Falk wanted to highlight a disjunction in US practice between ends and means: what it professed to believe and how it was prepared to act. In contrast to this, Tom Franck drew attention to the self-defeating character of that behaviour. He argued that one of major difficulties presented to US policy- makers in the aftermath of the Czechoslovakia crisis in 1968 was the US failure to realise that its critique of the so-called Brezhnev Doctrine that the Soviets had deployed to justify their interventions (namely, that intervention was justified as a matter of collective self-defence to protect the 'Soviet commonwealth' from anti-Soviet movements) was critically undercut by the fact that the US' own interventions in Guatemala, the Dominican Republic and Cuba had all been pursued on virtually identical grounds.[110]

What was missing, in Franck's view, was a necessary element of 'reciprocal thinking' – of the idea 'that one should act in accordance with the principles one expects of one's peers, and should eschew principles of conduct one seeks to proscribe in others'.[111] Only with such reciprocity might one envisage the development of those mutually shared expectations 'essential to the maintenance of the precarious peace and to the prevention of war by miscalculation among the superpowers'.[112] Perhaps a sort of moral Amero-Sovietism?

What both Falk and Franck advanced in their different ways was a straightforward demand that the United States should align its practice with the legal values that it sought to uphold. What they arguably both missed, though, was any sense (no doubt widely held in the Third World) that the US, or indeed the Soviet Union, for its part, might have been perfectly conscious of the contradictions in their ostensible position in each of these cases. They might also have been entirely conscious of the reciprocal 'signaling' to their ideological rivals that was being performed

[108] Ibid., 199.
[109] Ibid., 200.
[110] Franck and Weisband, 'The Johnson and Brezhnev Doctrines'.
[111] Ibid., 980.
[112] Ibid., 1014.

by their interventions in Czechoslovakia, Guatemala and Cuba, and they might have been entirely conscious of the idea that this was how the Cold War game was to be played. Indeed, the very fact that the US chose to undertake many of its activities under cover of secrecy was to suggest that awareness, itself, was not the problem.

The problem in all such cases was a tendency by the US or USSR to act precisely as if they were unaware – unaware either of the precedents they were setting internationally or of the apparently schizophrenic character of their policy-making and the evident disjunction between ends and means. The critical point here is not simply to decry or even observe the tendency to embrace this form of 'cynical reason', as Sloterdijk would call it,[113] but to notice that it was operationally institutionalised through a division of labour between the foreign services, on the one hand, and their intelligence counterparts, on the other. So divided, for instance, between the CIA and State Department, the Kremlin and the KGB, the British Foreign Office and MI6 – between, in other words, the agencies of secrecy and those of open public government, which allowed 'knowingness' to be divided and segregated and also allowed responsibility to be diffused – and muddied – through a compartmentalisation of knowledge.[114] After the end of the Cold War, the pattern of dealing with such dissonance by institutionalising a division of labour between the different faces of the US government arguably allowed the US, with a straight face, to claim moral and jurisdictional authority in one sphere even as it engaged in entirely contradictory behaviour in another.[115]

If the idea of 'ideological disavowal' was to find its ultimate expression in an institutional segmentation of foreign policy that allowed the 'State'

[113] Peter Sloterdijk, *Critique of Cynical Reason*, trans. Michael Eldred (London: University of Minnesota Press, 1987) 3–8.

[114] In a revealing memorandum sent by the legal advisor of the Department of State (Monroe Leigh) on 29 May 29 1975 to John Morrison, Deputy General Counsel of the CIA, it was pointed out that the CIA's arguments for the justification of espionage, electronic surveillance and covert action set out in a report of 1975 were not shared by the State Department: not everything, he was to suggest, could be justified by reference to the absolute priority of self-defence, or by reference to the US Constitution. Eleanor C. McDowell, *Digest of United States Practice in International Law 1975* (Washington, DC: Department of State Publication, 1976) 17.

[115] For a telling instance of such a split, see the video in which Bill Clinton, in his role as special envoy, speaks to Haitian rice farmers about his actions whilst president of the United States. 'Video: Bill Clinton's Trade Policies Destroyed Haitian Rice Farming, Now Haiti Faces Post-Hurricane Famine', *Democracy Now*, 12 October 2016, www.youtube.com/watch?v=RSE9wKUAMS8.

to maintain its apparent fealty to international law whilst 'feigning' an unawareness that any of its agencies might engage in its violation,[116] a vital supplement to it was the idea and practice of 'plausible deniability'. 'Plausible deniability' was a (sometime secret) term by which the US itself came to describe the limits of its own executive's power to engage in covert activities. But it could be taken as adescription of the logic of covert operations: in a context in which the rival powers were understood to have extensive capacity for espionage and surveillance, the key to such operations was not so much keeping them entirely secret but being able to deny attribution and hence responsibility.[117] After all, as Falk was to observe, the secret bombing of Cambodia 'was not being kept secret from the Cambodians, because they were on the receiving end'.[118] At best it was merely being kept secret from the American public and their allies. The point, however, was not just that some things were being kept secret from some people but that the condition of 'knowingness' itself was to be hidden behind a veil.

Underpinning the idea of 'plausible deniability' was thus the spectre of judgment – that governments might, in some way, be brought to account for their unlawful actions, that responsibility be assigned and blame apportioned. Not that courts or tribunals were in the habit of exercising that kind of jurisdiction. Indeed, with the notable exception of the *Nicaragua Case* from 1986[119] (and, to a lesser extent, the earlier *Corfu Channel case*),[120] covert operations of States were rarely, if ever, to be the

[116] See the footage of the interview with Allen Dulles in *Soundtrack to a Coup d'Etat*: Johan Grimonprez, *Soundtrack to a Coup d'État* (docu-essay, 150 min, France/Belgium/Netherlands, 2024). See also Dulles, *The Craft of Intelligence*.

[117] As Cormac and Aldrich point out, however, the British, in response to its operations in Yemen and Indonesia distinguished between 'untraceable' and 'deniable' operations. 'Untraceable' operations were those 'in which the hand of HMG at best will not even be suspected and at worst cannot be proved'. Deniable operations, by contrast, were those in which 'if, in spite of the probability that HMG connived [in] its execution and in spite of some tenable arguable evidence that HMG was officially involved, HMG considers it politically feasible to deny complicity in public statements eg in the House of Commons or the United Nations'. Rory Cormac and Richard J. Aldrich, 'Grey Is the New Black: Covert Action and Implausible Deniability' *International Affairs*, 94 (2018) 484.

[118] Falk, 'An Alternative to Covert Intervention', 199.

[119] *Military and Paramilitary Activities in and against Nicaragua (Nicaragua v USA)* (1986) ICJ Rep 14.

[120] *Corfu Channel (United Kingdom of Great Britain and Northern Ireland v Albania)* (1949) ICJ Rep 4. Carty reveals that the decision of the Court had been procured by the dissemination of a deliberate falsehood on the part of the British government. Anthony Carty, 'The Corfu Channel Case and the Missing Admiralty Order' *The Law*

subject matter of international legal proceedings. A handful of cases concerning aerial intrusions in the 1950s were brought to the attention of the ICJ, but none got even as far as the jurisdictional phase;[121] and in 1980, whilst examining the merits of US claims in relation to the Tehran hostages following the occupation of its embassy, the Court roundly dismissed the Iranian claims that the real dispute was the twenty-five years of US interference in its internal affairs following the CIA inspired coup d'etat of 1953.[122] In the Court's view, those events were simply part of a 'political context' that in no way detracted from its ability to determine the legal consequences of the US claims in relation to the occupation of its embassy. Judgment in the Amero-Soviet sphere was reserved largely for proceedings in domestic fora, in the courts, by the press or by public investigation/inquiry – and even then, they were frequently hidden behind doctrines of executive privilege or State secrecy/security[123] – or, more generally, before the 'court' of public opinion in the General Assembly of the United Nations. Needless to say, the imaginary of the trial (even if only the trial of public opinion) remained very much at the heart of what made covert operations covert, and in which plausible deniability could be seen to operate as part of a strategy to ensure that no judgment, or attribution of responsibility, might be made.

This was a matter of some significance for the International Court of Justice in the one key case from this era. In the *Nicaragua Case*, the Court was asked to determine whether the US could be held responsible directly or indirectly for a variety of acts of intervention in Nicaragua. It noted, however, that many of the events in question were shrouded in secrecy.

and Practice of International Courts and Tribunals, 3 (2004) 1–35. See also Michael Reisman and Chrstina Skinner (eds.), *Fraudulent Evidence Before Public International Tribunals: The Dirty Stories of International Law* (Cambridge: Cambridge University Press, 2014) 54–77.

121 *Treatment in Hungary of Aircraft and Crew of United States of America (USA v. USSR)* (1954) ICJ Rep 103; *Treatment in Hungary of Aircraft and Crew of United States of America (USA v. Hungarian Peoples Republic)* (1954) ICJ Rep 99; *Aerial Incident of 10 March 1953 (USA v Czechoslovakia)* (1955) ICJ Rep 6; *Aerial Incident of 7 October 1952 (USA v USSR)* (1955) ICJ Rep 9; *Aerial Incident of 4 September 1954 (USA v USSR)* (1958) ICJ Rep 158; and *Aerial Incident of 7 November 1954 (USA v USSR)* (1957) ICJ Rep 8; *Aerial Incident of 27 July 1955 (Israel v Bulgaria)* (1957) ICJ Rep 182; *Aerial Incident of 27 July 1955 (UK v Bulgaria)* (1957) ICJ Rep 190.

122 *United States Diplomatic and Consular Staff in Tehran (USA v Iran)* (1980) ICJ Rep 3, at 18–20, paras 33–38.

123 *Corfu Channel (United Kingdom of Great Britain and Northern Ireland v Albania)* (1949) ICJ Rep 4, at 30–31.

This made it considerably more difficult for the Court 'not only to decide on the imputability of the facts' but also to establish what the facts were. This was a problem only exacerbated by US refusal to participate in proceedings on the merits.[124] The Court remarked that:

> Sometimes there is no question, in the sense that it does not appear to be disputed, that an act was done, but there are conflicting reports, or a lack of evidence, as to who did it. The problem is then not the legal process of imputing the act to a particular State for the purpose of establishing responsibility, but the prior process of tracing material proof of the identity of the perpetrator. The occurrence of the act itself may however have been shrouded in secrecy. In the latter case, the Court has had to endeavor first to establish what actually happened, before entering on the next stage of considering whether the act (if proven) was imputable to the State to which it has been attributed.[125]

So, if an important element of a policy of plausible deniability was to involve a deliberate obfuscation of the evidentiary chains of causation or attribution, it had further effects upon the possibility of judicial 'knowing' itself. In part, these were necessarily linked.

As the *Nicaragua Case* itself exemplified, one of the ways in which the rival powers typically sought to avoid public responsibility and condemnation was by providing covert support or assistance (including military assistance and armaments) to agents of subversion elsewhere in the world. The contra rebels in Nicaragua or the PFLP in the Middle East are obvious examples. The routinisation of this practice led to persistent calls by some in the Western bloc[126] for a 're-interpretation' of the Charter rules on intervention – to allow, for example, intervention in support of preserving democracy, human rights or the rule of law.[127] Indeed, in the *Nicaragua Case*, the Court spent a considerable time debating whether the traditional rules prohibiting foreign intervention had, in fact, been modified by such practice in recent years.[128] The Court firmly shut the door on such a supposition, and indeed it emphasised that any kind of financial support, intelligence or logistical support to

[124] *Nicaragua v USA*, 38–39, para 57.
[125] Ibid.
[126] See, e.g., Richard Lillich 'Forcible Self-Help by States to Protect Human Rights' *Iowa Law Review*, 53 (1967) 325; Michael Reisman, 'Humanitarian Intervention to Protect the Ibos' in Richard Lillich (ed.) *Humanitarian Intervention and the United Nations* (Charlottesville: Virginia University Press, 1973) 167.
[127] See Chapter 2.
[128] *Nicaragua v USA*, 106–10, paras 202–9.

rebel groups would constitute unlawful acts of intervention.[129] But the very fact that the Court was fielding the question in the first place was an indication of the prevailing sense of dissonance between principle and practice.[130]

The real issue, however, was not so much the content of the rules governing intervention but the factual basis upon which an attribution of responsibility might rest.[131] The Court noted that, unlike the example of the *Tehran Hostages Case*, in which it was able to rely extensively upon public media coverage of the events, and in which the facts were not substantially in dispute, it had to be much more careful in case of Nicaragua. Not only were many facts contested, but 'widespread reports of a fact' did not give it any greater credibility. It observed that such a fact 'may prove on closer examination to derive from a single source' and therefore have 'no greater value as evidence than the original source'.[132] Ultimately, the Court devised an evidential rubric for determining what weight might be placed upon a particular fact. The greatest emphasis would be given to what might be called 'confessional' evidence – 'evidence of a party ... against its own interest'.[133]

What the Court did not spell out – apart from drawing attention to the absence of the US itself from proceedings – were the causes of its anxiety. One obvious difficulty was the documented habit of those engaged in covert warfare to circulate what might be called 'fictional truths': that Gary Powers' U-2 was a NASA weather reconnaissance aircraft, that the Soviet intervention in Czechoslovakia was a response to an 'invitation' on the part of the Czech government[134] or that the US intended 'no military intervention in Cuba'.[135] Lies (or 'disinformation') they may have been,

129 Ibid., 124, para 241.

130 The court was to note, for example, that the US 'have on some occasions clearly stated their grounds for intervening in the affairs of a foreign State for reasons connected with, for example, the domestic policies of that country, its ideology, the level of its armaments, or the direction of its foreign policy.' It was to assert, however, that 'these were statements of international policy, and not an assertion of rules of existing international law'. *Nicaragua v USA*, 109, para 207.

131 *Nicaragua v USA*, 38, para 57.

132 Ibid., 41, para 63.

133 Ibid., 43, para 69.

134 See Louis Henkin, 'The Reports of the Death of Article 2(4) Are Greatly Exaggerated' *American Journal of International Law*, 65 (1971) 547.

135 'Letter from President Kennedy to Chairman Khrushchev (Washington DC, 18 April 1961)' in *Foreign Relations of the United States, 1961–1963, Vol. VI, Kennedy-Khrushchev Exchanges*, Washington, DC: United States Government Printing Office, 1996) 10.

but in the context of the ideological Cold War, fiction was not so much non-non-fiction, as a stand-in for the truth. It was, after all, only through the circulation of would-be 'fictions' that the general public was to acquire much of its everyday 'virtual knowledge' of the workings of the intelligence services. Such accounts were often written by former members of the intelligence services themselves, and, in a sense, they stood in for the real thing and were believable at the level of their form if not in their actual content.[136]

But dissimulation was only part of a broader formation of what Sloterdijk calls the 'martial enlightenment'[137] that was to characterise the ideological Cold War. Psychological warfare programmes, propaganda campaigns,[138] the recruitment of the public media, universities and research institutions into the pursuit and defence of ideologically informed knowledge production tied knowledge to both 'interest' and 'enmity'. As Sloterdijk suggested, scientists lived under 'constant suspicion of being agents' or helpers of the powerful (e.g. Oppenheimer). Scientific knowledge and expertise itself became both an element of 'cultural diplomacy' and of spectacular rivalry (e.g. Sputnik). Enmity, for its part, channeled 'curiosity into a polemical course', producing specialised domains of research and epistemic interest[139] all linked to, or inseparable from, the waging of a covert form of total warfare. The breadth and scale of these activities – from nuclear science to the development of GPS or the science of weather modification – encouraged speculation, even at the time, that the space for 'disinterested' knowledge had radically shrunk if it had not disappeared entirely.

As Melley suggests, 'the postwar triumph of new mass media, strategic communications, and multinational capitalism' altered the essential 'conditions of public knowledge' in post-war Western societies, generating a 'pervasive skepticism about the public's ability to know what is real and true'.[140] This pervasive sense made it difficult, as the ICJ itself noted, for the Court to adjudge the 'covert activities' of the State. So, for instance, when the US was to claim that the *USS Pueblo* (a surveillance ship seized

[136] Melley, *The Covert Sphere.*

[137] Peter Sloterdijk, *Critique of Cynical Reason*, trans. Michael Eldred (London: University of Minnesota Press, 1987) 334.

[138] See generally, Kenneth Osgood, *Total Cold War: Eisenhower's Secret Propaganda Battle at Home and Abroad* (Lawrence: University Press of Kansas, 2006).

[139] Sloterdijk, *Critique of Cynical Reason*, 335.

[140] Melley, *The Covert Sphere*, 36. For the claim that it also underpinned the emergence of postmodernism in the US, see 36–39.

by the North Korean navy in 1968) was situated on the high seas at the time, and not 7.6 miles offshore as the North Korean authorities claimed, even the dissemination of apparently concrete evidence to that effect was met with a considerable degree of scepticism.[141] The same was true of the Soviet Union's claims that Korean Airliner 007 had penetrated Soviet airspace to engage in reconnaissance at the behest of the United States.[142]

As Derrida was famously to point out, the practice of secrecy and the dissimulation associated with it produced a particular effect upon the condition of public knowingness – and with it, the possibility of judgment:

> Wherever knowledge can only be supposed, wherever, as a result, one knows that supposition cannot give rise to knowledge, wherever no knowledge could ever be disputed, there is the production of a *secrecy effect*, of what we might be able to call a *speculation on the capital secret or on the capital of the secret*. The calculated and yet finally incalculable production of this secrecy effect relies upon a simulacrum . . . the risk of 'being deceived less by a secret than by the awareness that there is a secret'.[143]

In other words, the more that States were impelled towards an open practice of covert operations, in which both secrecy and dissimulation were key components, the less able they were to overcome the over-determining effects of such a practice: nothing they might say could be fully trusted, and no evidence adduced that was not itself tainted by the suspicion that it was, at best, only half true.

As we suggested above, the ICJ's response to this was to place the greatest emphasis upon 'confessional' evidence – evidence that States, or their agents, were to offer that, in one form or another, ran counter to their interests. In the process, the Court was to conclude that the US had violated the sovereignty of Nicaragua and breached the obligation of

141 See, e.g., William E. Butler, 'The Pueblo Crisis: Some Critical Reflections' *Proceedings of the American Society of International Law at Its Annual Meeting*, 63 (1969) 10, who noted that the US reports were 'inconsistent' and that there was evidence that prior to the Pueblo incident itself, US warships had penetrated as close as 3 miles offshore.

142 See generally, Craig A. Morgan, 'The Downing of Korean Air Lines Flight 007: Responses to Unauthorised Aerial Incursions' in W. Michael Reisman and Andrew R. Willard (eds.), *International Incidents: The Law That Counts in World Politics* (Princeton: Princeton University Press, 1988) 218–20.

143 Jacques Derrida, '"To Do Justice to Freud": The History of Madness in the Age of Psychoanalysis' *Critical Inquiry*, 20 (1994) 245.

non-intervention in the affairs of another State.[144] We can speculate about whether the Court itself had a clear handle on what might, or might not, be in a State's own 'interests' given that the language of 'interest' itself might allude to a terrain of knowledge that was both open and repressed. But the emphasis it placed upon the 'confession', or 'revelation', did suggest that 'true' knowledge, or knowledge that could be relied upon or trusted, was knowledge that started life as a 'secret' – knowledge that had somehow been stripped 'naked' and whose veracity was founded upon the act of its own unveiling. Sloterdijk puts the idea like this:

> What is naked is what was previously secret: the enemy, eavesdropped on in his own privacy; the hidden power here, the conspiracy there; the naked women, the genitals made visible; the confessions of the amoral; the true intentions, the real motives, the hard statistics, the relentless standards. Those who enlighten do not rely on what 'people say'; the naked facts will probably always be different from what 'people say'. The enemy is everywhere.[145]

For Sloterdijk, though, what is revealed in such moments is not a form of ideologically free knowledge but rather its opposite: an affirmation of '*the primary* connection between knowledge and polemical interest'. The naked facts 'ferreted out' by the intelligence services merely 'build the first solid layer of a cynical empiricism' because the content of that secret knowledge was always conditioned upon what was deemed necessary to 'keep the enemy in sight'. It was knowledge that both 'defined' the enemy and that was shaped and framed through the condition of 'enmity'. Secret knowledge was not knowledge stripped of polemical interest but knowledge infused by it, and whose 'laying bare' would simply constitute a further act of dissimulation (as being that of the agent who sees but who remains hidden).[146]

So, while the ICJ might not have had any reason to doubt the veracity of the 'confessional' information supplied to it for purposes of its own judgment in the *Nicaragua Case*, the rubric of the 'revealed' secret as the

[144] As Judges Oda and Schwebel pointed out, the court simultaneously appeared to ignore the evidence provided by the US Report of the Permanent Select Committee on Intelligence relating to Nicaraguan support for insurgents operating in El Salvador. *Nicaragua v USA*, 241, para 62 (dissenting opinion of Judge Oda), 324–25, paras 137–42 (dissenting opinion of Judge Schwebel).

[145] Sloterdijk, *Critique of Cynical Reason*, 335.

[146] Ibid., 336.

only form of knowledge that one might be able to trust spoke of a Cold War knowledge formation that was shaped or dominated by the secrecy effect. In other words, the suspicion that nothing was sacred and that no truth was to be spared.

7.4 The Spy

We have been describing how the ideological Cold War was a war fought under the banner of secrecy. At the heart of this were the intelligence agencies and the human and technological resources they brought into play (HUMINT, ELINT, SIGINT, IMINT, etc.).[147] As has already been noted, most of the post-1945 intelligence agencies could be traced back to wartime military agencies. And in the first instance, at least, they were invariably conceived as agencies concerned with military espionage and counter-espionage. The practice of military espionage has a history almost as long as the practice of warfare. But in the West, at the end of the nineteenth century, its practice in peacetime was the focal point of efforts to criminalise it, mainly as a supplement to the longer-standing crime of 'treason'. The central focus of various legislative initiatives was to punish individuals (whether or not they recognised themselves as spies) for disclosing (military) information that would be helpful to an actual or potential enemy. And even though the crime of espionage was not confined exactly to acts conducted in time of actual war (Captain Dreyfus, famously, was convicted of treason in 1894, having been suspected of passing military secrets to Germany),[148] it was conditioned by reference to a virtual state of warfare or preparedness for war. Disclosure of information to the 'enemy' was a common feature of most criminal codes.[149]

[147] Human Intelligence; Electronic Intelligence; Signals Intelligence; Image Intelligence. See generally, Fleur Johns, 'Shadowboxing: The Data Shadows of Cold War International Law' in Matthew Craven, Sundhya Pahuja and Gerry Simpson (eds.) *International Law and the Cold War* (Cambridge: Cambridge University Press, 2019) 137–58.

[148] In the US before 1954, the death penalty could only be imposed for a violation of the Espionage laws during wartime. The statute was amended, however, to make espionage a capital offence irrespective of whether it was an act committed in time of peace or war. See *US v Sobell*, 314 F.2d 314 (Fed Cir, 1963).

[149] For the US, see Espionage Act of 1917, which criminalises the communication of prohibited information to the advantage of any 'foreign nation'. Atomic Energy Act of 1954 s 224 prohibits violations of the act 'with intent to injure the United States, or with the intent to secure an advantage for a foreign nation'; Espionage and Censorship Statute of 1970, s 793(a) defines espionage as 'obtaining information respecting the national

This meant that in the background of these emergent rules were the rules of armed conflict sketched out in the Lieber Code[150] and the Declaration of Brussels of 1874[151] and later introduced into the Hague Conventions/Regulations of 1899/1907.[152] Those codes, and the gloss offered by commentators,[153] put two ideas in place. First, they introduced a distinction between legitimate reconnaissance (*ruses de guerre*), on the one hand,[154] and the perfidious act of spying, on the other. In other words, they drew a distinction between the criminal behaviour of the clandestine saboteur[155] and the privileged enterprise of the open reconnaissance party (or, in time of peace, of the diplomat). Spies – defined as

defence with intent or reason to believe that the information is to be used to the injury of the United States or to the advantage of any foreign nation'. Section 1 of the UK Official Secrets Act 1911 proscribes the making of any sketch, plan, model or note that could be useful to an enemy; the obtaining or communication to any person of any sketch, plan, model, article or note or other document or information, which could be useful to an enemy; and the approach to or entry into a prohibited place. See generally, David Williams, *Not in the Public Interest: The Problem of Security in Democracy* (London: Hutchinson, 1965) 26–38. See also French Penal Code articles 77–78; German Penal code s 109f, para 1(1); Soviet Criminal Code article 58-1a. See generally, Manuel R. Garcia-Mora, 'Treason, Sedition and Espionage as Political Offences as Political Offences under the Law of Extradition' *University of Pittsburgh Law Review*, 26 (1964–65) 79–83.

150 General Orders No. 100, (24 April 1863) arts 83 and 101. Article 88 stated that: 'A spy is a person who, secretly, in disguise or under false pretenses, seeks information with the intention of communicating it to the enemy. The spy is punishable with death by hanging by the neck, whether or not he succeed in obtaining the information or in conveying it to the enemy.'

151 Project of an International Declaration Concerning the Laws and Customs of War, Brussels, 27 August 1874, articles 19–22.

152 Convention (II) with Respect to the Laws and Customs of War on Land and Its Annex: Regulations Concerning the Laws and Customs of War on Land, the Hague, 29 July 1899, 32 Stat 1803, article 24. ('Ruses of war and the employment of measures necessary for obtaining information about the enemy and the country are considered permissible'); article 29, 1907 ('A person can only be considered a spy when, acting clandestinely, or on false pretences, he obtains, or endeavours to obtain information in the zone of operations of a belligerent, with the intention of communicating it to the hostile party. Thus, soldiers not wearing a disguise . . . are not spies.').

153 See, e.g., William Edward Hall, *A Treatise on International Law*, 8th ed. (Oxford: The Clarendon Press, 1924) 650; James Molony Spaight, *War Rights on Land* (London: Macmillan, 1911) 203–4.

154 Convention (IV) Respecting the Laws and Customs of War on Land and Its Annex: Regulations Concerning the Laws and Customs of War on Land, the Hague, 18 October 1907, 36 Stat 2277, article 24: 'Ruses of war and the employment of measures necessary for obtaining information about the enemy and the country are considered permissible.'

155 See, e.g., Ex parte Quirin, 317 US 1 (1942).

those wearing a disguise or acting under false pretenses[156] – could be put on trial or executed,[157] whereas members of a reconnaissance party kept their privileged status as combatants (or, again, in case of diplomats, their immunity).[158] Secondly, spies could be treated in the harshest possible manner,[159] but recruiting them, commissioning them or even deploying them was not prohibited.[160] In a sense, responsibility was individualised, attributed to the moral, or behavioural, failings of the spy him/herself. (S)he was understood characteristically to be motivated by treachery or private gain.[161] The spymaster, on the other hand, remained out of the reach of any moral or legal judgment.[162] As Oppenheim explained,

156 Henry Wager Halleck, 'Military Espionage' *American Journal of International Law*, 5 (1911) 598.

157 Espionage was commonly punishable by death. On 12 January 1950, for example, the Presidium of the USSR Supreme Soviet declared that the decree on the abolition of capital punishment (from 26 May 1947) would be 'inapplicable' to 'traitors to the motherland, spies and subversive diversionists'.

158 On the practice of declaring diplomats to be persona non grata as a consequence of espionage, see Eileen Denza, *Diplomatic Law: Commentary on the Vienna Convention of Diplomatic Relations*, 5th ed. (Oxford: Oxford University Press, 2025) article 9.

159 Green Haywood Hackworth, *Digest of International Law*, vol. II (Washington, DC: Government Printing Office, 1941) 304; Hall, *International Law*, 651. The standard rationale being that spies posed a 'special danger' and that violent deterrence was necessary. See, e.g., Richard R. Baxter, 'So-called "Unprivileged Belligerency": Spies, Guerrillas and Saboteurs' *British Yearbook of International Law*, 28 (1951) 329–30, 333.

160 See, e.g., H. W. Halleck, *International Law; or, Rules Regulating the Intercourse of States in Peace and War* (San Francisco: H. H. Bancroft & Company, 1861) §26, 406 ('The employment of spies is considered a kind of clandestine practise, a deceit in war, allowable by its rules'). The US Rules on Land Warfare (1956) provide, in article 77, that belligerents enjoy a 'well-established right' to 'employ spies and other secret agents for obtaining information of the enemy. Resort to that practice involves no offence against international law. Spies are punished, not as violators of the laws of war, but to render that method of obtaining information as dangerous, difficult, and ineffective as possible.'

161 See, e.g., Emer de Vattel, *The Law of Nations, or, Principles of the Law of Nature, Applied to the Conduct and Affairs of Nations and Sovereigns, with Three Early Essays on the Origin and Nature of Natural Law and on Luxury*, vol. III (Indianapolis: Liberty Fund, 2008; originally 1797) s. 179 ('a man of honour, who is unwilling to expose himself to an ignominious death from the hand of a common executioner, ever declines serving as a spy; and, moreover, he looks upon the office as unworthy of him because it can not be performed without some degree of treachery'). It is notable that the many accounts of Cold War espionage tend to identify a distinction between the 'ideological' spies, such as Philby, MacClean and Burgess, and the spies motivated by profit or gain.

162 Halleck was to suggest, however, that whilst the 'odium and punishment of the crime must fall upon the spy himself . . . it may be doubted whether the employer is entirely free from the moral responsibility of holding out inducements to treachery and crime'. Halleck, *International Law*, §26, 406. Delupis similarly argues in favour of sending State

espionage thus had a 'twofold character'. On one side, it was perfectly lawful for a belligerent to employ whatever methods it deemed necessary to obtain information about the enemy, including commissioning spies and traitors. 'But this right', as Oppenheim put it, stood 'face to face with the right to consider and punish such enemy individuals, whether soldiers or not, committing acts of espionage or treason, as war criminals'.[163] This resulted in an 'insoluble and inextricable conflict' within international law:

> On the one hand, International Law gives a right to belligerents to make use of espionage and treason. On the other hand, however, the same law gives a right to belligerents to consider espionage and treason within their lines, committed by enemy soldiers or enemy private individuals, as acts of illegitimate warfare, and consequently punishable.[164]

And so, one could neither say that espionage was unequivocally unlawful nor that States had a lawful right to engage in it. In part, this explains the different standpoints of the US and the Soviet Union in the case of Gary Powers: the US claimed a right to engage in acts of reconnaissance and the Soviet Union a right to treat those so engaged as spies.

The conditioning assumptions that lay behind the differentiation between 'reconnaissance', on the one hand, and espionage, on the other, were the existence or otherwise of a state of belligerency and whether or not the character of the action in question was open or covert ('deceitful'). Both conditions came under particular strain in the context of the Amero-Soviet Cold War. In the first place, as the very language of the Cold War itself suggested, the categories of 'peace' and 'war' were themselves strained by an ideological contestation that was marked by conditions of mutual enmity, but in which direct hostilities between the powers in their territories were held in suspense. There certainly were hostilities, but they were largely indirect, remote or by way of 'proxy'. And yet in relation to espionage at least, the Soviet Union and the US acted 'as if' they were at war.

In the second place, the 'total' character – and totalising effect – of the ideological Cold War was reshaping the practice of espionage itself. The industrial warfare of the twentieth century entailed the mobilisation of the total population – both for purposes of fighting in ways that needed

responsibility. Ingrid Delupis, 'Foreign Warships and Immunity for Espionage' *American Journal of International Law*, 78 (1984) 70–71.

163 Oppenheim, *International Law*, 267–68.

164 Ibid.

mass-conscription and to underpin the supporting economy of a technologically intensive form of warfare production.[165] Total mobilisation required that the populace be conscripted affectively, too, into supporting the war[166] and sacrificing their bodies in the national cause. This led to the development of State-led propaganda campaigns using the emergent instruments of the mass-media (film, television, radio, literature).[167] It also meant that activities that hampered efforts at conscription were criminalised. The effect was that the idea of enemy 'sabotage' was extended from acts that destroyed plant and facilities to acts (including 'utterances') that blocked the capacity of the armed forces to recruit or fight. As Galison points out, the crimes of 'sabotage' and 'espionage' were thus brought into line with the crime of sedition.[168] This shifted the focus away from an exclusive concern with information being passed to the enemy and opened up an entirely new front in warfare: combating the enemy within. This was the 'fifth column', whose allegiances were no longer defined (or subverted) by money or moral depravity but instead shaped by conscience and belief. So, every piece of knowledge became a potential secret, and every citizen became a potential traitor.[169] When ideology entered the field of espionage (and treasonable activities), it set the stage for the emergence of the 'ideological spy' – those, like Philby, Burgess and Maclean, who engaged in espionage on behalf of the Soviet Union as a consequence of their communist beliefs. It also led to the emergence of State activities to 'secure' potentially secret knowledge from disclosure by instituting procedures for 'vetting' those working in

165 Ernst Jünger, 'Total Mobilization' in Richard Wolin (ed.) *The Heidegger Controversy* (New York: Columbia University Press, 1991) 119–39.

166 Herbert Marcuse, *One Dimensional Man* (Boston: Beacon, 1964) 21. 'The main trends are familiar: concentration of the national economy on the needs of the big corporations, with the government as a stimulating, supporting, and sometimes even controlling force; hitching of this economy to a world-wide system of military alliances, monetary arrangements, technical assistance and development schemes; gradual assimilation of blue-collar and white-collar population, of leadership types in business and labour, of leisure activities and aspirations in different social classes; fostering of a pre-established harmony between scholarship and the national purpose; invasion of the private household by the togetherness of public opinion; opening of the bedroom to the media of mass communication.'

167 See generally, Andrew N. Rubin, *Archives of Authority: Empire, Culture and the Cold War* (Princeton: Princeton University Press, 2012).

168 Peter Galison, 'Secrecy in Three Acts' *Social Research*, 77 (2010) 950.

169 Shils, *The Torment of Secrecy*, 90–91.

'sensitive' occupations[170] and for classifying information for purpose of limiting access to it.[171]

And so the idea of secrecy, and secret knowledge, provided the operational frame for Cold War warfare. But it was the agents of secrecy – the spies – that became the most prominent objects of public discourse about the practice of secrecy. Spies were both celebrated and reviled in equal measure as the anti-heroes of an ideological rivalry in which espionage was understood to be a necessity, but whose conceptual moorings had become unhinged. None of the traditional operational distinctions that served to differentiate between the legitimate and illegitimate practice of information-gathering – between war and peace, the combatant and civilian, the open and the covert – were available as means of either justifying the practice or condemning it as unlawful. What emerged in its place was, on the one hand, a vast expansion of the criminalisable domain of espionage (i.e. an expansion of the numbers of people liable to be treated as spies through the classification of knowledge) and, on the other, an effort to delimit the legitimacy of reconnaissance/espionage by reference to its spatial demarcation. This takes us right back to the U-2 incident.

7.5 Spies in the Skies: The Making of Outer Space

The early years of the Cold War were dominated by stories of atomic espionage and the high-profile trials of those accused of passing of atomic secrets to other powers.[172] But by the time of the U-2 incident, the focal point of discussion had taken on an entirely new dimension – shifting

[170] See, e.g., Peter Hennesy and Gail Brownfield, 'Britain's Cold War Security Purge: The Origins of Positive Vetting' *The Historical Journal*, 25 (1982) 965–73; Walter Gelhorn, *Security, Loyalty, and* Science (Ithaca: Cornell University Press, 2019) chapter 4; Daniel Lomas, *The Secret History of UK Security Vetting from 1909 to the Present* (London: Bloomsbury, 2025).

[171] See, e.g., Alex Wellerstein, *Restricted Data: The History of Nuclear Secrecy in the United States* (Chicago: University of Chicago Press, 2021); Harold Relyea 'The Evolution of Government Information Security Classification Policy: A Brief Overview (1775–1973) in US Congress, House Committee on Government Operations, *Security Classification Reform*, hearings, 93rd Cong. 2nd Sess (Washington, DC: GPO, 1974) 505–97; Sam Lebovic, 'The Historical Presidency: Rethinking the Origins of National Security Classification' *Presidential Studies Quarterly*, 54 (2024) 259–70.

[172] For example, the trial of Klaus Fuchs, Alger Hiss and the Rosenbergs. On the former see Robert Chadwell Wiliams, *Klaus Fuchs: Atom Spy* (Cambridge, MA: Harvard University Press, 1987).

vertically towards the skies. By this time, the threat of aerial espionage had gained as much, if not more, importance than the terrestrial activities of the spy or secret agent. This shift towards a concern for aerial espionage was accompanied by a wider general movement in the modes of espionage from the human to the technological (from HUMINT to COMINT, ELINT, SIGINT and IMINT).[173] But alongside a technological change came a shift in legal attention from a focus on criminalising espionage in domestic law to framing espionage spatially within the field of international law.

At the beginning of the twentieth century, it was by no means clear that a State would be entitled to claim sovereignty over the space high above its territory.[174] In the debate that took place in the early decades of that century, the dominant concern was to strike a balance between two rival imperatives. The first imperative was to enable and facilitate the commercial opportunities of air flight that had opened out (mail, freight, passenger services and so on). The second – conflicting – imperative was to deal with the security implications associated with the unregulated passage of foreign aircraft over one's territory. In the ensuing dialogue, the old *mare liberum/mare clausum* debate was re-enacted in relation to airspace (the 'second battle of the books' as it was called)[175] with (occidental) jurists lining up on either side. Some, like Pradier-Fodéré and Nys, argued that airspace was incapable of being subject to sovereign control. Others, like Holtzendorf, Rivier, Von Liszt and Fauchille, argued that sovereignty extended into airspace, at least as far as the technology of policing enabled.[176] Two main solutions presented themselves: one being to declare the skies to be 'free', subject to a right of regulation in the name of security,[177] the other to declare airspace to be an intrinsic space of

[173] See note 147 for further references and where acronyms are explained.

[174] Harold Dexter Hazeltine, *The Law of the Air* (London: University of London Press, 1911) 6.

[175] Joseph F. English, 'Air Freedom: The Second Battle of the Books' *Journal of Air Law and Commerce*, 2 (1931) 356–72.

[176] See generally, Peter H. Sand, Jorge de Sousa Freitas and Geoffrey N Pratt, 'An Historical Survey of International Air Law before the Second World War' *McGill Law Journal*, 7 (1960–61) 24–42; Harold Dexter Hazeltine, *The Law of the Air* (London: University of London Press, 1911) 9–29.

[177] Paul Fauchille, 'Regime juridique des aérostats' *Annuaire de L'institut de Droit International*, 19 (1902) 32. 'L'air est libre. Les États n'ont sur lui en temps de paix et en temps de guerre que les droits necessaire à leur conservation. Ces droits sont relatifs à la repression de l'espionage, à la police douanière et aux necessités de la defense.'

sovereignty subject to a right of civilian overflight or 'innocent passage'.[178]

From as early as the Franco-Prussian War of 1870–71,[179] the question of espionage and the ability of 'enemy' States to obtain detailed information about defence installations by overflight was the subject of much debate.[180] Fauchille's particular solution was to propose the zoning of airspace above a State's territory by reference to technological capabilities of photography. An exclusive 'zone of protection against espionage' should be established, he suggested, limited to 1,500 meters above ground[181] from which all foreign aircraft would be excluded, save only those that were granted permission to enter. Nys, by contrast, argued that Fauchille's obsession with espionage was a 'dangerous mania'.[182] Not only was there an intrinsic international interest in promoting 'freedom of the air' to facilitate communication and commerce, asserting sovereignty over airspace for fear of espionage was also fundamentally obtuse. Such a claim was essentially premised upon the idea that foreign aircraft represented 'dangers to security', but it was also clear that the 'zone of protection' would actually have no meaning in time of war, when the question of security was most pressing. In those circumstances, overflight could not be prohibited: the passengers in an aircraft could certainly be treated as combatants, liable to be shot at, captured or treated as prisoners of war; but they would not be spies, as such, since aircraft, in his view, were incapable of 'dissimulation'.[183] The assertion of sovereign rights in relation to airspace was therefore built around a problem of espionage to which it provided no real answer.

[178] Westlake's solution. John Westlake, 'Régime des aerostats et de la têlégraphie sans fil', *Annuaire de L'institut de Droit International*, 21 (1906) 297–99.

[179] Haseltine was to note that from the time of the Franco-Prussian War of 1870–71, the main issue in contention was 'the right of espionage'. Harold D. Haseltine, *Law of the Air* (London: University of London Press, 1911) 3.

[180] Fauchille, 'Regime juridique des aérostats', 35. He recognised two other valid concerns relating to airspace – customs and sanitary regulations – but neither of these, he supposed, would justify the imposition of absolute restrictions on aerial overflight.

[181] Fauchille, 'Regime juridique des aérostats', 36. He assumed that, above that limit, photographic images would no longer be sufficiently clear to be useful. He later adjusted the height of the proposed zone to 500 meters. See Paul Fauchille, 'La circulation aérienne et les droits des états en temps de paix' *Revue Juridique Internationale de la Locomation Aérienne*, 1 (1910) 9–16.

[182] M. Nys, 'Rapport sur le régime juridique des aerostats' *Annuaire de L'institut de Droit International*, 19 (1902) 106.

[183] Nys, 'Rapport sur le régime juridique des aerostats', 108–9.

Ultimately, the terms of the 1919 Paris Convention on Civil Aviation, followed by the Ibero-American Madrid Convention of 1926, the Pan-American Havana Convention of 1928 and the 1944 Chicago Convention, all adopted a simpler and more categorical formula.[184] They proclaimed simultaneously that every State had 'complete and exclusive sovereignty over the air space above its territory'[185] and that there was a universal a right of overflight[186] but that both rights could legally be subject to limitations 'for reasons of military necessity or public safety'. There was no right of overflight for military/'State' aircraft[187] nor, significantly, under the terms of the Chicago Convention, for unmanned aircraft.[188] Contracting parties were also entitled to prohibit the overflight of certain areas and the use of photographic apparatus.[189]

The Chicago Convention was not ratified by Soviet governments until the late 1960s, but it performed one feat that was of more general significance. That was to stabilise, or cast as 'natural,' the idea that the State had exclusive sovereignty in relation to its airspace.[190] States party to the Chicago Convention (or the Paris Convention before it) asserted rights *in rem* (and hence *erga omnes*) and, in so doing, were asserting a general presumption that airspace was a space of sovereignty. These were rights putatively enjoyed by all in virtue of the very nature of sovereignty over territory. In the idiom of European international law, then, all States could thereafter claim authority to have exclusive control over their

[184] At which point McNair declared the 'important question of theory' to be 'closed'. Arnold D. McNair, *The Law of the Air* (London: Stevens & Sons, 1953) 4.

[185] Convention Relating to the Regulation of Aerial Navigation, Paris, 13 October 1919, 11 LNTS 173, article 1.

[186] Convention on International Civil Aviation, Chicago, 7 December 1944, 15 UNTS 295, article 5 (limited to 'non-scheduled flights').

[187] Convention Relating to the Regulation of Aerial Navigation, Paris, 13 October 1919, 11 LNTS 173, articles 30–32; Convention on International Civil Aviation, Chicago, 7 December 1944, 15 UNTS 295, article 3. Article 3(b) of the Chicago Convention defines State aircraft as including '[a]ircraft used in military, customs and police services'.

[188] Convention on International Civil Aviation, Chicago, 7 December 1944, 15 UNTS 295, article 8.

[189] Convention Relating to the Regulation of Aerial Navigation, Paris, 13 October 1919, 11 LNTS 173, article 27; Convention on International Civil Aviation, Chicago, 7 December 1944, 15 UNTS 295, article 36.

[190] The Air Code of the USSR 1935 reflected this. See John N. Hazard, 'The Soviet Union and International Law' *Soviet Studies*, 1 (1950) 196. See, e.g., United States Air Commerce Act of 1926, Civil Aeronautics Act of 1938, and Federal Aviation Act of 1958.

'sovereign airspace' and in the same measure assert the right to determine whether to allow aircraft of other States a right of innocent overflight.[191]

Rights in airspace were thus configured around the distinction between peace and war – military aircraft, the materialised embodiment of a condition of war, were prohibited from entering the airspace of another State in times of peace without express permission.[192] No such prohibition existed in time of war – for obvious reasons – and, whilst they were liable to be shot down, the pilots of the aircraft would enjoy an immunity from the jurisdiction of the territorial State so long as the aircraft and/or the pilot was suitably marked.[193] Whilst civilian aircraft from States party to the agreements enjoyed certain 'privileges',[194] that did not automatically mean they were entitled to enter the airspace of any another country in time of peace. Fauchille's analysis was to remain in play: peace simply suspended the privileges of combatancy through the attribution of 'permission': any aircraft could still be treated as engaging in unlawful espionage if it were to overfly the territory of another State without permission. Such permission, though, could be granted by generalised agreements in a treaty – whether that be the general terms of the Paris or Chicago Conventions[195] or the more specific terms of the bilateral air services agreements ('line' agreements etc.) that were to first make their appearance in the inter-war years.[196] And so even though the

[191] An unexpected corollary of the Chicago description of the 'innate' right to sovereignty over superjacent airspace was a recognition that all States were, by contrast, free to fly through the airspace over the high seas since there were no rights of sovereignty in play. This came to be implicitly recognised in article 3 of the Geneva Convention on the Continental Shelf, Geneva, 29 April 1958, 499 UNTS 311, in which it was stated that the rights of the coastal State over the continental shelf 'do not affect the legal status of the superjacent waters as high seas, or that of the airspace above those waters'.

[192] Convention Relating to the Regulation of Aerial Navigation, Paris, 13 October 1919, 11 LNTS 173, article 32; Convention on International Civil Aviation, Chicago, 7 December 1944, 15 UNTS 295, article 3(c). On the question whether this extended to aircraft in distress, see Oliver Lissytzyn, 'The Treatment of Aerial Intruders in Recent Practice and International Law' *American Journal of International Law*, 47 (1953) 559–89.

[193] See 'Rules Concerning the Control of Wireless Telegraphy in Time of War and Air Warfare', Commission of Jurists, December 1922–February 1923, article 3.

[194] The International Air Transport Agreement (1944) famously set out the 'five freedoms' but remained largely unratified. Its chief sponsor, the US, withdrew its assent in 1946. The International Air Services Transit Agreement (1944), dubbed the 'two freedoms' agreement, was more widely ratified by States in the West.

[195] Eg. Article 5, which provides for a right of non-scheduled overflight for civilian aircraft.

[196] See Robert Yewdall Jennings, 'International Civil Aviation and the Law' *British Yearbook of International Law*, 22 (1945) 191–209.

idiom of sovereignty over airspace seemed to envisage a generalised right of innocent passage, it was still a sovereignty written in the language of enmity, which then conditioned peacetime rights of overflight.

By 1945, it was relatively clear that aerial reconnaissance in peacetime was subject to the exclusive control of the territorial State and that any unauthorised overflight – whether of a military or civilian character – ran the risk of being forced down and the pilot prosecuted for espionage.[197] Such was the fate of Gary Powers, and a spate of similar incidents were to reaffirm the same (including, notably, the shooting down of the El-Al Flight 402 in 1955, the RB-47 incident of 1960[198] and Korean Airlines 007 in 1983).[199] What remained of the debate merely concerned the extent of any exceptions – whether aircraft in distress, for example, should be entitled to land,[200] whether civilian aircraft should be re-directed rather than shot down[201] – and whether third States might be held responsible for conniving in any unlawful acts of intrusion by allowing aircraft or balloons to be launched from their territory.[202]

On the face of it, then, the question of espionage and enmity had shaped the rules on aviation, and the rules on aviation in the Chicago

197 It is perhaps notable that in its memorial in the *Aerial Incident of 27 July 1955 (USA v Bulgaria)*, the US was to note that 'there is no existing treaty or international code which in terms prohibits a government from ordering the killing of innocent passengers in an innocent civil transport aircraft that has strayed without prior authorisation into the territorial air space of the killing government'. Memorial submitted by the Government of the United States of America (2 December 1958) 212.

198 See UN Doc. S/PV/880–83 (22–26 July 1960).

199 See Craig A. Morgan, 'The Downing of Korean Air Lines Flight 007: Responses to Unauthorized Aerial Incursions' in W. Michael Reisman and Andrew R. Willard (eds.), *International Incidents: The Law That Counts in World Politics* (Princeton: Princeton University Press, 1988) 202–37.

200 See, e.g., Oliver J. Lissitzyn, 'Some Legal Implications of the U-2 and RB-47 Incidents' *American Journal of International Law*, 56 (1962) 135–42.

201 Convention on International Civil Aviation, Chicago, 7 December 1944, 15 UNTS 295, annex II, appendix 2 envisages that a civilian aircraft might be intercepted as a 'last resort' and then only for purposes of providing it with 'navigational guidance'. It was on the basis of those provisions, that States reacted against the shooting down of Korean Airline Flight 007 in 1983. In the following year, the ICAO Assembly adopted article 3bis in which it was made clear that all States 'must refrain from resorting to the use of weapons against civil aircraft in flight and that, in case of interception, the lives of persons on board and the safety of aircraft must not be endangered'. See Gerald F. Fitzmaurice, 'The Use of Force against Civil Aircraft: The Aftermath of the KAL Flight 007 Incident' *Canadian Yearbook of International Law*, 22 (1984) 291–311.

202 See John Quigley, *Soviet Legal Innovation and the Law of the Western World* (Cambridge: Cambridge University Press, 2007) 161–63.

Convention (ratified ultimately by both Western and Soviet governments alike)[203] had, in turn, given the question of espionage (and secrecy) an entirely new spatial cast. As Nys had suggested, the defining features that marked out the spy – deceit and false pretenses – no longer shaped the field of regulation and, indeed, were scarcely relevant. Only in cases in which a civilian airliner might have obtained permission for overflight and then engaged in surreptitious surveillance might the question of deception be material. In all other cases, secrecy and security (or security through secrecy) were to be ensured by way of a spatial ordering in which the territorial State was granted an absolute right to control and regulate the overflight of aircraft (which might involve, at the same time, the restriction of any overflight over certain designated areas).[204]

Sovereignty thus came to be associated with a certain way of both 'seeing' and 'being seen'. What was being guarded against was being seen from above, not laterally, horizontally, from other States or from the high seas.[205] 'Observing the State' in its vertical extension intertwined a new way of thinking about sovereignty (as connoting a right to not be literally 'overseen' without permission) with a new conception of security (that envisaged 'enmity' to be a permanent condition given spatial meaning). And in the context of the Cold War, this was to animate a practice of dissimulation – the assertion of a right to see but not to be seen.

In his review of the U-2 incident, Quincy Wright, then editor of the *American Journal of International Law*, drew the broad and perhaps unsurprising conclusion that in authorising the U-2 flight over Soviet territory, the US had violated international law and that the Soviet Union was within its rights in forcing the U-2 down and prosecuting Powers under its criminal law.[206] In coming to those conclusions, however,

[203] See further, Air Code of 1932 of the USSR, Timothy A. Taracouzio, *The Soviet Union and International Law* (New York: The Macmillan Company, 1935) 401.

[204] Convention on International Civil Aviation, Chicago, 7 December 1944, 15 UNTS 295, article 9.

[205] It is notable that whilst rules existed for the control of surveillance from above, no such rules existed for surveillance of a State from adjacent territory or the high seas.

[206] Wright, 'Legal Aspects of the U-2 Incident', 853. The issues on which he had confidence were: (1) incursions by State agents into the territory of another State without permission were contrary to elementary principles of international law; (2) penetration of the airspace of States by unauthorised craft were similarly prohibited under the terms of the Paris Convention of 1919, the Havana Convention of 1928 and the Chicago Convention of 1944; (3) there was no recognised 'upper limit to a state's airspace' for such purposes; (4) neighbouring States were under an obligation not to allow their territory to be used for purposes of unlawful reconnaissance missions by third parties; (5) States were free to shoot down unauthorised planes penetrating their airspace with due warning; (6) States were entitled to prosecute under their criminal law the personnel of unauthorised planes

Wright drew attention to the apparent 'confusion between the status both of espionage and of aerial reconnaissance in times of peace and war'.[207] He noted that, whereas in wartime 'both are legitimate enterprises for belligerent governments', in time of peace both were 'illegitimate enterprises because they manifest a lack of respect for foreign territory'. In case of the latter, however, and echoing Eisenhower, a *tu quoque* argument was nevertheless available: 'While in principle all peacetime espionage in foreign territory is illegal, when all are engaging in it, it seems unreasonable to single out one state' for particular criticism.[208]

Wright reprised these arguments a year later in one of the few public discussions of the time about the lawfulness of peacetime espionage under international law. But by this time the debate had become charged by the public recognition that both the US and the Soviet Union had launched satellite reconnaissance programmes (in case of the former, as a partial replacement of the earlier U-2 programme). A key element of these programmes was that they sought to establish, by way of practice, the principle of free (and 'peaceful') use of outer space. In this context, Wright argued, following Baxter,[209] that whilst espionage in time of war was legitimate as a *ruse de guerre* (justified by the absence of any general obligation of belligerents to respect the territory or government of the enemy), in time of peace, it represented a violation 'of the rule of international law imposing a duty upon states to respect the territorial integrity and political independence of other states'.[210] Each State had the power and authority to criminalise espionage, sedition and subversion as it saw fit, and it was 'the duty of other states to respect such exercise of

violating their airspace; (7) aerial reconnaissance did not amount to an 'armed attack' so as to justify military measures in self-defence; (8) nor, in equal measure, could it be justified as an act of self-defence; (9) the violation of territorial sovereignty could give rise to legitimate demands for expression of regret and assurances against repetition. The issues in relation to which he was less clear were: (a) whether the misleading statements made by the US as to the purpose of the flight constituted acts of perfidy and (b) whether it constituted an 'act of aggression' (although the fact the U-2 was unarmed seemed to argue persuasively to the contrary).

207 Wright, 'Legal Aspects of the U-2 Incident', 849.

208 Ibid., 850.

209 Richard R. Baxter, 'So-called "Unprivileged Belligerency"', 329.

210 Quincy Wright, 'Espionage and the Doctrine of Non-intervention in Internal Affairs' in Quincy Wright, Julius Stone, Richard A. Falk and Roland J. Stanger (eds.), *Essays on Espionage and International Law* (Columbus: Ohio State University Press, 1962) 12. That conclusion, he added, could not be displaced, in case of the U-2 incident, by US claims to be acting in self-defence: 'Continual competition in arms, propaganda, subversion, and espionage between free democracies and totalitarian autocracies seems almost certain, in the atomic age, to spell the end of democracy, if not of humanity.' Ibid., 26.

domestic jurisdiction'.[211] And that was surely right as a matter of policy as well as law: subversion, infiltration, espionage, guerilla warfare and 'nibbling aggression' were practices to be associated with totalitarian dictatorships, not democracies, and it was only by abandoning them that democracy itself, if not humanity as a whole, might have a fighting chance.[212]

Wright's presentation was countered immediately by Julius Stone, who sought to set out how Wright was 'completely wrong on the basic matter'.[213] To his mind, the U-2 incident involved two different questions: one being the territorial intrusion, the other the act of peacetime espionage. On the first question, there was really no debate other than to ask why it caused such a commotion: whilst it was certainly wrong, 'the mere naughtiness of a territorial intrusion does not explain' the subsequent 'crisis'.[214] But once one separated the fact of intrusion from the practice of espionage, there was really no room for the view that espionage per se was wrongful.[215] After all, beyond putting on trial, or expelling those found to be engaged in espionage, States rarely pursued claims against the sending State for the fact of espionage alone. Separating the practice of espionage from collateral illegalities (such as territorial intervention) was of particular importance given the emergence of reconnaissance satellites. For in that context, there would be no illegality since there was 'no territorial intrusion when you're in outer space'.[216] Not only, then, was there 'no sufficient warrant' for saying that international law prohibits 'state-authorized espionage in peacetime',[217] there was no desirability for such a prohibition. Indeed, a mutual toleration of aerial espionage ('reciprocal espionage', as he puts it) would have a potentially salutary function of operationalising Eisenhower's *Open Sky* policy, warding off the possibility of surprise nuclear attack. Spying thus could serve a 'common interest' in those circumstances rather than the 'unilateral, selfish, self-regarding' interests with which it was commonly associated.[218]

211 Ibid., 13.
212 Ibid., 25.
213 Julius Stone, 'Legal Problems of Espionage in Conditions of Modern Conflict' in Quincy Wright, Julius Stone, Richard A. Falk and Roland J. Stanger (eds.), *Essays on Espionage and International Law* (Columbus: Ohio State University Press, 1962) 29–44.
214 Ibid., 32.
215 Ibid., 33. The only support for that view, he was to aver, was to be found in 'some dicta' in ex parte Quirin and in the Dutch case re Flesche.
216 Ibid., 34.
217 Ibid.
218 Ibid., 41.

Richard Falk, in turn, situated himself somewhere between Wright and Stone.[219] Drawing attention to the satellite reconnaissance programmes that had recently been launched by the US (Samos, Midas and Tiros), Falk was to argue that the standard rubrics of analysis offered by international law were largely indeterminate – rhetorically sustaining both the Soviet claim that surveillance from outer space was unlawful espionage[220] and the United States' claim that surveillance was an essential precaution against surprise attack.[221] Debating the question of the legality of espionage per se was not helpful: 'for espionage', much like prostitution in years gone by, had 'the peculiar quality of being tolerated, but illegal'.[222] States rarely, if ever, sought to exercise diplomatic protection in favour of a national being tried for espionage (the deafening silence of the Soviet authorities during the long trial of Colonel Abel attested to as much) but equally rarely did they admit their involvement (the U-2 incident, in that respect, was a rare exception). Whilst there was no doubt the Samos–Midas programme was a form of espionage, its illegality depended upon the motives lying behind it – whether it was for purposes of national defence or for aggression.[223] And the arguments were finely balanced on either side. Bearing in mind the possible thermonuclear consequences of an escalation of tension, Falk averred, the response had to be a prudential one: the US was best advised not to continue the programme for fear of escalating the stand-off.[224]

The differences between the three scholars, here, are on the face of it quite sharp. In many senses, they marked out the prevailing uncertainties about the legality or otherwise of the practice of espionage during the Cold War. Whereas Wright conceived the wrongfulness of espionage to be determined by the experience of the observed – all States were entitled to their secrets, at least in time of peace – Stone, by contrast, saw it to be dependent upon the location of the observer – there was no abstract right not to be subject to surveillance. Falk, in turn, regarded the matter as depending on the evidenced intentions – whether they could be shown to be defensive or aggressive in nature. Each brought into play different

219 Richard A. Falk, 'Space Espionage and World Order: A Consideration of the Samos–Midas Program' in Quincy Wright, Julius Stone, Richard A. Falk and Roland J. Stanger (eds.), *Essays on Espionage and International Law* (Columbus: Ohio State University Press, 1962) 45–82.

220 Ibid., 51–54, 58.

221 Ibid., 55–56.

222 Ibid., 57.

223 Ibid., 58.

224 Ibid., 74–75.

ways of thinking about the practice of espionage and the condition of 'peacetime enmity' that appeared to inform it.

But for all the apparent uncertainty, what was to become clear in the next few years is that the rival 'space-faring' powers (ie the Amero-Soviets) would join together to secure the formation of an entirely new legal space – outer space – through their mutual collaboration in the activities of the newly formed Committee on the Peaceful Uses of Outer Space (COPUOS).[225] COPUOS, which had been instructed by the General Assembly to produce a set of principles for purposes of the 'progressive development of international law pertaining' to outer space,[226] went on to draft a Declaration of Legal Principles Governing the Activities of States in the Exploration and Use of Outer Space, which was adopted by the General Assembly itself at its meeting in December 1963. This was a new jurisdiction asserted over something that had not (yet) been claimed and stabilised by the Amero-Soviet project. The first four paragraphs of Resolution 1962 (XVIII), banal as they might appear today, were as radical as any other Resolution it adopted at the time:

1. The exploration and use of outer space shall be carried on for the benefit and in the interests of mankind.
2. Outer space and celestial bodies are free for exploration and use by all States on a basis of equality and in accordance with international law.
3. Outer space and celestial bodies are not subject to national appropriation by claim of sovereignty, by means of use or occupation, or by any other means.
4. The activities of States in the exploration and use of outer space shall be carried on in accordance with international law, including the Charter of the United Nations, in the interests of maintaining international peace and security and promoting international cooperation and understanding.

Leaving aside the obviously problematic allusion offered in the first paragraph to the effect that the two Cold War rivals' activities in outer space were 'in the interests of mankind', the key performative feature of the Declaration was both to declare outer space to be situated beyond the realm of terrestrial sovereignty but at the same time to assert that a certain form of jurisdictional authority was operative in the heavens.

[225] UNGA Res 1472 (XIV) (12 December 1959).
[226] UNGA Res 1802 (XVII) (14 December 1962).

Both were in effect authorised by an assertion of sovereignty in a particular idiom of international law. Outer space was immediately to be distinguished from air space. Activities conducted in outer space, though still 'governed by international law', could not be condemned as a form of intervention or intrusion into the sovereignty of 'subjacent States'.

Immediately, then, the Declaration provided an answer to the problem of espionage with which Wright, Stone and Falk had grappled two years earlier. This was the idea that the orbital domain of satellite reconnaissance was external to the States whose territory was to be observed from afar, so there could be no case for arguing that such observation constituted a violation of the subjacent State's territorial sovereignty. What remained, at best, was Wright's hopeful dictum that the observing State ought to respect the legitimate desire of the subjacent State to retain its own secrets.

But if the Outer Space Declaration seemed to provide a spatial framework through which both rival Cold War powers might engage in the practice of satellite surveillance, it also prevaricated on the key question that Falk had put on the table – namely, as to whether such activity might be regarded as essentially aggressive or defensive in character. In its preamble, the Declaration referred to the 'common interest of all mankind in the progress of the exploration and use of outer space for *peaceful purposes*'. This was a concern that became much more explicit in the subsequent Outer Space Treaty of 1967. But beyond an insistence that outer space should not be used as a site of weapons of mass destruction, it was far from clear whether the use of satellite surveillance, for example, for the purposes of estimating the number or location of nuclear warheads ran counter to the Charter's prohibition on the threat of force. On one side, a claim that such information was necessary to ward off the threat of a surprise attack (as per Falk) was balanced out by the equally plausible conclusion that insofar as such information would be routinely used in missile targeting systems it could just as well serve as a measure preliminary to attack. Just as motive was incapable of being deduced from fact of surveillance itself, the injunction that all such measures should comply with the precepts of the Charter was largely an empty one.

7.6 Conclusion

There are three general observations we can make about the 'Cold War' and the apparently 'indeterminate' legal status of peacetime espionage.

These observations bear more generally upon the juridical dimensions of the Cold War. The first concerns the historic demarcation between war and peace. This is a demarcation that has structured Occidental treatises on international law since the early twentieth century,[227] but which became increasingly tenuous during the Cold War era. The language of the 'Cold War' itself, although not taken up by everyone, was suggestive of the way the habitual distinctions were being troubled. By invoking the idea of a state of ongoing hostilities in time of ostensible peace, the rhetoric of the Cold War alluded both to the fact that enmity was being channeled in new directions (into research establishments, cultural institutions, the media and the home), and to its geographical re-location (away from military confrontation in the North to fomenting 'proxy', wars in the South). Warfare was thus to become both more total and global, yet more simultaneously more local.[228]

In the second place, the debate over the permissibility of espionage brought into focus the relationship between technological development and the regulatory architecture of sovereignty. It has long been appreciated that the rules of warfare change in response to new technologies of warfare – the submarine, the aircraft, chemical weapons and nuclear warheads. This was clear at the time as well. What has perhaps been less frequently appreciated – and what we can see looking back from the present – is the way that such technologies also shape conceptions of warfare per se and rationalities of lawful ordering. So, the submarine, for example, gave expression to the idea of economic warfare regimented by rules of prize, contraband and neutrality. The long-range strategic bomber encapsulated the idea of total warfare regimented by rules governing the protection of 'civilians' and the bombardment of 'undefended sites'.[229] But more ambiguous technologies such as satellite reconnaissance gave expression to a conception of global policing through surveillance – a form of policing concerned with the accrual of an instrumental knowledge of the globe and all its physical and human attributes – with a view to its use in the ongoing struggle (physical, mental, moral and material) between the rival ideological blocs.

[227] See, e.g., Oppenheim, *International Law*.

[228] On the doctrine of 'local wars', see Istvan Kende, 'Twenty-Five Years of Local Wars' *Journal of Peace Research*, 8 (1971) 5–22.

[229] See generally, Christiane Wilke and Halyeh Doutaghi, 'Legal Technologies: Conceptualizing the Legacy of the 1923 Hague Rules of Aerial Warfare' *Leiden Journal of International Law*, 37 (2024) 88–110.

Thirdly, paying attention from the present to the phenomenon of peacetime espionage makes visible a 'Cold War' inscribed, jurisdictionally, in space. As we have seen, a central presupposition of the disagreement between Wright and Stone as to the legality of aerial reconnaissance was the question of whether satellite overflight impinged upon the sovereignty of the State underneath. This was a position that depended on a differentiation being maintained between the juridical status of airspace and that of 'outer space'. The Amero-Soviets led the world towards the recognition of 'outer space' as a new juridical domain that would seem to be 'beyond' the sphere of sovereignty. But it was of course through an assertion of sovereignty that this emplacement was made. And from the perspective of the world-making effect of Amero-Sovietism, this was also the putative assertion of jurisdiction over 'outer space' per se for one earth-bound and parochial system of law.[230] This has had consequences in the present for those companies that assert rights to commercialise outer space (and its resources). At the time, though, 'outer space' was a jurisdiction held together within the poles of antipathy, one in which the conduct of Amero-Soviet enmity operated at the margins of what was lawful/unlawful, blurring the recognised boundaries between war and peace, between legitimate reconnaissance and covert espionage. And it was from the vantage point of the 'high ground' of space, that the rival powers could visualise the terrain of that rivalry as being, in essence, the entirety of the globe.

[230] An example of this legacy in the present is the joint assertion of various 'rights' by companies such as Space X in tandem with the United States. See Cait Storr, 'Space is the Only Way to Go: The Evolution of the Extractivist Imaginary of International Law' in Shane Chalmers and Sundhya Pahuja (eds.), *Routledge Handbook of International Law and the Humanities* (New York: Routledge, 2021) chapter 22.

8

Nuclearism

Globalising the Cold War

8.1 Introduction: Going Global

In our story so far, we have described both the Amero-Soviet project and those of its rivals as operating in an internationalist mode. These involved contestation over the terms under which a new multilateral order might be established to govern the world. At the same time, the Amero-Soviet project of world-making was acting as midwife to the production of new forms of knowledge of an incipiently 'global' nature. The nuclear threat was at the heart of these initiatives. These emergent ways of knowing were shaping a new set of agendas that transcended the ideological divide and displaced local, national or regional divisions. They brought into play the languages of humanity, civilisation, one world, one planet and the commensurate labels for their end: Annihilation, Armageddon, and Mass Destruction. And as much as many States in the South sought to immunise themselves from the overdetermining effects of the Amero-Soviet Cold War – dis-aligning themselves, being neutralist, prefiguring other worlds, asserting rival internationalisms and international laws – the one feature of the Cold War they were never in a position to ignore was the rival hegemons' capacity to destroy all life on the planet. This effect was continuous with the Eurocentric tendency to claim for Europe an ability to speak for the 'world', for its interests to be everyone's interests and to assert its values as universal. But this time, the world-making effect of the Amero-Soviet Cold War was authorised by a quasi-legal monopoly on the ability to end the world.

We can understand this condition as the atomic, or nuclear, dimension of the Amero-Soviet Cold War. The Cuban Missile Crisis provides a window into that dimension and the imagined place of international law and institutions within it. We take up the story on 22 October 1962, the day that US President John F. Kennedy made a disquieting announcement to the American people broadcast on both television and radio.[1] He informed them that through its surveillance activities, the government had received 'unmistakable evidence' that a 'series of offensive missile sites [was] now in preparation' on the 'imprisoned' island of Cuba. 'The purpose of these bases', he continued, '[could] be none other than to provide a nuclear strike capability against the Western Hemisphere'.[2] Several of the sites contained 'medium range ballistic missiles capable of ... striking Washington DC, the Panama Canal, Cape Canaveral, Mexico City, or any other city in the southeastern part of the United States, in Central America, or in the Caribbean area'. Other sites, not yet complete, appeared to be designed for intermediate range ballistic missiles capable of travelling 'more than twice as far'. President Kennedy told his people that the 'urgent transformation of Cuba into an important strategic base – by the presence of these large, long range, and clearly offensive weapons of sudden mass destruction – constitutes an explicit threat to the peace and security of all the Americas'. 'We no longer live in a world', he went on, 'where only the actual firing of weapons represents a sufficient challenge to a nation's security to constitute maximum peril. Nuclear weapons are so destructive, and ballistic missiles are so swift, that any substantially increased possibility of their use or any sudden change in their deployment may well be regarded as a definite threat to peace.' 'Any nuclear missile launched from Cuba against any nation in the Western Hemisphere', he warned, would be regarded as an 'attack by the Soviet Union on the United States, requiring a full retaliatory response upon the Soviet Union'. He promised, therefore, to raise the matter before both the UN Security Council and the Organisation of American States (OAS).

The Security Council met the next day. Adlai Stevenson pressed the US case and accused the Soviet Union of creating 'a new and dangerous situation ... which imperil[led] the security of all mankind'[3] by introducing weapons into Cuba which were intrinsically 'offensive'.[4] He called upon the Security Council to condemn the Soviet initiative. Given the Soviet veto, anyone could have predicted that the call was destined to fail. And so Stevenson turned to the Organisation of American States to seek

[1] See 'Radio and Television Report to the American People on Soviet Arms Buildup in Cuba', 22 October 22 1962, JFK Library, www.jfklibrary.org/archives/other-resources/john-f-kennedy-speeches/cuba-radio-and-television-report-19621022.

[2] Ibid., para 1.

[3] UN SCOR, 17th sess, 1022nd mtg (23 October 1962) UN Doc. S/PV.1022, para 60

[4] Ibid., para 71.

authorisation for the US response.[5] On the same day as the Security Council meeting, the OAS Assembly[6] adopted a resolution calling for the withdrawal from Cuba of all missiles and other weapons with 'any offensive capability' and recommended the adoption of coercive or forcible measures to ensure that Cuba could not 'continue to receive from the Sino-Soviet Powers military materials and related supplies' including, in particular missiles with offensive capability.[7] Pursuant to the OAS resolution, the US declared its intention to institute, with the help of other regional powers, a 'quarantine' of Cuba (effectively a peacetime naval blockade) aimed at preventing the shipment of any further military material.[8] In that moment, the Soviets and the US came extraordinarily close to a nuclear exchange. But a public agreement was finally reached, brokered by the UN Secretary General, U. Thant.[9] The Soviets agreed to dismantle the weapons in exchange for an American assurance that it would not invade Cuba. A separate, secret, agreement was also reached between the US and the USSR in which the US agreed to dismantle its inter-continental ballistic missiles in Turkey.[10]

This episode provides a telling instance of the way the Amero-Soviet Cold War was juridically patterned and how nuclear weapons were woven into it. In the first place, Kennedy's speech, addressed first to Americans, but secondarily also to the world, was made against the juridified geo-political backdrop that the Cold War rivals imagined for themselves and projected outwards. This 'backdrop' entailed a formalised hegemony over their respective spheres of interest. On the Soviet side was the Warsaw Pact, in the Americas was the Rio Treaty of 1947. These arrangements, as we have already seen, recalled the old imperial spheres

5 See 'Minutes of the 506th Meeting of the National Security Council', Washington, DC, 21 October 21 1962, 2:30–4:50 p.m., https://history.state.gov/historicaldocuments/frus1961-63v11/d38.

6 See 'Rusk Speech and the Resolution Adopted by OAS' *New York Times*, 24 October 1962, www.nytimes.com/1962/10/24/archives/rusk-speech-and-the-resolution-adopted-by-oas.html; see also reflections by César Gaviria Trujillo, Secretary General of the OAS' OAS/UNESCO Symposium on Security for Peace', April 3, 1995, www.oas.org/en/media_center/speech.asp?sCodigo=02-0397.

7 Text in UN SCOR, 17th sess, 1022nd mtg (23 October 1962) UN Doc. S/PV.1022, para 81.

8 Jonathan Colman, 'Towards "World Support" and "The Ultimate Judgment of History": The American Legal Case for the Blockade of Cuba during the Missile Crisis, October–November 1962' *Journal of Cold War Studies*, 21 (2019) 150–73.

9 Walter Dorn and Robert Pauk, 'Unsung Mediator: U Thant and the Cuban Missile Crisis' *Diplomatic History*, 33 (2009) 261–92.

10 Martin Sixmith, *The War of Nerves* (London: Profile Books, 2021) 302–5.

of influence (most prominently the Monroe Doctrine) of the nineteenth century[11] and were given partial endorsement in both Chapter VIII of the UN Charter and in the provision for collective self-defence (article 51).[12]

By the time of the Cuban missile crisis in 1962, the US had already used the framework of the OAS to promote its anti-communist agenda in Guatemala (1954) and in the Dominican Republic (1965). Indeed, in January 1962 – some nine months prior to the 'crisis' – the US had persuaded the OAS to expel the government of Cuba from participation in OAS organs and had imposed an arms embargo upon it, even though Cuba had challenged the conformity of the measure with article 53 of the UN Charter.[13] The US objection to the missiles being placed in Cuba in the name of preserving the 'security of the hemisphere' was thus authorised by an institution whose existence had increasingly come to reflect the geopolitical division of the globe into regions coloured by particular ideological commitments and on the basis of a highly contested reading of the UN Charter.

In the second place, both Kennedy and Adlai Stevenson were forced to go to some lengths to explain the objectionable nature of the Soviet initiative. The United States had already installed ballistic missiles with nuclear warheads directed towards the Soviet Union at its bases in Germany, Italy and Turkey (not to mention elsewhere in Western Europe). So any objection towards the Soviet Union doing the same in Cuba had to emphasise the specificities of the Soviets' conduct. Here much ado was made of the 'deceitful' and 'clandestine' character of the Soviet deployment, which, in the view of the United States, revealed a hostile or aggressive intent on the part of the Soviets and a desire to disrupt the existing 'strategic balance' of nuclear forces.[14] The Soviet

[11] Akehurst was to specifically liken regional arrangements to a juridical form of the 'old hegemonic spheres of influence'. Michael Akehurst, 'Enforcement Action by Regional Agencies, with Special Reference to the Organization of American States' *British Yearbook of International Law*, 42 (1967) 225.

[12] The latter, which drew explicitly for its inspiration upon the terms of the Inter-American Reciprocal Assistance and Solidarity (Act of Chapultepec), Mexico City, 6 March 1945, TIAS No 1543.

[13] See generally, Nigel D. White, 'Ending the US Embargo of Cuba: International Law in Dispute' *Journal of Latin American Studies*, 51(1) (2019) 176.

[14] In truth, there was not much 'balance' of nuclear forces at the time, and it is speculated that the Soviets were largely interested in attempting to create a balance where none existed. Quite what might constitute a 'balance' in the context of a cumulative arsenal of nuclear weaponry that was capable of destroying the world several times over is only to be guessed at.

Union had indeed sought to keep its deployment of missiles in Cuba a secret, so the argument certainly had some plausibility. But it was less clear whether secrecy or deception alone was enough to colour as 'aggressive' what might otherwise be seen as the legitimate 'provision of arms' to a friendly government.

In the end, Kennedy and Stevenson relied upon a simpler, and probably more persuasive, argument. They argued that it was the character of the weapons being deployed that disclosed the Soviet Union's 'aggressive' intent. If the Soviet Union had chosen to deploy defensive anti-aircraft missiles, as Khrushchev had apparently promised, no objection would have been forthcoming. It was the decision to install intercontinental ballistic missiles (ICBMs), capable of striking cities across the hemisphere, that revealed the Soviet Union's malign intent. In the eyes (or at least the arguments) of Kennedy and Stevenson, such weapons were intrinsically 'offensive'. In his speech to the Security Council, for example, Stevenson condemned any pretence that such missiles could be anything other than offensive in nature:

> I should like to know what the Soviet Union considers "offensive" weapons. In the Soviet lexicon, evidently, all weapons are purely defensive, even weapons that can strike from 1,000 to 2,000 miles away. Words can be stretched only so far without losing their meaning altogether.[15]

But the more the US stressed the intrinsically hostile character of the Soviet weapons, the more difficult it became to explain their own possession and deployment of the same weapons. In characteristic Cold War style, the Americans relied on a background principle of distinction in which their own acts were glossed as benign, while those of the Soviets were cast as aggressive. But this undercut the very reciprocity upon which their account of international law itself seemed to depend. What was needed in order to explain away the idea of reciprocity at the heart of a system of sovereign equals was thus an act of faith amongst its audience: faith that US weapons would never be used except in self-defence, faith that the US was committed to the principle of no-first-use, faith that it would, in any case, comport itself in accordance with the law of armed conflict in distinguishing between legitimate and illegitimate targets.

Finally, both Kennedy and Stevenson asserted that the threat was not simply a localised one directed at the United States but one that

[15] UN SCOR, 17th sess, 1022nd mtg (23 October 1962) UN Doc. S/PV.1022, para 71.

potentially had both regional and global repercussions. Stationing weapons of 'sudden mass destruction' constituted a threat not only to the United States, nor 'just' to the security of the hemisphere, but to 'world peace' itself. What had appeared on the horizon was not a localised conflict but 'worldwide nuclear war'. The collective, and global, nature of the challenge was picked up by Stevenson in his final words to the Security Council at that 1962 meeting:

> I regret that people here at the United Nations seem to believe that the cold war is a private struggle between two great super-Powers. It is not a private struggle; it is a world civil war – a contest between the pluralistic world and the monolithic world – a contest between the world of the Charter and the world of communist conformity. Every nation that is now independent and wants to remain independent is involved, whether they know it or not. Every nation is involved in this grim, costly, distasteful division of the world, no matter how remote, no matter how uninterested.[16]

Whilst appearing to seek to unite the world against the threat posed by the Soviet Union, Stevenson's speech authorised another division of the world. As he saw it, this nuclear threat divided international politics between those – like the US and the Soviet Union – who were necessarily invested in a bipolar Cold War and its division of the globe. On the other side were those he regarded as irresponsible (like the Non-Aligned movement), who cast the great division as an internecine and provincial affair, a 'private war'. For Stevenson, this non-aligned group were asserting an impossible independence from the global distribution of force currently at large in the world. His 'regret' chimes, then, with the Amero-Soviet response to 'neutralisms' more generally[17] and their suspicion of those who refused to take sides in what the US considered to be a total, and totalising, division. He exhorted members to remember that 'the hopes of mankind are concentrated in this room. The action we take may determine the future of civilization .... Let [this day] be remembered not as the day when the world came to the edge of nuclear war, but as the day when men resolved to let nothing thereafter stop them in their quest for peace.'[18]

In retrospect, the Cuban Missile Crisis draws out two important facets of the atomic dimension of the Amero-Soviet Cold War, or what might

[16] UN SCOR, 17th sess, 1022nd mtg (23 October 1962) UN Doc. S/PV.1022, para 42.

[17] See Chapter 4.

[18] UN SCOR, 17th sess, 1022nd mtg. (23 October 1962) UN Doc. S/PV.1022, paras 82, 84.

be called the totalising effect of nuclear weaponry. One concerns the spatial projection of the Cold War, the other its modality. In the first place, nuclear technology seemed to totalise the space of prospective warfare. For the Amero-Soviets, this made a neutral detachment impossible since neither warfare, nor the effects of warfare, could be limited to the antagonists themselves. Both the US and the USSR pursued policies that expanded the prospective domain of warfare through the medium of nuclear submarines, through their installation of overseas missile bases and through efforts to partition the globe between them by way of regional military alliances. Even their desire to slow down, if not prevent, nuclear weapons being installed in outer space or in Antarctica reflected the same global imaginary, the same strategic theorisation of the prospectively unlimited nature of the nuclear battlespace.

Secondly, the nuclear missile as a modality of warfare seemed to swamp the means of war itself. It generated an imaginary that radically extended an idea of total war that had been emerging since the First World War. It blurred, and perhaps extinguished, the legal distinctions between combatant and civilian, between legitimate and illegitimate targets. Kennedy's warnings that a number of important US cities had been brought within the range of Cuban missiles made clear that the threat they posed was a threat to the civilian population in urban centres as much as (or indeed more than) to any armed forces located in their silos and bunkers. Whatever the legal and moral qualms about total warfare, the stark reality of nuclear weaponry was that it was uniquely designed and developed with that in mind: why else might one need a bomb with a 100-megaton capacity?

These two themes – the totalising methods of nuclear warfare and the totalisation of the space of nuclear warfare – produced a new global imaginary, a new way of thinking about the world as a unitary thing, a singular entity, a 'globe' or 'planet'.[19] It emerged first in theoretical terms and then in more material ways, coinciding with the production of images of the globe from space.[20] These ways of thinking, these imaginaries, were a hinge-point between past and future. They took up,

[19] See Joseph Masco, 'The Age of Fallout' *History of the Present: A Journal of Critical History*, 5 (2015) 137–68.

[20] 'EarthRise, December 24, 1968' and 'The Blue Marble' (NASA Photo AS17-22727) were released on 7 December 1972. See generally, Dennis Cosgrove, *Apollo's Eye: A Cartographic Genealogy of the Earth in the Western Imagination* (Baltimore: John Hopkins Press, 2001) 254–67.

continued and reshaped nineteenth-century imaginaries of 'humanity' and 'civilisation' and prefigured the forms of knowledge, processes of communication and material practices that would later come to mark the phenomenon of 'globalisation' in the 1990s. They were authorised by their ability to destroy. These forms were not only the offspring of the atom but progeny of the globalising tendencies of the nuclear threat and the associated efforts to control the possibility of a war of annihilation: the Armageddon, or end of worlds.

8.2 Total Warfare and the Legality of 'the Bomb'

Bernard Brodie, one of the most influential early American strategists of the nuclear age,[21] was to develop his theory of deterrence[22] based upon an arresting assertion. 'It is now physically possible', he said, 'for air forces no greater than those existing in the recent war to wipe out all the cities of a great nation in a single day'.[23] This is a striking image. But what we should notice, here, is not his claim concerning the destructive capabilities of atomic weaponry but the immediate, almost natural, association between 'the present bomb', as he put it, and the destruction of cities. This was neither an accidental association nor one he adduced simply for purposes of illustrating the kind of threat that would be posed to the United States if the USSR developed the same technology. The destruction of cities constituted the very rationale of 'the bomb'.

For Robert Oppenheimer, the architect of the bomb, this was more than obvious. As he was to put it, 'the pattern of the use of atomic weapons was set at Hiroshima'; 'aggression', 'surprise' and 'terror' were all 'as intrinsic' to atomic bombs 'as are the fissionable nuclei'.[24] In their very nature, atomic bombs were destined to be used to destroy cities, to deplete the morale of the civilian population and to spread terror and

[21] E.g. Barry H. Steiner, *Bernard Brodie and the Foundations of American Nuclear Strategy* (Lawrence: University Press of Kansas, 1991).

[22] Bernard Brodie, 'War in the Atomic Age, in Bernard Brodie (ed.), *The Absolute Weapon: Atomic Power and World Order* (Boston: Harcourt, 1946) 14.

[23] Ibid., 17. Interestingly, the book consulted was apparently the personal copy of President Eisenhower containing marginal inscriptions that may well have been his. The marginal inscription written alongside this particular sentence was: '?'.

[24] Oppenheimer, 'Atomic Weapons and the Crisis in Science' *Saturday Review of Literature*, 24 November 1945, 10.

fear.[25] Brodie developed his theory of retaliation (later framed within the language of 'deterrence') because he saw it as the necessary response to the inherently aggressive and indiscriminate character of nuclear weapons. But the impelling idea was that the threat posed by the development of nuclear weaponry was inseparable from the logic of a totalising inter-national warfare. This was not war imagined as taking place between combatants in the field of battle but one between nations engaged in a form of industrial, mechanised warfare entailing mass participation and in which the civilian population were the objects of legitimate violence as much as the infantry in the field. Much of the writing and thinking around Nagasaki and Hiroshima has this cast and was memorably captured by Robert Oppenheimer when he famously invoked the *Bhagavad Gita* around the time of the Trinity Test.

> We knew the world would not be the same. A few people laughed, a few people cried. Most people were silent. I remembered the line from the Hindu scripture, the *Bhagavad Gita* 'Now I am become Death, the destroyer of worlds.' I suppose we all thought that, one way or another.[26]

Total warfare was of course not an idea that began life with the Manhattan Project. It had its roots in the early twentieth century in the innovations of both aerial and naval warfare. The early (European) theorists of 'total warfare' – Douhet,[27] Daudet,[28] Ludendorff,[29] Jünger,[30] Liddell Hart[31] and Spaight[32] – had all observed a general shift in military strategy in the early twentieth century from a limited concern with the defeat of enemy forces on the field of battle to war aims that increasingly envisaged both the economy and the general population to be legitimate objects of coercive violence. For them, the logic was clear

[25] This was echoed by Truman who declared that it was wrong to think of the atomic bomb as 'a military weapon. It is used to wipe out women, children and unarmed people, and not for military use.' Lawrence Freedman, *The Evolution of Nuclear Strategy*, 2nd ed. (New York: St Martin's Press, 1989) 52.

[26] Robert Jungk, *Brighter Than a Thousand Suns: A Personal History of the Atomic Scientists* (Boston: Harcourt, 1958) 201.

[27] Giulio Douhet, *The Command of the Air*, trans Dino Ferrari (New York: Coward Mc-Cann, 1942; first published 1921) 5–9.

[28] Léon Daudet, *La guerre totale* (Paris: Nouvelle Librairie Nationale, 1918).

[29] Erich Ludendorff, *Der totale Krieg* (Steigra: Ludendorffs Verlag, 1935).

[30] Ernst Jünger, 'Total Mobilization' in Richard Wolin (ed.), *The Heidegger Controversy: A Critical Reader* (Cambridge, MA: MIT Press, 1991) 119–39.

[31] B. H. Liddell Hart, *Revolution in Warfare* (New Haven: Yale University Press, 1947).

[32] James Molony Spaight, *Air Power and War Rights* (London: Longman Green & Co., 1924).

enough. The more that warfare depended upon the industrial production of mechanised weaponry and the mass-mobilisation of the adult population, the more a country's potential for making war depended on directing the entirety of a nation's resources (people and supplies of raw material) to that end. This, in turn, legitimated targeting those 'resources' as part of a comprehensive military strategy.

In the context of total warfare, the distinctions that had come to shape the Hague Conventions of 1899 and 1907 largely evaporated: between combatant and non-combatant, between defended and undefended sites, between legitimate and illegitimate targets. In this logic, efforts to sap the morale of the enemy, to terrorise the population or convince them of the futility of their cause were equally rational, and equally legitimate, methods of warfare. As Spaight was to describe it in a passage typical of the literature:

> The huge army of passive defence, mainly civilian, must also be regarded as quasi-combatant. It is obviously illogical to drop incendiary bombs on your enemy's military objectives and then to spare the fire-brigade which tries to extinguish the conflagration or the demolition squad which tries to prevent it from spreading. The present war has witnessed an unprecedented increase in the number of civilian 'warriors' – those who make war material, those who transport it, and those who are otherwise engaged in services ancillary to active offence or defence. Modern war consumes enormous quantities of munitions and supplies of all kinds, and these have to be made in, and therefore conveyed from, places where the necessary labour is available. Mass-production of material cannot be organised without the concentration of the human agents of it in the large industrial centres. That is the sombre fact which has served to rob the great cities of a belligerent country of the virtual immunity which once they could claim. They have become an integrated part of the whole war-machine. They are part of the war. They do not stand aside from it.[33]

This was the logic that underpinned the widespread use of aerial bombardment on all sides throughout the Second World War, and which also led to the choice of two undefended cities in Japan as the appropriate locations on which to unleash the new 'weapon of mass destruction', the atomic bomb.[34] As Georg Schwarzenberger wrote in 1958, the organising distinction of the laws of war had been 'systematically set aside' during

[33] J. M. Spaight, 'Legitimate Objectives in Air Warfare' *British Yearbook of International Law*, 21 (1944) 162.

[34] Cf. Truman's famous utilitarian justification for dropping the atomic bombs on Hiroshima and Nagasaki.

the Second World War, and there was no reason to imagine it would be revived with the advent of nuclear weapons.[35]

In the immediate aftermath of the Second World War, the allied powers had relied upon the existing body of the laws of war as a standard of judgement against which the German high command were called to account. But few were blind to the obvious limitations of these laws given the general conduct of the belligerents. In the short term, calls for a revision of the laws of war led to a Conference convened by the ICRC and adoption of the four Geneva Conventions of 1949. These conventions sought to provide more detailed protection for those '*hors de combat*' and, in particular, rules for the treatment of civilians in case of belligerent occupation. But the conventions left open an equally important range of issues – particularly related to the modalities of both air and sea warfare – which commentators identified as needing further consideration. So almost immediately after the adoption of the Geneva Conventions themselves, a new chorus emerged for the further revision of the laws of war, led by jurists such as Kunz,[36] Schwarzenberger[37] and Lauterpacht,[38] which impelled the ICRC to convene a series of largely fruitless diplomatic consultations in the late 1950s concerning the limitations on indiscriminate warfare affecting civilians.[39]

These jurists identified two particular features of the Second World War as problematic.[40] The first related to the practice of unrestricted submarine warfare. This had already been the subject of extensive debate both during and after the first World War and was to become the central issue in the trial of Admirals Doenitz and Reader at Nuremberg.[41]

35 Sven Lindqvist, *A History of Bombing* (London: Granta Books, 2002).

36 J. Kunz, 'The Chaotic Status of the Laws of War and the Urgent Necessity for Their Revision' *American Journal of International Law*, 45 (1951) 37–61.

37 See Georg Schwarzenberger, 'From the Laws of War to the Law of Armed Conflict' *Current Legal Problems*, 21(1) (1968) 239–58; Georg Schwarzenberger, *The Legality of Nuclear Weapons* (London: Stevens & Sons, 1958).

38 See, e.g., Hersch Lauterpacht, 'The Problem of the Revision of the Law of War' *British Year Book of International Law*, 29 (1952) 360–82.

39 See Giovanni Mantilla, *International Humanitarian Law and International Armed Conflict* (Ithaca: Cornell University Press, 2020), 108–12

40 Baxter was sceptical of the possibility of legal control: Richard R. Baxter, 'The Role of Law in Modern War' *Proceedings of the American Society of International Law at Its Annual Meeting (1921–1969)*, 47 (1953) 94. 'The problems of submarine warfare, of aerial bombardment, of atomic weapons, and of guided missiles seem to be capable of no solution.'

41 Carl Schmitt, *The Nomos of the Earth in the International Law of Jus Publicum Europaeum*, trans G. L. Ulmen (New York: Telos Press, 2003 [1950]) 316.

Although the tribunal found both men guilty of war crimes for targeting neutral merchant vessels, and for giving orders not to rescue survivors from ships attacked by submarine,[42] it decided to set aside those elements of the indictment for the purposes of sentencing on the grounds that both the British and the US had engaged in similar practices in the Skagerrak and the Pacific, respectively. Despite the apparently unequivocal terms of the London Protocol of 1936, both axis powers and allies alike had been seduced by the military advantages of waging a largely unrestrained war against both military and commercial vessels on the high seas. Such strategies offered an ability to target the increasingly interwoven military and economic capacity of the enemy.

The second feature of the Second World War that concerned this group of jurists was aerial warfare and the apparent drift towards 'strategic' bombardment of civilian cities, or what was sometimes called 'target-area bombing'.[43] This tactic ultimately led not just to the fire-bombing of Tokyo but to the dropping of two atomic bombs on Hiroshima and Nagasaki. For many theorists of aerial warfare, the technology of flight had wrought a profound change in the methods and modalities of warfare for two different reasons. On the one hand, unlike warfare at sea or on land, aerial warfare was spatially unrestrained. Whilst the technology itself had its limits (the distance that war planes could fly without re-fueling for instance), it was otherwise unhampered by the geophysical constraints of land and sea. On the other hand, as Carl Schmitt observed, aerial warfare neither conformed to the logics of land warfare (namely, the miliary occupation of enemy territory) nor that of sea warfare (to blockade or interrupt commerce). Whilst it could operate as an auxiliary aid to both of those activities, its independent rationale lay in the purest acts of destruction – in the bombing of both military and civilian targets. As Schmitt put it:

> With air bombardment, the lack of any relation between military personnel in the air and the earth below, as well as with inhabitants thereon is absolute. Independent air war allows neither the one nor the other side a possibility to establish a relation. The airplane flies over and drops its bombs; low-flying pilots dive down and then fly up and away; both

[42] Order No. 154, 1939. This was supplemented by the 'Laconia order' of 1942.

[43] See Stephen Walker, '"You Don't Brag about Wiping out 60–70,000 People": The Men Who Dropped the Atomic Bombs on Hiroshima and Nagasaki' *The Guardian*, 22 June 2025, www.theguardian.com/world/2025/jun/22/atomic-bomb-hiroshima-nagasaki-author-stephen-walker.

> execute their destructive function, then immediately leave the scene, with all that has befallen men and materials on the ground, whose fate is in the hands of the sovereign of the surface state.[44]

Commentators were quick to point out that it was the Axis powers who had initially abandoned any pretense of differentiating between the aerial bombardment of military targets and the civilian population. But they did not suggest that allied strategic bombing consisted merely in acts of reprisal.[45] Spaight, for instance, had long championed the strategic importance of air power and for him it was the material constraints of air warfare that should determine the limits of any strategy. In the new industrialised warfare, not only was it logical to take the war to the cities, as '*places d'armes*', but it was also logical to engage in cascade bombing: 'the whole area containing the known objective has to be devastated, for it is usually studded with anti-aircraft guns, searchlights and locators, and putting them all out of action calls for a mighty bomb-splash'.[46] The use of 'huge bombs against urban centres of war production *is* militarily profitable. Of that there [is now] no . . . doubt'.[47] Spaight was joined by Lauterpacht,[48] Schwarzenberger[49] and Kunz,[50] each of whom came to the conclusion that the wartime practice of strategic bombing could be justified on either of two grounds. First, because the idea of what was, or was not, a 'military objective' had radically expanded in the context of total warfare and, second, because anti-aircraft installations were so

44 Schmitt, *The Nomos of the Earth*, 320.

45 See Lauterpacht, 'The Problem of the Revision of the Law of War'.

46 Spaight, 'Legitimate Objectives in Air Warfare', 163.

47 Ibid. It is curious to note, however, that Spaight nevertheless opposed the use of atomic weaponry in his 1947 book on *Air Power and War Rights*, where he argued that such weapons were essentially indiscriminate in a way that area bombing was not. He also made the point – in response to the argument that Hiroshoma and Nagasaki had shortened the war (and saved at least a million American lives according to Henry Stimson) – that not all war-shortening tactics were lawful: J. M. Spaight, *Air Power and War Rights* (London: Longmans, 1924) chapter 2. Around the same time, US and British officials were making the opposite argument at the ICRC debates about the Geneva Conventions. Civilian populations were to be protected from indiscriminate attack but there was powerful resistance among the Anglo-Americans to making nuclear weapons unlawful. Geoffrey Best, *War and Law since 1945* (Oxford: Oxford University Press, 1994) 111.

48 Lauterpacht, 'The Problem of the Revision of the Law of War'.

49 Georg Schwarzenberger, 'The Law of Air Warfare and the Trend Towards Total War' *American University Law Review*, 8 (1959) 1–18.

50 Josef Kunz, 'The Chaotic Status of the Laws of War and the Urgent Necessity for Their Revision' *American Journal of International Law*, 45 (1951) 37–61.

ubiquitous that there were few cities that could be declared to be 'undefended' according to the terms of articles 25 and 26 of the Hague Regulations.

These were the kinds of deliberations that framed discussions around the use of nuclear weapons. Whilst nuclear weapons wrought a quantum change in the scale of destruction available to military strategists in time of war, very few legal scholars were willing to develop an entirely new set of rules or frameworks of analysis. So instead of assimilating this shift, most legal scholars denied that nuclear weaponry was in any way 'exceptional' in relation to the available analytics of the laws of war.[51] And they continued to insist upon the possibility of legal control: that the deliberate targeting of civilian objectives, or the use of aerial bombardment (nuclear or otherwise) as a means by which the civilian population could be 'terrorised' were illegitimate.[52] But they did not – or could not – adjust the rules to accommodate the fact that nuclear weaponry largely made a nonsense of the distinctions on which they were based. If they had properly taken the material features of nuclear warfare into account, and measured them against the existing rules, the argument would logically have been an argument against war per se.[53]

Subsequent appraisals of the legality of nuclear weapons were superficially divided between those who regarded nuclear weapons as intrinsically illegal and those who sought to assess their legality by reference to the context in which they were deployed.[54] But the divide was not really material because neither side felt able to object to the continued possession of nuclear weapons by the existing nuclear powers. This was a kind of Gordion knot in which, given the context, the existence of nuclear weapons per se, produced weird logics of inevitability. In a sense, once they were created, nuclear weapons could not be un-invented, whether by physics or by international law. So, on the one hand, the Soviet leaders themselves advocated the view that nuclear weapons were or should be

[51] Gabrielle Hecht, *Being Nuclear: Africans and the Global Uranium Trade* (Cambridge, MA: MIT Press, 2012) 6.

[52] Hersch Lauterpacht, *Oppenheim's International Law*, 7th ed. (London: Longmans, Green & Co., 1952) 347–48; Robert W. Tucker, 'Rules Governing Weapons and Naval Warfare' *International Law Studies*, 50 (1957) 50–55; Myers S. McDougal and Florentino P. Feliciano, 'International Coercion and World Public Order: The General Principles of the Law of War' *Yale Law Journal*, 67 (1958) 831.

[53] This, as we shall see, was the essence of the Einstein–Russell Manifesto.

[54] See generally, Elliott Meyrowitz, 'The Opinions of Scholars on the Legal Status of Nuclear Weapons' *Stanford Journal of International Law*, 24 (1987–88) 111–77.

made illegal;[55] but they also asserted that their exceptional use by way of reprisal (in response, for example, to a nuclear attack directed against a civilian target) might be excusable.[56] It seemed only a fool would recommend that one's own side should be left undefended. According to this logic, the possession of nuclear weapons was both legal and legitimate insofar as they were necessary in order to deter aggression and maintain peace.[57] Meanwhile, the unanswerable question of whether nuclear warfare was more or less likely as a consequence of the growing number of available nuclear warheads hung like the sword of Damocles.

In contrast to the Soviet Union, the US government inclined to the view that nuclear weapons as mere instruments of destruction, were no different from any other and held out the possibility of their use in a suitably discriminating manner. In this latter environment, 'clean' nuclear weapons could be distinguished from the 'dirty' warheads of total warfare, 'tactical' weapons from 'strategic' weapons and so forth.

But at precisely the moment at which the Western lawyers were insisting that there was nothing per se indiscriminate about the use of such weaponry, nuclear strategists were moving in the opposite direction.[58] So while certain lawyers were arguing that the legality of nuclear weapons depended upon the specifics of their deployment, and their probable collateral effects upon the civilian population and the natural environment, the nuclear strategists were concluding that, in absence of a centralised agency capable of assuming control over the possession and use of atomic technology (such as proposed in the Baruch Plan submitted by the US to the UN in 1946) the only 'logical' response was to build up a system of deterrence to ward off the possibility of attack and to do so in a way that threatened 'massive retaliation'. What was envisaged in such a system, at least until the 1960s, was that if a State engaged in nuclear war, all its major cities would be targeted and destroyed in response ('countervalue targeting' as it was called).[59] It was this idea that seemed to

[55] See, e.g., Andrei Vyshinksky, Chair of the Soviet Delegation, speech at the UN General Assembly (Second Session, Plenary Meeting, 18 September 1947).

[56] Schwarzenberger, *The Legality of Nuclear Weapons*, 38–40; Nagendra Singh, *Nuclear Weapons and International Law* (London: Stevens & Sons, 1959), 222–23.

[57] Schwarzenberger, *The Legality of Nuclear Weapons*, 49–50

[58] Freedman comments that by the 1950s strategist believed that 'nuclear weapons, whatever their shape, size or ostensible purpose, could not be considered "just another weapon"'. He went on: 'But what sort of weapons these "tactical" nuclear weapons really were remained a mystery.' Freedman, *The Evolution of Nuclear Strategy*, 119.

[59] Freedman, *The Evolution of Nuclear Strategy*, 76–89.

underpin the Soviet initiatives in Cuba. And whilst the US later overtly abandoned its 'cities first' policy in the 1960s in favour of a more limited 'counterforce strategy', what ultimately emerged was the idea of 'mutually assured destruction',[60] the connotations of which were, at once, more equal, and proportionate but also more comprehensively annihilatory once the possibility of escalation was factored in.

It is tempting to see these two strands of argument as essentially antagonistic. On one side were the lawyers' arguments in favour of humanising warfare – insisting that nuclear weapons be used only for limited tactical purposes and be directed solely at military installations. On the other was a military strategy that insisted that the psychology of deterrence depended on a threat of massive (and necessarily 'inhumane') retaliation. This strategic argument appeared to push the lawyers to one side. Hans Morgenthau made this point in his critique of Robert McNamara's counterforce strategy. McNamara had declared that henceforth the US would focus on the 'destruction of the enemy's military forces, not of his civilian population'.[61] Morgenthau argued, however, that whilst a 'counter-city strategy, through the mechanics of mutual deterrence . . . expresses the inner logic of nuclear war' and minimises its possibility, a counter-force strategy, by contrast, 'puts a premium upon preventive war and thus stimulates not the desire to prevent nuclear war but rather competition for starting one'.[62] So for Morgenthau, the restraints called upon by some international lawyers to insulate the civilian population from the effects of nuclear war had the perverse effect of making nuclear warfare more, not less, likely.

But even if one could argue the niceties, in the end the two strands of argumentation were mutually sustaining. The lawyers were keen to bring nuclear weapons within the existing rubric of the laws of war. To do this they had to argue that they were not 'in essence' indiscriminate (and therefore illegal). Unless they wanted to give nuclear weapons away to the field of non-law, they had to argue that there was always the possibility that these weapons were open to deployment in suitably low-yield forms or as 'clean' bombs, in a manner consistent with the injunctions not to

[60] See generally, Freedman, *The Evolution of Nuclear Strategy*, 127.
[61] Robert S. McNamara, 'No Cities Doctrine', Commencement Address at the University of Michigan, 16 June 1962.
[62] Hans Morgenthau, 'The Four Paradoxes of Nuclear Strategy' *American Political Science Association*, 58 (1964) 30.

target the civilian population or cause unnecessary suffering.[63] Their position then had to be that 'mere possession', as such, was thus perfectly legitimate. Questions of legality could be centred, instead, on whether their 'use', in practice, was consistent with the relevant norms concerned.[64] But if this was the starting point, it was clear that any strategy of defence would not be confined by those rules. Even if strikes should, in principle, be limited to military targets (assuming they could), such a policy would not survive an attack on population centres, and hence the option of an annihilatory response had to be made strategically available. And here, once again, the lawyers would join the strategists in insisting that the legal rules would legitimise retaliation in kind following an (unlimited) nuclear attack.[65] One way or another, thus, Amero-Soviet legal and strategic discourses on nuclear weaponry pointed in the same direction – proportional response, the necessity of possession as deterrence and the maintenance of a 'balance of fear' – in which there could be no denying the possibility of possessing such weapons or using them in 'an extreme circumstance of self-defence' as the International Court of Justice was later to put it.[66]

Nuclear terror, thus, was always a regulated affair in the Amero-Soviet legal imagination. At almost every turn, the possession and use of nuclear weapons was controlled, (sometimes) authorised and often made legible through law. This was the rubric under which the totalising effects of nuclear weaponry were discussed in governmental circles in Europe and North America. It was counterpoised, nevertheless, by a very different account that was to develop in peace movements in both North and South. In this account, the indiscriminate character of nuclear weaponry, the fantasy that operational distinctions could be made between targets and non-targets and the irremediable collateral effects they would have upon the rest of humanity – were a mobilising force in an advocacy that linked their necessary abolition to the very survival of the human species.

[63] See, e.g., Tucker, 'Rules Governing Weapons and Naval Warfare', 50–54.

[64] Ibid., 54.

[65] Myers S. McDougal and Norbet A. Schlei, 'The Hydrogen Bomb Tests in Perspective: Lawful Measures for Security' *Yale Law Journal*, 64 (1955) 648–710.

[66] *Legality of the Threat or Use of Nuclear Weapons (Advisory Opinion)* (1996) ICJ Rep 226, 263, para 97. Schwarzenberger imagines a post-atomic world in which the ICJ is asked to determine whether war crimes have been committed by either side. 'The survivors of such a holocaust', he says, 'would probably have had more urgent calls upon their time'. G Schwarzenberger, 'The Misery and Grandeur of International Law' *Current Legal Problems*, 17 (1964) 202.

8.3 Anti-Nuclearism, Anti-Colonialism and Universal Death

In the late 1940s, various international peace movements began to attend to the dangers of nuclear weaponry;[67] but what dramatically mobilised anti-nuclear sentiment around the world was the Bikini Atoll incident of 1954, in which a Japanese fishing vessel called the *Daigo Fukuryu Maru* (the Lucky Dragon), was caught up in the fallout from a US hydrogen bomb test. The bonito boat had lost its nets and altered course toward the Marshall Islands where it was exposed to fallout from the 'Castle Bravo' nuclear test. The fallout of course radically exceeded what the US military had designated to be the 'danger zone'. All crew members immediately fell ill from radiation sickness.[68] What became clear was not simply that nuclear testing was dangerous but that radioactive fallout would have ongoing, global effects contaminating the atmospheric and marine environments for all.[69] In the years that followed, a variety of national and transnational groups were formed around the globe that both opposed further nuclear testing and called for general nuclear disarmament.[70]

In the West, the public profile of the anti-nuclear cause was raised by the Russell–Einstein 'manifesto' issued in London in July 1955, in which the British philosopher Bertrand Russell and the physicist Albert Einstein sought to give expression to the global character of of nuclear weapons and the resulting need to embrace the general cause of peace.[71] For them,

[67] See, e.g., Stockholm Peace Appeal 1950 of the Permanent Committee of the Partisans of Peace, which demanded the 'outlawing of atomic weapons as instruments of intimidation and mass murder' and held that any government that 'first uses atomic weapons . . . will be committing a crime against humanity and should be dealt with as a war criminal'.

[68] See James Yamazaki, *Children of the Atomic* Bomb (Durham: Duke University Press, 1995); Keith Parsons and Robert Zaballa, *Bombing the Marshall Islands: A Cold War Tragedy* (Cambridge: Cambridge University Press, 2017); Walter Pincus, *Blown to Hell: America's Deadly Betrayal of the Marshall Islands* (New York: Diversion Books, 2021).

[69] Toshihiro Higuchi, *Political Fallout: Nuclear Weapons Testing and the Making of a Global Environmental Crisis* (Stanford: Stanford University Press, 2020). The film *Godzilla* was in part inspired by these events. See Parsons and Zaballa, *Bombing the Marshall Islands*, chapter 5.

[70] For an account of the movements in the North, see Lawrence Wittner, *Toward Nuclear Abolition: A History of the World Nuclear Disarmament Movement, 1971–Present* (Stanford: Stanford University Press, 2003).

[71] The signatories of the document included, in addition to Russell and Einstein, Max Born, Percy Bridgman, Leopold Infeld, Frederic Joliot-Curie, Herman Muller, Linus Pauling, Cicil Powell, Joseph Rotblat and Hideki Yukawa. On the ensuing Pugwash Conferences, see Alison Kraft and Carola Sachse (eds.), *Science, (Anti-Communism and Diplomacy: The Pugwash Conferences on Science and World Affairs in the Early Cold War* (Leiden: Brill, 2020).

the avoidance of nuclear conflagration depended, not upon abolition of nuclear weapons per se but upon the abolition of war; and the abolition of war, in turn, depended upon rejecting a politics of difference embedded in the quarrel between 'Communism and anti-Communism'.

> There lies before us, if we choose, continual progress in happiness, knowledge, and wisdom. Shall we, instead, choose death, because we cannot forget our quarrels? We appeal, as human beings, to human beings: Remember your humanity, and forget the rest. If you can do so, the way lies open to a new Paradise; if you cannot, there lies before you the risk of universal death.[72]

The Russell–Einstein manifesto was animated by a commitment to a scientific, and politically neutral, concept of humanity as species beyond 'nation, continent, or creed' or, indeed, ideology. Elsewhere, however, anti-nuclearism found expression in the conjunction of a global peace agenda with anti-colonial and anti-racist activism. Beginning in the late 1940s, the black internationalist movement in the US and elsewhere had forged links not only between the struggles for racial justice and equality in the US and anti-colonial resistance elsewhere[73] but had begun to highlight the centrality of anti-nuclearism in the cause of global peace.[74] A similar idea was expressed at Bandung in 1955, where the Conference drew attention to the 'dangerous situation of international tension existing and the risks confronting the whole human race from the outbreak of global war in which the destructive power of all types of armaments, including nuclear and thermo-nuclear weapons, would be involved'. Accordingly, the conference recommended the 'prohibition of the production, experimentation and use of nuclear and thermo-nuclear

[72] Bertrand Russell and Albert Einstein, 'The Russell–Einstein Manifesto' *Impact of Science on Society*, 26 (1976) 15.

[73] See generally, Penny Von Eschen, *Race Against Empire: Black Americans and Anti-Colonialism 1937–1957* (Ithaca: Cornell University Press, 1997); Kevin Gaines, *African Americans in Ghana: Black Expatriates and the Civil Rights Era* (Durham: University of North Carolina Press, 2006).

[74] At the Fifth Pan African Congress in 1945, the delegates issued a final resolution that began with the words: 'The Delegates of the Fifth Pan African Congress believe in peace. How could they do otherwise when for centuries they have been victims of violence and slavery?' 'Selections from Declarations and Resolutions Adopted by the Fifth Pan-African Congress: Manchester, England, October 13–21, 1945' *Black Camera*, 13 (2021) 343. See generally, Jean Allman, 'Nuclear Imperialism and the Pan-African Struggle for Peace and Freedom: Ghana, 1959–1962' in Manning Marable and Vanessa Agard-Jones (eds.) *Transnational Blackness: Navigating the Global Color Line* (London: Palgrave Macmillan 2008) 333–54.

weapons . . . to save mankind and civilisation from the fear and prospect of wholescale destruction'.[75]

The link between anti-colonialism and anti-nuclearism was given more concrete impetus shortly after Bandung when France planned to initiate a series of nuclear tests in Algeria at the height of the war of independence. The First Conference of Independent African States in Accra, Ghana, in 1958, issued a significant sequence of pledges. They were:

> to recognise the right of the African peoples to independence and self-determination and to take appropriate steps to hasten the realization of this right; to affirm the right of the Algerian people to independence and self-determination and to exert all possible effort to hasten the realisation of their independence; to uproot forever the evil of racial discrimination in all its forms wherever it may be found; to persuade the Great Powers to discontinue the production and testing of nuclear and thermo-nuclear weapons; and to reduce conventional weapons.[76]

These were obviously not disconnected themes. For the nuclear powers, sparsely populated sites in Asia and Africa had become the privileged locale not only for sourcing uranium (such as the famous Shinkolobwe mine in the Congo) but also for nuclear testing (the Marshall Islands, French Polynesia, Kiribati, South Australia, etc.).[77] The implications rightly drawn by Asians and Africans were not only that the lives of those living near the testing sites were dispensable[78] but that a form of nuclear warfare itself was already being conducted in 'sacrificial sites' in the colonial or neo-colonial worlds. As Jacobs put it, 'for people living

[75] 'Final Communiqué of the Asian–African Conference', Asian–African Conference, Bandung, 24 April 1955, F.2.

[76] 'Conference of Independent African States, Declaration and Resolution IX: Accra, Ghana, April, 1958' *Black Camera*, 13 (2021) 9. It went on, in Resolution No. XII to call upon the 'Great Powers to discontinue the production of nuclear and thermos-nuclear weapons and suspend all tests not only in the interest of world peace but as a symbol of their avowed devotion to the rights of man' and strongly condemned 'all atomic tests in any part of the world and in particular the intention to carry out such tests in the Sahara'.

[77] The UK conducted tests in Emu Field, Maralinga and Motebello Islands, the US at Bikini Atoll and Enewetak Atoll and the French in Algeria, Moruroa and Fangataufa.

[78] A 'paradigmatic example of nuclear colonialism'. Alexis Vrignon, 'Pacifism and Anti-nuclear Protest in Polynesia at the End of the Cold War' in Luc-André Brunet and Eirini Karamouzi (eds.), *Beyond the Euromissile Crisis: Global Histories of Anti-Nuclear Activism in the Cold War* (New York: Berghahn Books, 2025) 199–216.

near atmospheric nuclear testing sites ... this was not an imaginary war – it was a limited nuclear war'.[79]

In the South, the practice of nuclear testing manifested itself as a potent symbol in the anti-colonial struggle.[80] In 1960 at the Positive Action Conference for Peace and Security in Africa in Accra, a Manifesto drafted by the International Sahara Protest Team was approved. It declared that:

> The action of France in developing its main base for nuclear and missile warfare in the Sahara, at the very time when colonialism and imperialism are being liquidated by the struggles of Africans for liberation, is an affront to the peoples of this entire Continent. It represents an effort by an overwhelming display of power to establish a nuclear imperialism which will be a constant massive threat to African unity and independence, as well as a constant menace to all Africa's peoples who will be the chief victims in any major war in which France may become involved.[81]

It called for non-violent positive action to mobilise a global campaign against the 'new barbarism of nuclear war' that threatened to undermine the anti-colonial programme. As Nkrumah put it, 'we in Africa wish to live and develop. We are not freeing ourselves from centuries of imperialism and colonialism only to be maimed and destroyed by nuclear weapons. We do not threaten anyone and we renounce the foul weapons that threaten the very existence of life on this planet.'[82] Even the idea of the possession of such weapons for purposes of 'defence' had to be renounced. Possession on such a basis meant in his view, 'no more than the ability to share in the honour of destroying mankind'.[83]

The theme of 'nuclear imperialism' also found its way, albeit in a more muted form, into the work of the non-aligned movement. At the 1961 Belgrade meeting of Non-Aligned Heads of State, the themes of world peace, decolonisation and general disarmament were brought together. Lasting peace, it was held, could only be ensured in a world

[79] Robert A. Jacobs, *Nuclear Bodies: The Global Hibakusha* (New Haven: Yale University Press, 2022) 14

[80] See generally, Vincent J. Intondi, *African Americans Against the Bomb: Nuclear Weapons, Colonialism, and the Black Freeodm Movement* (Stanford: Stanford University Press, 2015).

[81] 'Positive Action Conference for Peace and Security in Africa' (Accra, 7–10 April 1960), 'Appendix I: Resolutions and Manifesto', 18.

[82] 'Positive Action Conference for Peace and Security in Africa' (Accra, 7–10 April 1960), 'Speech by the Prime Minister of Ghana, Dr The Right Honourable Kwame Nkrumah', 5.

[83] Ibid.

in which 'the domination of colonialism-imperialism and neo-colonialism in all their manifestations is radically eliminated'[84] and in which the Great Powers commit themselves to general and complete disarmament. In case of the latter, it was declared that 'an agreement on the prohibition of all nuclear and thermonuclear tests should urgently be concluded' and that, in the meantime, a moratorium on the testing of all nuclear weapons should be observed by all countries.[85]

Later that year, the same group of States took the matter to the UN General Assembly. With the assistance of Soviet bloc, and by a vote of 55-20-26, they managed to force through a Declaration on the Prohibition of the use of Nuclear and Thermonuclear Weapons.[86] In that resolution, the General Assembly declared that the 'use of nuclear and thermo-nuclear weapons is contrary to the spirit, letter and aims of the United Nations and, as such, a direct violation of the Charter of the United Nations' and that their use 'is a war directed not against an enemy or enemies alone but also against mankind in general, since the peoples of the world not involved in such a war will be subject to the evils generated by the use of such weapons'. This 'ban the bomb' resolution,[87] as it was called, kept alive the globalist anti-nuclear agenda, but in the process its linkage to the theme of anti-colonial resistance began to fade away. What remained was a conception of a world knitted together through the perceived threat of its destruction, or at least of its irradiation, but a world also vainly struggling to persuade the nuclear powers to renounce their treasured armaments.

The limitations of the anti-nuclear agenda, more generally, were to be found in those sites in which it came to have greatest visibility. In the aftermath of the adoption of the Antarctic Treaty of 1959,[88] a series of agreements were concluded that sought to establish 'denuclearised zones', in which the manufacture, stationing, testing, possession or use of nuclear weapons (including, in some cases, the disposal of radioactive material) was prohibited. These included the Outer Space Treaty of

[84] 'Belgrade Declaration of Non-Aligned Countries, 1961', First Summit Conference of Heads of State or Government of the Non-Aligned Movement, Belgrade, Yugoslavia, 6 September 1961.

[85] Ibid., para 19.

[86] UNGA Res 1653 (XVI) (24 November 1961).

[87] Followed by UNGA Res 2936 (XXVII) (29 November 1972); UNGA Res 33/71B (14 December 1978); UNGA Res 34/83 (11 December 1979); UNGA Res 36/92I (9 December 1981); and UNGA Res 44/117C (15 December 1989).

[88] The Antarctic Treaty, Washington, DC, 1 December 1959, 402 UNTS 71.

1967,[89] the Treaty of Tlatelolco of 1967,[90] the Seabed Treaty of 1971,[91] the Moon Agreement of 1979[92] and the Treaty of Rarotonga of 1985.[93]

In all cases, these agreements were premised on the belief that whilst they were 'not an end in themselves' as the preface to the Treaty of Tlatelolco put it, they would nevertheless contribute to a general process of nuclear disarmament, 'reversing' the arms race and strengthening the conditions of world peace. Despite their declared purpose of immunising certain regions of the globe from the effects of nuclear warfare, it was clear enough that no such security could be ensured given the very global nature of the threat. No regional agreement could survive such a conflagration.

So, from the very beginning the treaties seemed to be conditioned upon an internationalist politics of disarmament that worried less about the legality of the weapons themselves and more about their aggregate number and the prospect of their proliferation in the hands of greater numbers of ('untrustworthy') States. The logic of that position – as came to be expressed in the phrase 'an acceptable balance of mutual responsibilities and obligations of the nuclear and non-nuclear States'[94] – was that the more States that possessed such weapons, the less sturdy and predictable would become the politics of deterrence and the less meaningful the ongoing efforts to 'stabilise', 'balance' or reduce the number of weapons on either side of the Cold War divide. Its unspoken premise was that nuclear weapons could not be wished away and that a certain number would necessarily be retained by the existing nuclear States, who, by implication, simply had to be trusted with them. At the same time, new obligations would fall upon non-nuclear States who would be asked to renounce any desire to obtain them.

[89] Treaty on Principles Governing the Activities of States in the Exploration and Use of Outer Space, Including the Moon and Other Celestial Bodies, Washington, DC, Moscow and London, 27 January 1967, 610 UNTS 205.

[90] Treaty for the Prohibition of Nuclear Weapons in Latin America, Mexico City, 14 February 1967, 634 UNTS 281.

[91] Treaty on the Prohibition of the Emplacement of Nuclear Weapons and Other Weapons of Mass Destruction on the Sea-Bed and the Ocean Floor and in the Subsoil Thereof, Washington, DC, Moscow and London, 11 February 1971, 955 UNTS 115.

[92] Agreement governing the Activities of States on the Moon and Other Celestial Bodies, New York, 5 December 1979, 1363 UNTS 3.

[93] South Pacific Nuclear Free Zone Treaty, Rarotonga, 6 August 1985, 1445 UNTS 177.

[94] GA Resn. 2028(XX), 29 November 1965.

8.4 Displacing Anti-Nuclearism: Non-Proliferation

The anti-nuclear and disarmament agendas that had begun in the late 1940s at the General Assembly took on a different life in the hands of the Amero-Soviets where it translated into the language of 'non-proliferation'. Non-proliferation pushed anti-nuclearism off the table by universalising a discriminatory regime – that had initially found expression in early peace treaties with former axis powers - that differentiated between the putatively 'rightful' possession of (nuclear) weapons on the part of the some, whilst prohibiting other (non-nuclear) powers from acquiring the same. This form of juridical parsing in lieu of prohibition was institutionalised within the structures of the United Nations.

It was apparent right from the opening session of the General Assembly in 1946 that the question of atomic technology would be at the centre of its concerns as an organisation. In its very first resolution, it resolved to create a Commission to deal with 'the problems raised by the discovery of atomic energy', which included 'the control of atomic energy to the extent necessary to ensure its use only for peaceful purposes' and 'for the elimination from national armaments of atomic weapons'. Foreshadowing the prospective challenges that it might face, the Commission was tasked with developing proposals for 'effective safeguards by way of inspection, and other means to protect complying States against the hazards of violations and evasions'.[95] At its first meeting in June 1946, the UN Atomic Energy Commission was presented with a plan drawn up by Bernard Baruch based upon an adapted version of the earlier report written by Dean Acheson and David Lilienthal.[96] The essence of the recommendations was that the development and use of all atomic energy and its raw materials should be placed under the control of an International Atomic Development Authority and, controversially, that the power of the veto (of the permanent five) over decisions of that authority be removed.[97] In presenting his plan, Baruch emphasised the global nature of the challenge:

[95] UNGA Res 1 (I) (1 February 1946).

[96] See 'A Report on the International Control of Atomic Energy' prepared for the Secretary of State's Committee on Atomic Energy (Washington, DC, 16 March 1946; Department of State Publication 2498).

[97] See 'Baruch Plan' (Presented to the United Nations Atomic Energy Commission, 14 June 1946), United Nations, *Official Records of the Atomic Energy Commission, First Year, Plenary Meetings* 4.

> Behind the black portent of the new atomic age lies a hope which, seized upon with faith, can work our salvation. If we fail, then we have damned every man to be the slave of fear. Let us not deceive ourselves: we must elect world peace or world destruction.[98]

So for Baruch, and for many others who would come to focus on the issue of atomic technology in subsequent years, it was not a matter that could be localised, or rendered in the normalised language of inter-State cooperation or solidarity, but was a problem both immediate and global in scale, uniting the entirety of the human population, if only in a state of common terror. But the debate over the type of international controls necessary to ward off the possibility of a future nuclear conflagration was immediately haunted by an essential incommensurability of ends and means. The threat posed by atomic or nuclear technology was undoubtedly global in character.[99] It threatened not just humankind but also the planetary environment.[100] But any operative means through which that threat might be addressed was determinately international. It had to be organised through the medium of multilateral diplomacy and accompanied by the conclusion of agreements between actual or prospective nuclear powers. Each such 'power' would have the right to accept or reject the proposals set before them. And in the context of an ideologically divided array of nuclear States, the prospect of any kind of unanimity was hard to imagine. This was true in relation to the legality of nuclear weapons themselves, as well as for the means by which their presence might be eliminated from international political life.

The Baruch Plan itself collapsed. It was not so much rejected, as not endorsed by its target audience, the Soviet Union.[101] As many suspected

98 See 'Baruch's Speech at Opening Session of UN Atomic Eenrgy Commission' New York Times, 5 June 1946, 4, www.nytimes.com/1946/06/15/archives/baruchs-speech-at-opening-session-of-un-atomic-energy-commission.html.

99 See, e.g., Eisenhower's 'Atoms for Peace' speech ('I need hardly point out to this Assembly, however, that this subject is global, not merely national in character.'): UN GAOR, 8th sess, 470th plen mtg (8 December 1953) UN Doc. A/PV.470, 450, para 86.

100 This was to become clear with the conclusion of the Limited Test Ban Treaty of 1963, which, as Masco argues, was the 'first nuclear weapons treaty and the first global environmental treaty'. Joseph Masco, 'The Age of Fallout' *History of the Present*, 5 (2015) 143.

101 For a critique, see, e.g., Korovin, 'American Imperialism: A Threat to the Sovereignty of Nations' in Evsey Rashba, *Materials Relating to Soviet Doctrines and Practices in International Law* (New York: New York University, 1959) 4. The Baruch Plan 'boils down to setting up an international atomic trust (with Anglo-American majority, of course). This trust is to have command over all varieties of atomic raw materials in

at the time, the Soviets had already embarked on their own atomic weapons programme and would not countenance the proposed removal of their veto power. The Soviet Union's response to Baruch was the 'Gromyko plan'. This contained its own proposals for a treaty prohibiting the production and use of atomic weapons together with a commitment to destroy all stockpiles within three months, which would be followed by the creation of an inspection regime to supervise the use of atomic energy.[102] This was rejected, in turn, by the Western members of the Commission on the grounds that it was 'completely unrealistic to expect any nation to renounce atomic weapons without any assurance that all nations will be prevented from producing them'.[103]

Even if not couched in such terms, it was fairly evident that the main objection to the Gromyko plan was the expectation that the US would dismantle its existing stockpile of atomic weapons while the Soviets were secretly developing their own. What was to become the mainstay of the subsequent 'disarmament' agenda, then, was the idea that the threat of atomic (later nuclear) weaponry would best be contained if kept in 'balance' by an equivalence in the destructive potential on either side (however large that might be). This continued to be the general dilemma for both Soviet and US policymakers in their negotiations with one another – underpinning, for example, SALT I and II, the ABM Treaty[104] – all of which authorised a politics of 'balance', conferring on

whatever country they may be. It is to control everywhere, through its international inspectors, production and uses of atomic energy except in the last stage, i.e., the making of atom bombs, in which the United States Government considers itself to have a monopoly.' See, too, Lindqvist, *History of Bombing*, para 246. 'Moreover, it is proposed to give the same international (more precisely, American) atomic trust the right to apply international sanctions, including military ones, to countries which may refuse to obey the orders of the United States, thereby circumventing the Security Council in which the United States is hampered by the requirement of unanimity among the Great Powers.'

102 Address by the Soviet Representative (Andrei Gromyko) to the United Nations Atomic Energy Commission, 19 June 1946' in *Documents on Disarmament 1945–1959, Vol 1, 1945–1956* (Washington, DC: US Department of State, 1960) 17.

103 Bertrand Goldschmidt, 'A Forerunner to the NPT? The Soviet Proposals of 1947: A Retrospective Look at Attempts to Control the Spread of Nuclear Weapons' *IAEA Bulletin*, (Spring 1968) 58, 64.

104 Interim Agreement on Certain Measures with Respect to the Limitation of Strategic Offensive Arms (SALT I) (Union of Soviet Socialist Republics–United States of America), Moscow, 26 May 1972, UNTS 944 3; Treaty on the Limitation of Anti-Ballistic Missile Systems (ABM) (Union of Soviet Socialist Republics–United States of America), Moscow, 26 May 1972, 944 UNTS 13; Treaty between The United States of America and The Union of Soviet Socialist Republics on the Limitation of Strategic

State parties the right to possess enormous numbers of nuclear weapons in the name of 'curbing the race in strategic offensive arms', setting the stage for nuclear disarmament and warding off the possibility of nuclear war.

Those demanding a balance or equivalence in nuclear capabilities were largely agnostic about the overall numbers of warheads collectively in operational deployment on the part of the Cold War powers. But the demands for equivalence did carry with them one essential proviso: that nuclear capability be exclusively contained within the respective Amero-Soviet blocs. This was cold comfort to States in the South, indeed to most of the world. But without such containment, many military strategists within the 'nuclear club' thought that the fragile architecture of deterrence, limitation and control through a reciprocity in threat and counter-threat would be undermined. This theme, indeed, made its first appearance in the conclusion of peace treaties with five former axis powers (Bulgaria, Finland, Hungary, Italy and Romania) in which each was bound to renounce possession, production and testing of atomic weapons.

Aside from signaling an early loss of faith in the prospect of a universal agreement on the subject of nuclear disarmament, the peace treaties heralded an approach to the question that would later find more general expression in the Non-Proliferation Treaty of 1968. Having been drafted, in large part, by the collaborative efforts of the US and the Soviet Union who dominated proceedings in the UN's 'Eighteen Nation Committee on Disarmament', the NPT received a lukewarm reception. Two nuclear powers (France and the PRC) were joined by a number of others including Argentina, Brazil, India, Israel, Pakistan, Saudi Arabia and

Offensive Arms (SALT II) (Union of Soviet Socialist Republics–United States of America), Vienna, 18 June 1979; Treaty between the United States of America and The Union of Soviet Socialist Republics on The Reduction and Limitation of Strategic Offensive Arms (START I) (Union of Soviet Socialist Republics–United States of America), Moscow, 31 July 1991, UN Doc. CD/1192; Treaty between the United States of America and the Russian Federation on Measures for the Further Reduction and Limitation of Strategic Offensive Arms (START II) (Union of Soviet Socialist Republics–United States of America), Moscow, 3 January 1993, UN Doc. CD/1194; Treaty between the Russian Federation and the United States of America on Strategic Offensive Reductions (The Moscow Treaty) (Russian Federation–United States of America), Moscow, 24 May 2002, 2350 UNTS 415; Treaty between the United States of America and the Russian Federation on Measures for the Further Reduction and Limitation of Strategic Offensive Arms (Russian Federation–United States), Prague, 8 April 2010, TIAS 11-205.

South Africa in refusing to ratify the agreement.[105] As many were aware, despite the terms of article VI, which committed State parties to 'pursue negotiations in good faith to cessation of the arms race . . . and to nuclear disarmament', it was more than clear that 'non-proliferation' was not a term concerned with reducing the overall numbers of nuclear warheads in deployment, or indeed with restricting their physical location in the world, so much as limiting the number of States capable of 'pushing the button', so to speak.

8.5 Globalising the Bomb and Transforming Politics

For many 'observers' at the time, and since, the advent of nuclear weapons changed everything.[106] This was not a view universally shared, however, and according to some contemporaneous commentators, the policy of deterrence was just an extension of patterns observable from the time of Thucydides;[107] Cold War nuclearism was simply the prolongation of history by other means. Within this historic frame, even nuclear war could be thought (and fought): it might be a shadow under which a conventional war takes place, there might even be a nuclear exchange at a relatively low level (a kind of signalling without the inevitable final 'spasm' of Armageddon).[108] It was this sort of thinking that led Mearsheimer to argue that it would have been safer to let Ukraine keep its nuclear capability after the fall of the Soviet Union. Or, as he puts it at one point: 'Nuclear weapons are a powerful force for peace because they are weapons of mass destruction.'

Others took a different view about nuclearity and the history of war and peace but agreed with the dissonant idea that nuclearism moved the dial towards peace. The physicist and military strategist Herman Kahn

[105] On the fate of the NPT, see generally, Michael Onderco, *Networked Nonproliferation: Making the NPT Permanent* (Stanford: Stanford University Press, 2021).

[106] See, e.g., Garry Wills, *Bomb Power: The Modern Presidency and the National Security State* (New York: Penguin Press, 2010); Itty Abraham, *The Making of the Indian Atomic Bomb: Science, Secrecy and the Postcolonial State* (London: Zed Books, 1998).

[107] Even looking backwards from the twenty-first century, some understand the Cold War as continuous with the long history and historical inevitability of war. John J. Mearsheimer, *The Tragedy of Great Power Politics* (New York: W. W. Norton & Co., 2014).

[108] See Herman Khan, *Thermonuclear War* (Princeton: Princeton University Press, 1960). On signaling, see John J. Mearsheimer, 'Nuclear Weapons and Deterrence in Europe' *International Security*, 9(3) (1984–85) 19–46.

(allegedly one of the inspirations for the character of Dr Strangelove)[109] had famously worried about 'thinking the unthinkable'.[110] But foreign policy realists and theoretically inclined neo-realists of the time not only encouraged one to think the unthinkable but to think of the unthinkable as a place of hope, or, at least, stability. This was because, as Kenneth Waltz argued, 'the absolute quality of nuclear weapons sharply sets a nuclear world off from a conventional one'.[111] And this 'setting off' was a positive development because, Waltz believed, nuclear weapons maintained peace by discouraging not just nuclear war itself but also conventional war of any sort. Nuclear weapons had defied or broken an iron cage of history that seemed to postulate the inevitability of war. Because traditional warfare was a rational enterprise conducted on the basis of poor information (the idea being to prevail at minimal cost but where the costs are not quantifiable or even knowable in advance), the nuclear combination of irrational war (there is no prospect of anything resembling a territorial 'gain', for example) and fully knowable costs strongly discouraged war.[112]

Alongside such debates in the North about whether nuclear weapons drove a wedge between past and present conditions of peace, there was a parallel conversation in a cognate milieu about the effect of atomic weaponry on international politics more generally.[113] In an influential account written in 1959, US State Department analyst John Herz argued that the conditions underpinning the modern State system had undergone 'such fundamental changes that the structure of international relations itself is different . . . and can no longer be interpreted in traditional terms'.[114] What had changed, as he saw it, was not just that a new type of weapon had been invented but that international politics had been transformed as a consequence of the pervasive possibility of civilisational

[109] Paul Boyer, 'Dr. Strangelove' in Mark C. Carnes, Ted Mico, John Miller-Monzan and David Rubel (eds.), *Past Imperfect: History according to the Movies* (New York: Henry Holt and Co, 1995) 266–69.

[110] Herman Kahn, *Thinking about the Unthinkable* (New York: Horizon Press 1962).

[111] Kenneth N. Waltz, 'Nuclear Myths and Political Reality' *American Political Science Review*, 84(3) (1990) 732.

[112] E.g. Waltz, 'Nuclear Myths and Political Reality'.

[113] Gary Wills argues that the atomic bomb fundamentally changed the US presidency, essentially putting the president outside the US Constitution. See Wills, *Bomb-Power.*

[114] John H. Herz, *International Politics in the Atomic Age* (New York: Columbia University Press, 1959) 11.

destruction.[115] No longer was it possible to rationalise international politics in the language of territorial sovereignty, independence and autonomous decision-making; everything rather had become 'permeable' and global in character.

> Permeability presages the end of the traditional protective function of state power and territorial sovereignty. The chief external function of the modern state seems to have vanished. Utmost power in the possession of one state goes hand in hand with utmost impotence to counter the like power that others have. In a symbolic way ... satellites circling the globe and penetrating the space above any territory of the globe, regardless of 'sovereign' rights over air spaces and duties of 'nonintervention', serve to emphasize the new openness and penetrability of everything to everybody.

In the convoluted rationalities of nuclear strategy, for Herz, the 'unlimited power to destroy would protect nothing except, possibly, itself, the machine of destruction'.[116]

Herz's gloomy prognosis was written as an argument for rethinking the standard analytical framework of international politics. But on the way, it was identifying a new subject of analysis. For Herz, a pervasive 'dread of annihilation' offered the possibility of thinking both concretely and 'realistically' in global terms – in the language of 'mankind', the 'human race', 'common interests' and common concerns. On one hand, it was apparent to Herz that an understanding of the world as a collection 'of protected national units possessing "territorial" power, no longer fit [ted] a situation in which neither "sovereignty" nor strategic superiority c [ould] protect nations from annihilation'.[117] On the other hand, in the calculus of rational interests, it was plausible to suggest that matters domestic and national 'are bound to recede behind – or at least only to compete with – the overriding interest of all in sheer survival'.[118] In other words, the destructive reach of nuclear weaponry transcended the capacity of a nation-state to secure itself and for its rulers to think in terms of logics of statecraft. This disrupted international politics by inaugurating a global frame linked to the potential for annihilation. Eurocentric thinking

[115] Ibid., 13. 'Since we are inhabitants on a planet of limited (and, so it now seems, insufficient) size, we have reached those limits within which the effect of the means of destruction has become absolute.'

[116] Ibid., 23.

[117] Ibid., 310.

[118] Ibid., 312. For similar, see Mary Kaldor, *New and Old Wars: Organised Violence in a Global Era*, 3rd ed. (Bristol: Policy Press, 2012): 'Do not nuclear weapons nullify the premise of modern warfare – state interest?'

had long claimed authority to speak for the international grounded in the asserted ability to 'civilise' it. Amero-Soviet Cold War thinking reasserted that claim for the 'global' through the possession of a monopoly over the ability to destroy it.

But even if there was an inaugural element in all this, a global consciousness was by no means simply a creation of the Amero-Soviet Cold War. Its roots could be traced back to two different ideas. On one side, 'mankind' (in the terminology of the day) appeared as a corollary of the emergence of the law of armed conflict in the late nineteenth and early twentieth centuries. Here mankind (and later humankind) was represented in the form of a global community of interest ('the interests of humanity'), which imposed moral demands on the conduct of hostile inter-State relations.[119] By 1918, as British Prime Minister Lloyd George was struggling at an Imperial War Cabinet meeting to articulate precisely what kind of crime the German Kaiser had committed by invading Belgium in 1914, the Canadian PM Robert Borden smoothly interjected: 'a crime against ... humanity'.[120] This global humanitarian eschatology was closely intertwined with the language of civilisation whose 'ever increasing requirements' were said to underpin that moral consciousness. It provided the grounds not just for the authority to criminalise violators of the laws of humanity (most visibly performed in Nuremberg and Tokyo) but for an emergent discourse of universal human rights as it was to take shape after 1945. It also paved the way for a new way of thinking about the character of war itself, no longer an inter-sovereign contest between two equally situated legal persons but instead a policing operation conducted against the enemies of 'humanity' by its authorised defenders.

On the other side, the threads of a globalist framework for imagining and understanding international politics could also be traced back to the emergence of the tradition of geopolitics in the late nineteenth century. There, in the hands of Friedrich Ratzel,[121] Johan

[119] Convention (II) with Respect to the Laws and Customs of War on Land and Its Annex: Regulations Concerning the Laws and Customs of War on Land, the Hague, 29 July 1899, 32 Stat 1803, preamble.

[120] William Schabas, *The Trial of the Kaiser* (Oxford: Oxford University Press, 2018) 21.

[121] German ethnographer and geographer. See, in particular, Friedrich Ratzel, *Politische Geographie* (München and Berlin: R Oldenburg, 1897 [1903]); Friedrich Ratzel, 'The Laws of the Spatial Growth of States' in Roger Kasperson and Julian Minghi (eds.), *The Structure of Political Geography* (Abingdon: Routledge, 2011); and Friedrich Ratzel, '*Lebensraum*: A Biogeographic Study', trans. Tul'si Bhambry, *Journal of Historical Geography*, 61 (2018 [1901]) 59.

Kjellén,[122] Halford Mackinder[123] and Karl Haushofer,[124] the emergent conditions of political and economic rivalry within the West had encouraged a conceptualisation of inter-imperial relations as one set within a global geophysical frame of reference. And the term given for that way of thinking was 'geopolitics'.[125] As a consequence, however, of its association with Nazi foreign policy (and the concept of 'lebensraum',[126] in particular) the language of geopolitics became ideologically suspect in the aftermath of the Second World War.[127] But many of its staple features provided the intellectual scaffolding for Cold War strategic thought.[128] Thus, in place of an imperial conceptual architecture of 'heartlands' and 'rimlands', 'shatterbelts' and 'imperial frontiers' emerged a parallel (ideological) conceptual architecture of 'containment', 'encirclement', 'dominos' and 'iron curtains'. These were 'geopolitical' concepts that envisaged a world of imperial rivalry, the pursuit of regional hegemony within global political space and the design of strategies to counteract the expansionist proclivities of rivals.[129] This was not lost on Kissinger himself who later re-introduced the language of geopolitics within the

[122] Swedish political scientist and geographer. See Rudolf Kjellén, *Staten som lifsform* [*The State as Lifeform*] (Stockholm: Hugo Gebers Förlag, 1916).

[123] British geographer and politician. See, e.g., Halford Mackinder, 'The Geographical Pivot of History' *The Geographical Journal*, 23 (1904) 421; Halford Mackinder, 'The Round World and the Winning of the Peace' *Foreign Affairs*, 21 (1943) 595–605.

[124] German geographer, diplomat and military historian. See, e.g., Karl Haushofer, *Geopolitik der Pan-Ideen* (Berlin: Zentral-Verlag, 1931).

[125] The term was coined by Kjellén (alongside 'biopolitics'). See Rudolf Kjellén, *Staten som lifsform* [*The State as Lifeform*] (Stockholm: Hugo Gebers Förlag, 1916). On Kjellén's work generally, see Ragnar Björk and Thomas Lundén (eds.), *Territory, State and Nation: The Geopolitics of Rudolf Kjellén* (New York: Berghahn Books, 2021).

[126] On which, see Ratzel, 'Lebensraum'; Schmitt, *Nomos of the Earth.*

[127] See, e.g., Hans Weigert, *Generals and Geographers: The Twilight of Geopolitics* (New York and Toronto, 1942); Derwent Whittlesey et al., *German Strategy of World Conquest* (New York: Oxford University Press, 1942); Andreas Dorpalen, *The World of General Haushofer* (New York: Kennikat Press, 1942); Johannes Mattern, *Geopolitik: Doctrine of National Self-Sufficiency and Empire* (Baltimore: Johns Hopkins Press, 1942); Dwight Flanders, 'Geopolitics and American Post-War Policy' *Political Science Quarterly*, 60 (1945) 578–85.

[128] For the relationship between German geopolitics and the emergence of 'realist' political thought in the US, see Matthew Specter, *The Atlantic Realists: Empire and International Political Thought between Germany and the United States* (Stanford: Stanford University Press, 2022). See also Or Rosenboim, *The Emergence of Globalism: Visions of World Order in Britain and the United States, 1939–1950* (Princeton: Princeton University Press, 2017).

[129] There were some in the US academy who continued to work in the tradition of geopolitics in their descriptions of the geography of the Cold War. See, e.g., Owen

West as a framework for understanding the strategic dynamics of Cold War global politics.[130] From the American perspective, this was to think of the space of the Cold War and the space of the globe as one and the same.

8.6 Surveillance and Planetary Production

The geopolitical inflection and incipient 'globalisation' of (international) politics was amplified by the emergent technologies of surveillance. As we saw in Chapter 7, the United States had developed a system of satellite reconnaissance that became effectively operational in 1960 as a replacement for the controversial U-2 programme of the late 1950s. An extensive system of land-based surveillance stations dotted around the globe from Turkey to the Marshall Islands worked together with the sea-going reconnaissance vessels and the new satellite programmes to provide the US with the means to accurately estimate the size and location of Soviet weapons. It also allowed the US to track and monitor whether new weaponry was being tested. The 'spies in the sky', as they were dubbed, were understood to be vital elements in the US defence system. It was partly in recognition of this fact that the US had pushed forward the creation of a new legal regime for outer space. As we have already seen, in proposing the formation of a Committee on the Peaceful Uses of Outer Space within the United Nations, the US (and the Soviet Union alongside it) sought general authorisation for the removal of 'orbital space' from the field of territorial sovereignty.[131] In the process, the US sought to achieve for space the same legal position that now rules in the high seas, that is, as a space free for all to 'use' and traverse. That included, in particular, an ability to use outer space for the purposes of the 'unlimited observation' of national territories.[132]

One of the main justifications offered by the US to the public for its reconnaissance programmes was not simply its own 'defensive' needs for accurate information about the capacities of Soviet forces but the need for a system of effective verification of any arms reduction agreements.

Lattimore, *Inner Asian Frontiers of China* (New York, American Geographical Society, 1951)

130 Henry Kissinger, *Diplomacy* (New York: Simon & Schuster, 1994) 713.

131 See Chapter 6.

132 Report by the Committee on Satellite Reconnaissance Policy, Foreign Relations of the United States, 1961–1963, Vol. XXV, Organization of Foreign Policy; Information Policy; United Nations; Scientific Matters, Doc. 421, 951–59.

This idea had been foreshadowed by Eisenhower in his 'Open Skies' proposal at the 1955 Geneva summit, at which he postulated that the aerial surveillance of military installations was an ideal technique by which to verify compliance with any arms control agreements as and when they were agreed. Khrushchev dismissed the proposal at the time as nothing more than an 'espionage plot'. But growing concern about the worldwide effects of nuclear fallout[133] led both powers to entertain the possibility of a prohibition on nuclear weapons testing and, alongside it, the creation of a 'system of control'. Over the years that followed, various proposals were mooted including the establishment of an international control commission with powers of on-site investigation, the creation of an extensive network of land- and shipborne-posts tasked with monitoring seismic events (the Geneva System) and the use of automatic recording stations for in-country verification.[134] Ultimately, the Limited Test Ban Treaty of 1963 prohibited tests in the atmosphere, the seas and outer space if these caused debris to be present outside the testing State's territory, but it specified no particular controls. It was already apparent, though, that both powers had already established extensive independent monitoring systems to detect nuclear explosions in the atmosphere. In the case of the United States, this 'Project Vela Uniform' led to the launch of a series of Vela Hotel and Vela Sierra satellites capable of detecting nuclear tests in both the atmosphere and outer space, complemented by the creation of a World-Wide Network of Seismograph Stations (WWNSS), which, by 1967, operated from 127 separate sites around the world.[135]

[133] In 1954, fallout from the US BRAVO test was found to have contaminated a Japanese fishing boat, causing the death of one man and serious illness to several others. Later in the same year, debris from a Soviet test fell over part of Japan This prompted the creation of the United Nations Scientific Committee on the Effects of Atomic Radiation (UNSCEAR) under mandate of General Assembly Resolution 913(X) of 1955, the main function of which was to compile data supplied by States as to the levels of ionising radiation and radioactivity in the environment and standardise data collection.

[134] See Paul G. Richards and John Zavales, 'Seismological Methods for Monitoring a CTBT: The Technical Issues Arising in Early Negotiations' in Eystein S. Huseby and Anton M. Dainty (eds.), *Monitoring a Comprehensive Test Ban Treaty* (Berlin: Springer, 1996) 53–81.

[135] See generally, Jack Oliver and Leonard Murphy, 'WWNSS: Seismology's Global Network of Observing Stations' *Science*, 174(4006) (1971) 254–61; Kai Henrik Barth, 'The Politics of Seismology: Nuclear Testing, Arms Control and the Transformation of a Discipline' *Social Studies of Science*, 33 (2003) 743–81; Carl Romney, *Detecting the Bomb: The Role of Seismology in the Cold War* (Washington, DC: New Academia Publishing, 2009).

By the time of the conclusion of the Anti-Ballistic Missile Treaty of 1972, the rival powers had come to accept that their respective systems of surveillance were sufficient to ensure compliance with the terms of the agreement. For the first time, the treaty included a clause (Article XII) that both authorised the use of such systems and imposed an obligation not to interfere or impede with such measures. The euphemism employed in the text was 'national technical means of verification' – a phrase elusive enough to obscure its precise implications. The same phrase was included in the SALT I (1972), the Threshold Test Ban Treaty (1974), SALT II (1979) and subsequently in the START I and START II agreements of 1991/93.[136]

But the significance of the new systems of surveillance and verification lay not only in the degree to which they accurately estimated compliance with various arms control obligations but in the way in which they contributed to the formation of new forms of global or 'planetary' knowledge. In the first place, the fact that many of the surveillance systems were located in the extra-atmospheric void – a space declared to be 'the province of mankind' outside the ordering powers of terrestrial sovereignty – was of no small significance. It shared with the seas the common idea that it was free from the possibility of enclosure. But outer space was different because it was neither a space for trade nor transportation, nor indeed for pursuit of a policy of economic warfare. Rather, and above anything else, it was a media(ted) realm: a realm of communication, of broadcasting, of seeing, listening and sensing. McLuhan's adage that 'the medium is the message' captured perfectly the significance of outer space at the time. What it projected was a spatial distinction between the terrestrial and the extra-terrestrial, a distinction between a world that was lived in and the place from which was observed, between the world of speaking and acting and the space of relays through which those activities might be both observed and communicated to one

[136] See Treaty between the United States of America and the Union of Soviet Socialist Republics on the Limitation of Underground Nuclear Weapons Test 1718 UNTS 216; Treaty between the United States of America and the Union of Soviet Socialist Republics on the Reduction and Limitation of Strategic Offensive Arms (signed 31 July 1991, entered into force 5 December 1994); Treaty Doc No 102–20, 16 UN Disarmament Yearbook, Appendix II 450; Treaty on Further Reduction and Limitation of Strategic Offensive Arms (Russia–United States of America) (signed 3 January 1993, entered into force 14 April 2000) reprinted in Stockholm International Peace Research Institute (ed.), *SIPRI Yearbook 1993: Armaments, Disarmament and International Security* (Oxford: Oxford University Press, 1993) 576.

another. And in the same sense, the medium was one through which an undifferentiated global space appeared or was bought to light – prefiguratively described in the images, 'Earth Rising' and 'Blue Marble' that were to capture the global public's imagination in the 1970s.

The new satellite surveillance systems seemed, in a very literal sense, to bring into view the existence of the planet as a whole. And relatedly, they also occupied the metaphorical vantage point of Amero-Soviet international law. What they produced, alongside the ground-based surveillance systems, was a concrete version of the same. Data from the WWNSS, for example, contributed to what has been described as a 'revolution' in the earth sciences, leading, amongst other things, to the emergence of the theory of 'plate tectonics', and a better understanding both of seismology and the earth's magnetic fields.[137] And, as Masco points out, the tracking of fallout from atmospheric nuclear tests was central to the formation of an understanding of the world as a biosphere. A new generation of earth scientists used the data generated from tracking radioactive contamination (strontium -90 and cesium -131) to map ecological flows through weather systems and food chains, developing an understanding of how atmosphere, earth and ocean interact in the process. Set alongside the emergent work on oceanography,[138] weather systems[139] and polar science[140] – much of which was informed by the

137 Described by Hallam as important as the theories of evolution and quantum mechanics 'in terms of its fundamental importance to our scientific understanding of the world'. Tony Hallam, 'The Great Revolution in Earth Sciences in the Mid-Twentieth Century' *Isis*, 105 (2014) 410.

138 Jacob Hamblin, *Oceanographers and the Cold War: Disciples of Martine Science* (Seattle: University of Washington Press, 2005); Samuel Robinson, *Ocean Science and the British Cold War State* (London: Palgrave MacMillan, 2018).

139 See, e.g., Roger Fleming, *Fixing the Sky: The Checkered History of Weather and Climate Control* (New York: Columbia University Press, 2010); Kristine Harper, *Weather by the Numbers: The Genesis of Modern Meterology* (Cambridge, MA: MIT Press, 2008); Matthias Dörrjes, 'The Politics of Atmospheric Sciences: "Nuclear Winter" and Global Climate Change' *Osiris*, 26 (2011) 19–223.

140 Peder Roberts, 'Scientists and Sea Ice under Surveillance in the Early Cold War' in S. Turchetti and P. Roberts (eds.), *The Surveillance Imperative* (New York: Palgrave Macmillan, 2014) 125–44; James Rodger Fleming, 'Polar and Global Meteorology in the Career of Harry Wexler, 1933–62' in Roger Launius et al. (eds.), *Globalizing Polar Science* (New York: Palgrave Macmillan, 2010) 225–41; Stephen Bocking and Daniel Heidt, *Cold Science: Environmental Knowledge in the North American Arctic during the Cold War* (London: Routledge, 2019).

respective demands of various branches of the military[141] – this accumulated knowledge underpinned the emergence of a new global environmental consciousness that was evidenced ultimately in the Stockholm conference of 1972 and subsequent international environmental initiatives (UNEP, IPCC, etc.).[142] Key insights of an emergent environmental science had already fed through into various foreign policy and international legal initiatives – including the launch of International Geophysical Year in 1957, the Law of the Sea Conference of 1958, the Antarctic Treaty of 1960 and the Limited Test Ban Treaty of 1963.[143] But such insights were sustained and advanced by data that was generated, from the 1960s onwards, by the various satellite programmes launched by the Cold War powers (such as ERTS, Landsat, Nimbus and TIROS) that provided the means by which global data on the geophysics of the planet, its atmosphere and weather systems, would be collected.[144]

8.7 Innocent (but Still Global) Knowledge

A central feature of the legal architecture underpinning the new systems of global surveillance was (as the preamble to the Outer Space Treaty emphasised) that they should be strictly peaceful in nature. But as the text of that treaty appeared to foreshadow, determining what activity was, or was not, 'peaceful' was a difficult task. On one hand, the commitment to 'use' outer space for 'peaceful purposes' appeared to ensure the strictly scientific, non-military, nature of outer space activity. Indeed, this was the gist of article 4 of the treaty, which prohibited sending nuclear weapons and other weapons of mass destruction into orbit and prohibited the establishment of military bases, installations and fortifications on the moon and other celestial bodies.

On the other hand, Article 3 of the treaty allowed – perhaps even instructed – States to 'carry on activities' in outer space in accordance

141 See, e.g., Ronald E. Doel, 'Constituting the Postwar Earth Sciences: The Military's Influence on the Environmental Sciences in the USA after 1945' *Social Studies of Science*, 33 (2003) 635–66.

142 See Aaron Wu, 'Bridging Ideologies: Julian Huxley, *Détente*, and the Emergence of International Environmental Law' in Craven, Pahuja and Simpson, *International law and the Cold War.*

143 See Barth, 'The Politics of Seismology'.

144 Beyond, and alongside the scientific knowledge itself, the surveillance systems developed on both sides of the Cold War divide were associated with the development of a number of related technological advances that were later to inform processes of 'globalisation' in the 1990s – including networked computer systems, GPS, satellite communication, etc.

with the UN Charter and 'in the interests of maintaining international peace and security'. Bearing in mind the general framework of the Charter concerning the use of force, 'peaceful purposes' was thus open to being construed in narrow terms, as excluding only aggressive, as opposed to defensive, military activities. This latter interpretation was the one proffered by the US. As Senator Gore was to put it when speaking before the UN First Committee in 1962:

> It is the view of the United States that outer space should be used only for peaceful – that is, non-aggressive and beneficial – purposes. The question of military activities in space cannot be divorced from the question of military activities on earth. To banish these activities in both environments we must continue our efforts for general and complete disarmament with adequate safeguards. Until this is achieved, the test of any space activities must not be whether it is military or non-military, but whether it is consistent with the United Nations Charter and other obligations of law.[145]

On this interpretation, there was nothing that prevented satellites being used for military reconnaissance purposes so long as those activities were not a prelude to an act of aggression.

But both of these interpretations were problematic for different reasons. In relation to the first, whilst the period of the Cold War was a time of significant scientific activity, it was always apparent that military interests had a profound effect upon the course of both basic and applied science. On both sides of the Cold War divide, the rival powers were actively pushing scientific endeavour in research institutes and universities in the direction of work that had potential military applications. As Fleming put it:

> Weapons systems of the past and current centuries have been based on science; they have also been increasingly lethal (especially to civilians), increasingly toxic, and increasingly pathological. Physics, chemistry, and biology have weaponized the atom, molecule, virus, and bacterium, while the geosciences have militarized the global environment in the air, under the seas, and in outer space. In the cold war era, it was presumed that clouds, storms, and even the climate, like any other natural phenomenon, could be controlled and weaponized.[146]

[145] UN First Committee, 'International Co-operation in the Peaceful Uses of Outer Space' (3 December 1961) UN Doc. A/C.1/PV.1289, 13.

[146] James Rodger Fleming, *Fixing the Sky: The Checkered History of Weather and Climate Control* (New York: Columbia University Press, 2010) 186.

In his view, it was not just that the military provided support for and patronage of the sciences but that there was an increasing 'interpenetration' of values and perspectives between the military, on the one hand, and the scientific community, on the other. So, for example, just as developments in meteorological knowledge seemed to offer the possibility of combatting droughts, improving agriculture or avoiding natural disasters, that same science supported the development of military communications and ballistic missile capabilities and, even more controversially, environmental modification.[147] As a consequence, the so-called neutrality of scientific research became an increasingly problematic idea,[148] and nuclear science, in particular, appeared to have paved the way for a suspicion on the part of many that prospective (military) utility drove basic science, not the other way round.

In relation to the second distinction – between aggressive and defensive surveillance – it was very clear from the outset that US claims that its satellite surveillance was purely defensive in character was, at best, a half-truth. As we have seen, the Soviets were initially adamant that satellite overflight not only violated their territorial sovereignty but constituted an aggressive measure on the part of the US. This was emphasised, in particular, by Zhukov writing in *International Affairs* in 1960. For him, satellite surveillance seemed to be designed 'to increase the efficiency of surprise attack, making it possible to knock out enemy missile bases at the very start and thereby to avoid a retaliatory blow'.[149] Even if this may not have been the explicit intention of the Eisenhower administration when designing the system, it was certainly clear that information gleaned from satellite surveillance would routinely be fed through into the targeting systems of the US Intercontinental Ballistic Missile control centres.[150] Perversely, then, the very same methods for verifying arms control agreements were methods that putatively enhanced first strike capabilities and, in so doing, seemed to contribute to the production of that which they were designed to forestall.

And yet the idea that atomic knowledge more generally could be 'split', as it were, between peaceful and aggressive purposes continued to

[147] See Convention on the Prohibition of Military or Any Other Hostile Use of Environmental Modification Techniques, 5 October 1978, 1108 UNTS 151.

[148] Naomi Oreskes and John Krige, *Science and Technology in the Cold War* (Cambridge, MA: MIT Press, 2014).

[149] Gennady Zhukov, 'Space Espionage Plans and International Law' *International Affairs*, (Moscow 1960) 53–57.

[150] William E. Burrows, *Deep Black: Space Espionage and National Security* (New York: Berkely Books, 1988).

circulate and to permit Amero-Soviet imaginaries that authorised the development and generalisation (and sale) of nuclear technologies with global effects, regardless of what 'others' thought. This was reflected in the terms of the Nuclear Non-Proliferation Treaty, which prohibited non-nuclear States from acquiring nuclear weapons, but which promoted and universalised – under supervision – the peaceful use of nuclear technology on the part of participating States. In this sense, the NPT tapped into a characteristic of Amero-Soviet world-making that had been flagged as early as 1946, when the Baruch Plan posited a division between the use of atomic technology for purposes of building warheads and its peaceful use as, for example, a source of power.

A central element of the Baruch Plan had been the establishment of an international atomic energy authority with managerial control both over the production of fissionable materials and over global supplies of uranium and thorium upon which they depended.[151] In addition to having sole and exclusive right to conduct research in the field of atomic explosives, it would also have been responsible for licensing the material and facilities for the production of power. The Soviet proposal of 1947 had similarly envisaged the creation of an international agency (the International Control Commission) to oversee 'all facilities engaged in mining of atomic raw materials and in production of atomic materials and atomic energy' for peaceful purposes.[152] In both cases, what was imagined was not just a tempering of their mutual rivalry through the creation of an architecture of international control but an assertion of rights in respect of global supplies of fissionable materials wherever they might be located (whether that be Canada, Czechoslovakia or the Congo).

These ideas were picked up by Eisenhower in his 'atoms for peace' speech of 1953 in which he proposed the creation of an International Atomic Energy Agency that would take charge of a bank of 'normal uranium and fissionable materials' with contributions to it by participating governments. Those materials would then be 'allocated to serve the peaceful pursuits of mankind'. As he described it:

[151] In the latter guise, it would be tasked with conducting 'continuous surveys so it will have the most complete knowledge of the world geology of uranium and thorium' in order to 'bring them under its dominion'.

[152] UN Security Council, 'Letter from the Chairman of the Atomic Energy Commission Addressed to the President of the Security Council, Dated 11 September 1947, Enclsoing the Second Report of the Atomic Enerby Commission to the Security Council', S/557, 90

> Experts would be mobilised to apply atomic energy to the needs of agriculture, medicine and other peaceful activities. A special purpose would be to provide abundant energy in the power-starved areas of the world. Thus the contributing Powers would be dedicating some of their strength to serve the needs rather than the fears of the world.

By 'splitting the atom', as he put it, the hope was to unify 'the entire divided world'.[153] Three years later, the International Atomic Energy Authority was created (its statute came into force in July 1957), which, alongside various activities dedicated to the promotion of nuclear energy production, ultimately took responsibility (under the terms of the NPT) for policing nuclear programmes via inspections to ensure that they were not 'diverted' into the production of new nuclear weapons.

As Hecht describes it, what this was to produce was the idea of the 'nuclear' being split, both culturally and politically, through the medium of two contrasting imaginaries. One imaginary was the dystopian nightmare of the nuclear apocalypse, the other was a utopia of limitless electricity, atomic-powered transportation, huge increases in crop yield and cures for diseases.[154] What held those global imaginaries together was not simply the common fact of nuclear science but the idea of its 'neutrality' in relation to the contrasting uses to which it might be put. This split was institutionally performed in the work of the IAEA whose central task under the NPT was to differentiate between 'military science' and 'peaceful science' and promote the globalisation of the latter whilst securing the localisation of the former.[155] It was a split whose generative effect was to secure, both affectively and programmatically, the

[153] The idea that nuclear energy might be tethered for peaceful purposes was endorsed by the Afro-Asian States at Bandung. There, it was stated that the use of nuclear energy for peaceful purposes 'would help answer the needs particularly of Asia and Africa, for what they urgently require are social progress and better standards of life in larger freedom. Freedom and peace are interdependent'. See Final Communiqué (24 April 1955).

[154] Hecht, *Being Nuclear*, 7–10.

[155] See generally Gabrielle Hecht, 'On the Fallacies of Cold War Nostalgia: Capitalism, Colonialism, and South African Nuclear Geographies' in *Entangled Geographies: Empire and Technopolitics in the Global Cold War* (Cambridge, MA: MIT Press, 2011) 77–81 (where she notes that the NPT 'made nuclearity a global "right," but left matters of safeguards and "technical assistance" to developing nations to the IAEA . . .. Together, the IAEA and the NPT thus enacted the technopolitics of global Cold War. Ideologically, they appealed to the highest possible moral purpose: the safekeeping of the human race and its planet. At the same time, they offered the possibility of reconciling this danger with the (also morally powerful) promise of unlimited modernity. They thus produced the "nuclear" as a mutual, but structurally unequal, engagement of the Cold War with the colonial and the postcolonial.').

globalisation of nuclear science in both senses – on the one hand, as threat, on the other, as promise.[156]

One of the consequences of this, as Masco points out, was that the US nuclear programme itself 'quickly turned the entire planet into an experimental theatre for nuclear science'.[157] On the military side, globality was advanced not only through the physical reach of intercontinental nuclear weapons (and their deployment in off-shore missile sites and on board nuclear submarines) but also via 'the extensive network of production and testing sites, which linked a global uranium industry, vast experimental laboratories and test sites with military support and delivery systems'.[158] This was complemented, on the civil side, by the work of the IAEA amongst others, in promoting 'peaceful uses' of nuclear technology in the fields of energy, food, healthcare, desalination and, ultimately, climate change. It was a major advocate, amongst other things, for the construction of small- and medium-scale nuclear power plants particularly in the developing world. It dabbled briefly with the idea – promoted more actively by the US Atomic Energy Commission in its Plowshare programme – of utilising nuclear explosives as an engineering tool.[159] But, and beyond this, what was to emerge from the early decades of the Cold War was a 'powerful vision of the biosphere as an integrated ecological space of complex interactions'[160] that came to be generated via the medium of an array of global surveillance technologies and institutions many of which were concerned with identifying and monitoring the testing, development and deployment of nuclear arsenals around the globe.

8.8 Conclusion

The atom was central to the way in which the Amero-Soviet Cold War globalised itself and turned itself in the process into a 'global civil war'. The two 'world wars' of the first half of the twentieth century had already

156 This, indeed, was to create a divide within the anti-nuclear movement more generally. On one side were those who regarded the separation between peaceful and military nuclear science to be at best illusory and at worst an ideological sleight of hand. On the other were those who saw in the possibility of cheap nuclear energy the prospect of rapid economic development.

157 Masco, 'The Age of Fallout', 144.

158 Ibid., 146.

159 See Fleming, *Fixing the Sky*.

160 Masco, 'The Age of Fallout', 147.

provided the template for a form of 'total warfare' – a warfare that evaporated the distinction between combatant and civilian, between those who might be the object of legitimate attack and those who could rightfully regard themselves as innocent bystanders. The atom bomb completed that process. However much lawyers and strategists sought to immunise the bomb from its association with total warfare in the aftermath of Nagasaki and Hiroshima, they were never able to shake off the possibility that it might be used, even quite legally, for purposes of laying waste to cities and whole populations. The bomb seemed to materialise the idea of total warfare in its very existence and contributed to emergent imaginaries of the global by way of the threat it posed to humanity as a whole. As a consequence of its potentially destructive effects, the atom bomb brought into view a new global subject – humankind. It was also the cause for the development of new forms of global knowledge, and new global technologies, that in its aftermath would come to be central to the globalising tendencies of the post–Cold War world.

And one way or another, global knowledge production fell under the shadow of a totalising Cold War advanced by what Eisenhower spoke of as a 'military industrial complex' guided by a 'scientific-technical elite'. In the process, the idea of politically innocent knowledge, of knowledge that was not already destined to be used or deployed in the furtherance of ideological ends, became harder and harder to identify, and that went as much for the natural sciences as it did for political knowledge and legal knowledge. The terrain was thus set for an enduring contestation over the politics of environmental science and the ability to act or speak in name of the 'globe' without assuming the posture of God.[161]

[161] See Bruno Latour, *Facing Gaia: 8 Lectures on the New Climactic Regime* (Cambridge: Polity Press, 2017) 136.

9

Fallout

Redescription, Periodisation and Aftermath

9.1 Redescription

One day in late 1946, a year after the end of the Second World War, the diplomat, financier and soon to be author of the *Baruch Plan for the Regulation of Nuclear Weapons*, Bernard Baruch, was sitting on a bench in Central Park when he overheard a homeless man refer to the post-war global scene as a 'Cold War'.[1] Baruch went on to use the phrase in public. It was popularised by the likes of George Orwell and Walter Lippman, and instrumentalised by Winston Churchill. Baruch's park bench savant had coined a term that entered the political consciousness and for nearly half a century became a description of the age.

This book was prompted by a desire to re-envision that age of the Cold War, not as object but as subject: as a particular project of world ordering, a style of world-making carried out in a variety of juridical forms originating in a broad array of geographical and diplomatic sites. Our experience of hearing experts and lawyers attribute this or that success or failure in international law, or transformation in institutions, to a monolithic, over-determining, usually North Atlantic, always bi-polar Cold War was an incitement to investigation. We quickly realised that although it existed everywhere as cause or effect, it was seldom made strange. It was a Cold War that was simply there, as an answer to every second question. Instead of having the Cold War explain us, we wanted to explain the Cold War, through disassembling and redescribing the truths our discipline took largely to be self-evident.

[1] Baruch first used the phrase in public on 16 April 1947. See Fred Halliday, 'The Ends of the Cold War' *New Left Review*, 180 (1990). Baruch was known for chatting to strangers on park benches. His biography was called 'Parkbench Statesman'. See Carter Field, *Bernard Baruch: The Parkbench Statesman* (New York: McGraw Hill, 1944) 5.

This quickly became a story about *international laws* and *Cold Wars.* It's already too long, but the book is not about everything that happened in the Cold War era. It doesn't even cover every international legal initiative of the period. But it has sought to bring out the plurality of international laws at play and the different ways in which what we might now think of as one international law was imagined, performed and constituted during the Cold War. At the same time, we have offered at least some, hopefully telling, examples of the very different Cold Wars that were experienced around the world in the post-war period and the forms of political and diplomatic life that Cold War practice and thought both closed off and left open for us, in our Cold War–inflected present.

One such remnant is felt through the putative effect of the many announcements of its demise. In 1995, Thomas Franck hailed the end of the Cold War as international law's post-ontological moment.[2] No longer would lawyers have to defend the existence of their discipline, he said, or even justify the set of rules that purport to be its subject. International law had found a safe landing, its authority confirmed at last. But this view of international law collapsed the period from 1947 to 1989 together, inventing an origin and tacitly imagining a Cold War international law that was absent, marginal, ineffectually humanitarian, univocal, always subordinated to the caprice of Great Power manoeuvring and ideological certitudes and, now, extinct.

In this book, we have sought to disrupt this framing of international law and the Cold War, in at least three distinct ways. First, by describing the multiple means by which the practice of international law organised, facilitated, accommodated and made the Cold War (or at least a particular kind of Cold War). Second, by bringing out the ways in which a variety of legal *forms* was integral to the administration of this Cold War world. Third, and perhaps most importantly, we have tried to dislodge received accounts by revisiting and redescribing the many substantive *laws* of the Cold War. Here the Cold War is understood as an encounter between different legal projects of world-making, different international laws and the reproduction of spaces of in-betweenness and improvisation in the interstices of this encounter.

[2] Thomas Franck, *Fairness in International Law and Institutions* (Oxford: Oxford University Press, 1995).

9.2 Periodisation

The Cold War is about itself.[3]

When we began this project of co-authorship, we had each already written around the 'Cold War' separately in different ways and in different styles, sometimes honouring it purely in the breach. Quite early on, we had to puzzle through the languages and questions we could share. We each knew we wanted to read and write against a common narrative of the Cold War as a long aberration or interruption in the development of international law, but it took much (much) longer for the project to settle around trying to rethink the Cold War as a time of rivalrous but constitutive accounts of the 'international', understood as a set of ideas, practices and intellectual and political manoeuvrings.

In doing so, we had to work through and to resist the siren song of a number of 'Cold Wars' and Cold War orthodoxies and to find ways to think about Cold War thinking. In particular, we soon realised we had to try to write about the relationship between the Cold War and international law without adopting the style of thought of its protagonists. On one hand, this meant maintaining a certain distance between the archive 'itself', as we crafted it, and the methodological or theoretical frames of reference through which we were trying to interpret it. But, on the other, it also meant treating the way that international law, Cold War and prevalent thematics were written about by different actors as itself part of the archive. To do this, we also had to position theory – and thought – as practice.

One kind of an analytical separation we tried to hold in place was between three different kinds of Cold War, each of which operates at a different level of generality or in a different genre or register. These are, first, the Cold War as a period of history that conventionally begins sometime in the early twentieth century (1945 or perhaps 1917) and ends in 1989/90; second, the Cold War as a description of the geo-political and ideological confrontation between East and West, more or less confined to relations between the Soviet bloc and the Western alliance; and third, the Cold War as a particular style of strategic thought and action – a mode of governmentality – that shaped and defined the outlook, and

[3] E. P. Thompson, (banned) Dimbleby Lecture (1981). See Edward Thompson, 'The Ends of the Cold War' *New Left Review*, 182 (1990) 139, 140.

operative priorities, of its main protagonists. These were principally scholars and statesmen in the US but could also be extended to those on the other side of the 'Iron Curtain' and sometimes beyond. We found that it was easy to slip between each of these registers – they are cumulatively concordant if read from one to three. But trying to hold them apart possibly helped us to think about the Cold War from something that approximated the 'outside', without internalising its own pathologies: to think about the Cold War other than in and on its own terms.

When we took up this exterior vantage point, three things seemed to emerge that turned out to be central to our project of re-reading and redescribing the Cold War and its relationship to international law. These 'things' concern periodisation, juridification and provincialisation. The book enacts the latter two themes by bringing out the juridical in Cold War practice/thought and by attending to the Cold War as a lawful event and by provincialising the North Atlantic Cold War and de-proxifying the Cold Wars of the South: the former no longer genesis, the latter no longer derivation.

Periodisation, we have said much less about: the familiar linear historiography characterises the Cold War as a specifiable period of global history with defined moments of origin and end.[4] But as soon as one holds apart the idea of the Cold War as an epoch in history from the idea of the Cold War as a particular set of practices and/or modes of thought, it becomes clear that the former is almost entirely parasitic upon the latter. The moment depends on the modes. In other words, the periodicity of the Cold War is dependent upon a description of its various operative sites (political, economic, legal, social, cultural, etc.). And so far as a description of what is or is not 'central' to any particular narrative is a matter of choice, it follows that periodisation is always an argument and never a fact.[5] Any straightforward description of the Cold War – including of its beginning or end – will depend upon the intellectual or geographic vantage-point from which it is examined or imagined. A geopolitical Cold War (beginning in 1945) might thus be contrasted with an

[4] We are participating in this characterisation ourselves in our editorship of the Cold War volume of *The Cambridge History of International Law.*

[5] Sundhya Pahuja and Cait Storr, 'Rethinking Iran and International Law: The Anglo-Iranian Oil Company Case Revisited' in James Crawford, Abdul Koroma, Said Mahmoudi and Allain Pellet (eds.), *The International Legal Order: Current Needs and Possible Responses: Essays in Honour of Djamchid Momtaz* (Leiden: Brill, 2017).

ideological Cold War (beginning in 1917), a Northern Cold War from a Southern Cold War (a distinction made explicit in 1956), a 'First Cold War' from a 'Second Cold War'. One's vantage, too, will determine whether one even chooses the term 'Cold War' in the first place. One might just as well describe these events as part of a history of racialised capitalism, or of white internationalism, or decolonisation or the crisis of late-empire – each of which will itself, adduce its own 'beginning' or end. All these rival accounts are alluded to, if not fully made out in these pages, and we offer them out as alternative ways of thinking about global events during the period conventionally understood as the Cold War.

But if we stay in the conventional Cold War itself, we might remember the French historian Marc Bloch who bemoaned the way in which historical periods are packaged retrospectively as 'centuries' and condemned the tendency of synchronic histories to narrate 'pell mell events whose only connection was that they happened around the same time'.[6] In international law, the conventionally rendered Cold War has been a victim of this tendency. Berlin is collapsed into the Cuban Missile Crisis or Bandung or détente or the murder of Patrice Lumumba or the law of the sea or decolonisation, simply because they each happened at around the same time. Often this lumping together takes place without much attention to the way in which such developments might cut against one another or be unrelated or distinct phenomena, or how they might be related other than synchronically. We tried to think – and talk – our way out of these rigid temporalities by attending to the longue durée of Cold War events (decolonisation as a history of Afro-Asian assertiveness, resistance, national liberation), US–Soviet relations as an arc of competing and shared modernities (their shorter, 'local' specificities [in the former case Angola or The Congo, in the latter case, say, Czechoslovakia or the NPT]). Perhaps, like so many things, the 'Cold War' begins when it is named. The christening attends the birth. If so, Orwell, Lippman, Baruch and his 'vagrant' can each claim some kind of parenthood.[7] Their announcements anticipated the events that marked

6 See Gerry Simpson, 'After Method: International Law and the Problems of History' in Annabel Brett, Megan Donaldson and Martti Koskenniemi (eds.), *History, Politics, Law: Thinking through the International* (Cambridge: Cambridge University Press, 2021) 102.

7 George Orwell, 'You and the Atomic Bomb' *Tribune*, 19 October 1945, quoted in Odd Arne Westad, 'The Cold War and the International History of the Twentieth Century' in Melvyn Leffler and Odd Arne Westad (eds.), *The Cambridge History of the Cold War* (Cambridge: Cambridge University Press, 2010) 3; Halliday, 'The Ends of the Cold War'.

the beginning of a series of splits in an always fragile wartime alliance. At the other end of the century, 1989 and 1991 represent plausible endings of something else: Gorbachev, *perestroika*, *glasnost*, the fall of the Wall, the reunification of Germany. . ..

But even this conventional chronology can be stretched or compressed. The Cold War might have begun in 1917 when two rival visions – Wilson's and Lenin's – of a 'post imperial' international order take shape as the Great War ends or, in 1885, when Europeans initiate a formal carve up of Africa or maybe in 1938 with the Molotov–Ribbentrop Pact (signalling Moscow's unreliability as an ally to the Western nations) or with the mandates system and the tentative beginning of decolonisation. And did it end (or resume) in 2001 when a new enemy emerged (or was brought into being) and a new comprehensive struggle to the death – a war on terror – was introduced into world politics? Or, perhaps, to adopt the usual European classifications of the Cold War, it may simply have gone into abeyance to be revived in 2008 (Georgia), 2014 (Crimea), 2021 (the Donbas, Kiev) by a more muscular, irredentist, Kremlin?[8] To perform the inverse and compress the chronology a little, it might be said that the war ended with Soviet defeat in Afghanistan or that it slowly receded as the Soviet Union stagnated under Brezhnev (and assorted successors) or that one Cold War ended with Cuba in 1962 and another began at the same time.

But we might also choose to think about the temporality of the Cold War through the lenses of continuity and discontinuity. Two theses come to mind. The first views the Cold War as having its own distinctive mood, one that can't be wished away by a recognition of its continuities with what came before and after. On this reading, Cold War particularities seem both descriptively and politically important. Descriptively, nuclear terror, for example – still with us but no longer apparently quite so terrifying – could well have had a peculiarly formative effect on the law: inviting the collapse of the stabilised categories of peace and war or giving meaning to the conception of a global community. Politically, the Cold War might also have represented a breathing space in the expansion of capitalism or of juridified humanity or late techno-capital. And in this breathing space there flourished ways of life and thinking that may no longer seem so possible or even imaginable from the present.

To read David Scott's *Omens of Adversity* on Maurice Bishop's Grenadan revolution, for example, is to be reminded that organised political

[8] See, e.g., Susan Richards, 'For Russia the New Cold War Has Begun' *The Guardian Weekly*, 22 May 2015, 18.

revolution was a signature of the Cold War and that this revolutionary form is now understood to have dissipated into counter-coup or is now read at least as spectacular (or mindless) violence or klepto-warfare. And it is also to be reminded that legal analysis of, say, 'the Grenada Intervention' was constituted in the West by a thin gruel of arguments about humanitarian intervention or the 'protection of nationals abroad': a form of discourse seemingly designed to divert one's gaze from other deeper projects of international ordering and disordering. The Cold War was different but a different form of different, different from the usual different, perhaps. That there were moments, places – let's adopt Jameson's idiom and call them 'enclaves' – where promising forms of resistance were present. Maybe in Conkary, maybe at Greenham Camp, maybe at the inception of the National Health Service, maybe in Havana, or St George's or Bandung or Belgrade or in Prague . . . . We have described others in these pages.

A second approach, though, might trace the grids, lines and contours of the present and the pre-1945 period back and forward to the Cold War. In this sense, we might choose to reject both '1989' and '1945' as natural bookends and argue instead that there was no rupture in the classic period (1945–90). On the contrary, 1945 was the culmination of forces already traceable in the late nineteenth century or the inter-war period; 1989 was not an ending but instead a re-gathering of irresistible, already-in-existence-forces. The Cold War – its terrors, its monstrosities, its mood, its friend-enemy core, its militant neo-liberalisms, its projects of juridical-techno-logical-governmental ordering – is here now, finally fully realised and not a gap or misfire in the long story of lawful progress from, say, 1918 to 1999.[9]

9.3 Aftermath

> Every regime needs it foes or in due course creates them.
>
> —Otto Kirchheimer[10]

[9] The Cold War contained a past, a present and a future. A past that represents revolutionary time; a present signifying a form of 'afterness' – after ideology, after revolutionary hope, after politics; a future without futurity, a long slow catastrophe displacing but not eliminating the eight minute warnings of our past. The present project belongs to an era, the final fragment of which we half remember. This is a plane of temporality closer to what David Scott calls 'biographical time'. One consequence of all this is that as writers we find ourselves checking 'experience' against 'reading'.

[10] Otto Kirchheimer, *Political Justice: The Use of Legal Procedure for Political Ends* (Princeton: Princeton University Press, 1961) 1.

Is this how we come to be where we are? The present – our present – is what history has bequeathed to us, or at least it is what we have authorised or permitted history to bequeath *to* us. Bloch again: 'a person cannot understand the past if he is totally ignorant of the present'.[11] We look around us first, then choose what to see in the past, so it becomes the present's 'usable' history. The Cold War, like other moments, has been the subject of an array of retrospectives each speaking to a particular circumstance or need, felt in the present. The histories of the Cold War written during its ascendancy, for instance, tended to reflect the imperatives of the moment. But in the immediate post–Cold War era, a certain amnesic view of the Cold War began to pervade the scene. Another way to put this is to say that there was a lot of forgetting to be done as from the perspective of the United States and its allies, 'new world orders' were inaugurated in print (Slaughter) and in practice (Bush I in Iraq). These hastily constructed edifices were like historical hoardings, or Potemkin orders. They needed a Cold War that was largely irredeemable, a thing to be left behind, and quickly, in an historiographical big bang, for the Cold War, in every sense, to be over.[12]

In this book, we have challenged this 'overness,' not by suggesting that the Cold War has been revived in the latest struggle between the United States and Russia in Ukraine, however much that conflict seems to reprise elements of Cold War orthodoxy, but instead by asserting that the Cold War has never disappeared. This inheritance is both prison-house and opportunity.

To qualify Bloch, we also need to know the present to ask good questions about the past. And so, through the book, we have traced the antecedents of some of our present disorders. To sketch just one example, in the case of non-alignment, the end of the Cold War also meant the end of a certain politics of space or 'thirdness' in international relations. With the Soviet Union gone, the 'other' could now be safely criminalised. Between humanity and its enemies there could be no neutral ground. And so, in the post–Cold War world, a roll call of racialised adversaries (Iran-Iraq-Serbia-Afghanistan-Libya) have been

[11] Marc Bloch, *The Historian's Craft* (Manchester: Manchester University Press, 1992) 36.

[12] For discussions of presentism, see François Hartog, *Regimes of History: Presentism and Experiences*, trans. Saskia Brown (New York: Columbia University Press, 2016). See, too, the work of Reinhart Kossalek, e.g., *Sediments of Time: On Possible Histories*, ed. and trans. Sean Franzel and Stefan-Ludwig Hoffman (Stanford: Stanford University Press, 2018).

subject to punitive sanction (war, the destruction of civil society). The treatment of Russia itself as an outlaw sovereign and the renunciation of the vestigial neutrality of the Scandinavians after the Ukraine War could be seen as the apotheosis of this trend. This sometimes feels like a return of Schmitt's 'Amity Line' where there could be no neutrality and where European civilisation battles 'native savagery' or Eurasian expansion.

All of this was prefigured during the Cold War in the idea, for instance, that all Algerians were to be rendered as combatants, or that 'privileged' warfare would be unevenly distributed, and it grimly foreshadows the war on terror and Israel's flattening of Gaza (and the idea that there are no civilians there). But it is also a redescription of the Cold War itself in which everyone in the world becomes a combatant and therefore target, taking us back in turn to Schmitt's prediction that anti-colonial warfare *beyond* the Amity Line would return to haunt Europe (the camps for the Boers, bombing the Libyans from the air in 1911).

The precedent for this, we might suggest, was the removal of people like Arbenz, Mossadeq and Allende who were liquidated not because they were communists but because they were not (each of them might plausibly be positioned as a social democrat). In the Global South, it sometimes seemed that only authoritarianism was permitted. People used to ask why socialism didn't exist in the United States, now they ask why democratic liberalism doesn't exist. One answer is that the move away from social democracy began in the Cold War and that US domestic politics now represents the embodiment of an introverted form of US foreign policy. In 1954, the CIA was initially looking for a 'soft-reformer' to replace Arbenz (why? he already was that person) but this gave way to the CIA installing a crack-pot-in-exile with such disastrous consequences that later, even the CIA was searching for social democrats to replace the string of right-wing dictators. They discovered too late that the contenders were all dead.

Maybe, though, and against some of this, we are seeing the renewal of non-alignment. The movement itself still exists in a depleted form. Some of the old ideas are hanging on. They are combining with new forms of resistance necessitated by Israel's ongoing efforts to incapacitate the Palestinian polity. The refusal of States to pass Vladimir Putin to the international criminal court marks a throwback to a form of non-belligerence. These 'neutral' States realise that the ICC has now become an arm of Western war-making masquerading as a beacon of juridical humanity. Switzerland's recent offer to host peace talks between Zelensky and Putin with the latter promised immunity from surrender to the ICC seems, then, to conjoin neutrality's past and future.

Through all this diagnosing, tracing and redescribing, thus, the book also became a project of retrieval. To paraphrase Gabrielle Hecht, we began with the idea of redistributing the political and legal history of the Cold War, and ended somewhere else.[13] Perhaps it became something like a paean – the Ancient Greek songs or lyric poems recited to express triumph or thanksgiving. But if it is a paean, it is also a call to arms, a plea to retrieve a lost world of legal experimentation, political non-alignment, spatial reconfiguration and revolutionary possibility.

[13] Gabrielle Hecht, *Entangled Geographies: Empire and Technologies in the Global Cold War* (Cambridge, MA: MIT Press, 2012) 7.

BIBLIOGRAPHY

Books/Articles

Abi-Saab, Georges, 'Wars of National Liberation in the Geneva Conventions and Protocols' *Recueil des cours*, 165 (2007) 1979.

Abraham, Itty, *The Making of the Indian Atomic Bomb: Science, Secrecy and the Postcolonial State* (London: Zed Books, 1998).

Adler, Jonathan L., 'The Unrecognized Government in the Courts of the United States' *Virginia Journal of International Law*, 5 (1964) 36–52.

Afsah, Ebrahim, 'Cold War (1947–91)' in *Max Planck Encyclopedia of Public International Law* (Oxford: Oxford University Press, 2009).

Ahn Cohen, Jerome, 'Chinese Participation in the United Nations: Changing Realities and the Imperatives of New Policy' *ASIL Proceedings*, 65(4) (1971) 1–8.

Akehurst, Michael, 'Enforcement Action by Regional Agencies with Special Reference to the Organization of American States' *British Yearbook of International Law*, 42 (1967) 175–228.

Alexandrowicz, C. H., *An Introduction to the History of the Law of Nations in the East Indies (16th, 17th and 18th Centuries)* (Oxford: Clarendon Press, 1967).

The Law of Nations in Global History, ed. David Armitage and Jennifer Pitts (Oxford: Oxford University Press, 2017).

Allman, Jean, 'Nuclear Imperialism and the Pan-African Struggle for Peace and Freedom: Ghana, 1959–1962' in Manning Marable and Vanessa Agard-Jones (eds.), *Transnational Blackness: Navigating the Global Color Line* (London: Palgrave Macmillan, 2008) 333–54.

Althusser, Louis, and Étienne Balibar, *Reading Capital*, trans. Ben Brewster (London: New Left Books, 1970).

Álvarez, Alejandro, *Le Droit International Américain: Son Fondement, Sa Nature D'après L'histoire Diplomatique Des Etats Du Nouveau Monde Et Leur Vie Politique Et Économique* (Paris: A. Pedone, 1910).

Monroe Doctrine: Its Importance in the International Life of the States of the New World (New York: Carnegie Endowment for International Peace and Oxford University Press, 1924).

Alvarez, Marcelo, '"Individual Opinion" in Conditions of Admission of a State to Membership in the United Nations (Article 4 of the Charter)' *Advisory Opinion, ICJ Reports*, 57 (1948) 71.

Anderson, Perry, 'Imperium' *New Left Review*, 83 (2013) 5–112.

Andrews, Kehinde, 'Beyond Pan-Africanism: Garveyism, Malcolm X and the End of the Colonial Nation State' *Third World Quarterly*, 38 (2017) 2501–16.

Anghie, Antony, *Imperialism, Sovereignty and the Making of International Law* (Cambridge: Cambridge University Press, 2005).

'Legal Aspects of the New International Economic Order' *Humanity: An International Journal of Human Rights, Humanitarianism, and Development*, 6(1) (2015) 145–58.

Antonopoulos, Constantine, *Non-Participation in Armed Conflict: Continuity and Modern Challenges to the Law of Neutrality* (Cambridge: Cambridge University Press, 2022).

Arendt, Hannah, *The Origins of Totalitarianism* (New York: Harcourt, Brace and Company, 1951).

On Revolution (New York: Penguin, 1963).

Aron, Raymond, 'The Diffusion of Ideologies' *Confluence*, 2 (1953) 3–12.

Asad, Talal, *On Suicide Bombing* (New York: Columbia University Press, 2007).

Attlee, Clement R., *As It Happened* (New York: Viking Press, 1954).

Aufricht, Ernst, 'Principles and Practices of Recognition by International Organizations' *American Journal of International Law*, 43(4) (1949) 695–98.

Balibar, Étienne, *Politics and the Other Scene* (London: Verso, 2002).

Bandyopadhyay, Pramathanath, *International Law and Custom in Ancient India* (Calcutta: Calcutta University Press, 1920).

Barkawi, Tarak, *Soldiers of Empire: Indian and British Armies in World War II* (Cambridge: Cambridge University Press, 2017).

Barth, Kai Henrik, 'The Politics of Seismology: Nuclear Testing, Arms Control and the Transformation of a Discipline' *Social Studies of Science*, 33 (2003) 743–81.

Baxi, Upendra, '"The Dust of Empire": The Dialectic of Self-Determination and Re-colonisation in the First Phase of the Cold War' in Matthew Craven, Sundhya Pahuja and Gerry Simpson (eds.), *International Law and the Cold War* (Cambridge: Cambridge University Press, 2019) 397–413.

Baxter, Richard R., 'The Role of Law in Modern War' *Proceedings of the American Society of International Law at Its Annual Meeting*, 47 (1953) 90–98.

'So-called "Unprivileged Belligerency": Spies, Guerrillas and Saboteurs' *British Yearbook of International Law*, 28 (1951) 323–45.

Bayandor, Darioush, *Iran and the CIA: The Fall of Mosaddeq Revisited* (London: Palgrave MacMillan, 2010).

Beard, Jennifer, *The Political Economy of Desire: International Law, Development, and the Nation-State* (Abingdon: Routledge, 2007).

Beaulac, Stéphane, 'The Westphalian Model in Defining International Law: Challenging the Myth' *Australian Journal of Legal History*, 8(2) (2004) 181–213.

Bedjaoui, Mohamed, 'Non-alignment et droit international' *Hague Recueil*, 151 (1976) 337–467.

Beirne, Piers, and Robert Sharlet (eds.), *Pashukanis: Selected Writing on Marxism and Law*, trans. Peter B. Maggs (Cambridge, MA: Academic Press, 1980).

Benjamin, Walter, 'Critique of Violence' in Peter Demetz (ed.), *Reflections: Essays, Aphorisms, Autobiographical Writings*, trans. Edmund Jephcott (New York: Schocken Books, 1978 [Preface 2007 (1921)]) 277–300.

Benton, Lauren, *Law and Colonial Cultures: Legal Regimes in World History, 1400–1900* (Cambridge: Cambridge University Press, 2002).

A Search for Sovereignty: Law and Geography in European Empires 1400–1900 (Cambridge: Cambridge University Press, 2009).

Bergson, Henri, *The Two Sources of Morality and Religion*, trans. R Ashley Audra and Cloudesley Brereton (Notre Dame: University of Notre Dame Press, 1935).

Berman, Nathaniel, 'Sovereignty in Abeyance' *Wisconsin International Law Journal*, 7 (1988) 51–105.

Bernays, Edward, *Crystallizing Public Opinion* (New York: Liveright, 1923).

Propaganda (New York: Liveright, 1928).

Beschloss, Michael R., *Mayday: Eisenhower, Khrushchev, and the U-2 Affair* (New York: Harper & Row, 1988).

Best, Geoffrey, *War and Law since 1945* (Oxford: Oxford University Press, 1994).

Bickers, Robert, *Ritual and Diplomacy: The Macartney Mission to China, 1792–1794* (London: Wellsweep Press, 1993).

Bischof, Günter, *Austria in the First Cold War, 1945–55: The Leverage of the Weak* (London: Palgrave Macmillan, 1999).

Björk, Ragnar, and Thomas Lundén (eds.), *Territory, State and Nation: The Geopolitics of Rudolf Kjellén* (New York: Berghahn Books, 2021).

Black, C. F., *The Land Is the Source of the Law: A Dialogic Encounter with Indigenous Jurisprudence* (London; New York: Routledge, 2010).

Blix, Hans Martin, 'Contemporary Aspects of Recognition' *Recueil des Cours*, 130 (1970), 587–693.

Bloch, Marc, *The Historian's Craft* (Manchester: Manchester University Press, 1992).

Blouin, Andrée, *My Country, Africa: Autobiography of the Black Pasionaria* (London: Verso 2005 [1983]).

Blum, Gabby, and Philip B. Heymann, *Laws, Outlaws, and Terrorists: Lessons from the War on Terrorism* (Cambridge, MA: MIT Press, 2010).

Blum, William, *Killing Hope: US Military and CIA Interventions Since World War II* (London: Bloomsbury, 2022).

Bocking, Stephen, and Daniel Heidt, *Cold Science: Environmental Knowledge in the North American Arctic during the Cold War* (London: Routledge, 2019).

Bogush, Gleb, 'Aron Trainin: The Legal Mind Behind a Soviet International Criminal Law Project' in Frédéric Mégret and Immi Tallgren (eds.), *The Dawn of a Discipline: International Criminal Justice and Its Early Exponents* (Cambridge: Cambridge University Press, 2020) 260–79.

Borgwardt, Elizabeth, *A New Deal for the World: America's Vision for Human Rights* (Cambridge, MA: Harvard University Press, 2005).

Borisova, Tatiana, and William B. Simons (eds.), *The Legal Dimension in Cold War Interactions: Some Notes from the Field* (Leiden: Martinus Nijhoff Publishers, 2012).

Borosage, Robert. 'Comments' *Proceedings of the American Society of International Law Annual Meeting*, 69 (1975) 203–6.

Bourne, C. B., 'The Federation of the West Indies', *University of Toronto Law Journal*, 13 (1960) 135–65.

Bowett, D. W., *Self-Defence in International Law* (London: Praeger, 1958).

Bowring, Bill, *The Degradation of the International Legal Order? The Rehabilitation of Law and the Possibility of Politics* (London: Routledge-Cavendish, 2008).

'Positivism versus Self-determination: The Contradictions of Soviet International Law' in Susan Marks (ed.), *International Law on the Left: Re-examining Marxist Legacies* (Cambridge: Cambridge University Press, 2008), 133–68.

'Yevgeniy Pashukanis, His Law and Marxism: A General Theory, and the 1922 Treaty of Rapallo between Soviet Russia and Germany' *Journal of the History of International Law*, 19 (2017) 274–95.

Boyd, William, *A Good Man in Africa* (London: Hamish Hamilton, 1981).

Boyer, Paul, 'Dr. Strangelove' in Mark C. Carnes, Ted Mico, John Miller-Monzan and David Rubel (eds.), *Past Imperfect: History according to the Movies* (New York: Henry Holt and Co, 1995), 266–69.

Brierly, James L., *The Law of Nations: An Introduction to the International Law of Peace*, ed. Humphrey Waldock, 6th ed. (Oxford: Clarendon Press, 1963).

Briggs, Herbert. 'Chinese Representation in the United Nations' *International Organization* 6 (1952) 192–209.

'"The Leaders" Agreement of Yalta' *American Journal of International Law*, 40 (1946) 376.

Brodie, Bernard, 'War in the Atomic Age' in Bernard Brodie (ed.), *The Absolute Weapon: Atomic Power and World Order* (Boston: Harcourt, 1946) 14–52.

Bronislavovich, Evgeniĭ, 'Pashukanis' International Law (1925–1926)' in Piers Beirne and Robert Sharlot (eds.), *Pashukanis: Selected Writings on Marxism and Law* (London and New York: Academic Press 1980).

Broughton, Bob, Donna Ah Chee, Jack Beetson, Deborah Durnan and Jose Le Blanch, 'An Aboriginal Adult Literacy Campaign Pilot Study in Australia Using Yes I Can' *Literacy and Numeracy Studies*, 21 (2013) 5–32.

Brown, Michael E., and Randy Martin, 'Left Futures' *Socialism and Democracy*, 9 (1995) 59–89.

Brownlie, Ian, *International Law and the Use of Force by States* (Oxford: Oxford University Press, 1963).

Brunet, Luc André, and Eirini Karamouzi, 'Introduction: Globalising the History of the Anti-nuclear Activism' in Luc André Brunet and Eirini Karamouzi (eds.), *Beyond the Euromissile Crisis: Global Histories of Anti-Nuclear Activism in the Cold War* (New York and Oxford: Berghahn Books, 2025) 1–20.

Buck-Morss, Susan, *Dreamworld and Catastrophe: The Passing of Mass Utopia in East and West* (Cambridge, MA: MIT Press, 2000).

Burke, Kenneth, *A Grammar of Motives* (Berkeley: University of California Press, 1969).

Language as Symbolic Action: Essays on Life, Literature, and Method (Berkeley: University of California Press, 1966).

Burrows, William E., *Deep Black: Space Espionage and National Security* (New York: Berkley Books, 1988).

Butler, William E., 'The Pueblo Crisis: Some Critical Reflections' *Proceedings of the American Society of International Law at Its Annual Meeting*, 63 (1969) 7–13.

Butler, W. E., 'Soviet Law and the Cold War' *Journal of Comparative Law*, 7 (2012) 334–41.

Buzan, Barry, and Ole Wæver, *Regions and Powers: The Structure of International Security* (Cambridge: Cambridge University Press, 2003).

Byrne, Jeffrey, *Mecca of Revolution: Algeria, Decolonization, and the Third World Order* (Oxford: Oxford University Press, 2016).

'The Romance of Revolutionary Transatlanticism: Cuban–Algerian Relations and the Diverging Trends within Third World Internationalism' in R. Joseph Parrott and Mark Atwood Lawrence (eds.), *The Tricontinental Revolution: Third World Radicalism and the Cold War* (Cambridge: Cambridge University Press, 2022), 163–90.

Byrnes, James F., 'Restatement of Policy on Germany' *Department of State Bulletin*, 15 (1946) 496–501

Cabral, Amilcar, 'Anonymous Soldiers for the United Nations' in *Revolution in Guinea: An African People's Struggle* (London: Love & Malcomson, 1969), chapter 3.

Caddell, Richard, 'Secret Treaties' *Max Planck Encyclopaedia of International Law* (2006) 1.

Callières, François de, *On the Manner of Negotiating with Princes* (Notre Dame: University of Notre Dame Press, 1963).

Carty, Anthony, 'The Corfu Channel Case and the Missing Admiralty Order' *The Law and Practice of International Courts and Tribunals*, 3 (2004) 1–35.

Cassesse, Antonio, *International Criminal Law*, 2nd ed. (Oxford: Oxford University Press, 2008).

Chakrabarty, Dipesh, *Provincialising Europe: Postcolonial Thought and Historical Difference* (Princeton: Princeton University Press, 2000).

Chai, Winberg, 'China and the United Nations: Problems of Representation and Alternatives' *Asian Survey*, 10 (1970) 397–409.

Chalmers, Shane, and Sundhya Pahuja (eds.), *Routledge Handbook of International Law and the Humanities* (Abingdon: Routledge, 2021).

Chamberlain, Paul Thomas, *The Cold War's Killing Fields: Rethinking the Long Peace* (New York: HarperCollins, 2018).

Chatterjee, Partha, *Nationalist Thought and the Colonial World: A Derivative Discourse?* (London: Zed Books for the United Nations University, 1986).

The Politics of the Governed: Reflections on Popular Politics in Most of the World (New York: Columbia University Press, 2004).

Chaumont, Charles, 'Nations Unies et neutralité: cours à l'Académie de la Haye, juillet 1956' in *Recueil des cours (Collected Courses of the Hague Academy of International Law)*, vol. 89 (The Hague: Nijhoff/Brill, 1956).

Nations Unies et Neutralité (Leiden: A. W. Sijthoff, 1956).

Chimni, B. S., *International Law and World Order: A Critique of Contemporary Approaches*, 2nd ed. (Cambridge: Cambridge University Press, 2017).

Chiu, Hungdah, 'The Right of the Republic of China and Its 21 Million Chinese People to Participate in the United Nations' John Marshall Law Review, 28 (1994) 247–57.

Chiu, Hungdah, and R. R. Edwards. 'Communist China's Attitude toward the United Nations: A Legal Analysis', *American Journal of International Law* 62(1) (1968) 20–50.

Churchill, Winston, *The Second World War: The Hinge of Fate* (Volume IV) (London: Cassell & Co, 1951).

The Second World War: Triumph and Tragedy (Volume VI) (London: Cassell & Co, 1954).

Ciobanu, Dan, 'Credentials of Delegations and Representation of Member States at the United Nations' *International and Comparative Law Quarterly*, 25 (1976) 351–81.

Clapham, Andrew, *War* (Oxford: Clarendon Press, 2021).

Claude, Inis, 'The OAS, the UN, and the United States' *International Conciliation*, 547 (1964) 3–67.

Cohen, Rosalyn, 'Legal Problems Arising from the Dissolution of the Mali Federation' *British Yearbook of International Law* (1960) 375–84.

Colman, Jonathan, 'Towards "World Support" and "The Ultimate Judgment of History": The American Legal Case for the Blockade of Cuba during the

Missile Crisis, October–November 1962' *Journal of Cold War Studies*, 21 (2019): 150–73.

Connell, Raewyn, *Southern Theory: Social Science and the Global Dynamics of Knowledge* (Cambridge: Polity Press, 2007).

Connell-Smith, Gordon, *The Inter-American System* (Oxford: Oxford University Press, 1966).

Pattern of the Post War World (London: Penguin Books, 1957).

Constantine, Dana, 'Korean War (1950–53)' *Max Planck Encyclopaedia of International Law* (2015).

Cooper, Frederick, *Citizenship between Empire and Nation: Remaking France and French Africa, 1945–1960* (Princeton: Princeton University Press, 2014).

Cormac, Rory, and Richard J. Aldrich, 'Grey Is the New Black: Covert Action and Implausible Deniability' *International Affairs*, 94 (2018) 477–94.

Corn, David, 'Public Interest Power Games: Turf Wars at the Fund for Peace' *The Nation*, 250(10) (12 March 1990) 342.

Cosgrove, Dennis, *Apollo's Eye: A Cartographic Genealogy of the Earth in the Western Imagination* (Baltimore: John Hopkins Press, 2001).

Cover, Robert, 'Nomos and Narrative' *Harvard Law Review*, 97 (1983) 4–68

Craven, Matthew, Sundhya Pahuja and Gerry Simpson, 'Reading and Unreading a Historiography of Hiatus' in Matthew Craven, Sundhya Pahuja and Gerry Simpson (eds.), *International Law and the Cold War* (Cambridge: Cambridge University Press, 2019), 1–24.

Crawford, James, *The Creation of States in International Law*, 2nd ed. (Oxford: Oxford University Press, 2006).

'The Right of Self-Determination in International Law: Its Development and Future' in Philip Alston (ed.), *Peoples' Rights* (Oxford: Oxford University Press, 2023), 7–67.

Cummings, Bruce, *Parallax Visions: Making Sense of American–East Asian Relations at the End of the Century* (Durham: Duke University Press, 1999).

Dalby, Simon, *Creating the Second Cold War: The Discourse of Politics* (London: Bloomsbury, 1990).

Dallin, Alexander, 'The Soviet View of the United Nations' *International Organization*, 16 (1962) 20–36.

Dao, André, Caitlin Murphy and Sundhya Pahuja, 'Bad States, Good Corporations? The Intersecting Histories of Business and Human Rights and International Investment Law' in Jochen von Bernstoff, Phillip Dann and Surabhi Ranganathan (eds.), *The Battle for International Law in the Neoliberal Era (1975–2000)* (Oxford: Oxford University Press, 2026).

d'Aspremont, Jean, *Formalism and the Sources of International Law: A Theory of the Ascertainment of Legal Rules* (Oxford: Oxford University Press, 2011).

Daudet, Léon, *La guerre totale* (Paris: Nouvelle Librairie Nationale, 1918).

Deák, Francis, and Philip Jessup (eds.), *A Collection of Neutrality Laws, Regulations, and Treaties of Various Countries* (New York: Carnegie Endowment for International Peace; Columbia University Press, 1939).

Dean, Jodi, *The Communist Horizon* (London: Verso, 2012).

Publicity's Secret (New York: Cornell University Press, 2002).

de Groot, Michael, *Disruption: The Global Economic Shocks and the End of the Cold War* (Ithaca: Cornell University Press, 2024).

Deeks, Ashley, 'A (Qualified) Defense of Secret Agreements' *Arizona State Law Journal*, 49 (2017) 713.

Deighton, Anne, *The Impossible Peace: Britain, the Division of Germany, and the Origins of the Cold War* (Oxford: Oxford University Press, 1993).

Delupis, Ingrid, 'Foreign Warships and Immunity for Espionage' *American Journal of International Law*, 78 (1984) 53–75.

Denza, Eileen, *Diplomatic Law: Commentary on the Vienna Convention on Diplomatic Relations*, 4th ed. (Oxford: Oxford University Press, 2016).

Derrida, Jacques, '"To Do Justice to Freud": The History of Madness in the Age of Psychoanalysis' *Critical Inquiry*, 20 (1994) 227–66.

Rogues: Two Essays on Reason (Stanford: Stanford University Press, 2005).

Deutschmann, David (ed.), *Che Guevara Reader: Writings by Ernesto Che Guevara on Guerilla Strategy, Politics and Revolution* (Melbourne: Ocean Press, 1997).

Dewerpe, Alain, *Espion: Une Anthropologie Historique du Secret d'État Contemporain* (Paris: Gallimard, 1994).

Diop, Cheikh Anta, *Black Africa: The Economic and Cultural Basis for a Federated State* (Chicago: Lawrence Hill, 1978).

Dixon, Paul, '"Hearts and Minds"? British Counter-insurgency from Malaya to Iraq' *Journal of Strategic Studies*, 32 (2009) 353–81.

Docauer, Victor, 'Communist Chinese Attitudes toward United Nations Membership 1945–1971: An Essay' Iustitia, 2(2) (1974) 14–27.

Doel, Ronald E., 'Constituting the Postwar Earth Sciences: The Military's Influence on the Environmental Sciences in the USA after 1945' *Social Studies of Science* 33 (2003) 635–66.

Donaldson, Megan, 'The Survival of the Secret Treaty: Publicity, Secrecy, and Legality in the International Order' *American Journal of International Law*, 111 (2017) 575.

Dorpalen, Andreas, *The World of General Haushofer* (New York: Kennikat Press, 1942).

Dörrjes, Matthias, 'The Politics of Atmospheric Sciences: "Nuclear Winter" and Global Climate Change'. *Osiris*, 26 (2011) 19–223.

Dorn, Walter, and Robert Pauk. 'Unsung Mediator: U. Thant and the Cuban Missile Crisis' *Diplomatic History*, 33 (2009) 261–92.

Dorsett, Shaunnagh, and Shaun McVeigh, 'Conduct of Laws: Native Title, Responsibility, and Some Limits of Jurisdictional Thinking' *Melbourne University Law Review*, 36(2) (2012) 470.

Jurisdiction (London: Routledge-Cavendish, 2012).

Douhet, Giulio, *The Command of the Air*, trans. Dino Ferrari (New York: Coward McCann, 1942 [1921]).

Du Bois, W. E. B., *Colour and Democracy: Colonies and Peace* (New York: Harcourt, Brace & Co, 1945).

Dudziak, Mary, *Cold War Civil Rights: Race and the Image of American Democracy* (Princeton: Princeton University Press, 2000).

Dugard, John, *Recognition and the United Nations* (Cambridge: Cambridge University Press, 1987).

'Towards the Definition of International Terrorism' *American Society of International Law Proceedings*, 67 (1973) 94–99.

Dulles, Allen W., *The Craft of Intelligence: America's Legendary Spy Master on the Fundamentals of Intelligence Gathering for a Free World* (London: Weidenfeld and Nicolson, 1963).

'U-2 Overflights of Soviet Bloc', Central Intelligence Agency CHAL 1138-60, 18 August 1960.

Duncanson, Ian, *Historiography, Empire, and the Rule of Law: Imagined Constitutions, Remembered Legalities* (Abingdon: Routledge, 2012).

Dunn, Peter M., *A Good Man in Africa* (London: Hamish Hamilton, 1981).

Duquet, Sanderijn, and Jan Wouters, 'Diplomacy, Secrecy, and the Law' in Claudio Barbieri and Christoph Friedrich (eds.), *Secret Diplomacy: Concepts, Contexts and Cases* (London: Routledge, 2016), 85–107.

Eden, Anthony, *The Reckoning: The Eden Memoirs* (London: Cassell, 1965).

Elleman, Bruce, *International Rivalry and Secret Diplomacy in East Asia, 1896–1950* (Abingdon: Routledge, 2019).

Ekbladh, David, 'The Interwar Foundations of Security Studies: Edward Mead Earle, the Carnegie Corporation and the Depression-Era Origins of a Field' *Global Society*, 28 (2014) 40–53.

Ellul, Jacques, *Propaganda: The Formation of Men's Attitudes* (New York: Vintage Books, 1962).

English, Joseph F., 'Air Freedom: The Second Battle of the Books' *Journal of Air Law and Commerce*, 2 (1931) 356–72.

Erickson, Richard J., *International Law and the Revolutionary State* (New York: Oceana, 1972).

Escobar, Arturo, *Encountering Development: The Making and Unmaking of the Third World* (Princeton: Princeton University Press, 1995).

Eslava, Luis, 'Development, International Law and the Cold War: A Long History of Disembedding' in Matthew Craven, Sundhya Pahuja and Gerry Simpson (eds.), *Cambridge History of International Law, Vol XI: International Law during the Cold War (1945–1990)* (Cambridge: Cambridge University Press, forthcoming).

Local Space, Global Life: The Everyday Operation of International Law and Development (Cambridge: Cambridge University Press, 2015).

Eslava, Luis, Michael Fakhri and Vasuki Nesiah (eds.), *Bandung, Global History and International Law: Critical Pasts and Pending Futures* (Cambridge: Cambridge University Press, 2017).

Estlund, David, *Utopophobia: On the Limits (If Any) of Political Philosophy* (Princeton: Princeton University Press, 2019).

Evatt, Herbert V., 'Risks of a Big-Power Peace' *Foreign Affairs*, 24 (1946) 195–209.

Falk, Richard A., 'An Alternative to Covert Intervention' *Proceedings of the American Society of International Law Annual Meeting*, 69 (1975) 195–200.

'Casting the Spell: The New Haven School of International Law' *The Yale Law Journal*, 104(7) (1995) 1991–2008.

'CIA Covert Action and International Law'*Society*, 12 (1975) 39–40.

'Space Espionage and World Order: A Consideration of the Samos–Midas program' in Quincy Wright, Julius Stone, Richard A. Falk and Roland J. Stanger (eds.), *Essays on Espionage and International Law* (Columbus: Ohio State University Press, 1962), 45–82.

(ed.), *The Vietnam War and International Law*, 4 vols. (Princeton: Princeton University Press, 1968–76).

Fanon, Frantz, *The Wretched of the Earth*, trans. Richard Philcox (New York: Grove Press, 2004 [1963]).

'Letter to Ali Shariati' in Jean Khalfa and Robert J. C. Young (eds.), *Alienation and Freedom*, trans. Stephen Corcoran, (London: Bloomsbury, 2018), 644–45.

Faturos, Arghyrios, 'Remarks by the Chairman' *Proceedings of the American Society of International Law Annual Meeting*, 69 (1975) 192–95.

Fauchille, Paul, 'La circulation aérienne et les droits des états en temps de paix' *Revue Juridique Internationale de la Locomation Aérienne*, 1 (1910) 9–16.

'Regime juridique des aérostats' *Annuaire de L'institut de Droit International*, 19 (1902) 19–86.

Featherstone, David, *Solidarity: Hidden Histories and Geographies of Internationalism* (London: Zed Books, 2012).

Fawcett, J. E. S., 'Intervention in International Law: A Study of Some Recent Cases' (Volume 103) in *The Hague Academy Collected Courses Online* (Leiden: Brill, 1961).

Feinberg, Norbert, 'L'Admission de Nouveaux Membres à la Société des Nations et à l'Organisation des Nations Unies' *Recueil des Cours (Hague Academy of International Law)*, 80 (1955) 297–393.

Fenwick, Charles, *International Law*, 4th ed. (New York: Appleton-Century-Crofts, 1965).

'The Old Order Changeth, Yielding Place to the New' *AJIL*, 47 (1953) 84.

Fergie, Dexter, 'Geopolitics Turned Inwards: The Princeton Military Studies Group and the National Security Imagination' *Diplomatic History*, 43 (2019) 644–70.

Field, Carter, *Bernard Baruch: The Parkbench Statesman* (New York: McGraw Hill, 1944).

Fifield, Russell, 'The Five Principles of Peaceful Co-Existence' *American Journal of International Law*, 52 (1958) 504–10.

Fitzmaurice, Gerald F., 'The Use of Force against Civil Aircraft: The Aftermath of the KAL Flight 007 Incident' *Canadian Yearbook of International Law*, 22 (1984) 291–311.

Fitzpatrick, Peter, *Law as Resistance: Modernism, Imperialism, Legalism* (Aldershot: Ashgate, 2008).

Modernism and the Grounds of Law (Cambridge: Cambridge University Press, 2001).

The Mythology of Modern Law (London: Routledge, 1992).

Flanders, Dwight, 'Geopolitics and American Post-War Policy' *Political Science Quarterly*, 60 (1945) 578–85.

Fleming, James Rodger, *Fixing the Sky: The Checkered History of Weather and Climate Control* (New York: Columbia University Press, 2010).

'Polar and Global Meteorology in the Career of Harry Wexler, 1933–62' in Roger Launius et al. (eds.), *Globalizing Polar Science* (New York: Palgrave Macmillan, 2010), 225–41.

Foden, Giles, *Last King of Scotland* (London: Faber & Faber, 1998).

Foucault, Michael, 'The Eye of Power: A Conversation with Jean-Pierre Barou and Michelle Perrot' in Colin Gordon (ed.), *Power/Knowledge: Selected Interviews and Other Writings 1972–1977* (Hampshire: Harvester Press, 1980), 146–65.

Fox, William, *The Superpowers: The United States, Britain and the Soviet Union – Their Responsibility for Peace* (New York: Harcourt, Brace and Company, 1944).

Franck, Thomas M., *Fairness in International Law and Institutions* (Oxford: Oxford University Press, 1995).

'Who Killed Article 2(4) or: Changing Norms Governing the Use of Force by States' 64 *American Journal of International Law* (1970) 809–37.

Franck, Thomas M., and Edward Weisband, 'The Johnson and Brezhnev Doctrines: The Law You Make May Be Your Own' *Stanford Law Review*, 22 (1970), 979–1012.

Franck, Thomas M., and Edward Wiesband, *Secrecy and Foreign Policy* (Oxford: Oxford University Press, 1974).

Franqui, Carlos, 'Che Guevara to Daniel [René Ramos Latour], 14 December 1957' in *Diary of the Cuban Revolution* (New York: The Viking Press, 1980).

Fraser, Lindley, *Propaganda* (Oxford: Oxford University Press, 1957).
Frazier, Robeson Taj, *The East Is Black: Cold War China in the Black Radical Imagination* (Durham: Duke University Press, 2015).
Freedman, Lawrence, *The Evolution of Nuclear Strategy*, 2nd ed. (New York: St Martin's Press, 1989).
Freire, Paulo, *Pedagogy of the Oppressed* (New York: Penguin, 1972).
Friedman, Jeremy, *Shadow Cold War: Sino–Soviet Competition for the Third World* (Durham: University of North Carolina Press, 2015).
Friedmann, Wolfgang, *The Changing Structure of International Law* (New York: Columbia University Press, 1964).
'Intervention, Civil War and the Role of International Law' *ASIL Proc.*, 59 (1965) 67–81.
Frucher, Norman, and Stuart Hall, 'Notes on the Cuban Dilemma' *New Left Review* (May/June 1961) 2–12.
Gaddis, John Lewis, *The United States and the Origins of the Cold War, 1941–1947* (New York: Columbia University Press, 1972).
'Was the Truman Doctrine a Real Turning Point? Reconsiderations' *Foreign Affairs*, 52 (1974) 386.
We Know Now: Rethinking Cold War History (Oxford: Oxford University Press, 1998).
Gaines, Kevin, *African Americans in Ghana: Black Expatriates and the Civil Rights Era* (Durham: University of North Carolina Press, 2006).
Galison, Peter, 'Secrecy in Three Acts' *Social Research*, 77 (2010) 941–74.
García Márquez, Gabriel, and Roberto Pombo, 'Subcomandante Marcos: The Punch Card and the Hourglass' *New Left Review*, 11 (2001) 69–79.
Garcia-Mora, Manuel R., 'Treason, Sedition and Espionage as Political Offenses under the Law of Extradition' *University of Pittsburgh Law Review*, 26 (1964–65) 65–97.
Gardner, Lloyd, *Spheres of Influence: The Great Powers Partition Europe, From Munich to Yalta* (Lanham: Ivan R. Dee, 1993).
Gavouneli, Maria, 'Neutrality: A Survivor?' *European Journal of International Law*, 23 (2012): 267–73.
Gearty, Conor, *Homeland Insecurity: The Rise and Rise of Global Anti-Terrorism Law* (Oxford: Polity Press, 2024).
Gelhorn, Walter, *Security, Loyalty, and Science* (New York: Cornell University Press, 2019).
Gerits, Frank, *The Ideological Scramble for Africa: How the Pursuit of Anticolonial Modernity Shaped a Postcolonial Order, 1945–1966* (Ithaca: Cornell University Press, 2023).
'"When the Bull Elephants Fight": Kwame Nkrumah, Non-Alignment, and Pan-Africanism as an Interventionist Ideology in the Global Cold War (1957–66)' *International History Review*, 37(5) (2015) 951–69.

Getachew, Adom, *Worldmaking after Empire: The Rise and Fall of Self-Determination* (Princeton: Princeton University Press, 2019).

Getachew, Adom, and Jennifer Pitts, *W. E. B. Du Bois: International Thought* (Cambridge: Cambridge University Press, 2022).

Gevers, Christopher, 'International Law in Africa during the Cold War' in Matthew Craven, Gerry Simpson and Sundhya Pahuja (eds.), *Cambridge History of International Law, Vol XI: International Law during the Cold War (1945–1990)* (Cambridge: Cambridge University Press, forthcoming).

'"Land[s] beyond the White World": (Re)imagining the International through Fiction' *Law & Literature*, 36 (2023) 241–64.

'Literal Decolonization: Re-reading African International Legal Scholarship through the African Novel' in Jochen von Bernstoff and Philipp Dann (eds.), *The Battle for International Law: South–North Perspectives on the Decolonization Era* (Oxford: Oxford University Press, 2019) 383–403.

'"News from Pan-Africa": Black Internationalism, Literature & International Law', 1900–1963', PhD thesis, Melbourne Law School, 2024.

'Refiguring Slavery through International Law: The 1926 Slavery Convention, the "Native Labor Code" and Racial Capitalism' *Journal of International Economic Law*, 25 (2022) 312–33.

'To Seek with Beauty to Set the World Right: Cold War International Law and the Radical "Imaginative Geography" of Pan-Africanism' in Matthew Craven, Sundhya Pahuja and Gerry Simpson (eds.), *International Law and the Cold War* (Cambridge: Cambridge University Press, 2019) 492–509.

'"Unwhitening the World": Rethinking Race and International Law' *UCLA Law Review*, 67 (2020–21) 1652–85.

Glees, Anthony, 'Open Secrecy' in Corneliu Bjola and Stuart Murray (eds.), *Secret Diplomacy* (London: Routledge, 2016) 108–31.

Gleijeses, Piero, *Conflicting Missions: Havana, Washington and Africa 1959–1976* (Chapel Hill: University of North Carolina Press, 2002).

Golan, Galia, *The Soviet Union and National Liberation Movements in the Third World* (Abingdon: Routledge, 1988).

Goldschmidt, Bertrand, 'A Forerunner to the NPT? The Soviet Proposals of 1947: A Retrospective Look at Attempts to Control the Spread of Nuclear Weapons' *IAEA Bulletin* (Spring 1968) 58–67.

Goldstone, Jack, et al., 'The State Failure Project: Early Warning Research for U.S. Foreign Policy Planning' in John L. Davies and Ted Robert Gurr (eds.), *Preventive Measures: Building Risk Assessment and Crisis Early Warning Systems* (Lanham: Rowman & Littlefield, 1998) 27–38.

Goodrich, Leland, *Korea: A Study of US Policy in the United Nations* (New York: Council on Foreign Relations, 1956).

Goodwin, Geoffrey L., *Britain and the United Nations*, Prepared for the Royal Institute of International Affairs and the Carnegie Endowment for International Peace (New York: Manhattan Publishing Company, 1957).

Goscha, Christopher, *The Road to Dien Bien Phu: A History of the First War for Vietnam* (Princeton: Princeton University Press, 2022).

Goyal, Yogita, *Runaway Genres: The Global Afterlives of Slavery* (New York: New York University Press, 2019).

Grabar, V. E., *The History of International Law in Russia 1647–1917: A Bio-Bibliographical Study*, trans. W. E. Butler (Oxford: Clarendon Press 1990 [1958 in Russian]).

Graeber, David, *Debt: The First 5,000 Years* (Brooklyn: Melville House, 2011).

Grandin, Greg, *The Last Colonial Massacre: Latin America in the Cold War* (Chicago: University of Chicago Press, 2004).

Empire's Workshop: Latin America, The United States, and the Rise of the New Imperialism (New York: Holt Paperbacks, 2006).

Grant, Thomas, *Admission to the United Nations: Charter Article 4 and the Rise of Universal Organization* (Leiden: Martinus Nijhoff, 2009).

'Hallstein Revisited: Unilateral Enforcement of Regimes of Nonrecognition Since the Two Germanies' *Stanford Journal of International Law*, 36 (2000) 221–52.

Gray, William, *Germany's Cold War: The Global Campaign to Isolate East Germany, 1949–1969* (Chapel Hill: University of North Carolina Press, 2003).

Green, Leslie C., 'Law and Administration in Present-Day Japan' *Current Legal Problems*, 1 (1948) 118–205.

Griffith, William, *The Ostpolitik of the Federal Republic of Germany* (Cambridge, MA: MIT Press, 1978).

Grosboll, John. 'Philip Jessup, The International Problem of Governing Mankind', *Michigan Law Review*, 46(1) (1947) 38.

Groves, Leslie, *Now It Can be Told: The Story of the Manhattan Project* (New York: Harper, 1962).

Grovogui, Siba N'Zatioula, *Beyond Eurocentrism and Anarchy: Memories of International Order and Institutions* (London: Palgrave Macmillan, 2006).

Sovereigns, Quasi Sovereigns and Africans: Race and Self-Determination in International Law (Minneapolis: University of Minnesota Press, 1996).

Grzybowski, Kazimierz, *Soviet International Law and the World Economic Order* (Durham: Duke University Press, 1987).

Soviet Public International Law: Doctrines and Diplomatic Practice (Leiden: A. W. Sijthoff, 1970).

Guevara, Ernesto Che, *Congo Diary: Episodes of Revolutionary War* in Che Guevara Studies Centre (ed.), *The Congo* (New York: Seven Stories Press, 2022).

Guevara, Che, *Guerrilla Warfare* (Nebraska: Bison Books, 1998 [1961]).

Gunther, John, *The Riddle of MacArthur: Japan, Korea and the Far East* (New York: Harper & Brothers, 1951).

Gupta, V. P., 'The Asian Concept of "Peaceful Coexistence"' *Philippines Law Journal*, 45 (1970) 623–33.

Gyallay-Pap, Peter, 'Regionalism and the Allied Debate on Postwar World and European Organization, 1940–1945', PhD thesis, The London School of Economics and Political Science, 1990.

Haas, Ernst, 'The Attempt to Terminate Colonialism: Acceptance of the United Nations Trusteeship System' *International Organization*, 7(1) (1953) 1–21.

Habermas, Jürgen, *Structural Transformation of the Public Sphere* (Cambridge, MA: MIT Press, 1989).

Hackworth, Green Haywood, *Digest of International Law*, vol. II (Washington, DC: Government Printing Office, 1941).

Hall, R Cargill, 'The Truth about Overflights' *Quarterly Journal of Military History*, 9 (1997) 24–39.

Hall, William Edward, *A Treatise on International Law*, 7th ed. Edited by A. Pierce Higgins. Oxford: Clarendon Press, 1918).

A Treatise on International Law, 8th ed. Edited by A. Pierce Higgins. Oxford: Clarendon Press, 1924).

Hallam, Tony, 'The Great Revolution in Earth Sciences in the Mid-Twentieth Century' *Isis*, 105 (2014) 410–12.

Halleck, Henry Wager, *International Law; or, Rules Regulating the Intercourse of States in Peace and War* (San Francisco: H. H. Bancroft & Company, 1861).

'Military Espionage' *American Journal of International Law*, 5 (1911) 590–603.

Halliday, Fred, 'The Ends of the Cold War' *New Left Review*, 180 1990) 139–146.

The Making of the Second Cold War (London: Verso, 1983).

Halliday, Paul, 'Laws' Histories: Pluralisms, Pluralities, Diversity' in Lauren Benton and Richard J. Ross (eds.), *Legal Pluralism and Empires, 1500–1850* (New York: New York University Press, 2013) 259–78.

Hamblin, Jacob, *Oceanographers and the Cold War: Disciples of Marine Science* (Seattle: University of Washington Press, 2005).

Harmer, Tanya, *Allende's Chile and the Inter-American Cold War* (Chapel Hill: University of North Carolina Press, 2011).

Hardt, Michael, and Antonio Negri, *Empire* (Cambridge, MA: Harvard University Press, 2000).

Harper, Kristine, *Weather by the Numbers: The Genesis of Modern Meteorology* (Cambridge, MA: MIT Press, 2008).

Hartog, François, *Regimes of History: Presentism and Experiences*, trans. Saskia Brown (Columbia: Columbia University Press, 2016).

Hatzky, Christine, *Cubans in Angola: South-South Cooperation and Transfer of Knowledge, 1976–1991* (Madison: University of Wisconsin Press, 2015).

Haushofer, Karl, *Geopolitik der Pan-Ideen* (Berlin: Zentral-Verlag, 1931).

Haynes, John Earl, and Harvey Klehr, *Early Cold War Spies: The Espionage Trials That Shaped American Politics* (Cambridge: Cambridge University Press, 2006).

Hazard, John N., 'Cleansing Soviet International Law of Anti-Marxist Theories' *The American Journal of International Law*, 32 (1937) 244–52.

'Communist States and International Law' *Problems of Communism*, 24 (1975) 36–43.

Law and Social Change in the U. S. S. R. (London: Stevens and Sons Limited, 1953).

'Pashukanis Is No Traitor' *American Journal of International Law*, 51 (1957) 383–85.

'The Soviet Union and International Law' *Illinois Law Review*, 43 (1948) 591–607.

'The Soviet Union and International Law' *Soviet Studies*, 1 (1950) 189–99.

Hazeltine, Harold Dexter, *The Law of the Air* (London: University of London Press, 1911).

Head, Michael, *Evgeny Pashukanis: A Critical Reappraisal* (Abingdon: Routledge-Cavendish, 2007).

Hecht, Gabrielle, *Being Nuclear: Africans and the Global Uranium Trade* (Cambridge, MA: MIT Press, 2012).

Entangled Geographies: Empire and Technologies in the Global Cold War (Cambridge, MA: MIT Press, 2011).

Henkin, Louis, *How Nations Behave: Law and Foreign Policy*, 2nd ed. (New York: Columbia University Press, 1979).

'The Reports of the Death of Article 2(4) Are Greatly Exaggerated' *American Journal of International Law*, 65 (1971) 544–48.

et al., 'Force, Intervention, and Neutrality in Contemporary International Law' *ASIL Proc.*, 57 (1963) 147–73.

Hennesy, Peter, and Gail Brownfield. 'Britain's Cold War Security Purge: The Origins of Positive Vetting' *The Historical Journal*, 25 (1982) 965–73.

Herbst, Jeffrey, 'Responding to State Failure in Africa' *International Security*, 21(3) (1996/97) 120–44.

Herman, Edward S., and Noam Chomsky, *Manufacturing Consent: The Political Economy of the Mass Media* (London: The Bodley Head, 1988).

Herz, John H., *International Politics in the Atomic Age* (New York: Columbia University Press, 1959).

Hevia, James, *Cherishing Men from Afar: Qing Guest Ritual and the Macartney Embassy of 1793* (Durham: Duke University Press, 1995).

Higgins, A. Pearce, 'The Monroe Doctrine' *British Yearbook of International Law*, 5 (1924) 103–18.

Higgins, Rosalyn, *The Development of International Law through the Political Organs of the United Nations* (Oxford: Oxford University Press, 1963).

Problems and Process: International Law and How We Use It (New York: Clarendon Press, 1994).

Higuchi, Toshihiro, *Political Fallout: Nuclear Weapons Testing and the Making of a Global Environmental Crisis* (Stanford: Stanford University Press, 2020).

Hilsman, Roger, *Strategic Intelligence and National Decisions* (Glencoe: The Free Press, 1956).

Hodges, Donald C., *The Intellectual Foundations of the Nicaraguan Revolution* (Austin: University of Texas Press, 1986).

Hoffman, Florian, 'Human Rights and the Cold War' in Matthew Craven, Sundhya Pahuja and Gerry Simpson (eds.), *Cambridge History of International Law, Vol XI: International Law during the Cold War (1945–1990)* (Cambridge: Cambridge University Press, forthcoming).

Hoffmann, Stanley, 'International Systems and International Law' *World Politics*, 14(1) (1961) 205–37.

Holdich, P. G. H., 'A Policy of Percentages? British Policy and the Balkans After the Moscow Conference of October 1944' *The International History Review*, 9 (1987) 28–47.

Hopkins, Benjamin, 'The Problem with "Hearts and Minds" in Afghanistan' Middle East Report, 255 (2010) 24–29.

Horn, Eva, *The Secret War: Treason, Espionage and Modern Fiction* (Evanston: Northwestern University Press, 2013).

Hourani, Albert, 'The Decline of the West in the Middle East – II' *International Affairs*, 29(2) (April 1953) 156–83.

Hoyt, Edwin, 'The United States Reaction to the Korean Attack: A Study of the Principles of the United Nations Charter as a Factor in American Policy-Making' *American Journal of International Law*, 55 (1961) 45–76.

Hrabar, V. E., 'Das heutige Völkerrecht vom Standpunkte eines Sowjetjuristen' *Zeitschrift für Völkerrecht*, XIV (1928) 188–214.

Huberman, Leo, and Paul Sweezy, *Cuba: Anatomy of a Revolution* (New York: Monthly Review Press, 1960).

Hudson, Manley, 'The Registration and Publication of Treaties' *American Journal of International Law*, 19 (1925) 273.

et al. 'The International Law of the Future: Postulates, Principles and Proposals for the International Law of the Future' *AJIL Supp*, 38 (1944) 41–50.

Hull, Cordell, *The Memoirs of Cordell Hull*, vol. II (New York: Macmillan, 1948).

International Preparatory Committee of the First Solidarity Conference of the Peoples of Africa, Asia and Latin America, Towards the First Tricontinental Conference (Havana 1966).

Intondi, Vincent J., *African Americans Against the Bomb: Nuclear Weapons, Colonialism, and the Black Freedom Movement* (Stanford: Stanford University Press, 2015).

Isaeva, Anna, 'History of Soviet Legal Doctrine', PhD thesis, University of Florence, 2016).

Jackson, John H., 'Sovereignty-Modern: A New Approach to an Outdated Concept' *American Journal of International Law*, 97(4) (2003) 782–88.

Jacobs, Robert A., *Nuclear Bodies: The Global Hibakusha* (New Haven: Yale University Press, 2022).

Jacobson, Harold, 'The Soviet Union, the UN and World Trade' *Western Political Quarterly*, 11 (1958) 673.

James, C. L. R., *The Black Jacobins* (London: Penguin, 2001 [1938]).

World Revolution, 1917–1936: The Rise and Fall of the Communist International (North Carolina: Duke University Press 2017 [1937]).

Jameson, Frederic, *Archaeologies of the Future: The Desire Called Utopia and Other Science Fictions* (London: Verso, 2005).

Jens, Erik, 'Cold War Spy Fiction in Russian Popular Culture: From Suspicion to Acceptance via Seventeen Moments of Spring' *Studies in Intelligence*, 16 (2017) 31–41.

Jennings, Robert Yewdall, 'Government in Commission' *British Yearbook of International Law*, 23 (1946) 112–41.

'International Civil Aviation and the Law' *British Yearbook of International Law*, 22 (1945) 191–209.

Jersild, Austin, *The Sino-Soviet Alliance: An International History* (Chapel Hill: University of North Carolina, 2014).

Jessup, Philip, *The Birth of Nations* (New York: Columbia University Press, 1974).

'Force under a Modern Law of Nations' *Foreign Affairs*, 25(1) (1946) 90–105.

The International Problem in Governing Mankind (Claremont: Claremont College, 1947).

'Should International Law Recognize an Intermediate Status between Peace and War?' *American Journal of International Law*, 48 (1954) 98–103.

Jhabvala, Farrokh. 'The Credentials Approach to Representation Questions in the U.N.' *California Western International Law Journal*, 7(3) (1977) 615.

Johns, Fleur, 'Shadowboxing: The Data Shadows of Cold War International Law' in Matthew Craven, Sundhya Pahuja and Gerry Simpson (eds.), *International Law and the Cold War* (Cambridge: Cambridge University Press, 2019) 137–158.

Joyce, Richard, 'International Law and the Cold War: Reflections on the Concept of History' in Matthew Craven, Sundhya Pahuja and Gerry Simpson (eds.), *International Law and the Cold War* (Cambridge: Cambridge University Press, 2019) 27–48.

Jünger, Ernst, 'Total Mobilization' in Richard Wolin (ed.), *The Heidegger Controversy* (New York: Columbia University Press, 1991) 119–39.

Jungk, Robert, *Brighter Than a Thousand Suns: A Personal History of the Atomic Scientists* (Boston: Harcourt, 1958).

Kaeckenbeek, Georges, 'The San-Francisco Charter as It Relates to International Law' *Hague Recueil*, 70 (1947) 109–330.

Kahn, Herman, *Thermonuclear War* (Princeton: Princeton University Press, 1960).
Thinking about the Unthinkable (New York: Horizon Press, 1962).
Kaldor, Mary, *New and Old Wars: Organised Violence in a Global Era*, 3rd ed. (Bristol: Policy Press, 2012).
Kalliney, Peter, *The Aesthetic Cold War: Decolonization and Global Literature* (Princeton: Princeton University Press, 2022).
Kantorowicz, Ernst, *The King's Two Bodies: A Study in Medieval Political Theology* (Princeton: Princeton University Press, 2016).
Karpov, Victor P., 'Soviet Concept of Peaceful Coexistence and Its Implications for International Law' *Law and Contemporary Problems*, 29 (1964) 858–64.
Kelsen, Hans, *Collective Security under International Law* (Washington, DC: United States Government Printing Office, 1954).
The Communist Theory of Law (New York: F. A. Praeger, 1955).
'The International Legal Status of Germany to Be Established Immediately upon the Termination of the War' *American Journal of International Law*, 38 (1944) 689–94.
The Law of the United Nations: A Critical Analysis of Its Fundamental Problems (New York: F. A. Praeger, 1951).
'The Legal Status of Germany according to the Declaration of Berlin' *American Journal of International Law*, 39 (1945) 518–26.
'Recognition in International Law' *American Journal of International Law*, 35(4) (1941) 605–17.
Kendall, Sara, 'Postcolonial Hauntings and Cold War Continuities: Congolese Sovereignty and the Murder of Patrice Lumumba' in Matthew Craven, Sundhya Pahuja and Gerry Simpson (eds.), *International Law and the Cold War* (Cambridge: Cambridge University Press, 2019) 533–58.
Kende, Istvan. 'Twenty-Five Years of Local Wars' *Journal of Peace Research*, 8 (1971) 5–22.
Kennan, George, 'Peaceful Coexistence: A Western View' *Foreign Affairs*, 38 (1960) 171–90.
Kennedy, David, *International Legal Structures* (Baden-Baden: Nomos Verlagsgesellschaft, 1987).
Kennedy, Paul, *The Parliament of Man: The Past, Present, and Future of the United Nations* (New York: Random House, 2006)
Kent, Sherman, *Strategic Intelligence for American World Policy* (Princeton: Princeton University Press, 1966).
Khrushchev, Nikita, *Khrushchev Remembers: The Last Testament* (New York: Little, Brown and Co., 1974).
'On Peaceful Coexistence' *Foreign Affairs*, 38 (1959) 1–18.
Kimball, Warren F., 'Naked Reverse Right: Roosevelt, Churchill and Eastern Europe from TOLSTOY to Yalta and a Little Beyond' *Diplomatic History* 9 (1985) 1–24.

Kimball, Warren, *Sword or Ploughshares? The Morgenthau Plan for Defeated Nazi Germany* (Philadelphia: J. B. Lippincott, 1976).

King, Frank. 'Allied Negotiations and the Dismemberment of Germany' *Journal of Contemporary History*, 16 (1981) 585–95.

Kinzer, Stephen, *The Brothers: John Foster Dulles, Allen Dulles and Their Secret World War* (New York: Times Books, 2013).

Kissinger, Henry, *Diplomacy* (New York: Simon & Schuster, 1994).

Kjellén, Rudolf, *Staten som lifsform [The State as Lifeform]* (Stockholm: Hugo Gebers Förlag, 1916).

Klapsis, Antony, et. al (eds.), *The Greek Junta and the International System: A Case Study of Southern European Dictatorships, 1967–74* (London: Routledge, 2020).

Knox, Rob, 'Marxism, International Law, and Political Strategy' *Leiden Journal of International Law*, 22 (2009) 413–36.

'Strategy and Tactics' *Finnish Yearbook of International Law*, 21 (2010) 193

Kolko, Gabriel, *Century of War: Politics, Conflict and Society Since 1914* (New York: The New Press, 1994).

Korovin, Eugene A., 'American Imperialism: A Threat to the Sovereignty of Nations' in Evsey Rashba (ed.), *Materials Relating to Soviet Doctrines and Practices in International Law* (New York: New York University, 1959).

Mezhdunarodnoe pravo perekhodnogo vremeni [International Law of the Transitional Period] (Moscow/Petrograd: Gosudarstvennoe Izdatel'stvo, 1923).

'The Problems of the International Recognition of the Union of Socialist Soviet Republics in Practice' *Iowa Law Review*, 19 (1934) 259–71.

'The Second World War and International Law' *American Journal of International Law*, 40 (1946) 742–55.

'Soviet Treaties and International Law' *American Journal of International Law*, 22 (1928) 753–63.

Sovremennoe Mezhdunarodnoe Publichnoe Pravo [Contemporary International Public Law] (Moscow: Gosudarstvennoe izdatel'stvo, 1926).

'The Society and the USSR' *American Journal of International Law*, 45 (1951) 779–80.

Koskenniemi, Martti, *The Gentle Civilizer of Nations: The Rise and Fall of International Law 1870–1960* (Cambridge: Cambridge University Press, 2001).

Kossalek, Reinhart, *Sediments of Time: On Possible Histories*, ed. and trans. Sean Franzel and Stefan-Ludwig Hoffman (California: Stanford University Press, 2018).

Kraft, Alison, and Carola Sachse (eds.), *Science, (Anti-)Communism and Diplomacy: The Pugwash Conferences on Science and World Affairs in the Early Cold War* (Leiden: Brill, 2020).

Kreijen, Gerard, *State Failure, Sovereignty and Effectiveness: Legal Lessons from the Decolonization of Sub-Saharan Africa* (Leiden: Martinus Nijhoff, 2004).

Kritsiotis, Dino, 'The Elusive Peace of Panmunjom' in Matthew Craven, Sundhya Pahuja and Gerry Simpson (eds.), *International Law and the Cold War* (Cambridge: Cambridge University Press, 2019) 49–78.

Krylov, Serge, 'Les Notions Principals Du Droit Des Gens (La Doctrine Soviétique Du Droit International)' *Hague Recueil*, 70 (1947) 407–73.

'Shifting the Blame' *American Journal of International Law*, 51 (1957) 771–73.

Kunz, Josef. 'The Chaotic Status of the Laws of War and the Urgent Necessity for Their Revision' *American Journal of International Law*, 45 (1951) 37–61.

Laclau, Ernesto, and Chantal Mouffe, *Hegemony and Socialist Strategy: Towards a Radical Democratic Politics* (London: Verso, 1985).

Lal, Priya, *African Socialism in Tanzania: Between the Village and the World* (Cambridge: Cambridge University Press, 2015).

Langer, William L., 'Scholarship and the Intelligence Problem' *Proceedings of the American Philosophical Society*, 92 (1948) 43–45.

Lapenna, Ivo, 'Legal Aspects and Political Significance of the Soviet Concept of Co-existence' *International and Comparative Law Quarterly*, 12 (1963) 737–77.

Lasswell, Harold D., *Propaganda Technique in the World War* (New York: Peter Smith, 1927).

'The Theory of Political Propaganda' *American Political Science Review*, 21 (1927) 627–31.

Latour, Bruno, *Facing Gaia: 8 Lectures on the New Climactic Regime* (Cambridge: Polity Press, 2017).

Lauterpacht, Hersch, *The Function of Law in the International Community* (Oxford: Oxford University Press, 1933).

Oppenheim's International Law, 7th ed. (London: Longmans, Green & Co., 1952).

'The Problem of the Revision of the Law of War' *British Year Book of International Law*, 29 (1952) 360–82.

Recognition in International Law (Cambridge: Cambridge University Press, 1947).

'Revolutionary Propaganda by Governments' *Transactions of the Grotius Society*, 13 (1927) 143–64.

Lawson, George, *Anatomies of Revolution* (Cambridge: Cambridge University Press, 2019).

Lebovic, Sam, 'The Historical Presidency: Rethinking the Origins of National Security Classification' *Presidential Studies Quarterly*, 54 (2024) 259–70.

Lee, Christopher, 'Afro-Asia as method Bandung, the Production of Postcolonial Space and the Cruel Optimism of the 1960s' *The Global Sixties* 15(1–2) (2022) 134–49.

(ed.), *Making a World after Empire: The Bandung Moment and Its Political Afterlives* (Athens: Ohio University Press, 2019).

Leffler, Melvyn, and David Painter, *The Origins of the Cold War: An International History*, 2nd ed. (New York: Routledge, 2005).

Lenin, V. I., *Imperialism, the Highest Stage of Capitalism: A Popular Outline* (New York: International Publishers, 2013 [1917]).

'The Revolutionary Proletariat and the Right of Nations to Self-determination' in Julius Katzer (ed.), *Lenin Collected Works*, vol. 21 (Moscow: Progress Publishers, 1964).

León, Blanca Mar, 'Revolutionary Diplomacy and the Third World' in Tanya Harmer and Alberto Alvarez (eds.), *Toward a Global History of Latin America's Revolutionary Left* (London: Routledge, 2021) 67–102.

Lerner, Warren, 'The Historical Origins of the Soviet Doctrine of Peaceful Coexistence' *Law and Contemporary Problems*, 29 (1964) 865–70.

Levebvre, Stéphane. 'A Brief Genealogy of State Secrecy' *Windsor Yearbook of Access to Justice*, 31 (2013) 95–114.

Levering, Ralph B., *The Cold War: A Post-Cold War History*, 3rd ed. (West Sussex: Wiley Blackwell, 2016).

Levi, Howard S., 'The Nature and Scope of the Armistice Agreement' *American Journal of International Law*, 50 (1956) 880–906.

Liang, Yuen-Li 'The Establishment of the Interim Committee of the General Assembly' *American Journal of International Law*, 42 (1948) 435–39.

'Recognition by the United Nations of the Representation of a Member State: Criteria and Procedure' *American Journal of International Law*, 45 (1951) 689–707.

Liddell Hart, B. H., *Revolution in Warfare* (New Haven: Yale University Press, 1947).

Lie, Trygve, *In the Cause of Peace: Seven Years with the United Nations* (London: Macmillan, 1954).

Lillich, Richard. 'Forcible Self-Help by States to Protect Human Rights' *Iowa Law Review*, 53 (1967) 325–51.

Lindqvist, Sven, *A History of Bombing* (London: Granta Books, 2002).

Lippmann, Walter, 'The Cold War' *Foreign Affairs*, 65 (1987) 869–83.

The Cold War: A Study in U.S. Foreign Policy (New York: Harper & Brothers, 1947).

Public Opinion (New Brunswick: Transaction Publishers, 1922).

U. S. War Aims (Boston: Little, Brown and Company, 1944).

Lissitzyn, Oliver J., 'Some Legal Implications of the U-2 and RB-47 Incidents', *American Journal of International Law*, 56 (1962) 135–42.

'The Treatment of Aerial Intruders in Recent Practice and International Law', *American Journal of International Law*, 47 (1953) 559–89.

Litvinov, M. M., *The Bolshevik Revolution: Its Rise and Meaning* (London: British Socialist Party, 1918).

Lomas, Daniel, *The Secret History of UK Security Vetting from 1909 to the Present* (London: Bloomsbury Academic, 2025).

Lorimer, James, *The Institutes of the Law of Nations: A Treatise of the Jural Relations of Separate Political Communities* (Edinburgh: William Blackwood and Sons, 1883).

Luard, Evan, *History of the United Nations: Vol 1, The Years of Western Domination, 1945–1955* (New York: St Martin's Press, 1982).

Ludendorff, Erich, *Der totale Krieg* (Steigra: Ludendorffs Verlag, 1935).

Lumumba, Patrice, *The Truth about a Monstrous Crime of the Colonialists* (Moscow: Foreign Languages Publishing House, 1961).

Lyon, Peter, 'Neutrality and the Concept of Neutralism'*Review of Politics*, 22(2) (1960) 255–68.

Mackinder, Halford, 'The Geographical Pivot of History' *The Geographical Journal*, 23 (1904) 421–37.

'The Round World and the Winning of the Peace' *Foreign Affairs*, 21 (1943) 595–605.

Maclure, Zofia, 'Soviet International Legal Theory: Past and Present' *The Fletcher Forum*, 5 (1981) 49–73.

Maher, Anne Garland, *From the Tricontinental to the Global South: Race, Radicalism, and Transnational Solidarity* (Durham: Duke University Press, 2018).

Maldoror, Sarah (dir.), *Sambizanga* (1972).

Mälksoo, Lauri, 'The Soviet Approach to the Right of Peoples to Self-Determination: Russia's Farewell to jus publicum europaeum' *Journal of the History of International Law*, 19 (2017) 200–18.

Russia, the Soviet Union, and Imperial Continuity in International Law (Oxford: Oxford University Press, 2025)

Mamdani, Mahmood, 'University Crisis and Reform: A Reflection on the African Experience' *Review of African Political Economy*, 20(58) (1993) 7–19.

Mamlyuk, Boris N., 'Decolonization as a Cold War Imperative: Bandung and the Soviets' in Luis Eslava, Michael Fakhri and Vasuki Nesiah (eds.), *Bandung, Global History, and International Law: Critical Pasts and Pending Futures* (Cambridge: Cambridge University Press, 2017) 196–214.

Mamyluk, Boris N., and Ugo Mattei, 'Comparative International Law' *Brooklyn Journal of International Law*, 19 (2011) 385–452.

Mann, F. A., 'The Present Legal Status of Germany' *Problems of Public and Private International Law*, 33 (1947) 119–45.

Mantilla, Giovanni, *International Humanitarian Law and International Armed Conflict* (Ithaca: Cornell University Press, 2020).

Marchetti, Victor, and John D. Marks, *The CIA and the Cult of Intelligence* (New York: Laurel Book, 1983).

Marcuse, Herbert, *One Dimensional Man* (Boston: Beacon, 1964).

Marks, Susan (ed.), *International Law on the Left: Re-examining Marxist Legacies* (Cambridge: Cambridge University Press, 2008).

Martinez, Carlos, *The East Is Still Red: Chinese Socialism in the 21st Century* (Glasgow: Praxis Press, 2023).

Masco, Joseph. 'The Age of Fallout' *History of the Present: A Journal of Critical History*, 5 (2015) 137–68.

Mastny, Vojtech, *Russia's Road to the Cold War: Diplomacy, Warfare and the Politics of Communism, 1941–1945* (New York: Columbia University Press, 1979).

Mattern, Johannes, *Geopolitik: Doctrine of National Self-Sufficiency and Empire* (Baltimore: Johns Hopkins Press, 1942).

Maurice, Frederick, *The Armistices of 1918* (Oxford: Oxford University Press, 1943).

Mazower, Mark, *Governing the World: The History of an Idea* (London: The Penguin Press, 2012).

Hitler's Empire: How the Nazis Ruled Europe (London: Allen Lane, 2008).

No Enchanted Palace: The End of Empire and the Ideological Origins of the United Nations (Princeton: Princeton University Press, 2009).

McDougall, Derek, and Antonia Finnane (eds.), *Bandung 1955: Little Histories* (Melbourne: Monash University Press, 2010).

McDougal, Myres S., 'Peace and War: Factual Continuum with Multiple Legal Consequences' *American Journal of International Law*, 49 (1955) 63–68.

McDougal, Myers S., and Florentino P. Feliciano. 'International Coercion and World Public Order: The General Principles of the Law of War' *Yale Law Journal*, 67 (1958) 771–845.

McDougal, Myres S., and Richard Goodman. 'Chinese Participation in the United Nations: The Legal Imperatives of a Negotiated Solution' *American Journal of International Law*, 60 (1966) 671–727.

McDougal, Myers S., and Norbert A. Schlei. 'The Hydrogen Bomb Tests in Perspective: Lawful Measures for Security' *Yale Law Journal*, 64 (1955) 648–710.

McDowell, Eleanor C., *Digest of United States Practice in International Law 1975* (Washington, DC: Department of State, 1976).

McGarr, Paul M., 'Tinker, Tailor, Soldier, Subversive: India, Pakistan and the Politics of Cold War Intelligence' in Leslie James and Elisabeth Leake (eds.), *Decolonization and the Cold War: Negotiating Independence* (London: Bloomsbury Academic, 2015) 285–302.

McKelvey, Charles, 'Reflections on the Communist Manifesto from Third World Socialism' *Sociological Review*, 52 (2018) 523–41.

McNair, Arnold D., *The Law of the Air* (London: Stevens & Sons, 1953).

McVeigh, Shaun, *Jurisprudence of Jurisdiction* (London: Routledge, 2023).

McWhinney, Edward, 'Changing International Law Method and Objectives in the Era of the Soviet–Western Detente' *American Journal of International Law*, 59 (1965) 1–15.

'Contemporary Soviet General Theory of International Law: Reflections on the Tunkin Era' *Canadian Yearbook of International Law*, 25 (1987) 187–217.

The International Court of Justice and the Western Tradition of International Law (Berlin: Grutyer, 1987).

The International Law of Detente: Arms Control, European Security and East-West Cooperation (Alphen aan den Rijn: Sijthoff & Noordhoff International, 1978).

'International Law Making in Times of Competing Ideologies or Clashing Civilizations: Peaceful Coexistence and Soviet–Western Legal Dialogue in the Cold War Era' *Canadian Yearbook of International Law*, 44 (2007) 421–36.

'The New Thinking in Soviet International Law: Soviet Doctrines and Practice in the Post-Tunkin Era' *Canadian Yearbook of International Law*, 28 (1990) 309–37.

'"Peaceful Coexistence" and Soviet–Western International Law' *American Journal of International Law*, *56* (1962) 951–70.

'Peaceful Co-existence' and Soviet–Western International Law (Leiden: A. W. Sythoff, 1964).

'The Renewed Vitality of the Five Principles of Peaceful Coexistence' *Chinese Journal of International Law*, 3 (2004) 382–83.

'Soviet and Western International Law and the Cold War in the Era of Bipolarity: Inter-Block Law in a Nuclear Age' *Canadian Yearbook of International Law*, 1 (1963) 40–81.

'The UN Declaration on Friendly Relations and the Systems of the Sources of International Law, by Gaetano Angio-Ruiz, Noordhoof 1979' *American Journal of International Law*, 75(1) (1981) 391–93.

Meaney, Thomas, 'The Winning Side' *New Left Review: Sidecar* (10 May 2024), https://newleftreview.org/sidecar/posts/the-winning-side.

Mégret, Frédéric, and Immi Tallgren (eds.), *The Dawn of a Discipline: International Criminal Justice and Its Early Exponents* (Cambridge: Cambridge University Press, 2020).

Mearsheimer, John J., 'Nuclear Weapons and Deterrence in Europe' *International Security*, 9(3) (1984–85) 19–46.

The Tragedy of Great Power Politics (New York: W. W. Norton & Co., 2014).

Melley, Timothy, *The Covert Sphere: Secrecy, Fiction and the National Security State* (Ithaca: Cornell University Press, 2012).

Meyrowitz, Elliott. 'The Opinions of Scholars on the Legal Status of Nuclear Weapons' *Stanford Journal of International Law*, 24 (1987–88) 111–77.

Mieville, China, *Between Equal Rights: A Marxist Theory of International Law* (Leiden: Brill, 2005).

The City and the City (New York: Macmillan, 2009).

'Commodity-Form Theory of International Law: An Introduction' *Leiden Journal of International Law*, 17 (2004) 271–302.

Mohandesi, Salar, *Red Internationalism: Anti-Imperialism and Human Rights in the Global Sixties and Seventies* (Cambridge: Cambridge University Press, 2023).

Mokhtefi, Elaine, *Algiers, Third World Capital: Freedom Fighters, Revolutionaries, Black Panthers* (London: Verso, 2018).

Moore, John Norton, *Law and the Indochina War* (Princeton: Princeton University Press, 1972).

Morgan, Craig A., 'The Downing of Korean Air Lines Flight 007: Responses to Unauthorized Aerial Incursions' in W. Michael Reisman and Andrew R. Willard (eds.), *International Incidents: The Law that Counts in World Politics* (Princeton: Princeton University Press, 1988) 202–37.

Morgan, Edward M., 'The Imagery and Meaning of Self-determination' *New York University Journal of International Law and Politics*, 20 (1988) 355–404.

Morgenthau, Hans, 'Diplomacy' *Yale Law Journal*, 55 (1945–46) 1067.

'The Four Paradoxes of Nuclear Strategy' *American Political Science Association*, 58 (1964) 23–35.

'To Intervene or Not to Intervene'Foreign Affairs, 45(3) (1967) 425–36.

Politics among Nations: The Struggle for Power and Peace (Chicago: University of Chicago Press, 1949).

Morgenthau Henry, Jr, *Germany Is Our Problem* (New York: Harper & Brothers, 1945).

Mosely, Leonard, *Dulles: A Biography of Eleanor, Allen and John Foster Dulles and Their Family Network* (London: Hodder and Stoughton, 1978).

Mosely, Philip E., 'Dismemberment of Germany: The Allied Negotiations from Yalta to Potsdam' *Foreign Affairs*, 28 (1950) 487–98.

Mueller, Wolfgang, *A Good Example of Peaceful Coexistence? The Soviet Union, Austria, and Neutrality, 1955–1991* (Vienna: Verlag der Österreichischen Akademie der Wissenschaften, 2011).

Murphy, Philip. 'Creating a Commonwealth Intelligence Culture: The View from Central Africa 1945–1965' *Intelligence and National Security*, 17 (2002) 131–62.

Mutua, Makau wa, 'Why Redraw the Map of Africa: A Moral and Legal Inquiry', *Michigan Journal of International Law*, 16 (1995) 1113–76.

Naimark, Norman, 'The Sovietization of Eastern Europe, 1944–53' in Melvyn Leffler and Odd Arne Westad (eds.), *The Cambridge History of the Cold War* (Cambridge: Cambridge University Press, 2010) 175–95.

Nanda, Ved, 'The United States Armed Intervention in Grenada – Impact on World Order' *California Western International Law Journal*, 14 (1984) 395–424.

Nayar, M. G. Kaladharan, 'Self-determination beyond the Colonial Context: Biafra in Retrospect' *Texas International Law Journal*, 10 (1975) 321–46.

Neff, Stephen, 'A Short History of International Law' in Malcolm Evans (ed.), *International Law* (Oxford: Oxford University Press, 2003) 31–58.

'A Three-fold Struggle over Neutrality: The American Experience in the 1930s' in P. Lottaz and H. R. Reginbogin (eds.), *Notions of Neutralities* (Maryland: Lexington Books, 2018) 3–28.

Nehru, Jawaharlal, 'Recollections of the Conference' in Sarvepalli Gopal (ed.), *Selected Works of Jawaharlal Nehru – Second Series: Volume 28: 1 February–31 May 1955* (Delhi: Jawaharlal Nehru Memorial Fund, 1995) 144–56.

Neocleous, Mark, *A Critique of Security* (Edinburgh: Edinburgh University Press, 2012).

Newton, Scott, *Law and the Making of the Soviet World: The Red Demiurge* (Abingdon: Routledge, 2014).

'Parallel Worlds: Cold War Division Space' in Matthew Craven, Sundhya Pahuja and Gerry Simpson (eds.), *International Law and the Cold War* (Cambridge: Cambridge University Press, 2019) 117–36.

Nietzsche, Friedrich, *On the Genealogy of Morals* (Penguin: Penguin Books, 2013).

Nijman, Jane, 'Cold War Bi-Polarity: ILP Hanging in the Balance' in *The Concept of International Legal Personality: An Inquiry into the History and Theory of International Law* (The Hague: T.M.C. Asser Press, 2004) 245–344.

Nixon, Richard, *The Memoirs of Richard Nixon* (London: Arrow Books, 1978).

Nkrumah, Kwame, *Africa Must Unite* (New York: F. A. Praeger, 1963).

Neocolonialism: The Last Stage of Imperialism (London: Thomas Nelson & Sons, 1965).

Nongbri, Brent, *Before Religion: A History of a Modern Concept* (New Haven and London: Yale University Press, 2013).

Nyerere, Julius K., *Freedom and Socialism/Uhuru na Ujamaa: A Selection from Writings and Speeches 1965–1967* (Oxford: Oxford University Press, 1968).

Nys, M., 'Rapport sur le régime juridique des aerostats' *Annuaire de L'institut de Droit International*, 19 (1902) 86–114.

Obregón, Liliana, 'Latin America During the Bandung Era: Anti-Imperialist Movements vs Communist States' in Luis Eslava, Michael Fakhri and Vasuki Nesiah (eds.), *Bandung, Global History and International Law: Critical Pasts and Pending Futures* (New York: Cambridge University Press, 2017) 232–47.

'Noted for Dissent: The International Life of Alejandro Álvarez' *Leiden Journal of International Law*, 19 (2006) 983–1016.

O'Connell, D. P., *The Law of State Succession* (Cambridge: Cambridge University Press, 2015).

'The Status of Formosa and the Chinese Recognition Problem' *American Journal of International Law* 50 (1956) 405–16.

Ofuatey-Kodjoe, W., *The Principle of Self-Determination in International Law* (Cambridge, MA: Nellen,1977).

Okoth, Kevin Ochieng, *Red Africa: Reclaiming Revolutionary Black Politics* (London: Verso, 2023).

Oliver, Jack, and Leonard Murphy. 'WWNSS: Seismology's Global Network of Observing Stations' *Science*, 174(4006) (1971) 254–61.

Oliver, Robert, *Why War Came in Korea* (New York: Fordham University Press, 1950).

Onderco, Michael, *Networked Nonproliferation: Making the NPT Permanent* (Stanford: Stanford University Press, 2021).

Oppenheim, Lassa, *International Law*, 8th ed.(London: Longman, 1955).

International Law: A Treatise, Vol. II: War and Neutrality, 2nd ed. (London: Longmans, Green and Co., 1912)

Oppenheimer, J. Robert, 'Atomic Weapons and the Crisis in Science' *Saturday Review of Literature* (24 November 1945) 10–12.

Oreskes, Naomi, and John Krige, *Science and Technology in the Cold War* (Cambridge, MA: MIT Press, 2014).

Orford, Anne, 'Beyond Harmonization: Trade, Human Rights and the Economy of Sacrifice' *Leiden Journal of International Law*, 18 (2005) 179–213.

Reading Humanitarian Intervention: Human Rights and the Use of Force in International Law (Cambridge: Cambridge University Press, 2003).

'Ritual, Mediation and the International Laws of the South' *Griffith Law Review*, 16 (2007) 353–74.

Osgood, Kenneth, *Total Cold War: Eisenhower's Secret Propaganda Battle at Home and Abroad* (Lawrence: University Press of Kansas, 2006).

Osgood, Robert, *NATO: The Entangling Alliance* (Chicago: University of Chicago Press, 1962).

Ougaard, Morton, 'The Origins of the Second Cold War' *New Left Review*, 147 (1984) 61.

Özsu, Umut, *Completing Humanity: The International Law of Decolonization, 1960–82* (Cambridge: Cambridge University Press, 2024).

Pach, Chester J., 'The Containment of US Military Aid to Latin America 1944–49' *Diplomatic History* 6 (1982) 232–34.

Padelford, Norman J., 'The International Non-intervention Agreement and the Spanish Civil War' *The American Journal of International Law*, 31(4) (1937) 578–603.

Padmore, George, *Pan-Africanism or Communism? The Coming Struggle for Africa* (London: Dennis Dobson, 1956).

Pahuja, Sundhya, *Decolonising International Law: Development, Economic Growth and the Politics of Universality* (Cambridge: Cambridge University Press, 2011).

'Laws of Encounter: A Jurisdictional Account of International Law' *London Review of International Law* 1 (2013) 63–98.

'Letters from Bandung: Encounters with Another International Law' in Luis Eslava, Michael Fakhri and Vasuki Nesiah (eds.), *Bandung, Global History and International Law: Critical Pasts and Pending Futures* (Cambridge: Cambridge University Press, 2017) 552–73.

Pahuja, Sundhya, and Cait Storr, 'Rethinking Iran and International Law: The Anglo-Iranian Oil Company Case Revisited' in James Crawford, Abdul Koroma, Said Mahmoudi and Allain Pellet (eds.), *The International Legal Order: Current Needs and Possible Responses: Essays in Honour of Djamchid Momtaz* (Leiden: Brill, 2017) 53–74.

Paranzino, Michelle D., '"Two, Three, Many Vietnams": Che Guevara's Tricontinental Revolutionary Vision' in R. Joseph Parrott and Mark Atwood Lawrence (eds.), *The Tricontinental Revolution: Third World Radicalism and the Cold War* (Cambridge: Cambridge University Press, 2022) 279–303.

Parrott, R. Joseph, 'Introduction: Tricontinentalism and the Anti-imperial Project' in R. Joseph Parrott and Mark Atwood Lawrence (eds.), *The Tricontinental Revolution: Third World Radicalism and the Cold War* (Cambridge: Cambridge University Press, 2022) 1–40.

Parsons, Keith, and Robert Zaballa, *Bombing the Marshall Islands: A Cold War Tragedy* (Cambridge: Cambridge University Press, 2017).

Pashukanis, Evgeniĭ Bronislavovich, 'International Law (1925–1926)' in Piers Beirne and Robert Sharlot (eds.), *Pashukanis, Selected Writings on Marxism and Law* (London: Academic Press, 1980) 168–83.

Pateman, Roy. 'Intelligence Agencies in Africa: A Preliminary Assessment' *Journal of Modern African Studies*, 30 (1992) 569–85.

Pechatnov, Vladimir, O., 'The Soviet Union and the World' in Melvyn Leffler and Odd Arne Westad (eds.), *The Cambridge History of the Cold War* (Cambridge: Cambridge University Press, 2019).

Peevers, Charlotte, *The Politics of Justifying Force: The Suez Crisis, the Iraq War, and International Law* (Oxford: Oxford University Press, 2013).

Percival, Mark, 'Churchill and Romania: The Myth of the October 1944 "Betrayal"' *Contemporary British History* 12 (1998) 41–61.

Peters, Anne, 'Introduction – a Century after the Russian Revolution: Its Legacy in International Law' *Journal of the History of International Law*, 19 (2017) 133–46.

Pettee, George S., *The Future of American Secret Intelligence* (Washington, DC: Infantry Journal Press, 1946).

Pincus, Walter, *Blown to Hell: America's Deadly Betrayal of the Marshall Islands* (New York: Diversion Books, 2021).

Platt, Washington, *Strategic Intelligence Production* (New York: F. A. Praeger, 1957).

Pocock, J. G. A., 'British History: A Plea for a New Subject' *Journal of Modern History*, 47(4) (1975) 601

Politis, Nicolas, *Neutrality and Peace* (Washington, DC: Carnegie Endowment for International Peace, 1935).

Popper, Karl, *The Open Society and its Enemies* (London: Routledge, 1945).

Poznansky, Michael, *In the Shadow of International Law: Secrecy and Regime Change in the Postwar World* (Oxford: Oxford University Press, 2020).

Prashad, Vijay, *The Darker Nations: A People's History of the Third World* (New Delhi: LeftWord Books, 2007).

Red Star over the Third World (New Delhi: LeftWord Books, 2017).

Preston, Andrew. 'Monsters Everywhere: A Genealogy of National Security' *Diplomatic History*, 38 (2014) 477–500.

Priestland, David, *The Red Flag: A History of Communism* (New York: Grove Press, 2009).

Prince, Charles, 'Current Views of the Soviet Union of the International Organization of Security, Economic Cooperation and International Law: A Summary' *American Journal of International Law*, 39 (1945) 450–85.

Qualter, Terence H., *Propaganda and Psychological Warfare* (New York: Random House, 1962).

Quigley, John, *Soviet Legal Innovations and the Law of the Western World* (Cambridge: Cambridge University Press, 2007).

'The Soviet New Thinking in International Law: An Opening to End the Cold War' *Wisconsin International Law Journal*, 9 (1989) 97–122.

Radpey, Loqman, 'Self-Determination during the Cold War' in Matthew Craven, Sundhya Pahuja and Gerry Simpson (eds.), *Cambridge History of International Law, Vol XI: International Law during the Cold War (1945–1990)* (Cambridge: Cambridge University Press, forthcoming).

Rahnema, Ali, *Behind The 1953 Coup in Iran: Thugs, Turncoats, Soldiers and Spooks* (Cambridge: Cambridge University Press, 2015).

Ramphal, Shridath, 'Not by Unity Alone: The Case for Third World Organisation' *Third World Quarterly*, 1(3) (1979) 43–52.

Ramundo, Bernard, *Peaceful Coexistence; International Law in the Building of Communism* (Baltimore: John Hopkins University Press, 1967).

Ratzel, Friedrich, 'The Laws of the Spatial Growth of States' in Roger Kasperson and Julian Minghi (eds.) *The Structure of Political Geography* (Abingdon: Routledge, 2011) 17–28.

'Lebensraum: A Biogeographic Study' [1901], trans. Tul'si Bhambry, *Journal of Historical Geography*, 61 (2018) 59–80.

Politische Geographie (München: R. Oldenburg, 1897 [1903]).

Rawls, John, 'The Law of Peoples' *Critical Inquiry*, 20 (1993) 36–68.

Reinsch, Paul S., *Secret Diplomacy: How Far Can It Be Eliminated?* (New York: Harcourt, Brace and Company, 1922).

Reis, Herbert, 'Legal Aspects of the Invasion and Occupation of Czechoslovakia' *Department of State Bulletin*, 59 (1968) 394–401.

Reisman, Michael, 'Coercion and Self-Determination: Construing Charter Article 2(4)' *American Journal of International Law*, 78 (1984) 642–45.

'Humanitarian Intervention to Protect the Ibos' in Richard Lillich (ed.), *Humanitarian Intervention and the United Nations* (Charlottesville: Virginia University Press, 1973) 167–87.

Reisman, Michael, and James Baker, *Regulating Covert Action* (New Haven: Yale University Press, 1992).

Reisman, Michael, and Chrstina Skinner (eds.), *Fraudulent Evidence Before Public International Tribunals: The Dirty Stories of International Law* (Cambridge: Cambridge University Press, 2014).

Relyea, Harold, 'The Evolution of Government Information Security Classification Policy: A Brief Overview (1775–1973)' US Congress, House Committee on Government Operations, Security Classification Reform, hearings, 93rd Cong. 2nd Sess. Washington GPO, 1974, 505–97.

Resis, Albert, 'The Churchill–Stalin "Percentages" Agreement on the Balkans, Moscow, October 1944' *American Historical Review*, 82 (1978) 368–87.

Rheinstein, Max, 'The Legal Status of Occupied Germany' *Michigan Law Review*, 47 (1948) 23–40

Richards, Paul G., and John Zavales, 'Seismological Methods for Monitoring a CTBT: The Technical Issues Arising in Early Negotiations' in Eystein S. Huseby and Anton M. Dainty (eds.), *Monitoring a Comprehensive Test Ban Treaty* (Berlin: Springer, 1996) 53–81.

Rist, Gilbert, *The History of Development: From Western Origins to Global Faith*, trans. Patrick Camiller, 3rd ed. (London: Bloomsbury, 2008).

Rittich, Kerry, 'Transformed Pursuits: The Quest for Equality in Globalized Markets' *Harvard Human Rights Journal*, 13 (2000) 231–61.

Roberts, Geoffrey, 'Ideology, Calculation, and Improvisation: Spheres of Influence and Soviet Foreign Policy 1939–1945' *Review of International Studies* 25 (1999) 655–73.

Roberts, Peder, 'Scientists and Sea Ice under Surveillance in the Early Cold War' in S. Turchetti and P. Roberts (eds.) *The Surveillance Imperative* (New York: Palgrave Macmillan, 2014) 125–44.

Robinson, Cedric, 'The Appropriation of Frantz Fanon' *Race & Class*, 35 (1993) 79–91.

Robinson, Samuel, *Ocean Science and the British Cold War State* (London: Palgrave Macmillan, 2018).

Rodney, Walter, *The Russian Revolution: A View from the Third World* (London: Verso, 2018).

Rogers, Asha, 'Review of *The Aesthetic Cold War: Decolonization and Global Literature*, by Peter Kalliney' *The Review of English Studies* 74(316) (2023) 772.

Rojas, Rafael, *Fighting Over Fidel: The New York Intellectuals and the Cuban Revolution* (Princeton: Princeton University Press, 2016).

Romney, Carl, *Detecting the Bomb: The Role of Seismology in the Cold War* (Washington, DC: New Academia, 2009).

Roosevelt, Franklin, *The Public Papers and Addresses of Franklin D. Roosevelt: The Year of Crisis, 1933 (Vol. Two)* (New York: Random House, 1938).

Root, Elihu, 'The Real Monroe Doctrine' *American Journal of International Law*, 8 (1914) 427–42.

Rosenberg, Justin, *The Empire of Civil Society: A Critique of the Realist Theory of International Relations* (London: Verso, 1994).

Rosenboim, Or, *The Emergence of Globalism: Visions of World Order in Britain and the United States, 1939–1950* (Princeton: Princeton University Press, 2017).

Rosenstock, Robert, 'The Declaration of Principles of International Law Concerning Friendly Relations: A Survey' *American Journal of International Law* 65 (1971) 713–35.

Ross, Alf, *Constitution of the United Nations: Analysis of Structure and Function* (New York: Rinehart, 1950).

Rousseau, Charles, *Droit International Public* (Paris: Recueil Sirey, 1953).

Rotfeld, Adam D., 'Legal Foundations of the West Berlin Status' *Polish Yearbook of International Law*, 6 (1974) 97–144.

Rubin, Alfred, 'The Concept of Neutrality in International Law' *Denver Journal of International Law and Policy*, 16 (1988) 353–75.

Rubin, Andrew, *Archives of Authority: Empire, Culture, and the Cold War* (Princeton: Princeton University Press, 2012).

Rusk, Dean, 'The Bases of United States Foreign Policy' *Proceedings of the Academy of Political Science*, 27 (1962) 98–110.

Russell, Ruth, and Jeannette Muther, *A History of the United Nations Charter* (Washington, DC: Brookings Institution, 1958).

Russell, Bertrand, and Albert Einstein. 'The Russell–Einstein Manifesto' *Impact of Science on Society*, 26 (1976) 15–20.

Ryn, Claes, *The New Jacobinism: America as Revolutionary State* (Bowie: National Humanities Institute, 1991).

S. R., 'Soviet Theories of International Law' *Soviet Studies*, 4 (1953) 334–38.

Sachs, Wolfgang (ed.), *The Development Dictionary: A Guide to Knowledge as Power*, 2nd ed. (London: Zed Books, 2010).

Said, Edward, *Orientalism* (New York: Pantheon Books, 1978).

Sainsbury, Keith, 'British Policy and German Unity at the End of the Second World War' *Historical Review* 94 (1979) 786--804.

The Turning Point: Roosevelt, Stalin, Churchill, and Chiang-Kai-Shek, 1943: The Moscow, Cairo and Teheran Conferences (Oxford: Oxford University Press, 1985).

Saksena, Priyasha, *Sovereignty, International Law and the Princely States of South Asia* (Oxford: Oxford University Press, 2023).

Sand, Peter H., Jorge de Sousa Freitas and Geoffrey N. Pratt, 'An Historical Survey of International Air Law before the Second World War' *McGill Law Journal*, 7 (1960–61) 24–42.

Satow, Ernest, *A Guide to Diplomatic Practice*, 4th ed. (London: Longmans, 1954).

Saunders, Frances Stonor, *Who Paid the Piper? The CIA and the Cultural Cold War* (London: Granta Books, 1999).

Sauvy, Alfred, 'Trois Mondes: Une Planète' *L'Observateur* (1952) 118.

Sayed, Hani, 'The Humanization of the Third World' in Luis Eslava, Michael Fakhri, and Vasuki Nesiah (eds.), *Bandung, Global History, and International Law: Critical Pasts and Pending Futures* (Cambridge: Cambridge University Press, 2017) 431–49.

Scarfi, Juan Pablo, *The Hidden History of International Law in the Americas: Empire and Legal Networks* (New York: Oxford University Press, 2017).

'Mexican Revolutionary Constituencies and the Latin American Critique of US Intervention' in Kathryn Greenman, Anne Orford, Anna Saunders and Ntina Tzouvala (eds.), *Revolutions in International Law: The Legacies of 1917* (Cambridge: Cambridge University Press, 2021) 218–41.

Schachter, Oscar. 'A Conversation with Oscar Schachter' *ASIL Proc.*, 91 (1997) 340–52.

Schindler, Dietrich. 'L'interdépendance des conventions' *Hague Recueil*, 121 (1967) 225.

Schindler, Dietrich, and Jiri Toman (eds.), *The Laws of Armed Conflicts: A Collection of Conventions, Resolutions, and Other Documents* (Leiden: Martinus Nijhoff, 1973).

Schmitt, Carl, *The Nomos of the Earth in the International Law of Jus Publicum Europaeum* (New York: Telos Press, 1984/2003).

Schoenborn, Benedikt, *Reconciliation Road: Willy Brandt, Ostpolitik and the Quest for European Peace* (New York and Oxford: Berghahn Books, 2020).

Schwarzenberger, Georg, 'The Impact of the East–West Rift on International Law' *Transactions of the Grotius Society*, 36 (1950) 229–69.

Schurmann, Franz, *The Logic of World Power* (New York: Pantheon Books, 1974).

Schwarz, Hans-Peter, 'The Division of Germany, 1945–1949' in Melvyn Leffler and Odd Arne Westad (eds.), *The Cambridge History of the Cold War* (Cambridge: Cambridge University Press, 2019) 133–53.

'From the Laws of War to the Law of Armed Conflict' *Current Legal Problems*, 21(1) (1968) 239–58.

'The Impact of the East–West Rift on International Law' *Transactions of the Grotius Society*, 36 (1950) 229–69.

'The Law of Air Warfare and the Trend towards Total War' *American University Law Review*, 8 (1959) 1–18.

The Legality of Nuclear Weapons (London: Stevens & Sons, 1958).

'The Misery and Grandeur of International Law' *Current Legal Problems*, 17 (1964) 184–210.

Schwebel, Stephen M., 'The Brezhnev Doctrine Repealed and Peaceful-Coexistence Enacted' *American Journal of International Law*, 66 (1972) 816–19.

Scobbie, Iain, 'Legal Theory as a Source: Institutional Facts and the Identification of International Law' in Samantha Besson and Jean d'Aspremont (eds.), *The Oxford Handbook of the Sources of International Law* (Oxford: Oxford University Press, 2018) 493–512.

'Voyaging towards Ithaca: Thinking about International Legal Theory' in Malcolm Evans (ed.), *International Law*, 6th ed. (Oxford: Oxford University Press, 2024) 53–90.

Scott, David, *Conscripts of Modernity: The Tragedy of Colonial Enlightenment* (Durham: Duke University Press, 2004).

Scott, Leslie, "Secret Intelligence, Covert Action and Clandestine Diplomacy' *Intelligence and National Security*, 19(2) (2004) 322.

Scrase, Gavin, 'The Balkans and International Politics in the 1940s: On the Eden-Gusev Pre-Percentages Agreement' *Journal of Southern Europe and the Balkans*, 2 (2000) 163–76.

Sen, Biswanath, *A Diplomat's Handbook of International Law and Practice* (The Hague: Martinus Nijhoff, 1965).

Seth, Michael, *A Concise History of Modern Korea: From the Late Nineteenth Century to the Present*, vol. 2, 2nd ed. (Lanham: Rowman & Littlefield, 2016).

Shaikh, Nermeen, *The Present as History: Critical Perspectives on Global Power* (New York: Columbia University Press, 2007).

Shaffer, Ryan, *African Intelligence Services: Early Postcolonial and Contemporary Challenges* (Lanham: Rowman & Littlefield, 2021).

Shatz, Adam, *Writers and Missionaries: Essays on the Radical Imagination* (London: Verso, 2023).

Shearer, Ivan (ed.), *Starke's International Law*, 11th ed. (London: Butterworths, 1994).

Shils, Edward Albert, *The Torment of Secrecy: The Background and Consequences of American Security Policies* (Glencoe: The Free Press, 1956).

Shimazu, Naoko, 'Diplomacy as Theatre: Staging the Bandung Conference of 1955' *Modern Asian Studies*, 48(1) (2013) 225–52.

Japan, Race, and Equality: The Racial Equality Proposal of 1919 (Abingdon: Routledge, 1998).

Shklar, Judith, *Legalism: Law, Morals, and Political Trials* (Cambridge, MA: Harvard University Press, 1964).

Simmel, Georg, 'The Sociology of Secrecy and of Secret Societies' *American Journal of Sociology*, 11 (1906) 441–98.

Simpson, Christopher, *Science of Coercion: Communication Research & Psychological Warfare, 1945–1960* (New York: Open Road, 1994).

Simpson, Gerry, 'After Method: International Law and the Problems of History' in Annabel Brett, Megan Donaldson and Martti Koskenniemi (eds.), *History, Politics, Law: Thinking through the International* (Cambridge: Cambridge University Press, 2021) 96–126.

Great Powers and Outlaw States: Unequal Sovereigns in the International Legal Order (Cambridge: Cambridge University Press, 2004).

Sinclair, Ian, *The Vienna Convention on the Law of Treaties* (Manchester: Manchester University Press, 1984).

Singh, Nagendra, *Nuclear Weapons and International Law* (London: Stevens & Sons, 1959).

Sixsmith, Martin Daniel, *The War of Nerves: Inside the Cold War Mind* (London: Profile Books in association with Wellcome Collection, 2021).

Slaughter, Joseph R., 'Hijacking Human Rights: Neoliberalism, the New Historiography, and the End of the Third World' *Human Rights Quarterly*, 40 (2018) 735–75.

Slobodian, Quinn, *The Globalists; The End of Empire and the Birth of Neoliberalism* (Cambridge, MA: Harvard University Press, 2020).

Sloterdijk, Peter, *Critique of Cynical Reason*, trans. Michael Eldred (London: University of Minnesota Press, 1987).

Snyder, Earl A., and Hans Werner Bracht, 'Coexistence and International Law' *International & Comparative Law Quarterly*, 7 (1958) 54–71.

Socher, Johannes, 'Introduction' in *Russia and the Right to Self-Determination in the Post-Soviet Space* (Oxford: Oxford University Press, 2021) 1–13.

'Lenin, (Just) Wars of National Liberation, and the Soviet Doctrine on the Use of Force' *Journal of the History of International Law*, 19 (2017) 219–45.

Soward, Frederic, *Canada and the United Nations* (New York: Manhattan Publishing Group, 1956).

Spencer, John, 'The Monroe Doctrine and the League Covenant' *American Journal of International Law*, 30 (1936) 400–13.

Spykman, Nichola, *America's Strategy in World Politics: The United States and the Balance of Power* (New York: Harcourt, Brace and Company, 1942).

The Geography of the Peace (New York: Harcourt, Brace and Company, 1944).

Squeff, Tatiana Cardoso, Natália Medina Araújo and Bianca Guimarães Silva, 'What about the Fourth World Self?' *Cadernos do Programa de Pós-Graduação*, 17 (2022) 87–105.

Stone, Norman, *The Atlantic and Its Enemies: A Personal History of the Cold War* (London: Allen Lane, 2010).

Stalin, Joseph, 'Questions and Answers: A Discussion with Foreign Delegates', Moscow, 13 November 1927.

Works, vol. 7 (Central Committee of the Communist Part of the Soviet Union, 1954).

Steil, Benn, *The Marshall Plan: Dawn of the Cold War* (Oxford: Oxford University Press, 2018).

Stone, Julius, *Aggression and World Order: A Critique of United Nations Theories of Aggression* (Berkeley and Los Angeles: University of California Press, 1958).

Stowell, Ellery C., *Intervention in International Law* (Washington, DC: John Byrne and Co., 1921).

Stourzh, Gerald, and Wolfgang Mueller, *A Cold War over Austria: The Struggle for the State Treaty, Neutrality and the End of East–West Occupation, 1945–1955* (Lanham: Lexington Books, 2018).

Strausz-Hupé, Robert, *The Balance of Tomorrow: Power and Foreign Policy in the United States* (New York: G. P. Putnam's Sons, 1945).

Geopolitics: The Struggle for Space and Power (New York: G. P. Putnam's Sons, 1942).

Stueck, William, *The Korean War: An International History* (Princeton: Princeton University Press, 2001).

Sumich, Jason, '"Just Another African Country": Socialism, Capitalism and Temporality in Mozambique' *Third World Quarterly*, 42 (2021) 582–98.

Suri, Jeremy, *Power and Protest: Global Revolution and the Rise of Détente* (Cambridge, MA: Harvard University Press, 2005).

Syatauw, J. J. G., 'The Relationship between the Newness of States and Their Practices of International Law' in R. P. Anand (ed.), *Asian States and the Development of Universal International Law* (Delhi: Vikas, 1972) 10–21.

Snyder, Jon R., *Dissimulation and the Culture of Secrecy in Early Modern Europe* (Oakland: University of California Press, 2009).

Spaight, James Molony, 'Legitimate Objectives in Air Warfare' *British Yearbook of International Law*, 21 (1944) 158–64.

War Rights on Land (London: Macmillan, 1911).

Specter, Matthew, *The Atlantic Realists: Empire and International Political Thought between Germany and the United States* (Stanford: Stanford University Press, 2022).

Steiner, Barry H., *Bernard Brodie and the Foundations of American Nuclear Strategy* (Lawrence: University Press of Kansas, 1991).

Stern, David S., Robert Borosage and Tom Farer. 'Covert Intervention and the Third World' *Proceedings of the American Society of International Law Annual Meeting*, 69 (1975) 200–16.

Stewart, Gordon, *The Cloak and Dollar War* (London: Lawrence and Wishart, 1953).

'Legal Problems of Espionage in Conditions of Modern Conflict' in Quincy Wright, Julius Stone, Richard A. Falk and Roland J. Stanger (eds.), *Essays on Espionage and International Law* (Columbus: Ohio State University Press, 1962) 29–44.

Storr, Cait, 'Space Is the Only way to Go: The Evolution of the Extractivist Imaginary of International Law' in Shane Chalmers and Sundhya Pahuja (eds.), *Routledge Handbook of International Law and the Humanities* (Abingdon: Routledge, 2021) chapter 22.

Sukovataya, Viktoria A., 'Spy and Counterspy as a "Cultural Hero" in the Soviet Cinema of the Cold War' *Diacronie*, 302 (2017) 1–18.

Taracouzio, Timothy A., *The Soviet Union and International Law* (New York: The Macmillan Company, 1935).

Tarling, Nicholas. 'Atonement before Absolution: British Policy towards Thailand during World War II' *Journal of the Siam Society*, 66(1) (1978) 22–65.

Taubman, William, *Khrushchev: The Man and His Era* (New York: W. W. Norton & Company, 2003).

Taussig, Michael, *Defacement: Public Secrecy and the Labor of the Negative* (Redwood City: Stanford University Press, 1999).

Telepneva, Natalia, *Cold War Liberation: The Soviet Union and the Collapse of Portuguese Empire in Africa, 1961–1975* (Chapel Hill: University of North Carolina Press, 2021).

Thompson, Edward, 'The Ends of the Cold War' *New Left Review*, 182 (1990) 139–146.

Tomashevsky, Dmitry G., *On the Peaceful Co-existence of States* (Moscow: Novosti Press Agency Publishing House, 1973).

Tomba, Massimiliano, *Insurgent Universality: An Alternative Legacy of Modernity* (Oxford: Oxford University Press, 2019).

Torrent, Mélanie, *Algerian Independence and the British Left: Solidarities and Resistance in a Decolonising World* (London: Bloomsbury Academic, 2024).

Traverso, Enzo, *Revolution: An Intellectual History* (London: Verso, 2021).

Triska, Jan, *The Theory, Law, and Policy of Soviet Treaties* (Redwood City: Stanford University Press, 1962).

Tsakaloyannis, Panos, 'The Moscow Puzzle' *Journal of Contemporary History*, 21 (1986) 37–55.

Tucker, Robert W., 'Rules Governing Weapons and Naval Warfare' *International Law Studies*, 50 (1957) 45–149.

Tunkin, Grigory, 'Coexistence and International Law' *Hague Recueil*, 95 (1958) 1–79.

Co-Existence and International Law (Leiden: Martinus Nijhoff, 1958).

'The Legal Nature of the United Nations' *Hague Recueil*, 119 (1966).

Politics, Law and Force in the Interstate System (Leiden: Martinus Nijhoff, 1989).

Theory of International Law (Cambridge, MA: Harvard University Press, 2013).

Tzouvala, Ntina, *Capitalism as Civilisation: A History of International Law* (Cambridge: Cambridge University Press, 2020).

Vaihinger, Hans, *The Philosophy of 'As If': A System of the Theoretical, Practical and Religious Fictions of Mankind*, trans. C. K. Ogden, 2nd ed. (London: Kegan Paul, Trench, Trubner and Co., 1935).

Vali, Ferenc. 'Legal Constitutional Doctrines on Germany's Post–World War II Status' *North Dakota Law Review*, 42 (1965) 20–45.

Vandenberg, Arthur, *The Private Papers of Senator Vandenberg* (Boston: Houghton Mifflin, 1952).

Vattel, Emer de, *The Law of Nations, Or, Principles of the Law of Nature, Applied to the Conduct and Affairs of Nations and Sovereigns, with Three Early Essays on the Origin and Nature of Natural Law and on Luxury*, vol. III (Indianapolis: Liberty Fund, 2008).

Verdross, Alfred, 'Austria's Permanent Neutrality and the United Nations Organization' *American Journal of International Law*, 50 (1956) 61–68.

Verzijl, J. H. W., *International Law in Historical Perspective: The Law of Neutrality* (Leiden: Brill Nijhoff, 1979).

Virally, Michel, *L'Administration Internationale de l'Allemagne: Du 8 Mai 1945 au 24 Avril 1947* (Paris: Pedone, 1948).

Vitalis, Robert, 'The Midnight Ride of Kwame Nkrumah and Other Fables of Bandung (Ban-doong)' *Humanity*, 4 (2013) 261–88.

von Dannenberg, Julia, *The Foundations of Ostpolitik: The Making of the Moscow Treaty between West Germany and the USSR* (Oxford: Oxford University Press, 2008).

Von Eschen, Penny, *Race Against Empire: Black Americans and Anti-Colonialism 1937–1957* (Ithaca: Cornell University Press, 1997).

Vrignon, Alexis, 'Pacifism and Anti-nuclear Protest in Polynesia at the End of the Cold War' in Luc-André Brunet and Eirini Karamouzi (eds.), *Beyond the Euromissile Crisis: Global Histories of Anti-Nuclear Activism in the Cold War* (New York: Berghahn Books, 2025) 199–216.

Vukadinovic, Radovan, *Non-Aligned Countries and Détente* (Beograd: Jugoslovenska Stvarnost, 1979).

Vyshinsky, Andrei, Speech at the UN General Assembly. Second Session, Plenary Meeting, 18 September 1947.

Wallerstein, Immanuel, 'The Curve of American Power' *New Left Review*, II(40) (2006) 41–55

Waltz, Kenneth N., 'Nuclear Myths and Political Reality' *American Political Science Review*, 84(3) (1990) 731–45.

Weathersby, Kathryn, 'Soviet Aims in Korea and the Origins of the Korean War: New Evidence from Russian Archives', Woodrow Wilson International Centre for Scholars Working Papers, 1993.

Weber, Max, *Political Writings* (Cambridge: Cambridge University Press, 1994).

Weigert, Hans, *Generals and Geographers: The Twilight of Geopolitics* (New York: Oxford University Press, 1942).

Weiss-Wendt, Anton, *The Soviet Union and the Gutting of the UN Genocide Convention* (Madison: University of Wisconsin Press, 2017).

Weizman, Eyal, *The Least of All Possible Evils: Humanitarian Violence from Arendt to Gaza* (London: Verso, 2011).

Wellerstein, Alex, *Restricted Data: The History of Nuclear Secrecy in the United States* (Chicago: University of Chicago Press, 2021).

Welles, Sumner, 'Preface' in Robert Oliver *Korea: Forgotten Nation* (Washington, DC: American Council on Public Affairs, 1944).

The Time for Decision (New York: Harper & Brothers, 1944).

Weng, Byron, 'Communist China's Changing Attitudes towards the United Nations' *International Organisation*, 20(4) (1966) 677–704.

Westad, Odd Arne, 'The Cold War and the International History of the Twentieth Century' in Melvyn Leffler and Odd Arne Westad (eds.), *The Cambridge History of the Cold War* (Cambridge: Cambridge University Press, 2010) 1–19.

Westadt, Odd Arne, *The Global Cold War: Third World Interventions and the Making of Our Times* (Cambridge: Cambridge University Press, 2007).

Westlake, John, 'Régime des aerostats et de la têlégraphie sans fil' *Annuaire de L'institut de Droit International*, 21 (1906) 293–328.

White, Nigel D, 'Ending the US Embargo of Cuba: International Law in Dispute' *Journal of Latin American Studies*, 51(1) (2019) 163–86.

Whittlesey, Derwent, et al., *German Strategy of World Conquest* (New York: Oxford University Press, 1942).

Whitton, John B., and Arthur Larson, *Propaganda: Towards Disarmament in the War of Words* (New York: Oceana Publications, 1964).

Whyte, Jessica, *The Moral of the Market: Human Rights and the Rise of Neoliberalism* (London: Verso, 2019).

Wilder, Gary, *Freedom Time: Negritude, Decolonization, and the Future of the World* (Durham: Duke University Press, 2015).

Wiliams, Robert Chadwell, *Klaus Fuchs: Atom Spy* (Cambridge, MA: Harvard University Press, 1987).

Wilk, Kurt, 'International Law and Global Ideological Conflict: Reflections on the Universality of International Law' *American Journal of International Law*, 45 (1951) 648–70.

'International Law and Ideological Realignment: Universality Re-examined' *New York University Journal of International Law and Politics*, 10 (1978) 463–90.

Wilke, Christiane, and Halyeh Doutaghi, 'Legal Technologies: Conceptualizing the Legacy of the 1923 Hague Rules of Aerial Warfare' *Leiden Journal of International Law*, 37 (2024) 88–110.

Wills, Garry, *Bomb Power: The Modern Presidency and the National Security State* (New York: Penguin Press, 2010).

Williams, David, *Not in the Public Interest: The Problem of Security in Democracy* (London: Hutchinson, 1965).

Williams, Susan, *White Malice: The CIA and the Covert Recolonisation of Africa* (New York: PublicAffairs, 2021).

Wilson, Woodrow, 'Let There Be Light' in *The New Freedom: A Call for the Emancipation of the Generous Energies of a People* (New York: Doubleday, Page & Company, 1913).

Winkler, Allan, *The Cold War: A History in Documents* (London: Routledge, 2011).

Wittner, Lawrence, *Toward Nuclear Abolition: A History of the World Nuclear Disarmament Movement, 1971–Present* (Stanford: Stanford University Press, 2003).

Wolfers, Arnold, 'Anglo-American Postwar Cooperation and the Interests of Europe' *American Political Science Review*, 36 (1942) 656–66.

Wright, Quincy, 'Espionage and the Doctrine of Non-intervention in Internal Affairs' in Quincy Wright, Julius Stone, Richard A. Falk and Roland J. Stanger (eds.), *Essays on Espionage and International Law* (Columbus: Ohio State University Press, 1962) 3–28.

'The Law of the Nuremberg Trial' *American Journal of International Law*, 41 (1947) 38–72.

'Legal Aspects of the U-2 Incident' *American Journal of International Law*, 54 (1960) 836–54.

Wu, Aaron, 'Bridging Ideologies: Julian Huxley, Détente, and the Emergence of International Environmental Law' in Matthew Craven, Sundhya Pahuja and Gerry Simpson (eds.), *International Law and the Cold War* (Cambridge: Cambridge University Press, 2020) 189–213.

Yaffe, Helen, *Che Guevara: The Economics of Revolution* (Basingstoke: Palgrave Macmillan, 2009).

Yamazaki, James, *Children of the Atomic Bomb* (Durham: Duke University Press, 1995).

Younis, Musab, 'Against Independence' *London Review of Books*, 39 (2017) 27–28.

Zemanek, Karl, '"Unconditional Surrender" and International Law' *Annual of the Association of Attenders and Alumni of the Hague Academy of International Law*, 26 (1956) 29–37.

Zhukov, Gennady, 'Space Espionage Plans and International Law' *International Affairs* (1960) 53–57.

Žižek, Slavoj, *First as Tragedy, then as Farce* (London: Verso, 2009).

In Defence of Lost Causes (London: Verso, 2008).

The Sublime Object of Ideology (London: Verso, 1989).

Zubok, Vladislav M., and Constantine Pleshakov, *Inside the Kremlin's Cold War: From Stalin to Khrushchev* (Cambridge, MA: Harvard University Press, 1997).

Cases/Treaties/Legislation

Abel v United States, 362 US 217, 80 S Ct 683 (1960)

Aerial Incident of 7 October 1952 (USA v USSR) (1955) ICJ Rep 9.

Aerial Incident of 10 March 1953 (USA v Czechoslovakia) (1955) ICJ Rep 6.

Aerial Incident of 7 November 1954 (USA v USSR) (1957) ICJ Rep 8.

Aerial Incident of 27 July 1955 (Israel v Bulgaria) (1957) ICJ Rep 182.

Aerial Incident of 27 July 1955 (UK v Bulgaria) (1957) ICJ Rep 190.

Aerial Incident of 4 September 1954 (USA v USSR) (1958) ICJ Rep 158.

Agreement on Basic Principles of Relations between the United States and the Soviet Union, Moscow, 29 May 1972.

Agreement between the Allies amending the Protocol of 12 September 1944, London, 14 November 1944.

Agreement between the Allies on Control Machinery in Germany, London, 1 May 1945, 5 UST 2072; TIAS 3070.

Agreement between the Allies on the Occupation Zones in Germany, London, 26 July 1945, 5 UST 2087; TIAS 3071.

Agreement between the Governments of the United Kingdom and the United States on the Economic Fusion of their Respective Zones, New York, 2 December 1946.

Agreement on Control Machinery in Austria, London, 4 July 1945, Cmd 6958.

Agreement on Control Machinery in Germany, London, 14 November 1944, 5 UST 2062; TIAS 3070.

Agreement on Cooperation in Environmental Protection, 852 UNTS 106.

Agreement governing the Activities of States on the Moon and Other Celestial Bodies, New York, 5 December 1979. 1363 UNTS 3.

Agreement on Trade and Intercourse between Tibet Region of China and India, Beijing, 29 April 1954.

Agreements concerning Control Machinery and Zones of Occupation in Austria and the Administration of the City of Vienna, Vienna, 28 June 1946, Cmd 6958.

Antarctic Treaty. Washington, DC, 1 December 1959. 402 UNTS 71.

Armistice Agreement with Bulgaria, Moscow, 28 October 1944.

Armistice of Cassibile, 3 September 1943.

Atomic Energy Act of 1954.

Austrian State Treaty (signed 15 May 1955, entered into force 27 July 1955) 6 UST 2369; TIAS 3298.

Basic Principles of Relations between the United States of American and the Union of Soviet Socialist Republics *American Journal of International Law*, 66 (1972) 920–22.

Basic Law (Grundgesetz) of the Federal Republic of Germany, 8 May 1949 (Germany).

Belgrade Declaration, 2 June 1955.

Brussels Treaty on Economic, Social and Cultural Collaboration and Collective Self-Defence, Brussels, 17 March 1948, 19 UNTS 304.

Cairo Declaration, 27 November 1943.

Case Concerning Military and Paramilitary Activities in and Against Nicaragua (Nicaragua v USA) Merits, Judgment, ICJ Reports 1986, 14.

Case–Zablocki Act of 1972, 1 U.S.C. § 112b (as amended).

Charter of the United Nations, San Francisco, 26 June 1945, in force 24 October 1945, 1 UNTS XVI.

Charter of the Allied High Commission for Germany, Paris, 20 June 1949.

China, Soviet Union: Treaty of Friendship and Alliance, American Journal of International Law Supplement, 40 (1946) 51–63.

Conditions of Admission of a State to Membership in the United Nations (Article 4 of the Charter), Advisory Opinion of 28 May 1948, Dissenting Opinion of Judge M. Krylov, ICJ Rep 107.

Constitution of the Republic of Korea, 12 July 1948 (South Korea).

Constitution of the Democratic People's Republic of Korea (North Korea).

Convention between the United Kingdom of Great Britain and Northern Ireland, the United States of America, France and the Federal Republic of Germany on Relations between the Three Powers and the Federal Republic of Germany (signed 26 May 1952, entered into force 5 May 1955) 331 UNTS 328.

Convention for the Prevention and Punishment of Terrorism, Geneva, 16 November 1937, 10 League of Nations – Official Journal (January 1938) 23.

Convention for European Economic Cooperation, Paris, 16 April 1948.

Convention for the Suppression of Unlawful Seizure of Aircraft, The Hague, 14 October 1971, 860 UNTS 105.

Convention for the Unification of Certain Rules for International Carriage by Air, Montreal, 28 May 1999, 2242 UNTS 309.

Convention on the Continental Shelf, Geneva, 29 April 1958, 499 UNTS 311.

Convention on the Duties and Rights of States in the Event of Civil Strife, Havana, 20 February 1928.

Convention on International Civil Aviation, Chicago, 7 December 1944, 15 UNTS 295.

Convention on the Rights and Duties of States, Montevideo, 26 December 1933.

Convention on the Use of Broadcasting in the Cause of Peace, Geneva, 23 September 1936.

Convention on the Prohibition of Military or Any Other Hostile Use of Environmental Modification Techniques, 5 October 1978. 1108 UNTS 151.

Convention to Prevent and Punish the Acts of Terrorism Taking the Forms of Crimes Against Persons and Related Extortion That Are of International Significance, Washington, DC, 2 February 1971, OAS TS No. 37.

Convention (II) with Respect to the Laws and Customs of War on Land and Its Annex: Regulations Concerning the Laws and Customs of War on Land, The Hague, 29 July 1899. 32 Stat 1803.

Convention (IV) Respecting the Laws and Customs of War on Land and Its Annex: Regulations Concerning the Laws and Customs of War on Land, the Hague, 18 October 1907, 36 Stat 2277.

Convention Relating to the Regulation of Aerial Navigation, Paris, 13 October 1919, 11 LNTS 173.

Corfu Channel (United Kingdom of Great Britain and Northern Ireland v Albania) (1949) ICJ Rep 4.

Covenant of the League of Nations, Versailles, 28 June 1919, 225 CTS 195.

Declaration Concerning the Entry into Force of the Occupation Statute, Bonn, 21 September 1949.

Declaration Concerning the Peaceful Coexistence of States, UNGAOR, 12th Session, Agenda Item 66, UN Doc. A/3673 (14 December 1957).

Declaration of American Principles, Lima, 1938.

Declaration of Paris (1856), 46 BFSP 137.

Declaration of the Government of the USSR, Moscow, 30 October 1956.

Declaration of Principles, Known as the Atlantic Charter (signed and entered into force 14 August 1941) 204 LNTS 381.

Declaration of Solidarity for the Preservation of the Political Integrity of the American States against the Intervention of International Communism *American Journal of International Law*, Supplement 48 (1954) 123–24.

Declaration of the Warsaw Conference of Foreign Ministers, Warsaw, 24 June 1948.

Declaration on Aid to Berlin, Bonn, 26 May 1952.

Declaration on the Inadmissibility of Intervention in the Domestic Affairs of States and the Protection of their Independence and Sovereignty, UNGA Res 2131 (21 December 1965).

Declaration Regarding the Defeat of Germany and the Assumption of Supreme Authority with Respect to Germany by the Governments of the United Kingdom, the United States of America and the Union of Soviet Socialist Republics, and the Provisional Government of the French Republic, Berlin, 5 June 1945, Cmd. 6648.

Declaration on World Peace and Co-operation, Bandung Conference, 24 April 1955.

Decree of 28 January 1918, RSFSR Laws 1917–18, No. 27, Article 353.

Espionage Act of 1917.

Espionage and Censorship Statute of 1970.

Ex parte Quirin, 317 US 1 (1942).

Finland–Soviet Union: Armistice, American Journal of International Law Supplement 39 (1945) 85–88.

Hungarian Armistice Agreement, Moscow, 20 January 1945, 59 Stat. 1321

Instrument of Surrender, Malta, 29 September 1943, 61 Stat. 2742.

Instrument of Surrender, Tokyo Bay, 2 September 1945, EAS No. 493.

Inter-American Reciprocal Assistance and Solidarity (Act of Chapultepec), 6 March 1945, 60 Stat. 1831.

Inter-American Treaty of Reciprocal Assistance, Rio de Janeiro, 2 September 1947, 21 UNTS 324.

Intermediate-Range Nuclear Forces Treaty, Washington, 8 December 1987.

International Military Tribunal (Nuremberg) Judgment of 1 October 1946.

Intelligence Organization Act, 106 Stat. 3188 (1992).

Intelligence Services Act 1994.

Inter-American Reciprocal Assistance and Solidarity (Act of Chapultepec) Mexico City, 6 March 1945. TIAS No 1543.

International Convention against the Taking of Hostages, New York, 17 December 1979, 1316 UNTS 205.

Interim Agreement on Certain Measures With Respect to the Limitation of Strategic Offensive Arms (SALT I), Union of Soviet Socialist Republics–United States of America Moscow, 26 May 1972. UNTS 944 3.

Joint Defence and Economic Co-operation between States of the Arab League American Journal of International Law Supplement 49 (1955) 51.

Legality of the Threat or Use of Nuclear Weapons (Advisory Opinion) [1996] ICJ Rep 226.

Letter Dated 19 January 1949 from the Acting Foreign Minister of the Republic of Korea to the Secretary-General Concerning the Application of the Republic of Korea for Admission to Membership in the United Nations and a Declaration Accepting Obligations Under the Charter, 19 January 1949, UN Doc. S/1238.

Letter Dated 11 February 1949 from the Representative of the Union of Soviet Socialist Republics Addressed to the President of the Security Council Concerning the Application of the Democratic People's Republic of Korea for Admission in the United Nations, 11 February 1949, UN Doc. S/1256.

Luther v Sagor [1921] 3 KB 532.

Memorandum on the Powers and Responsibilities of France, United Kingdom and United States Following the Establishment of the FRG, Washington, DC, 8 April 1949.

Military and Paramilitary Activities in and against Nicaragua (Nicaragua v USA) (1986) ICJ Rep 14.

Moscow Agreement, Moscow, 12 August 1970.

Moscow Memorandum, 15 April 1955.

Moscow Protocol, Moscow, signed 30 October 1943, formalised 1 November 1943, 3 Bevans 816.

National Security Act of 1947.

Neutrality Act, 26 October 1955 (Austria).

North Atlantic Treaty, Washington, 4 April 1949, 34 UNTS 541.

Occupation Statute of April 17, 1949, Official Gazette of the Allied High Commission for Germany, 23 October 1949.

Official Secrets Act 1911 (UK).

Pacific Charter, 209 UNTS 2819.

Potsdam Agreement, Protocol of the Proceedings, Potsdam, 1 August 1945.

Protocol Additional to the Geneva Conventions of 12 August 1949, and Relating to the Protection of Victims of International Armed Conflicts (Protocol I), Geneva, 8 June 1977, 1125 UNTS 3.

Protocol of Proceedings at the Yalta Conference (4–11 February 1945).

Protocol on Zones of Occupation in Germany and the Administration of 'Greater Berlin', 12 September 1944, 227 UNTS 279.

Roosevelt–Litvinov Agreements, Washington, DC, 16 November 1933.

South Pacific Nuclear Free Zone Treaty, Rarotonga, 6 August 1985. 1445 UNTS 177.

Southeast Asia Collective Defence Treaty, 209 UNTS 2819.

State Treaty for the Re-establishment of an Independent and Democratic Austria, 15 May 1955, 277 UNTS 222.

South West Africa cases (Ethiopia v. South Africa; Liberia v. South Africa) (Prelimiary Objections) (1962) ICJ Rep 319.

South West Africa cases (Ethiopia v. South Africa; Liberia v. South Africa) (Second Phase) (1966) ICJ Rep 6.

Treaty concerning Relations between the USSR and the GDR, Moscow, 20 September 1955, 226 UNTS

Treaty for an Alliance in the War against Hitlerite Germany and Her Associates in Europe, London, 26 May 1942, Treaty Series No 2 1942 Cmd. 6376.

Treaty of Friendship, Co-operation and Mutual Assistance (signed 14 May 1955, entered into force 6 June 1955) 219 UNTS 3.

Treaty of Peace with Finland, 1947, American Journal of International Law, Supplement 42 (1948) 203–23.

Treaty of Peace with Japan, San Francisco, 8 September 1951, 1832 UNTS 46.

Treaty of Peace with Romania, London, 10 February 1947.

Treaty on the Basis of Intra-German Relations, East Berlin, 21 December 1972.

Tripartite Declaration on Austria (Moscow, 1 November 1943).

Treaty between the Russian Federation and the United States of America on Strategic Offensive Reductions (The Moscow Treaty). Russian Federation–United States of America. Moscow, 24 May 2002. 2350 UNTS 415.

Treaty between the Russian Federation and the United States of America on Measures for the Further Reduction and Limitation of Strategic Offensive Arms, Russian Federation–United States. Prague, 8 April 2010. TIAS 11-205.

Treaty between the United States of America and the Russian Federation on Measures for the Further Reduction and Limitation of Strategic Offensive Arms

(START II), Union of Soviet Socialist Republics–United States of America. Moscow, 3 January 1993. UN Doc. CD/1194.

Treaty between the United States of America and The Union of Soviet Socialist Republics on The Reduction and Limitation of Strategic Offensive Arms (START I), Union of Soviet Socialist Republics–United States of America. Moscow, 31 July 1991. UN Doc. CD/1192.

Treaty between the United States of America and the Union of Soviet Socialist Republics on the Limitation of Anti-Ballistic Missile Systems (ABM), Union of Soviet Socialist Republics–United States of America. Moscow, 26 May 1972. 944 UNTS 13.

Treaty between the United States of America and The Union of Soviet Socialist Republics on the Limitation of Strategic Offensive Arms (SALT II), Union of Soviet Socialist Republics–United States of America. Vienna, 18 June 1979.

Treaty between the United States of America and the Union of Soviet Socialist Republics on the Limitation of Underground Nuclear Weapons Test. 1718 UNTS 216.

Treaty for the Prohibition of Nuclear Weapons in Latin America, Mexico City, 14 February 1967. 634 UNTS 281.

Treaty on Principles Governing the Activities of States in the Exploration and Use of Outer Space, Including the Moon and Other Celestial Bodies. Washington, Moscow and London, 27 January 1967. 610 UNTS 205.

Treaty on the Prohibition of the Emplacement of Nuclear Weapons and Other Weapons of Mass Destruction on the Sea-Bed and the Ocean Floor and in the Subsoil Thereof. Washington, Moscow and London, 11 February 1971. 955 UNTS 115.

Treatment in Hungary of Aircraft and Crew of United States of America (USA v. South Pacific Nuclear Free Zone Treaty. Rarotonga, 6 August 1985. 1445 UNTS 177. USSR*)* (1954) ICJ Rep 103.

Treatment in Hungary of Aircraft and Crew of United States of America (USA v. Hungarian Peoples Republic) (1954) ICJ Rep 99.

United States Diplomatic and Consular Staff in Tehran (USA v Iran) (1980) ICJ Rep 3.

US v Sobell, 314 F.2d 314 (Fed Cir, 1963).

United States - Great Briain - Soviet Union Armistice with Rumania American Journal of International Law, Supplement 39 (1945) 88–108.

United States v Coplon, 84 F Supp 472 (SDNY 1949)

United States v Melekh, 190 F Supp 67 (SDNY 1960)

United States v Egorov, 292 F Supp 106 (EDNY 1963)

United States v Valdik Aleksandrovich Enger and Rudolf Petrovich Chernyayev, 472 F Supp 490 (DJN 1978).

Vienna Convention on Diplomatic Relations, 1961, 500 UNTS 95.

Vienna Convention on the Law of Treaties, 1969, 1155 UNTS 331.

C Reports/Primary UN and Archival Documents

'Address by the Soviet Representative (Andrei Gromyko) to the United Nations Atomic Energy Commission, 19 June 1946' in *Documents on Disarmament 1945–1959*, Vol 1, 1945–1956. US Dept of State, 1960.

Adlai Stevenson's UN Security Council Address on Cuban Missiles (25 October 1962), www.britishpathe.com/asset/98254/.

Africa, Sandy, *Changing Intelligence Dynamics in Africa* (Birmingham: GFN-SSR, 2009).

Asian-African Legal Consultative Organization (AALCO), *Addendum to the Principles Concerning Treatment of Refugees*, 27 January 1970.

Principles Concerning Admission and Treatment of Aliens, 25 February 1961.

'Belgrade Declaration of Non-Aligned Countries, 1961', First Summit Conference of Heads of State or Government of the Non-Aligned Movement. Belgrade, Yugoslavia, 6 September 1961.

Bevin, Ernest, House of Commons Debates (5th series), cols. 1738–1739 (15 May 1947).

Castro, Fidel, 'At the Closing Session of the Tricontinental Conference' (Tricontinental Conference, Havana, 15 January 1966), www.marxists.org/history/cuba/archive/castro/1966/01/15.htm.

Letter to Nikita Khrushchev, 26 October 1962. Document 45, Cuban Missile Crisis, JFK Library. https://microsites.jfklibrary.org/cmc/oct26/doc2.html.

Churchill, Winston. 'The Sinews of Peace', International Churchill Society, https://winstonchurchill.org/resources/speeches/1946-1963-elder-statesman/the-sinews-of-peace/.

Committee on Aeronautical and Space Sciences, Soviet Space Programs, 1971–75 (Washington, DC: US Government Printers Office, 1976).

Conference of Independent African States, Declaration and Resolution IX: Accra, Ghana, April, 1958 *Black Camera*, 13 (2021) 9–12.

Conference of President Roosevelt, Generalissimo Chiang Kai-Shek, and Prime Minister Churchill in North Africa, *American Journal of International Law* Supplement 38 (1944) 8–9.

Current Documents: Resolution on Frontiers, Boundaries and Federations, *Current History*, 37 (1959) 41–46.

'Directive to the Commander in Chief of the United States Forces of Occupation', *Department of State Bulletin* 13 (1945) 596.

Documents of the United Nations Conference on International Organization, San Francisco 1945, Vols. 1–12.

Documents Relating to the Organization of a System of European Federal Union, LN Doc VII, 4 (1930).

General Assembly Resolution 197 A (III), 3 December 1948.

General Orders No. 100 (24 April 1863).

'Foreign Policy and Fund for Peace, Failed States Index 2005' *Foreign Policy*, July/August 2005.

Foreign Relations of the United States: Diplomatic Papers, 1945, General: The United Nations (Volume I) (Washington, DC: United States Government Printing Office, 1967)

Foreign Relations of the United States: Diplomatic Papers, 1945, The British Commonwealth, The Far East (Volume VI) (Washington, DC: United States Government Printing Office, 1969)

Foreign Relations of the United States: Diplomatic Papers, Conferences at Malta and Yalta 1945 (Washington, DC: United States Government Printing Office, 1955)

Foreign Relations of the United States, 1946: Eastern Europe; The Soviet Union (Volume VI) (Washington, DC: United States Government Printing Office, 1969)

Foreign Relations of the United States, 1948: Germany and Austria (Volume II) (Washington, DC: United States Government Printing Office, 1973)

Foreign Relations of the United States, 1948: The Western Hemisphere (Volume IX) (Washington, DC: United States Government Printing Office, 1972)

Foreign Relations of the United States, 1950: Western Europe (Volume III) (Washington, DC: United States Government Printing Office, 1977)

Foreign Relations of the United States, 1958–1960 (Volume IX). (Washington, DC: United States Government Printing Office, 1993)

Foreign Relations of the United States, 1961–1963: Kennedy-Khrushchev Exchanges (Volume VI). (Washington, DC: United States Government Printing Office, 1996)

Foreign Relations of the United States, 1961–1963: Organization of Foreign Policy; Information Policy; United Nations; Scientific Matters (Volume XXV) (Washington, DC: United States Government Printing Office, 2001)

Geneva Conference of Foreign Ministers on Korea and Indo-China, 27 April-15 June 1954, Geneva.

International Law Commission. *Draft Articles on the Law of Treaties* (1958) 2 YBILC 101.

International Law Commission, 'Memorandum on the Soviet doctrine and practice with respect to the law of treaties, prepared by the Secretariat' (21 November 1950) UN Doc. A/CN.4/37.

Kennedy, John F., 'Radio and Television Report to the American People on Soviet Arms Buildup in Cuba' (22 October 1962). JFK Library. www.jfklibrary.org/archives/other-resources/john-f-kennedy-speeches/cuba-radio-and-televi sion-report-19621022.

Kennan, George, 'Long Telegram', 22 February 1946, Moscow, National Archives and Records Administration, Department of State Records (Record Group 59), Central Decimal File, 1945–1949, 861.00/2-2246.

Kissinger, Henry, 'Central Issues of American Foreign Policy' (1969) Office of the Historian, https://history.state.gov/historicaldocuments/frus1969–76v01/d4.

Khrushchev, Nikita, 'Letter From Chairman Khrushchev to President Kennedy, October 27, 1962'. LS NO. 46236, JFK Library, T-94/T-24. https://microsites.jfklibrary.org/cmc/oct27/doc4.html.

'Letter to Fidel Castro', 31 January 1963.

Declaration on the Granting of Independence to Colonial Countries and Peoples (UN Doc. A/4502, 23 September 1960).

Legal Council. 'Scope of "credentials" in rule 27 of the rules of procedure of the General Assembly' UN Doc. A/8160, 11th November 1970, 25 UN GAOR, Annexes A.i.3.

'Exchange of Communications between the President of the United States and Maxim Litvinov of the Union of Soviet Socialist Republics, November 16, 1933' in *Public Papers and Addresses of Franklin D. Roosevelt. Volume 2* (New York: Random House, 1933) 471–86.

Fifth Pan-African Congress Report 'The Challenge to the Colonial Powers' (Manchester, 15–21 October 1945).

'Final Communiqué of the Asian–African Conference', Asian–African Conference. Bandung, 24 April 1955.

Guevara, Che, 'Message to the Tricontinental' (Organization of Solidarity with the People of Asia, Africa and Latin America, Havana, 16 April 1967), www.marxists.org/archive/guevara/1967/04/16.htm.

'Notes for the Study of the Ideology of the Cuban Revolution' (8 October 1960).

Lumumba, Patrice, 'Speech at Proclamation of Independence' (30 June 1960). Columbia University, www.columbia.edu/itc/history/mann/w3005/lumumba.html.

Maisky, Ivan, Memo of 11 January 1944, AVPRF, f.6, op.6, d. 147, II.14, 1–40.

Marshall, George, 'Address by the Chief of the US Delegation to the General Assembly' *Department of State Bulletin*, 17 (1947) 620.

Mao Tse-Tung, 'Peaceful Coexistence – Two Diametrically Opposed Policies: Comment on the Open Letter of the Central Committee of the CPSU (VI)', 12 December 1963.

McNamara, Robert S. 'No Cities Doctrine', Commencement Address at the University of Michigan, 16 June 1962.

Memorandum from Henry Morgenthau Jr., 'Suggested Post-Surrender Program for Germany', 1944.

Mont Tremblant Conference on the Problems of Peace in the Post-War World, Mont Tremblant, Quebec, 4–17 December 1942.

Morgenthau, Henry, 'Suggested Post-Surrender Program for Germany', 1 September 1944.

Moynihan, Daniel (United States of America), 'Address Delivered at 2327th Plenary Meeting' *Official Records of the United Nations General Assembly* (1 September 1975, New York).

National Security Council Directive on Office of Special Projects (NSC 10/2), 18 June 1948.

Nkrumah, Kwame, Speech before the House of Commons, London, United Kingdom (10 July 1953).

Novikov, Nikolae, Telegram to the Soviet Leadership, 27 September 1946, History and Public Policy Program Digital Archive AVP SSSR, f. 06. Op. 8, 45; 759.

Office of the Historian (US). 'Telegram From the Department of State to the Embassy in the German Democratic Republic' (Washington, DC, 22 January 1979, 1638Z), Foreign Relations of the United States, 1977–1980, Vol. XX, Eastern Europe, Doc. 124.

Organization of African Unity, 'Border Disputes Among African States' *Res*, 16(1) (17–21 July 1964).

'Peaceful Coexistence and the Struggle for World Peace' in Jan Triska (ed.), *Soviet Communism: Programs and Rules: Official Texts of 1919, 1952 (1956), 1961* (San Francisco, Chandler, 1962) 6367.

'Positive Action Conference for Peace and Security in Africa', Accra, 7–10 April 1960.

Position Paper Prepared for the Geneva Summit Conference, 18–23 July 1955, Foreign Relations of the United States, 1955–57, United Nations and General Matters, Vol. XI, Doc. 112.

'Proclamation Defining Terms of Japanese Surrender' *Department of State Bulletin* 13 (1945) 137–38.

Programme of the Communist International Adopted at its Sixth Congress, 1 September 1928, 'The 'Statement by Henry Cabot Lodge' *Department of State Bulletin*, 37 (1957) 693.

'Proposals for the Establishment of a General International Organisation' (Dumbarton Oaks Conference) (7 October 1944).

'Selections from Declarations and Resolutions Adopted by the Fifth Pan-African Congress: Manchester, England, October 13–21, 1945' *Black Camera*, 13 (2021) 343–51.

Strategy and Tactics of the Communist International in the Struggle for the Proletarian Dictatorship, Section VI.

Project of an International Declaration Concerning the Laws and Customs of War, Brussels, 27 August 1874.

Record of Meeting at the Kremlin, Moscow, 10 October 1944, 7 pm, Wilson Centre Digital Archive doc/123187.

Records of the Colonial Office, Commonwealth and Foreign and Commonwealth Offices, Empire Marketing Board and related bodies, UK National Archives, CO323/878.

Report by the Committee on Satellite Reconnaissance Policy. *Foreign Relations of the United States,* 1961–*1963,* Vol. XXV, Organization of Foreign Policy; Information Policy; United Nations; Scientific Matters, Doc. 421, 951–59.

Report of the Special Committee on the Problem of Hungary, UNGA, 11th session, Supp. No. 18 (A/3592) (5 July 1957).

Rules of Procedure of the General Assembly, UN Doc. A/520/Rev.19 (1984).

'Rusk Speech and the Resolution Adopted by OAS' *New York Times,* 24 October 1962. www.nytimes.com/1962/10/24/archives/rusk-speech-and-the-resolution-adopted-by-oas.html.

Rules of Procedure of the Security Council, UN Doc. S/96/Rev.7 (1982).

Secretary of State for Foreign Affairs to Parliament, 'Germany: An Account of the Events leading up to a Reference of the Berlin Question to the United Nations' (1948) Cmd. 7534.

Speech by First Secretary of the Soviet Union Leonid Brezhnev (13 November 1968).

Speech delivered by Joseph Stalin at a meeting of voters of the Stalin electoral district, Moscow, 9 February 1946, History and Public Policy Program Digital Archive.

Telegram from the Mission at the United Nations to the Department of State, *10 February 1959, in Foreign Relations of the United States, 1958–1960,* vol. II, Washington, DC: United States Government Printing Office, 1992).

Trend, Burke [Cabinet Secretary]. Memorandum to the Prime Minister, 'Anglo-American Nuclear Relations', 11 August 1972, Top Secret. National Security Archive, PREM 15/1362.

Tripartite Conference in Moscow *American Journal of International Law,* Supplement 38 (1944) 3–8.

Truman, Harry S., 'Address on Foreign Policy at the Navy Day Celebration in New York City', 27 October 1945.

'Inaugural Address' (January 20, 1949). www.trumanlibrary.gov/library/public-papers/19/inaugural-address.

Truman, Harry S., 'Special Message to the Congress on Greece and Turkey' (March 12, 1947) Truman Library, www.trumanlibrary.gov/library/public-papers/56/special-message-congress-greece-and-turkey-truman-doctrine.

United Nations Audiovisual Library of International Law, 'Declaration on the Granting of Independence to Colonial Countries and Peoples', https://legal.un.org/avl/ha/dicc/dicc.html.

United States Department of State Historical Office, 'The Record on Korean Unification 1943–1960: Narrative Summary with Principal Documents' (1960).

United States Department of State, Circular No. 175 (13 December 1955) para 3, 50 *American Journal of International Law* 784 (1956).

United States Diplomatic and Consular Staff in Tehran (United States of America v Iran) [1980] ICJ Rep 3.
United States, "Address by President Nixon to the United Nations General Assembly" (New York, 23 October 1970), Office of the Historian, https://history.state.gov/historicaldocuments/frus1969–76v01/d78.
United States, 'National Security Strategy for a New Century' (1998), https://history.defense.gov/Historical-Sources/National-Security-Strategy.
UN Doc. A/575, UNGAOR, 3rd Sess., Part I, Supp. No. 9 (1948).
UN Doc. A/583, UNGAOR, 3rd Sess., Supp. No. 10 (1948).
UN Doc. A/PV.470 (8 Dec 1953)
UN Doc. A/PV.925 (28 Nov 1960)
UN Doc. A/PV.935 (5 Dec 1960)
UN Doc. A/PV.939 (7 Dec 1960)
UN Doc. A/PV 944 (13 Dec 1960)
UN Doc. A/PV 947 (14 Dec 1960)
UN Doc. S/PV 410, (16 February 1949).
UN Doc. S/PV 423 (8 April 1949).
UN Doc. S/PV.857 (23 May 1960).
UN Doc. S/PV.1022 (23 October 1962).
UNGA Draft Resolution A/L.323 and Addenda 1 to 6 (1960)
UNGA Report of KPS Menon UN Doc. A/AC.18/28 (1948).
UNGA Res 1 (I) (1 February 1946).
UNGA Res 39 (I) (11 December 1946).
UNGA Res 97/1 (14 December 1946).
UNGA Res 111 (II) (13 November 1947).
UNGA Res 112(II) A & B (14 November 1947).
UNGA Res 195 (III) (12 December 1948).
UNGA Res 376 (V) (7 October 1950).
UNGA Res 377 (V) (3 November 1950).
UNGA Res 381(V) (17 November 1950).
UNGA Res 498 (V) (1 February 1951).
UNGA Res 500 (V) (18 May 1951).
UNGA Res 995(X) (14 December 1955).
UNGA Res 1131 (XI) (12 December 1956).
UNGA Res 1472 (XIV) (12 December 1959).
UNGA Res 1514 (XV) (14 December 1960).
UNGA Res 1541 (XV) (15 December 1960).
UNGA Res 1653 (XVI) (24 November 1961).
UNGA Res 1802 (XVII) (14 December 1962).
UNGA Res 1803 (XVII) (14 December 1962).
UNGA Res 2028 (XX) (29 November 1965).
UNGA Res 2138 (XXI) (22 October 1966).

UNGA Res 2625 (XXV) (24 October 1970).
UNGA Res 2936 (XXVII) (29 November 1972).
UNGA Res 3034 (XXVII) (18 December 1972).
UNGA Res 3050 (XXVIII) (18 September 1973)
UNGA Res 3201 (S-VI) (1 May 1974).
UNGA Res 3281 (XXIX) (12 December 1974).
UNGA Res 33/71B (14 December 1978).
UNGA Res 34/83 (11 December 1979).
UNGA Res 146 (XXXIV) (17 December 1979).
UNGA Res 36/92I (9 December 1981).
UNGA Res 44/117C (15 December 1989).
UNSC Res 21 (2 April 1947).
UNSC Res 82 (25 June 1950).
UNSC Res 85 (31 July 1950).
UNSC Res 1668 XVI (15 December 15, 1961).
UNSC Res 355 (22 June 1973).
US Department of State, 'A Report on the International Control of Atomic Energy', *Prepared for the Secretary of State's Committee on Atomic Energy.* Washington, 16 March 1946, Department of State Publication 2498.
US Department of State, 'Baruch Plan', Presented to the United Nations Atomic Energy Commission, 14 June 1946, United Nations, Official Records of the Atomic Energy Commission, First Year, Plenary Meetings, 4–18.
US Department of State, 'Baruch's Speech at Opening Session of UN Atomic Energy Commission' *New York Times*, 5 June 1946, 4, hwww.nytimes.com/1946/06/15/archives/baruchs-speech-at-opening-session-of-un-atomic-energy-commission.html.
US Department of State, 'Minutes of the 506th Meeting of the National Security Council', Washington, DC, 21 October 1962, 2:30–4:50 pm. https://history.state.gov/historicaldocuments/frus1961-63v11/d38.
United States, Commission on CIA Activities within the United States, Report to the President by the Commission on CIA Activities within the United States, Washington, DC, June 1975.
United States, Office of the Secretary of Defense Vietnam Task Force. Final Report of the Office of the Secretary of Defense Vietnam Task Force, Washington, DC,15 January 1969.
United States, Senate Select Committee to Study Governmental Operations with Respect to Intelligence Activities, Report of the Senate Select Committee to Study Governmental Operations with Respect to Intelligence Activities, Washington, DC, 29 April 1976.
US Note on Austrian Neutrality, *Department of State Bulletin*, 33 (1955) 1011–12.
US Department of State, 'Department of State Telegram Transmitting Letter From Chairman Khrushchev to President Kennedy, October 26, 1962', Moscow,

26 October 1962, 7 pm, https://microsites.jfklibrary.org/cmc/oct26/doc4.html.

World Bank, *World Development Report 1978* (Washington, DC: World Bank, 1978).

Yearbook of the United Nations (1950).

Yusuf, Shahid, et al., Development Economics through the Decades: A Critical Look at 30 Years of the Wilson, Woodrow, 'Fourteen Points as set forth in an address made before the joint session of Congress, January 8th 1918', Office of the Historian, www.archives.gov/milestone-documents/president-wo.

Wilson's Fourteen Points (8 January 1918).

World Development Report (Washington, DC: World Bank, 2008).

Online/Other

'Bevin Would Eradicate 38th Parallel, Unify Country as Solution for Korea', *The New York Times*, 30 September 1950.

DiResta, Renee, 'Process as Punishment: An American History of Political Spectacle' *Lawfare*, 14 April 2025, www.lawfaremedia.org/article/process-as-punishment–an-american-history-of-political-spectacle.

Falk, Richard A., 'CIA Covert Operations and International Law', 12 September 1974, www.cia.gov/readingroom/docs/CIA-RDP88-01315R000200030001-2.pdf.

Fitzpatrick, Sheila, 'Not Corrupt Enough' *London Review of Books* (2025) 15.

Gedeon, Joseph, 'Trump Signs Executive Order Rebranding Pentagon as Department of War' *The Guardian*, 6 September 2025, www.theguardian.com/us-news/2025/sep/05/department-war-defense-trump-executive-order-pentagon.

Gleijeses, Piero, '"We Wrapped the Guns in Plastic Bags"' *London Review of Books*, 39 (2017) 184–87.

Grandin, Greg, 'Don't Do What Allende Did' *London Review of Books*, 34(14) (19 July 2012) 3–4.

Grimonprez, Johan, dir. *Soundtrack to a Coup d'État*, Docu-essay, 150 min, France/Belgium/Netherlands, 2024.

Harding, Jeremy, 'I Am Only Interested in Women Who Struggle' *London Review of Books*, 46 (2024) 18–20.

Jacobs, Sean, 'Chop-Chop spirit' *London Review of Books*, 46 (2024) 9–14.

Letter to the Editor, *New York Times*, 16 July 1976.

'Letters' *Foreign Policy*, 90 (1993) 169.

National Security Agency/Central Intelligence Agency, 'Press Release: Declassified UKUSA Signals Intelligence Agreement Documents Available' (June 24, 2010), www.nsa.gov/Press-Room/Press-Releases-Statements/Press-Release-

View/Article/1629812/declassified-ukusa-signals-intelligence-agreement-documents-available/.

McVeigh, Shaun, and Adil Hasan Khan, 'Offices of the Southern Jurist-Diplomat' Melbourne Law School, https://law.unimelb.edu.au/centres/iilah/research/projects/offices-of-the-southern-jurist-diplomat.

Nesiah, Vasuki, 'The NIEO Against Racial Capitalism' *Progressive International* (2023), https://progressive.international/blueprint/30202c48-1324-4831-81e5–829f588d9492-nesiah-the-nieo-against-racial-capitalism/en.

Okoth, Kevin, 'Poison Is Better' *London Review of Books*, 45 (2023) 27–29.

Orwell, George, 'You and the Atomic Bomb' *Tribune*, 19 October 1945.

Peck, Raoul, *Lumumba: Death of the Prophet* (Velvet Film 1992).

Reynolds, John, and Noura Erakat, 'We Charge Apartheid' TWAILR Reflections (2021), https://twailr.com/we-charge-apartheid-palestine-and-the-international-criminal-court/accessed 20 September 2025.

Richards, Susan, 'For Russia the New Cold War has Begun' *The Guardian Weekly*, 22 May 2015, 18.

Runciman, David, 'The Great Political Films: Dr Strangelove & Fail Safe with Jill Lepore' *Past Present Future Podcast*, 3 November 2024, https://podcasts.apple.com/ee/podcast/the-great-political-films-dr-strangelove-fail-safe-w/id1682047968?i=1000675489492.

Storr, Cait, 'Mandates in International Law' *Oxford Bibliographies* (2020), DOI: 10.1093/OBO/9780199796953-0203.

Trujillo, César Gaviria, 'OAS/UNESCO Symposium on Security for Peace', 3 April 1995, www.oas.org/en/media_center/speech.asp?sCodigo=02-0397.

'Trump Administration Draft Order Calls for Overhaul of State Department' *New York Times*, 20 April 2025.

White House, The, 'Restoring the United States Department of War' (Executive Orders, September 5, 2025), www.whitehouse.gov/presidential-actions/2025/09/restoring-the-united-states-department-of-war/.

Walker, Stephen, '"You Don't Brag About Wiping Out 60–70,000 people": The Men Who Dropped the Atomic Bombs on Hiroshima and Nagasaki' The Guardian 22 June 2025, www.theguardian.com/world/2025/jun/22/atomic-bomb-hiroshima-nagasaki-author-stephen-walker.

Žižek, Slavoj, 'Knee-deep: Leftish Platitudes' *London Review of Books* 26(17) (2004) 3–6.

INDEX

CAMBRIDGE STUDIES IN INTERNATIONAL AND COMPARATIVE LAW

Recent books in the Series

200 *Rival Legalities: International Laws of the Cold War*
Mathew Craven, Sundhya Pahuja and Gerry Simpson

199 *Freedom of Information: Hegemony, Contestation, and International Law*
Wanshu Cong

198 *International Leviathans: Practices of Sovereignty by International Administrations*
Nicolas Lemay-Hébert

197 *Submarines in International Law*
Natalie Klein, Kate Purcell and Jack McNally

196 *The Classical Doctrine of Civil War in International Law*
Ville Kari

195 *Adjudicating over Anarchy: Judicial Remedies, Compliance, and Enforcement in International Law*
Geraldo Vidigal

194 *Regional Trade Agreements, Prosperity and the Global South: Normative Beliefs and Interests*
Yenkong Ngangjoh Hodu and Collins Chikodili Ajibo

193 *A Theory of International Organizations in Public International Law*
Orfeas Chasapis Tassinis

192 *The Individual in the Law and Practice of the International Court of Justice*
Yusra Suedi

191 *Ghosts of International Law: The Figure of the Foreign Fighter in a Cultural Perspective*
Alberto Rinaldi

190 *Merchants of Legalism: A History of State Responsibility (1870-1960)*
Alan Tzvika Nissel

189 *The Functions of International Adjudication and International Environmental Litigation*
Joshua Paine

188 *Demystifying Treaty Interpretation*
Andrea Bianchi and Fuad Zarbiyev

187 *International Law-Making by the International Court of Justice and International Law Commission: Partnership for Purpose in a Decentralized Legal Order*
Omri Sender

186 *The Rebirth of Territory*
Gail Lythgoe